THE **ORGANIC** COOK'S BIBLE

THE **ORGANIC** COOK'S BIBLE

HOW TO SELECT AND COOK THE BEST INGREDIENTS ON THE MARKET

Jeff Cox

JOHN WILEY & SONS, INC.

Copyright © 2006 by Jeff Cox. All rights reserved
Except where otherwise noted, photography copyright © 2006 Susanna Napierala-Cox.
Front cover © Leigh Beisch / Food Pix / Getty Images.
page A4: Crosnes, courtesy of Cécile Thomas, www.monmarchand.com; page C3:
Chestnut, Nevada, on the tree ready to harvest © Brian McCarthy and Carolyn Keiffer;
page C6: Borage and page C7: Lovage © Jerry Pavia

Published by John Wiley and Sons, Inc., Hoboken, New Jersey
Published simultaneously in Canada

For general information about our other products and services, please contact our Customer
Care Department within the United States at (800) 762-2974, outside the United States
at (317) 572-3993 or fax (317) 572-4002.

Wiley also publishes its books in a variety of electronic formats. Some content that appears
in print may not be available in electronic books. For more information about Wiley
products, visit our web site at www.wiley.com.

INTERIOR DESIGN AND COVER TITLE DESIGN BY DEBORAH KERNER / DANCING BEARS DESIGN

Library of Congress Cataloging-in-Publication Data:

Cox, Jeff, 1940-
The Organic Cook's Bible: how to select and cook the best ingredients on the market /
    Jeff Cox.
        p. cm.
    Includes bibliographical references and index.
    ISBN-13 978-0-471-44578-4 (cloth)
    ISBN-10 0-471-44578-9 (cloth)
1. Cookery (Natural foods) 2. Natural foods. I. Title.
    TX741.C72 2006
    641.5'63—dc22

                        2005032324

Printed in the United States of America
10 9 8 7 6 5 4 3 2 1

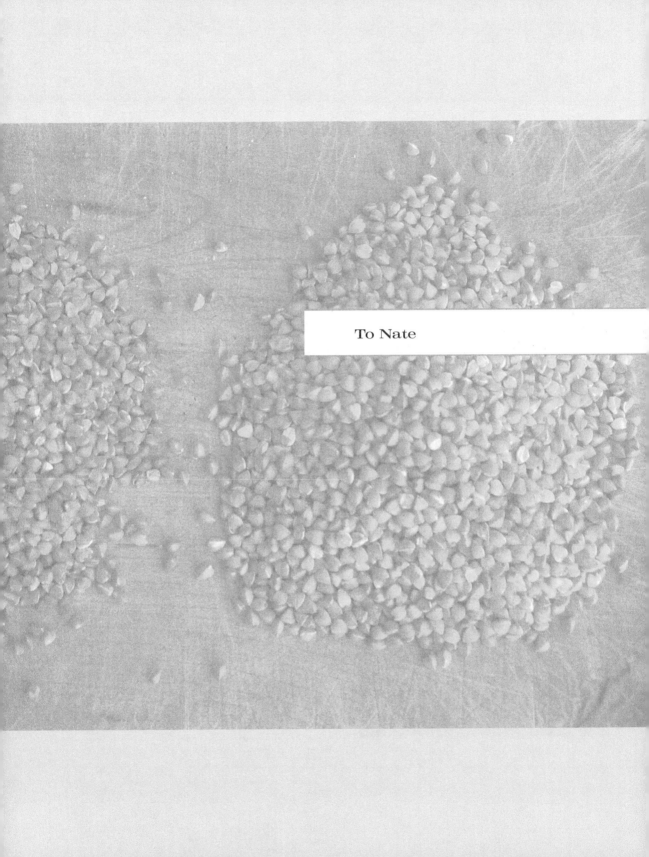

To Nate

Contents

Acknowledgments   ix

Introduction   x

How This Book Is Organized   xii

Discovering Organic Food   1

Why Go Organic?   21

Talking with Farmers   45

Vegetables   53

Fruits   215

Nuts, Seeds, Beans,
   and Grains 319

Herbs and Spices 377

Meats, Dairy, and Eggs 417

Kitchen Staples 451

Top Varieties
   of Organic Produce 479

Recipes by Category 511

Sources 517

Bibliography 527

Index 529

Sage

Acknowledgments

So many folks deserve recognition for the information in this book that it is not possible to list them all. But these people must be thanked:

Special thanks to the entire team at Wiley, especially editors Linda Ingroia and Adam Kowit, who labored hard to keep me focused, and to production editor Ava Wilder for her thorough management of every detail. Thanks to designer Deborah Kerner for making this wealth of information accessible and attractive. Thanks to my agent, Fred Hill, who got this ball rolling. Thanks to the folks at Oak Hill Farm in Glen Ellen, California, who gave generously of produce and time to make sure we got the photos we needed. Thanks also to J. Z. Cool, chef extraordinaire; Lynn Donches at Rodale Press; Anne Bertinuson, USDA; Gene Kahn, Cascadian Farms; Ben Faber, UC Davis; Elizabeth Mitcham, UC Davis Department of Pomology; Janet Caprile, UC Davis farm advisor; Louise Ferguson, UC Davis; John R. Clark, University of Arkansas; Allen Moore, USDA; Curt R. Rom, University of Arkansas; Adel A. Kader, UC Davis; Paul Vossen, UC Cooperative Extension; Chris Deren, University of Florida; Robin Siktberg, Herb Society of America; Dan Pratt, Organic Trade Association; John Duval, University of Florida; Dave Hill, Connecticut Agricultural Experiment Station; Robert Stebbins, Oregon State University; Chef John Ash; Dr. David G. Holm, Colorado State University; Greg Miller at Empire Chestnut Company; David Brenner, Iowa State University; Randy Wirth, Caffe Ibis; Glenn Roberts, Anson Mills; Jerry Tenenberg, The Great Spice Company; Gemma Claridge, Albert's Organics; Tricia Belcastro, Washington Apple Commission; Mark Farnham, PhD, USDA-ARS-U.S. Vegetable Laboratory; Eileen Weinsteiger, Rodale Research Institute; Manny Flores, Jaleo Restaurant, Washington, D.C.; Constance Jesser, Wine Country Cakes, Sonoma, California; Nancy Civetta, Civetta Communicazione; John Lewallen, Mendocino Sea Vegetable Co.; Stephanie Kimmell, Marche restaurant, Eugene, Oregon; Claire Criscuolo, RN, Claire's Corner Copia, New Haven, Connecticut; Birkett Mills, Penn Yan, New York; Nicolas and Laura Catena, Bodega Catena Zapata, Agrelo, Argentina; and all those who helped but aren't mentioned here.

A special acknowledgment to J. I. Rodale, whose organic epiphany started the movement.

Finally, thanks to my wife, Susanna Napierala-Cox, for her photos, her love and support, and her forbearance as I spent many a late night at my desk.

Introduction

The perfect dish requires perfect ingredients. That doesn't mean blemish-free produce. It means that the variety of fruit, vegetable, nut, or what-have-you is the right one for the dish being prepared, and that it's as ripe and full of flavor as it will ever get on the very day that the cook is inspired to use it.

And yes, it should be organically grown.

Why organic?

It tastes better. For the cook, organic produce sets the standard of quality. There are three reasons for this.

First, organic growers are primarily concerned with quality, so the varieties they select to grow are known for their flavor impact rather than their ability to ship well or keep well on the shelf.

Second, organic foods are grown in soil rich in all the nutrients plants need to develop maximum flavor nuances. The effect of organic farming techniques on the overall quality of plants and animals cannot be overestimated. A perfect dish needs the kind of intense expression of flavor that organic ingredients provide.

Third, organic food tends to be fresher, and food that's fresh contains the maximum amount of flavor and nutrition. Flavor and fragrance molecules begin to break down and disappear soon after most foods are picked from the field or tree, so one of the goals of organic farmers is to keep the distance between farms and consumers as short as possible. The increasing popularity of organic food sold at local farm stands, at farmers' markets, at specialty markets, and in supermarkets with organic produce sections means fresher food is becoming ever more available. More flavor to begin with and more of this flavor preserved because of freshness—that's a winning combination for any cook.

Another crucial factor about organic food is that it has been grown without agricultural chemicals; animals that produce organic meat, dairy, and eggs are not fed growth hormones or antibiotics; and genetic modification of crops is not allowed. The food is just good, clean food with the genes that nature gave it. That's reassuring, especially for families with small children who are more vulnerable than adults to the ill effects of agricultural chemicals and for anyone concerned about the effects of genetic manipulation of their foodstuffs.

This ain't just talk. I had my first organic garden in 1969. I've grown an organic garden just about every year since and have probably grown every type of crop imaginable. Having that abundance of good food at hand tempted me into the kitchen, where I began to remember the delicious meals my mom made when I was a kid. Slowly—and with many treks to the pizza parlor when my cooking didn't turn out very well—I learned to cook. Eventually, the increasing availability of organic food, coupled with a desire to create something delicious for my family, began to result in dishes even I was satisfied with. Cooking also became key to becoming a better gardener, because I learned which varieties of each crop tasted best in a given recipe, and so my garden more and more suited my taste.

I've spent most of my life—both at work and at play—acquiring the hard-won knowledge that this book represents. Sharing it with you feels very much like sending over a basket of fresh-picked produce from my garden. As you would with a gift basket, take what you want now and come back often to sample all the book has to offer.

—JEFF COX

How This Book Is Organized

A large portion of this book consists of entries covering over 150 foods grown, raised, or produced organically. Each entry covers the significance of the food's organic provenance. It discusses what farmers do to make sure the food is the cleanest, most nutritious, and most environmentally sound it can be.

Organic farmers select health-giving and tasty varieties of produce. They put a premium on raising healthy animals. They want the distance from farm to consumer to be as short as possible, and they know that food tastes best in season. They sell these products in a range of venues—organic aisles in supermarkets, farmers' markets, and even straight from the farms. With this in mind, the entries discuss when and where to find the foods, what to look for, and how to use them. Topping this off are recipes that show off the best aspects of top quality organic ingredients.

In addition, because organic farmers grow the healthiest and best-tasting produce varieties (many of them uniquely and deliciously flavored varieties you won't find in conventional supermarkets), I've created a Top Varieties section on page 479 that lists hundreds of the best varieties of vegetables and fruits. You'll find many of them at your local farmers' market or organic market, and more and more varieties are turning up in more places every day. I can't stress enough the importance of knowing which food varieties are going to give you the best gustatory payoff. Your insistence on the best

varieties will improve the food you put on the table and encourage growers to plant the better varieties.

Organizationally, you'll find vegetables in one section, fruits in another, the dry seeds of plants (grains, seeds, and nuts—and beans, too) in another, animal foods (meat, dairy, eggs) in yet another, and kitchen staples (oils, sweeteners, flavorings) in still another.

In some instances, I grouped like ingredients together. For example, while there are many Asian vegetables, they mostly tend to be members of the mustard family in various forms, and so I put them together in a section. Winter squashes share enough similarities that they needed to go together, and ditto for summer squashes. Citrus is a huge subject, so to simplify it, I put the various citrus fruits together in one section.

Some ingredients may be missing—coconuts for instance—because the state of organic farming has not yet covered these foodstuffs, as far as I can detect. Whenever possible I include either organic foods that I know can be procured or foods that I know are produced without the use of agricultural chemicals. If I can't find foods that meet those tests, I don't include them.

The organization of the food entries in each section of the book should be self-evident from the category names—The Organic Factor, Nutrition, Types, Seasonality, What to Look for, Storage, Preparation, Uses—and then recipes.

Each entry should give you a sense of what the ingredient is like when its quality is high, how you can use it in your cooking, and why you can feel good about eating its organic version.

A note on Types versus Varieties: Most of our vegetable kingdom foods are cultivated varieties of a particular kind of plant. These varieties can be classified by type (categories that are useful for the cook to know), such as size, color, nutritive content, and relative sweetness. Differing types might have different culinary uses, methods of preparation, or flavor; have different growing seasons; or simply appear differently at the market—such as green and purple figs (which actually taste similar). Where an ingredient listing has no Type, it is because the various forms of a food are similar in appearance and culinary use, although there still may be a number of specific varieties, each with its own unique flavor and personality.

The suggestions in this book for identifying fresh, high quality organic foods are meant to be guidelines, not hard-and-fast rules. We're talking common sense here, not rigid ideology. I'm sure many readers may want to eat only organic food, no matter what. Others may want to eat as much organic food as possible. Still others may be curious and want to try some organic food—just to see what all the talk is about. Personally, I try to eat as much organic food as possible and as much in season as possible, but if perchance the organic broccoli is sold out, I'll grab a head of conventional broccoli without worrying that I'm condemning myself to organic hell. But the more you know about conventional farming methods and the conventional food supply system, the more inclined toward organic you tend to become.

As I've worked on this book, I've kept you—the reader—in mind. I want you and your whole family—your kids, your grandkids—to thrive and grow healthy from your food. There are so many reasons to eat organic food, and they all point directly to you. *À votre santé*!

Olives

Discovering Organic Food

FARMERS' MARKETS, ROADSIDE STANDS, ON-FARM SALES,
SPECIALTY GROCERS, AND ORGANIC PRODUCE SECTIONS IN BETTER SUPERMARKETS

THE BEST APPLE I ever tasted was a Stayman Winesap. I bought it at a small mom-and-pop market in Hereford, Pennsylvania, one warm autumn afternoon years ago. It was prime apple time in the Pennsylvania Dutch dairy country.

The first bite hooked me. The skin was dark red, almost black on the shoulder, with a slight russetting where it had received the most sun. Each bite came off the apple with a satisfying crack, like chips from a flint. The flesh was snowy white, with a slight reddish tint just under the skin. It snapped and crunched as I chewed it, the juice spilling generously into my mouth. The flavor was sweet and sappy, with a tangy tartness that focused my attention.

That Stayman Winesap was the single best apple I've ever eaten in my life, right up to the present day. I don't suppose I'll ever find its like again—subsequent Winesaps from that store were disappointingly mealy or lacked the flavor punch. Fresh Braeburns come close but fall short. Cox Orange Pippins are wonderful and perfumey-flowery, but they don't have the flavor impact that the Winesap had. It's only in hindsight that such moments of perfection identify themselves, and then they become wrapped in associated memories and enshrined in one's personal mythology, whereupon it becomes ever more difficult to dislodge them from their pedestal.

Now compare that Winesap with a store-bought Red Delicious. No comparison. The proliferation of the inferior Red Delicious is due to two primary marketing factors. First, the apples have deep red skins and consumer preference tests show that people associate a deep red apple with quality, even if, as with Red Delicious, there's precious little quality to the flavor. Second, they are called "delicious" even though they aren't. What has caused the popularity of Red Delicious has nothing to do with how good they taste. Although today we see more flavorful apples showing up in stores—Gala and Fuji and Braeburn among them—Red Delicious still reigns.

There are over 8,000 varieties of apples in commerce around the world! Many if not most are far superior to even the best supermarket apples. In addition, scientists have recorded over 15,000 plants that have been used by human beings as food over the millennia, but there are only about 150 commercially important food crops worldwide these days. And in the large corporate food systems that provide foods to our supermarkets and big commercial stores, only a few of these 150 commodities are typically available to the consumer. These are chosen not because of their qualities of flavor or texture but mostly because of their ability to survive long-distance shipping and in-store display and still look good enough to eat.

Besides good cosmetic appearance and long shelf life, another goal of large food corporations is standardization of product. They want every Kraft Single to taste the same, every loaf of Iron Kids bread to taste the same, every Dole pineapple to taste the same. That way brand identification is assured. That's the way quality is "controlled." No matter where you are in the world, a Coke is a Coke is a Coke. Processing homogenizes food and creates a product that tastes the same year after

year. It also drains food of distinctive flavor and nutrition.

While the processing of food by huge corporations has been going on for a long time, it reached some kind of nadir with the advent of TV dinners over half a century ago. Mine was the kind of family where Mom always—*always*—cooked dinner from scratch, at least until TV dinners came along. Then home-cooked meals dwindled as we were given "pot pies," which I remember as being tasteless, with chalky crusts and scalding hot interiors. Or we might get frozen turkey dinners, whose only advantage was political: The fact that they were labeled "TV dinners" gave us a card to play as we argued with mom for permission to open folding tables and eat rubbery turkey while watching *Tom Corbett, Space Cadet*.

So-called TV dinners have come about as far from those days as *Star Wars* has from *Tom Corbett*. They're not just for TV anymore, and in fact, there are whole dinners—or goodly parts thereof—prepared and frozen for our convenience, easily nuked in a few minutes, or cooked in a regular oven in less than an hour's time. But who knows what lurks in those trays? Could be pesticides, fungicides, and herbicides. Might be genetically modified foods, or foods that have been sterilized with nuclear radiation. Many contain chemical taste enhancers, extenders, and texturizers. Might be meat grown with antibiotics and growth hormones. There will certainly be preservatives. And, if you read the labels, a lot of these frozen dinners are loaded with fats and salt.

Big food processing companies have every reason in the world to create food products that are convenient, at least tolerable to the taste buds, and cheap. If they have to use chemical flavorings, colorings, preservatives, texturizers, and such to do it, well, okay. If they load their products with sugar, fat, and salt, well, those substances taste good—in fact, they're almost irresistible. No wonder a burger and fries with a soda are the mainstays of the fast food industry: fatty meat, salty and fatty fries, and sugary soda pop. But as even a casual look around America will tell you, something's wrong with either our food or the way we eat, or both.

It's no secret that corporate agriculture and the commodification of our food have led to a diminution of flavor and aroma, texture, and overall quality. But for every action, there's a reaction. The reaction to low-quality, overprocessed, flavorless food has been the development of an artisanal food movement in many places around the world.

Slow Food, for instance, is an organization that developed in reaction to fast food, and has spread its "convivia," as it calls its chapters, around the world. It was founded in Italy's Piedmont region in 1986, and the international movement was founded in Paris in 1989. It now has 60,000 members on five continents and employs more than 100 people in its main office in the Italian town of Bra. Its manifesto has a simple message at its heart: Slow Food is a movement "for the protection of the right to taste." Its Ark of Taste Project identifies food products, dishes, and animals in danger of disappearing and gives economic support and media backup to groups and individuals pledged to save an endangered product, such as a fine local cheese that's being muscled out of the marketplace by large cheese factories.

Oldways Preservation and Exchange Trust, an American-based nonprofit educational organization founded in 1990, promotes alternatives to the unhealthy foods that fill the stores in industrialized countries. Its educational programs are based on current scientific evidence for healthy eating, organic and sustainable agriculture, and the traditional cuisines of indigenous cultures. Beginning in 1991, Oldways challenged the conventional wisdom about healthy diet. It questioned whether current science supported the twenty years of "low-fat" messages the government was promulgating and why this coincided with the emergence of the U.S. obesity epidemic. In the years 1993 through 1997, Oldways introduced a series of traditional healthy dietary pyramids: Mediterranean, Latin American, Asian, and Vegetarian. Finally, in June, 2000, new U.S. dietary guidelines reversed the low-fat message and recommended the moderate fat-eating patterns focusing on monounsaturated fats that Oldways had been urging. Now a whole series of Oldways initiatives—such as the Sensible Wine-Drinking Initiative, the Whole Grains Initiative, the Cheese of Choice Coalition, the Antioxidant Initiative, Continuing Medical Education for Physicians and Health Professionals, and the staging of conferences in Europe, North and South America, Asia, and Australia—are getting the word out about traditional eating patterns famous for their exquisite taste, their simplicity, and their ability to sustain lifelong good health.

FOOD WITH A TASTE OF A PLACE

Behind both Oldways and Slow Food is a simple but profound insight. Up until about 150 years ago when the railroads—and more recently, the automobile—arrived to give great mobility to the industrialized world, most people grew up, lived, worked, and died in the same area. Over centuries and sometimes millennia, local people had learned which crops and types of livestock thrived in their climate and on their soils. Those were the crops and breeds they farmed, steadily improving their quality by selecting for factors that improved taste, nutrition, and disease resistance.

Cooking techniques and recipes were for centuries very region-specific, and over time cooks in those areas learned how to make the most palatable dishes from unique local products. In the northern latitudes and higher elevations of Germany, cool springs and summers were the perfect climate for cabbage crops and pig farming, and long winters meant that the cabbage and meat had to be stored for the cold months. The result? Sauerkraut, pickled red cabbage, dried ham, and smoked bacon.

The French call these site-specific flavors *terroir*, or soil, which is a succinct way to describe the phenomenon that each specific place on the earth will express itself in the taste of the food that grows there. Each place on the earth has a unique climate, geology, and ecology, and these factors influence what foods will grow and what they will taste like.

Wine shows these intimate variations dramatically: A Cabernet Sauvignon from Paulliac in France is very different than one from the Napa Valley in California. We taste differences in onions from Walla Walla (Washington) and Maui (Hawaii) and Vidalia (Georgia), even though they may all be the same species of sweet onion. Cheesemakers know that morning milk from a given herd of cows is different in composition and taste from evening milk from the same herd. When I was a kid, we waited with great anticipation for the corn and tomatoes grown in southern New Jersey to arrive in our stores in Pennsylvania. Jersey corn and tomatoes were justly famous, for southern New Jersey's combination of hot, humid days and nights and loose, sandy soil creates the perfect conditions to bring out the flavor of the crops and make New Jersey "The Garden State."

ORGANIC FARMING ENCOURAGES TERROIR

Organic food especially will show *terroir* (region) because organic farming is designed to strengthen the ecological aspects of the land. The soil of an organic farm is made fertile through the addition of actively decaying organic matter, which can include manure, green cover crops that are plowed under, compost, and all sorts of plant detritus that rots. Although many people think of the process of rotting as something nasty, if plants could talk, they'd give us a far different story. They'd say that when microscopic soil organisms dismantle organic matter through the processes of rot and decay, they release nutrients into the soil that feed plants exactly what they like, in the form they need, and at the rate they want. By returning plant wastes and manures from the farm to the soil, the farmer allows biological recycling to take place, and with every turn of the cycle, the soil acquires more life, becomes richer and healthier, and strengthens the plants and animals that live off it.

Differences in flavor in foods show up because of differences in cultural—or specific growing—practices. This grower may raise her Charentais melons on a bed of straw while that one may train the melon vines up a trellis and tie strips of cloth as slings to support the melons that develop high above the ground. One tomato grower may remove all the suckers—the side shoots that arise in the leaf axils of the growing plant—from his plants, while another allows them to grow.

That's why it's important to know who grew your food, if that's possible. Almost every locality in the great expanse of the United States has local food resources. By sampling those resources, you soon learn who provides food to your taste—not to some taste panel or focus group at ConAgra headquarters but to your own personal taste. No matter what the tastemakers say you should eat, wear, or watch, or listen to, or drive, you and you alone must be the arbiter of your own taste. That sounds obvious, but a lot of folks forget that. The multibillion dollar advertising business is there to convince you that they know what you want, whether you really want it or not. I believe that the business of becoming a complete human being involves first acquiring a heart, then acquiring wisdom, and along the way acquiring a firm sense of your own taste and sticking to it. The real trendsetters and tastemakers, after all, are the people who don't care what anyone else says is good: They know what they like, and they live by it.

FINDING THE BEST FOOD

It's vitally important to know your growers and suppliers. Here are several correlates if you want truly great-tasting, fresh food. Like all generalizations, there are exceptions, but for the most part, these rules hold true:

The Smaller the Farm, the Better the Food • Chances are that at small family farms, more care will be taken with the produce, the meat and milk animals, and the farm itself. At very large factory farms, produce and animals are commodities. There's a machine designed expressly to machine-harvest every crop. Things are done by a schedule, including the application of agrichemicals. Small farmers, on the other hand, are much less regimented. They get "up close and personal" with their crops and animals. Their chickens are more likely to live in a pen by a henhouse, eat vegetable scraps and insects they find by scratching in the soil, and enjoy their lives than to live crammed together into cages under round-the-clock lights like agribusiness chickens. Which eggs do you think make the best omelets?

The Closer the Farm to Your Table, the Better the Food • The more local the food, the better, for a number of reasons. First of all, it's going to be fresh and in season; it's going to exhibit all the flavor it's capable of. Because it doesn't have to sit in trucks and railcars and on supermarket shelves for weeks, it can be one of those delicious but fragile varieties that doesn't ship well. It can be picked ripe, instead of harvested hard and green and then gassed into obtaining color (but not flavor) on the long journey to the super-market.

Also, the shorter the distance from the farm to your table, or at least to the market, the greater the chance you'll meet the person who actually grew the food. You'll be able to ask him or her questions about how the food is grown.

The Smaller and Closer the Farm, the Better the Effect on the Environment • There are environmental benefits to shortening those supply lines: Less fuel is used in transporting and storing the food. And local small farmers tend to be organic because they're farming their own land, and they don't want to expose themselves and their families to noxious chemicals. They also tend to be your neighbors and can be held accountable for their practices by their fellow citizens. If your neighborhood dairy is polluting the local creek by spreading raw manure on frozen soil (which allows it to run off into the local watersheds), you can do something about it. If your milk comes from cows penned on a thousand acres a thousand miles away, you won't even know about its environmental problems.

Small farmers who own their own land also have a deep relationship with that land and a regard for it. They know where the pheasants nest and may decide not to plow there during those times of year when the birds are raising their young. They can see the effects of their husbandry on the ecology of the natural world and the farm world as these worlds intertwine and affect one another. Factory farms tend to plow every inch that can be plowed, from fencerow to fencerow, without regard for the niceties of nature. Small farmers can be held accountable if there's something wrong with their produce. If there's something wrong with the crops from factory farms, and you try to talk to the person responsible, you'll be passed up the ladder of command until you reach someone who's either unavailable or surrounded by platoons of PR people to smooth-talk you or lawyers to sue you if you get too close.

Good luck.

The Shorter the Time from Harvest to Eating, the Better the Food • Although you may want to age your beef, cheese, and wine, and hang your game, most foods taste best and have the most nutrients when they're just picked or freshly killed. They taste better and have the most nutrients when it is allowed to develop fully on the plant it grows on. If you could graph the flavor development of a tree-ripened peach on a bell curve, the very highest point of the curve would be the moment it's picked dead-ripe from the tree. If that moment closely coincides with the moment you bite into it, well, it doesn't get any better than that. This doesn't hold true for every food. But we all know from experience that vine-ripened tomatoes taste better than supermarket tomatoes, and people who plant tomatoes in their gardens know that a tomato picked ripe and eaten on the spot tastes even better than a vine-ripened tomato from the store. Consumers put a premium on freshly picked corn because the moment an ear is snapped

off the stalk, it begins to lose sweetness and flavor.

Enzymes are the catalytic agents in fruits and vegetables responsible for these swift changes in flavor after picking. But enzymes are evanescent molecules without a great deal of persistence, especially after their work is done. One of the reasons fresh food tastes so bright and complex compared to food that's been trucked around for many days is the presence of enzymes, phenolics, and other plant substances that will wither away with every passing hour.

One of the best ways to shorten the distance and time from the farm to your table is to visit local pick-your-own operations. In Connecticut, a typical northeastern state, about 30 percent of the state's fruit and vegetable growers have pick-your-own plots. The crops from these plots are usually sold at reduced prices because the farmer doesn't have the expense of picking the crop. Over the past twenty-five years, there has been a gradual move by small farmers away from sales to wholesalers, who offer low prices for their crops, to direct-to-consumer marketing, where the growers get a fairer price (although higher for you, the consumer). A recent survey by the Connecticut Department of Agriculture identified about 560 state growers who market their produce through farm showrooms and roadside stands. Visit www.pickyourown.org for a list of such farms in every state.

VARIETY NAME MAKES A DIFFERENCE

One crucial aspect of knowing your grower is that your grower will know the variety of vegetable, fruit, or nut that he or she is selling. On a large conventional farm, decisions as to what to grow are often made by business people or by a farmer with his business hat on. His market is the whole-saler, and the wholesaler wants a low priced prod-uct that will not spoil during shipping. Just ten large supermarket chains control 50 percent of the fresh produce in this country, and what they say, goes. But the small-scale grower has the opportu-nity to grow varieties that taste good, because that's what his market —you and I—looks for.

There's no way you can identify your own per-sonal taste profile—that is, the foods that you like the best and want to seek out—unless you know the variety of foodstuff you're seeking. Once upon a time, when I would go to the market to buy potatoes, baking potatoes filled one bin and red "new" potatoes filled another. And that was about it. Toda, I can go to the market and find Yukon Gold, Yellow Finn, Burbank Russet, German Fin-gerling, Russian Banana, Kennebec, Red LaSoda, and so on. Because I can identify varieties, I know that Red LaSoda is my favorite for making mashed potatoes, that German Fingerlings excel in potato salad, that Kennebec and Burbank Russet have the best-tasting flesh for baking, that Yukon Gold develops a sweet flavor and crispy texture when peeled and pan-fried or roasted, and that Yellow Finn makes superb french fries. The point is that there is no such thing as "the potato." Every potato is one or another of the many dozens of cultivated varieties on the market, and every potato has a variety name.

IF YOU DON'T KNOW
THE VARIETY, ASK

It disappoints me to go to a market and find fruits and vegetables sold without variety names. Nec-tarines are a case in point. The best nectarine I ever tasted was Snow Queen variety, which I discovered at an exposition of farmers' market purveyors in Oakland, California, in 1987. I was astounded at the quality of this fruit. It looked pretty much like most nectarines, with cream-colored skin and blush-red areas, but its white flesh was smooth and very juicy, with a melt-in-your-mouth quality and a succulent flavor that surpassed any other nec-tarine of either white or yellow flesh that I'd ever eaten. I look for Snow Queen in vain these days, however, because when nectarine season comes around in late June, the fruit is invariably sold at supermarkets, farmers' markets, and even roadside stands without any variety name attached. If I were a nectarine farmer and had Snow Queen to sell, I'd want the variety name to accompany the fruit right to market, so that customers in the know could find it among the fifty-two varieties sold commercially in the United States.

I believe that as consumers, especially organic consumers interested in top quality flavor and freshness, we have the right to know the name of the variety of vegetable, fruit, nut, herb, or what-have-you that is being offered for sale. The variety name should be there every time in every market. As Steve Reiners, associate professor in Horticul-tural Sciences at Cornell University, told me, "There are many factors that determine the flavor of fruits and vegetables. The most important is probably the choice of variety."

One of the useful tools in this book is a list of top varieties of produce that are superior in flavor and texture (page 479). This list will help you identify varieties you would like to eat among those available at your grocer or, if unavailable, varieties you might request your grocer stock.

I encourage you to ask your food seller to name the varieties he or she is selling. Many supermar-kets have a place where you can make suggestions on a slip of paper, and keeping variety names attached to foods from farm to market is one good

How Plant Varieties Are Named

If you go to a nursery and ask to buy a daylily, the grower will point out that there are many kinds of daylily. Do you want one that's yellow, red, orange, or multicolored? If you say "yellow," she may point out that she carries Stella d'Oro, Hyperion, or several others. It all comes down to the variety name, called the *cultivar* by horticultural professionals. Cultivar is a contraction of "cultivated variety" and is the name of the particular plant.

Naturally occurring wild plants are named by their genus and their species: The naturally occurring form of broccoli is *Brassica oleracea*, with *Brassica* being the genus and *oleracea* the species. There are many different kinds of wild brassicas. Each kind is given a species name (in other words, a specific name) to differentiate it from others in its genus.

Over the years, growers and horticulturists have selected especially delicious or prolific strains of *Brassica oleracea* that come true to seed—meaning that if their seed is planted, it will produce the same strain as its parent. These are called open-pollinated varieties. Among types of broccoli, De Cicco, Italian Green Sprouting, and Umpqua are such open-pollinated varieties, and you might find them listed in catalogs like this: Brassica oleracea 'De Cicco'. "Heirloom varieties" are open-pollinated forms of crops that have been passed down through generations of home gardeners because of their high quality.

Horticulturists and plant breeders will often cross one open-pollinated variety with another to combine desired characteristics, producing hybrids, also known as crosses. These can be patented. If you plant hybrid seeds, you'll get the hybrid that the breeders intend. But if you let the hybrid plants go to seed and then plant those seeds, the subsequent generation will revert to a fairly random genetic mixture of the parents' characteristics, rather than more of the hybrids. Among broccoli, popular hybrids include Green Comet, Packman, and Premium Crop. Horticulturists use the symbol × (a cross) to denote a hybrid, so you might see a seed catalog with the following listing: *Brassica* × 'Packman'. Usually, however, seed catalogs forego all the botanical details and simply list plants by their cultivar names.

An easy way to think of these distinctions is to visualize a slot machine where the little windows with lemons and cherries and liberty bells represent a set of genes. Pulling the handle is like planting the seed. Wild plants will almost always produce the same pictures in the windows every time you pull the handle. So will open-pollinated varieties. Hybrids will produce the desired lineup of pictures only on the first pull of the handle. A second pull (equivalent to planting seed produced by a hybrid plant) will scramble the pictures, and you won't be able to say exactly what you'll get.

suggestion for helping you to identify high-quality produce. If your market has no suggestion box, call and ask for the manager's e-mail address and drop him or her the suggestion. The more of us demanding to know what we're buying, the more likely purveyors will be telling us.

Choice varieties vary from place to place across the United States. Not all garden crop varieties do well in all climates across this broad continent, so asking your local farmers which varieties they sell is a good way to regionalize your selection of foods. Be aware that for a conventional farmer, good yields are of primary importance, while the organic farmer is much more likely to choose varieties that taste great.

BUYING DIRECT FROM THE FARMER: OPPORTUNITIES AND ADVANTAGES

Now, knowing your grower and knowing the variety names of his produce is probably not going to happen at large grocers like Giant or Safeway, or even at an upscale market, at least not on a regular basis. But it may very well happen if you buy direct from a small farm, a roadside stand, or at a farmers' market. And it's more and more likely to happen at big markets such as Whole Foods. Still, farmers' markets are my first choice when shopping for organic ingredients for my cooking because they gather growers from an entire region in one convenient place. A farm may have a few items to sell, but a farmers' market represents dozens of farms with a panoply of items.

According to the U.S. Department of Agriculture (USDA), the number of farmers' markets in the nation has increased by 80 percent since the mid-1990s, totaling well over 3,000, with markets in every state. The number of farmers who sell at them more than tripled to close to 70,000. The USDA estimated that more than three million Americans a week buy their produce fresh at these markets, and much of it is organic.

Although more than $1 billion worth of food is sold at farmers' markets annually, most agriculture is still of the conventional sort. Total farm revenue in the United States is approximately $200 billion, and only 3.5 percent of the country's two million farmers sold any food directly to consumers. By way of contrast, the federal government pays out nearly $20 billion a year to subsidize factory-farmed commodity crops that head out into a glutted global market, but it offers no subsidies to help small farmers selling fresh, organic food at farmers' markets.

The growth of farmers' markets, while still small compared with big agriculture, is encouraging. Many readers of this book will remember the plight of family farmers in the late 1970s and 1980s, when thousands of long-established farm families were driven off their land by bankruptcies and foreclosures, with terrible social consequences. The number of farmers in the United States dropped by about half in the past forty years. The largest 2 percent of farms now produce 50 percent of our food supply. The romantic idea of a small farmer earning a decent living on his own piece of land by virtue of his knowledge and skill and hard work was a dream that dissipated over the past few decades. But the burgeoning farmers' markets offer at least some hope that small farmers—with all the social, economic, and environmental benefits they bring—may survive yet. Sometimes states help out. In Connecticut, the state agriculture department developed a network of sixty-five farmers' markets in cities and heavily populated suburbs. Close to 150 farmers sell well over $1 million worth of fruits and vegetables a year within this network.

Organic versus Sustainable Farming

At a typical farmers' market, there will be some farmers who are organic and some who aren't. Those who aren't may explain that, while not certified organic, they do practice sustainable farming. What is the difference? All organic farming is sustainable, but not all sustainable farming is organic.

Organic farms follow strict guidelines drawn up by certifying agencies like the California Certified Organic Farmers (CCOF) and, since the fall of 2002, the USDA. A sustainable farm may follow organic practices, but it isn't certified. It may therefore incorporate some farming practices that are banned under organic rules. But it may also be stricter than an organic farm in the environmental practices it follows. There's nothing pejorative about the term sustainable. It simply may be the route chosen by a small farmer who doesn't want the expense and paperwork of organic certification.

California leads the country in the number of farmers' markets with over 300, but New York State is not far behind with over 250. As for individual farmers, California has over 6,000 farms that market some or all of their crops directly to consumers. Pennsylvania is second with over 5,500, and Texas third with over 5,000. Then come Oregon and Ohio in the 4,000s. California is also first in the value of direct-marketed products, approaching $100 million. In terms of the average value of direct-market sales per farm, Rhode Island is first with almost $20,000; Massachusetts nearly that much; Connecticut nearly $15,000; New Hampshire over $13,000; and California almost $13,000. Some farmers report as much as $100,000 and more of yearly income from direct-to-consumer sales, even though there are months of off time during the winter.

SOCIAL BENEFITS

Supporting farmers through greenmarket purchases insures a supply of peak-season, superior quality foodstuffs for cooks. I think of my food dollars as ballots that can be cast either for agribusiness or for small farmers. Every dollar I can spend at a local farmer's stand helps to keep that farmer going.

Social benefits include more than the support of small family farmers. A typical example is Sacramento's Chavez Plaza Certified Farmers' Market. The "certified" means that the sellers are actual small farmers, not merely vendors who buy produce from wholesalers and resell it at stands in farmers' markets as though it's their own produce. (You have to watch out for that; USDA figures show that the larger the farmers' market, the more it will allow vendors to sell produce from wholesalers.) Sacramento's Wednesday market began in 1988 and was an instant success, revitalizing a plaza that was a haunt for drug dealers and other shady characters. The success of the market has spawned an educational program run by Renae and Don Best to teach low-income children about fresh fruits and vegetables. Before the program started, some of the children "didn't even know what a peach was," Renae says.

The social benefits of farmers' markets don't end with underprivileged children. Down in Margaret River, Australia, food writer Jane Adams told a group of local farmers who planned to open a market there that "people are becoming acutely aware that in this computer-driven society, we are losing touch with each other. At a farmers' market, people go to a place where they can meet other people and connect. Coffee shops do that, and so do farmers' markets."

The twice-a-week Ferry Plaza Farmers' Market on San Francisco's Embarcadero waterfront also has an education component, run by the Center for Urban Education about Sustainable Agriculture (CUESA). Every Tuesday and Saturday, over 100 regional farmers and 25 vendors including cheesemakers, fishermen, flower growers, bakers, chocolate makers, and many others get together to sell and to meet and greet their customers. Shoppers are dedicated to their favorite sellers. Each week there's a "Meet the Producer and Shop with the Chef" event. About sixty shoppers sit around an outdoor kitchen and listen to a farmer describe what's involved with growing his or her crop. Then they see a chef prepare that crop in a cooking demonstration. The shoppers get to taste the result and can take home a copy of the recipe. San Francisco is known for its foodies, and the Ferry Plaza Farmers' Market, started in 1993, and now housed in and around the newly remodeled historic Ferry Building, is a temple to their intense interest in good food and support of the people who make it.

I asked Greg Ptucha, Executive Director of CUESA from 2000 to 2003, if the market's farmers keep variety names with their produce. "Many of our farmers do," he says. "Having the variety name on the fruit or vegetable gives the produce a little more cachet."

With the rapid expansion of sustainable and certified organic farms in the Bay Area, CUESA has been recasting eligibility criteria for would-be vendors at the market. The organization goes through an annual process as to which farmers are granted selling privileges in its market. How close the farmer must be to the city is a big question. It allows organic but also noncertified sustainable farmers.

"Our bias," Ptucha said, "is clearly in favor of the small farmer." When there weren't so many organic farmers, CUESA used to let in some big growers, but now it can be more selective. Part of the rationale is to develop sales venues for the small farmers who need them, rather than the big farmers who don't. CUESA's goal is to try to insure that within the food-shed—that is, within a day's drive from a place like San Francisco—the well-grown products needed to sustain a healthy urban population have a venue where they can be sold. This helps the urban population understand the environmental and social consequences and benefits of nearby sustainable and organic farms.

THE RISE OF FARMERS' MARKETS

The same benefits that San Francisco enjoys are available to folks in every major city in the country nowadays, including New Yorkers. I remember living just east of Union Square on 14th Street in Manhattan in my wild oats days in the late 1960s. Union Square was an unsavory place—the park itself was a refuge for vagrants and drug dealers. In 1976, an urban planner named Barry Benepe pitched an idea to the city's Council on the Environment. Why not invite a bunch of upstate farmers to come to the park and sell their produce directly to New Yorkers? If Gothamites couldn't get out of town to the roadside stands, maybe the roadside stands could come to them!

The idea worked brilliantly and New Yorkers took to it with joy. The Union Square Greenmarket sparked a revolution in the way New Yorkers thought about food. Suddenly, instead of the anonymity of the supermarket produce aisle, they

Low-income pregnant women and mothers eat more fresh fruits and vegetables when they are allowed to use WIC coupons (the USDA's Special Supplemental Nutrition Program for Women, Infants, and Children) at farmers' markets, a recent University of California study showed. These coupons are in addition to food stamps and are aimed at encouraging low-income women and their children to eat a healthy diet.

Over half of all farmers' markets in the United States participate in WIC, food stamp, and local or state nutrition programs. In addition, 25 percent of the nation's farmers' markets are involved in gleaning programs that distribute food to needy families.

The Seniors Farmers' Market Nutrition Pilot Program is a new USDA program to provide coupons to low-income seniors that may be exchanged for eligible foods at farmers' markets, roadside stands, and community supported agriculture programs. The $10 million program will benefit an estimated 370,000 low-income seniors, providing them with transportation to and from the markets through a partnership with senior centers or arrangements with local growers to take their produce directly to senior housing.

---

could talk to the farmers who grew their food. They could ask questions. They could browse the stalls for the very freshest produce possible, for free-range brown eggs, for country cheeses. With the advent of the Greenmarket, a party atmosphere had come to New York's outdoor market. Within a few years, twenty more farmers' markets had sprung up around the city's five boroughs. Articles in newspapers and magazines devoted pages to the wonderful greening up of the concrete heart of the city. Some of the first folks to buy this sparkling produce were the city's chefs, many of whom invented ways to highlight the foods' best flavors and textures.

But wait, New Yorkers didn't invent the farmers' market. Of course, cultures from Europe to Africa and Asia have been doing this since time out of mind. In the Middle Ages, Paris was a city ringed with small farms. Their produce was carted into the city and sold at stands scattered along certain streets, a tradition that continues.

The development of open-air farmers' markets in New York in the 1970s had been predated by Los Angeles farmers' market, which opened in 1934, and Philadelphia, where the Reading Terminal Market grew up around the railroad terminal that brought fresh produce to the city from the Pennsylvania Dutch farms around Reading, Pennsylvania. The Reading Terminal Market has the air of something old, long-established, but perpetually renewed by the freshness of the meats and produce and the 10,000 other gastronomic wonders you can find there. Farmers' markets in major cities around the United States are nothing new, but small farmers growing organic produce and featuring it as such in local markets is a trend that started during the 1970s after the first Earth Day and the environmental movement began its rapid ascendancy in the public consciousness.

RURAL MARKETS
AND ROADSIDE STANDS

Whenever I can, I like to stop at farmers' markets in parts of the country I'm visiting. Each region of the United States has local specialties that show up at the farmers' markets and roadside stands but are virtually impossible to find elsewhere. While Philadelphia's Reading Terminal Market was a fine slice of Pennsylvania Dutch farm produce, it was at smaller markets out in the countryside where you could find the odd and the autochthonous. Zern's in Boyertown and Renningers in Kutztown had—and still have—local produce vendors and farmers but also stands selling fresh-killed chickens, pigs' feet, scrapple, smoky summer sausage, real iron-kettle-cooked apple butter, chow-chow (a medley of pickled vegetables), fresh-caught local fish, baked goods, used clothing and antiques, hand-crafted piggy banks, and you-name-it.

The best commercial strawberries I ever found were being sold in big boxes at roadside stands along Route 13 near Salisbury, Maryland. Down south, Georgia isn't called the Peach State for nothing, and tree-ripened peaches picked that day for the farmers' markets could be the best-tasting things on earth. Farther south, I've marveled at the flavor of citrus from roadside stands in Florida. I've run across antelope steaks in Texas (I've never had a tastier, leaner, or more flavorful meat than ranch-raised antelope), pine nuts fresh from the piñon trees in New Mexico, pawpaws (native mango-shaped fruit) in Kentucky, even salmonberries, cloudberries, blueberries, watermelonberries, smoked oysters, and smoked salmon in Alaska.

Besides farmers' markets, roadside stands, and direct sales from farms, organic foods are available from many mail order sources, and even perishable foodstuffs can be overnighted anywhere in the country using dry ice and a delivery service like Federal Express. See Sources (page 517) for an extensive list of organic foods available by mail.

COMMUNITY SUPPORTED AGRICULTURE

Another way to procure organic produce eliminates the middleman entirely. It's called Community Supported Agriculture, and the concept is simple: You join a group that supports a local organic or sustainable farm by agreeing to pay for the farmer's produce in advance; you then receive weekly deliveries of the freshest food possible directly from the farm to your door. The money and farm jobs are kept in the community. There's no overhead flowing out to maintain bricks-and-mortar supermarkets and all the expenses they incur. Nothing flows out of the community to faraway companies that may be owned by large agribusiness corporations; possible exploitation of foreign farmers is completely eliminated.

Community Supported Agriculture farms also offer fruit, herbs, flowers, and other products. CSA farms, as they are known, are getting some support from the U.S. Department of Agriculture and major support from the Sustainable Agriculture Network. If you're interested in Community Supported Agriculture, the Chelsea Green Publishing Company of White River Junction, Vermont, has published *Sharing the Harvest: A Guide to Community Supported Agriculture* (1999) by Elizabeth Henderson and Robyn Van En, an excellent resource with information about the idea and participating farmers. There are also web sites that can help you connect with local farmers who participate in CSA; see Sources, page 517.

A variation in the Community Supported Agriculture idea is a service that takes your orders for organic food and fills them for you by gathering your requested items from local farmers, then delivers the order to your door. One such service is Planet Organics of San Francisco, voted the best produce delivery service in the Bay Area by readers of *San Francisco* magazine. Owned by Larry Bearg, who has a PhD in clinical psychology, and Lorene Reed, a mental health counselor and licensed cosmetologist, Planet Organics touches the community in several positive ways. First, it supports local organic farmers. The service insures that produce is handled as little as possible as it is quickly consolidated into orders for delivery. Instead of 100 families making 100 round trips to the market for their groceries, one or two Planet Organics delivery trucks make long loops around the route, saving gas and oil. Subscribers plan their shopping lists online at the service's web site (www.planetorganics.com) using the site's "Build Your Own Box" feature. The service has instituted a scrip program that donates six percent of sales to designated schools and nonprofit organizations. It has also initiated a program that donates thousands of pounds of organic food each year to the San Francisco Food Bank to assist the needy. A number of these proxy-shopping services have sprung up in the United States in the recent past.

If you visit www.vividpicture.net, you'll find a web site devoted to nothing less than the transformation of the entire state of California's food industry toward a sustainable system. It's a project of the Roots of Change Fund (www.rocfund.org), a collaborative of foundations and leading experts that supports the transition to a healthier food system and healthier environment in California. The organic infrastructure is growing strongly, but without much coordination. The Vivid Picture project aims to give an overall direction and impetus to the changes going on.

THE RISE OF LARGE-SCALE ORGANICS

More and more, organic food is distributed locally through large chain stores, such as Whole Foods, and to conventional supermarkets with organic food sections. While supply lines to these large supermarkets often stretch just as far as for conventional foods, at least the food is organic, with the concomitant benefits for the consumer and the land where the food is grown.

The organic market segment has now grown large enough ($15 billion in 2005) to attract big players. While the nation's top ten supermarket chains have grown by less than 1 percent, organic-product sales sold outside the chains grew 38 percent in the past few years. That led General Mills Corporation to buy outfits like the Northwest's Cascadian Farms, makers of organic-food products.

The trend toward acquisition of natural and organic suppliers by global corporations has prompted the remark, "How long before we get an organic Twinkie?" We may already have one. Look at the recent yearly growth in these categories of organic products, according to *Natural Foods Merchandiser*: prepared food, 37 percent; nutrition bars, 35 percent; snack foods, 29 percent; nondairy beverages, 26 percent; and packaged grocery items, 23 percent. In addition, organic personal-care products grew 42 percent, and organic pet products grew 93 percent—ten times faster than conventional pet products. "People are aspiring to an organic lifestyle," says Jay Jacobowitz, president of Retail Insights, a marketing service in Brattleboro, Vermont. "It's no longer just highly educated, higher-income people who are interested in buying these products, but more middle-class consumers are aspiring to an organic lifestyle."

For years the organic food industry and the large conventional food producers were in very different camps. The organic camp looked at conventional producers as profit-mongers who cared little about the nutritional value of their products and the pesticide residues that might lurk in them—let alone the land where they were grown

Organic Ingredients Simplify a Chef's Job

"A chef's job is so much simpler when the ingredients are good," Allen Routt, executive chef at Brannan's Grill in Calistoga, California, at the north end of the Napa Valley, told me in an interview I conducted with him one day. "So much organic produce is fresh, seasonal, and raised well. You can always tell the difference between an ingredient that's raised well and one that's mass produced."

Part of being raised well, Routt says, is the quality of the soil the food plants are grown in. He said that organic ingredients are grown in soil full of the nutrients they need to express their optimum flavor. "A good organic carrot has that golden sweetness," he says. "By comparison, mass produced carrots are almost bitter. That's why I say good ingredients simplify my job. I just need to find ways to let their natural goodness come through." He does that through balance.

"The world of cooking is all about balance," he says. "To be a good cook you get your palate attuned and then balance textures, tones, and flavors, using contrasts."

He started learning those lessons early. Most Boy Scouts aren't spit-roasting game hens on campouts, but that was Allen Routt's passion at age 10. "My parents had no idea where this was coming from," said Routt, who grew up in Roanoke, Virginia. "They weren't exactly gourmets." He enrolled at the Culinary Institute of America (CIA) at 19. While at the CIA, Routt interned with Bradley Ogden at the recently opened One Market in San Francisco. "The quality and sheer variety of product Bradley was bringing into the kitchen every day boggled my mind. I had never seen so many different varieties of incredible organic and heirloom tomatoes," says Routt. "He really impressed upon me how important freshness and seasonality are to the end result on the plate."

After graduating in 1994, Routt landed a spot on the line at Patrick O'Connell's Inn at Little Washington. From there he took a job with acclaimed chef Jean-Louis Palladin. After a trip abroad in 1998 to eat his way through France, Spain, and Italy, Routt moved to Miami, Florida, to open Mark's South Beach with chef Mark Militello, a founding member of the "Mango Gang," along with chefs Allen Susser and Norman Van Aken. This group was at the fore of the South Beach culinary scene, which Routt cites as "one of the strongest markets for technique. Chefs there have been leading the trend away from heavy reductions into different dimensions such as refreshing salsas and purees."

On the recommendation of friends, Routt then set his sights on California's wine country. "It's very similar to Europe here," he says, "with the access to small local producers and farmers' markets, and of course the wine!" He landed a position at Kendall-Jackson winery in Sonoma County, which was something of a boot camp for a chef that was new to the wine country. "I would taste different wines in the morning and create a new dish every day with the three acres of organic gardens I had at my disposal," he says.

Routt uses modern techniques to lighten traditional American dishes for today's palate. In spring, he uses a cucumber and carrot juice reduction with steamed mussels and orange juice to give the bass notes of roast beets a tangy, bright flourish. "I like the minimalist approach of Asian cooking—the short cooking times using very high heat. I don't do fusion—I try for authenticity." Despite his obviously careful ruminations on the subject of cooking, he keeps a light perspective. "With cooking," he says, "it's easy to take it too seriously. It's just about nourishment—and pleasure."

Chefs Collaborative

The Chefs Collaborative is a nationwide group of more than 1,000 chefs, food professionals, and any persons interested in organic and sustainable cuisine that's local, seasonal, and artisanal.

Founded in 1993, the Collaborative helps its members run a foodservice business in a way that is environmentally sound. It encourages sustainable and organic farming. A key insight of the organization is that chefs' ingredient choices significantly affect the marketplace and consumer behavior. Chefs have educated people to, and created a demand for, foods like heirloom tomatoes, mesclun, and artisanal olive oil. People encounter these foods and then want to buy them for their homes; eventually they became mainstream products. The Collaborative is also dedicated to using the products of and promoting artisanal producers, such as cheesemakers, who preserve or establish valuable local traditions, and as well local growers, who provide restaurants and farmers' markets with fresh, seasonal produce. The Collaborative supports folks who are working toward sustainable, organic, or biodynamic agriculture and aquaculture and who practice humane animal husbandry and well-managed fisheries. And it backs conservation practices that lessen humans' impact on the environment.

The Collaborative's primary mission is the ongoing education of chefs and the public through newsletters, conferences, and seminars. Recent topics have included the proliferation of genetically modified organisms, the recrudescence of mad cow disease, and the development of sustainable fishing practices. The Collaborative also sponsors children's courses on basic cooking skills and how their food choices have an impact on themselves and their environment. The Collaborative, Stonyfield Farm (the world's largest organic yogurt maker), and the Odwalla company publish a Restaurant Guide that lists 160 restaurants around the country that belong to the Collaborative and are devoted to sustainable and organic cuisine.

---

or the farm workers who labored there. The big food corporations dismissed the organic food producers and consumers as eccentric and marginal. But by the late 1990s, the organic food segment was showing double-digit growth every year, and that caught the attention of companies like General Mills.

With conventional food conglomerates moving into the organic food business, green shoppers—those concerned about the environmental impact of the products they buy, including organic foods—should make a practice of reading labels closely. Eco-friendly sounding terms abound on products these days. I see the term "free range" applied to chicken, and this conjures up in my mind the picture of chickens happily scratching around the yard, giving themselves a dust bath, and in other ways doing what comes naturally to chickens, including laying eggs in a cage-free henhouse. To check my impression against reality, I visited the Consumers Union Guide to Environmental Labels at www.ecolabels.org, an excellent web site for the skeptical buyer. According to Consumers Union, to use the term free range "the government only requires that outdoor access be made available for 'an undetermined period' each day. That means that the door to the coop could be opened for five minutes a day, and if the birds didn't see the open door or chose not to leave—even every day—they could still qualify as free range." So this explains why, when I visited the production facility of a local chicken ranch that boasts its chicken are free range, I found them crammed beak to beak in pens the size of small rooms.

NEW DEVELOPMENTS IN FOOD CULTIVATION

The fruits and vegetables we will have tomorrow may be more nutritious than the ones we have today, because the development of more highly nutritious cultivars is ongoing at universities and research centers around the country. One of the leading centers of this research is the Vegetable and Fruit Improvement Center of the Department of Horticultural Sciences at Texas A&M University. The goal of the center is to develop new varieties of fruits and vegetables that taste better, look bet-ter, and contain higher levels of natural disease-preventing compounds, especially cancer preventives. In one of the most promising projects, scientists are searching for those fruit and vegetable varieties that have extra-high levels of flavor components, nutritive compounds, antioxidants, and substances that research has shown to have a preventive effect on chronic diseases. The scientists hope to move varieties to market that will taste so good, people will eat more of them; and as people increase their consumption of fruits and vegetables, their diet will become more healthful. Even if people don't eat more sheer weight of the new fruits and vegetables, they'll get greater health benefits because of elevated levels of nutrients and disease-preventing compounds. Education about the new and more nutritious varieties will be needed.

It may be possible to breed more nutrition into kale, for instance, but how much kale can you eat? I once asked Joan Gussow, a nutritionist at Columbia University, a rather simplistic question: Which vegetable is best for you? "Kale is probably the most nutrition-packed vegetable, but hardly anyone eats enough kale to get real benefits," she said. "So, I'd say, broccoli is best for you, because it's almost as nutritious as kale, and people eat enough of it to make a difference."

GROWING WHAT PEOPLE WANT

Research at state Agricultural Experiment Stations is revealing some important trends for people looking for fresh, organic food. In Connecticut, for example, the Connecticut AES for more than twenty years has been operating a New Crops Program. Connecticut sits astride one of the largest consumer markets for globe artichokes in the country. Forty percent of California's artichokes are sold in markets between New York and Boston. According to David Hill of the New Crops Program, writing in the Spring 2002,

Organic Sales for 2005 Jump 20 Percent

Sales of organic food in the United States reached $15 billion in 2005, up 38 percent from 2003, according to the Organic Trade Association.

Frontiers of Plant Science, "We learned how to grow artichokes in Connecticut by modifying their growth habit to shorten their normal biennial life cycle of two years down to just four months so we could produce an annual crop. Growers in Easton and Branford can attest to the popularity of locally grown artichokes whose flavor is superior to that of 10-day-old artichokes shipped from California."

The New Crops Program surveyed consumers and growers who attend farmers' markets to determine the kind of unusual fruits, vegetables, and herbs they would buy if they were locally grown. Leading the list of forty-five items were crops you wouldn't ordinarily associate with Connecticut: okra, leeks, sweet potatoes, *jilo* (a South American eggplant), and calabaza winter squash. The reason for these choices is the growth of new ethnic communities, such as the 15,000 emigrés from Brazil to the Danbury-Waterbury region who prize jilo, or the 350,000 Hispanics across the state who use calabaza in vegetable dishes, soups, and baked

goods. So the New Crops Program began to study these crops and found that okra, leeks, sweet potatoes, and jilo actually grew well in Connecticut if cultivars developed for northerly climates and cultural (growing) techniques to shorten the growing season were used. Now organic farmers in the state can grow these specialty crops and sell them at the open-air farmers' markets that are so culturally familiar to the Hispanic and Brazilian communities, and, increasingly, to the savvy mainstream markets.

GROWING MORE GENETICALLY-DIVERSE CROPS

Another benefit of small-scale agriculture compared to corporate agribusiness is the greater genetic diversity of open-pollinated crops typically grown by organic family farmers. You may remember the outbreak of disease that ravaged the American field corn crop throughout the Midwest in 1977. The problem was that almost all of the corn being grown was the same genetic hybrid. It grew well and produced good crops, but the hybrid was susceptible to a certain fungal disease, and the crop that year failed because of it. Farmers then saw the importance of planting a diverse set of cultivars with lots of genetic variation. If one hybrid gets a disease, another may not.

Genetic diversity is recognized as crucial now among field crops but perhaps less so among fruit and nut trees. Some U.S. fruit and nut industries are based primarily on one or two major cultivars: Bing and Royal Ann sweet cherries, Tilton and Blenheim apricots, Bartlett pears, Barcelona hazelnuts, Kerman pistachios, and Hayward kiwifruit, for some good examples. And a 400-year-old French cherry called Montmorency comprises 99 percent of the American sour cherry crop. Genetic diversity is important not just because it insures a certain level of disease resistance but it also creates many and varied flavors among fruits and nuts. When it comes to what people like in terms of flavor, *vive la difference*! Greater genetic diversity results in a wider palette of flavors, on which something for everyone will surely be found.

American fruit and nut breeding has been at a disadvantage because of the limitations of breeding stock. Yes, there are native American fruits and nuts, plus many imports from Europe, but the real repository of genetic diversity among fruits and nuts is the Caucasus Mountains eastward across the steppes of central Asia through Turkmenistan, Uzbekistan, Tajikistan, and Kazakhstan and into China. For many years in the 20th century, this region was off-limits to American scientists because it was behind the Iron or Bamboo Curtain. With more moderate policies in recent years, western scientists have been able to travel to these regions. What they discovered was a dazzling diversity of new wild varieties of produce. And when these new cultivars hit the greenmarkets of America, you can bet it will be the organic and sustainable growers who will be selling them.

Artichokes in Bloom

Why Go Organic?

W HEN I WORKED at *Organic Gardening* during the 1970s, the company had a lunchroom in a house on Main Street in Emmaus, Pennsylvania, called Fitness House. Clients and special guests were taken there to sample real organic food and healthy cooking. I remember it served the most unpleasant food imaginable: unsalted buckwheat groats, sweet potatoes without butter, potatoes boiled in milk, musty-tasting sprouts. At that time, organic food was thought of as good for you, good for the environment, clean and pure, and nutritious, but not much on the scrumptious side. (I usually passed Fitness House by and went to Richard's Market for a really delicious Italian hoagie or one of Richard's hot ham sandwiches on a sesame bun with horseradish sauce and melted cheese.) Granola and groats became synonymous with organic food in many places in the 1970s. I ate many an unpleasurable meal at back-to-the-land communes from Maine to California. Thank goodness that era is long gone. Nowadays organic food has also come to be appreciated for its richness of flavor, its freshness, and its purity. But as the years passed, I wondered if a special "organic cuisine" would develop, something that could truly be called organic cooking. And I wondered what it might be.

Would it be the gourmet-style of organic cooking found at some trendy restaurants? Writing in *The New Yorker* in 2003, Dana Goodyear describes the fare at Counter, an organic restaurant in the East Village in New York City:

This is a meat-and-potatoes kind of joint, if by meat you mean "meat loaf" made of portobello mushrooms ground up with almonds, macadamia nuts, and cashews in a porcini-mushroom-and-cabernet gravy—and by potatoes you mean cauliflower and pine nuts whipped into a fluffy cumulus and seasoned with parsley and a few shards of uncooked garlic....The menu attracts a loyal crowd of long-haired sirens so eerily happy-looking and outgoing they might be mistaken for members of a West Coast religion.

While these creative dishes can certainly be tasty, connecting such fabrications with organic food is limiting—this isn't how most people cook everyday at home, and it hardly reflects the range of organic cooking.

Organic cooking is real food for real people—good, solid, everyday food made with organic ingredients. It's no longer about faux potatoes made from whipped cauliflower and pine nuts or faux meatloaf made from portobello mushrooms, and you won't find recipes like these in this book. Good organic cooking can mean cooking in any style, if only because we live in an age where ingredients once found only in ethnic enclaves in America, or in the homelands of ethnic groups, are available to us fresh, seasonally, and often in organic form. In fact, organic cooking is most interesting when it is inclusive.

To understand how organic food can enhance any sort or style of cuisine, the organic cook needs to take a good look into the heart of the organic method of growing food, because it's there that the secret of its quality lies. So, please, bear with me as I condense the knowledge I've gained over thirty years of writing and gardening into a few paragraphs that I hope will be enlightening.

COMPOST

Healthy soil makes healthy plants makes healthy people.

OLD ORGANIC MAXIM

Put most simply, organic is a method of growing food using only naturally occurring substances. Properly done, it recycles all wastes and improves the soil as it increases crop yields. Its goal is to work with nature's laws and tendencies, rather than to counteract or defeat them. Practitioners of the method conceive of all life in the system as an interrelated whole to be strengthened, rather than as a group of creatures to be selectively supported, suppressed, or eliminated chemically.

Compost is the heart and engine of the organic method. It is—the rotted remains of what was once living tissue—is both the source and destiny of life. What was alive dies and decays to form a nourishing seedbed for new life. The concept is as old as life itself. Go into the woods and look closely at the forest floor. You'll see the leaves and twigs of past years decaying to form a rich, spongy duff that nourishes the trees and plants currently growing there, which will in turn eventually die, decay, and nourish yet another generation of plants. William Shakespeare articulated it well when the Friar in *Romeo and Juliet* proclaimed: "The Earth that's Nature's mother is her tomb/ What is her burying grave, that is her womb."

Compost is the perfect fertilizer, containing plant and animal remains, which naturally have the elements needed for the construction of new plants and animals. But compost is much more than just those elements. It is teeming with microscopic life of many kinds and functions. A teaspoon of fresh compost may contain billions and billions of living microorganisms. They tear apart and digest the remains of old plant, and multiply in a tumultuous explosion of life. A well-made compost pile can reach temperatures of 140 to 160 degrees Fahrenheit generated by the furious crescendo of microbial growth as these tiny bits of life colonize the feast of organic matter laid out for them.

Within each microorganism is a fluid that's slightly acidic. When these tiny single-celled organisms die, the acid fluid spills into the water in the soil. This acid dissolves elements in the soil, forming soluble mineral salts, which further enrich the compost. Some of these soluble mineral salts, such as potassium nitrate, are plant nutrients and get absorbed by root hairs; without the acid from the compost, much of the soil's mineral salt content would remain trapped in its insoluble state—of no benefit to plants.

Meanwhile, as the old plant matter (dead roots, leaves, and stems) is chewed up by the life in the soil, it eventually becomes a substance called humus. If you could be small enough for a particle of humus to seem as big as an automobile, you would see a dark, almost black lump with deep crevices, nooks, crannies, and channels creating an enormous surface area in a compact space. If you could stretch the particle out flat, the surface area would cover several acres. This humus particle is negatively charged, and it draws the positively charged ions to itself and holds them there.

Now nature, being the wonderful mother it is, has given the "soil solution" (as water in the soil is called) a remarkable property called the cation exchange capacity. As plant roots absorb and deplete positive ions from the soil solution, the cation exchange capacity replaces the ions to keep the cations at a fixed, balanced level. The replacement cations come from the humus particles, where they are stored on those negatively charged surfaces.

There's something else about the soil cations that's remarkable. Because they are the product of biological activity, their molecules are configured in a special way that soil scientists call "left-handed." This is exactly what growing plants require to build healthy tissues, because plants, being biological entities themselves, must have left-handed molecules to work with. Fertilizers made in a chemical factory, on the other hand, have a random mix of left- and right-handed

The Benefits of Good Soil ➤

In the not so distant past, people used to ingest beneficial soil- and plant-based microbes through the food they ate, food once grown in rich, unpolluted soil. During the past 50 years, however, our soil has been sterilized with pesticides and herbicides, destroying most bacteria both good and bad. Our modern lifestyle, which includes antibiotics, chlorinated water, agricultural chemicals, pollution, and a poor diet is responsible for eradicating many of the important beneficial microorganisms in our bodies.

Researchers have recently discovered that microorganisms found in soil influence maturation of the immune system. The lack of connection with these organisms through soil may be the reason why many of the allergies, bowel diseases, chronic fatigue, and other immune disorders are now reaching epidemic proportions.

Source: Better Nutrition,
October 2003

molecules, which throws a sort of chemical monkey wrench into the process.

As soil temperatures rise in the spring and plants start putting on rapid growth, they call for more nutrients from the soil solution and the cation exchange capacity doles them out as needed. Warmer temperatures also stimulate the growth of a whole range of soil microbes, such as nitrogen-fixing bacteria. These little guys live on the roots of legumes—a class of plants that includes beans and peas. Now get this: You may remember from high school chemistry that nitrogen comprises four-fifths of the atmosphere and that a nitrogen molecule is N_2, or two nitrogen atoms strongly linked together. Nitrogen-fixing bacteria have found a way to move an electron or two around and unhook the bond that holds the two nitrogen atoms together, like taking apart one of those metal Chinese puzzles. The free nitrogen atoms then combine with oxygen to form nitrates, and the nitrates feed the beans and peas. It's a neat, symbiotic arrangement that costs the farmer or gardener nothing. If, however, you fertilize your soil with chemical nitrogen fertilizer manufactured in a factory, using costly fossil fuel (and lots of it), the soil becomes flooded with nitrogen, which turns off the nitrogen-fixing bacteria permanently. You end up destroying a free, natural system and replacing it with a costly, pollution-causing system for which you pay dearly. And yet, this kind of wasteful substitution of industrial chemicals for natural processes happens all the time on factory farms.

To put it simply, compost feeds plants what they need, in forms they like, at just the rate they require. And nature is just full of simple cycles and processes like these.

FARMING WITHOUT AGRICULTURAL CHEMICALS

There are thousands of agricultural chemicals that fall into these categories: chemical fertilizers, herbicides, insecticides, fungicides, nematocides, and a few others.

According to the Environmental Protection Agency, 60 percent of all herbicides, 90 percent of all fungicides, and 30 percent of all insecticides are carcinogenic. The organic grower avoids using any chemicals that can harm people, the environment, or the ecology of diverse creatures that are part of it. Organic food is also free from genetically modified organisms, hormones, and antibiotics. Farming can be done—and is being done all over the world—quite well without these substances.

Importantly for the cook, organic food is "thrifty." That's not a reference to the cost of production. Thrifty is a grower's term that means the plant or animal is well-built, sturdy, and compact, without a lot of weak, watery, and excessive growth or spindliness. Thrifty plants and animals are healthy, because they get the care and nutrition that their natures require. Plants have proper color and well-developed roots from being grown in healthy soil fertilized with composted plant and animal residues. Animals are lively and lean, without being scrawny; their health derives from eating a nutritious diet of plants raised within this natural system. For people a healthy diet consists of organic grains, vegetables, fruits, nuts, fish, cheeses, milk, and meat that also are raised within the system.

The organic grower works within the natural system to strengthen and intensify it for the betterment of the crops. This leads to ecological diversity, among other benefits. The more participants in the growing system, the healthier the system becomes. One reason that organic growers can do without chemical pesticides is that a naturally occurring mix of insects will include beneficial insects and other animals that feed on the pests. Surviving pests target weak and sick plants first, just as a pack of wolves will target a weak or sick animal. This has the effect of culling the crop so that the strong and healthy plants survive and reproduce. The surviving healthy, organically grown plants tend to resist pests and diseases, just as healthy human beings resist diseases. One definition of health, after all, is freedom from disease.

Without pests, what would the beneficial insects eat? Without beneficials, who would pollinate the crops? Without compost plowed into the soil, what would the earthworms eat? Without earthworms, what would nourish the plants? Without the plants, what would the pests eat? And so the interwoven web of life forms circles within circles, great and small, that add up to health and—in the case of organic food—good eating.

Similarly, the reason that organic growers can do without fungicides (which, in the process of killing fungus, sterilize the soil) is that organically amended soil is so thoroughly colonized by beneficial microorganisms that disease-causing organisms like fungi can't gain much of a foothold. If a disease-causing organism of any kind lands in a healthy soil, it finds the competition can be too tough for it to gain a toehold. A myriad of other life forms destroy it or hold it in check, multiply and cause a problem.

Most herbicides target broad-leaved weeds, leaving grasses like corn and wheat a free field to grow in. This creates a monoculture of a single type of plant over broad acreage. So along comes a pest of that plant. "Oh boy," it says, "gonna be a feast for me tonight." Under organic culture, weeds are dealt with by tillage and by interplanting crops with many other crops. This confuses

the pests. Instead of a field filled with its favorite dinner, the pest needs to search in order to destroy, and the level of destruction is much lower. Much genetic engineering of crops has been done to make them able to grow in the presence of toxic herbicides.

CONVENTIONAL AGRICULTURE

Choosing organic food creates benefits in two directions. In one direction, the choice supports sustainable and beneficial farming practices that protect the environment and make for healthier, more varied, and tastier food. In the opposite direction, the dollars spent on organic produce will *not* support some pretty terrifying developments in conventional agriculture. Although nonorganic (conventional) farming practices are said to help provide more food to people at lower prices, the practices potentially pose various hazards, as described below.

GENETIC ENGINEERING

We're constantly being reassured by the biotech industry that genetically modified crops are safe and represent a boon to mankind. But experience gives us pause.

One genetic engineering technique causes new plant varieties to develop at evolutionary hyperspeed, which allows farmers to select for more "efficient" crop varieties faster than ever before. However, this technique is accomplished by splicing genes that cause colon cancer in humans into a plant's DNA, where they cause a chain of mutations that can produce thousands of mutated offspring at a fast rate. The offspring are then screened for useful characteristics.

Once these genetically modified varieties of plants (called genetically modified organisms, or

GMOs or just GMs) are introduced into a crop, their spread may be hard to control as their pollen can spread and pollinate non-GMO plants, turning their offspring into GMO plants. Genetically modified corn was inadvertently harvested along with soybeans for human consumption in Nebraska in 2001. That corn contained a gene to produce Aprotinin, which belongs to a class of substances called trypsin inhibitors that are known to cause pancreatic disease when fed to animals. It also acts as an insecticide, making the corn poisonous to insects.

In a separate incident, a strain of genetically altered corn was found to produce a glycoprotein found on the surface of two strains of HIV and the closely-related simian immunodeficiency virus. Injection of the glycoprotein into the brain of rats has been shown to kill brain cells, while injection into the human blood stream results in the death of white blood cells.

The U.S. government ordered this corn crop destroyed, but a day after that order was given, it was discovered that the biotech company that had developed the corn had additionally contaminated 155 acres of corn in Iowa. That, too, was ordered destroyed. "This is just the tip of the iceberg," read a release from the Institute of Science in Society. "The true extent of the contamination remains unknown owing to the secrecy surrounding more than 300 field trials of such crops since 1991. The chemicals these GM plants produce include vaccines, growth hormones, clotting agents, industrial enzymes, human antibodies, contraceptives, and abortion-inducing drugs."

One of the leading developers in GMO crops and other agricultural chemicals is a company called Monsanto. Monsanto sells dairy farmers a hormone that greatly increases cows' capacity to produce milk. An international committee has found that this genetically engineered bovine growth hormone (rBGH) may produce chemicals in the cows' milk that could cause breast or prostate cancer in humans who drink the milk (see Potential Dangers in Conventional Milk, page 438).

It's becoming harder and harder to get away from genetically modified crops. Corn, soybeans, and canola seeds available for sale to American farmers may have genetically modified (GM) seeds mixed in with them, according to a study released February 23, 2004, by the Union of Concerned Scientists, an independent nonprofit alliance of more than 100,000 concerned citizens and scientists that augments rigorous scientific analysis with citizen advocacy to build a healthier environment. The seeds studied were found to be contaminated with transgenic DNA at levels of roughly 0.05 to 1 percent. At these proportions, as much as 6,250 total tons of GM seeds entered the U.S. food supply without proper labeling. One GM variety, Star Link corn, which has been banned from human consumption, was found in more than 1 percent of samples submitted by growers and grain handlers in 2003–2004.

One result of the use of GM crops is that pesticide use has risen—probably the result of genetically engineering the crops to better withstand herbicides. A report by Charles M. Ben-brook in the Organic Trade Association's Winter, 2004 newsletter, states that "the planting of genetically engineered crops in the United States since 1996 has increased pesticide use by about 50 million pounds."

China, Zambia, India, and the European Union refuse to import GM foods from the United States. The EU has passed a labeling law stating that all GM foods must be so labeled. So far in the United States, the government has refused to allow labeling of GM foods as such. However, when foods carry the USDA Organic seal, or are certified organic by a legitimate certifying agency, you can be assured that they do not contain GM foodstuffs.

HERBICIDES

Herbicide manufacturers assure us that their products are safe "when used as directed." But news reports and scientific studies raise doubts.

For example, an herbicide called Roundup is 41 percent glyphosate weed killer; 15 percent "inert ingredient," which is identified as polyoxyethylene amine (POEA) that acts like a detergent, allowing the glyphosate to penetrate the waxy surfaces of leaves more easily; and other undisclosed ingredients. Japanese physicians investigating fifty-six cases of Roundup poisoning found that POEA is three times more lethal than glyphosate, according to the British medical journal *The Lancet*.

To increase sales of Roundup, the Monsanto corporation has developed "Roundup-Ready Lettuce," lettuce genetically modified to withstand applications of the company's glyphosate weed killer. Yet those herbicides aren't doing the environment—or us—any good. Herbicides may emasculate wild male frogs, according to *Science News*. And men living in rural areas have significantly lower quality sperm than men living in urban areas, most likely due to exposure to herbicides and fertilizers, according to the National Institute of Environmental Health Sciences. And it's not just males that can have their reproductive functions compromised.

Herbicides are ubiquitous, as they evaporate and contaminate moisture in the air. Herbicides occur in rainfall all around the world. In Canada, the herbicide 2,4-D was found in rainfall at levels potentially harmful to plants. The bottom line may be good for Monsanto's Roundup product, but it doesn't look so good for the rest of us.

ANTIBIOTIC-RESISTANT PATHOGENS

The widespread routine use of antibiotics in animal husbandry causes antibiotic-resistant strains of pathogens to develop. The result is that disease-causing bacteria may be developing more quickly than the drugs we use to fight them. For example, certain disease-causing bacteria found in meat, such as *salmonella* and *campylobacter*, are beginning to show up as antibiotic-resistant strains.

A Minneapolis study by the Institute for Agriculture and Trade Policy found that 95 percent of supermarket chickens tested were contaminated with *campylobacter* bacteria, and 45 percent of ground turkey was contaminated with *salmonella*. About 60 percent of each of these bacteria, which can cause infections in humans, were found to be resistant to one or more antibiotics, including Cipro and tetracycline. According to *WebMD Medical News*, an investigation by *Consumer Report*s that tested 500 whole broiler chickens from twenty-five cities around the country found nearly half the chickens to be contaminated by *salmonella* and *campylobacter*. "Investigators also found that 90 percent of *campylobacter* and 34 percent of the *salmonella* showed resistance to at least one antibiotic used to treat people. 'There is a growing consensus among the medical community that we have a problem with antibiotic resistance,' a spokesperson for the Institute for Agricultural Trade Policy told WebMD Medical News," the online medical site reported. If an agricultural trade group is admitting that, then you can bet it's an understatement.

The routine use of antibiotics is not allowed in organic animal husbandry—in fact, if an animal is treated with antibiotics to cure an illness or save its life, the animal may not be labeled organic until it has recovered and the antibiotics are out of its system.

PESTICIDES

Pesticides are ubiquitous around the world. Swiss researchers, for instance, found that much of Europe's rainwater is so contaminated with pesticides it would be illegal to sell it as drinking water, according to the Summer 1999 issue of *Analytical Chemistry*. But Europe is relatively clean compared to the United States. America is awash in pesticides. In the year 2000 alone, nearly a billion pounds of pesticides were sprayed, dusted, or dumped on America's farmlands and orchards. And this assault continues. About 20 percent of the U.S. food supply is contaminated with toxins from pesticide residues, according to the November 2002 issue of the *Journal of Epidemiology and Community Health*.

Many pesticides accumulate in fatty tissues, such as that found in female breasts. Breast cancer patients were found to be more than five times as likely as cancer-free women to have detectable levels of the pesticide DDT in their blood and more than nine times as likely to have detectable levels of another estrogen-modulating pesticide, hexachlorobenzene, according to a study of 409 women at Belgium's Sart Tilman University Hospital. Although DDT has been banned in the United States since 1972, its residues are stored in body fat and can remain in the body for decades. It is one of the organochlorine pesticides known as hormonal disrupters. Exposure to these chemicals has been implicated in birth defects, immune disorders, and certain cancers, according to WebMD.

There probably isn't a person in the United States who doesn't carry some pesticides in his or her body. That includes children who, because of their less-developed immune systems, developing

bodies, and lower weights, are more susceptible than adults to the effects of toxic pesticides.

A 2005 study by the Environmental Working Group showed an average of 287 contaminants in samples of umbilical cord blood—meaning that human fetuses are beginning life in a stew of toxic chemicals. The report was based on tests of umbilical cord blood taken by the American Red Cross. Among the 287 contaminants were mercury, fire retardants, pesticides, and the Teflon chemical PFOA (per fluorooctahoic acid).

In a full-page ad in the *New York Times* (June 5, 2002), physicians at the Center for Children's Health and the Environment at Mount Sinai School of Medicine in New York said in part:

We are deeply troubled that an estimated 12 million American kids suffer from developmental, learning, or behavioral disabilities. Attention deficit disorder affects three to six percent of our schoolchildren…certain pesticides cross the placenta and enter the brain of the developing fetus where they can cause learning and behavioral disabilities.… Exposures to organophosphate pesticides during pregnancy can result in abnormally low brain weight and developmental impairment.… A University of Arizona study found that children exposed to a combination of pesticides before birth and through breast milk exhibited less stamina, and poorer memory and coordination, than other kids.…There is much that parents can do to protect their children, beginning with the elimination of many pesticides both outside and in the home, and in the choice of a wise diet.

For more information, see:
www.childrenvironment.org.

How bad is the problem of pesticide accumulation in our bodies? Well, in May, 2004, the

Pesticide Action Network released a national study called "Chemical Trespass: Pesticides in Our Bodies and Corporate Accountability." The study found that children between the ages of six and eleven years old were exposed to the nerve-damaging pesticide chlorpyrifos at four times the level deemed acceptable by the U.S. Environmental Protection Agency (EPA). The report also said that women carry significantly higher levels than those the EPA considers acceptable of pesticides called organochlorines, known to reduce birth weight and disrupt brain development in infants.

Scientists have compared pesticide residues in the tissues of kids eating a conventional diet and those eating mostly organic food. One such study by a team of scientists at the University of Washington's School of Public Health and Community Medicine found that children on a conventional diet had 8.5 times higher average levels of organophosphate pesticide metabolites in their urine than children eating a mostly organic diet. The researchers concluded that "consumption of organic produce represents a relatively simple means for parents to reduce their children's exposure to pesticides."

CONVENTIONAL ANIMAL FARMING

The fact that organic meat animals are raised humanely would be reason enough for most compassionate people to eat organically—but there are still plenty of other reasons to eat organic meat.

Ninety percent of all nonorganic beef raised in the United States contains up to six growth hormones that are banned in Europe because of health concerns. One of those hormones, 17 beta-oestradiol, is considered "a complete carcinogen," the European Union's Scientific Committee on Veterinary Measures reported. And all of the hormones "may cause a variety of health problems, including cancer, developmental problems, harm

to immune systems, and brain disease. Even exposure to small levels of residues in meat and meat products carries risks," said the 139-page report. The U.S. Secretary of Agriculture called the report "unsubstantiated." Samuel Epstein, MD, a professor of environmental medicine at the University of Illinois, interviewed by the *Los Angeles Times*, said, "The question we ought to be asking is not why Europe won't buy our hormone-treated meat, but why we allow beef from hormone-treated cattle to be sold to American and Canadian consumers."

IRRADIATED FOOD

It seemed like such a good idea: bombard food with nuclear radiation and all microorganisms within the foodstuff will die. No microorganisms, no possibility of spoilage if the container remains unopened. Proponents of food irradiation claim that irradiation leaves no residue in the food. But the reason why nuclear waste (the substance used to irradiate food) kills pathogens—or mice, horses, humans, or any other living creature exposed to sufficiently high doses of it—is that the streams of radioactive particles from the waste literally tear molecules and atoms apart, leaving all sorts of residues, including free radicals that can cause cardiovascular disease, cancer, and other problems. Radioactive bombardment of foodstuffs also alters DNA and RNA in the foods' cells and creates a whole range of toxic substances —formaldehyde and formic acid among them— from what started out as perfectly wholesome and edible substances. No irradiated food can legally be sold as organic.

Had enough? These items are just a handful among literally thousands of news stories, scientific reports, magazine articles, and books all describing the dangers and decrying the abuses of chemical and biotech agriculture. Many more

Mad Cow Disease Not Found in Organic Beef

The discovery of cows infected with mad cow disease in the Pacific Northwest in recent years focused a huge amount of attention on the problem. People who eat organic beef need not worry.

Organic rules prohibit the feeding of bovine body parts to bovines for the purpose of increasing protein in their diet, which is the reason beef parts infected with bovine spongiform encephalopathy (BSE), or mad cow disease, have been recycled into the food supply of cattle. Infected beef can spread the disease to humans. But organically raised beef has no potential for spreading BSE to humans.

Not only that, organic beef is fully traceable from the market meat case all the way back to the animal's mother and the plot of land it was raised on. Traceability in conventional beef production is sketchy at best.

"The green and white 'USDA Organic' seal may be little, but it carries a big message: The organic product being purchased is fully traceable, has passed rigorous inspections, and, in the case of organic beef, has never been fed any animal by products in any form," says Katherine DiMatteo, Executive Director of the Organic Trade Association, the business association representing the $11 billion organics industry in North America.

While the retail price of organic meat is generally greater than conventional, to many consumers the greater peace of mind is priceless. Tighter regulatory practices that will be implemented over the long-term in the conventional meat industry will inevitably raise beef prices across the board. The price of organic beef already reflects the true cost of a production system that protects the health of animals and people.

The USDA's National Organic Standards, implemented on October 21, 2002, include rigorous standards for organic beef production. They state:

For an animal's entire life, organic practices prohibit feeding animal parts of any kind to any animals that, by nature, eat plants. While the practice of feeding mammalian protein in feed intended for cows and other cud-chewing animals was banned by the USDA in 1997, enforcement of the ban has lagged. Furthermore, byproducts of chickens and pigs that are fed mammalian protein are allowed in feed for conventionally raised cows. Beef sold as organic must come from animals raised organically from three months prior to birth. In other words, organic beef is born from animals that have received organic feed from at least the last third of gestation.

The organic production system provides traceability of each animal from birth to sale of the resulting meat. Each cut of organic meat and meat byproduct can be traced back to its origin. If there were ever a question about the safety of an organic meat product, removal from the food supply would be swift and efficient.

The guiding philosophy of organic production is to provide conditions that meet the needs and natural behavior of the animal. Thus, organic livestock are given access to the outdoors, fresh air, water, sunshine, grass and pasture, and are fed 100 percent organic feed.

Other practices allowed in conventional beef production are forbidden in the organic system. Forbidden conventional practices include: feeding plastic pellets for roughage, feeding formulas containing manure or urea, and the use of antibiotics and growth hormones.

studies and news reports are posted daily at the Organic Consumers Association web site, www.organicconsumers.org. This advocacy group is well worth investigating if you are interested in the on going struggle over the safety and cleanliness of our food supply.

AND NOW FOR SOME GOOD NEWS...

American agriculture is a huge business and, like most businesses, does what it must to protect itself from critics, especially lawmakers who would institute rules that would cost it money. But change—though slower than many would like—is happening.

The U. S. Congress now has an Organic Caucus, chaired at this writing by Representative Sam Farr of California. It was Farr who authored the nation's first organic standards, the California Organic Food Production Act of 1990, that became a model for the USDA standards. In North Dakota, State Senator Bill Bowman introduced legislation to allow farmers to sue biotechnology companies if their genetically modified wheat contaminates farmers' conventional or organic crops.

Americans are not just knuckling under to the GMO lobbyists. In Vedic City, Iowa, the city council unanimously passed a resolution making it illegal to sell genetically modified or any nonorganic food within the city limits. Mayor Bob Wynne said people can still buy conventional food outside the city and bring it in, but the town's two grocery stores henceforth must be all organic.

In Europe, the European Union Agriculture Council has agreed that no GM product will be allowed unlabeled into the EU market. All GM food, food ingredients, and animal feeds—including sugars, refined oils, and starches produced from GMOs—have to be clearly labeled. Another regulation sets up a traceability system to track food and food ingredients consisting of, containing, or produced from GMOs across all stages of

Organics Has Its Own Congressional Caucus

The Congressional Organic Agriculture Caucus, which held its initial meeting in Washington, D.C., on April 10, 2003, was formed as a bipartisan association of United States representatives to "enhance availability and understanding of information related to the production and processing of organic agricultural products."

At its formation, it included sixteen Democrats, five Republicans, and one Independent. "Organics is one of the fastest growing sectors in agriculture," said Representative Sam Farr (D-CA), who authored the nation's first comprehensive organic standards while he was a member of the California state legislature in 1990. "With new organic standards now in effect, consumers are demanding greater availability and farmers are seeking solutions to their organic production problems. This caucus will give us the chance to discuss ways of enhancing the standards to make them workable for producers and consumers."

"The formation of this caucus is a major step towards getting organic farmers their fair share of federal agricultural resources," says Bob Scowcroft, Executive Director of the Organic Farming Research Foundation (OFRF) based in Santa Cruz, California. "Organic farmers and their supporters should call their representatives and ask them to join the caucus. When it comes to Capitol Hill, there is strength in numbers," he added. For the current makeup of the caucus, visit the OFRF web site at www.ofrf.org and visit the policy page.

California County Bans GMO Crops

On Tuesday, March 2, 2004, Mendocino County, California, became the first county in the nation to ban genetically engineered crops and animals by passing a ballot measure backed by the county's organic farmers. Agriculture officials began to enforce the ban the day after voters approved it.

Some of the country's largest agribusiness interests spent more than a half million dollars locally to defeat the initiative, fearing that it could set a precedent. Their fears were well founded, as environmental groups in neighboring Sonoma and Humboldt counties immediately began preparing drives to qualify similar initiatives on the November 2004 ballot.

A consortium of agribusiness interests calling itself CropLife America spent $500,000 on a two-month campaign to defeat the measure. CropLife was supported by local and state farm bureau leaders and members of the county's conventional agricultural establishment. But a coalition of organic grape growers, businesses, and local political figures, which spent only about $70,000 on an educational campaign, convinced voters that they should take a stand against GMO crops.

CropLife refused to speculate about possible legal or legislative challenges to the ban. Mendocino County voters in the 1970s adopted an initiative to ban aerial spraying of pesticides, but within two weeks, the state legislature stripped counties of the right to institute such a ban. Supporters of the GMO ban said they are prepared for an assault on the ban by agribusiness. "We've had this ordinance reviewed by top lawyers, who say they're confident it will stand up to any challenge," said initiative spokesperson Laura Hamburg.

food delivery from farm to processor to market. "No GMOs can enter the European market unlabeled," said Lorenzo Consoli, Greenpeace Advisor on GMOs. "This sends a strong message to commodity exporting nations such as the United States of America, Canada, Argentina, and Brazil. The times when you could sneak millions of tons of GM soybeans and corn unlabeled into the food chain are definitely over." As of this writing, GM foods are still not allowed to be labeled as such in the United States.

United Natural Foods, one of the largest wholesale distributors of organic foods in the United States, sponsors "The Campaign to Label Genetically Engineered Foods" for the purpose of getting Congress and the president to pass and sign legislation that will require the labeling of GM foods here. If you're interested in aiding this cause, visit the web site at www.thecampaign.org.

There's no doubt that the production of organic foods is exploding. In 2001, worldwide sales of organic food reached $26 billion. It's estimated to reach $80 billion by 2008. Europe is leading the global push. Germany's goal is to make 20 percent of its farmland organic by 2010. Belgium, Holland, and Wales are shooting for 10 percent by then, and countries such as Italy aren't far behind. Organic farmland in the United States doubled in just five years between 1997 and 2002. In 2002, the USDA's National Organic Program issued strict rules for foods that can be given the Department's Organic seal. From a one-page flyer called "Organic Gardening in a Nutshell," distributed by the thousands in the 1970s, the rules for organic agriculture have ballooned to sixty-three pages of government regulations, covering every aspect of organic food production. What started in 1990 as the Federal Organic Foods Production

Act, sponsored by Senator Patrick Leahy of Vermont, has turned into a federally mandated program of nationwide rules defining organics and issuing seals of certification. Many small farmers are being left out, though, as big corporations, hand in hand with the USDA's huge bureaucracy, move forward to fill supermarket shelves with organic versions of everything from fresh vegetables to junk food.

ORGANIC STANDARDS AND CERTIFICATION, AND LARGE VERSUS SMALL PRODUCERS

The original goal of organic farming was to create sustainable local agriculture, where consumers know and trust the farmers, where farms protect the environment, where the supply lines from farm to table are short (the average distance food travels from farm to plate in America is 1,300 miles). Certification agencies like Oregon Tilth, California Certified Organic Farmers, and Northeast Organic Farmers Association (NOFA) began as regional groups dedicated to assuring the authenticity of local, seasonal organic foods. Today, certification agencies like Quality Assurance International in America and Eco-Cert in Germany are global in scope. Linda Baker, writing in the online journal *Salon* (July 29, 2002), described an American certification agent for Eco-Cert who found himself in Japan inspecting a food processor who was importing soybeans from China to process into goods for export to Europe. He said to Eco-Cert, "Isn't this a little unsustainable?" The expenditure of fossil fuels to move foods over long distances and fly certification agents around the world is expensive—and the cost of certification reflects this. It is not sustainable as environmentalists think of that term.

"Sustainability" had its genesis in a 1910 book, *Farmers of Forty Centuries*, which described how Chinese truck farms near large cities recycled every scrap of organic matter—including night soil—through composting processes, back to the land. By doing so, their farms remained fertile and productive year after year, for forty centuries. Sustainability became a goal of the organic movement as it developed through the 1950s and 1960s. If food production were kept local and organic wastes were captured and recycled, the terrible destruction of America's topsoil that was going on then (and continues on conventional farms) could possibly be halted and reversed. For my part, I started something called the National Soil Fertility Program in the mid-1970s that aimed to have the USDA identify all the sources of compostables in America and steer them to composting centers for eventual return to the land. I remember importuning the Texas Commissioner of Agriculture as he left a meeting in Washington, D.C. I wanted to hand him information about the program. He refused the copy and brushed me aside, saying, "I'm not interested in that [expletive][expletive]."

A deep conflict has arisen between the big organic producers who ship food globally and small, local farmers who find the cost of complying with the USDA and paying for certification prohibitive. (The organic certifier New Jersey NOFA, for instance, charges $285 the first year and $235 in subsequent years to certify farms grossing less than $5,000; farms grossing between $750,000 and $1 million pay $2,000 plus 2.5 percent of sales.) Many see that now that the government is in-volved in defining what's organic, the race to lower standards is on. Unless organic standards are kept strict, the term organic will become meaningless as more and more compromises are made. And lower standards will not apply only to the USDA's National Organic Standards, they will apply to every certification agency in the country. The enabling legislation is written so that no local group—such as the Maine Organic Farmers and Gardeners Association or California Certified Organic Farmers may impose stricter standards than those imposed by USDA. By contrast, most federal safety regulations set minimum standards. The Consumer Product Safety Commission, for instance, encourages manufacturers of products covered by its regulations to exceed federal standards and promote themselves to consumers that way.

Many small organic farmers, therefore, smell a rat. A big "problem in the long run is that the USDA program may so debase the meaning of organic that growers won't want to be involved unless they grow for markets that specifically require [the USDA seal], like big stores or processors," says Bill Duesing, president of the Northeast Organic Farmers Association Interstate Council (including NOFA chapters in Connecticut, Massachusetts, New York, New Jersey, Rhode Island, Vermont, and New Hampshire). "I think the federal takeover of 'organic' presents a very large challenge to define and communicate the values that are important to NOFA members and aren't addressed in the federal standards—local eating, family farms, low and solar energy use, labor issues, polyculture, sustainability, connection to community, knowledge, and control. Although it would be good if all food were grown organically, that won't address the above important issues if we just end up with industrial organic, which continues to put great distance between growers and eaters while increasing ignorance in the general population about our relationship with the earth." In England, by way of contrast, the Soil Association's organic standards are stricter than those in the United States—farmers can't use peat moss for fear of destroying the environment; they can't use dried blood because it's too high in nitrogen. For years the English have

USDA Backs Down on Organic Rule Changes

Big agriculture never stops trying to water down or chip away at the national standards for what constitutes organically grown food. The latest attempts came in April 2004, when officials in the National Organic Program (NOP) and Agricultural Marketing Service (AMS)–both agencies within the USDA–released changes to the organic standards. They included expansion of the use of antibiotics and hormones in dairy cows, allowing the use of more pesticides, and for the first time letting organic livestock eat potentially contaminated fishmeal. Administrators of the NOP also said seafood, pet food, and body care products could use "organic" on their labels without meeting any standards at all. These "Statements of Clarification" were issued without any public input.

The outcry against these "clarifications" from the public, from Congress, from the National Organic Standards Board (NOSB), Consumers Union, media outlets, and many other organizations and individuals around the country was so great that within a month, Secretary of Agriculture Anne Veneman rescinded the changes. She said the USDA was "awestruck at the size and the fury of the protest" against watering down organic standards in favor of nonorganic agribusiness practices.

The moral of this incident is that agribusiness will continue to try to deconstruct the organic standards and that the USDA can't be counted on to prevent that. Only the organic community–large and strong and growing stronger–can. Be watchful.

worried that long transportation of food, "excessive food-miles," will damage the environment.

Patrick Martins, the former head of Slow Food U.S.A. has long been an active communicator about this situation. He writes the following in *The Snail,* Slow Food's American news-letter:

One word that has been totally lost by the people who created it is the word 'organic.' Slow Food U.S.A. hopes we can soon return to a purer definition of the word—not a federal definition, but one that embodies the ideas of sustainability, preserving the land, and preserving the small independent family farm. With many Americans now demanding organic foods, huge factory farms have been quick to churn out products to accommodate. But are these foods what Americans are really clamoring for? While organic factory foods do fall under the umbrella of the new federal standards, we choose to support foods and companies that fit a more holistic definition of the word organic: one that embodies an ethic that doesn't exist on factory farms. This ethic is not motivated by profit, but by taste—a love of food....[We are] asking Americans to think about what 'organic' means to them—is it a formula or a philosophy? The future of our planet depends on the answer.

One effect of the movement of large corporations into organic agriculture is that many small farmers are looking to avoid the paperwork that comes along with federal regulated organic certification. "Certification is only necessary when you're not dealing directly with the consumer," according to Rose Koenig, a member of the National Organic Standards Board, the group that drew up the definition of what's organic and what's not for the USDA. Some organic farmers who do deal directly with consumers through farmers markets and Community Supported Agriculture are resorting to terms like "pesticide free," "natural," or "authentic" to describe their produce, rather than "organic," simply because by using "organic" without certification, they risk a $10,000 fine.

For most purchasers of organic food, the most visible aspect of this wrangling is the emergence of the USDA's green and white Organic seal. The USDA seal can be used on products that are 100 percent organic but also on foods that are only 95 percent organic. John Fromer, an organic farmer who operates Appleton Ridge Flower & Vegetable Farm in Appleton, Maine, asks, "What's the other five percent? Heavy metals? It's either 100 percent organic or it's not organic, if you ask me." And although large organic farms can use the seal, that doesn't say anything about freshness, says Eliot Coleman, a Maine grower and author of organic gardening books. "I don't care if elves and fairies grew it in California, it ain't fresh by the time it gets to Maine," he says. Coleman avoids certification and the use of the USDA seal altogether in favor of labeling his produce "authentic." But a spokesperson for the Organic Trade Association thinks creating another word is the wrong way to go. "There is no 'beyond organic,'" says Barbara Haumann of the Organic Trade Association. "That would totally confuse consumers."

Two others levels of "organic" have been set up under the USDA's National Organic Program. A package can state, "made with organic ingredients," if between 70 and 95 percent of the ingredients are organic, although the "USDA Organic" seal can't be used. And for products containing less than 70 percent organic ingredients, the organic ingredients can be labeled as such only on the ingredients panel. Again, the seal can't be used.

The standards set by the USDA's National Organic Program "aid larger farmers and retailers over smaller ones," agrees Bob Scowcroft of the Organic Farming Research Foundation. "Wal-Mart is one of the largest purveyors of organic foods in the country. Having a national standard allows large chain stores to buy year-round from many states and sources according to the same standard."

On the other hand, having national standards—and collecting fees for certification—also allows the USDA to fund organic research. In a press advisory dated April 16, 2004, Scowcroft wrote that in a historic development, the USDA announced the availability of $4.7 million in 2004 and $15 million through 2008 to fund projects designed to enhance the ability of producers and processors to grow and market certified organic food, feed, and fiber products. That USDA has funded organic agriculture at all shows what a sea change is underway. It's a far cry from the days when I had to conceal my *Organic Gardening* identity in the hallways of USDA just to get an interview with a plant scientist.

Scowcroft sees two tiers of organic produce developing side by side: the big guys and the family farmers. "In this new organic world, concerns over social justice and the distance the food has traveled lost out; taste and freshness came up as most important with the general organic food-buying public. This is going to spread to the entire general public. The taste and freshness possible with artisanal production is the next great wave in

Two Ways for Big Organic to Market Locally

One way to market organic milk is to do what the Horizon company has done: Create large dairies in several places in the country and move the milk to stores from there. It uses ultrapasteurization to prolong shelf life, but that destroys enzymes and "cooks" the milk. But another way is to do what Organic Valley has done: Form a co-op of 420 family farms in seventeen states that produce certified organic milk, cheese, butter, spreads, creams, eggs, produce, juice, and meats. The products are sold locally. The farmers in the co-op benefit from the overall marketing effort and publicity that the Organic Valley brand generates. George Siemon gets the credit for developing this idea, which supports family farming and rural communities as it protects the environment. Learn more at www.organicvalley.com.

food marketing, and it's coming soon to a much larger audience," he says.

Mark Dierkhising, executive chef at Sonoma State University in Rohnert Park, California, agrees. I asked him whether the kids at the university were asking for organic food. "The student demographic has changed enormously in recent years," he told me. "We're getting more kids from Southern California. They're well traveled, food savvy and are making demands for more sophisticated dishes than just burgers and pizza. We have pizza, of course, but it's made with fresh dough starter, not just powdered yeast. We make organic chicken, fresh ocean fish, prepared the way our better restaurants here in Sonoma County prepare them. But it's not just the kids. Everyone is demanding better organic food—the kids, the faculty, the staff, the workers."

The good qualities of organic food are being brought to the attention of larger audiences through marketing orders, which are essentially a tax on growers and producers of specific commodities used to advertise those commodities to the general public. The "Got Milk?" campaign is the result of the dairy industry commission's marketing order that has spent hundreds of millions of dollars to keep milk front and center in the American eye through print and TV commercials. Now that large companies and big agriculture are going organic, much more money can be garnered from them than from small family farmers. Scowcroft says that in the 1980s, the Table Grape Commission used marketing-order money to savage the notion of organic table grapes. A large California organic grower, Steve Pavich, was forced to pay into a fund used to denounce his growing method. But all in all, Scowcroft is sanguine. "USDA's $15 million for organic agriculture research," he says, "is just a drop in the bucket (0.1 percent of its research budget, according to some estimates) compared to conventional chemical agriculture, but it's a start. Still, it's obscene that land grant colleges (the big agricultural schools) don't do more organic research."

CURRENT RESEARCH

When I went to *Organic Gardening* magazine from the Allentown, Pennsylvania, newspaper, I was still in investigative mode. The magazine was great at telling people how to compost and grow tomatoes, but not much had been done to see whether there was a firm scientific base under the organic method. Over the next 10 years, I read books and research papers on soil science, entomology, molecular biology, mycology, ecology, plant pathogens, and other agricultural and horticultural sciences and discovered, to my surprise, that there was a ton of information that supported the basic tenets of the organic method—and even that expanded them to unforeseen areas. I was never at a loss for subjects for the articles I wrote.

Such scientific research continues today and bears on organic agriculture. The more mainstream organic becomes, the more research is underway. Here are just three from among dozens and dozens of studies I unearthed in a recent survey of ongoing organic research at large universities.

▪ At Michigan State, a Department of Entomology study carries the title, "Safe-guarding the Supply of Specialty Crops for Consumers." The goal of the project is to reduce the need for synthetic chemicals in the production of fruit, dry beans, and sugar beets. Specifically, "we will concentrate on reduced chemical input, good farming practices, and alternative pest control methods."

- At Cornell University, a study entitled, "Organic Farm and Food Systems Research" is underway to develop certifiable organic strategies for controlling weeds and pests in farm crops.
- At North Carolina State, horticultural researchers are studying "Farming System Sustainability and Research Support for Organic Agriculture Production." The goal is to determine the optimal strategy economically and biologically for making the transition from conventional to organic production.

RETAIL RULES

The advent of organic foods in supermarkets has created the need for some special rules. Retailers now have rules, defined by the USDA's National Organic Program (NOP), about displaying organic and conventional items together. Large chains like Whole Foods, Wild Oats, and Albert's Organics that carry both organic and conventional produce must present commingling of the groups of produce. Bulk products—such as bins of nuts or oatmeal, baskets of produce, or packaged goods—need to be separated by some sort of barrier. There should be an "organics only" area of the storage room for organic items, separate from the conventional storage area. When boxes have to be stacked on top of one another, the organic boxes should be placed on top so that no falling product or melting ice with pesticide residues will leak into the organic containers. Retailers are urged to hold on to their empty organic boxes to move organic produce, because as soon as organic produce goes into a conventional box, the produce is considered contaminated and can no longer be sold as organic.

NOP has laid down rules for cleaning and prepping organic greens and other produce. Before cleaning or prepping, the sink basin has to be washed with a cleanser to insure that any pesticide residues from conventional food items have been washed away. Tubs or trays used for storing the produce after prepping must be thoroughly cleansed as the retailer moves from conventional to organic items. The NOP requires that prep knives be cleansed after use on conventional produce before using them on organic produce. It recommends that the easiest method of complying will be to have separate tubs and knives for organic and conventional produce. It would be wonderful if these rules were followed and enforced, but one wonders how closely they'll be monitored.

Sticker Shock

You know those annoying little stickers you sometimes find on fruit at the supermarket? They are "price lookup" stickers. They're not mandatory and not used in all stores, but they contain some useful information. Conventional produce has a four-digit code. Organic produce has a five-digit code starting with 9. Genetically modified produce has a five-digit code starting with 8.

1 Organic products meet stringent standards. Organic certification is the public's assurance that products have been grown and handled according to strict procedures without toxic chemical inputs.

2 Organic food tastes great! It's common sense—well-balanced soils produce strong, healthy plants that become nourishing food for people and animals.

3 Organic production reduces health risks. Many EPA-approved pesticides were registered long before extensive research linked these chemicals to cancer and other diseases. Organic agriculture is one way to prevent any more of these chemicals from getting into the air, earth, and water that sustain us.

4 Organic farms respect our water resources. The elimination of polluting chemicals and nitrogen leaching, done in combination with soil building, protects and conserves water resources.

5 Organic farmers build healthy soil. Soil is the foundation of the food chain. The primary focus of organic farming is to use practices that build healthy soils.

6 Organic farmers work in harmony with nature. Organic agriculture respects the balance demanded of a healthy ecosystem: Wildlife is encouraged by including forage crops in rotation and by retaining fence rows, wetlands, and other natural areas.

7 Organic producers are leaders in innovative research. Organic farmers have led the way, largely at their own expense, to innovative on-farm research aimed at reducing pesticide use and minimizing agriculture's impact on the environment.

8 Organic producers strive to preserve crop diversity. The loss of genetically diverse, open-pollinated crop species on our farms is one of the most pressing environmental concerns. The good news is that many organic farmers and gardeners have been collecting and preserving heirloom seeds and growing unusual varieties for decades.

9 Organic farming helps keep rural communities healthy. USDA reported that in 1997, half of U.S. farm production came from only 2 percent of farms. Organic agriculture can be a lifeline for small farms, because it offers an alternative market where sellers can command fair prices for crops.

10 Organic abundance—Foods and nonfoods alike. Now every food category has an organic alternative. And nonfood agricultural products like wool and linen are being grown organically—even cotton, which most experts felt could not be grown this way.

Source: Organic Trade Association

BUT IS ORGANIC SAFE AND HEALTHY? AND HOW!

For more than three decades, I've tried my best to get the word out about the benefits of organic food production. Over all these years, the agribusiness line has not changed much: "Claims of organic superiority can't be substantiated." "If we farm organically, half the world will starve." "Organically-grown food is more dangerous than conventionally grown food." "Organic food is contaminated with *E. coli* bacteria." I even saw a chemical company flack drink what he said was a glass of water mixed with pesticide to prove its safety to the House Agriculture Committee. But over this time, the evidence for the actual superiority of organic food has steadily grown, and now the claims of industry seem pitiful and ludicrous. And I wonder how that guy who drank the pesticide is doing?

A telling report by the United Nation's Food and Agriculture Organization (FAO) has a reliable summation of the safety benefits of organic food production. Here are a few excerpts.

Cattle are ruminants naturally meant to eat grass, not grain. But most American cattle are "finished" on grain diets to add fat quickly. Virulent, disease-causing forms of *E. coli* develop in the stomachs of these cattle, but not in the rumens of grass-fed cattle. It's one of the most important goals of organic beef production to keep the nutrient cycles closed, and so the animals are fed on diets of hay, grass, and silage. "It can be concluded," the FAO said, "that organic farming potentially reduces the risk of *E. coli* infection."

Aflatoxin is a carcinogen produced by a grain fungus. According to the FAO:

Two studies found that aflatoxin levels in organic milk were lower than in conventional milk. As organically raised livestock are fed greater propor-

A Shopper's Guide to Pesticides in Produce

Stonyfield Farm, the country's largest maker of organic yogurt, in partnership with the Environmental Working Group (EWG), has published a wallet-size card that lists the twelve popular fresh fruits and vegetables that are consistently the most contaminated with pesticides and those twelve fruits and vegetables that consistently have low levels of pesticides.

The results take into account washing and peeling the items; that is, if people typically wash and peel a fruit or vegetable, that was done before the testing for pesticides was carried out. For those most contaminated crops, Stonyfield and the EWG recommend buying organic whenever possible. Here are the results:

HIGHEST IN PESTICIDES	LOWEST IN PESTICIDES
Apples	Asparagus
Bell Peppers	Avocados
Celery	Bananas
Cherries	Broccoli
Grapes (imported)	Cauliflower
Nectarines	Corn (sweet)
Peaches	Kiwifruit
Pears	Mangoes
Potatoes	Onions
Red Raspberries	Papayas
Spinach	Peas (fresh garden)
Strawberries	Pineapples

tions of hay, grass, and silage, there is reduced opportunity for mycotoxin contaminated feed (grain contaminated with the fungus) to lead to mycotoxin contaminated milk.... Organic agriculture's contributions to cleaner drinking water, for example in Lithuania's Karst area, UK's environmentally sensitive areas, and Germany's water protection areas, and to higher weed, insect, and bird diversity and general environmental quality, are positive values appreciated by consumers.... Organic farming enhances genetic biodiversity, including organisms living in the soil, wildlife, wild flora, and cultivated crops. Organic agriculture practices recover indigenous crop varieties and regenerate landscapes with distinct quality characteristics. The FAO Committee on Agriculture agreed in 1999 that properly managed organic farming contributes to sustainable agriculture and therefore has a legitimate place within the U.N.'s sustainable agriculture programs.

In Europe, where folks seem to be far ahead of the United States in implementing organic agriculture, more than 16,000 people were asked by the Eurobarometer polling organization whether they favored organic farming as a goal for the European Union's agricultural policy. Seventy-two percent said yes.

Organic foods are far safer than conventional, according to a study published in the peer-reviewed journal, *Food Additives and Contaminants*. The study team included analysts from Consumers Union, the publisher of Consumer Reports, and the Organic Materials Research Institute. The data covered more than 94,000 food samples taken through the 1990s and showed that about 80 percent of conventional foods showed pesticide residues, but only 27 percent of organic samples did, and that multiple residues were ten times more common in conventional foods. Where residues were found in organic produce, they were at much lower levels than in the conventional foods. Why any residues at all in organic food? The research showed that some were long-banned but persistent pesticides such as DDT, some contamination occurred from pesticides that were wind-blown onto organic acres, and some conventional items were possibly mislabeled as organic. Levels of minerals in organic produce were about twice those in conventional produce, according to a 1993 study by Bob Smith printed in the *Journal of Applied Nutrition*. And a recent review of all the available valid research comparing organic and conventional produce conducted by nutritionist Shane Heaton on behalf of the UK's Soil Association concluded, "Collectively, the scientific evidence supports the view that organically produced foods are significantly different in terms of food safety, nutrient content, and nutritional value. Consumers who wish to improve their intake of minerals, vitamin C, and antioxidant phytonutrients while reducing their exposure to potentially harmful pesticide residues, nitrates, GMOs, and artificial additives used in food processing should, whenever possible, choose organically produced food."

For years people scoffed at the idea that organic food could have more nutrients than conventional. "A plant doesn't care where it gets its nutrients," they'd say. "There's no difference in the foods produced by these growing methods." But Theo Clark, a chemistry professor at Truman State University in Missouri, discovered otherwise. Clark and his team of undergraduate students polled households in Miller, Missouri, to assess people's expectations of organic oranges. Eighty-five percent believed that organic oranges would have a higher nutritional content than conventional oranges.

Clark then decided to analyze organic and conventional oranges' vitamin C content because, as he told a Great Lakes Regional meeting of the American Chemical Society, the world's largest scientific society, "no one to our knowledge has thought to compare organic and conventionally grown oranges." Conventional oranges looked great—twice the size of organic oranges. When Clark and his team used chemical isolation and nuclear magnetic resonance to determine the vitamin C content, though, the organic oranges had 30 percent more of the vitamin than the conventional oranges, even though they were half the size. How could that be? "We speculate that with conventional oranges, farmers use nitrogen fertilizers that cause an uptake of more water, so it sort of diluted the orange. You get a great big orange, but it's full of water and doesn't have as much nutritional value."

A Bogus Organic Food Scare

"According to recent data compiled by the U.S. Centers for Disease Control, people who eat organic and natural foods are eight times as likely as the rest of the population to be attacked by a deadly new strain of *E. coli* bacteria," said the article by Dennis Avery in the Fall 1998 issue of *American Outlook*, a publication of Hudson Institute. *The Wall Street Journal*, along with many newspapers around the country, picked it up and published the following sentences:

"Consumers of organic foods are also more likely to be attacked by a relatively new, more virulent strain of the infamous *salmonella* bacteria. Organic food is more dangerous than conventionally grown produce because organic farmers use manure as the major source of fertilizer for their food crops. Animal manure is the biggest reservoir of these nasty bacteria that are afflicting and killing so many people."

Scary stuff, huh? But it's completely bogus. Dr. Mitchell Cohen of the CDC subsequently made a public statement that "the CDC has not conducted any study that compares or quantifies the specific risk for infection with *E. coli* through eating either conventionally grown or organic and natural foods." Sharon Hoskins of CDC added that the CDC did not have any such research currently in the works, nor was it planning to conduct any in the future because such research was "not warranted." She said that "We have tried to contact the magazine and have never been able to speak with anyone at *American Outlook*, including the editor. There has been no response."

Robert Tauxe, MD, chief of the Foodborne and Diarrheal Diseases Branch of the CDC, said that there is no such data on organic food production at their centers. He issued a statement saying he had called Avery and asked him to stop attributing such data to CDC and that Avery responded by telling him, "That's your interpretation, and I have mine." Avery then attributed the information to Dr. Paul Mead who works in Dr. Tauxe's branch. Absolute bunk, says Mead.

When investigators looked into funding for Hudson Institute, who showed up as the big backers? Monsanto, DuPont, DowElanco, Sandoz, Ciba-Geigy, ConAgra, Cargill, Proctor & Gamble, and on and on. What's scary is not foodborne illness from organic food—organic rules mandate composting and fallowing that destroy harmful bacteria—but that Avery's misinformation is picked up by newspaper editors and run under headlines like these: "Organic Just Means Dirtier, More Expensive," "Organic Food—Eight Times More Likely to Kill You," and "Organic Food Link to *E. coli* Deaths."

I don't think Clark's theoretical explanation is complete. Remember the concept of "thrifty" discussed on page 24? And how organic crops get the nutrients they need in the amounts they need at the time they need and in the form they need? Those plants are growing optimally, and whatever the biological limit on the amount of vitamin C—or other nutrients—they can produce, they are closing in on that limit.

A lot of this kind of information is finally breaking through now. Agribusiness can no longer stem the organic tide, or churn out disinformation about organics, and in many ways is starting to follow the old bromide, "If you can't beat 'em, join 'em." And so we have the spectacle of organic strawberries from California and Florida being sold in winter in the Northeast, grown by who-knows-who, but certified organic by Quality Assurance International.

It's heartening, though, to an old organic hand like me to see the whole national food system beginning to move toward organic. After all, organic acres are absolutely better in terms of clean grow-power and diverse ecology than conventional acres. But the best acres are the ones close enough for me to see with my own eyes ("Eat Your View" is a popular bumper sticker in Europe), farmed by a human being I can talk to. I most fondly remember the local farmers where I bought my eggs, bacon, and milk in Pennsylvania. And now here in California I meet the farmers at one of the many farmers' markets in Sonoma County. We can talk about how the hens are laying, whether the early lettuce got nipped by the late frost, or how the wild turkeys scratch up the broccoli seedlings. Many of the wine grape growers I respect the most are either organic or biodynamic. Robert Sinskey makes his own compost fertilizer by the tens of tons, and so does Mike Benziger, John Williams at Frogs Leap, and the folks at Fetzer, Frey, Lolonis, and on and on.

Tomatillos

Talking with Farmers

T'S IMPORTANT at farmers' markets to know whether you're dealing with an actual organic farmer, who will have grown the crop, or with a purveyor, who buys the crop wholesale and sells it retail. Not only does this guarantee that the food is organic, and that the profit will go directly to the farmers; it also means you can talk with the farmer about the food, how it's grown, and how to best prepare it. A farmer can tell you much about the food you're buying. A purveyor may be selling organic food but will probably not be able to tell you exactly why the food is organic and what makes it special.

The farmer will have produce that looks homegrown: Sizes and shapes will vary. You'll find some runty beets and some oversized ones because they aren't standardized for sale to supermarkets. Some tomatoes will have protuberances. You may spy the odd bug on the rib of a chard stalk. There may be several varieties of the same food. The name of the farm may be displayed. Farmers who sell their own products will often feature their oddball varieties—like the long, cylindrical Formanova beets, their grandma's heirloom tomato, or a box of Hansen's Bush Cherries. These aren't items that supermarkets are much interested in, but the farmer may like to grow them for better flavor, as well as other practical and sentimental reasons.

WHAT FARMERS CAN TELL YOU

When I grow my own food, I know everything about its growing conditions. These are the key factors:

- I know what varieties I have planted.
- I know how I fertilized and cultivated them.
- I know what problems I encountered growing them.
- I know how this year's crop reacted to the weather and climate.
- I know whether this year's crop is superior, ordinary, or inferior.
- I know when I harvested them.
- I know what the yield was this year.

Any farmer will know this information about his or her crops, and this knowledge forms the basis for questions you can ask the seller to determine the following:

- Did the seller actually grow the crop?
- Has the crop been grown organically?
- What cultural (growing) techniques have been used?
- Has anything been done to counteract climatic difficulties?
- Was this a good, ordinary, or poor year for the crop—and why?
- How was the crop handled after harvest?
- Is this a crop to be dried, frozen, or canned, or eaten fresh?
- What's a fair price for this crop?

The real farmer will be glad to talk with you about the different varieties he or she cultivates and how the crop was grown. As you read through the entry chapters in this book, you'll discover some interesting organic agricultural techniques that farmers use to make sure the crop is of the highest quality. You can use this information to start up a discussion with the seller.

IDENTIFYING AN ORGANIC FARMER

The farmer will tell you where the farm is located—and the nearer, the better. If they're organic, they'll be able to give you details on how they fertilize the land. Ask them whether they use green manures. All organic farmers know that green manures are crops grown expressly to be plowed under when they reach maturity in order to decompose in the soil and fertilize it. Clover, alfalfa, buckwheat, soybeans, annual ryegrass, and vetch are common green manures. Along with green manures, organic farmers will use compost to improve the soil. Ask the seller how hot his compost piles get. If they are true organic compost makers, they'll know that compost piles reach from between 140 and 160 degrees Fahrenheit. Both conventional and organic farmers will sometimes use farm animal manure on the land, but organic farmers will have composted the manure before spreading it. Manure left on the soil surface rapidly loses much of its fertilizing power as the nitrogen becomes ammonia that evaporates into the air.

Another way to tell an organic farmer is to ask if they've had any insect problems and how they've handled them. If the seller says he doesn't have insect problems, that's just not realistic. All farmers have insect problems, but organic farmers have a set of nontoxic ways of dealing with them. They may use Bt—*Bacillus thuringiensis*—a naturally occurring microbe that causes caterpillars to stop feeding and die. It has no adverse effects on other plants or animals, including human beings. It's been exceptionally useful in dealing with the caterpillar stages of common cabbage moths, tomato hornworms, tent caterpillars, and many others. In most cases, it's the moths and butterflies in the caterpillar or worm-like stage of their development that damages crops. Mature moths and butterflies tend to sip nectar. Genetic engineers have taken the gene that produces the Bt toxin from the microbe and inserted it into corn and cotton, so that the corn and cotton itself will kill any caterpillars or bollworms that come to feed on it. However, because it's built into the DNA of every cell in the plant, the Bt toxin is present in all the plant's tissues, including its pollen. In 2001, scientists found that the pollen from Bt corn was drifting into meadows near the cornfields and landing on weeds where monarch butterfly larvae (the butterflies' caterpillars) were feeding on milkweed, causing a massive die-off of the monarch butterfly population. By inserting the gene for Bt toxin into crops, the genetic engineers unwittingly hasten the day when insects will develop a resistance to the toxin and a perfectly useful organic control will be rendered useless.

Another fact of nature that farmers will be intimately familiar with is how variations in growing seasons produce fluctuations in the quality of crops. One year may be a banner year for apples, but the pears may not be so good. The next year, the pears may be wonderful—big, juicy, and relatively blemish free—but the apples will be runty or scabby. The same holds true for vegetable crops. A given year might produce a good growing season for tomatoes but a bad season for beans.

This effect generally varies from place to place and farm to farm, because it depends not only on the weather but also on how the climate interacts with the farmer's own cultural (growing) practices: If he plowed too early, that could harm the soil structure; if he plowed too late, that might affect which weeds become bothersome in July. Did he fertilize properly? Have the crops been given sufficient water? Organic farming involves taking many factors into account and managing them together to bring in consistently good crops. Even when everything is running most smoothly, there's usually some crop that's having an especially good year and another having an especially bad one.

Any organic farmer will know all these things and be happy to talk with you about them. That's what farmers do when they get together. I've been in more than one gathering of farmers where one will look at the ground, scuffle his shoe on a clod of soil, look up at the sky, and say something like, "Got a lot of stem borers in the squash." This is an invitation for another farmer to say something like, "I had 'em last year. Had to plow down the whole durn crop."

If an honest-to-goodness farmer at the farmers' market tells you he's organic but not certified, it's possible he's telling you the truth. Certification can be expensive, especially for small farmers. If you have doubts, ask him what he does about weeds. If he's truly organic, he'll be able to tell you when and how often he cultivates the soil to destroy weeds. Some organic farmers use tanks of propane mounted on the back of their tractors to generate flames that fry weeds in the rows between crops, but that's rare. What they won't use is herbicides.

PURVEYORS AREN'T FARMERS

Purveyors, on the other hand, tend to have fruits and vegetables that have been sorted by the wholesaler and look neatly identical. You won't find oddball varieties but rather the standard varieties that wholesalers sell to supermarkets. The purveyor may sometimes know the variety of foodstuff they are selling but most likely won't know the cultural details—where and how the crop was grown. The farmers' market may be a one-day event for a purveyor who's ready to move on to greener pastures tomorrow. The purveyor will act like a grocer, not a farmer. They usually won't have any business name displayed or a business card to offer. If they do have a card, it will say something like "John Smith, Farm Fresh Produce." (A farmer's card will usually feature the name of the farm: "Justa Farm, Organic Produce in Season, Paul Harps, Proprietor.") It's likely that a purveyor selling truly organic food will have documentation from a certifying agency. He'll be able to name the certifier and show you the agency's symbol. He may have the USDA's green and white Organic seal. I'm not saying you have to be paranoid about food fraud, but it pays to be suspicious if food sold as organic by a purveyor has no documentation.

The benefits of buying straight from farmers are manifold. First, farmers can pick their fruits and vegetables when they are at their peak. Vine-ripened berries don't last long. They soften when ripe, and tend to disintegrate before they reach the store's shelves. But a farmer can pick his berries in the evening and have them at the farmers' market the next morning. So many fruits develop amazingly delicious qualities only when they are picked ripe, and that goes for everything from avocados to watermelons. (There are exceptions to every rule, of course. Bartlett pears should be purchased when they are still hard and preferably green, for they turn to brown mush if left to ripen on the tree.)

Purveyors, even purveyors of organic produce, must buy the same wholesale fruits and vegetables that go to the organic sections of supermarkets. So their produce is bedeviled by the same problem as the big markets: It has to be picked early to ship well and to get the premium price that the first guy in with the crop can demand. And that means watery avocados, sour kiwifruit, and insipid melons. This problem doesn't much affect vegetables—they tend to be more delicate when picked on the young side. But it certainly does apply to fruit.

Some of the finest fruits, such as black raspberries, huckleberries, and wild strawberries, are actually found only at farmers' markets or roadside stands. Picked wild at peak ripeness, these astoundingly delicious fruits are incomparable; most won't keep for more than a day. I've grown any number of commercial black raspberries offered in the catalogs, and none of them comes close to the evanescent aroma and flavor of real black raspberries from wild bushes with their dusty violet, prickly stems. Growing up in Pennsylvania's countryside, I could tell the time of year by which wild fruits were available. The farmers' market lets us reestablish a link with the seasons.

FAIR PLAY FOR FARMERS

Besides the benefits to us as consumers of fine organic foods, buying from organic farmers is definitely a boon to the farmers. Conventional farmers often see only a few pennies of the dollars spent to buy their foodstuffs. The retailer takes a cut, the wholesaler takes a cut, the shipper takes a cut, and the government takes a cut at several stages along the way. Some commodities are sold below cost, and government price supports are needed to keep farmers from going under. In fact, with some crops, farmers do go under because of lack of price supports. Organic growers get a lot more of your dollar when they sell direct to you at farmers' markets, roadside stands, through Community Supported Agriculture, and straight from the farm. This helps create fair play for these farmers, because they don't get the backing of government programs that help out big agribusiness, such as USDA's daily pricing information for conventionally grown commodities.

But things are changing in favor of the organic farmer. In 2003, the Rodale Institute, a nonprofit organic research organization, launched the first wholesale price index of certified organic foods, called the New Farm Organic Price Index, which has been given the acronym OPX. OPX allows organic farmers to sell their products competitively, using prices for organically grown food being sold across their marketing region as a guide. The price data, updated weekly, draws from the best-available public and private sources. OPX is available free of charge on www.newfarm.org. The web site will be of interest to organic cooks and professional chefs as it details interesting angles on organic production, wholesale prices, techniques, markets, and agricultural news.

If you visit, you'll see that prices of organically grown and conventionally grown foods are listed side by side. OPX tracks organic foods in the same quality and packaging categories used by conventional foods, allowing for "apples to apples" comparisons. Also, buyers and sellers of certified organic food have regular pricing information from identified regions. These statistics take into account the quality, packaging, distance to market, value-added status, and relationships to buyers. The site managers hope that listing prices will help close the gap in price spreads between most organic and conventional foods and often among organic foods themselves.

OPX covers wholesale organic pricing in the New York–Boston corridor and the Pacific Northwest, two of the country's largest market regions for organic fruit and vegetables. Prices listed on OPX are average prices gathered at wholesale distributors and retail markets. The index includes fruits, vegetables, grains, dairy, and meat. Seasonal items will appear on the index as they become available in the markets.

Knowing how organic food is produced not only gives you fodder for intelligent discussions with farmers at the farmers' markets, but it helps to justify your choice of organic ingredients in your cooking.

It's hard to remember now, but it wasn't very long ago that our food choices were limited to standard varieties of the mainstays and staples of American cooking: potatoes, squash, corn, broccoli, chard, peppers, peas, and beans. Today small organic growers can deliver many kinds of interesting potatoes to their customers; baby squashes with the flowers still on; corn that stays sweet for days after you pick it; romanesco broccoli and broccoli raab as well as the standard big heads; chard with stalks in bright shades of white, pink, red, yellow, and tan; red, yellow, orange, and green sweet peppers along with five or six kinds of chilies; peas you can eat, pods and all; and slender haricots verts and other green beans with flavors far beyond mom's string beans. And that doesn't even begin to scratch the surface of all we have for organic ingredients these days. It has only been in the last thirty years that this transformation has taken place in America. One reason is that we have, as a people, traveled widely in the world and brought ideas home. Another is that progressive chefs like Alice Waters of Chez Panisse in Berkeley, California, and progressive foodies like Sibella Kraus, who worked with Alice, have pointed us in the proper direction.

But mainly it is the enormously hard work put in by a generation of farmers who took the organic idea and made it into a reality, for the betterment

Organic farmers may sell their beef, veal, lamb, pork, or poultry at farmers' markets. But are they really organic? If they display a USDA Organic certification seal, ask them who certifies their products. They should be able to give you a straight answer and identify where the certifier is located. If they don't have a certification seal, you may want to ask them the following questions:

How Much Grain, Silage, or Concentrate Were the Animals Fed and When? Ruminants (including cows, sheep, goats, deer, and bison) that graze exclusively on grass, clover, and other green plants have the highest levels of Omega-3, conjugated linoleic acid (CLA, which has anticancer and antiobesity properties) or CLA, beta-carotene, and vitamin E in their meat and milk. However, few farms have green pasture twelve months of the year. When grass isn't available, some alternative feed is required. The best way to preserve these desirable nutrients in the meat is to feed the animals stored forage, either in the form of hay or grass (not corn)

silage. Feeding of hay or grass silage causes a reduction in the nutritional value of the meat or dairy products, but not as much as grain or corn silage. When the animals are pastured again, the nutritional value of their meat rebounds in eight to twelve weeks. The most nutritious meat comes from an animal that has been on fresh or stored pasture all of its life and on grazed grass for at least three months before slaughter. Be aware that poultry and pigs aren't ruminants. They'll always be given grain or other feed supplements, which are important for their health.

Did the Ruminants Get any Grains or Other Feedstuffs While They Were on Pasture or Being Fed Hay? Some ranchers advertise their animals as "grass-fed" or even "grass-finished," but supplement them with grain or other products while on pasture. The meat will have lower levels of Omega-3 and CLA because of the grain. Kelp or vitamin and mineral supplements are okay—they don't detract from the nutritional quality of the meat.

However, meat from an animal that has been grass fed in its last few months of life—even if the animal has also been given some grain—is still nutritionally superior to feedlot beef. You might also want to ask how the farmer knows that supplemental grain isn't from GMO corn.

Were Pesticides, Herbicides, Antibiotics, or Hormones Used in the Production of These Animals? An unscrupulous producer or purveyor of conventional meat trying to pass it off as organic will probably deny using any of these. An honest conventional farmer will own up to using them. Your best safeguard against the unscrupulous is to ask to see her certification. If a farmer says something like, "We're all organic except we do use herbicides to keep down the broad-leaf weeds in our grass pastures," then she is honest but doesn't understand that you can't be a little bit organic. Either you follow the rules or you are not organic. And the rules don't allow for any of these substances.

of themselves, their land, their products, their customers, the environment, and society. They did it without the help of government programs and often in the face of governmental discouragement. And that's not overstating the case.

COOKING LIKE FARMERS DO

The final link in the chain from farm to consumer belongs to us: the cooks. The farmer can produce the finest ingredients in the world, but it is the cook who has the last chance to either glorify or spoil those ingredients. The organic cook has a few other considerations to think about besides turning out a fine meal. Because respect for the land and environment is such an important part of the organic approach, whether on the farm or in the kitchen, it's up to the organic cook to use his or her ingredients wisely and in full, if possible.

A simple example: When I make winter squash soup, I save the seeds, rinse them off, and dry them in the oven. The soup is made from the squash flesh and stock I've made from leftover vegetables and chicken, and maybe a small piece of serrano chile. Generally I make the soup the day before I serve it, for the time in the fridge gives the flavors of the soup time to marry. Before serving, I husk the squash seeds and give them a light toasting in the oven if they haven't developed that rich,

toasty flavor from the drying. Then I crush them. After I heat the soup and place it in individual bowls, I plop a spoonful of crème fraîche in the center and sprinkle on a small handful of the crushed, hulled, toasted seeds. The leftover squash skins and seed husks go into today's stockpot, and when I drain off the liquid later, the leavings go to the compost pile or—if I'm currently keeping chickens—over the fence to the chickens. In fact, when most people lived on small family farms, the farm animals were an integral part of the on-farm recycling process for the kitchen leftovers. Today that function might be reduced to the backyard compost pile, and having well made compost ready at hand is a very good thing.

One of the problems with cooking with conventional foods is the fear that husks, skins, shells, and outer parts of vegetables, fruits, and nuts are likely to be contaminated with agricultural chemicals and therefore must be thrown away. Who wants to make lemon zest with a pesticide-laden lemon? Who even wants to take the chance that a conventional lemon might contain pesticides, once you know the dangers of these chemicals? But when an ingredient is organic, new culinary uses open up.

In such ways, and in ways described throughout this book, your organic cooking will come alive.

Roma Tomatoes

Vegetables

VEGETABLES ARE THE HEART AND SOUL of organic cooking for several reasons. First, and most important, a good diet includes lots of vegetables as the main source of nutrients and energy for a healthy body. Second, organic vegetables have the potential to taste better than conventionally grown vegetables, because with organic gardening the plants' nutritional needs are fully met and the growing medium is optimal. Third, organic vegetables are safe and, unless contaminated from outside, contain no factory-produced insecticides, herbicides, fungicides, or chemical fertilizers; organic restrictions also outlaw genetically modified crops. Fourth, the organic production of vegetables improves the soil and builds topsoil as the vegetables grow. Farm waste is composted and returned to the soil. With every acre that goes under organic cultivation, the environment is made that much purer, and the ecology of wild and domestic plants and animals that share the environment is diversified and strengthened.

Working as a restaurant reviewer here in California's organic-minded wine country, covering Mendocino, Sonoma, and Napa counties for the Santa Rosa *Press Democrat*, I have reviewed over 500 restaurants in the past eleven years and acquired quite a few ideas for preparing organic vegetables. Plus, I asked the nationwide organization of organically-minded chefs—the Chefs Collaborative—to share recipes for this book, which many members graciously have done.

SHOPPER'S NOTE: *See Top Varieties (page 479) for best vegetable choices.*

Most important, as a cook and gardener myself for over thirty years, I know how great fresh organic vegetables can taste and have presented you with my best ideas for preparing them.

"All flesh is grass," the saying goes, and by that is meant that plants are at the bottom of the food chain, and all animal life depends on them for sustenance. Without the plants, there could be no herbivores, and without herbivores there could be no carnivores. We human beings are at the top of the food chain. That means that whatever toxins are used on farm crops works its way relentlessly toward us, either directly when we eat the crops or accumulated in the tissues of our meat animals. If all flesh is grass, we better make sure that the grass isn't contaminated with herbicides, pesticides, and fungicides.

Nature has fashioned a perfectly sound and pure way to grow vegetables. It requires no toxins. All it takes from us is to turn the great wheel of life a little faster than nature might. When your vegetables are grown organically, you are assured that your food is wholesome, that you are supporting an environmentally conscious farmer, that you are helping protect all the creatures that make up the farm's ecosystem, and that you are protecting the land itself through wise and sustainable practices. The sunlight remains as pure as ever. It's up to us to make all the rest of the steps in growing our vegetables pure, too.

Artichoke

CYNARA SCOLYMUS

ARTICHOKES are most likely a selected form of cardoon, which is a large thistle found wild in Italy and North Africa that has been eaten since the first person hungry enough to try one found out they tasted pretty good. The name comes from the Arabic *al-kharshuf,* thence to Spain where they became *Al Kharshofa,* and eventually to England where in 1531 it was written that a vendor "was bringing archecokks to the king."

A variety called Gros Vert de Laon was grown in the market gardens outside of Paris from the 1500s almost to the present, although the Parisians probably had to use mulching techniques similar to mine to get them to survive through the northern French winter. The French court of that early era especially desired artichokes because they were considered an aphrodisiac. Nowadays artichokes for northern European markets come up from the Mediterranean climates of southern Europe.

Artichokes arrived in America with the Italian immigrants who settled California's Monterey County coast in the late 1800s and found that the thistle (as well as Brussels sprouts) was eminently suited to the climate. Their popularity got a boost when Marilyn Monroe was crowned Artichoke Queen in Castroville, California, in 1948.

THE ORGANIC FACTOR ◆ The climate of northern California's Monterey coast, where almost all of America's artichokes are grown, is one of cool, sunny days and cool, foggy nights—perfect conditions for aphids, and for *botrytis* rot and fungus. And so commercial artichokes are usually sprayed with both pesticides and fungicides. That's why they are blemish-free, and you never see an earwig crawl out from the bracts (earwigs love to set up housekeeping in artichoke heads). So when you get your organic chokes home, tap them upside down in the sink to dislodge any hitchhikers. Or soak them in a large bowl of water to which you've added two tablespoons of salt and two of vinegar to chase away any earwigs or aphids.

NUTRITION ► Nutritionally, artichokes are low in calories and fat free and contain a good amount of vitamin C, folate, and potassium—but their real health benefits are in the phenolic compounds they contain. Polyphenols, as these compounds are more accurately known, are also found in high amounts in cranberry juice and red wine grapes and have a strong antioxidant effect and a high free-radical scavenging ability. And there's evidence that polyphenols inhibit the body's production of an enzyme that allows arterial plaque to form.

TYPES ► Today, almost all the artichokes sold coast to coast come from the Castroville area—the so-called Artichoke Capital of the World—and are either Green Globe, Green Globe Improved, Emerald, or Imperial Star varieties suited to the climate but all similar in flavor. That's too bad, because artichokes have a wonderful range of flavors, and are found in many fine varieties currently known mostly to Europeans—although here in the United States some small growers are beginning to sell them at farmers' markets. Some growers are introducing European-style varieties to large-scale production. Another good sign is that in California, artichoke culture is moving to the hot, dry interior, which is more suited to growing European purplish-green varieties than the conventional Green Globe variety. This is also good for organic farming because there will be fewer insects to worry about in this climate.

BABY ARTICHOKES ► I once grew Green Globe artichokes in my Pennsylvania organic garden (lots of mulch pulled them through the winter), but I was eventually disappointed when the thistly plant yielded only one large choke atop its central stem. All the rest of the chokes farther down the plant were runty little things that I didn't bother with.

Of course, as is true in many areas of life, my ignorance made me see difficulties where experience would have yielded treasure. I was accustomed to thinking of artichokes as big globes to be boiled and dipped in butter or, to be fancy, mayonnaise. In Italy, though, small chokes the size of jawbreakers from farther down the plant are choice. They are the canned artichoke hearts you find pickled in the supermarket. The Italians cook them and preserve them in olive oil or cut them in half and bake or grill them, then finish them in a pan with another pan set on top of them to press them down. *Carciofini alla Giudia* (little artichokes Jewish style) dates from ancient Rome, when Jews fried the small buds in olive oil—which popped open their leaves (or more properly, the leaflike bracts) prettily. I'm beginning to see small artichokes in local markets. This tells me that there's a growing market for them as people discover how to use them. Look for very small globes with tightly closed bracts (leaves).

SEASONALITY ► Artichoke season runs pretty much year round there, but the biggest crops occur from winter through spring.

WHAT TO LOOK FOR ► Whatever size or variety of artichoke you buy, the heads should be tight. Once the bracts start to separate seriously, the choke is over the hill. Sometimes there may be brownish or blackish areas on the outside of the bracts. This is frost damage and doesn't hurt the quality of the choke at all, although frost-damaged chokes may be marked down in price—which is good for the knowledgeable consumer.

PREPARATION ◦ I find scraping tiny bits of edible artichoke from the bracts with my front teeth to be tedious (although some people love it). Instead I go for the real meat of the matter straight away. I cut off most of the stem from the raw choke (leaving about ½ inch, peeled), cut the top off the choke, remove the remaining portion of the bracts, scoop out the thistly filaments from the top of the heart with a paring knife or tablespoon, and voila! I'm left with all meat. If I'm not going to use the heart immediately, I rub it with olive oil or dab it all over with lemon juice, because the hearts oxidize and turn an unappealing brownish-blackish color quickly.

USES ◦ In Italy and parts of France, artichoke hearts are eaten raw in salads. They're shaved or sliced ultra-fine and tossed with vinaigrette and shavings of good Parmigiano-Reggiano.

Artichoke hearts can also be baked, braised, marinated, roasted, steamed, grilled, or broiled; but please don't boil the life and flavor and nutrients out of them. I like to marinate raw chokes in oil, vinegar, and herbs, then grill them. Or steam them until they're soft, then use them with lemon, anchovies, garlic, and olive oil—their Mediterranean staple friends—as foundation partners. You can dice the chokes and mix them with bread crumbs to stuff a fish or a chicken breast. In Greece they make whole artichoke hearts au gratin with kefalotiri cheese. Polish cooks will braise artichoke hearts in white wine and garlic. I've had artichoke hearts cooked with onions, potatoes, lamb, and Moroccan spices in a tagine, and I offer a version of this wonderful recipe. This dish proved to me once again that foods indigenous to a region often make excellent culinary bedfellows. Be aware that some people find that artichokes don't pair well with wine. They say wine tends to intensify the astringent quality of the chokes. I personally don't find that to be true.

KEEP AN EYE OUT FOR KISS OF BURGUNDY ARTICHOKES

CHER AND TOM FAYTER, artichoke farmers of south Sacramento County, have bred a sweet, intensely flavored variety called Kiss of Burgundy (their green is partially diffused with dark red) that's coming into large-scale commercial production. "You see it at farmers' markets in Sacramento and San Francisco," Cher told me. I asked her whether Kiss of Burgundy was bred from some of the purple European varieties. "No, it came from a bunch of junk seed from Castroville. Artichokes aren't open-pollinated; they don't come true from seed, you know. If you plant a seed, you get a variety different from the parent. So we grew out this batch of seed and started making crosses, looking for a hybrid variety that could withstand our summer heat out here in the Central Valley, then we bred for a variety that could take the colder winters we have here, then for a large amount of meat, and then for flavor." What about the color? "God just threw that in," she said. "You know, they are really good. Some guys doing a cable show on farm produce were eating them raw."

MOROCCAN-STYLE ARTICHOKE STEW

SERVES 4

The artichokes sound a woodwind's note in the symphony of sweet and savory flavors found in this simple to make stew.

4 globe artichokes
Flour for dredging
Salt and freshly ground black pepper
1 pound boneless lamb leg or sirloin, cubed
1 anchovy fillet
2 tablespoons freshly squeezed lemon juice
1/2 cup olive oil
12 scallions, white parts only, cut into 1/2-inch pieces
1 red bell pepper, cored, seeded, and cut into
   1/4-inch-thick strips
2 large russet potatoes, peeled and cut into chunks
1 jalapeño pepper, seeded and diced
3 cloves garlic, diced
3 tablespoons black raisins
3 tablespoons golden raisins
1/4 cup slivered almonds
1 teaspoon ground cumin
1 teaspoon dried oregano
1 teaspoon ground coriander
1 cup chicken stock
Steamed Couscous (recipe follows)

1. Pare the artichokes down to the heart (see Preparation, page 56) and a bit of stem, and plunge into acidulated water. Season the flour with salt and pepper, and spread out on a plate. Dredge the lamb cubes in flour mixture. In a small bowl, mash up the anchovy fillet with the lemon juice and set aside.

2. Preheat the oven to 375°F. Pour 1/4 cup of the olive oil into a skillet and brown the lamb until surfaces are browned, then remove from heat. In a bowl, mix together the artichoke hearts, lamb, scallions, red pepper, potatoes, jalapeño, garlic, raisins, almonds, cumin, oregano, and coriander. Spoon the mixture into a 9 × 12–inch baking dish. Pour the chicken stock over. Drizzle the remaining 1/4 cup olive oil on top. Cover the dish with aluminum foil and bake for 45 minutes. Remove the foil and sprinkle the top of the stew with the anchovy and lemon juice mixture. Reduce heat to 325°F. Finish cooking the stew uncovered for 15 more minutes.

3. During this time, prepare the steamed couscous. When the couscous is ready, spoon stew over each plate of couscous. ▪

Steamed Couscous Steaming couscous is a much better method than boiling it, which can turn couscous mushy.

2 cups dry Moroccan couscous

Line a colander with a single layer of cheesecloth, keeping an equal amount of additional cloth handy, and set the colander in a stockpot; fill with water to just below the base of the colander. Add the couscous to the cheesecloth and fold the additional cloth over the top. Turn the heat to high, bring water to a boil, and steam the couscous uncovered (otherwise the condensation from the steam rains down on the couscous and makes it mushy) for 10 to 15 minutes, until it is tender and fluffy. Add more water periodically if necessary to prevent all the water from boiling away, but don't pour it through the couscous—add it down the side of the pot. ▪

ARTICHOKES SICILIANO

SERVES 4

Most people cook artichokes with the bract tips still attached. The Sicilians, though, have a unique way to serve them that's worth the effort and makes scraping the flesh off the bracts with your front teeth pleasurable indeed.

4 globe artichokes

½ cup olive oil

7 cloves garlic, minced

½ cup freshly grated hard Italian cheese, such as pecorino or Parmigiano-Reggiano

1 cup bread crumbs

2 anchovy fillets, mashed

1. Preheat the oven to 350°F. Prepare the chokes by using scissors or poultry shears to snip away the spiny tips of the bracts.

2. In a bowl, combine the olive oil, garlic, cheese, bread crumbs, and anchovy fillets, mashing and mixing the ingredients together. If it seems a little dry, add a tablespoon of water or two until the consistency is that of a paste. Pull the bracts open slightly with the tip of a butter knife, and insert a bit of the paste. Do this around each of the chokes for the inner 3 series of bracts.

3. Bake the chokes in an ovenproof glass baking dish for 45 minutes to an hour, or until a toothpick easily penetrates the stem end. ∎

Arugula

ERUCA VESICARIA subspecies
SATIVA

ARUGULA refers to a set of bitter leafy greens that have gone in and out of fashion over the centuries since colonists brought the first plants to North America from England. It was popular in Colonial days but went out of fashion in the 19th and much of the 20th centuries. It's wildly popular again now.

THE ORGANIC FACTOR ◦ Much of the arugula that's grown commercially in the western United States is organic, because it's not a plant that attracts many insects. The pepperiness of the leaves is probably a defense against insect attack. But in the eastern states, the common flea beetle bites tiny holes in the leaves. The presence of some round holes the size of a pinhead indicates that the plants weren't sprayed. Careful organic market gardeners have many tools to foil the flea beetles, but if they're around, a few usually find a way to leave their calling cards in the form of these holes.

NUTRITION ◦ Arugula is a great source of vitamin C and folate and a good source of calcium.

TYPES ◦ Arugula has so many common names, and so many different plants are called arugula that it takes a botanist to pick them apart, and even then the botanists give this versatile green a couple of names—something they rarely do. While the correct scientific name is *Eruca vesicaria* subspecies *sativa,* most plant scientists just call it *Eruca sativa.*

The Latin name Eruca has given rise to a slew of common names. In Greece it's *roka,* in France

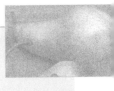

IF YOU'RE UP TO growing arugula, sow a flat of soil with seed and place it out on a deck or sunny porch. When the peppery seedlings show four leaves, cut them off and use like any other sprout. They're at their most tender and most mildly flavored as sprouts. Use them on sandwiches or in salads.

it's *roquette,* and in Italy over 2,000 years of cultivation have resulted in a bunch of monikers: *ruchetta, rughetta, regula,* and *rucola.* In England and America it's known as rocket, and in America it has still another name, arugula. You can hear the sound of the Latin name rattling around in all the common names. And there are at least three other, very different plants that aren't *Eruca* at all but are called arugula.

Besides true *Eruca,* two species of the genus *Diplotaxis* are sold as "wild arugula." One kind, *Diplotaxis erucoides,* is an herb that tastes very similar to true arugula and might be found in some farmers' markets. It's not hard to find in Italy, where it's often cooked with pasta or dry beans. In *The Cook's Garden Seed* catalog of organic seeds, it's listed as Selvatica Arugula. Another kind of wild arugula, *Diplotaxis muralis,* might also be found at the odd farmers' market or Italian market as "wild arugula." It also goes by the names rucola selvatica and sylvetta. And if you have a Turkish market near you, check for "Turkish arugula," which is really *Bunias orientalis.*

Yet another related plant, *Hesperis matronalis,* is known as dame's rocket. This is a pretty meadow and roadside weed that has naturalized in the eastern United States, but it's not a culinary item.

SEASONALITY ► Mid to late spring is a good time to find choice leaves for salads.

WHAT TO LOOK FOR ► Look for leaves about four inches long, which are at their peak of freshness.

USES ► In the spring, the young leaves have a mild peppery flavor and add zing and snap to a mesclun mix or lettuce-based salad. As hot weather arrives, arugula leaves become unpleasantly peppery and they get tougher in texture. At that stage, arugula is better used as a potherb or as a cooked green. Cooking reduces pepperiness but increases a pleasant bitterness that works well against savory and sweet flavors like beans and onions, but still, easy does it with mature, summertime leaves.

Although the peppery flavor diminishes after the plant flowers, the leaves are usually too tough then to make pleasant eating. The flowers, on the other hand, are a delight. Creamy-white little edible flowers have fine red veining and make a pretty garnish on salads, adding a light orange aroma that you can detect if you hold a handful of them to your nose. In ancient Rome, the seeds were used as a condiment, and in India and Pakistan today the seeds are pressed for jamba oil, as it's called there.

The wild arugulas and Turkish arugula are even more peppery than true arugula, and they have leaves that are more slender and finely toothed. They're usually eaten as a potherb or cooked with beans in their native country and in eastern Europe, where they're popular. Because fresh arugula gives off a warm, tingly smell, it makes a fine bed under ingredients like sun-dried tomatoes, slices of pear, radicchio, sliced chicken breast, shrimp, blue cheeses, carpaccio, pine nuts, pecans, and slivers of avocado drenched in lemon juice. Slice a piece of focaccia open and line it with a few arugula leaves, some crumbly goat cheese, and a slice of Italian deli meat for a fine sandwich. A few chopped leaves in potato salad alleviate the salad's mayonnaisey blandness.

Another interesting use for arugula is as an ingredient in creamed spinach. Make your creamed spinach as usual (see page 188), but add a cup of chopped, fresh arugula to the spinach before steaming it.

It's as a player in mesclun that arugula really shines, though, giving bite to what otherwise might be bland or bitter. Toss arugula and mesclun mix with some chopped, pickled artichoke hearts and the pickling solution from the jar, sprinkle on a few pitted oil-cured olives, then top with shavings of Parmigiano-Reggiano. Or try the following recipe.

ARUGULA AND MESCLUN SALAD WITH GRAPEFRUIT AND AVOCADO

The acidic grapefruit lends brightness to the earthy and peppery flavors of the arugula, while avocados give buttery texture and mangoes add sweetness.

FOR THE SALAD

1 bunch young arugula

1/2 cup pine nuts

1 white grapefruit

2 cups mesclun mix

2 avocados, pitted, peeled, and sliced

1 mango, peeled, pitted, and sliced thin

FOR THE DRESSING

1/4 cup olive oil

2 tablespoons balsamic vinegar

1 clove garlic, minced

Pinch ground cayenne

Salt and freshly ground black pepper

1. Trim off and discard the thick stems from the arugula. Wash the leaves in cold water until all grit is removed and drain thoroughly.

2. Toss the pine nuts in a small dry skillet over medium heat until toasted light brown. Set aside to cool.

3. Cut off the top and bottom of the grapefruit, then cut down along the sides to remove the peel and bitter white pith. Section the grapefruit into a bowl. Squeeze the juice out of the membrane and peel trimmings into a small cup and add any juice that collects in the bowl. If you don't have 3 tablespoons of juice, squeeze a section or two. Reserve this juice for the dressing.

4. Toss the arugula with the mesclun and the toasted pine nuts. Divide onto 4 plates. Lay grapefruit segments, avocado slices, and mango slices alternately in a circle on the salad. Whiz the dressing ingredients with the reserved grapefruit juice in a blender for a few seconds until it looks creamy, and immediately drizzle over the salads. ■

Asian Vegetables

various species

DOZENS AND DOZENS of varieties of Asian vegetables are available in the United States, and there are hundreds more around the world. Botanists have all sorts of trouble trying to classify them, but I take the commonsense approach: Forget the names and shop for what looks freshest. They're grouped together here in part because most are members of the mustard and cabbage family and because they appear in so many Asian dishes—Southeast Asian, Chinese, Korean, and Japanese.

THE ORGANIC FACTOR ‣ Many organic farms around the country grow Asian vegetables. You'll find them in stores from large organic supermarkets all the way down to roadside stands. One of the nation's largest organic suppliers of them is Purepak, Inc. of Oxnard, California (www. purepakinc.com), which contracts with organic growers on more than 5,000 acres to sell Asian vegetables under its PureVeg mark.

NUTRITION ‣ Most of these vegetables are rich storehouses of beta-carotene (the vitamin A precursor), folate, calcium, vitamin C, and many of the B vitamins.

TYPES AND USES ‣ Asian vegetables fall into several large groups. You'll notice the word *choi* or *choy* popping up in many of the names. (The spelling varies depending on who's doing the spelling.) Choy is the Chinese word for vegetable, and it's almost onomatopoeic when you think of chewing into a crunchy white stem of bok choy.

BOK CHOY ‣ Bok choy (*Brassica rapa chinensis*) is also known as *pak choi*; it includes leafy plants of varying sizes, shapes, and textures. The leaves of bok choy range from small to very large; some form heads, some are looseleaf. The succulent green to white leaf petioles (stalks) are universally used. In soups they add texture and bulk; in hot pots, they're a staple. They can be braised and stir-fried. They exude a mildly cabbagey redolence that instantly says Chinese cooking.

Chinese call young bok choy plants "chicken feathers." A form called "spoon type" has leaves and stalks that resemble the wide, flat-bottomed porcelain spoons used for Chinese soup. Chinese flat cabbage (sometimes called tatsoi) forms a low-growing rosette of thick, puckered, dark green leaves. Flowering bok choy has long shoots with yellow flowers and small buds.

These days I use a lot of *mei qing choy*, commonly called "baby bok choy." It's not really a baby but a smaller variety that matures at 6 to 8 inches tall (though it's often picked at 4 to 5 inches). It forms vase-shaped plants with a flavor and tenderness that surpasses the larger bok choy types. I like to place several in a covered pan with hot olive oil and some finely chopped scallions, turning them several times until they wilt and sweat and the onions caramelize a little, 5 to 8 minutes in all. Toward the end of this cooking, I toss in a minced garlic clove and some chicken stock, reduce the heat to simmer, replace the cover, and continue cooking for about 5 minutes more while I get the rest of the dinner to the finish line. The mei qing choy always comes out perfectly. For variation, I'll add a squirt of fish sauce or soy sauce or a few drops of toasted sesame oil during the final cooking.

CHINESE CABBAGE ► Chinese cabbage (*Brassica rapa pekinensis*) is also called Peking cabbage. There are two main types of this species of plant: the fat cylinders of fine, light green and white heads called napa cabbage, and the more elongated cylinders called *michihli*.

Most napa cabbage is found as barrel-shaped cylinders whose leaves curl in at the top, making the heads very tight. There's a pleasing savoy-like (crinkly) texture to the leaves, which vary in color from medium green to misty celadon to white. Their broad, grooved central white rib is a study in natural beauty. Braised napa leaves will wrap savory fillings for *holishkes*, too. But really, the flavor of napa cabbage is so delicious that using it raw in salads and slaw or lightly cooking it in a stir fry or braising until tender seems the right idea.

Besides these barrel types, there are lettucey types with more open heads that resemble romaine lettuce, as well as nonheading looseleaf varieties that yield succulent, crisp young leaves for raw salads and older leaves for the stew pot.

Michihli-type Chinese cabbage forms tight heads that are about 16 to 18 inches tall and about 4 to 5 inches in diameter. Its flavor is very mild, and so it will take on the characteristics of other foods it's cooked with. Long cooking doesn't destroy its flavor as it does napa cabbage, it just opens it to outside influences. And long cooking allows michihli to absorb pot liquors and thicken soups and stews.

CHINESE KALE ► (*Brassica oleracea, Alboglabra* Group) is also called Chinese broccoli and *gai lan*, among other names. Sturdy stems with strongly flavored, cabbagey leaves, clusters of buds, and a few white flowers are increasingly found in mainstream markets, not just Chinese specialty markets. Plants make a number of long shoots that are peeled, chopped, and stir-fried when mature. Look for tender, young shoots at the market. These will be no more than ½ inch in diameter, most of the flowers will still be in bud, and the stems and leaves will look and smell fresh and crisp, not fall limply and show brown on the cut end. The aggressive flavor of the leaves—bitter, cabbagey—softens somewhat when cooked. Stalks, leaves, and flower buds are steamed and stir-fried, or the flower buds can be dipped in batter and fried as tempura. If you're going to use Chinese kale in stir-fries or sukiyaki, it may be a good idea to blanch it first to soften and partially cook it, then add it to the wok. Served by itself as a side vegetable, it needs a sauce of some kind to bring it to life. Find the tender heart of a bunch of lemongrass and mince it finely. Mix it with a little canola oil, minced garlic, scallions, and lime juice, and pour this over the greens in their shallow dish. A simple splash of oyster sauce will do, too.

Look for a cross between Chinese kale and broccoli called Asparation (also known as broccolini; see page 76). It has loose, flowering stalks and was developed by Sakata Seeds near Gilroy, California. Besides being sweet and delicious, its dark green leaves are more nutritious than either broccoli or Chinese kale.

CHINESE SPINACH ► (*Amaranthus tricolor*) is also known as *hinn choy*. Actually, it is an amaranth, a relative of common redroot pigweed. Amaranth species grow all over the world (see Quinoa and Amaranth, page 361). The Chinese contribution to amaranth cultivation was this marvelous summer-season spinach substitute. Its leaves can be eaten raw, or they can be boiled, steamed, stir-fried, and used as a potherb or in egg foo young. If you find plants at the market with large leaves, blanch them and use them for wrapping up other ingredients.

MUSTARD GREENS ◂ (*Brassica juncea*) is also known as *gai choi*. The leaves vary in shape from curly-edged to flat, in surface texture from smooth to crinkled, in color from green to purple to red, and in pungency from mild to hot. Young leaves are often found in mixtures of spring salad greens and mesclun mixes. When mature, the long leaf stems are chopped for stir-fries and the leaves torn up for use as a potherb, that is, boiled greens. The Chinese pickle the mature stems and use varieties with swollen stems as a preserved vegetable.

SEASONALITY ◂ Like many in the crucifer, or brassica, family, Chinese vegetables are at their peak of quality in the fall through spring, although they are sold year around. They like the cool weather; in fact, frost actually converts some of their starch into sugar, making them sweeter.

WHAT TO LOOK FOR ◂ The fresher the better is the rule in much Asian cooking. Check the stems of Asian vegetables. They should be turgid and snap. The leaves should look bright. Heads of Chinese cabbage should have a clean, fresh appearance where they were cut from their roots.

KIM CHEE

MAKES 2 QUARTS

Kim chee is a kind of Korean sauerkraut flavored with chile peppers. It ranges from spicy to hot as hell and is absolutely delicious. You can buy it in jars in good grocery stores and Korean markets, but the homemade kind is more traditional, easy to make, and very tasty. It is served as a side dish at most Korean main meals.

1 head Chinese cabbage, cored and shredded
1 bunch scallions (white and green parts), chopped
1 cup grated carrots

½ cup grated daikon radish
3 garlic cloves, minced
1 teaspoon cayenne
2 tablespoons kosher salt
1 tablespoon grated fresh ginger
Unseasoned rice vinegar, as needed

1. Place everything except the vinegar in a strong bowl (I used a wooden bowl but a strong stoneware bowl would work). Using a wooden mallet, meat tenderizer, or the blunt handle of a large cleaver, pound everything together until cabbage is mashed and its juices are flowing.

2. Place the mixture in quart-size Mason jars—you'll probably need two. Use the mallet to press the mixture firmly into the jars until the juices cover the mixture and the top of the kim chee is about ³/4 inch below the lid. If you don't have enough liquid, either add more pressed-out cabbage juice or top with rice vinegar or water. Lightly screw down the lids just until they resist. Allow the jars to sit on the counter at room temperature for 3 days, then refrigerate. Use within 2 weeks. ▪

HALIBUT WRAPPED IN CHINESE CABBAGE LEAVES

SERVES 3

I'm always looking for delicate ways to cook fish—especially halibut, which overcooks easily. Here's a recipe that will have the fish lovers in your family standing up and applauding.

1 head Chinese cabbage
2 tablespoons whole grain Dijon mustard
1 tablespoon prepared Chinese hot mustard
Juice of 1 lemon
1 tablespoon grated fresh ginger
3 (8-ounce) pieces halibut fillet
½ cup chicken stock   *continued*

1. Get water boiling in a large, ovenproof skillet, select 6 of the largest unbroken leaves from the cabbage, using a knife to remove them at the base where they attach to the core. Braise 2 leaves at a time in the boiling water for about 6 minutes, until the wide central ribs of the leaves bend easily. Take them out of the water, spread out flat on paper towels, and let cool. Set them aside and repeat until all 6 leaves are braised and cooled.

2. In a small bowl, combine the mustards, lemon juice, and fresh ginger to make a thin paste. Return the skillet of water to high heat and start it boiling. Lightly oil a medium baking dish. Preheat oven to 300°F. Position a rack in the bottom third of the oven and a second rack in the top third.

3. Lay one braised cabbage leaf on a cutting board. Take a piece of halibut in one hand and with the other hand smear its surface with a teaspoon or so of the paste, then place the smeared side down on the leaf. Smear the top of the fish with another teaspoon of paste—but not more. Lay a second leaf on top pointed in the opposite direction, and tuck the ends of the bottom leaf under the ends of the top leaf. Repeat until all three pieces are wrapped, and gently lay them side by side in the prepared baking dish.

4. Place the skillet of boiling water on the bottom rack, and the baking dish with the halibut on the top rack of the oven. Bake for exactly 30 minutes. After 25 minutes, open the door and pour the chicken stock into the baking dish to keep things moist (although the halibut and cabbage leaves will have probably given up some of their juice to the pan). Serve immediately. ■

SUKIYAKI

SERVES 4

This traditional Japanese dish of simmering beef and vegetables has as much to do with togetherness and sociability as it does with nourishment. Just what our American culture needs.

1 cup sushi rice

1/2 cup tamari

1/2 cup sugar

2 tablespoons mirin (Japanese sweet rice wine)

2/3 pound Chinese kale

3 to 4 ounces beef fat, in 1 chunk

1 pound lean beef (such as sirloin), sliced very thin across the grain

1 pound firm tofu, cut into bite-size cubes

2 (8-ounce) cans bamboo shoots, drained and sliced thin

8 ounces fresh bean sprouts

8 fresh cremini mushrooms, sliced 1/4 inch thick

1 bunch scallions (white and green parts), cut into 2-inch lengths

1. About one hour before dinner, prepare the rice according to the instructions for boiling short-grain white rice on page 368. Don't remove the cover until you're ready to serve the rice.

2. To make the sauce: In a medium bowl, mix the tamari, sugar, 1 cup water, and mirin; reserve. Bring a skillet full of water to a boil and blanch the Chinese kale until it's a lively green, about 3 minutes; reserve.

3. To make the sukiyaki: Heat a large skillet until the fat sizzles when you touch it to the pan. Add the fat and move it around so the skillet is coated with melted fat. Place half the sliced beef in a corner of the pan and toss it a few times for a minute until it browns a little. Place about half of the tofu, bamboo shoots, bean sprouts, Chinese kale, and mushrooms each in their own spots in the pan. Drizzle half the reserved sauce over the meat and vegetables and

reduce heat to medium-low. Simmer for 5 minutes, then carefully turn each portion over. Make an empty space in the center of the skillet and put in half the scallions. Simmer 4 or 5 more minutes.

4. To serve: Have people seated at the table. Warm four bowls by adding warm water, then wiping dry with a towel. Using chopsticks (if you have them) serve each person one quarter of the cooked meat into his or her bowl, then give each person a quarter of the tofu and vegetables, but not the scallions. By the time everyone is served, the scallions should be done perfectly. Serve them equally. Accompany the sukiyaki with the cooked rice. Traditionally, each diner gets a bowl with a lightly beaten raw egg and dips mouthfuls of the sukiyaki in the egg to cool it off. These days we worry about salmonella so I leave out the raw egg. When folks are about halfway through the first round, begin to cook the rest of the sukiyaki by the same method. By the time they're done, it will be ready. ∎

Asparagus

ASPARAGUS OFFICINALIS

ASPARAGUS is a hardy plant that grows throughout the United States wherever the soil is well-drained. It prefers a loamy, sandy soil but will grow in almost any type except very alkaline desert soil. Because it needs regular water, it naturalizes only east of the Rockies, but needs irrigation in the desert Southwest and California. It's a perennial garden crop and will produce spears for many years if fed regularly with well-made compost.

THE ORGANIC FACTOR ◆ You should be able to find locally grown, organic asparagus in both supermarkets and farmers' markets throughout asparagus season, from spring through September. Because the standard varieties of asparagus are susceptible to asparagus beetles, red spider mites, rust, and fusarium wilt, conventional farms may spray both pesticides and fungicides. Certified organic asparagus will have none of that and will not need it if the variety is Jersey Knight, which is more disease resistant than the standard Washington State strains.

NUTRITION ◆ Green asparagus is a prime source of folic acid. Just ½ cup provides one-third of the recommended daily amount of this nutrient. The ghostly white blanched asparagus favored in Europe is not nearly as fully flavored nor as rich in trace elements like zinc, manganese, iron, and calcium as green or purple types.

Some people have a gene that imparts an unpleasant odor to their urine if they eat asparagus, and some are susceptible to dermatitis if they eat the vegetable raw, still others find the plants' little red berries that form on the ferny fronds of the mature plant poisonous. My advice is to leave the berries alone, whether you are susceptible or not.

TYPES ◆ In addition to green and purple asparagus, there is also white asparagus. I know gourmets just love white asparagus, but I find it lacks flavor.

SEASONALITY ◆ Fresh asparagus is the vegetable world's herald of true spring—the real, cottony, lush, flowery spring of April and May. Fresh, locally grown organic asparagus arrives in the stores and markets in most of the country then, and at an affordable price.

In addition to spring asparagus, summer and fall asparagus can be grown in most parts of the country. The asparagus plant doesn't care when you harvest its spears, as long as you only harvest them for three or four weeks and let the spears

PERHAPS THE BEST WAY to enjoy spring asparagus is to find patches of it growing wild. Birds eat asparagus seeds and deposit them along field edges and stream banks and in wild places that get at least five hours a day of sunlight, so these are all good places to look. A good guide to turn to for this is Euell Gibbons's book from the 1960s, *Stalking the Wild Asparagus*, a book about foraging wild food. I went foraging one fine spring day in 1970 in rural eastern Pennsylvania and came back to my friend's house with a bag full of wild asparagus and morel mushrooms (which can often be found growing near wild asparagus). If you forage for wild asparagus, be careful not to gather it near waste disposal sites, as asparagus has been shown to take up heavy metals from the soil.

grow as they will at other times. So growers may harvest only part of their beds in the spring, letting the rest grow into ferny tops, and later cut these tops off at ground level in June, July, or August. The plants in those newly cut beds will send up new spears that can be harvested for three or four weeks.

WHAT TO LOOK FOR ◆ What you want are sweet, succulent, tender spears, which raises the question of whether thick or thin spears are more tender. Going against common sense, the thicker the spear, the more tender it is. The reason is that each spear, no matter what its size, has a set number of tough fibers that run its length. In a small spear, they're crammed closer together and there's less of that juicy white meat between them. In the fatter spears, the fibers are farther apart, separated by more tender, sweet meat. While larger spears are more tender, the smaller spears have their flavor components packed in a smaller space and so can be more flavorful.

As an aside, the size of asparagus spears does not reflect their maturity but rather depends on following four factors: variety (for example, a new variety called Grande has been bred for size), the amount of water the plant gets (abundant water

equals large spears), planting depth (deeper planting means larger spears), and soil's organic matter (a rich compost-amended soil allows the plant to produce fat, tender spears).

PREPARATION ◆ Grasp the cut end in one hand and a spot a few inches from the tip in the other. Bend each spear until it snaps. That separates the tough part of the spear from the part that will prove tender enough to eat. (The tough ends can go into the soup pot.) Some people recommend peeling the lower ends of the spears with a vegetable peeler or sharp knife, but that's tedious busywork in my book. When they snap, the tip part is usually plenty tender from tip to the break.

USES ◆ Many people think that the only way to cook asparagus is to boil it and serve it steaming hot to the table. But that only begins to unearth the riches of this vegetable. Roasting does for asparagus what it does for beets—intensifies the flavor and gives it a bit of caramelized richness. Drizzle fat spears with olive oil, sprinkle some kosher salt over them, toss the spears until they're coated with oil, and roast in a 450°F oven for 5 minutes. At the end of 5 minutes, give the skillet a shake and turn the spears over with a spatula, then close the door for five more minutes. As they come out of the oven, squeeze the juice of half of a lime over them, and immediately serve as a side dish. Use thick spears for this method, as thin spears can toughen up in the hot oven.

If you haven't tried grilling the spears, you'll find that this method of cooking works nearly as well as roasting in terms of enriching the flavor. I use a grill basket with wire mesh, so the spears don't slip sideways and down between the grill's rods. Toss fat spears with oil and a little salt and grill them over a fire that's died down to a nice even medium heat. Grill for 12 minutes, turning them once about halfway through. Make sure they don't burn— burnt asparagus is bitter and unpleasant.

Steaming is a fine way to cook asparagus without boiling the nutrients out of them and is good for slender spears as it keeps them tender. Lightly steamed—about 4 or 5 minutes—thin asparagus gains a rich, sweet, green pea character. When I'm making asparagus risotto, for instance, I generally steam the tips, then add to the risotto as it nears completion. Lightly steamed asparagus can be pureed and made into a fine cold soup with a vegetable stock base. Swirl in a tablespoon of crème fraîche mixed with a teaspoon of lemon juice before serving.

If you choose to boil them, do it over medium heat in a covered skillet with ½ inch of simmering salted water. Check it frequently during a 10-minute boil to make sure the water doesn't boil away, and turn the spears once or twice. When properly cooked, they should be bright green. If the color goes dull and is more olive than green, they're overcooked. Asparagus should always have some turgidity in the finished spear.

Asian cooks cut spears on the bias and stir-fry them in hot oil, and sautéing is a way to achieve sort of the same result without using a wok.

Raw asparagus, served thinly sliced on a tray of crudités, has its virtues: a crisp texture and a green, herbaceous taste.

When asparagus comes into season in mid-spring, that's also when the morel mushrooms show up in abandoned apple orchards and woodland sites. Edibles that come into season together often go together on the plate, and asparagus and morels prove the point. Try tossing chopped, sautéed morels with your asparagus.

The old-fashioned German and Polish way to serve boiled asparagus is to dress the spears with bread crumbs browned in butter. Today we might use olive oil and bread crumbs or wheat germ. In the Czech Republic, spears are often baked in a casserole with milk, cheese, and nutmeg. Grated Gruyère, Cheddar, or kasseri cheese work well in this dish. Prepare 1 pound of spears and place them in a covered casserole. Melt ¼ pound of cheese in a saucepan over low heat. When melted, grate ¼ teaspoon of nutmeg into the cheese and pour over the asparagus. Bake covered in a 350°F oven for 30 minutes.

STEAMED ASPARAGUS WITH HOLLANDAISE SAUCE

SERVES 3 TO 4

Asparagus has such a delicate and subtle flavor that it's easily overwhelmed by too many other ingredients. But it always goes perfectly with three flavors: egg yolks, lemon, and butter. And when you combine those three other ingredients correctly, you get hollandaise sauce. One taste of this dish will reveal why hollandaise is the sauce that brings asparagus to life.

You can make hollandaise by hand in a double boiler, but I find the following method to be so much easier and really foolproof, that I've dispensed with the whisk and the worry.

continued

1 pound fresh asparagus, prepared

FOR THE HOLLANDAISE

3 egg yolks

2 tablespoons freshly squeezed lemon juice

Salt and freshly ground pepper

1 stick (¼ pound) butter

1. Steam the asparagus in a vegetable steamer for 4 to 5 minutes, until the spears are bright green and tender.

2. To make the hollandaise sauce, put the yolks, lemon juice, a pinch of salt and a single grind of fresh black pepper in the blender. Melt the butter in a saucepan over low to medium heat, until the butter foams, but don't let the butter brown. Put on the blender top and whiz on highest speed for a couple of seconds, then, with the blender running, uncover and pour in the melted butter in a steady drip of droplets—not a continuous stream. When most of the butter has been blended in, the sauce will be thick and creamy. Don't add the whitish residue in the bottom of the pan. If the sauce fails to thicken, pour it out into a cup, then pour it back into the whirring blender. The sauce should be the consistency of fluffy mayonnaise.

3. Immediately pour the sauce over asparagus on individual plates or in a serving dish, allowing some green to show against the beautiful light yellow sauce.

HEALTHY "HOLLANDAISE": Nothing can compare with the velvety smoothness of hollandaise, and I'd rather make the real thing and then avoid butter for the following few days, but if the sauce is just too much saturated fat for you, make a monounsaturated substitute by blending a ripe avocado with the juice of 1 lime, a few chopped basil leaves, 1 tablespoon of minced scallion (white part only), and a pinch or 2 each of salt and sugar. While the blender is whirring, drop in tablespoons of plain low-fat or nonfat yogurt until the mixture turns creamy. ▪

Avocado

PERSEA AMERICANA

THE AVOCADO is a one-of-a-kind fruit. Instead of ripening on the tree like most fruits, it ripens about a week or two after it's picked—like Bartlett pears. Instead of sweetening up like most fruits as it ripens, it fattens up, filling itself with precious avocado oil.

Its flowers are also unique in the plant world. Like many plants, they contain both the female part (stigma) and male parts (stamens). But unlike any other plant, they open once a day for two hours on two successive days, changing their sex in the process. The first day, the stigma will accept pollen from other avocado flowers, but not its own. Then it closes. The next day, its stamens shed pollen, but its stigma is now dormant. So effectively, it's a female flower the first day and a male flower the second day. Go figure.

The pre-Columbian peoples of the Americas grew avocados as far back as 5000 BCE, according to archeological evidence. When the Spanish arrived around 1500 CE, they found avocados growing from the Aztec Empire in Mexico to the Inca Empire in Peru and northern Chile. The Aztec word for avocado was *ahuacatl,* which meant both the fruit and human testicles, since the fruit grows in pairs. The Aztecs prepared a delicious dish from avocados that they called *ahuaca-mulli,* and which we today call guacamole. You can easily see the similarity between the names, especially when you know that the *g* in *guacamole* is pronounced like an aspirated aitch.

THE ORGANIC FACTOR ▪ Tons and tons of over 100 different chemicals are used on California avocados each year, so it behooves us to look for organic growers. They're out there. The California Certified Organic Farmers' web site (www. ccof.org) lists about sixty growers. Thanks to national outlets like Whole Foods, organic avocados are available around the country now.

NUTRITION ► While avocados have a high fat content, it's good-for-you fat: Avocado oil has a greater percentage of heart-healthy monounsaturated fat (primarily oleic acid) than olive oil and, for cooking, a higher smoking point (490 degrees Fahrenheit) than olive oil.

Beyond the fat, avocados are nutritional champions. In one study, subjects were given a half to one and a half avocados per day. Total blood cholesterol began to fall in one week. Body weight didn't increase. Although they can contain up to 30 percent fat, they average only 136 to 150 calories per half an avocado. They are good sources of vitamins, especially A, the B vitamins, C, and E. They're 1.5 times higher in potassium than bananas, and—unusual in a fruit—they have 2.4 grams of protein per 100 grams of flesh, and that is a complete protein with all the essential amino acids present. They're packed with soluble fiber— four and a half times more than apples! They're also rich in enzymes, especially lipase that reduces cardiovascular no-nos like blood fats and triglycerides to benign fatty acids and glycerol.

TYPES ► Avocado is native to the Americas and is the only important edible member of the laurel family. Three distinct branches give us the 500 or so varieties of avocado planted around the world today. The first is the West Indian avocado (*Persea americana* variety *americana*). In the United States, these are grown primarily in Florida, the Caribbean, and to some extent Hawaii. The fruits are large—from 2 to 5 pounds—and generally have less than 10 percent oil content. They have a

fruity flavor and can sometimes seem watery to people used to the rich California avocado. A second botanical variety is the Mexican avocado (*Persea americana* variety *drymifolia*), which is smaller, with anise-scented leaves and an oil content up to 30 percent. These have a nutty, buttery flavor. The third is the Guatemalan avocado (*Persea nubigena* variety *guatemalensis*), with an oil content up to 20 percent. It has a mild, buttery flavor. Most commercial avocados are hybrids between these botanical varieties.

The two dominant varieties in America, as well as South America, are the Hass and the Fuerte. The common summer avocado—available year round, although its California season is June to January—called Hass (formerly known as Haas), has a pebbly, brownish-greenish-black skin when ripe and is named after a Wisconsin mailman who escaped those cold winters and moved to Pasadena, California, where he crossed Mexican and Guatemalan avocados and came up with this variety, which now holds down over 70 percent of the avocado market in this country.

From January to June, markets display the leaf-green, pear-shaped Fuerte, a natural hybrid between the Mexican and Guatemalan races that appeared at Atlixco, Mexico, in the early 1900s. The Fuerte was once the leading California avocado and continues to be the leading variety in Europe. Its oil content ranges between 12 and 17 percent.

The Fuerte continues to be the major avocado in Chile. On a recent trip there, I visited the Bodega Errazuriz winery north of Santiago. The winery is surrounded by steep hills planted with Syrah and Cabernet Sauvignon on the lower part and Fuerte avocados on the topmost parts. The avocados harbor a predatory mite that preys on the red spider mites that attack the grape leaves.

Workers take leaves from the avocados and stuff them among the grape leaves to transfer the beneficial insects to the grapes.

SEASONALITY ◆ Different varieties of avocado alternate seasons, so avocados are available year round.

WHAT TO LOOK FOR ◆ Most avocados are still hard when offered for sale, and they will ripen quite easily on your kitchen counter. To determine ripeness, gently press on the stem end or gently squeeze the whole avocado. If there's any give, they're ripe. Avoid avocados with torn skin.

STORAGE AND REPARATION ◆ Cut the avocado in half, whack the pit lightly with the edge of a knife and twist to loosen it. The pit will come out on the knife edge. If the avocado is properly ripe, you can peel off the skin by hand, or scoop out the flesh.

If you're only using half of the avocado, spritz the cut side of the remaining piece with citrus juice and wrap as air-tight as possible with plastic wrap; otherwise the surface will discolor (not bad, just ugly).

USES ◆ The buttery texture and mild flavor of Hass and Fuerte avocados gives the cook opportunity to work the fruit into all kinds of dishes, contrasting it with sweet, spicy, sour, salty, and even savory flavors. Tropical and semitropical fruits such as citrus, pineapple, guava, banana, dates, and mango are natural partners with avocados. Grapefruit, with its sweet acidity, makes perhaps the best match of any citrus fruit, although limes aren't far behind. Condiments such as salt, vinegar (especially balsamic), and sugar all complement avocados. Slices of fresh chile peppers,

onions, and tomatoes work well. You can see that it's possible to construct all kinds of salads from these ingredients.

Ripe avocado will thicken soups, but incorporate the pureed flesh just before serving. Because of its tannin content, avocado turns bitter when cooked. It will give salad dressings a smooth, creamy texture without imparting a strong flavor to them.

A salted avocado, tortillas, and a cup of coffee might make an entire meal for Native Americans in tropical Central America. In Guatemala, a ripe avocado is set on the table along with a hot soup or entrée, and the diner scoops out the flesh and adds it just before eating. A gourmet breakfast there might be a half an avocado topped with scrambled eggs and anchovies. Brazilians think of avocado as a true fruit, using it in sorbets, ice cream, and milk shakes—but they add it to the ice cream mixes only after they have cooled so no cooking occurs. New Zealanders like avocado ice cream, too. They blend avocado, lemon juice, orange juice, orange zest, milk, cream, sugar, and a bit of salt, then freeze the mixture, beat it until it's creamy, and refreeze it. Hawaiians go local when they sweeten it with sugar and mix it with pineapple. In Java, avocado is sweetened and mixed with strong black coffee to make a dessert. In the United States, besides its use in salads and sandwiches, avocados are sometimes stuffed with seafood, such as shrimp or crab salad. Slices are routinely added to sandwiches.

EXTRA GOOD GUACAMOLE

MAKES ABOUT 2 CUPS

This recipe comes from quite a few years of fooling around with guacamole. Organically grown ingredients really make this guac sing with flavor.

2 ripe avocados, halved, pits removed, peeled
1 medium onion, chopped
1 serrano chile, minced
2 small tomatillos, husks removed, diced
Juice of 1 lime
Leaves of 3 sprigs cilantro
1/4 teaspoon salt

1. Mash one avocado and dice the other. Place 1/2 of the onion, 1/2 of the chile, the cilantro leaves, and the salt in a mortar and grind together.

2. Mix the mashed avocado with the tomatillos, lime juice, and the contents of the mortar, then gently fold in the diced avocado and the remaining onion and chile. Serve immediately. ▪

Beet

BETA VULGARIS

OUR MODERN BEET is descended from *Beta maritima,* a wild seashore plant that grew along the edges of tidal marshes and salty water inlets around the Mediterranean Sea and the Atlantic coast of southern Europe. The Romans ate the leaves and the slender roots. It wasn't until the 16th century that breeders managed to get the top part of the beet root to size up—but when they did, they really got it to grow. Our modern culinary beets are just one form of *Beta vulgaris*; another is the mangel-wurzel that grows to 60 pounds or more and is used as cattle fodder in Europe. Another form is the sugar beet, rare among root crops for its 8 percent sugar content. Yet another form is Swiss chard—probably close to the form that the Romans knew. These are all part of a larger family that includes spinach and the edible weed known as lamb's-quarters or goosefoot (*Chenopodium album*).

Beets' intensely red color, which remains even through hard cooking, is caused by an anthocyanin (a kind of pigment) called betanin. Betaxanthin gives the golden yellow color to golden beets.

THE ORGANIC FACTOR ► Root crops such as beets, because they are products of the soil rather than the growing tops above the soil, respond most actively to a soil rich in decaying organic matter such as compost. Because organic soils harbor a diverse array of soil life, pathogenic organisms are less likely to gain sway and attack the roots. Not only that, but the actively decaying organic matter continually bathes the roots in the nutrients they need, when they need them, and in the forms they can best use. The result: When beets are grown in a rich organic soil, their taste actually reflects different elements in the soil—similar to the concept of *terroir* in wine. Good, compost-amended soil imparts a clean, woodsy, forest-floor note to the roots instead of the dirty taste they can acquire from a worn-out soil low in organic matter.

The great thing about buying organic beets fresh from the farmers' market is that they're likely to have been picked within the day. Their tops and leaves will be intact—and the smallest, most tender leaves add a fine texture and flavor to salads. As with any leafy crop, the shorter the time from harvest to table, the higher the quality. Large beet leaves can be steamed or sweated like their relative, Swiss chard. Because they're organic, there's no worry about them containing agricultural chemicals.

NUTRITION ► Beets are very nutritious. The roots have good stores of calcium, magnesium, iron, phosphorus, carotene, B vitamins, and vitamin C, and the tops are even more nutritious than the roots.

TYPES ‣ They're all lumped together as beets, but this family has a lot of gustatory facets. Red beets have a dark, sensual earthiness and sweetness; golden beets have a brighter flavor; white beets have their decorative uses but aren't very flavorful; chioggias (the ones with the alternating red and white rings) have a delicate, sweet, almost candy-like flavor when roasted.

SEASONALITY ‣ Beets enter farmers' markets in early to mid summer, and then into the fall and early winter. But growers in very warm climates can supply organic beets to the markets year round through successive sowings and storage of the roots through the winter and spring months.

WHAT TO LOOK FOR ‣ Beets are sold as bunch beets (tops and leaves attached) or roots only. If you buy roots only, they should be very firm, with no softness. There should at least be stubs of the stems left on—if these are trimmed off down into the beet flesh, pass them by: It means the stem ends had started to disintegrate. Whether buying bunch beets or just roots, make sure the skin of the roots is smooth, without roughened spots that may indicate fibrous toughness underneath. Water stress due to drought brings about tough beets, even if they're small, as does overmaturity; so avoid very large roots unless they're the Lutz Greenleaf variety.

PREPARATION ‣ Cut off the green tops, leaving 1 inch of stem attached, and cut off the ratty-looking tail (the thin, tapering root). Wash and scrub with a vegetable brush under running water to remove loose soil.

USES ‣ If you haven't already discovered the glories of roasted beets, I'll bet that roasting becomes your favorite way of preparing them. Roasting concentrates their flavor, enhances and concentrates their sweetness, and gives them a nutty, smoky-toasty, charry, richly sweet caramel flavor no other form of cooking can impart.

To roast beets: Figure one beet per person for medium to medium-large beets (the size of tennis balls), two beets for smaller ones (the size of golf balls). Preheat the oven to 425°F. Lay a sheet of aluminum foil on a baking pan and set the prepared beets on the foil, then put it in the oven. (The beets will ooze some sweet juice during baking that would burn in the hot oven if it ended up directly on your racks—or the oven floor—making a smelly, smoky, sticky mess.)

Larger beets will take at least a good hour and a half to cook, the smaller ones proportionately less time. But it's their feel that tells you the beets are done. If you squeeze the surface of the beets and they are soft to the touch, they're not done. If you gently squeeze the skins and they collapse—revealing that the beets have shrunk away from the

KEEP AN EYE OUT FOR LUTZ GREENLEAF BEETS

I'VE GROWN MANY different kinds of beets, but Lutz was always a marvel to me. They could grow to the size of footballs without getting tough. Once, I retrieved a Lutz from the garden in late November. I cut it into sixteenths and steamed the pieces until tender. We ate about a quarter of the single root that night, and the rest became a few weeks' worth of pickled beets (see recipe, page 74).

A GREAT REASON TO HAVE A VEGETABLE JUICER

I'VE BEEN MAKING vegetable juice with a series of juicers for about 30 years, usually with organic produce pulled fresh from the garden: carrots, beets, beet greens, spinach, parsley, and kale, when these crops are in season. A foaming, sweet glass of vegetable juice makes me feel like I'm walking on air.

But there's another reason why a juicer is such a valuable instrument for the organic cook: Vegetable juices can enhance many dishes, replacing heavy cream and meat sauces with more delicate liquids. As an example, bake a piece of fish at 300°F for 30 minutes, and while it's cooking juice a couple of raw beets and pour the juice into a small saucepan. Add some freshly grated ginger, squeeze a clove of garlic through the press into the saucepan, toss in a tablespoon or two of diced celery, the juice of a lemon and a pinch of salt. Gently simmer this, reducing it to a syrup, and just before the fish is done, strain it. After you put the fish on a platter, pour the strained sauce around the outside of the fish, or drizzle it back and forth in a very thin stream over the fish. It will be a pretty visual addition to the fish, and the sweet-and-sour lemony flavor will upstage a fatty cream or butter sauce any day.

skins—they're done. The beets will be scaldingly hot in their jackets, so allow them to cool for about 15 minutes before trying to remove the skins. Take a beet in one hand and with your thumb, peel away a little of the flesh where the inch of stems was left. This opens up the skin and you can easily peel the rest away. Make sure you remove all the bits of skin.

Put a skillet on low heat on the stove. When it's hot, add a pat of butter. Transfer the whole beets to the skillet and shake the skillet back and forth so the beets roll in the butter and are covered. They'll acquire a beautiful dark red shine. At this point some people may cook down a little orange juice in the pan, or add a tablespoon of balsamic vinegar, a half teaspoon of maple syrup, or even Cointreau or Grand Marnier. Roasted beets are a perfect foil for intensely flavored meats such as duck, goose, guinea hen, and beef. If you're using dill, tarragon, or chives with other dishes on your plate, these beets will exalt them. Or let the beets cool, slice thin, and sprinkle them in a salad of fresh goat cheese, toasted walnuts, and spring greens tossed in a mild vinaigrette. Sure, their color prettifies the salad, but it's their deep flavor that gives the dish drama and verve.

When you've got a surplus of beets on hand, make pickled beets! My mom always had a jar in the fridge full of spicy-vinegary beets and raw onion rings that were pickled along with them. I give you my mom's recipe for pickled beets below. And don't think that pickled beets are old-fashioned. I recently had pickled beets, goat cheese, walnuts, and organic greens tossed together at a fancy San Francisco restaurant, and the dish was superb.

When buying beets from the farmers' market, you also get those tender greens. I braise them if they're large or steam the young, tender greens, give them a squirt of juice, and serve them alongside the beets. Where the beet roots are earthy and deeply sweet, the greens are meaty, minerally, and have a slight metallic flavor that contrasts beautifully with the roots.

Beets can be used to give pink, bright red, or even fuchsia coloring to other foods such as pastas, rice, or potatoes. Grated raw beets enliven the color of otherwise dull salads. If you're planning to serve baby beets as a vegetable to accompany a particularly nice cut of beef, make a color triumvirate from small red, baby golden, and little chioggia beets instead of all one color.

Because of their sweetness, beets balance sours, such as lemon, sour cream, and vinegar. They enhance the spicy and herbal, like nutmeg, cloves, cinnamon, dill, and anise. They create synergies with peppery and sharp flavors of arugula and horseradish. They absorb and reduce the saltiness of cured olives and anchovies. They marry their flavor with the fruitiness of citrus, especially oranges.

PICKLED BEETS

MAKES 1 QUART

The recipe could hardly be simpler or the results more delicious. Beets' natural sweetness complements the pickling solution's natural tartness. Use medium-size, tender young Formanovas fresh from the farmers' market, if you can find them, or any red beet if you can't. Formanovas are especially nice because slicing down their long cylinders yields many same-size slices from one root.

4 or 5 young red beets, washed and trimmed
1 medium onion, sliced thin and separated into rings
$\frac{1}{2}$ cinnamon stick
3 whole cloves
1 cup apple cider vinegar
$\frac{1}{4}$ cup sugar

1. In a large pot, place a steamer basket and an inch or two of water, and add the whole beets. Steam the beets for about 40 to 60 minutes, adding more water as it evaporates. When the beets are tender but not mushy, remove them from the heat and let them cool so they can be handled, then peel. Strain and reserve the liquor from the bottom of the steamer. Slice the beets into $\frac{1}{4}$-inch-thick rounds.

2. Place the beets, onion, cinnamon, and cloves in a 1-quart Mason jar. In a saucepan, combine the vinegar, sugar, and 1 cup of the beet-steaming liquor (add water to make 1 cup if you don't have enough). Heat over medium heat just until the sugar dissolves, then pour the liquid over the beets and onion rings. If it doesn't quite cover the vegetables, add more vinegar.

3. Screw down the jar lid to the point where the ring just begins to become tight but there's still the tiniest bit of play, and process in a boiling-water bath for 30 minutes, according to standard directions for canning acidic foods. Or, if you plan to use them up quickly, simply place the covered jar in the fridge for a day before serving. These pickled beets will keep that way for 2 weeks. ■

SERVES 6

This recipe is from Sam Gugino of New York City, author of *Cooking to Beat the Clock* and *Eat Fresh, Stay Healthy*.

1 small bunch each of red and golden beets, tops and greens attached

1 tablespoons minced shallots

1/4 teaspoon ground cloves

1/4 freshly squeezed orange juice

1/4 cup apple cider vinegar

2 tablespoons canola oil

Salt and freshly ground white pepper

1 orange, peeled, seeded, and sliced thin

4 ounces crumbled blue cheese (about 1 cup)

4 fresh chive spears, roughly chopped

1. Prepare the beets according to instructions under Preparation, reserving the green tops. Reserve the small leaves for the salad; save the larger leaves for another use. Steam beets as for Pickled Beets. When the beets are cool enough to handle, remove the skins and cut the beets into 1/4-inch-thick slices. Chill the slices in the fridge.

2. In a small bowl, combine the shallots, cloves, orange juice, vinegar, oil, and salt and pepper to taste. Line a platter with the fresh, small beet greens. Place the beets in an overlapping line down the center, alternating red and golden beet slices. Place orange slices around outside of the beets. Whisk the vinaigrette and when it's well mixed, pour it down the line of beets. Sprinkle with the crumbled blue cheese. Top with the chives. ∎

Broccoli

BRASSICA OLERACEA variety ITALICA

ALTHOUGH BROCCOLI was introduced to America in the late 18th century, it wasn't until the early 20th that Italian immigrants to the West Coast started growing the plant we recognize as broccoli and popularized it. In recent years, its popularity has soared because it not only tastes good but people realize how good it is for you.

THE ORGANIC FACTOR ▪ The best broccoli I ever tasted was grown by my two-year-old daughter in our organic vegetable garden. She put the seed in the soft, crumbly, early spring soil, and when the plant was a foot and a half tall, set her small plastic Mickey Mouse underneath its large leaves. The plant responded with the most resplendent head of broccoli I've ever seen, and man-oh-man was it sweet and tender.

That's because, like most crucifers (including cabbages, turnips, rutabagas, kohlrabi, cauliflower, Brussels sprouts, and radishes), broccoli is a heavy feeder: It takes lots of nutrients from the soil, especially nitrogen compounds but also major and minor elements like calcium, chromium, magnesium, and iron. It uses these elements to build flavor compounds in its tissues, among other beneficial substances. Evidence continues to mount that organic food, grown in soil that's well supplied with all the major and minor elements it needs, is able to build more of the compounds that make it taste good.

Conventional agriculture, by contrast, depletes soil of whatever varying nutrients happen to be present in a particular plot of land, and adds back only soluble forms of three major nutrients—

nitrogen, potassium, and phosphorus—yielding generic, similar-tasting crops bearing no mark of where they were grown.

Conventional farming also gives broccoli some nasty extras. The California Department of Pesticide Regulation lists five pages of agricultural chemicals and other substances used on broccoli. I'll take my broccoli from the organic farmer, thank you.

NUTRITION ◂ Broccoli is one of the most nutritious vegetables we can eat. Perhaps kale and parsley are more nutritious ounce for ounce, but how much kale and parsley will people actually eat? Yet we can—and many of us do—eat copious quantities of broccoli. Among its rich stores of nutritive elements are a plethora of cancer-fighting compounds. Many fruits and vegetables contain substances that seem to block cancer cells before they turn deadly, but broccoli tops the list with 30 different agents. There's more vitamin C in ½ cup of broccoli than a glass of orange juice (58 milligrams, two-thirds of our recommended daily allowance). Plus, it has good supplies of folic acid, B6, riboflavin, iron, carotenoids, calcium, phosphorus, potassium, chromium (which protects against diabetes), fiber, anticancer indoles, antioxidants like quercitin, and glutathione.

TYPES ◂ While the green varieties are standard, there are purple varieties. They tend to turn green during cooking and generally have a milder flavor than the green types. They add color to a plate of crudités.

Another variant, romanesco or broccoletti, is probably closer to cauliflower than broccoli (see Cauliflower, page 89). It has a gorgeous-looking lime green head with many spiral lumps in geometric patterns.

Another type, broccoli raab, is named after the Italian word for turnip, *rapa,* and in fact the Italians call broccoli raab *cime di rapa,* (top or height of the turnip). This is a strongly flavored, even bitter, plant with a flowering stem and large leaves. It's probably more closely related to a turnip than actual broccoli, but the name of broccoli raab has stuck. It's often used wilted and sautéed on pizza, in pastas, and such. If you find it too strong for your taste, blanch it before using it in other dishes. Keep a close eye on it as it cooks, because it overcooks easily.

In the spring, you may find broccolini, also called by its cultivar name Asparation, in stores. It's a hybrid between Chinese kale and broccoli and is an excellent potherb. I blanch it for a couple of minutes in boiling water, drain it, then stir-fry it in a wok over very high heat with olive oil, fleur de sel, and a little garlic. It emerges with tender, crunchy stems and wonderfully flavorful flowering heads.

SEASONALITY ◂ Broccoli is a winter vegetable. Peak season begins in late fall and lasts until the spring. Summer broccoli can be tougher than plants grown in the cool seasons because heat forces the plants to bolt (flower prematurely) and stimulates production of tough fibers.

WHAT TO LOOK FOR ◂ Make sure your broccoli has its full complement of nutrition by checking for absolute freshness. The masses of flower buds that make up the head should be tight, a lively dark green, with no separation and certainly no open yellow flowers.

The presence of even one flower means that the plant is quickly turning its sweetness to a woody substance called lignin. Check the cut on the stem end. It should look fresh and not dried out, and no fibers should be showing. The plant should be turgid, with no limpness.

PREPARATION ‣ In addition to the florets, broccoli's thick stems are full of nutrients, so it's a shame to toss them. Use a vegetable peeler and peel off the tough outer skin of the stems, then slice them lengthwise into ¼- or ½-inch strips and steam them along with the heads.

USES ‣ Broccoli is almost always steamed, which helps it retain its juiciness and nutrition. It can be boiled, although I don't like it prepared that way.

Broccoli has a sweet flavor all its own that doesn't really require much fiddling with. However, its flavor is enhanced quite a bit with a mixture of anchovies, garlic, olive oil, and lemon juice (see recipe below). Besides anchovies, lemon juice, garlic, and olive oil, broccoli has a flavor affinity for good Parmigiano-Reggiano, and for hollandaise sauce if you want to go retro.

BROCCOLI IN EXCELSIS

SERVES 4

This treatment really exalts the flavor of broccoli. If anyone in your family thinks he or she doesn't like broccoli, this recipe will change their mind.

4 anchovy fillets
2 tablespoons olive oil
3 cloves garlic, sliced thin
Juice of 1 lemon
1 head broccoli, reduced to florets

1. Place the anchovy fillets in a small, cold skillet and slowly heat over low heat. As the pan warms, you'll be able to mash the anchovies with a fork—

they'll actually dissolve. Don't let them sizzle or cook. Just delicately melt them. As soon as they've melted, set the pan aside.

2. In a separate pan, heat olive oil to just shy of the smoking point and add the garlic. Stir until the slices turn a light brown. Remove the pan from the heat and, using a fork, take the garlic slices out of the pan and drain them on paper towels.

3. Transfer the melted anchovies to a small bowl and add 1 tablespoon of the garlic oil and the lemon juice. Stir it until mixed.

4. Steam the broccoli over boiling water until just tender—no more than 5 minutes—and turn into a warmed bowl. Sprinkle with the fried garlic slices, then spoon over the anchovy-oil-lemon juice. ▪

PENNE WITH BROCCOLI AND FAVA BEANS

SERVES 4

This is straightforward and scrumptious spring fare. Fresh favas are available in March and April in most places. It's especially tasty if you can use your own tomato sauce. Serve this as a *primo piatto* before the main course. A thick veal chop or Italian chicken dish would be a fine follow-up. Or, if you're eating a light supper, this could be your main course.

1½ cups (2 to 3 pounds) shelled fresh fava beans
1 large head broccoli, reduced to florets
¼ cup olive oil
1 teaspoon minced garlic
⅛ teaspoon crushed red pepper flakes
½ pound penne pasta
3 cups tomato sauce
2 medium fresh tomatoes, seeded and chopped
½ teaspoon kosher salt
⅛ teaspoon freshly ground black pepper
¼ cup freshly grated Parmigiano-Reggiano

continued

1. Start a large pot of salted water for the pasta so it will be boiling when you need it.

2. Steam the shelled fava beans until they're tender, 8 to 10 minutes. If the favas are mature, set aside until cool enough to handle and slip off tough seed coats. If they're young, there's no need to do this—you can eat them seed coats and all.

3. Steam the broccoli florets until just tender but not quite finished cooking.

4. When the water is boiling, cook the penne until almost but not quite al dente.

5. Meanwhile, heat the olive oil in a large skillet over medium heat and add the garlic. Cook just until it's fragrant, 1 to 2 minutes. Don't let it color. Add the pepper flakes and the steamed broccoli florets, and sauté for a couple of minutes until the florets are tender but still bright green. To the skillet add the favas, tomato sauce, tomatoes, salt, and pepper and simmer for 3 to 5 minutes, until the mixture is hot and everything has finished cooking. When the penne is al dente, drain it and place it in a serving bowl. Toss it with the cheese. Pour on the contents of the skillet and toss again. ∎

Brussels Sprout

BRASSICA OLERACEA variety GEMMIFERA

ALTHOUGH THERE ARE references in the 13th and 15th centuries to plants that may have been Brussels sprouts, it's more likely they were actually developed from cabbage in the 18th century. Gardeners knew that if you remove the main head of a cabbage plant, or broccoli, smaller heads will develop around the cut stem as long as the root stays intact in the ground. This feature of cabbage plants was selected for and bred until the Brussels sprout was developed—a plant that forms a group of large leaves at the top of the stalk but develops small heads in each of the leaf axils that stud the elongated stalk (see insert photo, page A3).

They didn't really become a farmed crop until the early 20th century—before that, Brussels sprouts were edible oddities of home gardens. Thomas Jefferson, that indefatigable home gardener, grew them at Monticello in 1812, according to his notebook.

NUTRITION ◆ Brussels sprouts are a good source of fiber, antioxidants, and potassium. Just ½ cup contains about 50 milligrams of vitamin C; 12 percent of the daily requirement of folic acid; 6 to 12 percent of iron (6 for female plants and 12 for male); 11 percent of B6, plus good stores of vitamin A and thiamin.

TYPES ◆ There are many excellent varieties of Brussels sprouts (see Top Varieties, page 483), all cultivated varieties of the species.

SEASONALITY ◆ Brussels sprout season is fall and winter. The sprouts are especially good after a few hard frosts. Like kale and other hardy members of the cabbage family, a good stab of freezing weather sweetens them up. Sprouts are at their finest between Thanksgiving and the first day of spring.

WHAT TO LOOK FOR ◆ Like all the cabbage family members, Brussels sprouts contain a lot of sulfur in the form of sulforaphane, which turns them stinky if they're too old or overcooked. Any yellowing of stalk or sprouts means they're too old, with consequent bitterness and toughness. The solution is to buy young, small sprouts (⅔ to 1 inch in diameter) that are tightly formed and have a lively green color (whether blue-green, light green, or dark green).

The problem with shopping for Brussels sprouts is that it can be hard to find small, young sprouts at supermarkets, even in the organic department. Most Brussels sprouts are frozen and sold by packers, and they want sprouts that are between the standard ¾ and 1⅜ inches. Sprouts for the fresh market tend to be the frozen market's rejects—bigger, older, stinkier, and tougher.

The place to find those tender young sprouts is at the farmers' markets. These sprouts are likely going to be modern hybrids from the Netherlands and other northern European plant breeders— sweet, mild, tender varieties that have replaced the bitter packers' varieties. Many farmers' markets close for the winter just at the time when sprouts are best. But not all do, so it pays to look around for markets that are open all year. Also, large organic and natural food markets such as Whole Foods often carry organic produce in season, right through the winter.

Sprouts don't store well; they lose their sweetness and tenderness within a few days of being picked, so make sure those you buy are no more than an inch or slightly more in diameter. Check the cut where they were removed from the stem. It should look freshly cut, with no yellowing or drying.

PREPARATION ▪ To prepare Brussels sprouts for cooking, first soak them in salted water to which a bit of vinegar has been added—this dislodges any hitchhikers that may have come aboard in the organic garden. Then trim the cut end of the sprout to reveal fresh tissue. Some folks will cut an X with a paring knife in the cut end, supposedly to speed cooking, but I've never seen the

MY FAVORITE BRUSSELS SPROUTS

WHEN I WAS A KID, the sight of Brussels sprouts hitting the dinner table caused me to say (to myself so as not to cause my mother offense), "Oh, no." While Mom was generally a good cook, she had a blind spot with Brussels sprouts. Hers were invariably bitter and mushy, and aggressively cabbagey.

But when I was working for *Organic Gardening* magazine, I started keeping an organic garden, and even planted some Brussels sprouts, just to familiarize myself with growing them. To my delight, they were delicious cooked right from the garden—as most food is. But the best sprouts were those I picked one snowy day in early December. I went to the garden, brushed the new snow off the big, bug-chewed leaves at the top of the plant, and twisted off a meal's worth of small sprouts from near the top of the stalk. I prepared them by boiling them first and finishing them quickly in a skillet with olive oil and garlic, and I discovered then how sweet these little cabbage heads can be. I learned then that the fresher and smaller the sprout, the sweeter and more tender it will be. In retrospect, Mom's problem was simple: Her store-bought sprouts were large and over the hill. The variety she got at the store was probably a packers' variety, of inferior flavor but bred to mature all at once at a uniform size, instead of a home gardeners' variety that matures from the bottom of the stalk up, increasing in size as they mature so many different sizes are available on the stalks at once.

KEEP AN EYE OUT FOR SPROUTS ON THE STALK

SPROUTS STORE WELL on the stalk, lasting a couple of weeks or more if kept very cool. It may be hard to find sprouts on the stalk, but it's worth a try. If you do find them, the stalks should be green, with no yellowing.

need to do it. Sprouts can then be cooked whole, or cut into halves or quarters.

You can also detach Brussels sprout leaves and cook them separately—a nice way to prepare them if the sprouts are fairly large. In this case, slice each sprout in half to reveal the solid whitish core, then cut out the core and detach the leaves.

USES ▸ Brussels sprouts should be cooked quickly. Long, slow cooking, such as braising or stewing, turns them to an unpleasantly soft mush. The most common way to cook sprouts is by boiling them, which removes some of the cabbagey taste. Very small sprouts will be done in about 5 minutes, medium sprouts in about 8 minutes, and large sprouts will take about 12 minutes. However the real test is to taste. They should be just tender in the solid core. Steaming takes 5 to 10 minutes, depending on their size. They can be baked whole, which intensifies their flavor. Sautéing is good if you first halve or quarter them, or slice them lengthwise into thin slices to reduce their size so they'll cook fast.

Small sprouts can be boiled just until tender, then drained, shaken in a bag with flour, dipped in a beaten egg, rolled in panko (Japanese bread crumbs), and pan fried in a very hot pan with a generous amount of oil, shaking the pan periodically so the sprouts turn golden brown all over.

This gives a crunchy exterior and a soft and sweet interior.

Individual leaves can be quickly sautéed in a hot pan with a little olive oil, a diced shallot or clove of garlic (don't let the garlic burn and get bitter—add it toward the end), maybe a shake of crushed red pepper, a couple of tablespoons of stock added at the end to give some moisture, and a squeeze of lemon juice after the pan has been removed from the fire. Try a leaf to assess when they're done. I notice that more and more chefs are using detached Brussels sprouts leaves in rice, pasta, and noodle dishes.

Brussels sprouts are perhaps best when done simply and served on their own, not incorporated into other dishes. However, they do have an affinity for several flavorings and condiments that can be used to vary their taste subtly. Parsley, thyme and, surprisingly, nutmeg all go well with sprouts. Bacon and butter harmonize beautifully if you don't mind using some fat (render some diced bacon, lardons, or pancetta in hot butter until crispy, then add the sprouts and sauté). Garlic or onions can help a dish of sprouts, as can a squeeze of lemon juice. In Belgium and into northern France, chestnuts are often roasted or boiled and added whole or sliced to freshly cooked sprouts to make a delicious dead-of-winter pairing (see page 326 for information on cooking chestnuts).

BRUSSELS SPROUTS AND SHERRY SHRIMP

SERVES 4

Chinese cooking inspired this light, nutritious dish. The nutty flavor of good sprouts works well with sherry or even a tawny port.

1 pound Brussels sprouts (about 3 cups), soaked and
  trimmed (see Preparation)
3 tablespoons peanut oil
1 tablespoon butter
2 tablespoons diced scallions
1 pound medium shrimp, peeled and deveined (see Tip)
1/2 cup peeled, sliced water chestnuts
Juice of 1/2 lemon
Salt and freshly ground black pepper
1/2 cup dry sherry

1. Bring a large pot with salted water to a boil. Add the sprouts and boil for about 5 to 12 minutes, depending on their size, until just tender. Drain and place them on paper towels to absorb excess moisture.

2. Warm a serving dish in a warm (200°F) oven. In a large skillet, heat the oil and butter over medium-low heat until a bit of scallion sizzles when added, then add the scallions and sauté for about 1 minute. Add the shrimp and cook for about 4 minutes, flipping them often so both sides are cooked. Add the water chestnuts and Brussels sprouts, drizzle the lemon juice over them, and add salt and pepper to taste. Stir until everything is heated through. Turn the contents of the skillet into the warm serving dish. Deglaze the skillet with the sherry and turn up the heat so it boils, reduce by half, then pour it over the shrimp and sprouts and serve immediately.

TIP: There is a plastic device called a shrimp deveiner that peels and deveins shrimp in one swift motion; it is sold everywhere, and worth its weight in gold. ▪

Cabbage

BRASSICA OLERACEA
variety CAPITATA

WILD CABBAGE still grows along the Atlantic coast of Europe. It doesn't look much like the cabbage that we know, because its leaves don't form the big, round, tight ball we call the head. Instead, it's just a collection of lobe-shaped leaves. The ancient Egyptians and Greeks knew and ate this wild cabbage—the Greeks had the idea that cabbage sprang from Zeus's sweat, which may stem from the strong odor cabbage acquires when overcooked. Another Greek saying about cabbage is that "cabbage served twice is death." That is most likely a warning that cabbage doesn't make very good leftovers, which it doesn't.

The development of large terminal buds—the precursors of heads—probably started in northern Europe in the 1st century BCE. Pliny the Elder wrote about a head of cabbage a foot in diameter, although this was hearsay on his part and may have been an exaggeration. Cabbage as we know it probably originated in Germany in the 12th century, and it first came to the New World aboard Jacques Cartier's 1541 voyage to America. The first written record we have of cabbage being planted in North America is by Dutch and German immigrants in 1669.

From the 17th century, when northern and eastern European immigrants began arriving in America, to the 20th century, cabbage was one of the mainstays of the winter diet, either as fresh heads stored in the root cellar (they pulled up the whole plants, and hung them by the roots upside down from the ceiling, where they stored perfectly well for the entire winter) or as sauerkraut. Most folks in those agrarian times grew what they ate and ate what they grew. How thankful they must have been when the first fresh spring salad of dandelion greens and ramps arrived to alleviate the boredom of yet another dinner of dried apples, potatoes, pork, and sauerkraut.

THE ORGANIC FACTOR ▸ Lots of insects bedevil cabbage plants, which causes conventional growers to douse them with pesticides. But the chief pests—imported cabbageworms and cabbage loopers—can be easily controlled using organic methods like adding the bacteria *Bacillus thuringiensis* (Bt), which causes a caterpillar disease that's harmless to other forms of life. (The name "imported cabbageworm" refers to the fact that this pest crossed the Atlantic along with the northern Europeans and their heads of cabbage.)

Like most leafy plants, cabbage is a heavy feeder, meaning that it likes a soil rich in decaying organic matter—precisely the kind of soil organic gardeners and farmers strive to maintain. A soil rich in actively decaying organic matter produces the highest quality heads of cabbage.

NUTRITION ▸ The red types are quite nutritious: 3½ ounces of red cabbage contain 100 percent of a person's recommended daily allowance (RDA) of vitamin C, while a similar amount of green cabbage contains 35 percent.

Shredding and fermenting cabbage into the pickled form we call sauerkraut renders it even more nutritious than the fresh plant (see recipe, page 84). As with most fermented foods, the action of bacteria or yeasts add nutrition to the base food.

TYPES ▸ Centuries of breeding have given us numerous cabbage types—green, red, purple, white, and combinations of these colors; shiny leaves and tight, firm heads; light-green savoy-like heads (which have finely crinkled leaves) that are looser and are probably descended from the an-

cient Roman types; and Chinese types (see Asian Vegetables, page 62).

The flavor of cabbage changes from variety to variety, but the best raw cabbage is mild in flavor rather than pungently cabbagey, with a sweetness and delicate vegetal quality and a texture that is succulent and crisp, tender rather than leathery. When cooked, cabbage changes character, acquiring a stewed flavor that meshes beautifully with ham or corned beef.

Red cabbage is perhaps a little sweeter than green; green cabbage is more tender. Savoy-type cabbages, with their crinkled, frilled delicate leaves, are the mildest flavored.

SEASONALITY ▸ Even though it's available in our stores year round, winter is the best season for this staple food, when cabbage is at its sweetest.

WHAT TO LOOK FOR ▸ No matter what type of cabbage you're buying, check the stem end to make sure it's not dried out. The surface of any type should be clean and not bruised. Always toss out the wrapper leaves that have been handled in the journey from field to store.

USES ▸ The sweet flavor of cabbage makes it pair well with sweet, smoked meats, specifically sugar-cured ham and bacon, as well as with salty meats like sausage and corned beef and rich meats such as duck and pork. Cabbage makes a fine pairing with apples, onions, leeks, parsley, potatoes, and spinach. Condiments such as horseradish, mustard, juniper berries, and vinegar match up with cabbage's distinct flavor.

The most common method of cooking cabbage is boiling, but this does release those sulfur compounds that some folks find very unpleasant. Some say a sprig or two of parsley in the cooking water reduces the sulfurous smell, but I haven't found that to be true. If your tap water is alkaline, red cabbage will react to it by turning a bluish color. Vinegar, apples, and wine are all acidic and by adding one or more of them to the cooking water, you can avoid the unwanted color change. Another solution is to stir-fry the cabbage, which pretty much eliminates the odor problem.

NEW ENGLAND BOILED DINNER

SERVES 6 TO 8

A traditional stick-to-your-ribs dinner from when yeoman farmers worked the stony New England soil and found enough moxie to throw off the British yoke. Every American should try this dinner at least once in his or her lifetime.

2 pounds salt-cured ham, or fresh pork shoulder

4 pounds corned beef brisket

Bouquet garni (several sprigs of parsley, sage, and thyme tied together)

4 medium onions, peeled

6 medium potatoes, peeled

3 medium carrots, peeled

3 medium turnips, scrubbed

3 small beets

1 small head of cabbage, quartered and cored

Creamy horseradish sauce (homemade or store-bought)

1. If using ham, put it in a pot, cover with water, bring to a full boil, and then turn heat off and set it aside to cool.

2. Place the cooled ham or pork in a large pot with the beef brisket, cover with fresh water, and bring it to a boil. Boil for 10 minutes, skimming off any scum that accumulates on the surface of the water. Reduce heat, add the bouquet garni, cover, and simmer for 2 hours. At the end of this time, add the onions and potatoes and simmer for 15 minutes. Then add the carrots and turnips and simmer for 30 minutes more.

3. Meanwhile, in a small saucepan filled with water bring the beets to a boil and boil them until they are barely tender when stuck with a knife, 15 to 20 minutes. Drain, put them in a serving bowl, and keep warm in a 200°F oven.

4. When the meat and vegetables are done, remove the meat and vegetables from the broth, place the meat on a platter, slice it, and place the vegetables around the meat. Place the platter in the warm oven. Remove the bouquet garni and discard. Bring the broth back to a boil over high heat and add the cabbage quarters. Boil the cabbage for 5 to 7 minutes; drain and place in a separate serving bowl.

5. Serve the pork, beef, vegetables, beets, and cabbage along with a bowl of the hot cooking broth. Accompany with creamy horseradish sauce. ■

MIDWESTERN SWEET-AND-SOUR COLESLAW

SERVES 4

Hazel Hardebeck's (my mom's) coleslaw was always the best among family and friends. She hailed from Covington, Kentucky, and showed her German heritage in this dish. Alas, she never divulged her recipe. This version, the closest approximation, comes from Carlos at Nicola's Delicatessen in Calistoga, California. Hazel would have approved.

1 medium head savoy cabbage

1 carrot, peeled and grated

1/2 red bell pepper, minced

FOR THE DRESSING

1 1/2 cups mayonnaise

1/2 teaspoon celery seed

1/2 cup white vinegar

1/2 cup sugar

continued

1. Remove any coarse or damaged outer leaves from the cabbage. Quarter and core the cabbage, and slice it as thin as you possibly can, using a mandoline if you have one. Place the sliced cabbage in a large bowl of ice water for 1 hour.

2. Drain the cabbage and pat dry. Place in a large bowl and add the carrot and red pepper.

3. In a separate bowl combine the mayonnaise, celery seed, and vinegar. Slowly add the sugar, a little at a time. After each addition, mix until the sugar is dissolved, then taste. You've added enough when neither mayonnaise nor sugar dominates, but the whole becomes an integrated flavor.

4. Use half the mixture to dress the cabbage mixture and reserve the rest for the next batch. (It will last a week in the fridge.) Toss to mix thoroughly. Serve immediately. ▪

HOMEMADE SAUERKRAUT

MAKES ABOUT 3 QUARTS

Store-bought canned sauerkraut (German for "sour herb") is to homemade as canned spinach is to homegrown (although, truth be told, it is possible to buy some decent refrigerated sauerkraut these days). But it's hard to find real, honest organic kraut, which has just two ingredients, no additives, no agricultural chemicals, and plenty of goodness.

You can use regular green cabbage, savoy cabbage, or even Chinese cabbage, but don't use red cabbage as it turns an unappetizing color after fermentation.

10 pounds green, savoy, or Chinese cabbage
6 ounces (1½ cups) pickling salt or fleur de sel

1. Remove any tough outer leaves from the cabbage. Wash the cabbage and slice as thin as possible. If you have a mandoline, it will facilitate the process. Or you could use a food processor to shred the cabbage a bit at a time.

2. Mix half of the cabbage with half the salt in a large bowl and let it stand in the kitchen until the juice from the cabbage appears—about 15 minutes. Pack this into a 2-gallon crock or jar (an old fashioned stoneware crock is most satisfying) until the juice covers the cabbage. Then repeat with the second half of the cabbage and salt, adding that to the crock, also. The cabbage must be entirely submerged beneath the brine. To make this happen, thoroughly wash a plate that will fit into the crock and cover the cabbage, push it down, and set a large plastic bag filled with water on the plate to weigh it down. If you need to add more liquid, make a brine from 3 tablespoons of salt for each quart of nonchlorinated water.

3. Cover the top of the crock with a snug lid or second plate and a clean dish towel just so no insects can enter. Store the crock at a cool room temperature (ideally between 60 and 65°F). Long-time kraut makers say the cooler the temperature, the longer the fermentation takes and the better tasting the kraut will be. Some folks skim off any scum that forms on the surface of the brine on a daily basis, but that allows airborne yeasts and bacteria to enter, which would add unwanted flavors, so I let the crock ferment undisturbed for 3 weeks, at which point the fermentation should be finished. At this point, check the kraut to make sure bubbling has stopped, skim any scum off the liquid surface, pack it into quart jars, and store it in the fridge for no more than 3 months.

TIP: If the sauerkraut seems too sour for you, simply wash it in a colander. Many people eat the sauerkraut with no further fuss, but I think cooking it in a saucepan with some of its liquid for a couple of minutes enhances the flavor. ▪

Cardoon

CYNARA CARDUNCULUS

MY FIRST SIGHT of a mature cardoon was at Doug Gosling's fabulous organic garden in Occidental, California. The plant was as tall as I am and looked like an overgrown artichoke plant—long, bristly leaves with spiky leaf tips—that threatened to take over the world. Its resemblance to an artichoke on steroids stands to reason, since the wild Mediterranean thistle is the ancestor of our modern artichoke. Unlike the artichoke, which is grown for its flower buds (the globe we eat), the cardoon is grown for its wide, thick, flat stalks. They superficially resemble toothed celery stalks, but they are wider, thicker, longer, and flatter, with a dull silver-gray color.

Cardoons were considered a delicacy by the ancient Greeks and Romans but are infrequently found in markets today. When they are found, it's usually in markets and farmers' markets that supply ingredients to communities from the southern European and Mediterranean countries, where cardoons are still popular. In northern California, however, they are frequently found growing wild, because they've escaped from cultivation and naturalized in the same coastal regions where their cousins the artichokes grow so abundantly.

SEASONALITY ► Cardoon season is late spring through the fall, and they're available even into December in certain Italian markets (because their clientele look for it late).

WHAT TO LOOK FOR ► If you do find cardoon at the market, look for stalks that are small to medium in size, from 1½ feet to 3 feet long, rather than extra wide and large. The smaller they are, the more tender. Check out the cut ends. The cut ends will be discolored like the cut ends of artichokes, but that's okay. What's not okay is if the thick stalks are hollow inside, which means they're old and tough.

PREPARATION ► Remove all leaves and spines with a paring knife, slice off the ends to refresh them, cut each stalk lengthwise into two pieces and immediately place the stalks in a bowl of water acidulated with a squirt of lemon juice. (You might want to wear gloves to do this, as the spines can be very sharp, and the juices can turn your skin dark.)

To prepare for use, scrape off the strings, as you would with celery, using a vegetable peeler or a paring knife. Cut each stalk into 2- to 3-inch pieces, then immediately drop them into a pot of salted and acidulated boiling water (1 teaspoon salt and the juice of 1 lemon per quart of water) and boil for 15 minutes. Drain, fill the pot with fresh water, bring to boil, add cardoons, and boil another 10 minutes until they're tender.

USES ► Properly prepared, the cardoon has a subtle but delightful flavor—a little bit artichoke heart, a little bit celery, a hint of anise, and something of salsify. When they're meaty and tender, they can be used in many ways in combination with their taste mates: butter, lemon, garlic, hard Italian grating cheese, and vinegar. After preparing them for cooking, some folks sauté them in butter and garlic, others in bacon and flour to which cream is added, still others braise them, use them in stews and soups, or batter and fry them in olive oil. The French serve them in a Mornay sauce. Italians will brighten raw strips of cardoon with a garlic-anchovy dip called *bagna cauda*. But we seldom find cardoon picked young and tender enough for raw use. I like cardoons dressed Spanish style, which shows off their delicate flavor, as in the recipe below. Besides the leaf stalks, cardoon root is edible and can be prepared like any root crop, although it's rare to find the roots in markets. In the Balearic Islands, Italy, and Spain, the juice of the flower heads is sometimes used as a vegetable rennet to curdle milk for cheese.

CARDOONS, SPANISH STYLE

SERVES 6

The Spanish love cardoons, as do other southern European and North African nationalities. This version comes from Madrid.

6 cardoon stalks

3 tablespoons olive oil

3 small onions, finely chopped

2 tablespoons red wine vinegar

1/2 cup white wine

1 teaspoon flour

1/2 cup chicken stock

1 clove garlic, minced

1 bay leaf

Salt and freshly ground black pepper

1. Prepare the cardoons according to the preparation instructions (see page 85). During their second boil, heat a large skillet over medium heat, and add the olive oil. When hot, add the onions and cook until they are translucent but not brown, 3 to 4 minutes. Add the vinegar and wine and cook over medium heat until all but about 3 tablespoons of liquid have evaporated, about 5 minutes. Add the flour and stir thoroughly until any lumps are gone.

2. Drain and add the cardoons, stock, garlic, bay leaf, and salt and pepper to taste, and simmer, covered, for a couple of minutes, until the cardoons are tender. Take out the bay leaf and serve. ▪

Carrot

DAUCUS CAROTA variety SATIVA

ALTHOUGH THE WILD CARROT called Queen Anne's Lace grows just about everywhere in America, the vegetable we know as the carrot probably originated in Afghanistan, where the wild carrots are purple due to the presence of an anthocyanin, a phenolic coloring compound that functions as a coloring agent and a healthy antioxidant. From there, carrots were brought east to China and west to the Middle East, where the Romans called them *carota,* Latin for head or top (think carotid artery), and indeed used them for their aromatic leaves, much like we use chervil or parsley today. Their roots at that time were still small. The carrot traveled to North Africa and to Spain around 1100 CE. Before the 17th century, northern European carrots all had slender yellow or purple roots. An anonymous author in 1533 wrote (correctly): "Parsnepes and carettes . . . do nourishe with better juyce than the other rootes." It was the Dutch in the 17th century who bred carrots for size and for a rich orange color. Today plant scientists are breeding other colors back into carrots, and we can find carrots in colors such as maroon, purple, red, white, and yellow, as well as orange.

THE ORGANIC FACTOR ▸ When carrots are organic, you get to use their flavorsome thin skins, and not have to peel them away. If the carrots have been drenched in the usual array of pesticides— about 6 million pounds used on California carrots alone in 2001—you had better peel those carrots.

NUTRITION ▸ It's no fable that carrots are good for you. They contain 7 milligrams of betacarotene per 100 grams, which we metabolize into vitamin A. Just 2½ ounces of raw carrot provide the average person with 250 percent of his or her daily requirement of this important vitamin. Carrots are also sweet—they're 2 percent sugar—which is why fresh carrot juice is such a creamy, foamy, sweet treat.

TYPES ‣ We're used to eating long, tapered orange carrots, but good carrots come in all shapes and sizes from long to short to stubby little golf balls. They also come in a range of colors. And be on the lookout for baby carrots—not the stubs sold in bags (these so-called baby carrots are ground out of larger pieces by machine and taste like it) but miniature whole carrots bred to develop full color and flavor while still small. Farmers have also been breeding certain varieties of carrots with elevated levels of vitamin A so they can be grown in parts of the world suffering vitamin deficiencies.

SEASONALITY ‣ Carrots store well in the ground and so are available year around. But the peak season for carrots is midsummer through fall.

WHAT TO LOOK FOR ‣ If you can, try to locate a local farmers' market with fresh-pulled carrots available (just ask). If possible, avoid supermarket carrots; although carrots can be kept in the fridge for weeks, their ephemeral flavor and freshness will be gone after no more than a few days.

Look for carrots that still have their tops on. Examine the foliage; it should be a bright, lively green and have the smell of fresh carrots. If the foliage is limp, losing color, and stale-looking, then odds are that the carrot will also be past its prime. If the carrots are topless, avoid them. If you can't—because it's wintertime, for instance—check the place where the foliage attached. Make sure there's no mold. The root should be firm and not bend easily. If there are fine, white, hair-like rootlets growing from spots around the root, avoid that carrot. It's really old.

PREPARATION ‣ Organic carrots don't need to be peeled; just give them a quick washing.

USES ‣ Just about any way you can think to cook carrots has been tried successfully. They can be boiled, steamed, broiled, and sautéed. You can even bake them in a cake. Personally, I like to roast them: Their flavor is intensified, and, in addition, browning turns some of their starch to a form of sugar, intensifying their sweetness.

Try roasting carrots along with onions and potatoes and served with a tender, slow-cooked pot roast. I grate a little carrot into my cole slaw to add flecks of color. On the other side of the world, cooks in Iran grate some on their pilaf, and in China carrots are preserved in sugar as well as pickled. And carrot juice can be made into a sweet reduction sauce to enhance other vegetables.

IF YOU LIKE TO GARDEN

THERE'S NO OTHER WAY to get that perfect fresh carrot flavor than growing your own, and carrots aren't hard to grow in an 18-inch-deep container of compost or in loose, organic soil. Besides, carrot seed is so tiny that you inevitably grow plenty of extra seedlings, which you can use in creative ways, such as pureeing and adding them to soups or stews (see Uses above).

Carrots pair well with anise, chervil, cinnamon, cumin, dill, parsley, and tarragon. Chervil seems an especially good herb to sprinkle over sautéed, buttered carrots. I'll sometimes roll my cooked carrots in a little maple syrup or orange juice—or both—just to give them a glaze before serving. Carrots are a principal ingredient, along with celery, onions, parsley, thyme, and garlic, in the great and useful mirepoix of French cooking. But of all the ways to prepare or eat carrots, the best way has to be to pull one fresh from the garden, wash off the soil, and crunch on it.

If you have organic carrots, you might find ways to use their green tops. You could steam the foliage lightly and use it as a base for fish as you would dill (a close relative), or use it uncooked to present freshly shucked oysters.

CARROT-JUICE SALAD DRESSING

MAKES ABOUT 1 CUP, ENOUGH FOR 4 OR 5 SALADS

The creamy sweetness of carrots makes them useful for salad dressing. If your carrots are organic and very fresh, you might tear up some of the foliage to add to the salad. This dressing is creamy, yet bursting with sweet-sour-spicy flavor.

$1/2$ cup fresh carrot juice (from 1 or 2 carrots)

$1/4$ cup heavy cream

4 tablespoons tahini

1 tablespoon rice vinegar

1 tablespoon sugar

4 teaspoons Dijon mustard

$1/4$ cup canola oil

$1/4$ teaspoon sea salt

Place all the ingredients in the blender and whiz until smooth. ∎

CARROT SOUP WITH RICE (*POTAGE CRÉCY*)

SERVES 4

Potage Crécy is an old recipe from northern France for a delicious carrot soup with rice. Because of its sweetness and creamy texture, kids love it.

$1/3$ cup diced onion

1 strip of bacon, diced

3 cups thinly sliced very fresh carrots (Nantes if you can find them)

$1/4$ cup uncooked rice

5 cups chicken stock

1 tablespoon butter

4 tablespoons low-fat buttermilk

Salt and freshly ground black pepper

4 tablespoons cooked rice, optional

1. In a 2-quart saucepan over medium heat, fry the onion together with the bacon until the onion is translucent and tender, about 5 minutes. Add the carrots, raw rice, and chicken stock. Cover and cook over medium heat for 20 minutes.

2. Pour the mixture into a blender and whiz it to a puree that still has some texture, then return it to the pot. Bring it to a low boil and add the butter, buttermilk, salt, and pepper. Mix thoroughly and ladle into serving bowls. Top each bowl with a tablespoon of cooked rice, if desired. ∎

Cauliflower

BRASSICA OLERACEA
variety BOTRYTIS

Cauliflower is cabbage with a college education.

MARK TWAIN

CAULIFLOWER joins Brussels sprouts as one of those cabbagey vegetables that I disliked as a kid, but which became one of my favorites once I got a taste of them from my own organic garden. It changed my estimation of this vegetable entirely. No longer was it a smelly, boiled-to-mush chunk of white curd. Now it was a fancy treat, with delicate cabbage flavor, creamy, and nutty, with a pleasant crumbly texture.

THE ORGANIC FACTOR ▸ One of the problems with conventional cauliflower is the application of heavy doses of soluble nitrogen fertilizer. This causes the heads to lose their firmness and begin to form flower buds, which results in a loss of texture and quality. Organic cauliflower that gets a gentle feeding of nitrogen from the decay of organic matter in the soil is not as prone to rush toward flowering.

NUTRITION ▸ Cauliflower stems and florets are rich in vitamins and minerals stored for use in the flowers when they develop. I try to emulate the Chinese in peeling and slicing the stems thinly, then stir-frying them with other vegetables. A half cup of cauliflower contains 40 percent of the Recommended Daily Allowance of vitamin C, about 9 and 8 percent of vitamin B6 and folic acid respectively, 1.5 grams of dietary fiber, but only 12 calories.

TYPES ▸ In addition to white, cauliflower comes in green, purple, and even orange. Romanesco is a lime-green variety with a beautiful geometric pattern to its formation that's intermediate between broccoli and cauliflower, as is the pale green broccoflower. These colored cauliflower are choice types, stronger in flavor but also sweeter than either broccoli or cauliflower. Orange Bouquet and Marmalade varieties produce creamy orange curds rich in beta-carotene. (See Top Varieties, page 484, for more examples.)

SEASONALITY ▸ The secret of great cauliflower is to find a fresh head within a day or two of picking. Such a prize is most likely to be found at the farmers' markets from the fall through the dead of winter in relatively mild winter areas like the California coast and in the spring in colder regions, when certain hearty varieties that have lasted through the winter start to bear curds. These latter types, called the Walcherin, were first bred in Holland. They're planted in August and September and grow into large leafy plants that hold through cold—but not extremely bitter—winters and, depending on the strain, produce heads in March through May. Coastal regions of the Pacific Northwest are ideal for these strains.

WHAT TO LOOK FOR ▸ Most supermarket cauliflower, even organically grown, is trimmed of all its leaves and covered in perforated cellophane wrappers. You may see small browned areas on the creamy-white surface of such heads. Avoid these heads if you can. Look for heads that are still wrapped in their inner leaves. These are long green and white leaves that have either been tied up over the heads or naturally grown to cover them. Leaves keep direct sunlight from the curds, which can discolor them. If these leaves have a fresh, bright look and a turgid snap to their midribs, you can be sure the head is fresh. Also check the cut stem for drying or discoloration. The curd should not be ricey—where curds develop a velvety appearance and resemble a pot of boiled rice. When young and at its freshest, the curd is composed of tightly packed tips of offshoots from the thick stems. Only later, when the head is nearing maturity, do these tips differentiate into unopened flower buds, and, as the head matures even more, eventually into flowers themselves.

Avoid any cauliflowers with small green leaves appearing in the curd. This is due to the plant reverting to vegetative growth, rather than curd formation, because of warm temperatures. Curds that are excessively yellow rather than creamy white have been exposed to sunlight and will have a more pronounced cabbagey flavor and possibly more bitterness. If you find some pink color in the interior of the head, that's okay—it's due to excessively cool temperatures at harvest time and does not mean disease is at work. In many of the most popular types of white cauliflower, overmaturity or exposure to sunlight may cause a purple color to haze the surface of the curd.

PREPARATION ◂ Before cooking a head of organic cauliflower, I always soak mine in a bowl of water given a small handful of salt and a few tablespoons of cider vinegar for an hour, just in case one of those little green cabbage worms has set up shop in the interior.

USES ◂ Cauliflower is versatile. It's an excellent addition to a tray of raw vegetables, but it also can be baked, boiled, steamed, roasted, stir-fried, or sautéed and pureed after cooking to make a creamy sauce for grilled fish. I avoid boiling it, for that turns it to mush too quickly and brings out the cabbagey flavor. Chef Randy Lewis of Santa

Rosa simmers his cauliflower in almond milk—it turns the floret into the creamiest and loveliest vegetable imaginable. Cauliflower cooked with steam or dry oven heat—even microwaved—also produces good results.

When cooking colored varieties of cauliflower, be aware that cooking the purple types such as Violet Queen will turn their color to green. The pale green types will stay green, and the orange varieties will retain their color, too.

Because of its delicate flavor, cauliflower pairs well with more sharply flavored ingredients like cheeses, pepper, cumin, garlic, lemon, mustard, nutmeg, anchovies, and ham or bacon. Butter, cream, and bread crumbs are old-fashioned standard toppings.

Even without slathering on the butter, there are many ways to dress cauliflower for a starring role on the table. One of the ways Greeks handle this delicate vegetable is to separate the heads into florets, then steam them until just tender. They make a batter out of 2 egg whites beaten stiff, ½ cup of white wine, and ½ cup of flour, or a little more, whipped together to make a clingy batter. The florets are dipped in the batter then fried in a pan with hot olive oil until they're golden brown.

The Dutch and many other northern European nations like a little cheese on their cauliflower. In Holland they whisk 2 egg yolks with 1 tablespoon of butter and ¼ cup of flour, and heat this mixture in a double boiler or over low heat—but not hot enough to curdle and cook the yolks—until the mixture thickens. When the mixture is hot, add 5 ounces of gouda cheese and stir until it melts. Break a head of cauliflower into 4 or 5 pieces, steam until it is just tender, then place the pieces in a casserole, pour the cheese sauce on top, and bake in a preheated 350°F oven for 10 minutes, or until the cheese starts to brown. It serves five or six.

SPICY ROAST CAULIFLOWER

SERVES 4

Cauliflower is a favorite vegetable of the Indian sub-continent, although they use tropical varieties developed expressly for their climate. This spring recipe has exotic spices and spring vegetables guaranteed to wake your taste buds from their winter dormancy.

1 cup diced onion
1 head fresh cauliflower, reduced to florets
1 teaspoon minced garlic
1 tablespoon freshly grated ginger
1/2 tablespoon grated lemon zest
1/4 cup olive oil
1/2 tablespoon curry powder
1/2 tablespoon Garam Masala (see Tip)
1/2 tablespoon fennel seeds
1/4 teaspoon crushed red pepper flakes
Salt to taste
1 teaspoon freshly ground black pepper
1/2 cup shelled fresh garden peas
2 tablespoons chopped fresh parsley

1. Preheat the oven to 400°F. Place all the ingredients except the peas and parsley in a bowl and toss until the florets are coated. Place in a roasting pan and roast for 25 to 30 minutes, turning the cauliflower every 10 minutes so it browns evenly.

2. Just as the vegetables are finishing, lightly steam the peas for 3 to 5 minutes until just tender—don't overcook. Place the contents of the roasting pan in a serving bowl and add the peas and parsley. Toss to mix, and serve.

TIP: Garam masala can be found in stores, or you can make your own: Grind as fine as possible either with a mortar and pestle or in a spice grinder the seeds from 2 cardamom pods, 1 teaspoon whole cloves, 30 whole black peppercorns, 2 teaspoons whole cumin seeds, and one 2-inch piece of cinnamon. Store it in a tightly closed container in a cool, dark cabinet. ▪

LAMB AND CAULIFLOWER STEW

SERVES 4

A delicious Mediterranean-style dish that's perfect for a cold night.

2 pounds lamb sirloin cut into 1 1/2-inch chunks
1 cup all-purpose flour
2 tablespoons olive oil
1 cup roughly chopped shallots
2 cups tomatoes, peeled, seeded, and chopped
2 tablespoons Demi-Glace (page 453), or
    1/2 cup beef stock
1/2 cup red wine
1 slice of lemon
1 teaspoon dried oregano
Salt
1 head cauliflower, reduced to florets
Freshly ground black pepper
2 tablespoons chopped fresh parsley

1. Dredge the lamb chunks with flour, shake off the excess. Place the oil in a large skillet and heat it over medium heat, then add the lamb and brown on all sides, about 10 minutes. (You may have to do this in batches. Return all the meat to the skillet when done.) Add the shallots, stirring until they're slightly browned.

2. Add the tomatoes, demi-glace, wine, lemon slice, oregano, and salt to taste. Bring the skillet to a boil, cover it, reduce the heat to low and simmer it for 1 hour.

3. Add the cauliflower, mix it in, cover the skillet, and simmer for 20 or 30 minutes longer, until the cauliflower is tender.

4. Remove from heat. Add pepper to taste. Sprinkle with the parsley and serve. ▪

Celery

APIUM GRAVEOLENS
variety DULCE

FEW HOME GARDENERS grow celery, but the experience can help one understand the vegetable. For example, I learned that if you grow celery in hot summer weather out in the strong summer sun, it turns a rich green and produces a bitter compound called apiin. And yet, it needs sunlight on its leaves to mature properly. With enough trial and error, you learn that celery needs warm sun coupled with cool air, such as the conditions found along the seashore, especially the shorelines of cold oceans. And indeed, it appears that celery is a plant that grows wild near the oceans of Europe and Asia.

You also learn (if you grow your own celery) that if you don't routinely flood it with water, it stays small and spindly, and those strings that run the length of the stalk crowd together and turn it impossibly chewy.

Those indefatigable gardeners, the British, figured out how to grow it properly. They dig a trench and enrich the soil in the bottom of the trench with compost, then flood the trench and plant their celery starts down in the muck at the bottom of the trench. The plants elongate to find the sun, which makes for good, long stalks, and either adds soil to the trench as the stalks elongate, or fills the trench with last fall's bagged, dead leaves, allowing the celery's green leaves to appear above the leaf level in the trench. The compost feeds the celery, which likes lots of nutrients to grow large and succulent. The cool earth keeps the stalks cool. The brown leaves keep the stalks shaded. The sun can blast the celery's green leaves all it wants. And the trench can be frequently drowned in plenty of water to keep things marshy down where the roots are. British gardeners have a whole class of celeries called trench celery, usually with names that include the words pink or red, and when these varieties are grown this way, their blanched stalks have a pinkish hue. These are seldom seen in the United States, but keep an eye out for them in farmers' markets.

THE ORGANIC FACTOR ► It's especially important to find organic celery, either at the farmers' market or a store. The agricultural chemicals used on celery run to three single-spaced pages in the 2001 Annual Pesticide Use Report for the state of California. Of the 150 tons of pesticides, some of the largest applications were for acephate, chlorothalonil, malathion, oxamyl, and permethrin, with lesser amounts of methyl bromide, paraquat, and other very toxic substances.

NUTRITION ► Celery has between 10 and 15 percent of our daily need for vitamin C, potassium, folate, and soluble fiber, plus trace elements like molybdenum and manganese—but hardly any calories.

TYPES ► In addition to stalk celery, there is also Chinese celery. This is the same species, but it hasn't been selected for size like European types. It's closer to wild celery, with slim stalks and a strong flavor. It's invariably cooked with other vegetables as a steamed or stir-fried mixture and is sometimes sold in Asian markets.

In some farmers' markets, you can also find wild celery. The progenitor of both our stalk celery and celery root, it has thin stalks and very leafy tops and was used in ancient times as a medicine and flavoring. It's still occasionally sold in France as *céleri à couper* and used for flavoring soups and stews, and it is used in Italy to flavor *ragù* or meat sauce. It's very strongly flavored, not to be used as a raw salad vegetable.

SEASONALITY ◄ The peak season for garden- or farm-grown celery is midsummer to fall in the Midwest and Northeast, winter on the West Coast, and winter through spring in Florida. Because of these staggered seasons, we can find celery in our stores at every time of year.

WHAT TO LOOK FOR ◄ Sometimes at farmers' markets you'll find small, thin-stalked heads looking like cute, or baby, celery. This just means they have been improperly grown, unless the farmer is selling wild celery. For fresh eating and as a salad vegetables, you want fat, massive stalks—the more massive, the more tender they'll be. They should be rigid, never flaccid. And look for a pale green rather than a darker green color.

PREPARATION ◄ Sometimes soil will splash up from rains or irrigation flooding of celery trenches and lodge where the stalks attach to the base. Check that area and wash it well if soil is present.

USES ◄ Celery doesn't star in many recipes. It's an indispensable supporting actor, though. What would Thanksgiving turkey stuffing be without celery and sage? Soups without celery would be bland affairs indeed.

When it does star, it's usually eaten alone, cold, and raw. It's the vegetable that refreshes the palate when a tray of crudités is served. I like to remove the outer stalks from a head of celery, cut off the tough base, and devour the heart—it's refrigerator-cold, crunchy, and herbaceous, with a sort of spiciness in the leaves.

In the kitchen, celery has a hundred uses as an ingredient in savory dishes and salads. It has a liking for its fellow umbelliferous plants: parsley, fennel, and dill. It also blends well with lemon and sharp cheeses. I find lots of uses for celery leaves and always buy celery that has leaves still attached if I can. Chopped finely, they make a fine addition to soups, salads, stews, stuffings, even rice dishes like risottos.

CELERY AND SEAFOOD CONSOMME

SERVES 4

This soup can be made with any shellfish, but I think it's best with lobster or crabmeat, especially eastern blue crab lump crabmeat. We used to make this with freshly caught crab at the New Jersey shore on late summer days long ago, but it's not just nostalgia that keeps it in my repertoire.

6 cups fish or chicken stock
4 cups coarsely chopped celery stalks and leaves
1 medium onion, coarsely chopped
Salt and freshly ground black pepper
2 whole stalks celery
2 slender carrots, peeled
1 cup cooked crabmeat, lobster, or chopped shrimp (see Tip, page 94)
2 tablespoons minced celery leaves

1. In a large pot, mix the stock, chopped celery, and onion and bring to a boil. Reduce the heat to medium-low and cover. Simmer for 30 minutes.

2. Strain through a colander into a clean pot. Press out the juices from the vegetables; discard the vegetables.

3. Julienne the whole celery stalks and carrots. Blanch them in boiling water for 2 minutes and

continued

drain. Add the seafood and the julienned vegetables to the consomme and reheat quickly to serving temperature. Sprinkle the top of each bowl with a pinch of minced celery leaves.

TIP: If you cook your own seafood—which I recommend—you can reserve up to 1 cup of the cooking liquid and add that to the stock. ■

Celery Root

APIUM GRAVEOLENS

variety RAPACEUM

CELERY ROOT, or celeriac as it's sometimes called, is celery that has been bred to grow an enlarged root—usually about the size of a softball—with a rough, brownish surface pitted, pocked, and studded with rootlets. The leaf stems that are the edible portion of ordinary celery are small and usually bitter in celery root and not the prized portion here, although they can be used to flavor soups.

Celery has been known since time immemorial—Homer called it *selinon*, from which word our modern name derives. Celery root is a relatively modern innovation, first developed as a separate vegetable in the 16th century. The wild progenitor of both stalk celery and celery root is a marsh plant used in rituals and as a flavoring in ancient times. In the Middle Ages, wild celery was known as smallage, and its root was eaten, and it was a delicacy in the Arab world. Because the enlarged roots store water, celery root does not require the soggy conditions necessary for growing stalk celery. Although celery root became very popular in continental Europe, it was never popular in Britain and America until recently, when it was discovered by chefs who understand its gourmet qualities.

THE ORGANIC FACTOR ▸ As opposed to celery, which is liberally doused with agricultural chemicals by conventional growers, almost all the chemicals used on celery root are snail and slug baits spread on the ground around the plants rather than sprayed on the plants themselves, and then only a couple of tons are used in the whole state of California. Which is good to know, because organically grown celery root can be hard to find, especially when most farmers' markets close for the winter months.

NUTRITION ▸ Like celery, celery root is rich in Vitamin C, potassium, and phosphorus. A half cup has only 25 calories.

SEASONALITY ▸ Late fall through winter.

WHAT TO LOOK FOR ▸ Some say that small roots are better, but I say that by the time you peel them, there's hardly anything left. I look for larger roots, the size of a softball or larger, that are firm and feel heavy in the hand, with no "give" when squeezed. They should be especially firm at the top where the stalks emerge.

PREPARATION ▸ Set the celery root on a cutting board and go at it with a serrated knife, slicing deep enough into the flesh to cut out all the pockets and depressions in the root surface. I work around the root, slicing off the surfaces of the top third piece by piece, then cut off a band of the surfaces around the middle. I turn the root upside down and slice off the surfaces of the bottom third all around. I'm left with a snowy white, vaguely ball-shaped root with many flat surfaces.

USES ▸ For years I simply avoided celery root, because I had no idea what to do with such an outlandish-looking thing. Did one boil it? Eat it like an apple? Fry it? Actually, one can do any of those things, as well as steam, bake, grate, pickle, shred, julienne, braise, sauté, roast, and microwave it. Its flavor and aroma combine that of parsley (a fairly close relative), parsnip (a more distant one), and celery. These aromatics are what's attractive about celery root and make it an intriguing addition to many types of dishes, from turkey stuffing to minestrone.

The French have made a culinary cliché out of celery root salad with remoulade—but for good reason. Remoulade's flavors of mayonnaise, capers, gherkins, herbs, anchovies, Dijon mustard, and lemon juice make it a sassy accompaniment to finely shredded celery root's snowy white color and refreshing flavor. Besides remoulade, celery root finds common cause with potatoes, onions, winter squash, lemon, carrots, caraway seed, and cream.

Eastern Europeans have found dozens of uses for it, and some of its variety names suggest the countries that love it: Large Smooth Prague, for example. Include it in a medley of roasted root vegetables such as potatoes, turnips, parsnips, rutabagas, carrots, and even salsify and *scorzonera*. It can be grated fresh in a salad, although be aware that the fresh root can take over a salad despite its mild flavor.

Celery root's real charm is as an adjunct to soups, stews, braised meats, purees, and as a partner with mashed potatoes—especially garlic mashed potatoes. The urge to make a beef stew usually comes over me in late fall when days turn cold, and I want something warm and filling. Celery root contributes fine-textured chunks that yield a lovely aromatic essence. If I have leftover celery root, I'll steam it until it softens, then puree it in the blender, pour it into ice cube trays, and

freeze it. When frozen, I bag the cubes. In my winter soups, a cube or three of pureed celery root not only adds its aromatics but also thickens and intensifies the soup. It never seems to interfere with other flavors but simply exalts them, the way parsley will exalt so many dishes for which it is the final touch.

When braising, I cut long strips of celery root and add them to the liquid along with meats such as lamb shanks or other vegetables like Belgian endive. The strips then become a side dish when the braised food is served.

CELERY ROOT AND RICE, BULGARIAN STYLE

SERVES 4

This recipe combines some ingredients from Eastern Europe with some from the Mediterranean regions near Bulgaria. The result is delicious.

1 medium to large celery root, trimmed and cut into
   $1/2$-inch cubes
5 tablespoons olive oil
$1/3$ cup Arborio rice
1 tablespoon tomato paste
1 tablespoon chopped fresh parsley
Salt and freshly ground black pepper
$1/4$ cup freshly grated Parmigiano-Reggiano

Place the olive oil into a medium skillet over medium-low heat, then add the celery root and sauté until nearly soft, about 7 minutes. Add the rice and cook over low heat for 5 minutes, stirring frequently. Add the tomato paste, parsley, $1 1/2$ cups hot water, salt, and freshly ground pepper. Cover and simmer gently for 20 to 30 minutes, until the rice is done and the liquid mostly absorbed. Sprinkle on the cheese and serve. ■

GARLIC MASHED POTATOES AND CELERY ROOT

SERVES 4

Garlic mashed potatoes are great, but when celery root joins the party, they're exquisite!

1 pound red potatoes, peeled and quartered

5 cloves garlic, peeled

1 whole celery root (roughly, about 1¹/₂ pounds), trimmed and quartered

2 tablespoons unsalted butter

¹/₂ teaspoon kosher salt

4 grinds of black pepper

¹/₂ cup warm whole milk

Paprika

1. Bring a large pot of water to a boil, add the potatoes, garlic, and celery root. Reduce heat to medium and cook until the potatoes and celery root are very soft, about 30 minutes.

2. Pour off the water, returning any ingredients to the pot. Add the butter, salt, pepper, and milk and mash together with a potato masher. If too thick, add a splash more milk and mash again. Transfer to a serving bowl and lightly dust the top with paprika. Serve immediately. ■

Chard

BETA VULGARIS variety CICLA

BOTANICALLY chard is a subspecies of ordinary garden beets, bred for its leaves rather than its root, and packs the same kind of nutritional punch. The name "chard" comes from the French *chardon,* or thistle, although chard is not a thistle (the name came about because chard has a wide midrib similar to the cardoon, which is a thistle, and because of this physical resemblance the French word for thistle came to be applied to chard as well).

For some reason, chard also goes by the name of Swiss chard. While the vegetable is commonly grown in Switzerland, among other northern European countries, it's the French and Italians, not the Swiss, who have done the most with chard, with the Spanish and Greeks running a close second. In southern Spain and out on the Balearic Islands, it's cooked much as the Arabs of North Africa use it, with spices and hot chiles, or cooked with sweetmeats. In fact, chard's history is long, going back before Rome (its subspecies name, *cicla,* refers to *sicula,* the ancient name of Sicily), before Greece, back to ancient Babylon. Various theories have been proposed for why the country of Switzerland has been associated with chard, but none of them seem worth repeating. I just call the vegetable chard and leave it at that.

THE ORGANIC FACTOR ✦ Make sure your chard is organic. The high-nitrogen chemical fertilizers used in conventional agriculture can cause the plants to take up too much nitrate, which can change within the human digestive system to cancer-causing nitrites. Organic soils feed chard their nitrogen from natural sources, at just the rate the plants need it.

NUTRITION ‣ Just ½ cup of cooked chard provides 30 to 40 percent of the daily requirement of vitamin A, 20 percent of vitamin C, 20 percent of magnesium, 13 percent of potassium, 5 percent of calcium, and 25 percent iron for males and 11 percent for females. While you sometimes see chard recommended as a salad ingredient, use it sparingly because raw chard contains oxalic acid, enough of which can cause gastrointestinal upsets and block the body's ability to absorb iron and calcium. Cooking disarms the oxalic acid.

SEASONALITY ‣ When grown in cold winter climates, chard is ready to harvest in late spring or early summer and will continue to produce stalks until hard frosts in November. In warm winter areas, winter is its preferred season with best growth and largest yields.

WHAT TO LOOK FOR ‣ Look for stems that are crisp, not limp, and inspect the cut ends; they should look freshly cut, not dried or shriveled. The leaves should be fresh and glossy. Reject any bunches with leaves that have begun to decay.

PREPARATION ‣ While it's certainly possible to cook chard leaves and stems together, the leaves will be done long before the stems finish cooking, so it makes more sense to cook the two separately (the exception is if they're going into a soup, stew, or braising pan that will cook for a long time). To separate leaves from the stems, lay a leaf on a cutting board and cut along either side of the rib.

To prepare chard stems for cooking, check the fibers that run up the back of the stems. If the stems are wide and older, their fibers may be unpleasantly chewy: Use a paring knife to peel the fibers from the stem, as you would with celery. Fresh young chard stems—even big ones—may not need to be de-strung. Give them a tooth test to see how chewy they are.

USES ‣ Chard is as versatile in cooking as just about any vegetable. The leaves have a delicious earthy tang and the stems are succulent, bittersweet, and have a hint of salsify and cardoon in their flavor. The leaves and stems are functionally two kinds of vegetables from the same plant.

CHARD LEAVES ‣ Chard leaves can be steamed and served like spinach, made into a quiche (see recipe, page 99), or used like spinach. The substantial leaves also make excellent wrappers, dolma-style, for ground meats, grains, or nuts to be baked *en casserole*.

IF YOU LIKE TO GARDEN

IN ADDITION TO BEING a versatile vegetable in cooking, chard is one of the more ornamental plants that you can grow in a vegetable garden; tuck a few plants into your flower garden. The variety called Bright Lights, for instance, produces stems in yellow, gold, pink, orange, crimson, lavender, and purple—and shades in between. If you let it go to seed, it will come back for you again and again. Years ago someone in the San Francisco area let plants of an heirloom Italian variety of chard go to seed, and it has been volunteering around the margins of the bay ever since. I planted chard in my garden in Sonoma County the first year I moved here, and as long as I let a plant go to seed, it comes back regularly and grows all year around.

CHARD STEMS ▪ Chard stems take a little more work, but they're worth it. The white midribs of Lucullus and Argentata varieties are my favorites.

The prepared stems can be braised, or parboiled and then finished in any number of ways, such as simmering in stock or deep frying. To parboil, cut the stems into two- to three-inch pieces and boil in lightly salted water acidulated with a tablespoon of lemon juice for about five to seven minutes. Then rinse them in cold water.

After parboiling, simmer the pieces in stock with a splash of lemon juice until they are tender. They can be served as is or gratinéed. My favorite way to prepare the parboiled stems is to squeeze them dry between paper towels, dip them in batter made of 2 eggs mixed with 3 tablespoons of milk, dredge them with spicy bread crumbs, and fry them in a skillet in olive oil (turn so that both sides become crunchy and golden).

TACOS OF CREAMY BRAISED CHARD

MAKES 16 TO 18 TACOS

Rick Bayless, the renowned chef and owner of Frontera Grill and Topolobampo in Chicago, gave me this recipe, writing, "There's something about this creamy combination of greens and green chiles that I want to taste time and again."

4 medium-large fresh poblano chiles (about 3 ounces each)

1 tablespoon olive oil

1 medium white onion, sliced 1/4 inch thick

2 cloves garlic, chopped fine

1/4 teaspoon dried oregano, preferably Mexican

1/8 teaspoon dried thyme

16 to 18 corn tortillas (plus a few extra, in case some break)

3/4 cup chicken stock

3 medium red potatoes (about 10 ounces), cut into 1/2-inch cubes

1 (12-ounce) bunch chard, leaves only, sliced 1/2 inch thick (6 cups, loosely packed)

2/3 cup heavy cream or crème fraîche

1/2 teaspoon salt, or to taste

2/3 cup crumbled Mexican queso fresco or pressed, salted farmer's cheese

1. Roast the chiles directly over a gas flame or 4 inches below a very hot broiler until blackened on all sides, about 5 minutes for open flame or 10 minutes for broiler. Remove from the heat, cover with a kitchen towel and let stand 5 minutes. Peel, pull out the stem and seed pod, then rinse briefly. Slice into 1/4-inch strips and reserve.

2. In a 10- to 12-inch skillet, heat the oil over medium heat, then add the onion, stirring often until nicely browned but still a little crunchy, about 5 minutes. Add the garlic, oregano, and thyme, toss a minute longer, stir in the chile strips, and remove from heat.

3. To warm the tortillas, set up two vegetable steamers with 1/2 inch of water under the steamer basket; bring to a boil. Make two stacks of the tortillas and wrap them in heavy kitchen towels, lay them in the steamers and cover tightly. Heat for 1 minute, then turn off the heat and let stand without opening for 15 minutes.

4. While the tortillas are steaming, prepare the filling. In a small saucepan, combine the chicken stock and potatoes, cover, bring to a simmer and cook over medium-low heat until nearly tender, about 15 minutes. Pour the potatoes and stock into the pan with the chiles, mix in the chard, bring to a boil over medium-high heat and cook until the stock has evaporated, about 4 minutes. Mix in the cream and continue to boil, stirring regularly, until the cream is reduced enough to coat the mixture nicely. Taste and season with salt.

5. Scoop the mixture into a deep, warm serving dish, sprinkle with the cheese and serve immediately with the warm tortillas. Your guests can assemble the tacos for themselves at the table. ▪

WINTER GREEN SLAW WITH WARM BACON DRESSING

SERVES 4

The folks at Planet Organics (www.planetorganics .com) came up with this low-fat, nutritional power-house. Use small and tender Lacinato kale leaves (see page 135), fresh, tender beet greens, and ten-der chard leaves to avoid producing a chewing marathon.

1 teaspoon olive oil
$1/2$ cup sliced onion
$1/4$ cup cream cheese, softened
$1/4$ cup fat-free milk
2 teaspoons white wine vinegar
1 teaspoon Dijon mustard
$1/2$ teaspoon dry dill
$1/2$ teaspoon honey
$1/8$ teaspoon freshly ground black pepper
2 cups thinly sliced ($1/4$-inch) kale
2 cups thinly sliced beet greens
2 cups thinly sliced chard leaves
2 strips of turkey bacon, cooked and chopped

1. Heat the oil in a pan over medium heat. Add the onion and sauté until tender and browned. Reduce heat to low, add the cream cheese, milk, vinegar, mustard, dill, honey, and black pepper. Stir until all is well blended then remove from heat.

2. Place sliced greens in a bowl, pour on the cream cheese mixture, and toss until the greens are evenly covered. Divide on plates and top with chopped bacon. ▪

SAVORY CHARD NO-CRUST QUICHE

SERVES 8

Break out the Gewürztraminer to serve with this sa-vory custard. If you like, make a partially baked pas-try pie shell (see page 211; make dough and then follow step 3 of "Pumpkin" Pie recipe to bake the shell), and use this recipe as the filling for a quiche.

You'll need a 9-inch round baking dish, 4 to 5 inches deep.

4 tablespoons butter, plus extra for buttering the
    baking dish
1 tablespoon canola oil
1 cup chopped onions
2 bunches chard, leaves only
1 pound ham, sliced thin
$1/4$ pound coarsely grated provolone (about 1 cup)
$1/4$ pound coarsely grated mozzarella (about 1 cup)
$1/4$ cup grated Parmigiano-Reggiano
$1/2$ cup ricotta
$1^2/3$ cups whole milk
6 eggs, beaten
Salt and freshly ground black pepper

1. Butter the baking dish, and line the bottom with a piece of parchment paper cut to fit. Butter the paper. Preheat the oven to 350°F.

2. In a 12-inch skillet, heat the canola oil and 2 tablespoons of the butter over medium heat, then add the onions and sauté until translucent, about 5 minutes. Add the chard leaves and turn heat to high. Cook, stirring continually, until the leaves are well wilted and any moisture is evaporated (don't let the leaves scorch). Remove from heat and reserve.

continued

3. Slice the ham into strips about 1/2 inch wide and cook them in a medium skillet in the remaining 2 tablespoons of butter, turning them several times until they're lightly browned, about 5 minutes. Reserve.

4. In a bowl, mix together the provolone, mozzarella, and Parmigiano-Reggiano. Puree the ricotta with the milk in a blender, then pour into another bowl. Whisk the eggs into the wet ingredients. Season this custard mixture to taste with salt and pepper (remember, the cheese and ham are salty, so easy on the salt, but don't skimp on the pepper!).

5. Place a third of the dry cheeses in the baking dish and drizzle a small amount of the custard on top. (You're going to make a stack of nine layers, each drizzled with custard, so use it accordingly.) Make layer with a third of the ham and drizzle that with custard. Make a layer with a third of the chard and drizzle with custard. Repeat this layering sequence 2 more times. The layers should not quite reach the top of the dish.

6. Cover the dish with aluminum foil. Place the dish in a roasting pan with enough boiling water to reach halfway up the side of the baking dish. Gently place this in the oven and bake for 1 hour, then turn the heat to 400°F and bake for 20 minutes. Remove the foil so the top will brown and bake for 10 minutes more. The custard is done when it pulls away from the sides of the dish and a knife inserted in the center comes out clean and dry.

7. Remove from the oven and place on a cooling rack until you can handle the baking dish, about 20 minutes or more. Run a knife around the edges of the dish, then place a large plate over the top of the baking dish and carefully invert. Remove the paper. Select a serving dish and place it on top of the custard, then invert once again. ∎

Chicory and Endive

CICHORIUM INTYBUS and CICHORIUM ENDIVIA

THIS GROUP of related vegetables includes chicory, Belgian and curly endive (*frisée* in French), Italian radicchio, and Batavian escarole. The flavor of all the chicories has an edge of icy-sweet bitterness that helps the cook create a contrast with sweet, savory, or salty flavors. Salads of these greens come to life when set off by apples, blue cheese, figs, ham, pears, nutmeats, or citrus wedges.

The edible chicories are related to the wild chicory we see growing along roadsides and in weedy places just about everywhere in America. This is the plant that develops a flower stalk a foot or two tall with pure blue daisy-like flowers. Don't try making food out of the wild plants, though.

THE ORGANIC FACTOR ▸ Conventionally grown varieties of chicory and endives get a lot of agricultural chemicals applied to them, so it's wise to seek out the organic versions. Belgian endive is a separate story. According to Richard Collins, president of California Vegetable Specialties, Inc., the largest producer of Belgian endive in the world, "The Belgian endive is never treated with any pesticides, nor does it need to be washed for any reason."

NUTRITION ▸ All the chicories and endives have good stores of kaempferol, one of the flavonoids, plus vitamin C. Flavonoids are antioxidants found in many foods and have a beneficial effect on several aspects of human health, such as cancer prevention, antiaging effects, and cardiovascular health.

TYPES ‣ Both chicories and endives are members of the genus *Cichorium*. Chicory varieties are perennials and part of the species *intybus* while the endives and escaroles are biennials of the species *endivia*.

Chicories and endives have dozens of types that are grown around the world. Here are the kinds most often grown in Europe and the United States.

BELGIAN ENDIVE ‣ Belgian endive is actually one of the chicories (*Cichorium intybus*), which is shown by its other common name, Witloof Chicory.

Use Belgian endive the same day you buy it, if at all possible, for its crisp freshness is its best feature. The roots of certain varieties of chicories are roasted and ground as a coffee substitute or an addition to regular coffee. One can do this with the roots of Belgian endive, if you're growing them at home.

SUGARLOAF ENDIVE ‣ Leafy forms of *Cichorium intybus* are called chicory in England, and usually called Sugarloaf endive in the United States. The same plant goes by the name *pain de sucre* in France. It has thick, crunchy leaves that make a fine addition to salads or can be used to protect meats and fish during cooking.

RADICCHIO ‣ Radicchio (*Cichorium intybus*), once just an Italian obsession, shows up in salad mixes across America these days. There are two types. The forcing type is grown in spring and the leaves are cut off just above the crown in late summer. These forcing types then resprout, some with a red-leaved and white-veined ball-like head, while others form a more elongated, cone-shaped head similar to the *chicon* of a Belgian endive (as the forced heads are called), and yet others form a loose head resembling a strikingly red romaine.

ESCAROLE ‣ Escarole (*Cichorium endivia*) is a large-leaved form, often found as Batavian Full Heart. Its green leaves acquire an unpleasant bitterness, so it's most often blanched and sold with a pale yellow to cream-colored center that combines sweetness with the little bit of bitterness that aficionados prefer. When escarole reaches about a foot across, growers tie up the outer leaves over the centers to blanch them. The outer leaves of escarole can be harvested as a cut-and-come-again crop, but usually only in spring or fall when the weather is cool. Add leaves to soups and add the

MY FAVORITE CHICORY

GROWING MY OWN BELGIAN ENDIVE was a revelation, because, alone among the gardeners I knew, I was the only one harvesting fresh garden vegetables in the middle of January. It made my tired winter salads come to life. I sowed the seed in the spring, grew out the plants over the summer, and when the weather turned cold in the fall, pulled out the plants, trimmed the tops off the big roots, and buried the roots in a deep pit filled with leaves and hay to keep the roots from freezing. Then in January, when the ground was frozen solid and covered with snow, I opened the pit and took the roots into my dark basement, where I set them upright in boxes filled with wet sand. In about three weeks, I was harvesting homegrown, organic *chicons*. They had that icy-bitter flavor with a touch of sweetness that marks the chicories.

mild inner leaves to salads. The bottom knob of solid flesh holds the leaves in place. Stuff between the leaves with bread crumbs and grated Parmigiano-Reggiano, then tie up the leaves with string and simmer the head in chicken stock.

FRISÉE ► Curly endive (*Cichorium endivia*), also known as frisée, is one of the few endives suitable for cutting in the summer months, but it needs sun protection in hot climates. It produces very finely cut, frizzy leaves that show up as part of mesclun mixes, as garnishes, and as beds under entrees like fish. Use it in salad mixes, or dip in boiling water until it wilts, then drain, pat dry, and drizzle with olive oil and vinegar.

SEASONALITY ► When chicories and endives become exposed to warm weather and light, they turn impossibly bitter. For this reason, fall and winter are the best seasons for all these vegetables.

WHAT TO LOOK FOR ► Leafy chicories, endives, and escaroles should be crisp and fresh, with no browning at the cut ends. Browning of either leaves or cut ends means the produce is quickly losing freshness. When shopping for Belgian endive at the farmers' market, look for leaves with white to pale yellow color and no green showing. Green color means it has been exposed to light and begun to turn bitter. If buying frisée at the market, check to make sure there's no brown burn at the leaf tips.

KEEP AN EYE OUT FOR PUNTARELLA

"YOU KNOW WHAT'S the most expensive dish in a Roman restaurant?" asked my friend Luciano Zamboni. We were sitting at the kitchen table at Victorian Gardens, his bed and breakfast on the Mendocino coast.

"No idea," I said. "What?"

"*Puntarella*," he said. He took me out back to his organic garden. One of the raised beds was crowded with broad-leaved plants whose young, undeveloped flower stalks stood a foot or two above the leaves. "You have to pick these stems when they're still tender," he said, and he showed me how to squeeze them to tell whether they were tender or had grown tough and hard. He gathered a few handfuls of the most tender stalks and took them back to the kitchen.

I'd never heard of puntarella, so I watched, fascinated, as he peeled each stalk, cut it into 1/4-inch-wide strips, and cut them into 2- to 3-inch lengths. The work was painstaking, slow, and tedious. "This is why it costs so much," he said. "It takes forever to make enough for one serving." After he prepared the little strips, he placed them in a bowl of cold water, tossed in a few ice cubes, and placed the bowl in the fridge. Several hours later, he drained the strips, which had rolled up into little curlicues, and dressed them with a mixture of olive oil, vinegar, and mashed anchovies. The puntarella had a flavor somewhat similar to asparagus, but with an appealing crunchiness and slight bitterness. I had no idea what sort of vegetable it was until I found it in a seed catalog: Puntarella is *ciccoria di Catalogna*—Catalonian chicory, a variety of *Cichorium intybus*.

A related form of Catalonian chicory is known as *dentarella*. It's the red-ribbed Red Dandelion that one finds in the farmers' markets in the early spring, with toothed leaves and smoky red midribs.

PREPARATION ◂ As escarole grows, it traps soil in the base of the leaves, so trim off the bottom where the leaves come together and rinse the leaves well. The other chicories and endives simply need refreshing with a rinse of cold water. Belgian endive doesn't even need that.

USES ◂ Leafy chicories and endives are great raw in salads. Belgian endive can also be braised, used raw, or wrapped in thin slices of ham. Escarole is sometimes sliced into ribbons, added to boiling chicken stock, and served in a soup, *escarole in brodo*. It is also sautéed with raisins and pine nuts, much like spinach.

BRAISED BELGIAN ENDIVE

SERVES 4

Braising Belgian endive transforms its bittersweet fresh quality into something deliciously savory—a great accompaniment to roast pork and baked apples.

2 tablespoons olive oil
4 heads Belgian endive
Juice of 1 lemon
Generous pinch of salt
1 teaspoon sugar

1. In a Dutch oven or other heavy lidded pot, heat the olive oil over medium-high heat. When oil is hot, add the endives and cook for 1 1/2 minutes until brown, then turn them over and cook another 1 1/2 minutes to brown on the other side. They'll spit and pop in the hot oil.

2. Add the lemon juice, salt, and sugar. Turn the endives to coat. Reduce the heat to low, put on the lid, and simmer for 30 minutes. ▪

RED AND WHITE SALAD

SERVES 4

The sweet toasted pine nuts contrast remarkably with the bitter red and white salad ingredients.

FOR THE DRESSING
3 cloves garlic, chopped
Juice of 1 lemon
1/2 cup olive oil
1/2 cup freshly grated Parmigiano-Reggiano
Salt and freshly ground black pepper

FOR THE SALAD
1/2 cup pine nuts
1 head frisée (about 6 to 8 ounces)
1 small head radicchio (about 4 to 6 ounces)

1. To make the dressing: puree the garlic and lemon juice in the blender. With the blender running, slowly pour in the olive oil until the dressing is smooth. Add the cheese and blend until thick and smooth. Adjust the seasoning and refrigerate.

2. To make the salad: Toast the pine nuts in a dry skillet set over medium heat, stirring, until they brown and turn aromatic, about 2 to 3 minutes (do not let them burn). Remove the outer green leaves from the frisée and save for another use. Tear up the tender, white, inner leaves of the frisée into a bowl. Thinly slice the radicchio and toss with the frisée and the salad dressing. Sprinkle the pine nuts over the salad and lightly toss again. ▪

Chile Pepper

CAPSICUM, various species

AMONG THE MANY GIFTS of the New World to the Old, fiery chile peppers may be the most valuable. On Columbus's first voyage across the Atlantic, the natives he encountered offered him tiny, red, wild berries that looked to him like the red peppercorns grown in India and had a similar pungent spiciness. That led him to believe he'd found India. And so Native Americans became Indians, and those small red berries became peppers.

The small wild berries (*Capsicum annuum* variety *aviculare*), now called pequins or chiltepins, weren't the only chiles growing in the Americas at the time, though. Native Americans in South and Middle America had been cultivating chiles for 7,000 years. Despite their vast differences in size, shape, pungency, and flavor, most of the world's cultivated chiles today are *Capsicum annuum.* The most familiar exceptions are the tabasco pepper (*Capsicum frutescens*) and the habanero (*Capsicum chinense*).

Within a few years of Columbus's first voyage, chiles were being planted in Europe and North Africa, and it wasn't long before they were planted around the world. They slipped easily and quickly into cuisines as diverse as Spanish, African, Southeast Asian, Indian, and Chinese. Everywhere they went, they had a profound effect on the dishes they entered, enlivening them, turning bland to grand, and providing an abundance of good flavor.

The substance that makes chiles so spicy hot is called capsaicin. The heat is measured in Scoville units. While a typical jalapeño measures about 2,000 Scoville units of pungency, a habanero—one of the hottest peppers in the world, if not the hottest—measures 200,000 to 300,000. Some argue that pungency ought to join sweet, sour, salty, bitter, and umami (the so-called "yummy" taste) as one of the basic tastes, but I think pungency is more a sensation than a flavor.

Capsaicin is produced in glands on the placenta of the fruits—the whitish substance in the interior of the pod to which the seeds are attached. Seeds do not produce pungency, but because of their proximity to the placenta and the fact that bits of placenta may cling to the seeds, they can absorb capsaicin and effectively be quite hot. No other part of the chile produces capsaicin. The "burn" we experience from an abundance of capsaicin in our mouths stimulates the body to produce natural endorphins—pain killers our bodies make that create a good feeling. Eating a hot pepper just may be the high point of your day.

THE ORGANIC FACTOR ▸ Insects tend to avoid capsicum. So, most chiles are not sprayed. (In fact, gardeners use hot chiles to make a bug-repelling spray.) But choose organic chiles for their superior culinary quality.

NUTRITION ▸ A green chile pod contains three times the vitamin C of a Valencia orange and the entire minimum daily requirement. When the pods ripen and turn red, the provitamin A levels increase to twice that of a carrot. Even when they're dried, chiles retain their nutritional power and their pungency. Just ½ tablespoon of red chili powder furnishes the minimum daily requirement of vitamin A.

TYPES ▸ The different types of spicy chiles available these days give the organic cook a wide palette of flavors to choose from. But these just scratch the surface. There are over 200 types of chiles in cultivation today—100 in Mexico alone.

All the chile peppers, whether mild, medium, hot, or very hot, have something to offer the cook besides their level of pungency.

Dried poblanos, which are called anchos, have a sweetish flavor; mulatto has a chocolatey taste. Mirasol is fruity; chipotle is smoky (because they are jalapeños that have been dried over a smoky fire). For my money, the chile with the best flavor is the habanero (sweetly aromatic, fruity, and luscious), but it's so darn hot that it's difficult to taste anything when your mouth feels like its being blasted by a flamethrower. I've eaten a whole habanero at one go, but I do it by seeding it, mincing it, and topping a hamburger with it. Putting even the tiniest sliver by itself into your mouth is a revelation of the power of capsaicin.

Hot chiles are one of the few types of vegetables (botanically, they are actually berries) that are ranked less by their quality of flavor than their appropriate use. No one would say that a little serrano is better than an Anaheim if your purpose is to make stuffed peppers. Here's a cook's take on the most common types of hot chiles.

Anaheim—Long, narrow, mild pepper, often stuffed.

Ancho—A dried poblano, reddish brown, medium to very hot.

Bird—Another name for Thai chile.

Caribe—A yellow, very pungent chile named for the Caribbean tribe.

Cascabel—Small, round, dark red chile of medium heat, rich flavor.

Cayenne—Slender, bright red chile of powerful pungency.

Charleston Hot—A new cayenne type found at farmers' markets.

Cherry Pepper—Small, round, bright red chile of mild to medium heat.

Chilaca—The fresh form of pasilla, brown when ripe, medium heat.

Chipotle—A dried smoked jalapeño with sweet, smoky flavor, medium heat.

Fresno—A stubby, green to red chile of medium to hot pungency.

Guajillo—A dried chile, deep shiny red, very hot, long and narrow.

Habanero—Small, blocky yellow to orange pepper of extreme pungency.

Hungarian Wax—Greenish-yellow chile of medium heat, almost a hot-wax flavor.

Jalapeño—Short, stubby, versatile, green to red chile of medium heat.

Jamaican Hot—Very hot, bright red chile of irregular, narrow shape.

Mulatto—A dark brown, fruity chile that's used to make mole.

Pasilla—Richly flavored, black-brown, long and narrow dried chilaca.

Peperoncini—Sweet, pungent peppers usually sold green and pickled.

Pequin—Tiny, oval chiles of fiery pungency and a sweet, smoky flavor.

Poblano—Blackish-green chile of medium heat used for chiles relleno.

Santa Fe Grande—Small, tapered, medium-hot chiles from yellow to red.

Scotch Bonnet—Similar to the habanero in appearance and pungency.

Serrano—A very hot little cylindrical chile with green, red, or yellow skin.

Thai Chile—Very small, narrow chile that packs a pungent wallop.

Togarashi—A small, red Japanese chile of medium-hot pungency.

People are continuing to breed new kinds of chiles for a variety of uses, but the destruction of the wild plants' habitat also means that breeders may lose valuable germ plasm to work with. Dr. Kevin Crosby at the Texas A&M Vegetable Research Center says novel fruit types, such as sweet jalapeños, are being developed and peppers with more quercetin—a beneficial antioxidant— are being evaluated.

WHAT TO LOOK FOR ◆ When buying fresh chiles, make sure they are glossy, firm, and sound, with no soft spots, pitting, or overall softness when given a gentle squeeze. Check the stem end, which should look fresh cut. With dried chiles, there's less to check. Just make sure they smell good and have no mold.

PREPARATION ◆ When working with chile peppers, protect yourself. Use rubber gloves to prevent having the capsaicin in the peppers get onto your fingers and under your nails.

I always wear my glasses when cutting fresh chile peppers, because I've had the merest dot of juice squirt out of a pepper into my eye, and that's no fun. Be especially cautious when working with extremely hot peppers such as Thai chiles, Scotch bonnets, and habaneros. I've found that cooking habaneros on the stovetop can release enough capsaicin into the air to cause burning and choking in the throat.

If capsaicin causes such pain to the mucous membranes, what does it do to our stomachs? Scientists have used long tubes with optical tips to look into the human stomach after the ingestion of chile peppers to see if any damage is done, and it turns out that chile peppers, even very hot chile peppers, cause no trauma at all to the stomach. They are in many ways beneficial to our systems, causing a healthy perspiration and acting as a vermifuge, that is, an agent that dispels worms from the intestinal tract.

USES ◆ Fresh chiles can be used to add heat to dishes in many ways, from a faint glow to a real burn. Here are some ways to add a pleasant heat to your cooking.

Cut up a jalapeño and add it seeds and all to a small bottle of cider vinegar, store for a week, and then use on salads, on strong ocean fish like bluefish or salmon, or on cabbage. Similarly, slice a couple of serranos and add them to a cruet of olive oil, store for a week, then use the oil for sautéing onions or shallots, to sauté shrimp or scallops, to replace butter on popcorn, to brush onto bruschette or crostini, or even to cook a fried egg. A hot chile sliced open, seeded, and its hot placental material scraped into melted butter and cooked over low heat just until the butter melts, then chilled, produces a chile butter that turns bread and butter into something truly special. Use chile butter to grease a pan and sear a filet mignon before finishing it in a 350°F oven. Once you start getting creative with that light mouth glow, you'll miss it unless you feel it at every meal.

Dried chiles give different flavors based on how they are prepared. Grinding the dried pods in a mortar and pestle or *molcajete* (see recipe at right) gives a strong, assertive pungency when added to a salsa or other sauce. Toasting chile pods before grinding gives them a sweeter, richer flavor. (To toast the pods, bake them in a 300°F oven for 10 minutes.) Soaking dried chiles in water for half an hour to soften them before grinding results in a more aromatic taste. Dried peppers can be soaked and stuffed or pureed to add to soups and sauces, and ground dried chiles can be worked into sauces for enchiladas.

SALSA MOLCAJETE

MAKES ABOUT 1 PINT

A *molcajete* is a heavy granite mortar in which salsa ingredients are traditionally ground. You can use a blender pulsed a few times to approximate the chunky texture a molcajete gives.

5 ripe medium Roma or plum tomatoes
3 jalapeño peppers
1 small white onion, chopped
1/2 cup cilantro leaves
2 cloves garlic, peeled
Salt to taste

1. On a grill or in an iron skillet over high heat, sear the tomatoes and jalapeños, turning them a few times until they are soft and all sides are charred. Remove from heat and allow them to cool.
2. Remove the tomato skins. Remove the stems from the jalapeño peppers and then their skins by rubbing them with a paper towel. Place the peeled tomatoes, chiles, onion, cilantro, garlic, and salt in a molcajete and pound until chunky and blended. If using a blender, pulse to roughly chop the ingredients.

GREEN SALSA (SALSA VERDE): Follow the recipe above, replacing the tomatoes with 1/2 pound of tomatillos, husks removed, chopped, and cooked in a skillet over medium-low heat for 15 minutes. Add 1/2 teaspoon of sugar.

EXTRA HOT SALSA: To increase the pungency of the salsa, add 5 seeded, chopped serrano chiles or 1 habanero. The serranos and habanero can be used raw, as grilling is impractical and may release choking, burning fumes. ■

HARISSA

MAKES ABOUT 1 CUP

This hot sauce originated in Tunisi but has become the staple flavoring agent for many North African dishes. You can buy it canned or in tubes at many Middle Eastern markets, but it tastes best when homemade and will last in the fridge up to six months. You can vary the level of pungency by choosing different varieties of chiles. For a good, hot harissa—the way the Moroccans like it—use dried pasillas or chipotles, and if you want to maximize the burn, include a dried habanero or two.

12 dried chiles, sliced in half, seeds removed, and roughly chopped
1/2 cup extra-virgin olive oil, plus extra for storage
1 teaspoon ground cumin
4 cloves garlic, coarsely chopped
Salt to taste

1. Soak the pieces of chile in warm water for 30 minutes, until they soften. Drain and place the chiles in a blender with the olive oil, cumin, garlic, and salt.
2. Blend until a smooth paste is formed. Put the paste into a small jar and float 1/4 inch of olive oil on top. Cap and refrigerate. ■

MOROCCAN CHICKEN

SERVES 4

Here's a way to use some of that Harissa (page 107) you've made from scratch in a traditional Moroccan dish. The chicken is rubbed with a harissa and spice paste, then stewed, and finally broiled. Serve with couscous studded with golden raisins and dried currants. (Prepare the Steamed Couscous as on page 57, adding a handful of raisins and currants before steaming.)

FOR THE HARISSA PASTE

2 tablespoons caraway seeds
4 cloves garlic, peeled
1/2 teaspoon saffron threads
1 piece peeled fresh ginger, about the size of your thumb
2 tablespoons Harissa (page 107)
2 tablespoons ground coriander
2 tablespoons ground cumin
2 tablespoons freshly squeezed lemon juice
1 tablespoon sweet paprika
1 tablespoon olive oil
1 tablespoon salt

2 (3-pound) chickens, cut in half, backbones removed
4 tablespoons butter
3 cups diced onions
1/4 cup chopped fresh cilantro

1. To prepare the harissa paste: Heat the caraway seeds in a dry skillet over medium heat for 1 minute, until they're fragrant. Put them in a blender, then add the other harissa paste ingredients. Blend to a rough paste.

2. Wash the chicken halves and dry well with paper towels. Rub the chicken halves with the harissa paste, slipping a little under the skin here and there.

3. Melt the butter in a Dutch oven or heavy lidded pot over medium heat and add the onions. Sauté until the onions are translucent and soft, about 5 to 10 minutes.

4. Add the chicken halves to the pot and almost cover with water, about 4 or 5 cups. Bring to a boil, then reduce to a simmer. Cover and simmer 45 minutes, turning the chickens once during that time, until chicken is tender. Remove the chicken from the pot to a baking sheet. Add the cilantro to the liquid in the pot and boil about 20 minutes, until the liquid is reduced to about 2 or 3 cups.

5. While the liquid is reducing, preheat the broiler and broil the chicken skin side up until golden brown, about 5 minutes. Transfer the chicken to a platter. Correct the seasoning in the reduced juices, if necessary, and pour the juices over the chicken. You can strain the liquor if that pleases you aesthetically, but it's traditionally served unstrained. ▪

Corn

ZEA MAYS

CORN HAS COME a long way since a Mexican annual grass called teosinte crossed with another wild grain (scientists don't know which or when, but it was probably sometime well before 6000 BCE) and the resulting hybrids began to sport small, 3/4-inch heads studded with seeds. The first evidence of cultivation of this plant by Native Americans was discovered in the Tehuacan Valley of Puebla, Mexico, and dates to 5500 BCE.

By the time Columbus arrived 6,992 years later, the plant had changed into its modern form—dependent for its survival on human hands to pull the seeds off the cobs and plant them individually a foot or so apart.

THE ORGANIC FACTOR ▸ As of this writing, about 60 percent of the corn planted in the United States has been genetically modified to be able to grow well in an herbicide-drenched environment or to incorporate a gene from a bacterium that expresses a caterpillar toxin, making the corn generate its own pesticide. So, besides avoiding the pesticides conventional farmers spray for insect pests, organic corn will be free of such unnatural additions to the corn genome.

NUTRITION ▸ Native Americans long ago learned to boil their corn in water into which they threw wood ashes. Today we know that niacin—a necessary vitamin in the human diet—is present but locked up and unavailable in corn. Societies that depend on corn for the bulk of their protein are liable to develop pellagra, a particularly nasty disease caused by niacin deficiency. Adding ash to cooking water, however, alkalizes the water and converts the niacin into a form that can be assimilated by humans—a process scientists call nixtamalization. Today corn is just a part of our diet rather than the central foodstuff, and we get plenty of niacin from other sources.

TYPES ▸ Sweet corn is a natural mutation of Indian or field corn—the starchy corn used mainly for cattle fodder in the United States. A mutant gene slows the conversion of sugar to starch, keeping the corn sweet—but only until the ear is picked. As soon as it is picked, the corn begins turning its sugar into starch. For maximum sweetness, then, you have to get the corn to the pot of boiling water immediately.

In recent decades corn breeders have come up with corn that contains the so-called sugary enhanced gene (se), which produces added sugar in the kernel. We're not talking genetic engineering here, but just regular, old-fashioned selection of superior strains.

Eventually breeders found corn with the so-called shrunken gene (sh2), which slowed the conversion of sugar to starch so completely that this corn, known as Xtra Sweet, will stay sweet for two weeks after it's picked.

I'll say this for Xtra Sweet corn: it's really sweet. So sweet that some people find it cloying. I'm on the edge: If it's fresh-picked, fine. Then it's crisp, juicy, and sweet. But don't let it sit for two weeks. It'll still be sweet, but it will also have lost many of

SEE ANY EARWORMS?

CORN EARWORMS ARE those fat gray grubs that chew into the kernels at the tips of corn ears. The presence of earworms is a minor inconvenience, says nothing about organic versus conventional farming practices, and simply means that the farmers aren't rotating their crops. If the earworms have been there for a while, they can chew their way down toward the midlength of the ears, but that's rare and really indicates that the corn is too old. Despite their rather grubby appearance and the trail of frass they leave in their wake, earworms are natural. Usually they are found just in the tips of the ears and the tips can be broken or cut off easily and discarded, earworm and all.

A good organic farmer will never grow corn in the same field year after year. His or her corn will be relatively earworm-free because of good management. And more nutritious, too.

the enzymes that make fresh corn taste so good. Treat it like any other corn: eat it as soon as possible.

There is another kind of corn coming on the market that you may find at farmers' markets or roadside stands called Triple Sweet or Sweet Breed™. Each ear of this corn contains standard sugary (su), sugary enhanced (se), and Xtra Sweet (sh2) kernels on the same ear. I haven't tried it yet, but it sounds like an advance over the heavily sweet types. You get sweetness, but also old-fashioned corn flavor from the standard kernels.

BABY CORN ‣ When I was learning to grow vegetables organically, I planted my first corn crop in soil so poor I had to open up a 4-inch-deep channel in the brick-hard earth with a pick. I planted the seeds a foot apart in five rows 3 feet apart, like the seed packet said, and pretty much forgot about the corn. Later that summer I found spindly little stalks about 18 inches tall growing among weeds. They had 2-inch ears, which I dutifully harvested. I thought they looked like the baby corn that was showing up in Szechuan dishes in Chinese restaurants, so I tasted one—hmm, sweet and tender. So I harvested the bunch of them—got maybe two handfuls from the whole darn patch—and wokked them into a stir-fry. That's how I discovered that Chinese baby corn is just that—immature corn picked very young and not a separate kind of corn.

SEASONALITY ‣ Ideally, corn is a summer annual, with a peak season of August and September in the Northeast, with the season extending earlier and later than that in warmer climates.

WHAT TO LOOK FOR ‣ Ideally corn laid out for sale should be iced down in summer heat. I remember sweet corn vendors coming to Pennsylvania from southern New Jersey, the back of

their trucks loaded with sweet corn covered in ice. Cold water ran in rivulets from the bottoms of their flatbeds. The corn had been picked that morning and was perfect. You could tell because the cut stem ends were still green or whitish green, and juicy-crisp when nicked with the thumbnail. When corn gets old, the cut ends are white and fibrous looking, and feel dry when nicked. When really old, they're brown.

Way back, nobody ever thought of stripping the husks open to inspect each ear of corn the way people do now. It astounded me when I first saw shoppers pulling down the husks from ear after ear, tossing ones they didn't like back on the pile—for later poor suckers to buy, I suppose. You can feel through the husks when an ear is full and fat and when it's not. You can pull open just the very top of maybe an ear or two and give it the fingernail test: If the kernel expresses clear juice when it's pressed open with a thumbnail, it's too young. If it expresses a milky fluid, it's just right. If the kernel is dry and doughy, it's too old.

PREPARATION ‣ To husk corn, peel the husks back just to the stem end, like peeling a banana, then grasp all the husks with one hand and the ear with the other and twist the husks off with a breaking motion. When grilling corn in the husks, remove the tough outer husks and soak the partially husked corn in cold water for a half hour before grilling. Otherwise the husks dry and burn before the corn is properly grilled.

USES ‣ Sweet, tender, creamy corn is so luscious simply boiled on the cob that it's hard to believe it could be better. But when someone takes the time to dig a pit in the seashore sand and burn a driftwood fire, reducing it to a bed of red-hot coals, then load in wet seaweed, a few bushels of corn, lobsters, and soft-shelled clams, and top it with more seaweed and wet burlap until the corn and seafood are all roasted and steamed, right there could be your first dinner in paradise.

Think of all the things that corn gives us. Bourbon! (My folks were from Kentucky, "where the corn is full of kernels and the colonels are full of corn.") But also tortillas, tamales, scrapple (a Pennsylvania Dutch pudding made of corn meal and ground up parts of pigs that is sliced and fried in lard), popcorn, hominy grits, polenta, hush puppies, corn pone, corn bread, hoe cakes, johnny cakes, spoon bread, and—hallelujah!—corn smut. This is a fungus that invades corn and looks like a gray and blackish-purple alien growth, but which is treated as a delicacy called *huitlacoche* in Mexico, where it's steamed or fried.

Corn has many culinary affinities, among them bacon, butter, cayenne, cheese, lemon, lime, onions, black pepper, and salt. It's as versatile and delicious a vegetable and grain as we have.

HUMITA CASSEROLE WITH CORN HUSKS

SERVES 4

I first ran into *humita* at a restaurant called Grand-ma's House near Mendoza, Argentina, and was delighted at its richness and delicate flavors. In subsequent days eating at a variety of restaurants, I saw that humita—a mild and tender preparation made with freshly grated corn kernels—is a national dish in Argentina, often accompanying great portions of grilled beef.

Under different names, humita is known throughout the Americas, especially Spanish America. A sweetened version is preferred in the northwestern parts of Argentina and is made with cheese, onions, lard, and sugar and spiced with cinnamon and nutmeg, or anise. But the following is my favorite.

Even though they are not edible, the corn husks (called *chalas* in Argentina) enhance the fresh corn aroma of the humita; they are the main seasoning for this very special dish.

12 ears corn in their husks
Salt
1 cup milk
1 tablespoon cornstarch
1/4 cup olive oil
1 large onion, chopped
1 teaspoon ground cumin
1 teaspoon anise seeds
2 tablespoons brown sugar
Freshly ground black pepper

1. Bring a large pot of water to a boil. Remove husks from the corn and add them to the pot along with 1 teaspoon salt, and blanch for 3 minutes. Take the pot off the heat, drain the husks, and reserve.

2. Prepare corn kernels as follows: Cut kernels off cobs. Squeeze remaining corn milk out of cobs with the back of a knife, or slice down through the rows of kernels of a few of the ears with a sharp knife and then scrape out the milk and flesh with the back of a knife, then slice off the remaining kernels. Place this in a blender and whiz to a grainy consistency, not a fine puree.

3. In a small bowl, dissolve the cornstarch in the milk. Preheat the oven to 300°F.

4. In a large skillet, heat the oil over medium heat. Add the onion and cook for about 3 minutes, or until translucent and softened. Add the cumin, anise seeds, the corn puree, and milk with dissolved cornstarch in it. Bring to a boil and simmer gently until mixture thickens, about 4 to 5 minutes, stirring constantly to prevent sticking. Remove from the heat, stir in brown sugar, and salt and pepper to taste.

5. Butter or oil a Dutch oven with a heavy lid and carefully line it all the way around inside with the

continued

parboiled husks, first the sides and then the bottom. Use scissors to trim husks for the bottom to fit the pot's dimension. Husks on the sides must be placed with the pointed ends upwards, so they can later be folded over the top of the humita. Pour the humita into the husk-lined pot, fold the pointed husk ends over the top of the mixture and cover completely with additional husks. Place the lid on the pot and bake for about 1 1/2 hours, until the humita is tender and fluffed up.

6. For maximum drama and fun, bring this to the table hot from the oven still covered. Remove the cover and the husks on top, then open up the folded-in husks with a large spoon. ▪

INDIAN PUDDING

SERVES 6

One taste of this sweet and spicy pudding and you're back with the Pilgrims eating wild turkey and oyster pie on the shores of Cape Cod Bay. It's a delight when the weather turns cold, and there's a fire in the fireplace.

1/2 cup stone ground cornmeal
4 cups whole milk
1/2 cup blackstrap molasses
4 tablespoons unsalted butter plus extra for the casserole
1/2 teaspoon salt
1 teaspoon ground ginger
1 teaspoon ground cinnamon
1 large egg, well beaten
2 tablespoons sugar

1. Preheat the oven to 275°F. Place the cornmeal in a 1 1/2- to 2-quart saucepan, stir in 1 cup of the milk, turn the heat to medium, and add another cup of milk, stirring to avoid lumps. As the milk comes to a boil, slowly add the remaining milk, stir-

ring as you do so. Cook for 3 minutes, then reduce the heat to low and simmer for 15 minutes.

2. Add the molasses and stir until entirely dissolved. Remove the saucepan from the heat and let cool for while you grease a 2-quart casserole. Stir the 4 tablespoons of butter, the salt, ginger, cinnamon, egg, and sugar into the batter. When it's well incorporated, pour the batter into the casserole. Bake uncovered for 2 1/2 to 3 hours. ▪

CHEESY CORN SOUFFLÉ

SERVES 4

When corn is in season, I can't get enough of it. Here its savory flavor merges beautifully with fontina cheese in a light and fluffy soufflé.

2 cups corn kernels and cob scrapings, prepared as for Humita Casserole (page 111, Steps 1 and 2)
1/2 cup shredded fontina cheese (about 2 ounces)
6 eggs, separated plus 2 extra egg whites
4 tablespoons finely chopped chives
Salt and freshly ground black pepper
1/4 teaspoon cream of tartar

1. Preheat the oven to 425°F. Grease an ovenproof 2-quart soufflé dish.

2. In a mixing bowl, blend together the corn, cheese, 6 egg yolks, chives, salt, and pepper. Place all 8 egg whites in a separate bowl; add the cream of tartar, and beat them to soft peaks. Using a rubber spatula, fold the whites into the corn mixture until they're well incorporated. Pour the mixture into the soufflé dish, and bake uncovered for 10 minutes. Reduce the heat to 375 and bake for 30 minutes more. ▪

Crosnes

STACHYS AFFINIS

ALTHOUGH *CROSNES* (a French word, pronounced "crones") are a relatively new item in markets around the United States, they've been enjoyed in Europe and Asia for years. In Asia they are called *chorogi*, Chinese or Japanese artichokes, or knotroot. Crosnes are a perennial member of the mint family, in the same genus as woolly-leaved lamb's ears. They're tubers, about the size of your little finger, and have ridges around their circumference like the Michelin man. And they have a sweet, nutty taste and crunchy texture, something like a water chestnut or the nutty roots of field sedges, with a bit of the juiciness of a Jerusalem artichoke.

THE ORGANIC FACTOR ‣ Crosnes are very much a specialty crop—the kind small organic farmers like to grow.

NUTRITION ‣ Crosnes have lots of crunch but not much nutrition—or many calories. Three ounces contain about 2½ grams of protein and 17 grams of carbohydrates.

SEASONALITY ‣ Crosnes are harvested mostly in the fall, so that is the best time to find them in markets.

WHAT TO LOOK FOR ‣ Crosnes should be creamy white without brown spots, and crisp in texture without soft spots.

Crosnes are popping up more and more frequently at organic markets, specialty shops, and farmers' markets. Additionally, there are a number of sources for crosnes for eating as well as planting. (See Sources, page 517.)

PREPARATION ‣ Because crosnes are tubers that grow underground, they need to have any clinging soil washed away. Snip off any brown tips.

USES ‣ I made my first acquaintance with crosnes on a visit to the restaurant at the Domaine Chandon winery in the Napa Valley. Chef Ron Boyd made a vegetarian plate of salsify and crosnes with black trumpet mushrooms and green garlic in a black mushroom sauce, with smoked onion and French lentils on the side. I had to ask what the lumpy little tubers were.

Crosnes can be washed well and served raw with crudités or in salads. They add crunch in stir-fries.

IF YOU LIKE TO GARDEN

CROSNES ARE EASY TO GROW as long as you have good organic soil that's amended with compost and kept moist, especially during summer hot spells. Like lamb's ears, they'll form a mat of leaves in the summer. In the fall, when the leaves turn brown, the tubers are ready to harvest by gently turning over the soil and picking through it by hand to find the lumpy little crunchies. Don't harvest them all—the tubers you leave in the ground will sprout new top growth next spring and make more roots.

They can be pickled or steamed and tossed in butter sauce. Because they're in short supply but so useful, they're currently bringing very high prices in gourmet and specialty markets. That's sure to change as more growers get in on the bonanza.

CROSNES, PEAR, AND HAZELNUT SALAD

SERVES 4

This recipe was shared by Cheryl Long, the editor of *Mother Earth News,* who published an article on the tubers in her magazine's February–March 2004 issue.

1 cup raw crosnes

2 cloves garlic, crushed

Juice of 1 lemon

3 tablespoons hazelnut oil

5 tablespoons rice vinegar

Salt and freshly ground black pepper

4 cups mixed salad greens

2 ripe Anjou or Bosc pears, halved, cored, and sliced thin

1/2 cup toasted hazelnuts, coarsely chopped

1. Clean the crosnes and remove any brown tips. Bring 3 cups of water to a boil in a saucepan. Add the crosnes, garlic, and lemon juice. Reduce heat and simmer for 2 minutes. Remove the pan from the heat and let the crosnes and garlic sit in the water for 5 minutes more. Drain the crosnes and pat dry on paper towels. Discard the garlic.

2. To make the dressing, whiz together the hazelnut oil, rice vinegar, and salt and pepper to taste in a blender. Divide the salad greens among 4 plates. Arrange the sliced pears and crosnes on top. Sprinkle with chopped nuts. Drizzle with the dressing and serve immediately. ■

Cucumber

CUCUMIS SATIVUS

WHEN WE IN AMERICA think of cucumbers, we usually think of those smooth, dark green jobs in the supermarkets that have thick, tough skins covered with a waxy film that's put on the cukes after harvest. These are American Slicers. Their thick, waxed skins slow down the transpiration of water through the cucumbers' skin so they have extended shelf life in the markets, but during that extended time the fresh, delicate flavors and aromas dissipate. Instead of crisp, juicy flesh, these usually old cucumbers have soft, watery flesh and are often filled with overly-mature, hard seeds. Additionally, a substance called cucurbitacin develops just under the skin and at the stem end to make these market cukes unpleasantly bitter and difficult to digest.

Breeders have been hard at work of late, however, and new hybrids tend to produce less cucurbitacin. New varieties are often grown in greenhouses on trellises; these varieties are self-pollinating and seedless, sweet rather than bitter, and very digestible.

THE ORGANIC FACTOR ◆ Cucumbers have not one but two insects that are so hell-bent on feeding on them that they have the word "cucumber" appended to their names: striped and spotted cucumber beetles. To find their host plants, these beetles home in on the cucurbitacin present in the cucumber. Shady conditions, cool nights, and too little water cause an excess of cucurbitacin in the cucumbers.

Conventional growers spray pesticides against the beetles, because these insects carry fungal and bacterial wilts that infect the vines as they feed. The wilts produce a thick, viscous substance that clogs the vines' intricate plumbing systems, which have evolved because cucumber fruits are 97 percent water. The clogged vines eventually die.

Among organic growers, the chief line of defense against the wilts are physical barriers to the cucumber beetles, such as fine-mesh row covers. And most organic growers interplant their cucumbers with a variety of other crops, avoiding the monoculture of cucumbers that floods the fields with the cucurbitacin that attracts the beetles. Finally, organic farmers look for fungus and wilt-resistant varieties of cucumbers. All this means that organic growers can grow their cucumbers without having to spray for striped or spotted cucumber beetles. I never grew cukes without noticing some of the beetles hanging around, but they were never plentiful enough to cause trouble.

NUTRITION ◆ Because cucumbers are almost all water, there isn't a lot of nutrition in them, except for about 3 to 5 milligrams of vitamin C in a 3-ounce serving.

TYPES ◆ There are many types of cucumber out there other than American Slicers—for instance, Pickling Cucumbers (see Top Varieties, page 486). For years when I was a beginning gardener, I thought pickling cucumbers should only be used for pickles. But over time I discovered that they are simply a cucumber variety with thin skins, little bitterness, and a firmer, crisper, sweeter flesh— ideal for pickling but also for eating. Cornichons are miniature cucumbers and also ordinarily pickled, but they can be eaten raw as well.

Eventually, I found European Greenhouse cucumbers in the markets. These are the long, slender cukes that come wrapped tightly in plastic, and they are excellent. Their crisp flesh tastes mild but coolly refreshing. They lack any bitterness.

They have no seeds. Their ribbed skins are so thin they don't need peeling. And they are very digestible. Middle Eastern types also have ribbed skins and thin skins. They are my preferred sort for Greek salad.

And don't forget about Asian types—those used by sushi chefs to make matchstick cukes for rolled sushi. They are extra flavorful and crisp and can substitute for other types in a wide variety of dishes.

SEASONALITY ◆ Just when the weather turns hot, here comes the new crop of fine cucumbers to cool things off. Lie on the couch with a cold, wet washcloth across your forehead and slices of cucumber on your eyes and the hot weather will blow away in the cucumber's cool breeze.

WHAT TO LOOK FOR ◆ When looking for cucumbers at roadside stands, farmstands, or farmers' markets, don't buy any that are waxed. That's a sure sign of low quality. Warty cukes are fine— they're probably high-quality pickling cukes. Cukes that have prickly spines are also to be sought after. The spines come off easily by rubbing the cuke with a dish towel. In all cases, they should be a nice, green color all the way around. If they have a yellow patch on one side, that means they are overly ripe and probably contain large numbers of hard seeds. Make sure the cukes are very firm, with no "give" when you squeeze them.

PREPARATION ◆ Thin-skinned cucumbers don't require peeling.

USES ◆ It's the rage right now to cook cucumbers, but I'm so enthralled by their cool, fresh flavors that I have a hard time putting them to the flame. I like them raw in Thai salad, where they combine well with chiles and lemongrass. Occasionally on very hot days I may make an Indian raita—a refreshing relish made with yogurt and chopped or pureed cucumbers, flavored with mint, cumin, lemon juice, and a bit of spicy chiles. On hot days when you just can't cook, buy some cold, precooked salmon and serve it topped with finely diced cucumbers. At tea time, serve those precious little tea sandwiches made of cucumber slices on buttered crustless bread.

You can also make pickles. When you find organic pickling cucumbers, slice them lengthwise in quarters and put them in a jar with a small handful of dill seeds, a few coriander seeds, and a tablespoon of kosher salt and fill the jar with white vinegar. Let it stand on the kitchen counter uncovered for two or three days, then screw the lid on and put it in the fridge. Shake the jar every few days. In about two weeks, you'll have your own organic pickles.

TZATZIKI

SERVES 6

In Greece, this thick cucumber-yogurt dip is served with almost everything. It is great as a spread with pita bread, as a sauce for seafood, chicken, roast lamb, or goat, or as a dip for grilled slices of summer vegetables. Greeks drain excess liquid from their yogurt to thicken it; otherwise, the tzatziki will be too watery.

1 quart plain yogurt
1 medium pickling cucumber, peeled and grated
3 cloves garlic, minced
1 tablespoon red wine vinegar
1 tablespoon chopped fresh mint
2 tablespoons extra-virgin olive oil
Salt and freshly ground black pepper

1. Place the yogurt in a double layer of cheesecloth, tie it up in a bag, and let it hang for 2 hours, until well drained and thickened. Press the grated cucumber between paper towels to remove as much liquid as possible.

2. In a bowl, mix together the drained yogurt, cucumber, garlic, vinegar, mint, and olive oil, and season with salt and pepper to taste. Place in a serving dish, cover with plastic wrap, and refrigerate for several hours to give the ingredients time to integrate. ■

GREEK SALAD

SERVES 4

As long as we're going Greek with the cucumbers, I'm including a recipe for Greek salad. No lettuce, please. And the tomatoes should still be warm from the garden and the cucumber firm and juicy rather than limp and watery. If you aren't growing the ingredients in your garden, make the salad the same day you buy the ingredients fresh from a farmstand. This is real Greek salad, as encountered by my wife and son on a five-week tour of Greece.

3 ripe tomatoes, preferably heirlooms
1 top-quality cucumber, peeled and cut into 1/4-inch slices
1 cup cubed feta cheese (1/2-inch cubes)
3 tablespoons olive oil
GARNISHES, OPTIONAL
1/2 green bell pepper, seeded and cut lengthwise into thin strips
1 anchovy fillet, mashed and tossed with the basic ingredients
1/2 cup pitted kalamata olives
1 small red onion, cut in half lengthwise, sliced 1/4 inch thick and separated
1/2 teaspoon dried oregano

1 tablespoon vinegar
1 tablespoon capers
Salt to taste

Lay out the tomatoes and cucumbers on a platter and sprinkle with the feta, and drizzle olive oil on top. These ingredients alone form the basic Greek salad. However, even in Greece cooks will add a little something else for flavor. Add any combination of garnishes that you like. However, I suggest you use either the vinegar or the capers but not both, and reserve the right to use neither. ■

Edible Flowers

NOT ALL FLOWERS that are edible are palatable. Also remember that not all flowers are edible. Some are poisonous. You must know for certain that any flower you are putting on a plate or into a salad is indeed safe to eat. Be aware that some edible flowers, if eaten in a large quantity, can cause stomach upsets or diarrhea, so it's wise to limit the use of any edible flower to small amounts.

THE ORGANIC FACTOR ▸ It's imperative that they be organic. Never use flowers from a florist, a flower stand, or a nursery, as these invariably have been sprayed with pesticides. The best place to gather edible flowers is from your own or someone else's organic ornamental garden or from the wild if you know the area hasn't been sprayed. Be wary of roadside flowers—even if they haven't been sprayed, they may contain burned hydrocarbons from vehicle exhaust.

TYPES ▸ Many flowers are quite safe to eat, and they can brighten up the look of a dish or salad, as well as add spicy herbal notes. The following flowers can safely be eaten.

Alliums—This includes the blossoms of onions, leeks, chives, and garlic chives. Separate the florets and sprinkle them on salads to add a hint of onion or garlic flavor.

Angelica—Its flowers range from light lavender to rose and carry a licorice-like flavor. A fine garnish for ocean fish.

Anise hyssop—Lilac-blue flower spikes can be pulled apart and the anise-scented flowers used as a garnish. A few of the tender top leaves add a similar flavor to salads.

Apple blossoms—A few apple blossoms in springtime add beauty to a fruit dish, ice cream, or sorbet dessert.

Basil—Basil flowers range from white to pink and lavender and carry the same clove-like scent as the leaves. Pull florets from the flower spikes and use them to pretty up light pasta dishes.

Beebalm—The garden varieties (*Monarda didyma*) have red or pink circular blossoms that can be pulled apart, while wild beebalm (*Monarda fistulosa*) has a heady spicy scent from pale lavender flowers.

Borage—Borage flowers are a pretty true blue and taste like cucumber. Excellent sprinkled in a salad or as a garnish for tall drinks.

Calendula—Pull the petals from the composite blossoms and sprinkle on salads, soups, pasta, and rice dishes. Shower over a frosted cake. The flavor may be spicy or tangy.

Dianthus—Carnations or dianthus species have clove-scented flowers in a variety of colors. Trim the petals away from the bitter core of the flower and use them in salads or to decorate cakes.

Chamomile—The tidy composite flowers with raised centers make a decorative addition to cakes and desserts.

Chervil—Sprinkle their anise-flavored, small white flowers on salads or use as garnish for lamb.

Chicory—Cool blue petals in summer have an endive-like taste because they are in the endive family.

Chrysanthemum—Petals often used in Asian cooking. Use the petals only as the base is bitter.

Cilantro—The pinkish white, small flowers have the same strong flavor as the leaves of this parsley-like plant.

Citrus—Use a few of the waxy flowers to add a heavenly scent as a garnish with fruit dishes.

Clover—Crimson clover has deep, rich crimson color. Use sparingly. Little white Dutch clover has a sweet taste. Pull florets off flower head to use in salads.

Cornflower—Sky blue flowers have a spicy, clove-like flavor. Use as a garnish or to decorate icing.

Dandelions—Pull the yellow florets off just-opened flowers. They have a warm, honey-like flavor. Sprinkle on salads, pastas, rice.

Daylilies (*Hemerocallis* species only)—Cut the petals away from the thick, juicy base just as they open and tear up to sprinkle on salads. They taste sweet and pleasant.

Dill—Tear fresh umbels and use the flowers anywhere dill is called for, such as in soups, in tartar sauce, with pork dishes.

Elderberry—The blossoms make an excellent addition to pancake batter. Use only the blossoms themselves as all other parts of elderberry are very poisonous, even the stems that hold the flowers.

Fennel—Yellow fennel flowers have a strong, dill-like flavor and can be used with fish and on salads.

Fuchsia—Great as a decorative garnish, but an insipid flavor makes them useless as food.

Gardenia—Flowers project a strong and beautiful scent. Use as a garnish.

Geranium (*Pelargonium* species only)—A few of the flowers of different species of scented geraniums are best used as garnish or sparingly in salads. They are also used in jellies.

Gladiolus—The petals don't have much flavor but make a strong color splash torn up and used in salads.

Hibiscus—Tangy and tart blossoms can be used whole as a striking garnish, or the petals can be torn into bits for use on salads. Dried, these are the basis for a popular West Indian and Mexican beverage.

Hollyhock—Not much taste in the petals, but useful as garnish.

Honeysuckle—As you probably found out as a kid, the flowers of Japanese honeysuckle (*Lonicera japonica*) are pointedly sweet. Use sparingly in salads. The berries are poisonous.

Impatiens—A few flowers of the "busy Lizzie" can add color as a garnish.

Jasmine—Highly fragrant flowers are usually used for scenting tea but can also be used on rice after it's cooked.

Johnny-Jump-Up—This pretty, diminutive viola is easy to grow and self-seeds (hence its name). Use as garnish or a few blossoms in salads.

Lavender—Strongly-scented blossoms can be scraped off flower heads and sprinkled on lamb, used in salads, in crème brulée and custards, and a flower head adds a whimsical scent and flavor to sauvignon blanc.

Lemon verbena—Use the citrusy, lemony, whitish blossoms to flavor custards, and use in salads.

Lilac—Use pretty, scented florets in salads.

Marjoram—The small white flowers have the same scent and flavor as the oregano-like herb. Use as you would the herb.

Mint—The mint-scented and -flavored white to pinkish flowers are a pretty addition to tabbouleh and can be brewed with tea.

Mustard—Yellow flowers in spring can be added to early spring salads. Some people are allergic to mustard.

Nasturtiums—Unopened buds can be pickled and used like capers. Flowers are strongly colored and have an interesting, snappy, peppery flavor. Chop petals and use in salads. Whole flowers are a common garnish.

Okra—One of the prettiest of the vegetable flowers. Use flowers as a garnish.

Oregano—Purplish-pink blossoms carry light version of leaf flavor. Use as you would leaves in Italian, Greek, Provençal, and Spanish dishes.

Pea—The white to faintly colored blossoms of garden peas are excellent in salads. The gaily-colored ornamental known as Sweet Pea is poisonous; don't use.

Petunia—Not much flavor but makes a pretty garnish.

Primrose—Slightly sweet but essentially flavorless. Best used as a garnish on cakes and desserts.

Radish—The white and lilac flowers have the peppery bite of radishes and help dress up salads. The young seed pods that follow can be pickled.

Rosemary—Garnish rack and leg of lamb with sprigs of rosemary in full bloom. Use the tiny blue fresh flowers on all sorts of savory dishes, especially meats and shellfish.

Sage—Flowers of various varieties range from white to pink to bright red to violet to an almost midnight blue. They're small, with a light sage flavor, and are clustered on a terminal flower spike. Use spikes as a garnish. Use florets to enliven vegetable dishes like succotash or ratatouille. Also good with savory meats, especially chicken.

Savory—Both summer and winter savory flowers are edible. Summer savory's are white to rose, while winter savory's are white to lilac. Both have a slight medicinal flavor that is just right with green beans or cooked shell beans.

Scarlet runner beans—These climbing beans produce red flowers with the taste of green beans. Toss some in the salad.

Squash blossoms—The petals of yellow-orange squash blossoms can be sliced into thin strips and used in corn and bean dishes. Whole flowers can be stuffed and fried, battered for tempura, or used as a wrapping for little packets of freshly cooked vegetables. (See page 191 for a recipe.)

Sunflower—Flower buds can be steamed like artichokes. After they open, use the petals as you would calendula or chrysanthemum petals.

Sweet woodruff—Tiny white flowers have a warm, vanilla-like scent and a sweet, herbaceous flavor. Used in Germany to flavor May wine.

Thyme—The flower heads have thyme's familiar scent and resinous flavor. Use the flower heads as garnish or pull off florets and sprinkle on soups, salads, pastas, and chicken.

Violet—Freeze the sweet-scented little flowers of wild violets in ice cubes. Or toss a few into salads. They have a sweet, mild taste. Use flowers to decorate cakes, cupcakes, ice cream desserts.

SEASONALITY ◦ Edible flowers are available year around in the warm climates, during the growing season in colder regions.

WHAT TO LOOK FOR ◦ Freshness is the key; the flowers should not look limp or faded.

PREPARATION ◦ Washing delicate flowers will mar their beauty. Remove any ovaries—small lumps of tissue where the petals attach—and stems.

USES ◦ Flowers are mostly used as garnish or to add a bit of color to green salads or other dishes. They are also used to flavor sorbets and ice creams and may be candied for garnishes to desserts or turned into jellies, as here.

VIOLET JELLY

MAKES ABOUT 8 HALF-PINT JARS

This jelly has a most delicate flavor and color. It makes a fine accompaniment to tea cakes and English muffins. Or use it as a pastry glaze.

1 cup dark purple violet flowers
1/2 cup chopped mint leaves
4 cups sugar
2 tablespoons unseasoned rice vinegar
3 ounces liquid pectin

1. Place the violets and mint leaves in a small saucepan with 2 cups of water. Bring the mixture to a full boil, remove from the heat, and let it steep for 20 minutes.
2. Strain through a fine sieve into a larger saucepan and add the sugar and vinegar. Turn heat to medium-high, bring the mixture to a boil, and

cook, stirring frequently, until sugar is entirely dissolved, about 3 to 4 minutes. Add the pectin and bring the mixture back to a boil for 1 minute, then take the pan off the fire.
3. Skim any foam from the top, then pour the mixture into 6 to 8 sterilized jelly jars, leaving 1/2-inch head space. Put on lids. Allow to cool completely and freeze, or process in boiling water bath according to jar manufacturer's instructions and store in a cool, dark place. ▪

Eggplant

SOLANUM MELONGENA

EGGPLANTS are members of the *Solanaceae* family and are related to tomatoes, peppers, potatoes, ground cherries, and tomatillos, as well as some dangerously poisonous and addictive plants, including tobacco, belladonna, jimsonweed, and black nightshade. Although it's grown as an annual in the temperate United States, the plant is a tropical perennial.

Of the edible *Solanaceae*, eggplant is the only one native to the Old World. Scientists believe it originated in either India or Burma and was carried east to China and west to Arabia. The Moors introduced it into Spain and from there to rest of Europe in the 8th century. Before the arrival of its New World relatives with Columbus, eggplant was as much a staple crop in southern Europe as the potato later became. In Italy, it was originally thought to be poisonous and was called *mela insana,* or insane apple. Today the Italian word for eggplant, *melanzana*, is a corruption of the phrase. In the rest of Europe it's known as aubergine, a term that has come down a convoluted path from its original Sanskrit. With good old American bluntness, we know it as eggplant, and if you have ever seen the variety called Osterei, which means Easter egg, you'd think you were looking at a white egg.

THE ORGANIC FACTOR ➤ Conventional growers spray eggplant with fungicides for phomopsis blight and with pesticides for an array of insects including lace bugs, blister beetles, flea beetles, and Colorado potato beetles. Organic growers control these pests with physical barriers like row covers, with sticky traps, and, for potato beetles, a strain of *Bacillus thuringiensis* that's harmless to other forms of life.

NUTRITION ➤ Many recipes combine eggplant with other Mediterranean ingredients in various ways, along with lots of heart-healthy olive oil. Eggplant is heart-healthy in other ways, too—it's one of the top ten vegetables in antioxidant content.

TYPES ➤ Besides the familiar raven-dark, purple-black common eggplant seen in supermarkets, there are eggplants varieties that vary in size from ping-pong balls to two-foot ropes and in color from orange-red to pinkish lavender to celadon green to ivory white. These you'll most likely find at specialty markets, farmers' markets, and roadside stands—or in your own gardens.

If you are already familiar with the common purple types of eggplant, I suggest looking for pale green types that are exceptional in quality; smaller Asian types (such as Japanese and Chinese) with thinner skins and very delicate flavor; white types with tough skins but an earthy, mushroomy flavor, and the violet to pink and white Italian types, especially Rosa Bianco (also sold as Rosa Bianca), which is very meaty, texturally fine, and has a choice, delicate flavor.

SEASONALITY ➤ You'll find the choicest eggplants at farmers' markets in August and September in most of the country.

WHAT TO LOOK FOR ➤ To obtain the highest quality eggplants, growers should harvest them at about two-thirds of their full, mature size. Full sized eggplants have a tendency to turn overly bitter and their seeds ripen and become hard and bothersome. The bright gloss of their skin dulls. They soften and turn watery and puffy. When pressed with a thumb, the indentation remains. Smaller eggplants, when perfect, have skins with a high gloss and when pressed with a thumb have a little "give" that rebounds when the pressure is lifted. Their green cap and stem are bright and freshlooking. And the best eggplants will feel heavy in the hand—like citrus fruit.

Because of its tropical nature and its short shelf life, don't store eggplants in the fridge. Just set them on a cool counter space and use within a day or two after buying.

IF YOU LIKE TO GARDEN

EGGPLANTS ARE RELATIVELY EASY TO GROW and having your own eggplant fresh from the garden will give you a benchmark for quality that you can use when buying them. Eggplant is a very ornamental plant, with pretty purplish and yellow flowers and showy fruits that dangle under the wide leaves.

USES ‣ Eggplant adds texture and bulk to dishes along with its sappy flavors. It's used around the world in a variety of regional and ethnic dishes. In the Middle East, baba ghanoush joins hummus as a preferred dip for pita bread. In Sicily, caponata relish is made by cooking eggplant, onions, tomatoes, anchovies, olives, pine nuts, capers, and vinegar in olive oil. In Spain, tiny white eggplants are pickled. In Greece, moussaka is a national dish. In France, ratatouille and aubergine au gratin are standard fare. In Russia, they make eggplant caviar from a cooked, peeled, and finely chopped eggplant mixed with grated onion, garlic, minced peeled and seeded tomato, a little olive oil, and salt and pepper.

No matter what color eggplant you start with, cooking is going to turn the skin a shade of gray-brown.

MIDDLE EASTERN STUFFED EGGPLANT (*IMAM BAYILDI*)

SERVES 2

Across the Muslim world there's a dish known as *Imam Bayildi*, which translates as "the priest fainted." One school of thought has it that he fainted from the sheer pleasure of the dish, and another that he fainted when he found out how much expensive olive oil his wife used to make it. This recipe is easily doubled to serve four people, but you'll need a larger dish for the final baking.

1 large black eggplant
1 small onion, chopped
1/2 cup plus 2 tablespoon olive oil
1/2 teaspoon cumin seed
3 cloves garlic, chopped
1 ripe medium tomato, peeled, seeded, and chopped
1 teaspoon tomato paste

Salt and freshly ground black pepper
1/2 cup dried bread crumbs
1/2 cup freshly grated Parmigiano-Reggiano
2 cups boiling water
2 tablespoon minced Italian flat-leaf parsley

1. Cut the eggplant in half lengthwise and score the flesh with a knife, spooning out the flesh into a bowl, leaving a 1/2-inch thickness of flesh and skin for later stuffing.

2. Preheat oven to 400°F.

3. Heat 1/2 cup of the olive oil in a medium skillet over medium heat. Add the onion and the eggplant flesh, and fry about 5 to 7 minutes, until the onions are tender and translucent and the eggplant is tender. Add the cumin, garlic, tomato, tomato paste, and salt and pepper to taste, and mix thoroughly. Reduce the heat to medium-low and simmer the mixture for 3 to 4 minutes, turning several times so everything is well mixed and almost all the moisture is absorbed.

4. Stuff the eggplant shells with the mixture, top them with the bread crumbs and grated cheese, and drizzle them with the remaining 2 tablespoons of oil. Place the stuffed shells in a 9 × 9-inch baking dish and pour the boiling water into the dish, making sure it doesn't come close to the top of the shells. Cover the dish with aluminum foil and bake for 40 minutes. Sprinkle the tops of the stuffed eggplant shells with the parsley and serve. ■

INDIAN EGGPLANT AND POTATO STEW (*SALNA*)

SERVES 6 TO 8

The spicy flavors of India transform two members of the *Solanaceae* family—eggplant and potatoes—into an exotic stew with a bright yellow color. It's a fabulous side dish with curried lamb.

2 pounds Japanese or Italian eggplants, quartered

1 pound red potatoes, peeled and quartered

2 serrano chiles, halved lengthwise and seeded

2 teaspoons minced garlic

1 tablespoon minced fresh ginger

1 tablespoon Garam Masala (see Tip, page 91)

1 teaspoon mustard seeds

1/2 teaspoon ground turmeric

1/4 cup olive oil

2 tablespoons chopped cilantro

2 tablespoons chopped scallions

Preheat the oven to 400°F. Place the eggplant, potatoes, chiles, garlic, ginger, garam masala, mustard seeds, turmeric, and oil in a large bowl and toss to thoroughly coat the vegetables with the oil and spices. Place in a baking pan large enough to hold everything in a single layer. Bake for 45 minutes, turning every 15 minutes. The stew is done when the potatoes are cooked through and golden brown on the outside, and the eggplant is soft. Serve garnished with the cilantro and scallions. ■

RATATOUILLE

SERVES 6 AS A SIDE DISH

Ratatouille is a late summer dish that begs to be made when the tomatoes and eggplants are at their flavorful best. Despite its simple ingredients, it bursts with flavor. Make a batch the evening before a day when you don't plan to cook, as it gains charm in the fridge overnight. On hot days, serve it cold with cold meats, such as a rotisseried organic chicken.

1/2 pound eggplant, your choice of type

1/2 pound very young zucchini

3 tablespoons olive oil, plus more if needed

1 1/2 cups thinly sliced onions

1 cup red, yellow, or green bell peppers slices

2 cloves garlic, chopped

Salt and freshly ground black pepper

1 1/2 cups peeled, quartered, and seeded tomatoes

3 tablespoons minced fresh parsley

1. Peel the eggplant, unless it is a very thin-skinned type. Slice lengthwise into 1/2-inch slices, and cut these into about 1-inch-wide strips. If the eggplant is watery, sprinkle with salt, set aside for 30 minutes, press, rinse, drain, and pat dry. Cut the zucchini to strips about the same size.

2. In a skillet, heat the olive oil over medium heat. Add the eggplant strips and sauté for 1 minute on each side. Repeat with the zucchini. Set aside both vegetables.

3. In the same pan, add the onions and peppers, adding a little more oil if necessary, and cook for about 10 minutes, until they're softened but not browned. Stir in the garlic, and add salt and pepper to taste. Cut the tomato quarters into 1/2-inch-wide strips and place them on top of the onions and peppers. Cover the pan and cook on low heat for about 5 minutes, until the tomato juice starts to run.

4. Remove the lid and spoon some of the pan juices over the tomatoes, then turn up the heat to medium and let the juice reduce until it's almost all gone, about 5 minutes. Remove from the heat.

5. Spoon about one-third of the tomato-onion-pepper mixture into a flameproof casserole, and sprinkle 1 tablespoon of the parsley over it. Cover this with half the zucchini and eggplant strips. Spoon half the remaining amount of tomato mixture over the strips and sprinkle another tablespoon of parsley on top. Top with the remaining zucchini and eggplant strips. Finish with the last of the tomato mixture on top and the last tablespoon of parsley.

6. Cover the casserole and cook over low heat for 10 minutes. Remove the lid and spoon the

continued

juices over the vegetables, then cook uncovered on medium-low heat for another 15 minutes. Correct the seasoning. Spoon the juice over the vegetables several more times until it is almost entirely gone, but be careful not to let it all evaporate or the vegetables might scorch. ■

Fennel

FOENICULUM VULGARE
variety DULCE

FENNEL is a member of the *Umbelliferae* tribe—an aromatic group that includes dill, cumin, caraway, coriander, carrots, parsley, celery, and angelica, among others.

Italian immigrants may have first brought wild fennel to California, where it escaped from cultivation many years ago, or the wild fennel here may have crossed over as Florence fennel, which then escaped and reverted to a stronger, wild, bulbless form. In any event, it's a ubiquitous weed in California and the Pacific Northwest now, used by cooks much as it is in Europe—as a vegetable, and its seeds as a flavoring, especially for salmon and other seafood caught fresh from the Pacific.

A form of fennel known in the Mediterranean is called bitter fennel because of the intensity of its licorice-flavored, bitter sap. Bitter fennel may, in fact, be the plant that has naturalized on the West Coast. When fennel is mentioned in antiquity, it's bitter fennel that's being referred to—sweet fennel appeared about 900 CE, and bulbous Florence fennel didn't appear until the 16th or 17th centuries. Bitter fennel, for example, is mentioned several times in the Roman cookbook by Apicius. In Greek mythology, when Prometheus stole fire from the gods to give to

mankind so that people could emerge from their brutish state, he supposedly hid the flame in a fennel plant—a strange tale until you see wild fennel in the fall when it's beginning to senesce. Its stalks turn a range of beautiful, warm colors: pink, reddish, cream, yellow, and salmon. It looks as though it might conceal fire somewhere deep within itself.

THE ORGANIC FACTOR ▸ Most commercial Florence fennel sold in the United States is grown in California or the Deep South, and its distinctive aroma seems to discourage most insects. Even in California, where conventional farmers pour chemicals on their crops just to prevent insects from wandering into their fields, only two and a half tons of all types of agricultural chemicals and other substances were used on fennel in 2001 in the whole state. That means that the fennel you get at farmers' markets is most likely free from harmful chemicals—but, of course, that's not the same as a certified organic crop with all the benefits that accrue to the environment, the farm, and the vegetable's flavor and nutritive value.

NUTRITION ▸ Three ounces of Florence fennel provide about 12 to 14 percent of a person's minimum requirement of vitamin C for a day and good amounts of calcium and potassium.

TYPES ▸ You'll sometimes see this vegetable called anise due to its light anise-like aroma and flavor, but true anise is another plant altogether. And I've seen it called "sweet fennel" at farmers' markets, but here in northern California the name sweet fennel is reserved for the wild fennel that's a familiar sight (and smell) along roadsides and pathways in the countryside. The same wilding is also found in southern France and in Italy, where its strongly anise-scented and -flavored feathery fronds are used in soups and sauces and for stuffing fish, poultry, and rabbit.

The bulbous fennel we see in most markets is Florence fennel or finocchio, as it's called in Italian markets. The bulb of Florence fennel isn't an enlarged root but, rather, enlarged petioles—leaf stems where they attach to the crown. As such, they overlap, and the outer petioles conveniently protect the inner ones when soil is mounded up around the swelling bulbs to blanch them in the garden or field.

If you're growing it in your garden, allow a few plants to head up and go to seed—the seeds carry a sharp fennel flavor of an essential oil, *anethole*, that can be used in making bread, pastries, confections, and sausage and to flavor seafood. In earlier times, cranky babies were given "gripe water," in which fennel seeds and herbs like chamomile were steeped. Seeds of Florence fennel are readily available in most markets.

SEASONALITY ✦ Florence fennel is a summer through fall crop. Fennel seed is available year round.

WHAT TO LOOK FOR ✦ Fennel that's locally grown in rich organic soil develops a tender crunchiness that's succulent, aromatic, and refreshing. The feathery leaves have some turgidity and stand up straight. I can usually tell commercial fennel sold in supermarkets—whether organic or conventional—by its marred surface (from long farm-wholesale-retail handling) and its dull look and limp leaves.

If you're buying Florence fennel, try to find bulbs with as many of the feathery leaves still attached as you can. If you're buying at a farmers' market, ask your farmer if he or she will bring some fennel with all the fronds attached next time—then plan to stuff your salmon or trout with the chopped fronds (see Uses, below).

PREPARATION ✦ When separating the fronds from the bulbs of Florence fennel, leave about an inch of the stalks at the top of the bulb.

USES ✦ Fennel's celery-like crunch and light anise (almost dill-like) flavor are irresistible. Its anise character, already mild, is lessened by cooking, so some cooks looking to maintain its flavor will add fennel seeds or *pastis*, as the French call their anise-flavored liqueurs such as Pernod. I like the attenuated anise character of cooked Florence fennel and don't find a need to increase it.

Fennel definitely has an affinity for fish, especially salmon, and its flavor merges beautifully with lemon juice, cucumbers, niçoise olives, bourbon, and good Parmigiano-Reggiano. I buy a half pound of fresh sausage loose at the market, mix it with a heaping tablespoon of fennel seed and an ounce or two of bourbon, and fry it in patties for Sunday breakfast of eggs and sausage.

COOKING WITH FENNEL FRONDS ✦ Whole fish stuffed with a bunch of the fronds is aromatic bliss. To prepare a whole fish that weighs 3 pounds or less, use a 500°F oven; for a fish heavier than 3 pounds, such as a whole salmon, use a 450°F oven. Make three or four diagonal slashes on each side of the fish. Separate the feathery fronds from the fennel stalks. Line a roasting pan with aluminum foil to facilitate cleaning up and lay the stalks down on the foil. If you are using wild fennel, blanch the fronds for 30 seconds before stuffing the fish. Coarsely chop the fennel fronds and stuff into the whole fish. If any are left over, lay them on the stalks. Place the fish in the roasting pan and bake at the temperature indicated.

A fish under 3 pounds will take from 25 to 35 minutes, depending on size. A large fish may take 45 minutes or even more. Check doneness by pulling one of the slashes apart with a fork held in each hand. When the flesh is opaque right down to the bone, the fish is done. Whiz the coarsely chopped bulb in the blender with a peeled and seeded cucumber and a bit of salt. When the fish is finished, serve it with the pureed fennel-cucumber sauce.

Try making pesto with fennel fronds instead of basil. If using Florence fennel, they can be used fresh. If using wild fennel, blanch the fronds for 30 seconds, then drain. Chop the fronds fine. Squish a couple of cloves of garlic through your garlic press into the chopped fronds. Mash two anchovy fillets in some olive oil and stir the mixture into the pesto. Mash a small handful of pine nuts (taste them first to make sure they taste sweet and lightly piney; so often pine nuts taste rancid) in a mortar and stir them in. Toss with fresh pasta.

COOKING WITH FENNEL STALKS • This is the part between the bulb and the fronds in cultivated fennel. Wild fennel has no bulb, just stalks and fronds. In Provence, cooks will grill fish over a fire of dried sweet fennel stalks. If you want to try this, gather the stalks in summer when they're still juicy; they lose their fennel flavor when they dry naturally after they senesce for the winter. Try some fresh, young, spring stalks in dishes like braised fennel. Get them shortly after they emerge, for they toughen and become woody by late June. Peel the stalks until you're down to the juicy centers, then cut them into 3-inch lengths. Pan fry them in a little garlic and olive oil for about 10 minutes, turning them frequently, then add ½ cup of fish stock, cover the pan, and braise them for about 20 minutes until tender.

FENNEL AND TOMATO SALAD

SERVES 4 TO 6

In high summer or early fall, when tomatoes are at their garden-fresh finest, use the best you can find—heirloom or good old Beefsteaks, whatever is perfectly ripe—to make this luscious salad.

2 or 3 medium dead-ripe tomatoes
1 fennel bulb, leaves attached
2 tablespoons freshly-squeezed Meyer lemon or orange juice
Freshly grated zest of 1 Meyer lemon or small orange (well scrubbed if not organic)
2 tablespoons olive oil
1 tablespoon apple cider vinegar
Salt and freshly ground black pepper

Slice each tomato into 8 wedges. Cut off the stalks and feathery leaves from the fennel, reserving the leaves. Very thinly slice the fennel bulb. Toss the tomatoes and fennel with the citrus juice and zest, oil, vinegar, and salt and pepper to taste. Chop the feathery fennel leaves very fine and garnish the salad with a generous tablespoon of them. Toss and serve. ▪

Garlic

ALLIUM SATIVUM

THE ANCIENT EGYPTIANS imbued garlic and onions with divinity and took their oaths on them. In Numbers 11:15, we read that the Israelites, wandering in the desert after their escape from Egypt, fondly recalled the garlic they had eaten there. Among the other treasures in King Tutankhamen's tomb were heads of garlic. The wild progenitors of garlic were native to south-central Asia and the central Asian steppes. It's likely the plant made its way west to the Middle East and the Mediterranean on the caravans that plied the Silk Road in deep antiquity. Certainly garlic seems to have remained unchanged since the days of ancient Egypt, probably because it is propagated vegetatively by planting cloves rather than sexually through seeds.

THE ORGANIC FACTOR ◆ You would think that garlic, with its pungency and antibacterial properties, would be the last crop to need heavy applications of agricultural chemicals. But in California—where much of the country's commercial garlic is grown—the crop is drenched with 25 tons of chemicals a year, much of it to fumigate the soil against root-destroying worms known as nematodes.

It makes sense, therefore, to find a local source for organic garlic, either at a farmers' market, roadside stand, or your own backyard. Because it's easy to grow, many organic truck farmers and market gardeners grow it. You can also find it fresh from online suppliers.

NUTRITION ◆ Allicin is a major factor in the considerable health benefits of garlic. It thins the blood, is important in preventing heart attack and stroke, dissolves blood clots, raises the level of good (HDL) cholesterol, lowers the level of bad (LDL) cholesterol, lowers triglycerides (fats in the blood), lowers blood pressure, and protects against colon cancer. It also kills or stuns bacteria, fungus (especially yeast), internal parasites, protozoa, and some insects.

TYPES ◆ The white-skinned garlic you find at most supermarkets, and sometimes see braided into long strands, are usually California Early and California Late types. They're what's called "soft-neck" varieties, and they usually have white or silver skins. When the heads of soft-neck types are harvested and the leaves dry out, they are pliable and easy to braid. Hard-neck varieties, which tend to have darker red or purple striped skins, are generally more pungent and when their tops dry, they are stiff and difficult to braid. But the hard-neck varieties are also hardier and can be grown in the

IF YOU LIKE TO GARDEN

ONE OF THE NICE THINGS about growing your own garlic is that you have lots of different varieties to choose from instead of being stuck with the conventional varieties called California Early and California Late. Not far from me in the little village of Occidental, California, lives Chester Aaron, the garlic maven of all garlic mavens. He grows over 60 different varieties of "the stinking rose," as garlic is sometimes lovingly called, and has written *The Great Garlic Book* and *Garlic Is Life*.

northern states, and their flavors are more varied than the soft-neck types. If you find a source for organic garlic who knows the names of the varieties he or she sells, you've found a true garlic aficionado.

Besides these true garlics, a number of other plants are often lumped in with garlic (see Top Varieties, page 487).

SEASONALITY ✦ Although garlic is in the stores all year around, it definitely has a season of peak quality—and that's summer. Garlic is day-length sensitive, as are many members of the onion family. That means that the heads swell and grow to size until the sun turns south after the summer solstice, at which time they ripen. Most garlic, being hardy and able to withstand winter's frozen months, is planted in the fall as single cloves from the head. Each clove will make a new head next year. The small garlic plants overwinter and start growing again when the soil warms up in the spring. Along about mid-May, you may start seeing fresh, young heads of garlic at the farmers'

markets. These are easy-to-peel, immature heads of mild flavor and are quite nice sliced and added to salads, baked on a pizza, and added to soups.

By the end of June the heads have reached their full size and slowly ripen, their outer layers becoming the papery husks we're familiar with. By fall, the garlic flesh begins to shrink and dry a bit. When the weather turns cold, the garlic cloves ready themselves for winter by sprouting a small green shoot inside each clove. These shoots are meant to lie dormant in the soil until spring calls them forth. But they also have an unpleasant bite and harsh flavor. During the late fall and winter, slice your garlic cloves open and remove the green sprouts if their taste becomes bothersome to you.

WHAT TO LOOK FOR ✦ When buying garlic, what you don't want to see is any green sprouts showing from the tips of the cloves. The heads should be perfectly firm, with no softness. Give the heads a gentle squeeze. There should be no "give."

ROASTED GARLIC

ONE OF MY FAVORITE WAYS to use garlic is to roast several whole heads in a moderate oven (too hot an oven turns the cloves to a brownish, pungent, bitter mush), about 375°F. Put about 1/2 inch of water in a casserole and set the heads upright, the way they grew. Cover and roast about 30 minutes, then test a clove to see if it's soft. If it's soft, it's done. If still firm, uncover and give the heads 5 or 10 more minutes. When done, I let the cloves cool until I can handle them, then shear off the tops of the cloves with my poultry shears and squeeze the soft, garlicky paste into a bowl. This stuff is a precious ingredient to have on hand. Mix it into mashed potatoes, mix it with olive oil and salt to brush on toast, drop a dollop into soups and stews, spread some on the top of your omelet before folding it over, make soft polenta with mascarpone cheese and whisk in 1/2 cup of the roast garlic—you'll find plenty of ways to use this garlic mush, as I call it.

PREPARATION ◆ Garlic is odorless until you peel the skin from the cloves. Then enzymes work on the garlic flesh to produce a compound called allicin that gives the cloves their pungency. Over a fairly short period of time—less than an hour— further enzymatic action degrades allicin, reducing its punch, although it increases the healthful properties of garlic. Cooking also reduces the pungency of allicin. When cooking, use freshly peeled cloves for the best flavor. Be aware, though, that the more finely you chop or mash garlic, the more allicin is created and the stronger the pungency will be. Garlic presses, therefore, yield the most intense flavor, whereas the use of whole cloves or coarsely chopped or sliced cloves yield proportionately less.

Another tip about using garlic: It really does become nasty if it burns or scorches, and it burns and scorches easily. When adding chopped or minced garlic to fried or sautéed dishes, add it during the last minute, the exception being when you rub meat with mashed garlic before roasting.

USES ◆ All over the world, cultures use garlic to enhance savory dishes (and then there are the folks in Gilroy, California, who make garlic ice cream). Many of the traditional sauces, marinades, and rubs for meat and fish in diverse cuisines of the world contain garlic. In Cuba, garlic is combined with lime juice and cumin to make *mojo*, a marinade for grilled chicken, pork, or firm-fleshed fish. In Russia, garlic is pickled. In the countries of Southeast Asia, it's combined with lemongrass, ginger, soy sauce, cilantro, and hot chiles.

Think of the sauces and dips we find in restaurants everywhere these days, such as the garlicky mayonnaise from southern France called aioli. Italians pound basil, garlic, pine nuts, cheese, and olive oil together to make pesto. Greeks make the sauce and dip called *skordalia* from pureed baked potatoes, garlic, lemon juice, olive oil, vinegar, parsley, and bread crumbs or ground nuts. *Persillade* is parsley and garlic. *Gremolata*, traditionally sprinkled on osso buco, is made from minced parsley, lemon peel, and garlic. Rouille is the hot and spicy mix of fiery chiles, garlic, bread crumbs, and olive oil mashed into a paste. It's used as a garnish with seafood stews like bouillabaisse and mixed with fish stock to give the stock a wallop. This just begins to tap the troves of garlic sauces and dips.

Garlic seems to inspire passion in the kitchen. I was taught an old Italian way to dress pasta with garlic by a friend in Rhode Island. He took a dozen whole heads of garlic and broke them into cloves that he whacked with the flat blade of a butcher knife to break open their papery skins. He then shucked the fleshy cloves and chopped them coarsely on his cutting board. He put a good ¼ inch of olive oil in his largest skillet, heated it on medium-low and when the oil reached medium heat, he dumped in the garlic. Stirring it constantly to avoid any scorching he removed the pan from the fire when the garlic turned a light golden color and achieved a degree of chewiness. He'd timed a large pot of spaghetti to be ready just at this point and drained it and turned it into a large serving bowl, then poured the oil and garlic over the pasta, gave it a quick toss, and we ate. And ate. And ate—it was so good. Sounds simple until you have to peel the cloves from a dozen garlic heads. I was tempted once—only once—to buy those already peeled garlic cloves at the supermarket to make this dish, but the already peeled cloves had lost a lot of their perfumey, pungent goodness.

ANCIENT GREEK GARLIC SAUCE

MAKES 1 CUP

There's evidence in the archaeological record that ancient Greeks used some version of this sauce on their esteemed fish slices (considered then to be the pinnacle of gastronomy). I like it as a dip for pita bread along with hummus, accompanied by oil-cured olives.

1 slice whole-wheat bread, crust removed
1 head garlic
1/2 cup blanched almonds
Salt to taste
1/4 cup olive oil
1/4 cup red wine vinegar

Soak the bread in a dish of water. Separate and peel the garlic cloves, and mash them in a mortar with the almonds and salt until a thick paste forms. Squeeze the excess water from the bread and add it to the paste, along with the olive oil and vinegar. Mash and mix thoroughly. Correct the salt if necessary. Stores in the fridge for up to 1 week. ■

GARLIC RUB FOR MEAT

MAKES ENOUGH TO RUB ONE RACK OR ROAST

ABOUT 1/2 CUP

Rub this on a rack, shoulder, or leg of lamb; on a rolled boneless pork roast; or on a beef roast before cooking.

4 cloves garlic, peeled
2 teaspoons freshly ground black pepper
1 tablespoon each minced fresh parsley, sage, rosemary, and thyme (just like the Simon and Garfunkel song)
1/2 teaspoon kosher salt

Mash everything together in a mortar with a pestle or pulse briefly in a food processor and rub over the surface of the meat before roasting. ■

Green Bean

PHASEOLUS, VIGNA, VICIA,
GLYCINE, various species

WHEN WE SEE the term "green beans," most of us think of the common snap bean (*Phaseolus vulgaris*). That's just the surface of the world of fresh beans, though. Beautifully streaked and colored horticultural beans, flat pods, shell beans, slender filet beans, favas, soybeans, and limas all qualify as green beans, whether the whole pods or just the fresh beans inside the pods are eaten.

In Latin bean is *faba* and refers to the fava bean (*Vicia faba*) known in ancient Europe. In Slavic, fava beans are *bobu* and in German, *Bohnen*. A thousand years ago in Old English *bean* was pronounced BAY-ahn. But these were all favas or lentils. Green beans as we know them have their heritage in Central and South America. There's archaeological evidence that they were cultivated in Peru 5,000 years ago, and lima beans (*Phaseolus lunatus*) were indeed first encountered by westerners when the Conquistadors entered Lima, Peru, in the 16th century. The Aztecs called green beans *ayecotl*, which has been carried into French as *haricots*.

THE ORGANIC FACTOR ▸ Cooks interested in quality should be glad that organic green beans in season are becoming widely available, because the alternative isn't very appetizing. Along with strawberries and peppers, green beans are one of the most heavily sprayed crops in conventional agriculture. And that's because beans are as attractive to insects and diseases as they are to us. Organic growers have a variety of methods for dealing with insect pests like the Mexican bean beetle: planting soybeans as a trap crop, covering bean plants with fine-mesh row covers, releasing parasitic wasps that destroy the beetles' larvae, and spraying the plants with the extract of the neem tree—a harmless substance that repels insects.

NUTRITION ◆ Green beans have just a trace of fat and no cholesterol and are a good source of protein—although it's not a complete protein. That's why Native Americans long ago planted corn, beans, and squash together, calling them the Three Sisters. Proteins from those three vegetables combined have all the amino acids that make up complete protein. Besides, they grow so well together. The corn grows tall, creating a pole for the beans to climb while the squash runs in the rows, its big leaves shading the ground and keeping down weeds. The beans, being a legume, add nitrogen to the soil through the action of nitrogen-fixing bacteria that colonize their roots, and nitrogen is exactly what corn needs to produce a bountiful crop.

The nutritional champion among beans is the lima bean—it has four times the amount of carbohydrates and folic acid of snap beans and three and a half times as much potassium. Beans are whole seeds, so they belong with whole grains and seeds on the new food pyramid.

TYPES ◆ Beans can be classified in any number of ways. The green beans eaten whole are classified by how they grow, by their fibrosity, and by size.

Common green beans—which are eaten whole—are first named by how they grow—they are called either bush beans or pole beans. Bush beans grow on short bushes; pole beans are climbing vines that grow on poles or trellises or some other support. Bush beans are easier to grow, but pole beans produce greater yields.

They are further categorized by fibrosity: String beans have indigestible strings running the length of the pods, while snap beans have had the strings bred out of them. Most green beans on the market today are snap beans.

Further, these green beans are grouped by size. The smallest beans are called filet or French beans (*haricots vert*), and they are slender, tender, and delicious. Yard-long beans and asparagus beans are tender when very young but tough when they grow to their foot-long-plus mature size.

Wax beans are so named because they have a succulent waxy texture, and they are ordinarily yellow whole beans you eat pod and all. Shell beans—which must be removed from their pods before cooking and eating—usually have specific names, which are then classified as either fresh or dried, depending on how they're prepared.

SEASONALITY ◆ Other than bush snap beans, which are available pretty much year round, other green beans are highly seasonal, appearing at farmers' markets and organic grocery stores from early summer through midfall.

WHAT TO LOOK FOR ◆ You can test the freshness of a snap bean by bending one. If it's dull in color, rubbery and limp, it's past its prime. If it's a bright lively green, bends a little, and then breaks in half, it's fresh. The pods should be straight and smooth, without the obvious lumps of the beans inside showing. Common snap beans like Blue Lake will be tender at 6 inches or so and start toughening up when longer than that.

Most green beans are best on the young side. Haricot verts, the slender French filet beans, should be just 2 to 3 inches long—any longer and they get tough fast. These beans are more flexible than regular snap beans, so don't expect them to snap in half. The asparagus bean (*Vigna unguiculata* subspecies *sesquipedalis*), also called the yard-long bean, should never be allowed to grow to size, or it will be like eating rope. They should be young and no more than 6 or 7 inches long. Flat-podded pole beans like Romano are tender at 6 to 8 inches, but don't buy them if they're longer. With shell beans, on the other hand, we want the beans inside to be full grown or near to it, since we're not going to eat the pods. And so, look for clean, supple pods, with no damage or disintegration—that show the obvious lumps of the beans inside.

PREPARATION ► A word of warning right up front: Don't nibble raw shell beans while you're shelling them out of their pods or otherwise preparing them for cooking. They contain glycosides that can produce hydrocyanic acid in the human digestive system, and there are cases of children dying from eating raw beans. Just a few minutes of cooking detoxifies them. To be on the safe side, boil shell beans for a few minutes, then pour out the water and add fresh water. Return to a boil to finish cooking. Soybeans and favas don't contain the glycosides, but they taste better cooked anyway.

To remove favas' tough seed coat, boil the favas in their pods for 10 minutes, run cold water over them, then open the pods to reveal the beans. Slip them out of the pods with your thumb. Each bean will have a small green area at one end. With your thumbnail, nick open the seed coat at the end opposite the green part. Holding the bean by the green part, squeeze it gently and the nice, bright

green bean inside will slip out. I do this no matter what their size, even though small beans won't yield much.

One more word of warning: It's rare, but some people, mostly of Mediterranean descent, lack an enzyme to break down fava beans and can have a serious reaction to them. If that's your heritage, nibble a little fava before you launch into a plateful or have your doctor give you the test for favism.

And while sprouting makes beans' starch and protein more digestible, raw sprouted beans—except mung beans—contain a substance that inhibits trypsin, a digestive enzyme. So sprouted seeds of green beans should be cooked, such as in a stir fry.

USES ► Snap beans have a long running love affair with toasted almonds and, for some reason, with anchovies. Italians dredge them in flour and fry them in olive oil until they're golden brown and crispy. In India, they haul out heavy spices for snap beans: turmeric, cumin, cayenne, and mustard among them. Eastern Europeans tend to sauté them with onions and flavor them with dill, garlic, nutmeg, and a little beef stock. In Greece and Bulgaria, they may add tomatoes, carrots, bell peppers, and thyme to the sauté pan. Here in America, we have tended to cook them and serve them plain—as if their natural flavor were flavor enough.

Favas have a delightfully subtle, green taste and a silky texture, so look for ways to showcase their delicate flavor, such as dressing boiled favas with just a little olive oil and fleur de sel. Go Mediterranean with favas, sautéing them with olive oil, spring onions, thyme, oregano, rosemary, and garlic and giving them a flavor bump with a teaspoon of olive tapenade mixed in—although you'll lose some of their delicacy this way. Favas also have an affinity for pancetta, pecorino cheese, and the breath-freshening herb called savory.

Fresh limas, black-eyed peas, and other shell beans have a more vigorous flavor than favas, so think of simple ways to use them: in broth, or boiled in salted water and served at room temperature (like green Japanese soybeans called *edamame*), or as an accompaniment for delicate fish like halibut or sole. Think dill or just a bit of nutmeg to enliven their flavor, with maybe a dash of cream. Large limas have a more generous, earthy flavor, while small ones are not only harder to shell out but have a greener, more herbaceous flavor.

BUTTERBEANS AND COLLARDS

SERVES 3 TO 4

Beans don't get much more down home than in this dish. Look for fresh butterbeans in high summer at Southern farmers' markets. If you can't find them, use fresh lima beans as a perfectly good substitute. These ingredients allow the sweet, slightly herby flavor of the beans to come through, enhanced by a hint of savory.

1 cup fresh butterbeans or limas, rinsed (about 1 pound in the pod)
1/2 cup white wine
1 sprig fresh thyme
1 sprig summer savory
1/2 teaspoon olive oil
1 small onion, chopped
1 bunch collards (2 dozen leaves)
1 jalapeño pepper, seeded and minced
Salt and freshly ground black pepper
Dash of white wine vinegar

1. Rinse the beans and add them to a pressure cooker along with the wine, thyme, and savory, plus enough water to just cover the beans. Turn the heat to medium, but don't put on the cover. Let the beans gently cook for 10 minutes.

2. Meanwhile, heat the olive oil in a skillet, add the onion, and sauté until translucent, about 5 minutes. Rinse the collards and lay them on top of each other in a stack, then roll them up tightly and cut across the roll to produce 1/4-inch, nicely shredded strips of leaves. Add the onion, jalapeño, shredded collards, and salt and pepper to the pot of beans and stir everything together.

3. Put on the lid and bring up to full pressure for 3 minutes. Cool the cooker under running water, and turn the contents into a serving bowl. Remove the thyme and savory sprigs. Add a dash of white wine vinegar and toss, then serve immediately. ∎

Ground Cherry

PHYSALIS PRUINOSA

ONE OF THE GREAT JOYS of growing up in the country was the discovery of good things to eat that grew wild. One of my favorites was ground cherries.

Ground cherries are found in old fields, meadows, along roadsides, and in waste places throughout the East, from Canada to Florida. They're borne prolifically on trailing, lanky stems that weave through summer's tall grasses and herbs—up to 300 fruits per plant. They are related to the tomatillo (*Physalis philadelphica*) and the Cape gooseberry (*Physalis peruviana*), and indeed, they resemble miniature yellow-brown tomatillos but are more flavorful.

NUTRITION ✦ These small fruits are good sources of vitamins C and A.

TYPES ✦ Ground cherries are the wild species, although they have many relatives of different species.

SEASONALITY ✦ Ground cherries are hard to spot until fall, when other plants die back. That's when you see the lacy, beige, papery husks and inside each one, a berry the size of a blueberry.

WHAT TO LOOK FOR ✦ Few farmers grow them, as wild ground cherries are fairly ubiquitous east of the Rockies. Because of that, I have seen wild-picked pint baskets of them offered for sale at farmers' markets and roadside stands on warm October days. They should be bought ripe; they will stay fresh for extended periods (four to six weeks) as long as their papery husks are not breached.

PREPARATION ✦ Peel away the husk, and you'll find a small, tomato-like, sweet-tart fruit. Until they ripen, ground cherries are green and inedible. When yellowish, yellow-brown, or yellow-spotted brown, they're ripe and ready to eat raw or baked. In spite of their name, they do not have stones like regular cherries.

USES ✦ The tomato-like tangy, sweet, earthy flavor of ground cherries is wonderfully appealing. The Pennsylvania Dutch folks who lived around my home in the Poconos and in the Lehigh Valley to the south made pie from them, and it is an intense piece of pie, existing somewhere between sweet and savory. Once a season is usually plenty of exposure to ground cherry pie, due to the strength of the flavor.

The berries can also be used raw: Chop them and add to salads or mix with onion and hot chiles

to make a salsa. They're also made into preserves and dried for addition to winter dishes later on.

GROUND CHERRY PIE

MAKES ONE 9-INCH PIE

I've this recipe from a Mennonite woman from around Huff's Church, Pennsylvania. She topped her pie with a flour-sugar-butter crumb crust, but I prefer it with either a regular pie crust or lattice top. Use your favorite recipe for a double pie crust; or double the recipe on page 211; or if you want a crumb top, mix three tablespoons of flour with an equal amount of white sugar, cut in two tablespoons of chilled unsalted butter until reduced to crumbs, and scatter the mixture on top.

4 cups ripe husked ground cherries
1/2 cup packed brown sugar
2 teaspoons instant tapioca
1/4 teaspoon salt
2 tablespoons all-purpose flour
2 tablespoons butter
Pastry for a double crust 9-inch pie

1. Preheat the oven to 450°F and place a rack in the middle of the oven.

2. Mix the ground cherries, sugar, tapioca, salt, and flour in a bowl and let stand while you roll out or prepare the bottom pie crust and line the 9-inch pie pan.

3. Stir the mixture and pour it into the pie pan, then dot the top with little pieces of the butter. Place the other crust on top, crimp the two crusts together, and prick the top well to allow steam to escape; or make a lattice top.

4. Bake for 10 minutes; reduce the heat to 350°F and bake for 40 minutes more, until golden brown. ■

Kale

BRASSICA OLERACEA

variety ACEPHALA

KALE is closer to the urbrassica—the native wild cabbage of Europe's cold shores—than any of the other members of the cabbage family we cook with today, including broccoli, cauliflower, kohlrabi, and head cabbage—except perhaps for collard greens, which are simply a flat-leaved version of curly kale.

Kale was the staple green of ordinary people during the Middle Ages and as such kept the peasant farmers in better health than their lords and masters, who dined principally on meat. Simple meals of kale, potatoes, and black bread sustained the poor farmers of northern Europe and Russia through long, harsh winters—as kale would grow when no other fresh greens were available.

Kale is so winter hardy that it persists quite nicely through most European winters—and if things get really frosty, you can just mound snow over it and it will keep fine. Not only that but kale becomes sweeter and more tender when hit by hard frosts.

THE ORGANIC FACTOR ✦ Like most dark green, leafy vegetables, kale will take up and concentrate nitrogen from the soil in its tissues. In excess, certain of these compounds can form carcinogenic nitrosamines in the intestines. One of the hallmarks of conventional agriculture is its overuse of quick-acting, soluble nitrogen fertilizers, which gives the soil an excess of nitrogen. That's why it's important to find a source of organic kale. Under organic cultivation, the soil is fertilized with compost rather than flooded with chemical nitrogen. Compost is buffered by the action of microorganisms and delivers to plants only the amount of nitrogen they need for their health—and ours.

NUTRITION ✦ Of all our foods, kale is one of the nutritional champions. It's chock full of calcium, iron, and health-promoting antioxidant carotenoids. Just 1 cup of boiled, chopped kale provides two-thirds of our daily requirement of vitamin C and all of our vitamin A.

Kale tends to be chewy stuff unless it's cooked slowly for a long time, so most people don't eat a great deal of it. I grow it in the garden by the armful and put it through my juicer along with carrots, parsley, and beets. I may not get all the roughage, but I get the minerals and vitamins in the sweet juice.

TYPES ✦ Kale is usually categorized by leaf shape and color. There are red kales, green kales, and black kales like *laciniato* (also called *cavolo nero*, see Top Varieties, page 488). Some kales have extra curly leaves, while others have wavy edges.

Besides its use as an edible vegetable, kale makes a fancy garnish. The colored varieties used as ornamental plants in the warmer zones of the country during the winter—red on green or white on green—make pretty beds for whole baked fish or roast meats.

SEASONALITY ✦ Kale is definitely a cool-weather crop. Hot summer sun turns its leaves bitter. And so the best time to buy kale is in fall through the winter into early spring. Farmers' markets are likely to be closed in the winter, but organic food stores will stock it.

WHAT TO LOOK FOR ✦ Look for a rich green color with no wilting, brown spots, or yellowing leaves.

STORAGE AND PREPARATION ✦ For a while, I kept kale in the crisper along with the apples and noticed that within a few days, the green of the leaves had turned a blanched-out yellow. I believe that's due to the ethylene gas given off by the apples. Best to keep kale away from any fruit that gives off ethylene gas as it continues to ripen—apples, stone fruits, bananas, and the like.

All kale has a tough midrib in the center of the leaf. To remove this, I lay each leaf flat on my cutting board and run a sharp knife down either side of the midrib, cutting away the relatively more tender leaf parts. Instead of just chucking the midribs, I tie them in a bundle and use them to flavor soup or stew. Or sometimes I'll simmer them in a little water—the longer the better, to retrieve as many nutrients as possible—reduce and reserve the mineral-laden water. I use this kale stock as part of the stock for soups and stews, mix it with a can of chicken stock to make the liquid for risotto, or use it straight for poaching fish or cooking rice or barley. Kale's just too full of nutrients to be wasted.

USES ✦ The leafy greens can be sautéed in olive oil with a pinch of salt over medium heat. Or, if I'm frying meat that yields its fat, like sausage or bacon, the kale greens cook nicely in the rendered fat. Either way, they are chewy-sweet and very palatable. I have tried microwaving them, but I don't like the results.

Kale's earthy flavor marries well with garlic, lemon juice, and olive oil. Add it to cooked onions, potatoes, shellfish (especially clams), and smoky and spicy meats like bacon, smoked ham, and sausage.

Kale's green leafy parts become tender with long, slow cooking. I toss some in the slow

SECRET MEANINGS IN THE WORD KALE

THE ROOT OF THE WORD kale is Greek *kaulos,* meaning stem. This root word echoes throughout the cabbage family of brassicas, especially in the cognate English word kale. The Scottish word *kail* also means the vegetable, but kale is so ubiquitous at a Scottish table that the word has been stretched to mean dinner, so that you might be invited by the MacTavishes to kail.

You can hear the Greek root in the German word for cabbage: *kohl,* as in the German red cabbage, *rotkohl.* It's less obvious but still there in Italian *cavolo,* very present in Spanish *col,* as it is in Swedish *kal.* It's there in French *chou,* even though the final *l* has been lost. And it's easy to hear in Dutch *kool.*

Coming back to English, there it is, influenced by Dutch, in coleslaw and Old King Cole. It's up front in kohlrabi, collards, and cauliflower. An alternative English name for kale is *borcole,* which was taken over from the Dutch *boerkool,* meaning "farmer cabbage." (The *boer* part means farmer or peasant, as the cognate *bauer* does in German. That word has come into English as the pejorative boor—meaning a person with rude, clumsy manners, like a peasant.) But if kale has been looked down upon as rough, peasant food, it certainly sustained and strengthened those who produced the fancier foods for royalty's tables.

cooker—yes, the slow cooker. In the morning, into the pot go an onion, a couple of potatoes, a few leaves of kale, a carrot, a stalk of celery, three or four chicken thighs, a few peppercorns, maybe a handful of barley, a tied-up bundle of parsley and sage, and a bottle of white wine. I cover the pot, turn it on low, and when I get home dinner will be waiting.

Finally, Black Tuscan kale (*laciniato*) can be steamed and used in place of grape leaves for dolmas, or stuffed grape leaves.

PORTUGUESE KALE SOUP (*CALDO VERDE*)

SERVES 8

I first had this Portuguese staple in New Bedford, Massachusetts, when my fraternity brother Armand Fernandes Jr. took me to a Portuguese restaurant. I never forgot it, and I still make it today. It has a wonderful smoky, earthy, and rich flavor that makes you think of Portuguese fishermen spooning down quantities of this hot soup to bolster themselves against the penetrating cold of the North Atlantic. This is just one version of the soup, but a good one. Serve it with cornbread. Note that you should start this soup a day before you plan to serve it.

²/₃ cup dry white cannellini beans

1 smoked ham hock

½ pound chouriço or chorizo sausage, removed from its casing

²/₃ cup dried split peas

1 teaspoon salt

6 cups deribbed and finely shredded kale leaves

2 cups peeled and chopped potatoes

2 cups finely chopped head cabbage

1. Place the beans in a 3-quart saucepan and add water to cover them by ½ inch. Bring to a boil, cook uncovered for 3 minutes, then cover and let stand overnight.

2. The next day, brown the ham hock and the sausage in a skillet, then add them to the beans and water along with the peas, salt, and kale. Bring to a boil, reduce the heat to low and simmer, covered, for 2 hours, adding more water if the soup seems to be getting too thick. Pull the meat from the ham hock bone and return the meat to the pot. Add the potato and cabbage and simmer covered for 30 minutes or more, until the potatoes and cabbage are tender. ■

Kohlrabi

BRASSICA OLERACEA
variety GONGYLODES

To MANY AMERICANS, kohlrabi is an oddity. It does have a strange look. The stem just above ground level swells into a globe from which petioles bearing sparse collard-like leaves protrude at jutting angles. But despite its creature-from-outer-space appearance, it is a delicious, versatile crop—woefully underappreciated in this country. On the other hand, kohlrabi is very much appreciated in Eastern Europe from Germany down to Hungary and on the Indian subcontinent, Southeast Asia, and in China, where it is a staple vegetable.

The name kohlrabi combines the German *kohl*, meaning cabbage, with *rapa*, the species name of *Brassica rapa*, or turnip. This would suggest that kohlrabi is a cross between these two types of brassicas, but it's not, although it does combine the taste and texture of cabbage and turnip. It's classified as part of the *gongylodes* group of brassicas, a name taken from the Kashmiri word for a small red turnip, *gongolou.* (You often see that suffix *-odes* or *-oides* on botanical names; it means "-like," as in "like a gongolou.")

Where did this strange vegetable originate? Pliny the Elder (circa 20 to 79 CE) makes a reference to a "Corinthian turnip" that grew above ground and sounds like it might be a kohlrabi, but he wrote about so many fabulous—and chimerical—creatures both animal and vegetable that it's hard to trust him on that. It next shows up in 14th-century France as a fully formed kohlrabi, so it's a good bet that peasant farmers kept saving seed of bulbous-stemmed strains of *Brassica oleracea* throughout the Dark Ages and Middle Ages, simply because there was something tender and good there to eat. Today it's still around, just waiting for Americans to get with the program.

THE ORGANIC FACTOR ► Kohlrabi is attacked by the same wide range of insects and diseases that attack cabbage, including cabbage loopers, imported cabbage worms, root maggots, and flea beetles, along with downy mildew, black rot, and fusarium yellows. Organic growers have a full battery of nontoxic controls for all these problems. Conventional growers use chemicals.

NUTRITION ► Kohlrabi is packed with nutrition. A cup of boiled kohlrabi provides the full daily requirement of vitamin C and more than 25 percent of a person's daily potassium needs.

TYPES ► You can pretty much divide the kohlrabi you'll see into two types: large and small. Which to buy? It all depends on the variety. Go large if it's a variety like Gigante, Superschmelz, or Grand Duke that doesn't get woody or pithy and stays tender and crisp even when it grows to large sizes, because you'll lose relatively less flesh when peeling it. If you don't know the variety, however, the safest bet is to stay small. You may lose more flesh, but you'll be assured of a more tender vegetable.

SEASONALITY ► Midsummer to fall.

WHAT TO LOOK FOR ► If you're buying kohlrabies at the farmers' market, look for bright, fresh-looking leaves. If the leaves are fresh, the globes will be perfect. Be aware that in Asian markets, the leaves are usually cut away before the kohlrabies are displayed.

USES ▸ Kohlrabi is at its mildest and sweetest eaten raw. You can peel one and eat it like an apple—it's crisp and juicy and tastes like a mild Tokyo Cross turnip (see page 204) with hints of raw broccoli stem, cucumber, Jerusalem artichoke, celery root, and cauliflower. Its texture is crunchy, like water chestnuts. Peeled and thinly sliced, it makes a fine addition to a tray of crudités and can be grated raw into a salad or incorporated in a slaw—it is a "cole crop," after all. In Europe, some cooks get variety in their homemade fermented sauerkraut by replacing regular shredded cabbage with the peeled, shredded Gigante variety of kohlrabi—a type that grows to 10 inches in diameter without turning woody.

But kohlrabi shines as a cooked vegetable, too, because cooking intensifies its turnip-like flavor. It can be cooked like potatoes and prepared like a German potato salad. Julienned, it can be stir-fried in a little butter with herbs and spices, and it has a true affinity for nutmeg. Its flavor also merges seamlessly with butter and cream, lemon, parsley, and rice vinegar. In India, kohlrabi is used in numerous ways, but I like it peeled, boiled, pureed, and made into a hot soup with curry spices and cumin.

Like small turnips, it can be peeled and added to stews. Also like turnips, it can be cooked with potatoes and smashed together with them to add tang. If you like Moroccan cooking, try adding peeled, sautéed, small kohlrabies to spiced lamb or chicken *tagines*. And get creative—think of other ways to use kohlrabis as you would cabbage or turnips. The leaves—but not the fibrous, tough leaf stems—can be cooked and eaten, and they have a sharp tang, sort of like spinach. Many kohlrabi dishes include the leaves, such as steamed kohlrabies tossed with their sautéed leaves and flavored with lemon and butter.

AUSTRIAN-STYLE KOHLRABI

SERVES 6

Austria is kohlrabi country, and the Austrians have a simple way of preparing the globes that allows their delicate flavor to come through.

2 pounds kohlrabies
3 tablespoons unsalted butter
1/2 teaspoon sugar
3 tablespoons all-purpose flour
1/2 teaspoon chopped fresh parsley
1/2 cup vegetable stock
Salt to taste

1. Bring a large pot of lightly salted water to a boil. Add the kohlrabies and boil for 15 to 20 minutes, or until soft through when pricked with a fork. Drain, let cool, then peel.

2. Melt the butter in a skillet over medium heat, add the sugar and stir until the sugar browns slightly. Blend in the flour and parsley. When the flour is well saturated and bubbling with hot butter (a minute or two), add the stock and bring to a boil.

3. Add the peeled kohlrabies and stir until they're heated through. Serve immediately. ▪

Leek

ALLIUM AMPELOPRASUM
variety PORRUM

LEEKS have a more delicate onion flavor than regular onions, with a mineral aftertaste that adds a perfect touch to savory soups.

The wild progenitor of leeks is a wild onion found all over Europe, around the Mediterranean, and even out on the Cape Verde islands in the Atlantic. The ancient Egyptians and Romans loved them. Nero thought leeks improved his singing voice, which earned him the popular name of *porrophagus*, or leek eater. In about 640 CE, the Welsh fought and won a battle with invading Saxons by wearing leeks in their hats to identify friend from foe, and the leek has been a symbol of Wales ever since. The word leek dates to Anglo-Saxon times, when *leac* in Old English meant any member of the onion clan, including *gar-leac* (garlic), which meant spear-onion.

THE ORGANIC FACTOR ▸ As members of the onion family, leeks are prone to many of the diseases that attack onions. Growing them in rich, compost-amended soil, as organic gardeners and farmers do, makes for healthy leeks that resist most of the diseases without the need for toxic sprays.

NUTRITION ▸ Leeks are low in sodium and very low in saturated fat and cholesterol. They're a good source of dietary fiber, vitamin B6, folate, iron and magnesium, and a very good source of vitamin C and manganese.

SEASONALITY ▸ During the summer, look for slender young leeks. About the size of your thumb or forefinger, these are simply leeks that haven't yet sized up—they may be any variety. They're great for grilling. The best fully grown leeks are found from late September through March.

WHAT TO LOOK FOR ▸ At the market, look for leeks with a long length of usable white to light green stem, fresh-looking leaves, and white, plump, fresh-looking roots. The stem should be slightly limber, not stiff or unyielding, which would indicate toughness.

PREPARATION ▸ Because the hilling, or lengthening, of leeks is done by slowly mounding up soil around the stalk, leeks have to be carefully washed to remove any grit that may have gotten into the stems. Here's my method for trimming and washing them:

Cut off the bottom ¾ inch or so of the leek where the roots are attached. (This sole plate, as it's called, can be replanted in the garden and will often sprout a new plant. Leeks are one of those crops that, once you have them, you'll always have them. If you're not gardening, still trim off the sole plate, as it's tough and fibrous.) Then trim off the green leaves down to the place where the stem becomes cylindrical and tight. I use my thumbnail to slit the outer layer of the leek lengthwise down the cylinder and remove just the outer layer.

If there's no visible grit in either cut end or under the outer layer, there probably won't be any elsewhere in the leek. Simply wash the cylinder under cold water. If there is grit, insert a sharp knife through the cylinder about two inches up from the base and draw it up the cylinder to the top. Holding the leek under running cold water, gently riffle through the layers, making sure each layer is washed.

USES ► While our markets usually offer leeks, they are inexplicably not a particularly popular vegetable in the United States. Once you start using them in your cooking, however, that will change for you.

Leeks can be steamed, and also grilled; baby leeks can be brushed with olive oil and grilled which makes a delicious finger food. Leeks especially like a liquid environment when being cooked, and they are excellent braised in stock or used in soups (including the famous vichyssoise) and stews. Slicing leeks ¼-inch-wide crosswise produces lots of fluffy ringlets to be tossed into a soup pot. They will add more body than shallots or onions, but a milder flavor. Or use them as an aromatic flavoring when making vegetable stock.

Leeks' refined flavor dovetails nicely with thyme and parsley, bacon, potatoes, mustard, olive oil, and roux.

LEEKS À LA GRECQUE

SERVES 6

Vegetables prepared in the Greek manner are usually served cold. The French seem to prefer fat leeks to skinny ones, so use plenty of big fat leeks in this dish.

10 fat leeks, white parts only
Salt to taste
³/₄ cup vegetable stock
³/₄ cup dry white wine
¹/₄ cup olive oil
2 tablespoons freshly squeezed lemon juice
6 whole black peppercorns
1 sprig parsley
¹/₄ teaspoon dried chervil
¹/₄ teaspoon dried French tarragon
1 bay leaf

1. Bring a large stainless-steel saucepan of water to a boil and add salt. Cut the leeks into 2-inch pieces and place them in the boiling water. Cover the saucepan and boil over medium heat for 3 minutes, and drain.

2. Return leeks to the saucepan, and add the remaining ingredients. Cover the saucepan, reduce the heat, and simmer about 20 minutes, until the leeks are just tender. Set the covered pan aside with the leeks still in it and let cool to room temperature. Leaving the liquid and herbs in the pan, fish out the leek pieces and serve them with a few tablespoons of the cooled liquid spooned over them. ∎

Lettuce

LACTUCA SATIVA

IT HASN'T BEEN very long since fine looseleaf lettuces began showing up in our markets and stores. Time was, a salad meant a wedge of head lettuce, such as iceberg, a slice of tomato, and maybe a little raw onion, all given a plop of Russian dressing. Three factors have wrought major changes in the lettuces we see in today's salads.

The first is that the culinary customs of the Europeans have jumped the Atlantic and completely changed our thinking about salads. The second is that organic gardeners and farmers, ever searching for higher quality and better taste, have grown and popularized the many different European and Asian varieties of salad greens—especially lettuces—and brought them to farmers' markets nationwide. And the third reason is the work of very talented and pioneering people like Alice Waters at Chez Panisse in Berkeley, California; Sibella Kraus of San Francisco, whose organizational skills brought organic produce to the public's attention, and Renee Shepherd, who founded a seed company devoted to great-tasting varieties of lettuce.

More than anyone, it was Alice Waters who popularized the French love of mesclun. Mesclun, meaning a mixture of wild greens, was traditionally gathered in the spring when new shoots and leaves were emerging and country folks needed something fresh and green after a winter of pickles and stored foods.

THE ORGANIC FACTOR ▸ Although lettuce is cooked in many places around the world, it's almost always eaten raw in the United States. This makes it doubly important to seek out organic lettuce that's free from harmful agricultural chemical residues. And, boy, are they ever used on lettuce.

Massive use of agricultural chemicals would be unnecessary were lettuce grown organically. I've grown lettuce on both coasts and found it an easy crop to grow. All lettuce required was a rich, crumbly soil with a lot of decayed organic matter in it, cool weather, plenty of water, sunshine, and a good weeding from time to time. I've never had to use any pesticides, but I did need to set out slug and snail traps made from jar lids filled with beer and set into the soil at 10-foot intervals. The slugs crawl in, but they don't crawl out.

NUTRITION ▸ Romaine is the nutritional champ among lettuces. Just ½ cup raw and shredded is high in potassium and provides about 10 percent of our daily needs of vitamins A and C and folic acid.

TYPES ▸ There are five basic types of lettuce that have been cultivated since the 16th century (earlier varieties of cultivated lettuce date back to ancient Egypt). The types are classified according to their leaf shape and texture.

Butterhead or Boston lettuce has loose rosettes of leaves, with a creamy yellow-green center and a soft, buttery texture.

Batavian lettuce is a sturdy type that forms shaggy heads with cream-colored centers of fine, sweet flavor and crispy texture.

Romaine lettuce is familiar to everyone as the crunchy tall heads used to make Caesar Salad (see recipe at right).

Looseleaf lettuces don't make heads but make a loose collection of leaves from a central growing point. They come in dozens of varieties— green, reddish, and speckled; smooth-edged, wavy-edged, pointy-edged, lobed, ruffled, slender, wide, and everything in between.

Crisphead lettuces are the cabbage-like ball heads often called Iceberg, although Iceberg is just one of many cultivars of this type of lettuce. Crispheads don't have much flavor or nutrition, but they do provide a very refreshing crunchiness.

SEASONALITY ▸ Lettuce is a cool-weather crop, but that doesn't prevent growers in various parts of the country from growing lettuce year-round by using such things as shading devices on hot summer days. In cold winter, lettuce is grown in Florida and California's warm Imperial Valley. The growers find ways to meet the constant demand.

WHAT TO LOOK FOR ▸ The chief quality to look for in lettuce is freshness. A leaf should snap into two crisp pieces when bent, rather than bend limply. The outer leaves should be as crisp as the inner ones and not be beat up by wear and tear during shipment. Check the growing point (the place where the leaves emerge)—it should be moist and white. If you're buying mesclun or spring mix that consists of individual leaves, make sure they are crisp and not flabby.

PREPARATION ◆ Most lettuces need nothing more than a rinse. In the case of the looser lettuces, a thorough rinse may be needed to remove the rich earth caught between their leaves.

USES ◆ Because of its mild flavor, lettuce makes a great foil for stronger flavors, such as anchovies, blue cheese, garlic, vinegar, and bacon (what would a BLT be without lettuce?). Tomatoes, lemon juice, nut oils, and avocados also enjoy the company of lettuce.

I use lettuce leaves to protect fish—like halibut—from drying out during slow cooking. Blanch the leaves in boiling water until flexible, then wrap them around the fish. Blanched lettuce leaves can be used in place of grape leaves making dolmas. The raw leaves of butterhead types are usually flexible enough to be given a tablespoon of hummus and rolled up, or fill them as Thai cooks do with dried shrimp, lime, crushed peanuts, cucumber, sweet sauce, and a little grated ginger. Italians sauté lettuce in olive oil and garlic—this method works best with the sturdy Batavians and romaines—until the leaves are tender and wilted.

THE TRUE CAESAR SALAD

SERVES 2

I've reviewed hundreds of restaurants, and it seems like I've been served as many versions of Caesar salad. Here's the classic version as created by Caesar Cardini at his restaurant in Tijuana, Mexico, many years ago. You can add anchovies if you wish, but the classic Caesar didn't have them.

1 loaf Vienna-style French bread or Italian bread
1/2 cup plus 2 tablespoons extra-virgin olive oil

continued

KEEP AN EYE OUT FOR CELTUCE

A VARIETY OF LETTUCE called celtuce is full of the bitter milky sap that has been bred out of most modern lettuces. (The wild progenitor of modern lettuce, *Lactuca serriola*, has bitter, milky sap present in all its parts, and in fact our word lettuce comes from the Latin for the genus *Lactuca,* whose root is *lac,* or milk, referring to the milky sap produced in the flower stalk.)

A clever seed company concluded that, because this kind of lettuce grows a tall stem, it must be a cross between celery and lettuce and gave the lettuce its new name, but it is no such thing. It is a specific variety of regular lettuce. I grew it…once. When the crop reached full size, I found the leaves far too bitter to eat, and likewise the stems. "There must be a way to eat this," I thought, "or why would they sell it in the seed catalogs?" Finally I tried peeling the stems and was left with a semi translucent, light green, cucumber-like (except no seeds) piece of limber vegetable with a mild flavor of lettuce. I understand that the Chinese love this vegetable and pickle it, as well as pop it into their stir-fries. I'm sure that's a fine way to use it. But I've never grown it since, nor do I ever see it at the markets. If you see the stems, try them, but peel them first.

2 cloves garlic, peeled

1 head romaine lettuce

1 teaspoon salt

1 egg, coddled or boiled for 1 minute

Juice of 1 lemon

1/2 cup freshly grated Parmigiano-Reggiano

Dash of Worcestershire sauce

Freshly ground black pepper

1. Preheat the oven to 350°F.

2. To make the croutons, cut two 3/4-inch-thick rounds from the bread, remove the crusts, and toast them on a baking sheet for 10 minutes. Brush both sides with 2 tablespoons of olive oil and rub them with a garlic clove cut in half, then return them to the oven for 10 minutes until crisp and lightly browned. Cut the rounds to your desired size of crouton (1/2-inch squares are traditional but any size will do).

3. Remove the outer leaves from the lettuce (save them for another use) and select the inner leaves—those about 7 to 8 inches long and a pale celadon green. Rinse these leaves until they're free of grit, then gently pat dry with paper towels.

4. Chop the other garlic clove, then mash it into the salt (grind it with the side of a heavy knife). Place the mashed garlic in a small bowl and incorporate the remaining 1/2 cup of oil, stirring with a fork.

5. Just before serving, place the romaine leaves in a large bowl, drizzle with the oil mixture, and toss to coat. Break the egg into the salad and toss again until it's well incorporated. Sprinkle on the lemon juice and toss. Add the Parmigiano-Reggiano, the dash of Worcestershire sauce, and pepper to taste, and toss. Finally, add the croutons, toss, and make 2 portions in oval bowls. ■

LOOSELEAF LETTUCE AND ROASTED BEET SALAD

SERVES 6

This simple salad is extraordinarily delicious. A mixture of looseleaf types gives a nice appearance along with the beets. A small amount of creamy blue cheese dressing would make a perfect topping. It's a favorite salad in Italy.

3 medium red beets

3 medium yellow beets

1/2 pound mixed looseleaf lettuce

1 small red onion, sliced thin

Leaves from 4 sprigs watercress

1/2 cup walnut pieces

1/4 cup pine nuts

Blue Cheese Dressing (recipe follows)

1. Roast the beets, let cool, and remove their jackets according to the instructions on page 72. Cut into quarters.

2. While the beets are roasting, spread the walnuts on a baking sheet and toast in the oven until lightly browned and fragrant. Toss the pine nuts in a small dry skillet over medium heat until toasted light brown. Set both nuts aside to cool.

3. Place mixed lettuces on 6 serving plates. Place 2 red and 2 yellow beet quarters on each plate. Add some onion rings and sprinkle on watercress leaves, walnuts, and pine nuts. Drizzle equal portions of the dressing across the top of each salad. ■

Blue Cheese Dressing

1/2 cup crumbled blue cheese (about 2 ounces)

1/2 cup mayonnaise

1 shallot, minced

1 clove garlic, minced

1 tablespoon red wine vinegar

1 teaspoon Dijon mustard
Splash of whole milk
Freshly ground black pepper

Place all ingredients in a bowl and mix well to combine. ∎

Lima Bean

PHASEOLUS LUNATUS

AS THEIR NAME IMPLIES, lima beans originated in Peru, and there's evidence in Lima that they were in use as long ago as 5000 BCE (or even 7000 BCE, according to *The Oxford Companion to Food*). After Europeans came to the Americas, it didn't take long for lima beans to spread around the world.

As a child, I detested lima beans. My parents, who grew the plants on long poles formed into a tipi, would pick the beans when they were big and over-ripe and then boil them into mush. I didn't like their insipid flavor or their mealy texture. I carried this impression until I started working at *Organic Gardening* magazine. Growing my own crops there revealed to me the joys of organic foods picked and cooked at their peak of freshness. So, inspired, I grew lima beans in rich soil and picked the beans when they were young and tender, cooked them gently, and wondered where these beans had been all my life.

THE ORGANIC FACTOR ‣ Cool, wet weather can cause downy mildew to get started in lima beans. The nontoxic organic treatment is a simple application of lime-sulfur spray.

NUTRITION ‣ Lima beans help sustain people across the globe, because they are such a good source of nutrients. Dried limas are ground to flour and added to bread in the Philippines. They're used to make bean paste in Japan. And they're a staple across Africa. No wonder: ½ cup of boiled limas contains 109 calories, 7.3 grams of protein, 19.7 grams of complex carbohydrates, and 6.8 grams of dietary fiber. That ½ cup also provides about 20 percent of a person's daily requirement of folic acid, 30 percent of a male's iron needs and 12.5 percent of a female's, 13 percent of our thiamine requirement, 10 percent each of our need for magnesium and zinc, and 478 milligrams of potassium, so necessary for strength and muscle function.

TYPES ‣ There are two types of lima beans: bush limas, which grow on bush-type plants and need no support to climb on, and pole limas, or climbers, which do. While the plants differ, however, the flavors are similar.

SEASONALITY ‣ Lima bean season is short—it runs from late summer to early fall.

At any time of the year, however, you'll find dried limas—sometimes called butterbeans—and frozen, organic baby lima beans at your organic foods supermarket. Lima beans freeze well and frozen beans can be substituted for fresh without an enormous loss of quality.

WHAT TO LOOK FOR ‣ Even in season it may be difficult to find fresh-picked lima beans at farmers' markets, organic food stores, or roadside stands. But keep your eyes peeled. The pods of fresh-picked beans should be filled out but not lumpy and bulging. The tips of the pods should feel a bit spongy. If you can open one, check to make sure the beans are young and tender, not large and mealy. *Don't* eat them raw: Raw limas

LIMA BEANS ARE EASY TO GROW. The climbing types will cling to anything—not just poles, but a trellis, tight strings, even up your garage drainpipe. Just make sure to harvest the beans young, when they are about two-thirds full size, to ensure the most tender beans.

contain glycosides that generate poisonous hydro-cyanic acid in the human digestive system; the poison is destroyed by boiling. But you can safely bite into a raw bean to check the taste and texture—a little nibble won't have enough glycoside to hurt you.

PREPARATION ▸ If you're lucky enough to find them fresh in their pods, shell them and boil them for about 3 minutes, drain to pour off the unwanted glycosides, and boil again in fresh water for another 3 minutes until just tender.

To use dried limas, soak 1 cup of the beans for 6 to 8 hours, changing the water halfway through. Drain them and put them in a pot with 3 cups of fresh water and a pinch of salt and simmer them for about 2 hours. They won't be very different from other beans after this treatment.

USES ▸ Treat them simply with just a dab of butter so you can enjoy their real, uncompromised flavor. Try them in a succotash (recipe at right).

Like other beans, they combine well with bacon and butter, with mild or sharp Jack or Cheddar cheeses, with garlic, mushrooms, olive oil, and tomatoes.

LIMA BEAN SUCCOTASH

SERVES 6

A fabulous way to get your veggies in a focused, savory way. It makes a splendid side dish to roast pork or grilled veal chops. It's absolutely at its best when you can use fresh baby lima beans. The ingredients speak of the bounty of late summer and early fall.

2 cups shelled fresh baby lima beans (about
    2 pounds in the pod)
2 tablespoons diced onion
1 strip of bacon
1 cup peeled, seeded, and chopped fresh tomato
    (about 2 medium tomatoes)
2 cups corn kernels, freshly cut off the cob
    (2 medium ears)
1 teaspoon butter
Salt and freshly ground black pepper

1. Bring a small pot of water to a boil, add the lima beans, and boil for 4 minutes; drain the beans, refill the pot with fresh water, bring to a boil, add the beans, and boil for 3 more minutes or until just tender. Drain and reserve.

2. Put the onion and bacon in a 2-quart saucepan or skillet with 1 cup of water. Bring the mixture to a boil, reduce heat to low, cover, and simmer for 20 minutes. Add the tomatoes and corn and simmer for 10 more minutes, adding the limas for the last 3 or 4 minutes. Remove the bacon, add the butter and salt and pepper to taste, and stir well. ▪

Vegetables

ARTICHOKE • Imperial Star, top bud
(full size) and side bud (baby)

ARTICHOKE •
reen Globe,
bloom
bove)

ARUGULA

ASIAN VEGETABLES • Bok Choy • Joi Choy, Mei Qing
Choy, a.k.a. baby bok choy

IAN VEGETABLES • Bok Choy • Chinese Flat Cabbage, a.k.a. Tat-soi

ASIAN VEGETABLES • Chinese Kale • Asparation

WHEN NO VARIETY NAME APPEARS, FOOD IS THE ORIGINAL SPECIES

A1

ASIAN VEGETABLES • Chinese Cabbage • Burpee's Two Seasons (napa type)

AVOCADO • Hass

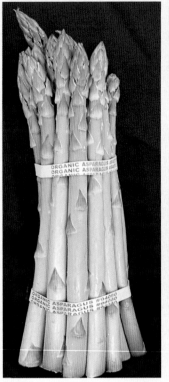

ASPARAGUS • Martha Washington

BROCCOLI • Broccolini

BEET • Chioggia

BEET • Detroit Dark Red

RUSSELS SPROUT • Oliver, sprouts on the stalk

CABBAGE • Red Type • Ruby Ball

CARDOON • Gigante di Romagna, stems

CAULIFLOWER • Romanesco

CAULIFLOWER • Self-Blanche, Snow Crown, leaves attached

CARROT • Touchon

CELERY • Victoria

CELERY ROOT • Giant Prague

CHARD • **Bright Lights**

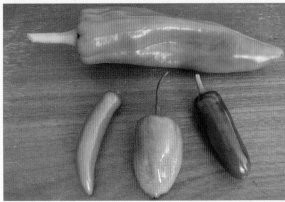

CHILE PEPPER • **Anaheim** (top) and from left: **serrano, habanero, jalapeño**

CHICORY AND ENDIVE • Radicchio • **Rossa di Verona**

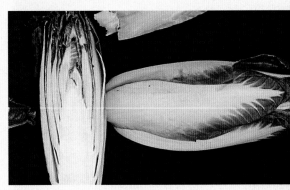

CHICORY AND ENDIVE • Belgian Endive • **Red**

CHICORY AND ENDIVE • Frisée • **Tres Fine**

CUCUMBER • **Holland** (European greenhouse type, top), **Sweet Slice** (slicing type)

CORN • **Super Sweet Jubilee**

CROSNES

CUCUMBER • **Lemon**

EGGPLANT • from left: Little Fingers (Japanese type), Black Beauty, Pingtung Long Improved (Chinese type)

FENNEL • Zefa Fino

GARLIC • Soft-Neck Type • California, Early with shoots

GREEN BEAN • Scarlet Runner (pole snap), on the vine

GREEN BEAN • Snap Bean • from left: Fin de Pagnois (filet), Purple King (pole), Blue Lake (bush), Kentucky Wonder (wax), Romano (flat-pod)

GROUND CHERRY • Cape Gooseberry

GREEN BEAN • Fava Bean • Aprovecho Select

KALE • Redbor

KOHLRABI • Early Purple Vienna

LETTUCE •
Romaine •
Verte
Maraichere

LEEK • Blue de Solaise   LEEK • ramp

LETTUCE • Butterhead • Butterking

MÂCHE • Vert de Cambrai

MUSHROOM • clockwise from top left: shiitake, morel, cinnamon cap, hen of the woods, a.k.a. maitake

ONION • Red Torpedo

POTATO • starchy • top from left: Yukon Gold, Russet Nugget; waxy • bottom from left: All Red, German Fingerling, French Fingerling

OKRA • Clemson Spineless

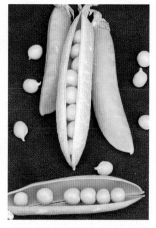

PEA • English (Garden) • Laxton's Progress

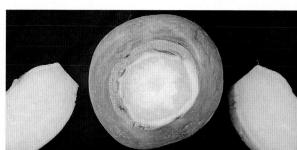

RUTABAGA • Laurentian

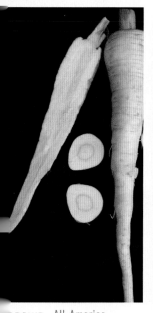

PARSNIP • All-America

RADISH • Western type • French Breakfast

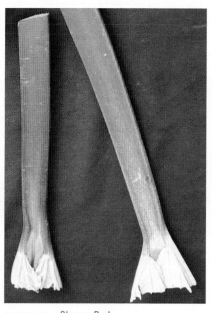

RHUBARB • Cherry Red

SHALLOT • French Red

SALSIFY • oyster plant

SPINACH • New Zealand

SWEET POTATO • Orange Type • Jewel

SUMMER SQUASH AND ZUCCHINI • Zucchini • clockwise
from top left: Gold Rush, Caserta, Burpee Fordhook, Tatuma

SUMMER SQUASH AND ZUCCHINI •
Patty Pan • clockwise from top left: Peter
Pan Hybrid, Early White Bush, Sunburst

SWEET PEPPER • medley of yellow and red bell, Ivory bell, Italia
frying (large, curved), Turkish (small, sickle-shaped)

Mâche

VALERIANELLA LOCUSTA

MÂCHE (pronounced *mahsh*) is also known as lamb's lettuce or corn salad. This plant has been gathered wild across Eurasia since time immemorial, but it was only brought into cultivation in the 1500s. Carried to North America by Europeans, it quickly naturalized in regions with mild winters.

THE ORGANIC FACTOR ► As a fresh, raw salad ingredient, it's important that it be grown without toxic sprays. Mâche is a specialty crop often found at organic markets.

NUTRITION ► Mâche is rich in vitamins A and C, calcium, and iron.

TYPES ► The first time I grew mâche in my own organic garden, I wasn't sure I liked the flavor—it had an odd, weedy taste. So I stopped growing it.

Now, however, I've rediscovered it through two varieties that have a fine, mildly herbal, slightly bitter flavor and show nothing of the weediness I objected to thirty years ago. They are Coquille (also known as Coquille de Louviers) and Vit. Coquille makes a pretty, upright rosette of small, spoon-shaped leaves, while Vit is a small, mild-flavored form that's excellent picked young as baby mâche, to use in salads. The mâche sold in grocery stores in clear plastic clamshell packs is probably Vit.

SEASONALITY ► Mâche is at its most tender and fine-flavored from late fall through winter and into early spring. You may find it in year-round

farmers' markets or organic supermarkets. The early spring crop that starts growing again after the soil warms up past 50 degrees Fahrenheit is the choicest of the year. That goes as well for the similar Italian species, *Valerianella eriocarpa,* which like mâche is native to the Mediterranean basin.

WHAT TO LOOK FOR ► The leaves of mâche should be crisp, turgid, and a bright green, without blemish. Look underneath the little head where it was cut from the root. The cut should look fresh, not dried out.

USES ► The small, spoon-shaped leaves of this plant are crisp and succulent, with a slightly bitter, mildly herbal flavor reminiscent of arugula and radicchio. Mâche is chiefly used fresh in salads or as part of a mesclun mix. If grown in the garden, the leaves can be harvested ½ inch above the crown and the plant will send out a new rosette of leaves.

"SPRING TONIC" SALAD WITH SWEET DRESSING

SERVES 2

When I lived in the Northeast, winters seemed endless. But then there'd come a precociously warm day in April when the promise of summer could be felt in the waxing power of the sunlight. Balmy air carried the smells of growing and flowering plants. Then I'd pick my spring tonic salad, as I called it.

Watercress would be starting to leaf out in the boggy place below the springhouse, so that went in the basket. White and purple violets were blooming in the woods, so I'd toss a few of their flowers into the mix. Bitter dandelion leaves were young and perfect. I'd tear up a few young spears of wild onions. In my garden, I'd uncover young spinach plants that

continued

had wintered over under the mulch and toss a few tender leaves to the salad. I'd pull a carrot, which had been sleeping dormant under the ice and snow since last fall, to grate and add some color. But the star of the spring tonic salad was the mâche that had wintered over under mulch and now was in exactly the right condition for good eating.

Now we can hunt and gather the ingredients for this pick-me-up salad at the better organic stores and farmers' markets instead of scouring the wild meadows for them. I'm not sure it's as much fun as gathering wild food, but the flavors are similar.

If you can't find all these ingredients, substitute other seasonal greens or eliminate some. If gathering dandelion greens from a lawn area, make sure the lawn hasn't been treated with chemicals.

FOR THE SALAD

1 bunch mâche
3 sprigs watercress, torn
3 fresh chive spears, chopped
1 scallion, white parts only, chopped
3 leaves Belgian endive, torn
2 cups spring mix or mesclun
2 tablespoons pepper cress leaves
3 young dandelion leaves, torn up
5 wild violet flowers

FOR THE DRESSING

1/3 cup walnut oil
1/2 cup black Muscat dessert wine (see Tip)
Pinch salt
1/2 teaspoon fresh thyme leaves
1/2 teaspoon fennel seed

1. Combine the salad greens in a large bowl.
2. Whisk the dressing ingredients together thoroughly in a small bowl and pour an amount to your taste over salad (tastes vary as to how much dress-

ing to use, so start with a little, then add more). Toss and serve immediately. Store leftover dressing covered in refrigerator for up to 2 weeks.

TIP: If you can't find black Muscat dessert wine, substitute any sweet, late-harvest red dessert wine. ▪

Mushroom

various species

MUSHROOMS have been held in high culinary esteem since classical times. The ancient Romans called them *cibum diorum*, the food of the gods. The word "mushroom" comes from the archaic French *mousseron,* usually held to be a derivative of *mousse,* or "moss"—I suppose because, like moss, mushrooms are found on the forest floor.

Most mushrooms important in cooking are different species of mycorrhizal fungi. Organic farmers and gardeners may recognize that name, because a major tenet of the organic method is to incorporate lots of actively decaying organic matter into the soil in part to stimulate the growth of mycorrhizal fungi. The term is from *mycor,* which refers to mushrooms (hence a mycologist is a mushroom scientist) and *rhizal,* which refers to rhizomes, or roots. In a neat bit of symbiosis, the fungus colonizes the roots of certain plants and lives on the sugary substances that exude from the roots. The fungus has no chlorophyll and so can't make these nutrient-rich sugars itself. In return for the sugary sap, the fungus extends its hyphae (filamentlike projections) far into the soil, absorbing precious phosphorus compounds and bringing them back to the plant roots, which absorb them. This greatly enhances the plant's ability to secure this major nutrient, which is often in short supply in the soil.

THE ORGANIC FACTOR ▸ Mushrooms grown organically and commercially in caves or insulated dark sheds are required to be grown on organic substrates, that is, on manures and materials that have not been chemically treated. If compost is used, it can only be sterilized by heat, not by chemicals. These mushrooms grow on a substrate of wood, shredded paper, sawdust, or composted straw and manure, depending on the type of mushroom grown. These are usually mushrooms that grow naturally on decaying wood, in fields, or in composted garden soil, such as enoki, oyster, and shiitake mushrooms.

To prevent other fungi and molds from contaminating their substrates, conventional growers often sterilize the compost as well as use sterilizing chemicals on the shed walls and floors, but these chemicals are usually dissipated before inoculation with the desired species' spores. The best way to ensure the purity of your mushrooms is to buy mushrooms that have organic certification or have been harvested from the wild. Or harvest them yourself.

NUTRITION ▸ Mushrooms of all types are high in niacin and riboflavin and in the protective antioxidant selenium.

TYPES ▸ My local organic market carries common white button mushrooms, and because of their reasonable cost I still use them in my everyday cooking. But I can also choose from an array of gourmet "wild" mushrooms—called wild but oftentimes grown by mycologists who have learned how to produce them commercially.

Depending on the season, I can find fresh morels, chanterelles, black trumpet mushrooms,

KEEP AN EYE OUT FOR WILD-HARVESTED MUSHROOMS

FINDING WILD MUSHROOMS that have actually been picked in the wild, often referred to as "wildcrafted mushrooms," is not difficult. I see them sold at our local farmers' market; your own local farmers' market may well have a table run by a mushroom forager, too.

You can also find wildcrafted mushrooms in dried form in organic supermarkets, but their provenance can be uncertain. According to LocalHarvest, an online site (www.localharvest.org) devoted to putting buyers together with local sellers of mostly organic products, wild-harvested American mushrooms are sometimes shipped to Europe for packaging and then sold as dried European wild mushrooms, and some packages of dried morels sold as French morels were identified as being harvested in northern India and smoked over dung fires to preserve them. If you can afford it, it's better to buy fresh wildcrafted mushrooms at a farmers' market where you can meet the forager face to face.

Foraging for your own mushrooms is a great activity, and there are plenty of books available on the subject. But a word about eating mushrooms you've picked from the wild: A mistake can kill you in a particularly agonizing way. I knew a young man with a bright future who died this way, and it was a tragic end to a promising life. I also knew the composer John Cage, who loved to hunt mushrooms. He put himself in the hospital several times experimenting with new types. I hunt mushrooms, too, but here's my personal rule: Unless I'm 100 percent positive that the mushrooms I've found are edible and harmless, I don't pick them and I certainly don't eat them. By 100 percent, I mean that I would feed them to my kids. A great basic guide for anyone interested in foraging for wild mushrooms is David Arora's *All That the Rain Promises, and More.*

shiitakes, matsutakes, creminis, oyster mushrooms, enokis, and the big, dark-gilled caps of portobellos.

A word about portobellos. Once upon a time, when common button mushrooms were left too long in the mushroom houses and grew to their mature size, they were considered worthless and discarded. Then one day a marketing genius decided to give these overgrown button mushrooms the name portobello and sell them as gourmet mushrooms, and the rest is history. Not that they're bad for you or bad tasting (they're meaty and delicious), but they are simply the common white mushroom all grown up.

Many of the mushrooms that are associated closely with certain kinds of trees and grow naturally on the forest floor are difficult to grow commercially, because they need their natural environment. These include boletes, chanterelles, morels, and black trumpet mushrooms—although mycologists are making progress growing these commercially.

To list names of mushroom varieties (see page 490), I've divided mushrooms into two categories, those that grow naturally on the forest floor and those that grow in fields, in compost, or on decaying wood. These divisions separate the types of mushrooms by their substrates—there are certainly wonderful mushrooms in both divisions.

SEASONALITY ✦ Mushrooms like to appear in cool weather after lots of rain. Prime mushroom season in the wild is in fall when soil is moist and frosts are arriving as well as during similar conditions in the spring. Commercially grown mushrooms are produced year-round because these conditions are reproduced in the insulated mushroom houses.

WHAT TO LOOK FOR ✦ Select mushrooms that are pristine, not bruised or broken. Check the end where they were attached to their substrate—it should look fresh and moist, not dried out or woody.

PREPARATION ✦ Fresh mushrooms usually need only a brushing with a soft-bristled brush to remove any of the growing medium that clings to them. Washing is generally unnecessary and only makes the mushrooms soggy. Dried mushrooms should be soaked in warm-to-boiling water or other liquid to soften and reconstitute before being added to a dish. This soaking liquor will add flavor to the dish, but it should be strained thoroughly to remove any dirt and grit that was dislodged.

USES ✦ All mushrooms impart an essential earthiness to dishes, as well as a luscious, meaty texture. But flavors vary greatly from species to species, so it is best to refer to the individual mushrooms to get a sense of each variety's textures and uses.

BEEF STEW WITH PORCINI

SERVES 4 TO 6

This stew is a fall favorite at our house, but since the mushrooms are dried, it can be made any time of the year. It's definitely comfort food. Serve over noodles.

2 ounces fresh or 1 ounce dried porcini mushrooms

2 pounds lean beef, cut into 2-inch cubes

Kosher salt and freshly ground black pepper

2 large plum tomatoes, peeled, seeded, and coarsely
    chopped

1 tablespoon butter

1 tablespoon extra-virgin olive oil

1 medium onion, peeled and diced

2 medium carrots, diced

1 stalk celery, diced

2 cloves garlic, chopped

1 bay leaf

1 sprig Italian flat-leaf parsley

1 sprig thyme

1 tablespoon flour

2 cups dry red wine

1. If using fresh mushrooms, halve or quarter, depending on their size. If using dried, reconstitute the mushrooms by placing them in a bowl and pouring boiling water over them just to cover. Set the bowl aside for 20 minutes.

2. Place the beef in a bowl and sprinkle with just a little salt and pepper.

3. Heat the butter and olive oil in a large Dutch oven over medium-high heat. Add the meat in small batches (the cubes should not touch one another) and sear so they are evenly browned on all sides, 5 to 7 minutes per batch. Remove each batch to a dish before adding the next.

4. When all the meat is browned, reduce the heat to medium-low and add the onion, carrots, tomatoes, celery, and garlic. Stir, scraping any browned bits off the bottom of the pot. Cook, stirring frequently so vegetables are coated with fat, for about 5 minutes.

5. Return the meat to the pot. Tie the bay leaf, parsley, and thyme sprigs together with a bit of kitchen string and add to the pot. In a little bowl, mix the flour with a couple of tablespoons of the wine, stirring so there are no lumps. Add this along with the rest of the wine to the pot. Stir and cover, and simmer over low heat for 2 hours.

6. After 2 hours, add the fresh mushrooms. If using dried mushrooms, carefully lift them out of their soaking liquor. If they still feel gritty, rinse them lightly under running water and pat dry. Chop the mushrooms and add them to the pot. Slowly pour in the liquor, making sure you don't add any of the sediment that may have settled at the bottom. Cover and simmer another hour. Remove the bundle of herbs, correct the seasoning, and serve immediately. ■

Okra

HIBISCUS ESCULENTUS

OKRA is a relative of the hollyhock and the ornamental mallows. It is native to Ethiopia, although it found an enthusiastic welcome in the cuisines of West Africa. The pretty flowers, resembling small hibiscus or hollyhock blossoms, are followed by seed pods with a very mucilaginous sap. Besides the young pods, in Africa the seeds are eaten as a sweetmeat and roasted and ground as a coffee substitute. It came to North America with African slaves, and so gained its toehold in the American south. Today one can hardly imagine southern regional cooking—especially in the Creole and Cajun cooking of Louisiana—without gumbos and stews thickened with the clear liquid okra exudes.

Both the words okra and gumbo are also of West African origin. "Okra" derives from the word Accra, the capital city of Ghana, and "gumbo" comes from *ngombo,* an Angolan word for a similar dish.

THE ORGANIC FACTOR ► The organic cook should make an effort to find organically grown okra. This member of the mallow family is related to cotton and is afflicted by many of the same pests. When grown in commercial agriculture, the two crops are often treated with the same pesticides, especially in the cotton-growing areas of the south. California growers are moving toward using neem extract—an effective insect-repelling substance derived from a tree native to the Indian subcontinent.

NUTRITION ◆ Okra is a good source of vitamin C. Just one-half cup of cooked okra contains 2 grams of soluble fiber in the form of gum and pectins. It also contains good stores of insoluble fiber that helps protect against colorectal cancer. That half cup contains about 10 percent of the recommended daily doses of vitamins B6 and folic acid.

TYPES ◆ Okra pods come in one of three shades. The most common is a medium green, but there's also a pale, lime green type with much the same flavor. The best type of all for flavor and texture, in my opinion, is a reddish type that keeps its color when cooked.

SEASONALITY ◆ The plant likes hot, humid weather and produces its top yields during high to late summer.

WHAT TO LOOK FOR ◆ Always select pods that are between 2 and 3 inches long. Although some pods stay tender at longer lengths, many do not, and it's sometimes hard to know which variety you're dealing with unless the grower is on hand to tell you. By sticking with small pods, you're guaranteed of getting them young and tender. They should have no bruises or discolorations and have a pleasant, velvety feeling.

PREPARATION ◆ Trim off the tough stem ends and rinse the pods.

USES ◆ The flavor of okra recalls various herbaceous plant flavors—a little asparagus, a hint of artichoke, and a touch of sweet pepper. Its salient feature is the sticky liquid its pods exude when cut, and it's this substance that makes it so useful in enriching and adding body to rice-based stews.

I love the flavor of okra, but simply boiled, its sliminess is a little off-putting to my taste. I prefer to pan-fry it, which sizzles the mucilage, makes it crunchy, and intensifies its flavor. The method for this can be as simple as frying sliced rounds of the pods in olive oil over medium heat, but it becomes

IF YOU LIKE TO GARDEN

ASIDE FROM PRODUCING tasty pods, okra plants produce beautiful flowers that are pretty enough to star in the ornamental garden and certainly add color and pizzazz to the vegetable garden. Okra likes lots of heat and sunlight. Think Louisiana. But it can be grown farther north. It was grown in Philadelphia in the 18th century. It responds to plenty of nutrients in a rich organic soil and plenty of moisture. Keep picking those pods while young and tender, because if a plant is allowed to mature its pods (and the seeds inside), it considers its work finished for the season and you get no further flowers or pods.

extra special when treated in the North African style and given a little help from cumin, tomato, and lemon (see page 153).

Okra makes a good partner with other high- to late-summer crops like garlic, onions, tomatoes, and sweet peppers; with spices like cumin and coriander; and with flavorings like lemon and parsley. In fact, this is pretty much a listing of the ingredients that would go into a good gumbo, along with rice, andouille sausage, and a few pieces of chicken (recipe follows).

OKRA, NORTH AFRICAN STYLE

SERVES 2 TO 3

A quick, flavorful side dish.

1/2 teaspoon cumin seeds
1 tablespoon olive oil
7 to 9 okra pods, sliced into 1/2-inch rounds, stem ends discarded
1 teaspoon tomato paste
1 teaspoon freshly squeezed lemon juice
Salt and freshly ground black pepper

1. Heat the cumin seeds in a dry skillet over medium heat for 30 seconds or so, until they become fragrant. Then transfer them to a mortar and, when they're cool, grind them up with a pestle.

2. Heat a skillet over medium-high heat, add the olive oil, and when hot add the okra. It only takes a few minutes for the okra to tighten up and acquire a little crunchy browning. Once this happens, add the tomato paste and lemon juice, the ground cumin, and salt and pepper to taste. Reduce the heat to medium-low and continue cooking for another minute or so, stirring occasionally, until the okra is fully tender and coated with the tomato mixture. ■

CHICKEN FILÉ GUMBO

SERVES 4 TO 6

This recipe takes a bit of prep time (begin two days ahead to give the flavors time to marry), but it's worth it. The result is an authentically rich, glistening, fragrant, and luscious bowl of gumbo just like you'd get at a Louisiana shotgun shack down on the bayou. Serve with ice cold beer.

Do the prep work before starting the recipe, except for chopping the chives; do that just before serving.

2 teaspoons cayenne
2 teaspoons kosher salt
1 teaspoon freshly ground black pepper
1 tender young chicken (about 3 pounds), cut into 6 pieces (2 thighs, 2 legs, 2 breasts; see Tip)
2/3 cup extra-virgin olive oil
1 cup all-purpose flour
1 cup sliced okra pods
1/2 cup chopped celery
1/2 cup chopped onions
2 tomatoes, peeled, seeded, and quartered; juice strained and reserved
1/2 cup chopped green bell pepper
7 cloves garlic, minced
2 quarts fat-free, low-salt chicken stock
12 ounces raw andouille sausage
1 cup cooked long-grain white rice
1/2 cup chopped scallions
Tabasco sauce, optional
1 teaspoon filé powder (powdered sassafras)
A few fresh chive spears

1. Put the cayenne, 1 teaspoon of the salt, and the black pepper into a paper bag with no holes. Wipe the chicken pieces with a piece of paper towel lightly dipped in the olive oil, then add the chicken

continued

pieces to the bag, and shake. Open the bag and add $1/2$ cup of the flour and shake again.

2. Pour about 4 tablespoons of olive oil into a cast-iron skillet and heat to a gentle medium heat—if the oil smokes, it's too hot. Take the chicken pieces from the bag, shaking off any excess flour, add to the skillet, and brown the chicken pieces on all sides, 5 to 10 minutes, being careful not to let the flour on the chicken burn. When the pieces are a nice golden brown, remove them from the skillet and set them aside. Now add the okra and fry it, turning the pieces with the spatula, until it's sizzling and looks heated through, about 3 to 5 minutes. Remove from the skillet and set it aside.

3. Now add the remaining olive oil to the skillet, scraping up the browned bits with the spatula so they're loose and can be incorporated into the roux. Reduce heat to medium-low and add the remaining $1/2$ cup of flour to the skillet, stirring constantly with a wooden spoon so the flour doesn't stick to the bottom of the pan. Stir the roux as it bubbles. Keep the heat gentle and watch the color. It will turn light brown and then a light reddish brown over the next 5 or so minutes. When the color reaches a medium brown—not too dark—remove the skillet from the heat, add the chopped celery, onions, tomatoes, bell pepper, and garlic to the skillet, and stir for a minute or two, until the roux stops bubbling.

4. Using a spatula, scrape all the contents of the skillet into a soup pot. Add a cup or two of the chicken stock to the skillet and stir it around with the wooden spoon to deglaze, lifting up and incorporating any brown bits attached to the bottom; pour this into the soup pot. Add the remaining chicken stock to the pot and whisk to mix thoroughly.

5. Bring the pot to a boil on high heat, stirring with the whisk, then reduce the heat to a simmer. Add the okra, and the chicken pieces and simmer for about 45 minutes.

6. Remove the chicken pieces from the pot and set them aside. Slice the andouille sausage into thin coins and add to the soup pot. Add the cooked rice to the pot and simmer until the sausage is cooked through, about 10 to 15 minutes. While this is simmering, separate the chicken meat from the skin and bones and gristle. Pull the meat into bite-size pieces.

7. When the sausage is cooked through, add the chicken meat and the scallions to the pot. Stir and taste. Adjust the salt. If the spiciness is too mild, add a few shakes of Tabasco sauce until the gumbo gives a gentle glow in the mouth.

8. Cover the soup, turn off the heat, and let cool to lukewarm. Refrigerate until you're ready to serve it, preferably for 2 days to let the flavors marry.

9. Just before serving, add the filé powder and reheat over gentle to medium heat, stirring often so it doesn't stick and burn on the bottom, until it's nice and hot. Finely chop a few long spears of fresh chives. Garnish each bowl with a pinch of the freshly chopped chives.

TIP: Simmer chicken back, wings, and giblets with an onion and a few black peppercorns to make chicken broth. ▪

OKRA-MIRLITON SLAW

SERVES 3 TO 4

Jan Birnbaum, formerly of Catahoula Restaurant in Calistoga, California, and Sazerac in Seattle, Washington, gave me this recipe for a quick and easy okra slaw that comes straight from his Louisiana heritage. He says, "This slaw is a great accompaniment for fish. A catfish dipped in buttermilk and dredged in a mixture of half flour and cornmeal then pan fried would be a perfect match." Mirliton is also called chayote or vegetable pear.

FOR THE DRESSING

Juice of 4 lemons

1 tablespoon Dijon mustard

1 tablespoon champagne vinegar or white wine vinegar

1 teaspoon kosher salt

Pinch freshly ground black pepper

$1/3$ large shallot, peeled and minced

$1/3$ garlic clove, minced

Freshly grated zest of 1 large lemon (well scrubbed
   if not organic)

1 cup olive oil

FOR THE SLAW

15 small okra pods, sliced thin in cross-sections, stem
   ends removed

1 red onion, sliced very thin

1 mirliton, halved, seeded, and cut into fine matchsticks

1 red bell pepper, cut into $1/2$-inch dice

3 tablespoons chopped cilantro

1 jalapeño pepper, seeded and finely julienned

1. To make the dressing, place all ingredients except the zest and oil into a blender and mix 5 seconds on medium speed. Add the zest and oil and pulse until well incorporated, just a few seconds.

2. Combine the okra, onion, mirliton, red pepper, cilantro, and jalapeño in a large stainless-steel bowl. Toss the vegetables with the dressing. ■

Onion

ALLIUM CEPA

A WISE COOK once said that every good meal begins by chopping an onion. The maxim has stuck in my mind because it is so true. I cook the evening meal most nights at our house, and I'd say nine times out of ten I start by peeling and chopping an onion. Onions give a sweet flavor and add texture to all kinds of dishes, from risottos to stews to burritos. It also means that every good meal begins with a good cry because of onions' irritant qualities.

Onions are members of the *Allium* genus, which also includes leeks, chives, garlic, shallots, *cippolini*, topset onions, *rocambole*, ramps, and many other species and cultivars grown all over the world from the tropics to the polar circles.

The name "onion" is usually reserved for large-bulbed varieties of *Allium*. We get our word "onion" from pearl onions. *Unio* is the Latin word for unity, but it is also a name for a large white pearl. It became a nickname in the Roman street for small white onions. But onion eating far predates the Romans. The original ancestor of our bulb onions has long disappeared, but its wild relatives still grow in central Asia where plant scientists believe it originated.

THE ORGANIC FACTOR ◆ Slicing any onion may make you cry, but an organically grown onion may bring about a greater stream of tears than a conventional one due to the abundance of sulfur and other minerals the onion will have taken in from the compost-enriched soil (see Crying Onion Tears, page 156). The sulfur compounds do more than cause weeping. The organic advantage comes when these sulfur-rich compounds in the onions are stabilized through cooking into delicious flavor compounds.

Because conventional onions are so heavily sprayed, many cooks throw the papery skins away. But with organic onions, you can use those papery skins to give color to broths. The onion-skin hue looks especially nice in clear soups.

NUTRITION ‣ In ancient times, onions were used to treat intestinal parasites and gastroenteritis. In modern times, they are thought to have a beneficial effect on high blood pressure and heart disease and are used for their antibacterial, antifungal, and antitumor properties. Additionally, onions have some antioxidants, such as quercetin and anthocyanins, and vitamins B6 and C.

TYPES ‣ Although there are many classifications for onions, I think the simplest and most accurate way is to group them into just two kinds: pungent and mild.

Many of the mild types are often called sweet onions, although in most cases they are no sweeter—or even less sweet—than the pungent types. They seem sweeter because the onions' mildness allows their sugar content to register on the palate, whereas the bite of the pungent types

obliterates the sensation of sweetness. Most mild onions are known as "short day" types, suitable for growing at 37 degrees latitude or south. These types thrive on 12 hours of sunlight a day, but they don't develop properly with the longer days found farther north.

Pungent types are usually more suitably grown above latitude 37 degrees where crops get 15 to 16 hours of sunlight as the summer solstice approaches and is passed. (If it seems counterintuitive that more northerly areas get more hours of sunlight, remember that the Arctic Circle is the "land of the midnight sun.")

In general, pungent types are best for cooking and mild types are best for fresh uses like slicing to cover a hamburger or tossing into a salad. Pungent onions store well, but mild ones don't last long and should be used fairly quickly.

The familiar large-bulbed onions—whether sweet or pungent, red onions, white onions, Spanish onions—are all cultivated varieties of *Allium cepa*.

Besides large bulb onions, there are a few other major types available:

There are the slender onions without bulbs, which go by many names. Some call them scallions, others call them green onions or green

CRYING ONION TEARS

ONIONS CONCENTRATE SULFUR in their tissues as pyruvate, which is the negative ion of pyruvic acid, a naturally occurring acid found in foods. When an onion is cut, enzymes at the cut area immediately go to work on the pyruvate to produce allicin, a sulfur-containing compound. The more cutting, the more allicin is produced and released. Allicin-bearing fumes meet the moisture film on our eyes and dissolve into it, producing H_2SO_4—sulfuric acid. No wonder our eyes burn and our tear ducts start washing the irritant away. That's why a simple splash of cool tap water on the eyes will stop the burning and tears—you're just hastening and intensifying the rinsing away of acid.

ONIONS ARE EASY TO GROW. Start the seed indoors under lights in February and transplant to a garden bed around the first of April. Keep the bed well weeded. Most pungent onions are day-length sensitive, meaning they'll enlarge their bulbs until the summer solstice, then ripen over the next few weeks. Many mild onions are not day-length sensitive and can be planted to overwinter in the garden or ripen in the late summer.

When I grew pungent storage onions (the Northern Oak variety) in my organic garden in Pennsylvania, they'd ripen in mid-July. I let the tops dry out, then braided them and hung them from the rafters in the cool, dark, dry upstairs room of the house. Stored under those conditions, they'd last through the winter into the following spring.

bunching onions, still others are white-stalked or white bunching onions, or Japanese, Chinese, or Oriental bunching onions. Almost all, however, are variations of *Allium fistulosum.*

If slender onions are allowed to grow past the slender stage, they become known as spring onions. If you see what appear to be oversized scallions with slight bulges at the base, they are spring onions: snap them up. Brushed with a little oil and laid on the grill to cook until soft, they make a succulent side dish to grilled meats.

Pearl onions are small, red, white, and yellow-brown skinned onions, also called boilers, creamers, or baby onions. The Italian *cippolini* are a flat form of pearl onion, and all are miniature versions of *Allium cepa* that have been selected for their small size and grown in tightly packed groups to keep them small and firm.

In summer you may find red torpedo onions or Egyptian Topset onions at farmers' markets or roadside stands. The former are medium-pungent *Allium cepa* onions with an elongated shape, but the latter are truly unique, making several small bulbs at the base and a cluster of small, squiggly-tailed, edible bulbils (small, tadpole-shaped repro-

ductive structures) at the top of the green stems. The bulbils can be used raw in salads or pickled. These topset onions are a cross between *Allium cepa* and *Allium fistulosum.*

It's rare to find "potato onions," but they are occasionally seen at farmers' markets. Planting a small bulb yields one or two larger bulbs. Planting a large bulb produces eight to 12 small bulbs in a cluster underground. By using some and replanting some, these multiplier onions, as they are also known, can be kept growing continuously in the garden or in pots all year round. Shallots are a particular type of these so-called "multiplier onions." They are *Allium cepa,* but in a special subset known as the *Aggregatum* Group.

SEASONALITY ◂ Day-length sensitive onions reach peak season shortly after the summer solstice. Onions that are not day-length sensitive can be found year-around in markets.

WHAT TO LOOK FOR ◂ Hard, pungent onions with thin necks store best, and that's something to look for when selecting onions from a bin. Make sure there are no soft or moldy spots.

PREPARATION ◆ To chop a large bulb type onion for cooking: Using a sharp knife, cut the tip off the top of the onion, then score a circle around the roots. Draw the point of the knife through just one or two thin outer layers from the top down to the circular score mark. Leave the roots attached. With your fingers, peel away the skin and top layer or two of the onion.

Holding the onion straight up, make ½-inch-wide cuts down through the onion as deep as you can without touching the root. After you've made cuts across the bulb, turn the bulb 90 degrees and, holding it firmly, again make ½-inch cuts down through the onion.

Now turn the onion on its side and, starting at the top end, cut away ½-inch-wide slices across the bulb until you reach the root. You can either chop these remaining bits by hand or toss the root end in the stock pot.

To peel pearl or other small onions, place them in a bowl and pour boiling water over them, then keep them underwater. After 5 minutes or so, drain and cover with cool water. You'll find that a paring knife used to nick open the white skin at the root end will allow you to easily peel the onions.

USES ◆ The one characteristic that all onions share is their sweetness. It is the presence of sugar that makes onions so useful in all forms of cooking; this vegetable can be baked, broiled, boiled, roasted, braised, fried, grilled, sautéed, steamed, or eaten raw.

Their sugar allows them to pair with almost anything savory, including bacon, sharp cheeses, garlic, tomatoes, and vinegar. Onions also make a match with Provençal culinary herbs such as oregano, sage, and thyme. It's as if onions and its partners are the bass and drums for the melody and harmonies played by a dish's main ingredients.

I roast small onions like those delicious flat cippolini. Roast them whole (about 6 to 8 per person) in a 450°F oven for 15 to 20 minutes until they become tender to a knife point. When they cool, they'll peel easily. Then sauté them in a skillet with a tablespoon of olive oil over medium heat until they're hot and slightly browned. All they need is a little salt and pepper to make a fine side dish.

PICO DE GALLO

MAKES ABOUT 4 CUPS

This traditional Mexican salsa should be spicy enough to make you sit up and take notice, if you want it to be authentic, but you can adjust the heat to taste. Top your taco with it, or serve with plain tortilla chips.

1½ cups diced ripe tomatoes
1 cup chopped onion (a mild bulb onion if possible)
1½ cups diced ripe avocado
3 serrano chiles, minced
3 tablespoons freshly squeezed lime juice
¼ cup chopped cilantro
Salt and freshly ground black pepper

Combine all ingredients in a bowl and refrigerate for two hours for the flavors to marry. ■

SCALLION FRITTATA

SERVES 4

A frittata is a type of Italian omelet that's an easy and tasty way to start a weekend morning. Here scallions play a major role in the flavoring along with their friends, the tomatoes.

8 eggs
1/2 cup freshly grated Pecorino Romano
Leaves from 1 sprig fresh sage, finely chopped
Salt and freshly ground black pepper
1 tablespoon extra-virgin olive oil
6 scallions, trimmed and sliced thin (white and green parts separated)
18 grape tomatoes, halved

1. Whisk the eggs until well mixed. Stir in the cheese, sage, and salt and pepper to taste.

2. Place the oil in a medium to large nonstick skillet over medium heat. When hot, add the chopped scallions, reserving 1 tablespoon of the chopped green ends. Stir until the scallions are wilted, about 2 minutes.

3. Preheat the broiler. Add the egg mixture to the skillet and reduce heat to medium-low. Cook for 2 to 3 minutes, pulling the cooked eggs toward the center with a spatula and allowing the uncooked portion to run underneath. Sprinkle the tomatoes evenly over the top and continue cooking another 2 to 3 minutes until the eggs are almost set through but the top is still runny.

4. Sprinkle the top with reserved scallions and pass under the broiler for about 1 minute, until the top sets and is lightly brown. Loosen the frittata and carefully slide it onto a warm serving plate. Cut into wedges. ▪

Parsnip

PASTINACA SATIVA

HOW TO DESCRIBE parsnip's flavor? It's aromatic, smelling of equal parts parsley and carrot, with something slightly sweet and musky that's all its own. Not everyone cares for parsnips because of their unusual taste, but they're missing the point in my opinion. Its unusual taste is what's intriguing about this root.

The name parsnip has an interesting etymology. The botanical Latin name for the genus, *Pastinaca,* comes from the Latin word *pastinare,* meaning "that which is dug up," and originally referred to both parsnips and carrots. By passing through French, the root *pas-* acquired an *r* to make it *pars-.* The *-nip* suffix is from Anglo-Saxon *naep,* which in turn descended from Latin *napus,* meaning a root crop.

THE ORGANIC FACTOR ▸ Most of the unique flavor of a parsnip lies just under its skin, which gives an organic parsnip a great advantage over a conventionally grown one in that you don't have to peel the root, so all that flavor may be retained.

NUTRITION ▸ Parsnips are nutritious. A half cup of boiled, sliced root gives you 6 percent of your daily magnesium, 12 percent of vitamin C, 11 percent of folic acid, and 8 percent of the daily potassium requirement.

SEASONALITY ▸ The highest quality parsnips are found in early winter, when the fall crop is still young and firm but has endured frost. According to the received wisdom, frost will turn some of the root's starch to sugar, making them sweeter. Once, as an experiment for *Organic Gardening* magazine, using a hand refractometer that measures sugar in juice, we took a sugar reading of the juice of parsnips in September, before the hard frosts had come, and it read 6 Brix (Brix is the percentage of sugar). We let the parsnips stay in the ground, then took another reading around mid-December after the really hard freezes had descended on the garden. We found the Brix had risen to nearly 9 percent—not a huge rise, but noticeable.

Those who grow parsnips know that they keep perfectly well in the ground over winter with just a light mulch, but they must be harvested before they wake up in the spring because they are biennials, and as soon as they start spring growth, their cores turn woody and fibrously tough.

WHAT TO LOOK FOR ◆ Make sure they're firm, white, undamaged, and of medium size (9 to 11 inches long) rather than super large or beginning to sprout new top growth, which turns them tough. This is especially true if you are looking for parsnips in the spring.

USES ◆ I find that parboiled parsnips (boiled for only about 5 to 7 minutes) can be finished by any number of methods: baking, braising, breading and then sautéing in butter, pureeing, steaming, or grilling. I'll also boil one part parsnips to two parts potatoes, then mash them with milk, butter, and salt. And I'll always cut up a parsnip and add it to beef stew.

Parsnips sing baritone in the quartet of roasted root vegetables that also includes turnips, carrots, and celery root—or sometimes rutabagas and potatoes. I dice them, toss them with a little olive oil, and roast them in a 400°F oven for 30 to 40 minutes, turning them occasionally and making sure they don't burn. They're done when the outside of the cubes is crisp and lightly caramelized and the inside soft and tender.

Another pairing I like is parsnips poached in fresh coconut milk. Poach quartered roots in barely simmering coconut milk until almost tender, then finish by sautéing them in a little butter with a pinch of salt, and at the end add a splash of coconut milk from the poaching liquid and reduce it until it glazes the roots.

Try contrasting parsnips' sweetness with sour, salty, or bitter. The musky flavor pairs with fellow umbelliferous herbs, including chervil, dill, and parsley. It also goes with nutmeg, oranges, butter, and nuts such as almonds, hazelnuts, and walnuts.

The last time parsnips had a real vogue was the late 19th and early 20th centuries. In 1898, the *Boston Cooking-School Cook Book* by Fanny Farmer advised readers to boil and mash parsnips with butter, salt, and pepper, then make small cakes from them, dredge them in flour, and sauté them in butter. You'll find more modern treatments of this crop in the recipes.

TEMPURA ROOTS IN OHSAWA SAUCE

SERVES 4

Simone Parris, a friend from Cape Cod, raises macrobiotic cooking to a delicious art. In this recipe, the root vegetables are fried as tempura, then simmered so that the crisp coating dissolves into a sauce. *Kombu* and bonito flakes are becoming readily available at natural and whole foods stores, although you can certainly find them in any Japanese market. Serve this sauce over soba or udon noodles.

1 (3 × 8–inch) piece dried kombu seaweed

1 fresh shiitake mushroom

1/4 cup dried bonito flakes

1 pound or more combination of carrot, parsnip, and burdock root, cleaned and trimmed

2 cups or more safflower oil

¹/₂ cup arrowroot powder
¹/₂ cup all-purpose flour
Pinch salt

1. Make a broth by filling a medium saucepan with 3 quarts water, adding the *kombu*, shiitake mushroom, and bonito flakes. Bring to a simmer (do not let boil), and simmer for 20 to 30 minutes. Pour through a strainer, return the liquid to the saucepan, and place over medium heat.

2. Cut the carrots, parsnips, and burdock diagonally into 2- to 3-inch lengths. Add them to the simmering stock and cook lightly, about 8 minutes, removing the roots while still firm. Drain vegetables and let cool.

3. Heat the oil in a heavy skillet over medium-high heat until hot. While it's heating, make the tempura batter: Combine the arrowroot powder, flour, and salt in a bowl. Stir just enough water to make a thick batter.

4. In batches, dip the roots in the batter and deep fry in the safflower oil until golden, about 3 minutes per batch.

5. Add the tempura-fried vegetables to the broth and simmer slowly, covered, for an hour or more, until a thick gravy is formed. ▪

SAUTÉ OF PARSNIPS, CHESTNUTS, AND BRUSSELS SPROUTS

SERVES 4

Ann Cashion, owner of the no-frills-named Cashion's Eat Place in Washington, D.C., provides this wonderful recipe that glorifies the parsnip. Parsnips and chestnuts have an affinity for one another not only because they peak in the same season but also because both have a natural sweetness.

15 fresh chestnuts
2 cups chicken stock
1 stalk celery
1 carrot
Salt and freshly ground black pepper
1 pound parsnips
¹/₂ pint Brussels sprouts
1 tablespoon olive oil
1 tablespoon chopped Italian flat-leaf parsley

1. Peel the chestnuts by scoring the outer shell with a sharp knife. Place in cold water in a saucepan and bring the water to boil. When the water boils, drain the chestnuts and peel off the husks. If the chestnuts are fresh this should pose very little problem.

2. Add the chicken stock to the saucepan, along with chestnuts, celery, carrot, and salt and pepper to taste, bring to a simmer, and cook 10 to 12 minutes, until the chestnuts are just tender. Remove the chestnuts and reserve. Discard the celery and carrot; save stock for another use.

3. Cut the parsnips into batons, removing the tough inner core. Cut the Brussels sprouts in half, or leave them whole if they're very small.

4. Film a skillet with the olive oil and place over medium heat. Add the parsnips and Brussels sprouts, cover, and cook 8 to 10 minutes, turning the vegetables from time to time until they begin to turn pale gold in spots and are cooked through. You may add a little water to the pan to facilitate the cooking process and prevent overbrowning. After 4 to 5 minutes, add the chestnuts so that they can heat through and pick up color. Season with salt and pepper if needed. Toss with the chopped parsley and serve immediately. ▪

Pea

PISUM SATIVUM

THE MOMENT peas are picked, they begin to lose their sweetness and their herbaceous, garden-fresh flavor. For that reason alone, I encourage lovers of organic foods to grow their own, just to experience the joyful pleasure of eating the new growing season's first main crop fresh from the vine (see If You Like to Garden, below). Peas right off the vine are incomparably better than frozen peas.

THE ORGANIC FACTOR ◆ While conventional pea farmers use chemicals on their vines, organic farmers must find alternative methods of dealing with diseases and pests. Most pea crops planted in compost-amended soil will produce just fine without the need for pest and disease controls, but occasional problems can occur, including aphids, symphylans, and mildew. Aphids can be rubbed off or washed away with a hose. Symphylans are soil-borne pests related to cen-

tipedes that damage the roots of many crops, including peas. Organic growers can amend their soil with diatomaceous earth, the sharp-edged skeletal remains of ocean-dwelling diatoms (one-celled algae). The sharp edges puncture the skin of the symphylans, killing them.

Mildews seldom affect peas, but if they do, organic growers spray vines with a solution made of one tablespoon of baking soda dissolved in a gallon of water. The alkaline environment produced by the baking soda discourages mildews.

NUTRITION ◆ As with most other seeds, and especially legumes (beans, lentils, etc.), peas are very nutritious. One half cup of boiled peas contains 67 calories but no cholesterol, 12 grams of carbohydrates, 4 to 5 grams of protein, 2 to 3 grams of dietary fiber, 13 percent of the daily requirement of vitamin C, 18 percent of thiamine, 13 percent of vitamin B6, 13 percent of folic acid, 8 percent of iron, 11 percent of niacin, 10 percent of riboflavin, 8 percent of magnesium, and 6 percent of needed potassium. That's a heap of nutrition for a half-cup of any food.

IF YOU LIKE TO GARDEN

WHEN MY CHILDREN were preschoolers, our vegetable garden included a 25-foot trellis for growing Laxton's Progress English peas. When they'd get hungry for lunch, the kids would wander up to the pea patch and pick fat pods off the vines, nimbly prying them open and gobbling up the sugary peas inside. If you have the garden space and small children, give them this experience. They'll remember it the rest of their lives.

If you don't have a trellis, consider making a teepee from six long garden stakes tied together at the top. Grow peas up each stake, leaving an opening for kids to crawl in. Once inside, they'll find pea pods hanging within arm's reach in their edible bower.

What if you have only a small yard? Peas grow vertically, so all you really need is a space 8 feet long by 1 foot wide. Two sturdy uprights 7 feet tall and 8 feet apart hold a crossbar on top from which you can run lengths of twine at 6-inch intervals down to a piece of twine tied horizontally across the bottom.

KEEP AN EYE OUT FOR PEA SHOOTS

THESE LOOK LIKE little packets of folded leaves, flower buds, and tendrils that grow at the tips of pea vines. They are common ingredients in Chinese cooking and can sometimes be found in Chinatown markets during pea season. If you grow your own peas, you see them growing at the tips of the vines—snip off the outermost two or three inches of these tender tips. Cut them here and there from the vines so you leave plenty of growing tips to produce peas.

Pea shoots can be stir-fried with a few drops of toasted sesame oil and a pinch of salt, and perhaps some crushed almonds. Or you can steam them and serve them with a touch of butter and some fresh chervil. A pinch of salt and a shake of mirin (Japanese sweet rice wine) is another satisfying way to dress steamed pea shoots.

TYPES ► English or garden peas are the familiar peas we find fresh in their inedible shells. They must be shelled before they can be used. Dishes with the names *Saint-Germain* and *Clamart* refer to French pea varieties called *petits pois*. These diminutive English peas have a firm texture and a delightfully rich flavor.

Snow peas—flat-podded peas favored by Chinese cooks—can be eaten whole and are very useful in vegetable medleys or with rice or meat stir-fries.

Sugar snap peas were first released to the public in 1976, when Calvin Lamborn, a talented plant breeder, working with centuries-old and modern strains of plant material, perfected an edible-podded pea called the snap pea. Lamborn's advance was to breed an edible pea pod that was fat, sweet, and succulent (like the peas inside) and didn't have a tough parchment lining. It did, however, have a tough string running down one side (and sometimes both sides) of the pea pod. So the first edible-podded peas from Lamborn were much like string beans. However, marketing people being what they are decided to call them sugar snap peas. Over the ensuing years, those bothersome strings have been bred out of the pea pods and today we have snap peas that need no stringing.

SEASONALITY ► Whether they're home-grown, bought at the farmers' market, or store-bought, fresh (and fresh-picked) peas are worth putting up when the season is in high gear, which is usually in late May or early June. Peas like cool weather—they're typically planted around St. Patrick's Day in much of the country. Summer heat will cause them to stop producing pods. You should be able to find English (garden) peas at farmers' markets in your region at the height of the season.

WHAT TO LOOK FOR ► Look for vivid green pods with a glossy surface, no yellowing, and juicy stems where they were picked rather than dried stem ends. To be truly choice, peas have to be absolutely fresh. The peas inside need to be developed but not overdeveloped.

The way you tell whether English or sugar snaps are developed to the proper size is to open a pod and look. If the peas are plump but not touching each other, that's perfect. Now take a pea and squeeze it between your thumb and forefinger. It should mash, rather than split into two halves. If it does mash, you've got the peas at their peak.

Snow peas are best when the peas inside are still juvenile—barely making a lump in the pod. The

pods should be on the small side and very thin, even translucent if held up to a strong light. They're tender and sweet if not overcooked, so cook them gently.

STORAGE AND PREPARATION ◆ Snow peas still have a string down one side, so zip the strings off before cooking them in a stir-fry or by steaming them. They can be used whole or sliced on a diagonal. English peas simply need to be popped out of the pods, and sugar snaps need no prep at all. Dried whole peas will cook more evenly and quickly if they are first soaked overnight.

One way to preserve the fresh taste of late spring peas is to freeze them at the peak of their season. You can find frozen-fresh organic peas in the freezer section of your organic market, but peas taste the sweetest when you put them up yourself, especially following this method.

Peas are best blanched and frozen still in their pods. This stops the enzymatic action that can create off flavors in frozen food. The pods help preserve the delicate flavor of the peas inside. Blanch English or sugar snap peas still in their pods, plunging them in boiling water for about a minute. Drain and run them under cold water to stop the cooking. The pods should be bright green. Then spread the pods out on cookie sheets and freeze them. When they're frozen solid, put a cup's worth of peas (1 pound) into individual freezer bags, twist-tie the bags shut, and store in the freezer.

When it's time to thaw them out, float the freezer bag in a bowl of hot water about an hour before dinner so they will defrost gently. Turn the peas into a saucepan, discarding the pods (even sugar snap pea pods are inedible after being frozen). Make sure there's enough liquid in the saucepan to heat the peas (add a little water if necessary), and turn the burner to low. Cover the pan and heat the peas just until heated through. These peas will carry something of summer's evanescent goodness, and I guarantee they will be the best peas you'll have ever eaten in January.

USES ◆ Peas are wonderfully versatile. You can take advantage of their versatility if you have some growing at home. Fresh-picked green peas are wonderful tossed raw into salads or lightly cooked, but that's just the beginning. With sugar snaps and snow peas, you also have edible pods, which are great in stir-fries and vegetable medleys with other early summer vegetables such as squash. You can sprout organic pea seed in flats (see If You Like to Garden, page 162) and harvest the little sprouts for fresh salads.

Peas partner with a wide range of other ingredients. James Joyce, in *Ulysses,* admonishes us to "Mint your peas!" The combination of flavors is classic—but easy on the mint. Mushrooms, nutmeg, onions, and rice—especially risotto—pair beautifully with peas. The French boil garden peas, drain them, add a pinch of powdered sugar, and toss them with butter.

If you grow your own peas, you can also allow peas to mature and dry on the vine, then shell them out to store as dried peas for winter soups. If you do this, make sure the peas are very dry. Tie up a couple of tablespoonfuls of salt in a piece of paper towel, and include this in each storage jar. The salt will absorb any moisture still in the pea seeds, which otherwise might cause mold.

BAKED SUGAR SNAP PEAS

SERVES 4

Garden-fresh snap peas are perhaps best eaten raw from the vine, but lacking a garden source, here's a way to highlight the flavor of peas fresh from the market.

1 pound sugar snap peas
2 tablespoons olive oil
2 tablespoons minced shallots
2 teaspoons chopped fresh thyme
Salt

Preheat the oven to 450°F. Mix peas and oil in a bowl until peas are coated, then turn onto a medium baking sheet in a single layer. Sprinkle them with the shallots, thyme, and salt to taste. Bake 7 minutes until tender but still firm. ∎

PEAS BRAISED WITH LETTUCE AND ONIONS

SERVES 2 TO 3

This is a classic French dish and certainly one of the most delicious ways to eat cooked peas. The French typically use petits pois, but English garden peas can also be used.

8 white pearl onions
1 head Boston or butterhead lettuce
3 tablespoons butter
1/4 teaspoon salt
Freshly ground black pepper
2 cups shelled fresh garden peas
1 tablespoon sugar
6 parsley stems, tied in a bouquet

1. Bring a small saucepan of water to a boil, add the pearl onions, and boil for 5 minutes; set aside. When cool, remove their skins and cut a small X in their root ends so they will cook in time with the other ingredients.

2. Cut the lettuce into quarters and tie each quarter around its middle with kitchen string so it holds together while cooking.

3. In a large heavy saucepan, add 1/3 cup of water, the butter, salt, and a grind or two of black pepper. Bring to a boil so the butter melts and the salt dissolves, then reduce heat to low, add the peas, tossing them so they're covered with the liquid. Add the sugar. Snuggle the parsley down among the peas. Place the lettuce quarters over the peas and baste with the liquid. Sprinkle the onions over the lettuce.

4. Place a bowl or deep plate concave side up over the top of the saucepan to act as a lid and place a handful of ice cubes in it. (When the water boils the steam will condense on the under surface

continued

of the cold bowl and rain back on the contents of the saucepan.) Bring the pan up to a slow boil, reduce heat to low, and cook slowly for about 20 minutes, until peas are very tender. Remove the bowl several times during the cooking and pour off the melt water, gently stir the ingredients in the pan, then replace the bowl and add more ice cubes.

5. When the peas are tender, most of the cooking liquid should have evaporated. Remove the parsley and the strings from the lettuce. Place the lettuce quarters around the edge of a heated serving dish. Pour the peas and onions into the center of the serving dish. Serve immediately, while steaming hot. ■

SCANDINAVIAN PEA SOUP

MAKES 3 QUARTS

Organic supermarkets usually carry organic dried peas in bulk. This hearty Danish-style soup is inexpensive to make and wonderful for lunch or on a cold winter's evening.

2 cups dried peas
8 small leeks
1 smoked ham hock
$1/2$ teaspoon dried thyme
$1/2$ pound celery root
4 carrots
Salt and freshly ground black pepper

1. Place the peas in a large bowl and cover 2 inches deep with water. Soak overnight at room temperature.

2. The next day, drain the peas. Wash the leeks well and drain, then chop coarsely. In a large, heavy soup pot, combine the peas, leeks, ham hock, thyme, and 3 quarts of water. Bring to a boil, then

reduce heat and simmer for 30 minutes until the peas are very tender. While this is cooking, peel the celery root and dice into $1/4$-inch cubes. Cut the carrot lengthwise into quarters, then cut into thin strips; reserve.

3. When the peas are tender, puree the soup in batches in a blender (leave the ham hock in the pot), then return it all to the soup pot.

4. Add the celery root and the carrots to the soup, bring to a simmer, and cook 20 to 30 minutes, stirring occasionally, until these are tender.

5. Remove the ham hock, remove the meat from the skin and bones, chop the meat coarsely and return it to the soup; discard the remainder. Add salt and pepper to taste. If the soup is too thick, thin with water. Serve hot. ■

Potato

SOLANUM TUBEROSUM

POTATOES have kept whole cultures alive. Not only the Incas, who first cultivated the tuber, but (after potatoes reached Europe in the 16th century) also many countries in the northern parts of Europe. Potatoes were a staple of the Irish, at least until a bacterial blight decimated the Emerald Isle's crops in the mid- to late-1840s, causing starvation and necessitating emigration.

The word *potato* comes from the Carib Indian word *batata,* which actually referred to the sweet potato. The Spanish conquistadors who arrived in the New World pronounced it *patata* and used it also to refer to the white potato because of its similar appearance. Eventually the word became *papas* in Spanish. Like other New World crops, such as peppers and tobacco, potatoes soon conquered Europe and then the world. The Italians first thought of potatoes as a kind of truffle, because they both grow under the ground, and called them *tartufo bianco*, or white truffle. That became *taratufflo*, which the Germans heard as *kartoffel*. The Russians heard the German name and gave it a Slavic twist by calling them *kartochki*.

THE ORGANIC FACTOR ‣ The flavor and texture—even the color—of the same variety of potato can change dramatically depending on where it's grown and the soils and climate in that place. But no matter where they're grown, few foods are better than potatoes pulled fresh from dark, crumbly organic soil and cooked within minutes. They have an earthy, comforting flavor, probably from delicate esters and other flavor compounds that disappear in storage. They also have a smooth, rich texture, perhaps due to the contrast with conventionally grown potatoes whose cell division has been chemically altered. If you can't grow potatoes where you live, by all means seek out real organic spuds at the farmers' markets or organic supermarket. You'll also be more likely to find some of the superior if somewhat unusual varieties listed on page 493 at farmers' markets.

Because we get the full benefit of potato nutrients only when we leave the skins on, it's extremely important that we eat only organic potatoes, which don't have to be peeled. Two toxic chemicals are sprayed on much of the nation's $2.5 billion conventional potato crop each year, both in the field and in storage, to inhibit sprouting; and anyone who cooks with conventional potatoes would be wise to peel them to remove the bulk of the chemical residue. Maleic hydrazide is applied a few weeks before harvest. It inhibits cell division in the tubers but not cell expansion—therefore, besides stopping the formation of sprouts on the potatoes, it also produces tubers with large, watery cells. So the buyer gets less taste along with his chemical-treated potato. A second chemical, chlorpropham, is applied to potatoes when they are being stored, before they go to market.

That's just the sprout inhibitors. Other chemicals are used in the processing of potatoes for potato chips, instant potatoes, and other potato products. I am reassured about the benefits of organic food every time I cook organic potatoes skins and all.

NUTRITION ‣ While the bulk of the potato tuber is made up of starches—energy-packed complex carbohydrates—most of a spud's generous stores of nutrients are in a thin layer just under the fibrous skins. Just 7 ounces of baked potato, with skin, gives you 4.7 grams of protein. While that's not a huge amount, it is usable, as potatoes

KEEP AN EYE OUT FOR NEW POTATOES

REAL NEW POTATOES are harvested from the plant's trailing underground roots while the plant is still growing. They tend to be small and their skins are thin and flaky. They are prized for their fine, delicate flavor, so if you find them—usually when the first early summer crop is still weeks from harvest and again when the second crop in September is still weeks from harvest—nab them. I've never seen them sold anywhere but at farmers' markets and roadside stands, but they may start appearing in specialty markets.

are higher in lysine than the other top starches of the world—wheat, corn, and rice. Those 7 ounces also provide 50 percent of our Recommended Daily Allowance of vitamin B6, 30 percent of vitamin C, from 15 percent (females) to 30 percent (males) of our daily iron needs, 20 percent of niacin, 20 percent of thiamine, 15 percent of magnesium, 5 percent of folic acid, and 42 percent of our potassium.

TYPES ⬩ It used to be that potatoes were generic, and either brown or red skinned. The reds were sometimes called "new potatoes," but that was a misnomer—they were simply a smaller variety, while new potatoes really are new, or immature (see Keep an Eye Out for New Potatoes, page 167). Red potatoes have a flesh that's classified as waxy, while the big Idaho bakers in the stores are starchy. Waxy potatoes take to boiling better than the starchy types that tend to become too soft and watery. For that reason, I prefer red potatoes for mashed potatoes, while starchy potatoes are best for baked potatoes. Either type makes good french fries.

Nowadays you can find many other kinds of potatoes in various shapes like thumbs, fingers, and crescents, and in colors from red to pink to yellow to purple and violet. The Peruvian Purple potato is a starchy type that arrived in America in the 1970s and caused everyone to ooh and aah—it's now one of the 200-plus varieties grown in the United States. I love the French or German fingerlings, with their dense, waxy, rich flesh, and luscious flavor. I like to cut them on the diagonal into thirds, fry them in a heavy skillet in a little olive oil, just until they start to brown (about 8 minutes over medium heat), add a chopped onion, salt, and fresh ground black pepper and finish them for 20 minutes in a 350°F oven. They are perfect for

boiling with their skins on and then slicing cold into salads, especially the tangy German-style ones. They make great mashed potatoes. You see a lot of the varieties called Yukon Gold and Yellow Finn in stores these days. These are intermediate between the waxy and starchy types, and Yukon Golds have a sweeter flavor and sap that caramelizes easily when pan-fried.

SEASONALITY ⬩ Potato crops come in from summer through fall. Winter potatoes are either taken from storage or are grown in mild climates.

WHAT TO LOOK FOR ⬩ When choosing potatoes, first of all make sure there's no green showing through or just under the skin. When potatoes are exposed to light, even artificial light, they produce a green substance called solanine. It's a poisonous alkaloid and should never be eaten. You can peel it away, but better, don't buy green potatoes.

See that your spuds (the word spud is a corruption of the word spade, which you use to dig the tubers) are free of black, rough, scabby spots. They should have no soft spots or cuts in the skin, no discolored spots, no moldy pits, and they should be firm, even hard. The presence of dried soil on organic potatoes is actually a good sign, since soil shows that the tubers haven't been washed, which exposes them to mold and rot spores and to bacteria. You can always brush them clean at home.

In the old days, farmhouses had root cellars where potatoes for the winter were stored. The root cellar was dark, the air was mildly moist, and the temperature a natural year-round 58 degrees Fahrenheit. Those conditions remain ideal for potatoes; but since most of us don't have root cellars, it's enough that we store potatoes in the dark at room temperature. If you put them in the fridge, the cold causes the tubers' starches to change into sugars, giving them a weirdly sweet, off flavor.

USES ▸ Potatoes are champions at enhancing and holding the flavors of other foods. Cooked with celery root or turnips or garlic and mashed with cream, butter, and salt, they are exalted. Potatoes with bacon or with onions or leeks are irresistible combinations.

POTATO SOUFFLÉ

SERVES 4

This is an old German recipe that shows off the taste of good potatoes. Make sure all your ingredients are fresh, young, starchy potatoes like White Rose or russet.

1 pound baking potatoes, peeled
4 eggs, separated
2 tablespoons butter
1/2 teaspoon freshly grated nutmeg
Salt and freshly ground black pepper
1/3 cup grated Gruyère cheese

1. Fill a large pot with water and add the potatoes. Bring to a boil, salt lightly, reduce to a simmer, and cook for 20 to 30 minutes, or until the potatoes are tender. Drain well.

2. Preheat the oven to 375°F. Mash the potatoes with the egg yolks, butter, nutmeg, and salt and pepper to taste.

3. Beat egg whites until soft peaks form. Fold into the potato mixture. Pour into a buttered shallow 9 × 9–inch baking dish and sprinkle the top with the cheese. Bake for 12 minutes. ■

FINGERLING POTATO AND CHANTERELLE GRATIN

SERVES 6

Here's a wonderful update on the potato gratin, a confabulation of flavors that's intense, luscious, full of sinful fat, and perfect for holiday feasting.

1 1/2 tablespoons butter, plus extra for the pan
5 ounces blue cheese, at room temperature
2 1/2 cups half-and-half
Salt
1/2 teaspoon freshly ground black pepper
1 pound chanterelle mushrooms, coarsely chopped
1 1/2 teaspoons chopped fresh thyme, or 1 teaspoon dried
2 pounds German or French Fingerling potatoes, sliced into 1/4-inch rounds

1. Preheat the oven to 400°F. Butter a 9 × 13–inch baking dish.

2. Put the cheese and 1/2 cup of the half-and-half in a bowl and mash them into a coarse paste with salt and the pepper. Add the remaining 2 cups of half-and-half and mix thoroughly.

3. In a heavy pot, melt the 1 1/2 tablespoons butter over medium high heat. Add the chanterelles and thyme. Sauté until the mushrooms are tender and the liquid is mostly reduced, about 7 to 9 minutes.

4. Place half of the potatoes in the buttered baking pan. Ladle 3/4 cup of the cheese sauce over the top. Top with all the mushroom mixture, then with another 3/4 cup of the cheese sauce. Place the remaining potatoes on top and cover them with the remaining cheese sauce. Cover the baking pan with aluminum foil and bake for 30 minutes. Remove the foil and continue baking for 30 minutes more, until the potatoes are tender and the top is golden brown. Remove from the oven and let stand 10 minutes before serving. ■

SCANDINAVIAN POTATO PANCAKES

MAKES ABOUT 16 PANCAKES, SERVING 6 TO 8

This is a traditional Scandinavian recipe for potato pancakes that puts the blush in those Norwegian, Swedish, Danish, and Finnish cheeks. You can find barley flour in most natural and whole foods stores.

4 medium baking potatoes

6 tablespoons barley flour

3 tablespoons all-purpose flour

1/2 teaspoon salt

8 tablespoons (1 stick) unsalted butter

2 tablespoons minced fresh parsley

1. Coarsely shred potatoes with a grater or the grater attachment on a food processor. Place the shredded potatoes in a large sieve and run under cold tap water until water runs clear; let drain.

2. Mix the barley and all-purpose flours and the salt together in a large bowl Add the grated potatoes and toss to coat them completely. Let stand for 15 minutes.

3. Preheat the oven to 300°F. Take 1/4-cupfuls of the potatoes and pat them into cakes 1/2 inch thick and 3 to 4 inches in diameter, then place them on waxed paper.

4. When all the potatoes have been formed into cakes, melt 1 tablespoon of the butter in a 12-inch skillet over medium heat, add 4 pancakes and cook about 3 minutes, until the undersides are golden brown. Add another tablespoon of butter to the pan, turn the pancakes, and cook another 3 minutes until the other sides are golden brown.

5. Transfer the finished pancakes to a baking sheet and set in the warm oven; continue with the remaining cakes. When all the cakes have been fried and are on the baking sheet, test one to make sure they are done through and the potatoes inside are soft and not crunchy. If not quite done, increase oven temperature to 350°F and bake for 5 to 10 minutes, then recheck. When the cakes are done, transfer to a serving platter and garnish with parsley. ∎

Radish

RAPHANUS SATIVUS

BEFORE THE Culinary Institute of America set up shop in St. Helena, California, the Greystone building was used for varied purposes. Once when I visited it was hosting a trade show put on by purveyors of foodstuffs from Thailand. One stall displayed the Thai art of vegetable carving. All sorts of colorful vegetables had been carved into elaborate shapes, but the gem of the exhibit, I thought, was an exquisite, pinkish-red, heart-shaped vegetable faceted like a diamond. Its green and white skin was peeled back like a flower in full bloom, and its red flesh seemed to glow from within. "What kind of vegetable is that?" I asked the stall keeper. "Radish," she said. And that's when I first discovered there is more to the lowly radish than I had ever imagined.

The source of our modern radishes is thought to be Central Asia, although the actual wild progenitor plant is no longer found. Modern radishes, though, have been known since ancient times. In the fifth century BCE, Greek historian Herodotus described an inscription on the great pyramid of Egypt that told of the slaves who built the monument eating great quantities of radishes, along with onions and garlic.

While the wild progenitor of modern radishes has gone missing, another species of wild radish (*Raphanus raphistrum*) grows across the North American continent. It is especially abundant in the cool, wet spring here in northern California, where its white and magenta flowers join yellow mustard in coloring up the vineyards. I like its crunchy, pungent, young seedpods in spring salads, but you have to get them right after they form or they develop tough strings.

You'd think that the name radish derives from the genus name, *Raphanus*, but that's not the case. It comes from the Latin *radix*, meaning root, and hence is related to the word "radical."

THE ORGANIC FACTOR ◦ When buying small radishes at farmers' markets, inspect the leaves. If they have an abundance of tiny shot holes in them, it's a good bet they were made by flea beetles—a difficult-to-control pest. If flea beetles are making holes, that signifies that the crop is most likely organic, or at least not sprayed. If the leaves are without blemish, inquire further as to how the grower controls flea beetles. An organic grower will lament the presence of this bug, possibly saying he puts out yellow cards coated with stickum. The beetles are attracted to that color and get stuck. A conventional grower will tell you which pesticide he or she uses. Beware the grower whose radishes have perfect leaves and who tells you he's organic and doesn't have a problem with flea beetles. This pest is ubiquitous, although a moderate infestation doesn't harm the edible portion of the plant or do much to slow down radishes' rapid growth.

NUTRITION ◦ Just ½ cup of sliced radish gives us 20 percent of our daily requirement of vitamin C—although not much else in the way of nutrition.

TYPES ◦ The familiar red globes we know as radishes are the most familiar of the many kinds that are available.

Asian or winter radishes are usually planted to mature in the fall and keep through the winter. Some, like the daikon, are white cylinders up to 18 inches long, with myriad uses. That beautifully carved radish I saw at the Thai expo was most likely the oriental radish called *Xin Li Mei*, Chinese for Beauty Heart, and sometimes sold as Red Daikon. Others may be green skinned or have green shoulders or flesh. These can be sweet rather than pungent.

While these are the two most widely grown sorts of radishes, there are yet other kinds. Black radishes are favored in Eastern Europe and Russia. These large radishes have skin that's black with grayish overtones and a heavy kick of earthy, rooty pungency.

While leaf radishes are used in some countries as fodder, in other places their hairless leaves are used as a potherb to add snap to soups.

Then there are the rat-tailed radishes of Asian countries that produce long seed pods—up to a foot in length—that are eaten raw, cooked, or pickled.

IF YOU LIKE TO GARDEN

RADISHES ARE AMAZINGLY QUICK GROWING. The seeds go into pure compost as soon as it warms to 50 degrees Fahrenheit. Three or four weeks later, I'm pulling fat little red globes the size of jawbreakers and slicing them into the first spring salads of dandelion greens, violet flowers, and wild onions.

SEASONALITY ◆ Radishes like short days and cool weather—midspring conditions—but return for a fall reprise that's become a part of Oktoberfest: In the beer halls of Munich, the brews are accompanied by black bread, salt, and thin slices of pungent radishes called *Münchner Bier*. The long days of summer throw radishes into reproductive mode, whereupon they send up flower stalks and toughen their roots. Hot weather turns their delightful sweet-and-zingy pungency—sort of like a well-behaved horseradish—unpleasantly intense.

WHAT TO LOOK FOR ◆ All fresh radishes should be firm to the touch, not soft. Reject any with splits, cracks, or evidence of a cut-off seed stalk. The leaves—even if flea beetle-bitten—should be fresh looking, not yellowed or dried out. Radishes sold without tops in little plastic bags are to be avoided.

USES ◆ While all radishes are delicious raw, they can also be stir-fried, braised, steamed, or boiled in stews and soups. Cooked, they'll lose their pungency and function more like turnips—to which they're closely related—in texture and taste.

Whichever of the bulbous root radishes you find, they all are versatile. Take a slice of black bread or pumpernickel—or if you can find it, a slice of German *Landbrot*—and spoon on some quark (a kind of unripened soft cheese similar to thick yogurt), top with a layer of minced pungent radishes, garnish with chopped chervil or thyme, then grind a pinch of coarse sea salt on top.

Slice daikons into rounds and use them as a canapé base instead of a cracker for smoked salmon, pickled herring, caviar, or *fromage blanc*. Grate or shred them to accompany sashimi. Julienne them for inclusion in sushi. Add chopped daikon to soups and sauces or cook them with meat—they soften, absorb juices, and add texture. Pickle daikon or other Asian radishes as the Koreans do in their kim chee (add some to the recipe on page 64).

RADISH SALSA

MAKES ABOUT 1½ CUPS

The radish adds a different kind of pungency to the peppery heat of a typical salsa. It also adds a nice crunch and color when the red radishes are young and crisp.

Use as a topping for chicken, pork, or fish tacos; as an addition to meat, rice, and beans in burritos; or eat with chips.

½ cup finely diced small red radishes
½ cup seeded and diced ripe plum tomato
   (1 large tomato)
¼ cup finely chopped scallions (white parts only)
1 teaspoon minced garlic
2 tablespoons freshly squeezed lime juice
1 teaspoon minced jalapeño or serrano pepper
2 tablespoons roughly chopped cilantro
2 tablespoons olive oil
Salt and freshly ground black pepper

Gently stir all ingredients together in a serving bowl. ■

DAIKON STIR-FRY

SERVES 4

Simple, but it makes a fine accompaniment to highly flavored Asian dishes.

1 tablespoon peanut oil
¾ pound daikon radish, scrubbed and sliced thin

Salt to taste

1/2 teaspoon sugar

1 tablespoon minced fresh parsley

2 tablespoons minced chives

2 tablespoons toasted sesame seeds

1. Heat the oil in a wok on high heat. Add the daikon and toss to cover with oil, then add salt. Cook, stirring occasionally, for 3 minutes. Add the sugar and continue to cook 5 minutes more.

2. Remove the wok from the heat, add the parsley and chives, toss, then sprinkle sesame seeds on top. ▪

Rhubarb

RHEUM RAPHONTICUM

aka RHEUM RHABARBARUM

RHUBARB'S sour tang and earthy flavor make it especially welcome in the spring when it joins asparagus and radishes among the first crops of the new year.

One of my earliest food memories is of the dishes of stewed rhubarb my mom would set beside the main plate at the dinner table. I liked the way it looked—all reddish and off-white. It was sweet from the sugar she added, but it had the most wonderful tang.

THE ORGANIC FACTOR ► Rhubarb from the market or store is not likely to be contaminated with agricultural chemicals—only two pounds of chemicals were used on the entire California crop in 2001—because rhubarb is usually pest and disease resistant. The amount of conventionally grown rhubarb fluctuates, but usually hovers somewhere around just 1,000 acres in the whole country, with most production in northern states, including Washington and Oregon.

Organic rhubarb is likely grown in the field as part of mixed organic crops.

NUTRITION ► Citric, malic, and oxalic acids give rhubarb stalks their acidic flavor, although a superabundance of oxalic acid makes the leaves poisonous. Oxalic acid binds with iron, rendering it unavailable in the bloodstream, and so can cause anemia. The long leaf stalks, or petioles, have only about as much oxalic acid as spinach and chard and are the only edible part of the plant.

TYPES ► Most of our edible rhubarb is *Rheum raphonticum,* because, while there other types commonly grown in China, Mongolia, Siberia, and Italy, they are seldom seen here in the United States.

SEASONALITY ► You'll find the choicest stalks in midspring, when the tender young leaves

IF YOU LIKE TO GARDEN

SOME YEARS AGO, when I was designing ornamental and edible gardens for clients, I discovered that rhubarb's big leaves and red stalks make a bold landscaping as well as culinary statement, and they are as striking as any perennial in the garden. If you have an ornamental garden, mix in just one perennial rhubarb plant, and you'll not only have its good looks as a foil for finer-leaved plants but you'll probably have more than enough stalks for your kitchen use.

have unfurled and the stalks are ready for picking. The stalks toughen up as summer comes on, usually losing enough quality by late July that picking stops.

WHAT TO LOOK FOR ✦ When choosing rhubarb at the market, check both ends to make sure they aren't dried out. Many varieties are stringy and need to be peeled, others are tender and need no peeling. See the Top Variety section (page 494) to find tender varieties.

STORAGE AND PREPARATION ✦ Blanched rhubarb freezes wonderfully, so there's no need to buy it off season. Blanch spring-grown stems (which are low in oxalic acid and high in quality) for about 1 to 2 minutes in boiling water, chill them in ice water, then cut them into 1-inch-long pieces and freeze on baking sheets. When frozen through, transfer to freezer bags and store.

USES ✦ Because it tastes sweet-tart like fruit, it is usually classed as fruit, although botanically it is a vegetable. Indeed, rhubarb has an affinity for fruit. Rhubarb and strawberry pie is a classic. Rhubarb and huckleberry pie is even better, if you can find huckleberries, or substitute rhubarb and blueberry pie instead. Make a fruit crisp with rhubarb, strawberries, and plums, sweetened with brown sugar and baked in ramekins.

Rhubarb's acid quality allows it to pair well with and enliven low-acid fruits, such as gooseberries, elderberries, and mulberries. It's also made into jam. Chilled rhubarb soup can be refreshing on hot summer evenings, and at the restaurant Chez Panisse in Berkeley, California, rhubarb-strawberry sorbet can sometimes be found on the menu. Ginger, angelica, and orange all make particularly nice flavor harmonies with rhubarb, and its sour flavor also works seamlessly with cinnamon, brown sugar, and plums.

Besides its use as a partner for fruit, think of it as a sour ingredient in sauces to provide contrast in sweet meat dishes using pork and chicken. Or let its acid content cut through the fattiness of oily fish like salmon or of poultry like duck or goose.

STEWED RHUBARB

SERVES 3 TO 4

Of all the uses of rhubarb, I like the comfort of my mom's stewed rhubarb best. It's so simple to make and tastes like a sweet-and-sour fruit.

2 to 3 cups of cranberry-red rhubarb stalk, cut into
    1-inch pieces
1 teaspoon grated fresh ginger
1/4 cup honey

Combine the rhubarb, ginger, and honey with 1/4 cup water in a medium stainless-steel saucepan. Cover, bring just to a boil, then reduce the heat to a simmer. Cook until the rhubarb falls apart, about 10 minutes, adding a little more water if necessary. Serve chilled. ∎

RHUBARB-HUCKLEBERRY PIE

MAKES ONE 9-INCH PIE; SERVES 6 TO 8

Freeze your springtime rhubarb (see Storage and Preparation above) until late July, when huckleberries reach their juicy peak—as do blueberries, if you can't find huckleberries.

This pie is worth the effort of planning ahead in this way, and it would make a perfect midsummer conclusion to a meal. If you want to serve this pie à la mode, coconut gelato is a fabulous accompaniment.

Pastry for a double-crust 9-inch pie (double the recipe on page 211)

$1/2$ cup all-purpose flour

$1^{1}/_{2}$ cups sugar

3 cups huckleberries or blueberries (if using blueberries, add 2 teaspoons freshly squeezed lemon juice)

3 cups fresh or frozen rhubarb, cut into 1-inch pieces

2 tablespoons unsalted butter, diced into pea-size bits

1. Roll the dough into two 12-inch rounds between sheets of waxed paper, and chill in the fridge.

2. Preheat the oven to 425°F. In a medium bowl, mix the flour and sugar. In a large bowl, toss the huckleberries with rhubarb (and lemon juice if using blueberries). Add the dry ingredients to the fruit and toss gently.

3. Line the pie plate with one of the crusts, trimming the dough so there's at least a $1/2$-inch overhang over the edge of the pan. Fill the pan with the filling and evenly dot the surface with the diced butter.

4. Place the second round of dough on top. Working along the edge of the pan, tuck the excess of the top crust under the $1/2$-inch edge of the bottom crust, then crimp together with the back of a fork. Cut three or four 2-inch vents in the top crust with a sharp knife.

5. Bake for 15 minutes, then reduce heat to 375°F. Bake for another 45 to 60 minutes, until the crust is golden brown and the juices are bubbling through the vents. Allow the pie to cool until it's just warm and serve. ∎

Rutabaga

BRASSICA NAPUS, NAPOBRASSICA GROUP

THE MUCH-MALIGNED rutabaga—isn't that the purplish- and-dun-colored, wax-covered lump in the supermarket bin? Don't the Scots traditionally serve "bashed neeps" with their hideous haggis, and isn't neeps short for tur-neeps, by which they mean rutabagas? Well, yes, yes, yes, and yes. But here's a secret I discovered along the way: rutabagas are delicious.

Before refrigeration, rutabagas were prized, especially in northern Europe and the colder regions of North America, because they kept so well in a root cellar over winter. The English, in fact, call rutabagas swedes, with a lower case s. And indeed the name rutabaga comes from the Swedish *rota bagge,* which means red bags.

Rutabagas have a rare quality—their color deepens slightly when cooked.

THE ORGANIC FACTOR ‣ As members of the cabbage family, rutabagas are susceptible to the same pests and diseases as its cousins. Healthy soil produces healthy rutabagas that are not prone to the yellowing diseases, wilts, and fungi that can attack roots grown in deficient soil. Cabbage pests can also be controlled by effective organic techniques.

NUTRITION ‣ Rutabaga seeds are rich in oil, but unfortunately they are also rich in toxic substances. But plant breeders have bred the toxic substances out of certain strains, and these are grown for their oil seeds, especially in Canada. We know this oil as canola.

SEASONALITY ▸ Rutabagas are at their peak in fall and winter.

WHAT TO LOOK FOR ▸ Rutabagas come in too late for most roadside stands. But farmers' markets that continue well into the fall and winter are most likely to sell unwaxed roots, which is what you want. Most large, commercial sources of rutabagas wax them to improve storage ability, but wax may also seal rot and mold organisms against the skin, where they can soften and degrade the quality of the yellow flesh underneath.

STORAGE AND PREPARATION ▸ Rutabagas keep for a few weeks' storage in the fridge's vegetable crisper or a cold cellar; as they sit their flavor becomes more and more radish-like, mild and earthy. Rutabagas need to be peeled before use.

USES ▸ Rutabagas are excellent raw. They have a firm but smooth texture. Try julienned rutabaga when serving vegetable crudités—but don't tell anyone what they are. Their sweet and mildly radish-like crunchiness will win converts. Then you can tell people they're rutabagas and be met with raised eyebrows. They can also be marinated in red wine vinegar to give them a tangy nuance. Or grate them raw into salads.

I use rutabaga in a fall root vegetable medley to go around a pork roast. Dice into small cubes a rutabaga, parsnip, turnip, celery root, a carrot or two, even a potato, and toss with just a little olive oil, salt, and pepper; then roast the mix in a single layer on a baking sheet in a 350°F oven, stirring occasionally, until the surfaces are chewy-crisp and the insides of the cubes are tender, about 40 minutes or so. Spoon these roasted root vegetables around the roast on a serving platter with sprigs of parsley for garnish.

Swedes and Finns fry cubed rutabagas in butter with salt and sugar until they're browned and serve them as a side dish. They also bake them in a casserole with eggs, nutmeg, bread crumbs, cream, butter, and salt. Rutabaga flesh has a drier, finer-grained texture than turnips, which makes it superior for mashing (or bashing, as the Scots would say), alone or with potatoes.

Along with parsnips, I'll toss a rutabaga, peeled and cut into quarters, into a beef or lamb stew. And the root can be microwaved or steamed until tender, then pureed in the blender and added to soups to thicken them.

BASHED NEEPS (RUTABAGAS), SONOMA STYLE

SERVES 3 TO 4

A delicious take on the Scottish dish. The scent of this dish is alluring, the flavor truly incomparable. In the finished dish, the rutabagas lose their radishy flavor but acquire a bit of spicy heat. If you've shied away from rutabagas, this dish will be a revelation.

2 rutabagas medium size, about 2¹/₂ to 3 pounds

³/₄ cup nonfat yogurt

2 tablespoons unsalted butter

1 tablespoon fresh thyme

1 teaspoon dried herbes de Provence

1 tablespoon freshly ground nutmeg

¹/₂ teaspoon kosher salt

Freshly ground black pepper

1. Peel and cut rutabagas into eighths. Steam them in a basket over boiling water until tender, approximately 30 minutes. Add more water as necessary to avoid boiling away the water.

2. Turn the finished rutabagas into a warmed bowl. Add all the other ingredients and mash with a potato masher. ▪

Salsify

TRAGOPOGON PORRIFOLIUS, SCORZONERA HISPANICA, and SCOLYMUS HISPANICUS

THREE DIFFERENT PLANTS—all root vegetables—share the name of salsify, probably because all three plants have straight, long edible roots (shaped something like a narrow carrot), which can be used in somewhat similar ways. All can be hard to find at markets, but they are becoming increasingly available.

THE ORGANIC FACTOR ◂ If you do find any of these salsifies, it is most likely to have been grown organically—or even harvested from the wild, for salsify long ago escaped cultivation and grows wild throughout much of the United States and Canada.

NUTRITION ◂ Salsify has good stores of calcium, iron, vitamin C, and fiber.

TYPES ◂ The salsify that you're most likely to find (*Tragopogon porrifolius*) is a straight white root, occasionally branched. It is a biennial, meaning it grows a root and tops its first year, then produces flowers and seed and dies in its second.

This salsify goes by several other names, including oyster plant—supposedly because the boiled roots taste like oysters, although I've never found this to be true. It does have a sheen that might recall a slippery oyster, however. The plant is also known as goat's beard, which is the straight translation of *tragopogon* from the Greek. (But don't confuse it with another goat's beard, *Aruncus dioicus,* which is a common garden perennial ornamental with a tall wand of frothy white flowers.) The species name of this salsify, *porrifolius,* means leek-leaved, and its leaves do recall those of a leek, although they are typically more slender.

If you enjoy foraging for wild plants, you can identify this plant in the wild by its spearhead-like flower buds and its purplish composite flowers (like a daisy or aster). If you do find it—and it's not hard to find—take great care digging the tender roots, as they break easily. Several new hybrid tragopogons have appeared recently in the Pacific Northwest—crosses occurring naturally in the wild between tragopogon's species.

A second salsify is commonly called black salsify (*Scorzonera hispanica*). As the name suggests, the roots have a black skin but white flesh within. They are long and blunt-ended, shaped rather like some carrots, but not as tapered. Native to a wide region of Europe and Asia, black salsify has a finer texture and more flavor than white-rooted salsify, and is worth looking for. There's a suggestion of coconut and artichoke about its taste, and it's

sweeter than white salsify. The sweetness comes not from sugar but from inulin, the same compound that gives Jerusalem artichokes (sunchokes) their sweetness. Inulin, while tasting sweet, is safe for diabetics (although it can give rise to flatulence). Its roots are even more easily damaged than white salsify.

Although I've never seen it sold in the United States, a third kind of salsify, *Scolymus hispanicus,* (Spanish Salsify), is popular in Spain. It is a type of thistle with branched roots that have a hard woody core. Folks peel the white flesh from the core, cook it, and mash it.

SEASONALITY ✦ The best season for any salsify is summer through fall.

WHAT TO LOOK FOR ✦ Look for firm, unblemished, and fresh-looking roots. If they're flabby or soft, they haven't been stored properly and they've most likely lost their delicate flavor.

PREPARATION ✦ Before cooking, any type of salsify should be scrubbed hard to remove soil particles and any little rootlets. You can peel the skins while they are raw. If you have black salsify you can also remove the skin by blanching the salsify for 2 to 3 minutes, after which the skin will peel off especially easily. (Overcooking, however, will cause the skins to cling to the flesh.)

USES ✦ Whether you're eating the roots raw or cooking them, always plunge them in acidulated water (water with the juice of a lemon or two) as you peel or cut them, because the cut surfaces quickly discolor when exposed to air. The same substance that discolors the root will stain your fingers, so you might want to wear rubber gloves.

The roots of both oyster plant and black salsify can be eaten raw, sautéed in a little olive oil, or boiled just until tender and then mashed. They can be roasted like chicory root and used as a coffee substitute. Give salsify a flavor kick by blanching the pieces in boiling acidulated water for a couple of minutes, marinating them in lemon juice with salt and pepper, chopped parsley, and a little olive oil for an hour, then dipping them in tempura batter and deep frying until the root is tender and the batter turns golden brown.

Salsify—both black and white—is commonly baked as an accompaniment to meats, boiled then whizzed in the blender and added to soups, or sliced thin and sautéed as a side with light meats like chicken or fish.

Whichever way you cook salsify—and its flavor intensifies and becomes creamier when cooked—finish it with onions, shallots, olive oil, cream, butter, lemon juice, nutmeg, bechamel sauce, or Parmigiano-Reggiano.

SALSIFY GNOCCHI

SERVES 4

This astoundingly delicate and lovely dish takes some preparation but is well worth it.

1 pound oyster plant or black salsify
6 tablespoons butter
2 tablespoons minced chives
2 tablespoons minced fresh parsley
Pinch of freshly grated nutmeg
Salt and freshly ground black pepper
1 cup all-purpose flour
4 large eggs
1/2 teaspoon freshly squeezed lemon juice
Whole milk, if needed
1/3 cup grated Parmigiano-Reggiano

1. Peel the salsify and immediately drop the pieces into a saucepan with enough water acidulated with a little vinegar or lemon juice to cover them all. Begin cooking over low heat.

2. Meanwhile, in another saucepan, combine the butter, chives, parsley, nutmeg, salt, pepper, and 1 cup of water, bring to a boil, and cook until the butter has melted. Remove from the heat and add the flour all at once. Beat the mixture with a wooden spoon to incorporate everything smoothly, then return the pan to a moderately high heat and continue beating for a minute or two, until the mixture leaves the sides of the pan and forms a mass.

3. Remove the pan from the heat, let cool for a minute, and make a well in the center of the mass. Break 1 egg into the well and beat to incorporate, then make another well and repeat the process until all 4 eggs have been beaten into the mixture and thoroughly incorporated. Reserve this paste, or *pâte à choux* as the French call it.

4. Turn up the heat on the pan with the salsify and acidulated water and cook until the salsify is very tender and able to be mashed. Drain the salsify and mash it or puree in a blender with the lemon juice. If more liquid is needed to make a thick puree, use a little whole milk.

5. In a bowl, combine 1 cup of the warm paste and the cheese with the salsify, beating it all together until smooth. (Freeze leftover paste for future use as profiteroles, éclairs, cream puffs, or timbales for savory fillings.) Take large spoonfuls of this mixture and roll them with your palm on a lightly floured board, forming rolls about 1 inch in diameter and 2 1/2 inches long.

6. Prepare a deep skillet of salted water that's almost simmering—not boiling, or the gnocchi may fall apart. Slip the gnocchi into this barely simmering water and cook for 15 to 20 minutes. When they've almost doubled in size and roll easily in the water, they're done. Remove them with a spoon and drain on paper towels. You can serve them as is or place them in a buttered baking dish, sprinkle with a little more cheese, and pass under the broiler until the cheese melts. ▪

Seaweed

various genera and species

PEOPLE WHO EAT a lot of processed foods unknowingly eat seaweed all the time in the form of fillers and extenders and texturizers such as agars, carrageenans, and alginates—all seaweed extracts. But many varieties of whole seaweed—either fresh or dried—form a staple of a healthy organic diet and can be used in endless ways, from a seasoning to a main ingredient.

Seaweed are marine algae that grow in the tidal zones or shallow ocean water where sunlight can penetrate. Although they're simple organisms, loosely classified as plants, there are 6,000 red, 2,000 brown, and 1,200 green species. They're found around the world in salt water, and none is known to be poisonous.

Seaweed is collected in parts of the world where the water is pure. In addition to the bays of northern Japan, seaweed is collected from the wild along the coast of northern California up into Washington, on the east coast along Maine and the Canadian Maritimes, and in Europe along the coast of Ireland and up into Scandinavia.

THE ORGANIC FACTOR ◆ In addition to its healthy culinary uses, seaweed provides a range of agricultural benefits to the organic gardener. Organic gardeners and farmers who live near the ocean can use salt hay—the marsh grasses that grow in tidal swamps—as easy-to-harvest mulch, and seaweed mixed with salt hay makes mineral-rich compost that supplies trace elements in abundance to a garden.

Seaweed is used to make liquid extracts that inland growers can apply to the leaves of their fruits and vegetables (in a technique called foliar feeding); the nutrients are absorbed through the leaves. These extracts are also used as a drench to the plants' roots. Because seaweed grows in seawater filled with minerals, it can return elements to the soil that may have been leached out by acid rain or farmed out over years of soil abuse by conventional farmers. Everything does, finally, return to the sea, and the use of seaweed in organic culture is a way of recycling scarce nutrients back to crops so they can grow healthy tissues.

We then become beneficiaries of this nutrient recycling when we eat these organic foods grown in such a garden, with their panoply of nutrients supplied by the sea.

NUTRITION ◆ The Japanese have long incorporated seaweed in their diet—and they have notably good health to show for it.

Scientists say that the blood in our bodies has about the same mineral and salt content as the primordial seawater out from which our ancestral life forms crawled to begin life on land. Consuming seaweed allows our blood to be replete with the minerals we need for optimal health. They are the oldest family of plants on earth.

Seaweed may also help protect us against one of the newest dangers on earth—radioactivity. Kelp, for instance, contains iodine-127. This beneficial isotope of iodine floods the thyroid gland, where iodine accumulates. This prevents the body from absorbing radioactive iodine-131, which is released into the atmosphere during so-called normal operations of nuclear power plants and weapons facilities. Kelp also contains sodium alginate, which can bind with radioactive strontium-90 and cesium-137, as well as heavy metals, and aid the body in excreting them.

TYPES ‣ See below.

KELP ‣ Also commonly known by its Japanese name *kombu*, this is probably the most familiar seaweed to most people. Roasted, dried, and ground into flakes, it's used as a seasoning and salt substitute. But it can also be purchased as a dried whole vegetable to add to soups and other vegetable dishes. Kelp is gathered in Japan and on the coast of Mendocino, California, where it's dried in the sun. Kelp's most common and important use is in the preparation of dashi. The Japanese basic stock for soups, stews, and sauces. Soak a 6-inch piece of *kombu* in 4 cups of water for 2 hours, then slowly bring to a boil. Just before the water boils, remove the kelp from the water, turn off the heat, and let the broth cool. The dashi can be used as a delicious vegetarian broth in Japanese and other dishes.

Kelp is also good when sliced and used as an ingredient in soups, stews, and vegetable and bean dishes. The Japanese commonly use kelp to enhance the flavor of the brine that's used to marinate pickles. Sometimes, the kelp itself is one of the ingredients to be pickled.

According to my friend John Lewallen, who operates the Mendocino Sea Vegetable Company, kelp can be simmered along with other foods to impart its flavor. Once simmered, it can be cut in strips and used in a wide variety of vegetable dishes. John suggests stirring a few strips of dried kelp in a pot of rice as it's cooking (lay a sheet of kelp underneath the rice, then cook as you normally would). "Kelp does magic things with all types of beans," he says, "speeding cooking time, softening the beans, and thickening the broth. Kelp strips in beans become translucent, tender, and tasty." A 4- to 6-inch-long strip of dried kelp is sufficient for one pound of beans.

Sea whip fronds are another form of kelp and the most tender of all sea vegetables; they're sweet and salty, good raw and in soups.

NORI ‣ This black seaweed—used to wrap sushi—is often bought in sheets, but the best nori is dried in leaf form. It can be used as is, lightly roasted, or even fried as tempura. Roasted nori can be crumbled over grains and vegetables as a condiment. (To roast nori, place on a dry skillet on medium heat for 15 seconds on a side.) It's nutritious: about one-third pure protein.

DULSE ‣ Another common seaweed is dulse. The best of these is a red algae variety labeled Grand Manan, which comes from an island of that name in the North Atlantic. Shaped like the palm of a hand, it has the texture of thin rubber; both the amount of branching and size (ranging from 5 to 16 inches) vary. Growing on rocks, mollusks, or larger seaweeds, dulse attaches by means of disks or rhizomes. It is commonly dried and eaten raw by North Atlantic fishers; the flavor becomes evident after prolonged chewing. Dulse is eaten also with fish and butter, boiled with milk and rye flour, or used as a relish.

The gelatinous substance contained in dulse is a thickening agent and imparts a reddish color to the food with which it is mixed. It's zesty dried or cooked, with an underlying sweetness. Dulse from the west coast of North America is fiercely salty and powerful. Finely chopped dulse becomes a multifaceted condiment used in place of salt. Its flavor accents eggs, vegetables, rice, casseroles, chowders, and—especially—potatoes. It can be used on pizzas like anchovies and in omelets like bacon. Cooked in a soup, dulse gradually softens and disintegrates into the liquid, flavoring it.

OTHER SEAWEED ►

Arame is a mild seaweed and cooks in about half the time of *hiziki* (below). Both hiziki and *arame* are Japanese imports and fairly easy to find at natural food stores.

Bladderwrack, known as rockweed on the East Coast, is used as a healing tea and also in soups. At Maine clambakes, it's used to steam lobsters and steamer clams.

Grapestone is a seaweed resembling a deep red, exotic mushroom; it's excellent in stir-fries.

Hiziki is exceptionally nutritious—full of trace minerals and known as a blood strengthener. It has a strong flavor and sturdy texture, and it takes about 10 minutes to cook.

Sea lettuce is called *ao nori* by the Japanese and is a bright green seaweed used as a condiment.

Sea palm fronds are unique to the Pacific Northwest, from San Francisco to Vancouver, British Columbia. They're used raw, sautéed, and in soups and salads.

Wakame is a sweet, relatively tender seaweed that's a standard addition to miso soup. It has an appealingly clean, salt-air aroma. Use it in soups, stir fries, or in salads (see recipe at right).

USES ► Seaweed is not much used in American cooking, but it's an important part of the diet in Japan, in maritime Ireland and Scotland, and in Iceland, Norway, France, and eastern Canada. Because of its nutritive value, seaweed has probably made more inroads into organic and macrobiotic kitchens than the kitchens of most other segments of American society, save for those of Japanese Americans and Japanese restaurants. Once you start to use seaweed, however, you begin to wonder how you got along without it. It imparts a true flavor of the sea to everything from soup bases to omelets.

WAKAME ORANGE SALAD

SERVES 3 TO 4

This recipe is from Simone Parris, a private chef, who cooks for celebrities in the Los Angeles area. The celebs like to stay slim and healthy, and her dishes help them achieve both goals. This salad combines the sweet flavor of cucumbers and oranges with a salty matrix of seaweed and soy sauce and adds a spicy kick from the ginger and cayenne.

1 medium slicing cucumber
1/2 teaspoon sea salt
1 tablespoon wakame flakes (purchased precut)
2 medium oranges
1/4 cup raw sesame seeds
1 piece fresh ginger, about the size of your thumb
1 teaspoon mirin (Japanese sweet rice wine)
   or maple syrup
2 teaspoons soy sauce
2 teaspoons unseasoned rice vinegar
1 teaspoon toasted sesame oil
Dash of ground cayenne
Freshly ground black pepper
2 scallions, chopped fine

1. Peel stripes down the length of the cucumber, slice it in half lengthwise, then cut in half-rounds 1/8 inch thick. Place the cucumbers in a bowl with the sea salt and combine them. Place a plate on top of the cucumbers and a weight, such as a gallon jug of water, on the plate, and let sit for 20 minutes. This procedure takes some of the water from the cucumbers and breaks down cell walls, making them easier to digest.

2. Soak the wakame flakes in enough water to cover until they're soft, about 10 minutes, then squeeze out and discard the water.

3. With a sharp knife, cut the tops and bottoms

from the oranges deeply enough to remove the white, then do the same all around the sides of the oranges. When all the white is removed, slice the orange into quarters, remove any seeds and the white core, and cut the quarters into $1/2$-inch pieces.

4. Wash the sesame seeds in a fine mesh strainer and let drain. Heat a small skillet over medium heat, add the sesame seeds, and toast, stirring continuously with a wooden spoon. If they start jumping around, the heat is too high. When you can easily crush a seed between your thumb and ring finger, the seeds are done. Be careful not to overcook. As soon as they're done, transfer them to a small bowl.

5. Grate the ginger until you have 1 heaping tablespoon; press the gratings by placing them in a soup spoon and pressing out the juice into a small dish with the back of a second spoon. You should extract about 1 teaspoon of juice.

6. Prepare the dressing by whisking together the ginger juice, mirin, soy sauce, vinegar, toasted sesame oil, cayenne, and black pepper.

7. Rinse and gently squeeze liquid out of the cucumbers and combine them with the oranges and wakame in a medium bowl. Toss with the dressing and garnish the top with a sprinkling of toasted sesame seeds and scallions. ▪

BRAISED HIZIKI WITH VEGETABLES

SERVES 3 TO 4

Here's another recipe from Simone Parris. The savory flavor of toasted sesame oil envelops the vegetables in a very elegant way.

1 cup dry hiziki
2 medium carrots
1 large or 2 small onions

$1/2$ cup shelled peas
1 tablespoon toasted sesame oil
$1/2$ teaspoon sea salt
$2/3$ cup fresh or frozen sweet corn kernels (1 large ear)
1 tablespoon soy sauce
1 tablespoon mirin (Japanese sweet rice wine) or maple syrup
2 tablespoons chopped scallions

1. Soak the hiziki in 3 cups water until soft, about 10 minutes; strain and discard water. Slice the carrots $1/2$ inch thick on the diagonal, then cut into matchsticks. Peel the onion, cut it in half from top to bottom, then slice into thin half-rounds. String the peas and slice in half on the diagonal.

2. Heat a deep covered skillet over medium-high heat. Add the sesame oil. When oil is hot, add onions and sauté until translucent, 5 to 7 minutes. Add the hiziki and sauté another 5 minutes. Layer the carrots on top and add $2/3$ cup water, sprinkle on the sea salt, cover, and reduce the heat to medium-low. Cook for 45 minutes, checking occasionally and adding more water if necessary to prevent burning.

3. Add the corn and the soy sauce and cook 5 more minutes. Remove the lid, add the mirin, and turn heat to medium-high. Cook off the liquid, and just before liquid is gone, add the peas, replace lid and cook for 2 minutes. Taste and add more soy sauce if necessary. Garnish with the spring onions. ▪

Shallot

ALLIUM CEPA, AGGREGATUM GROUP

WHY NOT JUST use onions? They may look similar, but shallots are different from other onions, and certainly from garlic. They have a unique flavor that's more delicate, with a pungency specifically their own, and a lovely tenderness that allows them to soften quickly and easily during cooking. The glassy membranes between the thin growth rings are just a film, not nearly as tough as onions. The more I use them, the more I like them.

Shallots are a form of multiplier onion: As with garlic, bunching onions such as scallions, and lilies (which are relatives of the onion family), a single shallot clove planted in good, rich, organic soil will produce many new shallots joined together at the base. (Indeed, the words *shallots* and *scallions* are cognate, derived from the same Greek word *askolonion,* a name for bunching onions dating back to 300 BCE.)

THE ORGANIC FACTOR ◆ Shallots are very hardy in the garden, resistant to pests and diseases, and make fine crops for organic market gardeners to grow.

NUTRITION ◆ Shallots, like large bulb onions, contain antioxidants such as quercetin and anthocyanins, plus vitamins A, B6, and C.

WHAT TO LOOK FOR ◆ Look for mature shallots that are firm, unbruised, with skins intact, no soft spots, and no mold. They should feel heavy for their size.

Once shallots mature, they are good keepers if stored in a dark, airy place, but I try to use them up within a week or two nevertheless. Don't remove their papery skins until just before using.

USES ◆ Shallots are a great addition to soups and stews, as they flavor and thicken them. Combine them in an all-onion medley with onions, garlic, and leeks, then roast or sauté them to use around meats. Or braise them along with veal or lamb shanks. They can also be creamed as you would cream pearl onions. Whole shallot cloves can be tossed with a little oil and baked at 350°F for about 30 minutes, until they are caramelized, then served with grilled or roasted meats. Shallots also make a fine pickle.

Shallots are part of many classic rich French sauces. But shallot sauces do not have to be heavy and can be made quickly during the process of

KEEP AN EYE OUT FOR TOP-ON SHALLOTS

IT'S REALLY ONLY in the past couple of decades that shallots have become widely available, and even today most of our large market shallots are imported from Europe. If you do find an organic source at a farm, roadside stand, or farmers' market, encourage the grower to bring you some young early summer shallots with their tops still attached. Until the tops begin to yellow and wither, they can be used much like scallion greens, while the young bulbs will be even more tender and delicate than older imported bulbs. Once the young bulbs begin to size up, they can be pulled and used anytime, but their youthful delicacy in early summer only adds to their charm.

deglazing a pan that has been used for roasting or sautéing meats.

Here's how to do it: While the meat is finishing cooking, mince 3 shallots and have them ready along with some beef stock and red wine for red meats, white wine and chicken stock for white meats, or dry vermouth for either. When the meat is done, remove it to a platter to rest. Pour off all but a teaspoon of fat from the pan and place it on a burner at medium heat. Add the shallots, and sauté them for about 1 minute. Add ¼ cup of wine or vermouth and ¾ cup of stock. Turn up the heat until the mixture boils and stir, scraping up any pan drippings or congealed bits. As the liquid reduces to the consistency of a thick sauce, turn down the heat to prevent scorching. When the mixture is thick enough to coat the back of a spoon, pour it over the meat and serve. Chefs at this point will often beat in a tablespoon of butter or two to enrich the shallot sauce, but I find the sauce needs nothing more than perhaps a grind or two of black pepper to be perfect.

We think of shallots as something particularly French, but their appeal extends to Thailand and Southeast Asia and, these days, around the world.

VEAL SCALLOPS WITH SHERRY-SHALLOT SAUCE

SERVES 2

Instead of Wiener schnitzel or breaded veal cutlets, try this delicious version of veal scallops. Get organic veal to insure that it has been humanely raised.

½ cup all-purpose flour
Salt and freshly ground black pepper
6 (2-ounce) veal scallops, pounded very thin
2 eggs, lightly beaten
2 tablespoons extra-virgin olive oil
1 tablespoon minced shallot
⅓ cup dry sherry (Amontillado or similar)
1 tablespoon freshly squeezed lemon juice
1 tablespoon unsalted butter
2 teaspoons minced fresh parsley

1. Season the flour with salt and pepper to taste, place on a shallow plate; place the eggs in a separate plate. Dredge the veal in the flour mixture, shake off the excess, and lay on a third plate or waxed paper. Don't stack them or let them overlap.

2. Preheat the oven to 200°F. Heat 1 tablespoon of the olive oil in a skillet over medium heat until hot but not smoking. One by one, dip the floured veal scallops in the egg, coating both sides and allowing excess egg to drip off. Add the veal scallops to the pan and sauté for about 1 minute on each side, until golden. Place finished veal on a platter in the warm oven.

3. When all the veal has been sautéed, add the remaining oil to the pan, and add the shallots and sherry. Ignite it with a match (to be safe, use a long match). Reduce the heat and stir constantly until the flames go out. Add the lemon juice and butter and stir until the butter is melted and incorporated in the sauce. Pour the sauce over the veal scallops and sprinkle the parsley on top. ▪

Spinach

SPINACIA OLERACEA

EAT SPINACH on a regular basis—if it's organic, that is. Spinach is what growers call a heavy feeder—it pulls a lot of nutrients from the soil to stoke its quick growth, and when that soil is organic and full of all necessary minerals, spinach can be one of the most nutritious foods on earth.

Spinach is a member of the goosefoot family, so named for the shape of the leaves, which resembles the imprint of a goose's foot.

Spinach is native to Iran, where the species still grows wild. It made its way east to China in the first millennium, probably along the Silk Road, and west to Arabia and then to Spain with the Moorish invasions and on to the rest of Europe. The name comes from the Old Persian *aspanakh*, and the root *span* has entered Greek in the names of spinach-based dishes such as spanakopita.

THE ORGANIC FACTOR ◆ Because spinach is a heavy feeder, it will absorb an excessive amount of whatever is present in the soil—pesticides, fungicides, and chemical fertilizers as well as nutrients. In the conventional farming of spinach, using chemicals to solve one problem usually creates another, which demands yet another chemical. For example, using chemical fertilizers can force abnormally quick growth of spinach leaves, but without a rich, nutritive soil to grow from, the leaves tend to have weak tissues and be especially prone to mildew and mold. On top of this, the sterilized soil used to grow the spinach lacks the natural organisms that would have suppressed mold growth. And so farmers must apply additional fungicides to prevent mold. And in the case of spinach, boy, do they pour the chemicals on.

Although the effects of agricultural chemicals on consumers of spinach needs further documentation, they're not likely to be good. The sheer number of chemicals that go into cultivated spinach reminds us once again why one might want to choose organic produce.

NUTRITION ◆ Spinach is a nutritional powerhouse. Just ½ cup of boiled spinach gives us 2 grams of dietary fiber, 80 to 100 percent of our daily requirement of vitamin A, 32 percent of our folic acid, 40 percent of iron if you're male and 20 percent if you're female, 20 percent of magnesium, 20 percent of potassium, 18 percent of riboflavin, 16 percent of vitamin B6, and 10 percent of calcium.

The leaves' dark green color—meaning there's plenty of chlorophyll—and rich stores of carotenoids contribute to spinach's cancer-blocking abilities. Studies show spinach lowers blood cholesterol in lab animals. According to Dr. Frank Dainello at the Vegetable and Fruit Improvement Center at Texas A&M: "Spinach has a high antioxidant activity. It contains high amounts of xanthophylls, lutein, and zeaxanthin that are strongly associated with reduced risk of age-related macular degeneration.... Spinach is one of the best sources of folic acid, a compound that's been shown to reduce the risk of birth defects, heart disease, and stroke."

The raw leaves of the crinkly kind of spinach contain the most oxalic acid, which binds with some of the calcium and iron to render them unusable. Cooking, however, reduces much of the oxalic acid. The sweeter Asian leaf spinaches have less oxalic acid—another reason beside their tender, sweet taste to use them in salads. Or buy a variety called Monnopa that is low in oxalic acid and so is good even for baby food.

TYPES ‣ There are two types of spinach found in today's organic markets. The old-fashioned savoy types have large crinkled leaves; they are usually sold in bunches (one bunch serves three people, as a rule of thumb). They're best when cooked. Asian types are smaller-leaved, oval in shape, thinner, more tender, and sweeter. They're generally sold as individual leaves (sometimes labelled as baby spinach) by weight, and are best eaten raw in salads. Additionally, several varieties of amaranth (including *Amaranthus tricolor*; see page 361) are grown for their nutritious leaves, which have even more iron than spinach and are sometimes sold as "summer spinach." Amaranth leaves, while more nutritious, are not as tender or tasty as spinach.

SEASONALITY ‣ Spinach is one of the first plants to germinate or start growing again in spring if overwintered in the garden or field. As soon as the soil temperature reaches 50 degrees Fahrenheit, spinach breaks dormancy and starts growing. It likes cool weather, and so is at its best in early spring and midfall. A spinach plant will grow from seed to mature size in six or seven weeks at these times of the year.

WHAT TO LOOK FOR ‣ When buying spinach, make sure the leaves are glossy and crisp, with no limpness or yellowing. The small leaves of the Asian type should also be crisp and fresh. Check the cut end of the leaf stem. It should look freshly cut, not blackened. There may be the odd hole in organic spinach leaves where a bug has had first dibs—take this as a good sign that the plant has indeed been grown organically.

Spinach tastes best when it is grown quickly in rich, compost-laden organic soil, and forms large, crisp leaves. Spinach that stays small or is set back in its growth due to water or heat stress tends to be inferior. Ask your farmer how he or she prevents leaf miners, which leave those squiggly white trails in the leaves. The organic answers will be: "I cover the rows with netting," or "I pull off any affected leaves as soon as I see them."

PREPARATION ‣ You can eat spinach with the stems attached, but I find it coarse that way. It doesn't take long to strip the tender leafy parts of the leaves from the stems. Just take the whole leaf in one hand and with your other, strip off the green parts by running your closed fingers up the stems. Then plunge the leafy parts in cold water and wash them thoroughly to make sure there's no grit on them. The savoy types, especially, can catch soil splashed up by rains.

USES ‣ Besides its significant nutritional benefits, spinach has an amazing ability to blend well with a wide range of ingredients, especially curry spices, vinegar, eggs, anchovies, cheese, garlic, mushrooms, olive oil, onions, tomatoes, yogurt, and nutmeg.

Spinach is a joy to cook with. When I'm in a hurry, I simply toss the leaves in a steamer, steam them until they're collapsed, turn them into a warm bowl, give them a squeeze of half a lemon, and maybe a pinch of salt, toss, and serve.

But sometimes it's fun to gussy them up a little. Then I'll toss spinach with a few tablespoons of gremolata, a mixture of finely minced garlic, lemon zest, and finely chopped parsley.

In India, hot, spicy foods are served with raita—a salad of chopped vegetables like spinach, cucumbers, potatoes, or eggplant, and seasoned with Garam Masala (see Tip, page 91), or with cooling herbs like chervil, tarragon, cilantro, mint, or parsley, all mixed with cold yogurt.

Here's a simple vegetarian use for spinach: Take a Dutch oven, sauté a diced small onion in it, then add a bunch of clean, stemmed spinach and pour ½ cup of rice over that. Add ½ cup of diced tomato, 1 finely chopped garlic clove, and salt and pepper to taste. Finally, add 1 cup of hot water, cover, and simmer for 1 hour.

CREAMED SPINACH

SERVES 4 TO 6

As a child, I loved spinach—especially my mom's creamed spinach, but I wondered if something was wrong with me because in the cartoons, comic books, movies, and radio programs, spinach was the butt of jokes about how terrible it tasted. Popeye was a role model because spinach gave him super powers, but I knew this was just a way to convince kids to eat their spinach. I didn't understand the revulsion that spinach was supposed to cause until one day I tasted canned spinach.

Creamed spinach made from fresh savoy-type leaves stripped of their stems is ambrosial. Here's the recipe Mom used.

2 pounds (about 2 bunches) large savoy-type spinach
1 teaspoon freshly squeezed lemon juice
1 clove garlic, smashed

3 tablespoons butter
2 tablespoons minced shallot
2½ tablespoons all-purpose flour
Salt
1 cup half-and-half
½ teaspoon freshly grated nutmeg

1. Strip the leaves from the stems and wash them well, then steam in a basket until collapsed, 3 to 5 minutes.

2. Placed the spinach in a bowl (so as to catch the liquid) with lemon juice and chop it into tiny pieces with two knives. Some people force it through a coarse strainer, but using two knives seems more honest to me.

3. Rub a skillet with the garlic. Heat the skillet over medium-low heat, add the butter, and let it melt.

4. Add the shallots and stir in the flour. Add salt to taste. Cook for about a minute. Slowly stir in the half-and-half and cook until the sauce has become smooth, 3 to 4 minutes.

5. Add the spinach, stir and blend it in well, and cook for 3 minutes. If it seems too thick, add a little milk or water. It should have a thick consistency, neither pasty nor soupy. Add the nutmeg, stir well, and serve. ■

Summer Squash and Zucchini

CUCURBITA PEPO

TENDER SUMMER SQUASHES are mildly flavored, slightly nutty, slightly sweet, and great combined with other foods, as they won't interfere with other, more highly flavored meats and vegetables. Summer squashes—zucchini being the most familiar—are delicate, perishable, and soft-skinned, so different from the more robustly flavored, hard shelled and hard fleshed winter squashes. Summer squashes don't keep for more than a week in top condition, while winter squashes improve from fall into winter.

Summer squash developed early in the history of agriculture in the Western Hemisphere, with the oldest remains of squashes found between 5500 and 7000 BCE. Originally, squashes of both kinds were one of the famous Three Sisters of the pre-Columbian Native American diet, joining beans and corn to make a complete protein (containing all 20 essential amino acids)—a meatless diet that could sustain life in a healthy, tasty, and energy-packed way.

It used to be that the only summer squash you'd see on the market were green zucchini and their yellow crookneck equivalent. More and more frequently, organic growers are taking advantage of new varieties of summer squash and displaying them at farmers' markets and roadside stands. We've truly entered a golden age of summer squash.

NUTRITION ◆ According to the USDA, ½ cup of boiled, sliced summer squash has good stores of minerals, 1.3 grams of dietary fiber, and provides 6 percent of our daily requirement of vitamin C, 6 percent of our magnesium needs, and 9 percent of our potassium. Well, it's a good thing the department's skills at nutritional analysis are more refined than their culinary ability, for all squashes are rendered unpalatable by boiling. They're already watery and need dry heat to retain or improve flavor and texture.

The seeds of summer squash, if allowed to mature completely and then shelled, are wonderfully nutritious, containing 45 percent unsaturated fat, 25 percent protein, a range of minerals, and B-complex vitamins.

TYPES ◆ Summer squashes occur in an appealing variety of shapes. The simplest may be the zucchini—a long, cylindrical squash that can be green or yellow and begs to be sliced into coins or split lengthwise and grilled. All zucchini are summer squash, but not all summer squash are zucchini. Others include golf-ball-sized patty pan squashes, which are round, with a wavy, scalloped edge; crookneck squashes, usually yellow, with a bulbous bottom and an elongated neck that curves gently toward the stem end; and even summer squashes that are shaped like eggs.

SEASONALITY ◆ As their name indicates, summer squash are high summer crops that keep producing into late fall in warm regions.

WHAT TO LOOK FOR ◆ When buying summer squash at the markets, bigger is not better. Picture there being a finite amount of flavor in each squash: With increasing size comes a decrease in flavor, as well as bigger—and harder—seeds. Choose small, brightly colored, shiny squashes with fresh looking cut ends. Nick the skin with a thumbnail. It should nick easily, with little resistance. Choose straight squashes, crookneck, and yellow squashes when they are 6 to 8 inches

IF YOU LIKE TO GARDEN

WHEN I BECAME A GARDENER, zucchini was one of the first crops I planted because it was so prolific and easy to grow. I grew huge zucchinis, and since I didn't always know what to do with them, I would deliver the thumping vegetables to friends who didn't know what to do with them either.

While I still plant zucchini, I plant just 3 seeds in a hill and thin to the strongest-looking plant. One is plenty as long as you harvest flowers for stuffing and frying, and pick the fruits daily at 6 to 8 inches long. And if I can't use them right away, friends don't mind being given a trio of small zucchini with the blossoms still attached.

If you have any room for a small sunny garden, or even a large pot with good drainage that you can fill with purchased compost, one zucchini plant will keep you in plenty of flowers all summer, as long as you keep the fruits picked off. Male flowers are probably the best for stuffing. The petals emerge from a long, thin stem. Female flowers have an ovary behind the flower petals that is like a miniature squash. This adds a fleshy textural effect to the flowers that might interfere with the diaphanous petals. Both types of flower, though, have the same subtle taste.

long; Tromboncini (*Zucchetta rampicante*) at from 8 to 10 inches; and round and patty pan types when they are the size of golf balls.

USES ► To me the best way to prepare summer squash is to grill them. In the summer, when my big gas grill is going full blast, I cut small squash fresh from the garden into halves, brush them with olive oil, and grill them on both sides so they acquire some delicious charring and a tender interior. They really don't need anything else.

The Greeks layer slices of fresh summer squash in an oiled baking pan with bechamel sauce, finish the top with *kefalotiri* cheese and bread crumbs mixed with a little melted butter, then bake at 325°F for 30 minutes. If you have a mandoline, you can make ultrathin slices of long squash and layer them in vegetable casseroles. Or roll them up with a filling made of Parmigiano-Reggiano and ground almonds, set the little cylinders in a baking dish, top them with bread crumbs, and bake at 350°F for 20 minutes.

Squash blossoms (often called zucchini blossoms)—big, satiny, deep golden, and evanescently luscious—add to the fun of summer cookery. They can be stuffed and baked, stuffed and served raw, battered and fried (see recipe at right), used as wrappers, and cut into thin strips to garnish soups.

ANGEL HAIR PASTA WITH SUMMER SQUASH

SERVES 6

This recipe is from Jesse Cool, one of the country's finest organic chefs. She suggests making this in the summer, when just-harvested summer squash has wonderful flavor and an almost creamy texture.

1/4 cup olive oil

1 small red onion, thinly sliced

1 pound summer squash (patty pan, yellow or green zucchini, or crookneck), cut into bite-size pieces

2 cloves garlic, minced

1 (2-ounce) can anchovies, drained and chopped fine

1 tablespoon capers

1 tablespoon chopped green or red chile

1/4 cup white wine

1 pound angel hair pasta (capellini)

1 cup coarsely chopped fresh basil

Freshly ground black pepper

Freshly shaved or grated Parmigiano-Reggiano

1. Bring a large pot of salted water to a boil.

2. Meanwhile, in a large sauté pan over medium heat, warm the olive oil. Add the onion and cook until translucent, about 4 minutes.

3. Add the squash and cook until the squash is just al dente, about 5 minutes. Add the garlic, anchovies, capers, chile, and wine. Set aside.

4. When the pot of water reaches a boil, add the pasta and boil until al dente. Drain pasta and toss with the zucchini mixture, basil, and pepper. Put on a large platter or on six individual plates and top with the cheese. ▪

BATTERED AND FRIED SUMMER SQUASH

SERVES 6

After grilling, this is my favorite way to prepare summer squash. It's so simple—and so good.

1/2 teaspoon salt

1 cup all-purpose flour

1 pound summer squash, sliced 1/8 inch thick

Canola oil

1. Preheat the oven to 200°F. Mix the salt with the flour. In a bowl, put 1 1/2 cups water and gradually sift in the flour, stirring constantly so the batter stays smooth. When all the flour is incorporated, the batter should have the consistency of loose yogurt or crème fraîche. If more flour or water is needed, add it.

2. Pour canola oil into a deep heavy skillet to a depth of 1 1/2 inches and place over high heat. When the oil is very hot—but not smoking—drop about 6 slices of the squash into the batter. Using a fork, lift out one at a time and slip it into the hot oil. Allow it to sizzle until a golden crust forms on one side, 2 to 3 minutes, then flip each piece and fry until the golden crust forms on the other side, another 1 to 2 minutes.

3. Remove from the oil and place between paper towels. Place in the warm oven while you repeat with remaining squash. Serve as soon as all the squash slices are cooked. ▪

STUFFED SQUASH BLOSSOMS

SERVES 4

This recipe is from Rhonda Carano of Ferrari-Carano Vineyards and Winery in Sonoma County. The fresher the squash blossoms, the better the final result. Male squash blossoms also make a better result because they don't have the lump of hard squash ovary behind the blossom.

12 male squash blossoms

1 1/2 ounces prosciutto, sliced paper thin

1/2 cup shredded mozzarella cheese (about 2 ounces)

1 tablespoon chopped fresh basil

Freshly ground white pepper

1/2 cup all-purpose flour

1/4 cup cornstarch

1/2 teaspoon baking powder

3/4 cup cold nonfat milk

1 tablespoon extra-virgin olive oil

2 cups canola oil

2 egg whites

4 tablespoons grated Parmigiano-Reggiano

4 tablespoons diced fresh tomato

continued

1. Preheat the oven to 200°F.

2. Clean the squash blossoms by gently swishing them in a bowl of cold water. Shake them dry. With scissors, snip out the anthers or style and trim the stem from the base of the blossoms.

3. Trim fat from the prosciutto and dice what remains. Mix the prosciutto, mozzarella, basil, and pepper; set aside.

4. In a large bowl, sift together the flour, cornstarch, and baking powder. Make a well and add the milk, working it gradually and not too completely into the dry ingredients. Drizzle in the olive oil. Do not overmix. The batter should still appear lumpy.

5. Heat the canola oil in a deep medium skillet. In a small bowl, beat the egg whites to soft peaks, then fold in the prosciutto-cheese mixture. Stuff each blossom with a tablespoon of this mixture. Secure the ends of the petals with a toothpick.

6. In batches of four, dip the blossoms in the batter and immediately fry in the hot oil, turning them once when they become golden brown. Drain on paper towels and place in a warm oven until all the blossoms are cooked.

7. To serve, place 3 blossoms on each of 4 plates, sprinkle Parmigiano-Reggiano on top and place a tablespoon of diced tomato alongside. ■

Sweet Pepper

CAPSICUM ANNUUM

ORGANICALLY GROWN, colorful, ripe sweet peppers at the farmers' market in the summer and fall are usually priced well below what the big markets—even the organic ones—charge.

And organically grown sweet peppers set the standard for flavor. Because organic farmers have less interest in high-volume turnaround, they are more likely to choose varieties of peppers that are meant to color up and ripen to their full flavor potential, rather than typical conventional peppers more often bred to be picked green and immature. If you think you don't like peppers, it might be because you're thinking of green bell peppers, which have a bitter, vegetative, almost metallic edge to their taste. Red, yellow, and other colorful peppers, by contrast, are wonderfully sweet.

THE ORGANIC FACTOR ✦ Conventional growers use fertilizers comprised chiefly of the mineral salts of nitrogen, phosphorus, and potassium, with no organic matter or trace elements. Flooding the soil with these soluble nutrients causes the peppers to grow extra large and the plants to produce more fruits. But researchers have found that pepper plants manufacture a fixed amount of flavor compounds in their peppers, so larger fruits and more of them mean less flavor per pepper. The nitrogen, especially, pushes the pepper plants and its fruits into large but ultimately watery growth that lacks flavor.

Organic growers are more likely to be interested in planting nutrient-improved varieties. At Texas A&M's vegetable improvement center, scientists are working to develop varieties that contain more of the healthful antioxidants like vitamin C, quercitin, and luteolin. Organic growers' focus is on flavor and health-giving characteristics; conventional growers typically focus on varieties that look good and ship well. Organic peppers avoid the burden of toxic agricultural chemicals lavished on peppers. Many of these chemicals were extremely toxic and damaging to the environment.

NUTRITION ► As peppers ripen, the walls of the peppers thicken and they become twice as sweet as green peppers. They also become much more nutritious. A half cup of chopped raw red bell pepper has double the vitamin C (158 percent of the recommended daily allowance) and vitamin A (30 percent of the RDA) of an unripe green bell.

TYPES ► Most sweet peppers are green when immature and turn color only as they ripen. So the blocky green bell peppers at the supermarket are actually unripe peppers of inferior flavor (and they're priced that way), which would have ripened to red, yellow, orange, or brown.

Not all sweet peppers are the blocky bell type. Some are tapered, some look like horns, some have a conical shape, and some have irregular twisty shapes. These nonblocky peppers are choice because you can bet they are grown to ripen fully— you seldom see these other types sold green. A rich red color will indicate the best flavor. Orange or yellow varieties are sweeter than other colors, and have a smooth taste. Here is a list of bell peppers you'll see on the market, both in their unripe and ripe states. The rule of thumb is that unripe peppers have a sharper, less sweet taste than ripe peppers, no matter their color.

IMMATURE COLOR	RIPE COLOR
Green	Red, yellow, orange, or brown
White	Ivory turning lilac turning red
Brown	Dark red
Purple	Dark red

SEASONALITY ► Summer into fall.

WHAT TO LOOK FOR ► Look for peppers with a deep color that are shiny and wrinkle-free, that are firm but not stiff (which would indicate immaturity), that have bright green stems, and— most important—that seem heavy for their size. This means they have matured, their walls have thickened, and they'll be extra sweet.

USES ► Ripe peppers are sweet and succulent raw, as crudités or in salads. I always add ripe sweet pepper to my risottos, and they have a real affinity for tomatoes, onions, and olive oil—staples of Italian cooking.

IF YOU LIKE TO GARDEN

SWEET PEPPERS JUST LOVE the moderate Mediterranean climate here in coastal California, where they develop their best flavor over a long season. When I grew them in Pennsylvania, I planted them close together and mulched them well. That way their leaves touched, forming a canopy of dense shade over the mulch. Then I'd make sure the mulch was continually moistened so that on warm summer days, there was warm humid air under and within the pepper plants' canopy. This simulated the tropical conditions of Central America where this plant is indigenous, and I never failed to have a superior crop.

Roasting red sweet peppers is one of the best ways they can be prepared for optimum flavor. I have a gas grill that does it beautifully, but you can also use a charcoal grill, the broiler element in the oven, the gas flame of the stove top, or even a stovetop electric element turned to high. The idea is to blacken and blister all sides of a pepper. Turn the peppers every minute or two and the process should take about 20 minutes total. You want the skin to blister up without cooking the flesh underneath any more than is necessary.

When the peppers are properly blackened and blistered, including the tops and bottoms, immediately place them in a paper bag or covered bowl—anything that will hold the steam coming from the peppers. Steaming further loosens the skins. After about 10 minutes, the skins should come off easily. If bits of skin stick to the pepper flesh, flick them off with the edge of a paring knife. Don't rinse the peeled peppers or you'll rinse away flavor. Now the peppers can be cut open and the seeds removed. Try not to remove the white veins—the placental material—where the seeds attach to the pepper wall. This contains abundant amounts of beneficial bioflavonoids, substances important in maintaining capillary health.

If you're using charcoal, you'll get the best flavor from your peppers because the coals will add a slightly smoky taste and aroma that complements the peppers' flavor. Roasting by any method will concentrate the sweetness, caramelize some of the sugars, and destroy some of the bitter phenolic compounds in the raw peppers. Keep the grill about 3 inches above coals that have burned down so they're completely gray and the fire is moderately hot instead of blazing hot.

I cut roasted peppers into thin strips and put them into a bowl with some olive oil and salt and pepper for a half hour's rest. I drain off the oil, dredge the strips in flour, dip them into well-beaten eggs, and fry them in hot olive oil until they're golden brown. Scrumptious. Three large sweet red peppers will serve four people.

I make a savory, salty paste by squashing and melting several anchovy fillets in olive oil over medium heat, then adding peeled and seeded fire-roasted red sweet peppers. I cook them until they soften and can be mashed with the back of a fork, then mash everything together. Add 2 or 3 minced garlic cloves and 1 very ripe chopped tomato, then reduce the heat and simmer until the tomato is softened. Spoon this over pasta for a simple, quick, easy lunch or dinner.

PASTA WITH HUNTER'S SAUCE

SERVES 6

Claire Criscuolo, chef, and owner of Claire's Corner Copia in New Haven, Connecticut, prepares this sauce using plump red, yellow, and green organic bell peppers. She says it's one of the most popular selections at her vegetarian restaurant, which has been keeping Yalies and townies happy and healthy for three decades.

¼ cup extra-virgin olive oil

8 large cloves garlic, coarsely chopped

5 large bell peppers, assorted colors, seeded and coarsely chopped

1 large red onion, coarsely chopped

1 pound mixed mushrooms, sliced

2 teaspoons fennel seeds

½ teaspoon crushed red pepper flakes

1 tablespoon fresh rosemary leaves, chopped

Salt and freshly ground black pepper

2 (28-ounce) cans Italian whole peeled tomatoes, crushed with your hands

1 pound rigatoni, penne, or other pasta

1. Put a large pot of salted water on to boil.

2. Heat the olive oil in a heavy pot over medium-low heat. Add the garlic and cook for 2 minutes, stirring frequently, until softened. Add the peppers, onion, mushrooms, fennel seeds, red pepper flakes, rosemary, and salt and pepper.

3. Cover, raise the heat to medium and cook for 15 minutes, stirring frequently, until the peppers are softened. Add the tomatoes. Bring to a boil, reduce the heat, and simmer for 30 minutes, uncovered, stirring frequently, until the sauce reduces by about one quarter. Taste and adjust seasonings. Keep the sauce warm.

4. About 10 minutes before the sauce is done, add the pasta to the boiling water, and cook according to the package directions. Drain and turn into a warm serving bowl. Spoon one quarter of the sauce over the top and toss to coat the pasta. Spoon the remaining sauce over the top. Grind additional black pepper over the top if desired. ▪

SWEET PEPPER AND SAUSAGE FRITTATA

SERVES 6

This delicious dish is quintessentially Italian. It's perfect for lunch at an outdoor table on a cool day on a fall weekend.

$^{1}/_{2}$ pound sweet Italian sausage, casings removed
2 ripe sweet peppers, red or yellow, cut into very thin 2-inch strips
1 large red onion, cut in half, sliced thin, and separated
8 eggs
$^{1}/_{4}$ cup chopped Italian flat-leaf parsley
Salt and freshly ground black pepper
1 cup shredded mozzarella cheese (about 4 ounces)

1. Preheat oven to 350°F. Crumble and cook the sausage in an ovenproof, nonstick skillet over medium heat until cooked through, about 5 minutes. Remove and drain on paper towels.

2. Add the peppers, onion, and $^{1}/_{2}$ cup of water to the skillet and cook over medium heat for about 12 minutes, stirring every couple of minutes, until the peppers are tender and the water has evaporated.

3. In a bowl, beat the eggs, parsley, salt, and pepper. Stir in the mozzarella and sausage, then pour this mixture over the vegetables in the skillet. Cook over medium heat about 3 minutes, until the egg mixture begins to set around the edges. Place skillet in the oven for about 12 minutes, until the frittata is set. Loosen the frittata and slide it onto a warm serving plate. Cut into wedges. ▪

Sweet Potato

IPOMOEA BATATAS

THE ROOT we know as the sweet potato is, in fact, not related to the common white potato at all, but is a tuberous form of morning glory of the genus *Ipomoea*. It's easy enough to see the relationship when you see the plant's vines climbing up a trellis and opening small, rosy-pink, morning glory–like flowers.

As far as names go, sweet potatoes are actually the original "potato." When Columbus reached the New World, the Native Americans he encountered showed him the sweet potato and called it *batata*, hence its species name. When Spanish adventurers later discovered the white potato, it bore a resemblance to *batata,* or *patata* as they sometimes called it, and the name was transferred by the Spanish to white potatoes.

The word "sweet" was bestowed by the English as a way to tell it apart from white potatoes. It was a sweet potato, with the emphasis on potato. But since the English language has a tendency to move emphasis to the front, over time emphasis shifted to the word sweet, and eventually people started thinking of sweet potatoes as distinct food.

Although the Spanish brought sweet potatoes to the Philippines in the mid-1500s (and thence to China and the rest of Asia), they had already been grown on the Polynesian islands of the South Pacific and as far west as New Zealand for hundreds of years. This was one of the clues that led Thor Heyerdahl to posit that people from the Americas sailed in reed rafts across the Pacific. Another clue was that the ancient Peruvian word for sweet potato, *kumar*, was found in languages of the Pacific islanders as *kumala, gumala*, and *umala*.

A more contemporary naming confusion relates to the difference between a sweet potato and a yam—many Americans think they are the same thing. In fact, the sweet potato bears no relation to any of the yam species (of the genus *Dioscorea*) grown in Africa and Asia. Our tendency to use the word yams to refer to extra sweet, yellow- or orange-fleshed forms of the sweet potato is an artifact of the slave trade, when slaves being transported to the New World were fed true yams during their trans-Atlantic voyage, and the name was then transferred to the tropical New World native *ipomoea*.

THE ORGANIC FACTOR ‣ Scientists are hurriedly trying to develop disease resistance in and otherwise "improve" the sweet potato through genetic engineering. A project at Fort Valley State College in Georgia looks to add foreign genes to sweet potatoes, supposedly to create plants with "superior horticultural traits." All the more reason to locate and eat organic sweet potatoes. The scientists at Fort Valley don't say what "foreign genes" will be inserted into sweet potatoes, nor do we know how the additions can affect sweet potato

agriculture or the potato consumers. I for one like sweet potatoes just the way they are, without having to wonder whether they contain frog or chicken genes.

NUTRITION ‣ Sweet potatoes have a nutritional edge over regular potatoes due to their rich stores of beta-carotene, which colors their flesh yellow and orange and converts in our bodies into vitamin A. This conversion is stimulated when fats are ingested, which makes it wise to have a bit of butter with your sweet potatoes. They contain about 16 percent starch and 6 percent sugar, but the level of enzymes that convert starch to sugar increases when they are held in storage after harvest. That's why, although they are a tropical native and grow over a long, warm summer, the season for the best roots is from November to March. That's when conversion of starch to sugar is maximized and flavor is best. They also contain good amounts of dietary fiber, vitamin B6, magnesium, and 23 milligrams of vitamin C per 100 grams (about three ounces) of sweet potato.

TYPES ‣ Depending on the variety, sweet potato skins can be white, yellow, red, tan, brown, or purplish red. The flesh varies from white to orange.

Having said that, as a rule of thumb, sweet potatoes can be divided into two main types. The first type has orange flesh and is moist, creamy, and squash-like when cooked. These are the sweet potatoes that came from North and South America as well as Australia. This is certainly the more common type in the United States.

The second type, which tends to have whiter flesh, is a dry, starchy type, with a sweet aroma, that cooks up fluffy. These types came originally from Asian and Caribbean sweet potato varieties. Although these are less often seen in the United States, in other parts of the world (like Japan), where sweet potatoes are a staple food, people tend to prefer this less sweet variety, which tastes like a cross between white potatoes and pureed chestnuts.

SEASONALITY ◂ Sweet potatoes are ready for harvest in late summer and early fall. They store well after harvest, and so are available through late fall and early winter in their best shape.

WHAT TO LOOK FOR ◂ At the market, look for firm, fat, unblemished, heavy roots.

STORAGE AND PREPARATION ◂ Although sweet potatoes look rather sturdy, they are very perishable and should be used within a few days of purchase. Store them at room temperature, not in the fridge, where cold makes them deteriorate faster. When peeled raw, they discolor rapidly, so either immediately cover them with water or cook them in their jackets and remove the skins later.

USES ◂ Baked sweet potatoes are easy to make: Bake in a 400°F oven for an hour or until the very center of the root is soft and creamy as disclosed by the point of an inserted knife. Be aware that sweet potatoes will often exude a syrupy sweet liquid during baking that will fall to the bottom of your oven and burn. To prevent this, wrap the roots in aluminum foil before baking.

I like sweet potatoes with meats such as pork and duck. I pair them with winter flavors like maple syrup, apples, cinnamon, nutmeg, sherry, and dried apricots. Sweet potato puree can be enhanced with any—or all—of these ingredients. Try mixing the baked sweet potato with baked acorn squash, then accenting the combination with a little butter and maple syrup.

Some people prefer candied sweet potatoes. To make these sweet treats, parboil three roots in their jackets for 10 to 15 minutes. Remove the skins, cut sweet potatoes into 1-inch-thick rounds, lay them in a greased baking dish, pour on about 1 cup of orange juice and sprinkle on 1 cup of brown sugar, a little salt, and a pinch or two of ground ginger. Dot the top with smidgens of butter and bake at 375°F for 45 minutes.

SWEET POTATO AND SPINACH FLAN

SERVES 6

I got the idea for this recipe from Rhonda Carano of Ferrari-Carano Vineyards and Winery in Sonoma County, California. When I tried it, I was amazed at its silky texture and the rich and tangy taste. Aromatics like Marsala, orange zest, and nutmeg lift the dish out of the realm of the ordinary.

2 large sweet potatoes
3 tablespoons olive oil
1/4 cup bread crumbs
1 tablespoon butter
1 clove garlic, minced
1 tablespoon Marsala
1 cup chicken stock
1 bunch fresh spinach, washed, dried, and stemmed
1/2 cup freshly grated Parmigiano-Reggiano
4 eggs
2 teaspoons freshly grated orange zest (well scrubbed if not organic)
1/2 teaspoon freshly grated nutmeg

1. Bring a pot of water to a boil. Add the sweet potatoes and parboil for 5 minutes. Drain, peel, and cut into 1/2-inch slices, then into 1/2-inch-wide strips.

2. Preheat the oven to 350°F. Lightly grease a 6-cup muffin pan or 6 ramekins with 2 tablespoons of the olive oil. Coat each with bread crumbs.

continued

3. Heat the remaining olive oil and the butter in a sauté pan, add the sweet potato, cover and cook, turning often, until tender, 15 to 20 minutes. Add the garlic during the last few minutes.

4. Uncover, add the Marsala and cook until it evaporates, then add the chicken stock and spinach and cook until the liquid has almost evaporated and the ingredients are soft, 8 to 10 minutes. Let the mixture cool slightly and blend or process in a food processor until smooth.

5. Empty into a bowl and add the cheese, eggs, orange zest, and nutmeg. Stir until well blended, then pour into muffin tin or ramekins. Place these in a roasting pan with 1 inch of warm water. Bake for 35 to 40 minutes. Cool for 10 minutes. Run a knife around the edges of each flan, then invert on a plate and serve warm. ■

Tomatillo

PHYSALIS IXOCARPA

ALTHOUGH THE TOMATILLO is just now coming into widespread distribution and use in the United States, it has been known for ages in Mexico, where it was a staple part of the diet in Aztec and Mayan times, was cultivated even before the tomato, and remains an important food there to this day.

Tomatillos are members of the genus *Physalis*, a group of plants whose fruits are enclosed in papery husks. As such, it's related to the ground cherry (*Physalis pruinosa*) and to the Cape gooseberry (*Physalis peruviana*) as well as to the inedible ornamental Chinese Lanterns that are garden annuals.

THE ORGANIC FACTOR ► Many tomatillos sold in the United States are grown in Mexico or simply harvested from wild plants, so it's hard to tell how much, if any, pesticide is used in their production. Some are grown in California, and in the entire state, only about 60 pounds of chemical pesticides were used in their production in 2001. I have not found organic certification on any tomatillos so far, but their increasing popularity and the expansion of the organic food business means there's an opportunity for growers to fill this niche and sell certified organic fruit at farmers' markets and to large organic grocery stores.

NUTRITION ► Nutritionally, 3 ounces of tomatillo supply about one-third of our daily requirement of vitamin C, plus good stores of magnesium, phosphorus, and potassium. They are high in beta-carotene, the precursor of vitamin A, and especially in the antioxidant lutein.

TYPES ► There are over a hundred varieties of tomatillos in Mexico, with a wide range of flavors, colors, and sizes, but only seven varieties are sold in the United States, the top five of which I've included here (see Top Varieties, page 479).

SEASONALITY ► Late summer through fall and winter are the best seasons, although they are grown year-round in Mexico and sold here.

WHAT TO LOOK FOR ► A plus for organic-minded buyers are the papery husks that cover the tomatillos. If any chemicals are applied in or near the tomatillo patch, they will settle on the husks, and so look for tomatillos with husks intact. The fruits should be firm, not soft and squishy.

STORAGE AND PREPARATION ► These fruits have thin skins but will store well for many weeks if their papery husks aren't removed. When you are ready to use them, remove the husks and rinse the tomatillos well; they tend to be sticky on the outside.

USES ◂ Tomatillos are usually used somewhat underripe to make salsa verde and mole verde, and to add an acid snap to sauces and Mexican dishes. If allowed to ripen fully, they acquire a yellow cast and become milder and sweeter with a light citrusy flavor, when they are good for chutneys and preserves. A few razor-thin slices add a mouthwatering essence to salads. Cooked by boiling for 3 to 5 minutes, depending on their size, they soften in both texture and flavor. Roasted in a hot 450°F oven for 10 to 15 minutes, they gain concentration of flavor, but be conservative in cooking time; if they go too long, they can burst. Cool before pureeing.

SALSA VERDE

MAKES ABOUT 1½ CUPS

This spicy green sauce is a specialty of Michoacan on Mexico's west coast. It's particularly good as an accompaniment to chicken, and the tanginess of tomatillos adds zing to ocean fish like seared ahi and black grouper. I spoon it on soft tacos, burritos, enchiladas, tamales, and sometimes on grilled steak.

5 fresh serrano chiles
8 to 10 tomatillos (about ⅔ pound), husks removed
1 pickled serrano chile, seeds and stem removed, reserving pickling juice
1 clove garlic, peeled
½ teaspoon salt
½ cup coarsely chopped cilantro
⅓ cup minced onion
1 avocado, pitted, peeled, and cubed

1. Bring a large saucepan of water to a boil. Add the fresh chiles and boil for 5 minutes. Add the tomatillos and cook 3 minutes more. Remove and drain the chiles and tomatillos. Stem the chiles.

2. In a blender, combine the chiles, tomatillos, pickled chile, 1 tablespoon of the pickling vinegar, the garlic, and salt, and puree well. When pureed, add the cilantro and blend with two or three 2-second bursts.

3. Transfer to a serving bowl, add the onion and avocado, and mix. Serve immediately. If you plan to serve it later, refrigerate the puree and add the onion and avocado just before serving. ▪

GREEN GAZPACHO WITH SHELLFISH

SERVES 4

Susan Spicer, the chef and owner of restaurant Bayona in New Orleans, Louisiana, gives a Mexican twist to Spanish gazpacho by using tomatillos. This flavorful dish is best prepared by making the gazpacho and shellfish ahead of time so all are thoroughly chilled by serving time. Dice the radishes and avocado just before serving.

6 tablespoons olive oil, plus extra for the seafood
2 cups diced onion
2 poblano peppers, diced
8 tomatillos, husks removed, quartered
2 medium slicing cucumbers, peeled, seeded, and diced
1 bunch scallions, chopped
Leaves of 1 bunch cilantro, coarsely chopped
1 jalapeño pepper, seeded and minced
1 teaspoon minced fresh garlic
½ teaspoon ground cumin
Juice of 6 limes
Salt and freshly ground black pepper
Dash of Tabasco
½ pound cooked lump crabmeat
12 medium shrimp, peeled and deveined
1 small ripe avocado, pitted, peeled, and diced
2 small red radishes, finely diced *continued*

1. Heat 2 tablespoons of the olive oil in a skillet to medium-hot. When hot, add the onion, poblanos, and tomatillos. Toss and cook for about 3 to 4 minutes, until the vegetables are wilting and the tomatillos are starting to break down. Remove from the heat, let cool for a few minutes, then spoon into a blender and pulse to mix.

2. Take 2 tablespoons of the diced cucumber and dice it even finer. Reserve this for garnish. Add to the blender the remaining cucumbers, the scallions, cilantro, jalapeño, garlic, cumin, half the lime juice, the Tabasco, salt, pepper, and the remaining olive oil and blend to a slightly lumpy consistency, rather than a smooth puree. Taste and add more lime juice if it needs more tang. Pour into a container and chill.

3. Pick over the crabmeat and mix it with the remaining lime juice and a dash of olive oil. Sauté the shrimp in a little olive oil in a skillet over medium heat until just cooked, about 3 minutes. Chill the crab and shrimp.

4. To serve, ladle 3/4 cup of the gazpacho in each of 4 soup bowls. Place a quarter of the crabmeat in the center and three of the shrimp around that. Sprinkle with the diced avocado, diced cucumber, and diced radish. ∎

Tomato

LYCOPERSICON LYCOPERSICUM

OUR MODERN TOMATOES are the result of many generations of selection, starting with pea-sized cherry tomatoes that still grow wild in Peru, Ecuador, and other places in South America. This wild species was domesticated in Mexico, where the Aztecs called them *xitomatl* (the root *-tomatl* means plump fruit). The Spanish dropped the prefixes and the final *l,* and the name became *tomate.* It was taken over into English as tomato, its vowels pronounced as in the existing word "potato." Tomatoes, potatoes, and peppers, along with the eggplants already known in the Old World, and along with tobacco, are members of the *Solanaceae* family—the nightshades. Sixteenth century Europeans thought tomatoes were poisonous (although they had no such qualms about sweet and spicy peppers) and grew them as ornamental plants. Later they were thought to be an aphrodisiac and became known as "love apples," or *pomme d'amour* in French and *pomodoro* in Italian.

The sensual nature of the tomato is celebrated wildly in Spain these days at La Tomatina in Buñol during the Festival of San Luis Bertran the last Wednesday of August. At La Tomatina, thousands of people gather in the town. Truckloads upon truckloads of tomatoes are brought in as ammunition, and the celebrants hurl tomatoes at one another until the people, the streets, and everything is one sticky, gooey, sweet mess.

Despite La Tomatina, Spain is not the top tomato-producing country in the world. That honor goes to Russia, followed by the United States, Egypt, and Italy. Perhaps the Mediterranean countries have perfected the use of tomatoes, though. A perfect lunch might be a piece of good bread topped with a crushed ripe tomato, a clove of garlic sliced on top, a pinch of sea salt, and a quick drizzle of olive oil.

THE ORGANIC FACTOR ▸ The best way to get the full effect is to grow them yourself, but barring that, visit an organic farm and pick a basket yourself, or at least buy them vine-ripened from an organic grower at the farmers' market or the organic food store. Watch out for conventional tomatoes. Not only are agricultural chemicals used, but genetic engineers have been able to reduce the amount of cell-wall softening enzymes in certain tomato strains so they stay harder longer, allowing longer shelf life in the supermarkets. You get none of that when you buy organic.

NUTRITION ▸ In addition to its cancer-fighting properties, just 4 ounces of raw tomato give us 30 percent of our daily need for vitamin C, 10 percent of vitamin A, 7 percent of iron for men and 3 percent for women, and almost 5 percent of folic acid, along with beta-carotene, lycopene, and minerals.

TYPES ▸ There are three main types of tomato: cherry or grape cluster tomatoes, which are either round or pear-shaped and up to the size of golf balls; regular tomatoes that can grow up to eight or nine inches in diameter but are usually half that size; and Italian plum tomatoes that are meatier than other types. They can also be categorized by skin color: white, red, green, purple, multicolored, black, orange, and yellow.

SEASONALITY ▸ When the peak tomato season of mid to late August ends, you are left with meager choices: Roma tomatoes from Mexico; bright red but tasteless and expensive cluster tomatoes grown hydroponically in Holland; local hydroponic tomatoes; commercial tomatoes from Florida gassed with ethylene to turn red (although not ripe); and relatively tasteless winter tomatoes grown organically in the warmer parts of southern Florida, Texas, Arizona, and California. So in the off season I go for canned low-salt or no-salt certified organic tomatoes. I know these are grown and canned at peak season, meaning peak flavor. Tomatoes can beautifully, and I highly recommend canning your own if you are able.

WHAT TO LOOK FOR ▸ Because the true essence of tomato is only found when they are vine-ripe and garden-fresh, their quality peaks about the same time that summer does in mid to late August. Their texture ranges from sloppy-juicy to dry and mealy. Tomatoes can be on the mild and sweet side, like the yellow pear or plum-shaped varieties, or on the acid side like Beefsteaks, or a nice balance of the two, like Brandywines. They can be found in sizes ranging from as small as a pea to as large as a softball, from round to flattened to pear-shaped and irregular.

STORAGE AND PREPARATION ▸ The tomato's culinary properties surpass almost any other vegetable in the pantry—just make sure they are kept in the pantry rather than the refrigerator, where they quickly lose quality. Tomatoes need no preparation beyond a quick rinse. But some people prefer to peel them before using them raw or in cooked dishes. To peel, cut out the core at the stem end, score a shallow X at the other end, blanch in boiling water for 15 to 30 seconds, then dunk in ice water or hold under running cold water until the skins loosen.

If you choose to seed your tomatoes, do so over a sieve placed over a bowl; the liquid is flavorful and a good addition to whatever you're cooking.

USES ▸ They can be grilled or griddled, fried, broiled, baked, roasted, stewed, sautéed, or eaten raw. You can stuff them; turn them into a condiment (ketchup); make a juice or a sauce; add them to main dishes like ratatouille; smear them on pizza; eat them raw in salads; top a burger with a slice. Mix them with their natural partners: basil, garlic, onion, thyme, oregano, peppers, cheese, meats, eggs, parsley, olives, and many other ingredients.

For a great lunch, try a tapa I had at Jaleo in Washington, D.C. Chef Jose Andres tops a very thin slice of toasted bread with a thin layer of grated and drained tomato and very thin slices of manchego cheese, then sprinkles the whole with a little olive oil and serves it warm. It's simple and delicious.

One way to make tomatoes even more versatile is to roast them the way Tom Colicchio of New York's Gramercy Tavern does. He shared his technique in *Food & Wine* magazine. He rinses ripe tomatoes, stems them, slices them in half crosswise, and places them cut side down in rows on a baking sheet. Then he tosses on a couple of heads' worth of unpeeled garlic cloves, a handful of fresh thyme sprigs, and drizzles ½ cup of olive oil over the tomatoes, seasoning them with a little salt and black pepper. The pan goes into a 350°F oven for 20 minutes. He pours off and reserves the released juice, pulls the skins off the tomato halves, and returns the sheet of tomatoes to the oven for about 2½ hours longer. During this roasting, about every 20 minutes or so he pours off and saves the liquid that escapes the tomatoes. After the roasting, he lets the tomatoes cool, removes the thyme sprigs, and packs the roasted tomatoes into one container, the roasted garlic cloves in another to be peeled as needed, and the collected juice into another, and stores them all in the fridge. This yields three

passionately-flavored ingredients to be used in sauces, braised meats, and many other ways.

My wife Susanna and I make our own spaghetti sauce by blanching and peeling about 20 pounds of our organic tomatoes and putting them into our largest stainless-steel pot. We add 3 diced onions, 6 heads of peeled, roughly chopped garlic cloves, the leaves of 2 bunches of basil, 1 bunch of Italian flat-leaved parsley, a handful of chopped fresh oregano and half that amount of thyme, and 1 cup of olive oil. This mixture sits uncovered on low heat for several days, stirred whenever we walk by, until it's reduced in volume by at least a third, even better by one half. (But I'm careful not to let the sauce scorch on the bottom.) When it has been reduced, we pack it into canning jars and pressure-cook five jars at a time for 20 to 30 minutes. If you do this, follow canning directions carefully.

UNTRADITIONAL GAZPACHO

SERVES 4

Chef Greg Hallihan of Stella's Café in Sebastopol, California, tweaks classic gazpacho into something refreshingly new and delicious—a sort of Spain-meets-Thailand cold vegetable soup.

4 large ripe tomatoes
1 medium slicing cucumber
1 bunch lemongrass
1 piece fresh ginger, about the size of your thumb
Juice of 4 limes
Salt to taste
1 teaspoon superfine sugar
1 small white onion, peeled
1 ripe avocado
1 lemon

1. Bring a saucepan of water to a boil, add 3 of the tomatoes and blanch for 1 minute. Remove and rinse under running water until the skins slip off easily. Wrap in plastic wrap and place in the refrigerator for 1 hour or until thoroughly chilled.

2. Quarter and seed the 3 peeled tomatoes over a bowl; strain and reserve any juice. Peel, seed, and coarsely chop the cucumber. Remove the woody outer layers of the lemongrass until you reach the whitish heart; very finely mince the tender heart. Peel and coarsely chop the ginger.

3. In a blender, combine the quartered tomatoes and strained tomato juice, cucumber, lemongrass, ginger, lime juice, a pinch of salt, and the sugar and whiz until blended and smooth. Refrigerate.

4. Seed and finely dice the remaining tomato, the onion, and 1/2 teaspoon of the avocado and combine. Set aside. Remove the peel of the lemon with a vegetable peeler, but leave on the white material under the peel; and cut the lemon into 1/4-inch-thick rounds, removing any seeds.

5. Pour the chilled gazpacho into four bowls. Add a tablespoon-size scoop of avocado to each bowl and set a tablespoon of the tomato-onion-avocado salsa on the avocado scoop. Float a lemon slice on the surface of the soup. Serve at once or chill until serving. ∎

TABBOULEH

SERVES 4

Tabbouleh is perfect with homemade hummus, pita bread, and cooked lamb entrees.

1 cup bulgur wheat
2 large ripe tomatoes
5 tablespoons freshly squeezed lemon juice
1/4 teaspoon salt
2/3 cup finely chopped scallions
1 cup chopped fresh parsley
1/2 cup chopped fresh mint
1/3 cup olive oil
1/2 teaspoon ground allspice
Freshly ground black pepper

1. Place the bulgur in a bowl and cover with cold water for 1 hour. While the bulgur is softening, halve the tomatoes, gently squeeze out the juice and seeds, and chop the remaining pulp fine. Toss the chopped tomatoes with 1 tablespoon of the lemon juice and the salt and set aside.

2. Drain and squeeze the bulgur in paper towels to soak up any excess water, then transfer to a serving bowl. Fluff it with a fork and add the tomatoes, scallions, parsley, and mint. Combine the remaining lemon juice and the oil and mix it into the wheat mixture. Add the allspice, and pepper and mix through. Adjust the seasoning. Place this mixture in the refrigerator for at least 1 hour, or until cold. ∎

Turnip

BRASSICA RAPA, RAPIFERA GROUP

THE TURNIP was once a winter staple of the yeoman farmer's table because it could be stored in the root cellar throughout the cold months. The standard way to serve turnips then was to mash them up with butter, cream, salt, and pepper. Today's cooks are more creative.

THE ORGANIC FACTOR ‣ Because turnips are such an early crop, they avoid the worst of the summer insect pests, which makes them attractive to organic farmers.

NUTRITION ‣ On a visit I took to an organic winery in Bordeaux, France, the owner, Robert Amoreaux, proudly showed me his vineyards. "In the fall and winter, I grow turnips between the rows of vines," he said. "Turnips have long tap roots that grow deeply into the soil and haul minerals and nutrients to the surface. In the spring when the vines begin to leaf out, I gather and chop the turnips and dress the soil under the vines with the chopped roots. That feeds the vines naturally."

For the same reason, turnips are nutritionally rich root vegetables that supply us with 10 to 20 percent of our daily need for vitamin C, high in calcium and potassium, high in folic acid, and an excellent source of dietary fiber and cancer-fighting glucosinolates.

TYPES ‣ Green and purple-top turnips are most common, although there are pure white, red, and yellow types, too. In addition, some types of turnips are grown for their leaves, which can be stewed.

SEASONALITY ‣ Because cool weather makes them grow quickly (they're native to northern Europe and originally hailed from Scandinavia or Russia as long ago as 2000 BCE) turnips are at their absolute peak in the spring and fall, with mild-flavored, tender, sweet flesh.

The springtime's first young, fresh organic turnips should not be missed. Because they are young, they have a delicate flavor that makes them excel as crudités as well as in cooked dishes. High quality young turnips just a couple of inches in diameter will reappear in the fall after the days again turn chilly. Hot summer days, on the other hand, turn them strong and pithy. The larger, tougher-skinned turnips about 4 or 5 inches in diameter you see in stores at all seasons with their tops cut off have been in cold storage and are older, perhaps harvested in summer, and not as good as young turnips. Make sure the remnants of their tops look fresh, with no mold or softening. These are best used in cooked dishes, to bolster stews and to thicken soups.

WHAT TO LOOK FOR ‣ At the market, try to find turnips with their greens still attached. If the greens aren't fuzzy and they look healthy and fresh,

KEEP AN EYE OUT FOR TOKYO CROSS TURNIPS

THEY LOOK LIKE WHITE RADISHES, and they are icy-sweet and crisp as radishes but without the pungent bite. They are best eaten raw but can be used in cooking. As with all turnips, don't overcook them if they are to be a featured vegetable. Cook until they are just tender but not mushy.

you can use them and make two dishes from the same vegetable. Or if the turnips are small (say 2 to 3 inches in diameter) you could steam them whole—roots, tops, and all.

PREPARATION ◂ Young turnips don't need peeling, but the big ones do.

USES ◂ The flavor of turnips complements that of potatoes, and one of the most popular ways to serve turnips is to peel and boil them with potatoes and then mash both together. I use two parts potatoes to one part turnips (and I never use garlic because I find garlic and turnips do not make a good match).

Turnips add a delicate, earthy-sweet note to mixtures of roasted root crops, such as celery root, rutabagas, carrots, yellow beets, and parsnips. Roasting converts starch into caramelized sugars and sweetens the root. A mixture of diced roots roasted at 350°F, turned often, for about 45 minutes, makes an excellent bed for braised lamb shanks.

Throughout Asia, turnips are pickled and colored by the addition of a bit of red beet to the pickling solution. In China, turnips are often roasted. Ironically, the least palatable way to serve turnips—boiled and served plain—is the one most commonly practiced worldwide, which keeps this lovely vegetable on the sidelines of culinary favorites. Simply by combining it with ingredients that give it life, turnips can come in out of the cold. Some pleasant combinations can be made with bacon, apples, cheese, mustard, onions, sherry, and vinegar.

Save your best young turnips to sauté until browned and add to the roasting pan for the last 15 to 20 minutes of roasting a whole duck.

SAUSAGE AND TURNIPS IN THEIR SHELLS

SERVES 3

Here's a way to make the lowly turnip the center of attention. Select turnips the size of juice oranges.

3 medium round purple-top turnips
1/2 pound bulk fresh pork sausage
1 teaspoon minced fresh onion
Salt and freshly ground black pepper
1/4 cup bread crumbs
2 tablespoons melted butter
Salt to taste

1. Preheat oven to 350°F.
2. Scrub the turnips under cold running water with a vegetable brush. Cut off the taproot, leaving a flat spot. Cut a thin slice off the top. Carefully scoop out and reserve the centers of the roots from the top, making sure not to pierce the walls or the bottom, producing empty shells with walls about 1/3 inch thick.
3. Bring a small saucepan of salted water to a boil. Place the shells in the saucepan and cover them with the water. Bring the water back to a boil and boil the shells for 5 minutes, uncovered. Drain and transfer the shells to a baking pan. Put the turnips' centers in a saucepan with 1/2 inch of water, add a pinch of salt, and cover. Turn heat to medium and cook until the turnips are soft, 5 to 10 minutes. Drain and mash them.
4. Meanwhile, heat a skillet over medium heat until hot. Add the sausage and cook until lightly browned, about five minutes, adding the onion near the end. Add the sausage and onion mixture to the mashed turnips, correct the seasoning, and mix thoroughly. Stuff this mixture into the turnip shells. Combine the bread crumbs and butter; sprinkle over the top of each turnip. Bake for 25 to 30 minutes. ■

Watercress

NASTURTIUM OFFICINALE

AS THE botanical name shows, watercress is the official nasturtium; while it shares a spicy, peppery quality with the brightly colored garden flowers we call nasturtiums, those garden flowers are *Tropaeolum majus,* botanically a different plant. Watercress is a member of the mustard family along with cabbage, kale, kohlrabi, broccoli, cauliflower, and other common herbs and vegetables. Most of these mustards have the pungent quality that makes watercress such a pick-me-up in salads.

Watercress grows just about everywhere in North America that water flows, and foraging for your own leaves can be a wonderful way of getting the freshest, crispest organic leaves imaginable (see My Favorite Watercress below). Be aware that watercress will grow just fine in polluted ditches along roadsides and farm fields, so if you are gathering from the wild, make sure that the water in which it grows is pure. It can also be grown in the garden as long as the soil is kept well moistened.

THE ORGANIC FACTOR ‣ Like the other members of the *brassica,* or mustard, family, watercress is attacked by flea beetles, among other insects, and conventional growers will spray pesticides to keep them from eating holes in the leaves. Organic growers use traps, nontoxic repellant sprays, and mesh row covers or other physical barriers to keep the insects away. The B&W Company, which sells watercress to Europe as well as the United States, is the largest supplier of certified organic watercress in the country.

NUTRITION ‣ Fresh watercress is a nutritious plant. Just 3 ounces (a small bunch) gives us 200 percent of our daily requirement of vitamin C, and it's also rich in calcium, beta-carotene, iron, and the antioxidant selenium. It stimulates the production of the enzyme glutathione-S-transferase, which protects the colon's mucosa from cancer-causing foodstuffs like nitrites and charred meat.

SEASONALITY ‣ Watercress is a perennial whose roots survive the winter in all but the coldest regions of the country. Watercress can get too

MY FAVORITE WATERCRESS

I KNOW A PLACE in the deep woods of Pennsylvania where a spring bubbles up out of the ground. Someone long ago built a small cobblestone house about the size of a doghouse over the spring, and to the front fixed a door with a screen to keep out insects. The water exits through a small sluice below the door and runs away down a gentle slope. Along the first 20 feet or so of its length, watercress grows. As the spring comes on, first a few leaves appear, then more, then more, until by June there's a big bank of it. In the cool and pretty month of May, the cress is at its finest—juicy, crunchy, and slightly peppery, with a clean, refreshing flavor that's the vegetative equivalent of the spring water itself.

This is my memory of that place, and I drank there often as a boy and enjoyed a few leaves of watercress, plain and raw. It's been many decades since I've been there, and I hope it hasn't changed a wink, since the world needs places like that for boys and girls to find and to know the taste of pure, natural spring water bubbled fresh through subterranean rocks, and the watercress that grows in it.

peppery fairly quickly in the spring, so early spring is the prime time for this leafy green. I find that by the time watercress starts blooming, it's too pungent and is past its prime.

WHAT TO LOOK FOR ◆ The best watercress shows no blooming stalks or even unopened flowers. Its leaves are small and its stems delicate and juicy. When picking over watercress at the market, avoid any with thickened or tough stems, or with leaves that have started to yellow.

PREPARATION ◆ Wash your watercress carefully, inspecting both sides of the leaves, as small snails and a particular sort of little black beetle enjoy the cress, too. If the stems are thick, you might want to remove and only use the leaves on the thinnest stems, especially in salads.

USES ◆ Use watercress as soon as possible after you get it home, as it quickly loses its fresh, sweet quality. Watercress stars in salads, providing pungency to brighten the mild flavor of lettuce. Try crisp watercress instead of lettuce in your next sandwich. Puree raw watercress with a bit of liquid to make a quick and easy sauce to stir into soups (such as vichyssoise) right before serving.

WATERCRESS, BEET, AND ORANGE SALAD

SERVES 4

The flavors in this salad are remarkable in the way they harmonize and complement each other. The roasted beets will need time to chill, so make them a day ahead.

3 small beets, with root tip and 1 inch of stem left attached

2 tablespoons red wine vinegar

$1/8$ teaspoon salt

$1/4$ teaspoon dry mustard

6 tablespoon olive oil

$1/8$ teaspoon freshly ground black pepper

Pinch of fresh or dried thyme

1 bunch watercress, washed well and drained

1 small head butterhead lettuce, rinsed and dried in paper towels

1 head Belgian endive

1 mandarin orange, peeled and segmented (other sweet citrus can be used, but remove tough membranes and seeds)

$1/4$ cup coarsely chopped walnuts

1 tablespoon coarsely chopped Italian flat-leaf parsley

$1/2$ cup soft goat cheese (2 to 3 ounces)

1. Preheat oven to 425°F. Roast the beets on a sheet pan for about 1 hour, until the beet flesh shrinks away from its skin. Let cool, peel, place in a plastic bag and refrigerate until cold, 3 hours or overnight.

2. In a jar with a screw cap, combine the vinegar, salt, mustard, olive oil, pepper, and thyme, and shake vigorously for half a minute.

3. Quarter the beets. Pick through the watercress, removing large stems, yellowed leaves, and roots.

4. In a salad bowl, make a bed with the lettuce leaves. Cut the endive in half lengthwise, then cut each half into thirds. Separate these and sprinkle over the lettuce. Scatter the watercress over the salad, then the beets, the orange segments, and the walnuts, and sprinkle the top with the parsley. Finally, make dots of goat cheese over the surface of the salad. Shake the vinaigrette vigorously once more, then sprinkle over the salad. No need to toss, as the dressing will coat the salad as it is served. ■

WATERCRESS SOUP

SERVES 2

One of the few traditional ways to cook watercress is as the main ingredient in a soup. This soup is good by itself, but it also adds an herby note and interesting color when half a cup is given one quick swirl through a serving of butternut squash soup.

1 bunch watercress
1 small onion, minced
1 clove garlic, minced
1 teaspoon olive oil
1¼ cups chicken or vegetable stock
½ teaspoon minced fresh parsley
Salt and freshly ground black pepper

1. Separate the tender leaves and small stems from the tough main stems, wash them well, and drain. As they are draining, sauté the onion and garlic in the olive oil in a medium saucepan over medium heat, being careful not to burn the garlic.

2. Add the chicken stock, bring to a simmer, and cook for 5 minutes. Add the parsley and simmer for 5 minutes more. Remove from the heat and add the watercress. Let it stand for a few minutes so the watercress wilts, then puree the mixture in a blender or food processor. Strain the soup through a sieve. Add salt and pepper to taste. Reheat slowly, bringing it just to the desired temperature; don't let it boil. It's important not to cook the watercress or it will lose its pleasant bite. Serve hot. ■

Winter Squash

CUCURBITA MOSCHATA and CUCURBITA MAXIMA

SQUASH is another of the New World's great gifts to the Old. The name "squash" is an abbreviation of the Narragansett Indian word *asquutasquash,* with the prefix *asq* meaning uncooked or raw. Along with corn and beans, it is one of the Native Americans' Three Sisters, three vegetables that were often grown together, and which together formed a staple diet complete in all necessary proteins.

NUTRITION ▸ Winter squash are intensely rich in vitamin A—1 cup provides 150 percent of our daily needs, plus 30 percent of our need for vitamin C, 25 percent of our potassium, much of our manganese and folate, and good amounts of many other trace elements.

TYPES ▸ The types of winter squash seem endless. There are acorn, buttercup, butternut, hubbard, kabocha, spaghetti, pumpkin, and more (see Top Varieties, page 479).

SEASONALITY ▸ The season for winter squash runs from late August through March, but the very finest squashes are found from October through January—the heart of this season.

WHAT TO LOOK FOR ▸ During those years when I don't plant butternut squash in my garden (giving a crop a rest every third year helps deter the buildup of pests), I buy them from the local farmers' markets. They start appearing in August and are offered for sale until the market shuts down for the winter. I make sure to ask the seller if the butternut is a bush type or is grown on a long, vining plant. If she says she doesn't know, then I know she didn't grow the squash herself, and I'll ask more questions to see if she's a purveyor. If she says they were grown on a bush-type plant, then I thank her and maybe consider buying some. But if she says, "These were grown on big, rambling vines that just about smothered my carrots," I know she's got the real goods. Now I ask if these are the Waltham strain. If she says yes, I can be sure I'm bringing home not only my favorite winter squash, but also the very best variety of that squash.

On one of my last trips to the farmers' market before it folds its tent up for the winter, I buy some butternuts to store for the wintertime. If a squash is going to be cooked right away, there's no reason to watch out for nicks, but if they're meant for winter storage, I make sure that each squash is firm and sound, with its tough dried stem intact and its skin totally uncut.

STORAGE AND PREPARATION ▸ Winter squash can be baked whole—just remember to poke them with a knife in a few places so the squash doesn't explode. You can also cut them in half and empty out the seeds and fibers before baking. If you are going to cut the squash into chunks to steam it, peel it first.

Butternuts store perfectly well for the winter on newspapers spread on the floor of my garage, where it doesn't freeze. You might wonder why I store some myself, rather than just buying butternuts from the supermarket during the winter. The main reason is to make sure my squash are organically grown. Another reason is because when they're stored in a cool, dry place, they tend to sweeten up as the cold weather comes on, reaching

KEEP AN EYE OUT FOR DELICATA AND SWEET DUMPLING

IF ANY WINTER SQUASH can challenge butternut for top quality honors, it's delicata. This heirloom variety makes a loaf-shaped squash about 7 to 9 inches long and 3 to 4 inches wide. It's a pretty thing, with a light creamy white to yellowish background and dark green stripes and flecks down its ribbed surface. Its flesh is very finely textured, light orange, and nutty-sweet with a hint of caramel in the flavor when baked just a tad past done so the surface browns up a bit.

Another squash to look out for is the Sweet Dumpling, which is about 3 to 4 inches wide and about 3 inches high and weighs about 8 ounces. It has the same pretty white and green striping as the delicata, but the inside is hardly more than a morsel by the time the seeds are scraped out and the top discarded.

A roasted Sweet Dumpling, however, is great for serving a hot dish in an eye-catching container for special occasions. If a knife is inserted near the stem at an angle slanting inward, and then cuts a circle so the top comes off like a lid, the top can be replaced on the squash without it falling into the interior. Save the top, scrape out as much of the seeds and flesh as you can so the little squash becomes a container, then add filling and set the top snugly back on. A hot squash soup or a medley of baked squash chunks with diced ham and potatoes make good fillings, but my favorite filling for little Sweet Dumplings is a hot Crab and Squash Soup (see recipe, page 212).

MY FAVORITE SQUASH

ONE SUMMER when I lived in Pennsylvania, I would pass a large field every day as I drove to work. It wasn't until the leaves died away in September that I could see the big, round, bumpy, red-orange skins of winter squashes. It seemed funny, because I'd never seen that kind in the markets around there and wondered what they were used for. I got my answer a few days later. They were being loaded onto a truck painted with a large sign that read, "Mrs. Smith's Pies." Mrs. Smith's pie factory was located in nearby Pottstown, so it didn't surprise me that local farmers were growing crops for her pies—but what kind of pie would she make from big old red squash? I stopped and asked the foreman about it. "These here are Golden Hubbards," he said. "We make pumpkin pies out of them."

"Yeah?" I said. "Why don't you use pumpkins?"

"Pumpkins don't make very good pies. These are much better," he said. I told him I'd like to try that, and cadged a small Hubbard from him. Hacked in two on my kitchen counter, it showed good color—not quite as rich as butternut but an inviting yellow orange. After baking, the flesh was sweet, though a bit coarser and stringier than butternut. Then I got out my mom's old pumpkin pie recipe, and made me a pie. It was luscious—certainly better than any I'd made from the kind of pumpkins they sell for jack-o'-lanterns at Halloween. But it got me thinking. If Mrs. Smith made good pumpkin pies from Hubbards, why couldn't I make brilliantly wonderful pumpkin pies from Waltham butternuts? That Halloween I tried it, and we've been making our pumpkin pies with the Waltham variety of butternut squash ever since (see recipe at right).

a peak of sweetness about November and then keeping that quality or even improving it over the duration of the winter. Who knows what conditions supermarket butternuts have endured? My home-stored organic Waltham butternuts are far sweeter and tastier than any I've found at the chain stores.

USES ◆ Even the richest-flavored of the winter squashes is still mild compared to highly-flavored vegetables like garlic or tomatoes. That means that squash can successfully absorb a wide range of other flavors. Think of squash flavored with

cheeses like Cheddar and fontina, or with ginger, or leeks, oranges, sage and thyme, maple syrup, sherry, curry powder—the list can go on; squash's forgiving flavors can work so many different ways.

The classic way to treat winter squash is to roast it. Just cut the squash in half. Scoop out the seeds and place them cut side up in a shallow pan of water. If it's a less sweet variety like the acorn squash, plop on a bit of butter and some maple syrup in the holes where the seeds had been—sweeter squash like butternut don't need anything. Then roast at 400 degrees F for 1 hour. That's it.

"PUMPKIN" PIE MADE WITH BUTTERNUT SQUASH

MAKES ONE 9-INCH PIE

Because pumpkin pie filling is so wet, it's a good idea to prebake the piecrust before filling it.

1 large or 2 small butternut squash (about 4 pounds)
Single Crust for a 9-Inch Pie (recipe follows)
3 eggs, separated
1 1/2 cups heavy cream
6 tablespoons brown sugar
2 tablespoons white sugar
1/2 cup dark corn syrup
2 tablespoons blackstrap molasses
1 teaspoon ground cinnamon
1/2 teaspoon ground ginger
1/4 teaspoon ground cloves
1/4 teaspoon freshly grated nutmeg
1/4 teaspoon ground allspice
1 teaspoon vanilla extract
1/2 teaspoon salt

1. Preheat the oven to 350°F. Cut the squash in half. Remove the seeds. Place the halves cut side up in a baking pan with 1 inch of water in the bottom, and lightly place aluminum foil over the squash. Bake for 1 1/2 hours or until the squash is soft and falling apart. While the squash is baking, prepare the dough for the pie crust and refrigerate for 1 hour.

2. Remove the squash from the oven and raise the temperature to 425°F. When the squash is cool enough to handle, remove any tough browned or burnt skin that may have formed on the surface, spoon out 2 cups of the soft meat and reserve (save the rest for another use).

3. Roll the dough into a circle about 1/8 inch thick and 12 inches in diameter. Transfer to a 9-inch pie pan. Trim the edges 1/2 inch larger than the edge of the pan and crimp with the back of a fork.

Poke holes here and there with a fork. Line the dough with wax paper, then fill with pie weights or dry beans to weight down the dough. Bake for 10 minutes. Remove the weights and wax paper, return the crust to the oven and bake for 3 to 4 minutes, until the crust is a golden brown.

4. While the crust is baking, prepare the filling. In a large bowl, combine the 2 cups squash, the 3 egg yolks, cream, brown and white sugars, corn syrup, molasses, spices, vanilla, and salt and mix well with a whisk.

5. Using an electric mixer, beat the whites until they form soft peaks. Fold them into the squash mixture. Fill the prebaked crust to within 1/2 inch of the top of the crust. If any pie filling is left over, pour it into a ramekin and bake it alongside the pie.

Bake the pie for 45 minutes to 1 hour, until a butter knife inserted in the center of the pie comes out clean. Remove from the oven and let cool. ■

Single Crust for a 9-Inch Pie

MAKES ONE CRUST FOR A 9-INCH PIE

1 cup all-purpose or pastry flour
1/4 teaspoon salt
4 tablespoons butter, chilled
2 tablespoons canola oil, chilled
1/4 cup cold water

1. Mix the flour and salt together in a bowl. Cut the butter into 4 pieces and add them into the flour along with the 2 tablespoons of canola oil. Using 2 knives or a pastry cutter, cut the butter into the flour until the pieces of butter are smaller than peas and the mixture resembles coarse meal.

2. Add 3 tablespoons of water and toss the mixture lightly using two forks. Add more water if needed so that you can press the mixture together into a ball that retains its shape. Refrigerate for at least a half hour before rolling. ■

CRAB AND SQUASH SOUP

SERVES 6

This recipe involves serving a sweet-tasting Delicata squash soup in cute little containers made from Sweet Dumpling squash (of course you can also use bowls if you can't find the squash).

If you're up to cooking crab (which isn't hard to do, and picking out the meat is fun), I suggest using Eastern blue crab, western Dungeness crab, or Alaskan king crab (in that order), or you can go with high-quality store-bought lump crab meat.

The soup itself doesn't take long to assemble. First cook the crab. Then while the squash is cooking, pick the crabmeat and prepare the containers.

1 or 2 blue crabs, 1 Dungeness crab, 1 king crab leg,
   or 2/3 cup cooked lump crabmeat
1 9- to 10-inch Delicata or other fine-fleshed squash
6 Sweet Dumpling squashes, or other small squash that
   will hold a 1 cup serving of soup
5 cups fish or chicken stock
2 egg yolks
1 cup half-and-half
4 tablespoons butter
4 tablespoons all-purpose flour
Salt and freshly ground black pepper

1. If preparing the crab at home, ask your fishmonger to clean and crack blue or Dungeness crabs. Blue crabs should be cooked in a steamer, covered, with 2 to 4 cups water for about 5 minutes until opaque and cooked through, then picked and refrigerated until needed. Dungeness and king crab generally come precooked, so simply need to be picked. Refrigerate crab until needed later.

2. Preheat the oven to 375°F. Cut the Delicata squash in half, place in a baking pan with 1 inch of water in the bottom, and cover with aluminum foil. Bake the halves for 1 hour or until the squash is soft and falling apart.

3. While the Delicata squash is cooking, pick out 2/3 cup of crabmeat if you are preparing it at home.

4. Cut off the tops of the Sweet Dumpling squash with the knife angled in so the tops will stay on when they're put back. Using a tablespoon, scrape out as much of the seeds and stringy interior as possible. Set the containers and tops aside.

5. When the Delicata squash is done, spoon the squash meat into a blender and puree, adding a little of the stock to make it blend. Reserve the pureed squash.

6. In a small bowl, blend the egg yolks well with the half-and-half.

7. Melt the butter in a saucepan, remove from heat and stir in the flour. Return to medium heat and cook, stirring constantly, until the mixture is golden, about 3 to 5 minutes; this is a roux. Remove the roux from the heat and add the stock (the mixture will bubble up), stirring constantly to combine the stock and roux. Return the pan to the heat and cook until the roux is entirely dissolved and the mixture thickens, about 3 minutes.

8. Again remove the soup from the heat and add the pureed squash and the egg yolk–half-and-half mixture. Return to medium-low heat and cook for 3 to 4 minutes until lightly bubbling. Adjust the seasoning. Add the crab and immediately spoon the soup into the Sweet Dumpling squash containers. Put on their tops and serve immediately on individual plates. ∎

SPAGHETTI SQUASH WITH TOMATO AND BASIL

SERVES 4

Few dishes could be simpler, healthier, or tastier than this one. The fresher the ingredients, the better the dish. When prepared, spaghetti squash looks like glistening rice noodles. It has a mild squash flavor and slick texture that needs enhancing from the tomatoes and basil.

1 spaghetti squash, about 2 pounds
1/4 pound fresh plum tomatoes
4 cloves garlic
1/4 cup extra-virgin olive oil
1/2 teaspoon salt
3 or 4 basil leaves, finely shredded
Crushed red pepper flakes

1. Place a rack in the middle of the oven and preheat the oven to 375°F.

2. Stab the spaghetti squash in 5 or 6 places with the point of a knife to allow the steam to escape, then set the whole thing in a baking dish or on a piece of aluminum foil placed on the middle rack of the oven. Bake for about 1 hour, until the squash is tender when pierced with a skewer or thin knife.

3. While the squash is cooking, bring a small saucepan of water to a boil. Add the tomatoes, blanch for 1 minute, then run under cold water. Slip off the skins. Cut tomatoes in half, remove seeds, and finely dice the tomatoes.

4. Roughly chop the garlic cloves. Heat the olive oil over medium heat. Add the garlic and cook for 1 minute, stirring in the salt toward the end; remove from the heat.

5. When the squash is finished, let set until cool enough to handle, cut it in half lengthwise, remove the seeds, and separate the strands of the "spaghetti," which is actually the tender but fibrous inner flesh of the squash, with a fork. Place the strands in a bowl. Add the tomatoes and shredded basil leaves. Sprinkle on the crushed red pepper and pour on the garlic-oil mixture. Toss well with two forks and serve. ■

Apple Espalier

Fruits

OW IS IT SO THAT MANY PLANTS hide their seeds inside sweet, juicy casings? Is it really so that animals such as birds and raccoons and human beings will eat the fruits, seeds and all, and then deposit them somewhere else, conveniently embedded in nutrient-rich droppings? One can see that this strategy has evolutionary value—plants that adopt it are more likely to thrive than plants that don't. But there's another factor: The sugar in fruits that fall from the plants stimulates the growth of soil microorganisms over the plants' roots, which in turn feed the plants. Sweet fruit is a self-fertilizing device as well as a means of insuring seed dispersal.

Whatever the plants' reasons for placing its seeds inside sugary fruits, there's no denying the attractiveness of fruit, or its contribution to our health. We humans are programmed from birth to like sweet foods, and fruit is a big part of a healthy diet, providing energy as well as protection from the diseases of modern civilization: cancer, heart disease, and autoimmune disorders. The antioxidants in fruits play a potent role in the prevention of disease caused by volatile, unstable, and toxic molecules called free radicals. These are a by-product of normal metabolic processes, and they're also produced in our bodies by environmental pollutants such as car exhausts and tobacco smoke, as well as X-rays and ozone. These radicals have oxygen atoms in their make-up that bind with DNA, cellular molecules, even the material of our cell walls, and distort or destroy them—literally burn them up. Antioxidants render the free oxygen powerless by neutralizing its ability to bind with cell contents.

SHOPPER'S NOTE: *See Top Varieties (page 479) for best vegetable choices.*

FRUITS BY SEASON

WHETHER YOU WANT in-season, local, organic fruits for fresh eating or to put up, they are never cheaper or better than when their season arrives. Most fruits are available year-round, but they have either been kept in climate-controlled storage, trucked in from far away, or shipped in from other countries (like Chile and Australia that have their summers during our winter). In all of those cases, the fruit loses quality. It may not be organic. And it is sure to be expensive compared to its price in season. That's why canning or freezing in-season organic fruit makes economic as well as gustatory sense.

SPRING	SUMMER		FALL
Cherimoyas	Apples (early	Nectarines	Apples
Cherries	varieties)	Papayas	Dates
Loquats	Apricots	Passion fruit	Figs
Papayas	Blackberries	Pineapples	Kiwifruit
Pineapples	Blueberries	Peaches	Persimmons
Strawberries	Currants	Plums	Pomegranates
	Figs	Raspberries	Raspberries
	Gooseberries	Strawberries	Strawberries
	Huckleberries	Watermelons	Grapes
	Mangoes		Pears
	Mulberries		Quinces
	Melons		Cranberries

Vitamin C is one such antioxidant, and it's found in many fruits such as strawberries, citrus, and cantaloupes. Another is beta-carotene, the precursor of vitamin A; it protects against lung cancer by neutralizing a free radical called singlet oxygen. Fresh and dried apricots are particularly rich in beta-carotene. Red grapes contain an antioxidant called anthocyanin and another called quercitin—and these are available not only in the fresh fruit but in red wine. Quercitin protects arteries and discourages blood clots and blocks cancer both in its early single-celled stage and in later stages when tumors have formed. Strawberries, blackberries, raspberries, blueberries, cranberries, grapes, and apples all contain ellagic acid. This antioxidant helps block four different kinds of cancer-causing substances, including aflatoxin mold and nitrosamines.

Many scientific studies have shown that people who eat the most fruits and vegetables have lower odds of developing cancer and other diseases than folks who eat a lot of processed, high-fat, sugary foods. The National Academy of Sciences recommends that people eat five or more servings of fruits and vegetables every day. Because cooking can diminish the potency of some antioxidants, detoxifiers, and anticancer agents, it's important to eat plenty of raw fruit.

Fruit also protects us from chronic diseases such as cardiovascular disease. Blueberries, pomegranates, apples, red grapes, strawberries, pineapples, bananas, peaches, lemons, oranges, pears, grapefruit—all these delectable fruits and many others keep us healthy as well as please our palates.

Not only that but fruit is visually beautiful—often the subject of still-life paintings, photographs, and sculpture. Fruit marks the seasons and gives us something to look forward to: the first really sweet white Florida grapefruit at the beginning of the year, the first local strawberries of June, the stone fruits of high summer, and the crisp apples of fall.

Unfortunately, we are not the only creatures who like ripe fruit. There's a world of competition for each piece of fruit in the orchard—from animals such as raccoons and deer to birds to insects, to the simplest forms of life such as rots and molds. Organic orchardists and fruit growers have devised ingenious ways to bring in a harvest without poisoning their crops and land. For example, apple fruit fly larvae, which burrow through the flesh of apples and plums, develop in the skin of apples after the adult flies lay their eggs in skin cracks in late June or early July. An excellent organic control for this pest is to coat red, apple-sized, plastic balls with stickum and hang three or four in every apple tree. When the flies emerge from the soil and fly up to lay their eggs, the red balls are most attractive to them, and they become stuck. It works as well as pesticide, but with no damage to the rest of the environment.

Every piece of organic fruit you buy is another vote for this kind of life-affirming, joyful, and humane farming. Besides, fruit is delicious, and good health through good taste is at the heart of an organic diet.

Apple

MALUS DOMESTICA

FOR ALL THEIR goodness, apples have figured in some deeply rooted and nefarious stories, from Adam and Eve in the Garden of Eden to the poisoned apple in *Snow White and the Seven Dwarfs.* All those dark associations were dispelled for me when I grew my own apples in Pennsylvania: varieties like Northern Spy, Rhode Island Greening, Smokehouse, and Cox's Orange Pippin. My homegrown apples were the fruits of my soil, my sunshine, my rain, and my work—totally benign and absolutely delicious.

THE ORGANIC FACTOR ► Organic growers tend to focus on great taste, but they also tend to pick varieties that are resistant to apple scab and other diseases so they don't need fungicidal sprays. All apples are prone to attack by serious apple pests such as apple fruit fly and codling moth, but instead of coating the orchard with insecticides, organic producers use natural methods of protecting the fruit: Tanglefoot, a proprietary tar-like goo smeared on paper round the trunk of trees to catch insects; tillage under the trees to disrupt the life cycle of insects; and red balls coated with stickum to lure and capture apple fruit flies. They'll also plant "cover crops" in the orchard—crops that attract and host beneficial insects, which then attack the apple pests.

A five-year study by Washington State University reported in *Nature* compared organic and conventional apple production systems. It found that both systems had comparable yields, but the organic system "had higher soil quality and potentially lower negative environmental impact than the conventional system" and that "the organic

MY FAVORITE APPLE

COX'S, OF COURSE. Well, it's one of my favorites. I planted Cox's because it bears my name, but also because of the beautiful way this apple came about. In the 1830s in England, a Mrs. Richard Cox, a parson's wife, walked out of her house one day and saw an apple tree in full bloom. She stopped to consider this lovely sight when she noticed a bee working a particular flower and was struck with the magnificent yet humble way in which God's world works. She marked this epiphany by tying a piece of yarn to the spur that carried that blossom and later harvested the apple that developed from it.

Now, apples don't come true to variety from seed. This means that if you plant the seeds of an apple variety, each will develop into a different kind of apple—almost always bitter, runty, and worthless (so Johnny Appleseed planted a lot of bad apples). If you want more of a certain variety, you must cut scion wood from the existing tree and graft it to a rootstock. But Mrs. Cox planted the seeds from her apple. Five trees grew. When they bore fruit, four of them were worthless, but the fifth was wonderfully delicious, with a flowery essence and a rich, winey flavor. It acquired the name Cox's Orange Pippin and within fifteen years was the most popular apple in England. To this day it's one of the most popular apples in the world.

system produced sweeter and less tart apples, higher profitability, and greater energy efficiency."

NUTRITION ➤ Apples—especially their pectin—promote bowel health and regularity, help to lower bad cholesterol, decrease risk of stroke and heart attack, and promote the excretion of toxic substances from the bloodstream. The optimum amount of apple consumption? The old saying about "an apple a day" isn't wrong.

TYPES ➤ I've seen figures that there are anywhere from 1,400 to 7,000 named apple varieties being sold. Yet only a handful are found in our major marketplaces. Just try finding a good variety of apple in a supermarket. You'll find a lot of tasteless Red Delicious, maybe some pretty good Galas and Fujis, and if you're lucky, some really good Braeburns.

The best chance we have of finding wonderfully delicious apple varieties is at farmers' markets and roadside stands, and especially from organic

KEEP AN EYE OUT FOR JAZZ APPLES

TRICIA BELCASTRO, who works at a the Washington State Apple Commission, and knows about new apple varieties before most of us do, is currently raving about a new apple variety out of New Zealand called Jazz. "It has aromas and hints of flavors that I've not tasted in an apple before. Some people say there's a hint of honey taste in it, and I would agree." If you can't find Jazz, she suggests looking for a tart and sweet apple called Pink Lady that's popping up in orchards. Check out the Washington Apple Commission's site at www.bestapples.com.

growers. Apples are grown in just about every state (and many countries around the world—they originated in the steppes of Central Asia), so buy local organic apples whenever you can, especially if you live in New England, where the very best apples come from. You're not only getting the best flavor but you're supporting local farmers and a whole ecology that thrives on an organic farm.

SEASONALITY ▸ The earliest apples of the new season start arriving in early August, but the main crops occur in the fall, even into early December.

WHAT TO LOOK FOR ▸ Apples should look plump and shiny, or at least not dull. They should be firm when pressed on the shoulder by the stem, without any "give." They certainly should show no bruises, cuts, or blackened patches of apple scab. Check the blossom ends for black frass—the excrement of codling moths and apple maggots. The blossoms ends should be blemish-free.

STORAGE ▸ Apples keep very well in the fruit crisper of the fridge, but don't store kale with them. The ethylene gas that escapes from the apples quickly turns kale yellow. Apples that are harvested late in the season—in October and November—are the best keepers, and they will often last the winter in a cold fridge.

USES ▸ Apples are excellent for eating just as they are, but the cooking varieties are superb as sauce, charming as chutney, and, of course, perfect in pies, crisps, betties, and other kinds of pastries. Diced apple makes a nice addition to morning dry or cooked cereals. You can puree peeled apple slices and make fruit leather from them. Follow the fruit leather recipe under Uses on page 222.

Apples are at their best when firm and crisp, before they soften and lose their bracing acidity.

TARTE TATIN

SERVES 4

This upside-down apple tart is at its best served hot. Try it with very flavorful apples that cook well, such as Gravenstein, Empire, or Pound Sweet.

FOR THE DOUGH

$1/2$ cup all-purpose flour

Pinch of salt

1 teaspoon sugar

2 tablespoons butter, chilled

2 teaspoons canola oil, chilled

1 to 2 tablespoons cold water

FOR THE FILLING

2 pounds crisp apples (5 to 6 medium apples)

$1/2$ cup sugar

$1/2$ teaspoon ground cinnamon

Butter for the pan

3 tablespoons melted butter

1. To make the dough, combine the flour, salt, and teaspoon of sugar in a bowl. Use two knives to cut in the butter until the mixture looks grainy. Sprinkle on the canola oil and 1 tablespoon of water and mix with your hands until the dough forms a ball that just sticks together. If the dough doesn't hold together, add a little more water. (Work quickly so as not to let the butter melt from your hands' warmth or the kitchen's heat.) Place the dough in the fridge for 1 hour.

2. Preheat the oven to 375°F. Position a rack in the lower third of your oven.

3. Peel the apples, cut them into quarters, and core them. *continued*

Slice lengthwise about $1/8$ inch thick. Place them in a bowl with $1/4$ cup of the sugar and the cinnamon. Toss to coat the apples.

4. Butter a 6- or 7-inch ramekin or any ovenproof baking dish about 6 to 8 inches in diameter, making sure the bottom is especially well greased. Sprinkle 2 tablespoons of the remaining sugar into the bottom of the ramekin, then place a third of the apple slices on top. Drizzle with 1 tablespoon of the melted butter. Repeat with 2 more layers of apples and butter, and sprinkle the remaining sugar on top.

5. On a floured surface, roll out the dough about $1/8$ inch thick and cut it into a circle that will cover the contents of the ramekin. Place it loosely on top of the filling and cut 5 small vents in the dough so steam can escape. Bake the tart in the lower third of the oven for 50 to 60 minutes. If the dough seems to be browning too rapidly, cover lightly with aluminum foil. Tilt the tart slightly so you can see the liquid that has formed. When it's caramelized brown rather than lightly colored, the tart is done. Remove it from the oven, run a knife around the inside wall of the ramekin, place a serving plate upside down on top of it and quickly turn the whole thing upside down, then remove the ramekin. Be careful not to let any hot sugar spill onto your skin when you flip it. ▪

AMERICAN APPLE PIE

MAKES ONE 9-INCH PIE; SERVES 6 TO 8

There is a store not far from my home called Mom's Apple Pie with a real mom (Betty Carr) and real apple pie. It used to be surrounded by Gravenstein apple orchards that supplied the year's first fresh apples to all of America, until the bottom fell out of the market due to controlled atmosphere storage in Washington State—but Mom's Apple Pie remains and the pies are as good as ever.

Pastry for double-crust 9-inch pie (double the recipe on page 211)

6 medium apples

$1/2$ cup brown sugar

1 tablespoon cornstarch

$1/8$ teaspoon salt

$1 3/4$ teaspoon ground cinnamon

$1/8$ teaspoon freshly grated nutmeg

$1 1/2$ tablespoons butter

1 tablespoon freshly squeezed lemon juice

$1 1/2$ teaspoons white sugar

1. Prepare the pie dough, divide in half, and chill in the fridge for 1 hour.

2. Peel, quarter, and core the apples, and thinly slice pieces lengthwise. Place the apples in a bowl. Combine the sugar, cornstarch, salt, $1/4$ teaspoon of the cinnamon, and the nutmeg, and add them to the bowl. Toss the apple slices gently with the dry ingredients until they are evenly coated.

3. Preheat the oven to 450°F. Place a sheet of aluminum foil on the oven rack to catch any drips.

4. Roll out one of the balls of pie dough and line a 9-inch pie pan. Place the apple mixture in the shell and sprinkle it with the lemon juice, then dot the top with the butter. Roll out the second ball of dough, place on top and trim off the excess. Crimp the top and bottom crusts together along the rim of the pie pan with the back of a fork. Mix the remaining $1 1/2$ teaspoons of cinnamon with the white sugar. Very lightly sprinkle the top of the pie with the cinnamon sugar mixture. Prick the dough in 5 places with a fork.

5. Bake for 10 minutes, then turn the heat down to 350°F and bake for 45 to 60 minutes, until the crust is golden brown and the juices are running. Remove from the oven and cool on a wire rack. ▪

Apricot

PRUNUS ARMENIACA

APRICOTS, like peaches, originated in China. Today there are over 2,000 varieties of apricots in that country. Like so many fruits and vegetables from that region, apricots were carried west along the ancient Silk Road, reaching Persia and the Middle East, then Europe, being finally brought across the Atlantic to the Americas.

Apricots are freestone fruits, meaning the pits come out easily (unlike cling fruits—such as certain peaches—where the flesh binds tightly to the pits). Don't be tempted to eat the apricot kernels inside the pits as many varieties contain an enzyme that produces poisonous prussic acid in the human digestive tract.

THE ORGANIC FACTOR ◆ Apricots, like their close relatives peaches and nectarines, host a wide range of diseases and pests. Organic growers are faced with the same problems as conventional farmers but use nontoxic controls such as planting disease resistant varieties, using parasitic wasps and sex pheromones to interrupt the mating of the oriental fruit moth—a major pest—and spraying the developing fruit with elemental sulfur, among other methods.

NUTRITION ◆ Apricots are nutritious; about 3½ ounces—two apricots—contain 2,612 international units of vitamin A and 10 milligrams of vitamin C, along with 296 milligrams of potassium and 2½ milligrams of dietary fiber.

TYPES ◆ Today there are a few dozen varieties sold in the United States—see Top Varieties, page 499, for those varieties that set the standard of quality. But keep an eye out for new varieties of apricot, which are continually being bred.

MY FAVORITE APRICOTS

ONE SUMMER DAY, walking down a quiet back street in Emmaus, Pennsylvania, I saw a 30-foot-tall apricot tree practically weighed down with ripe fruit. A low branch hung within easy reach, so I climbed a little way up into the tree and spent an unforgettable fifteen minutes eating one after another perfectly ripe apricot. Their flesh was orange and full of sweet juice. They had a rich perfume and a luscious flavor that became my standard of apricot quality ever since.

Some years later, I grew two apricot trees on my own property—a Moongold and a Sungold. Each year they flowered and each year brown rot took all the fruit before it ripened. But that same apricot in Emmaus (about 10 miles away) would be full of spotless ripe fruit! Why hadn't the brown rot infected it? Then one year, my two apricots unexpectedly bore crops of healthy fruit. Hooray—but why?

After some sleuthing, I discovered that the conditions in Emmaus—with yards of grass and asphalt streets—gave the brown rot fungus no place to build up, whereas my country property was a cleared meadow surrounded by woods where the fungus was plentiful. I also found out that apricots must ripen on the tree. If wet weather settles in when that fruit is ripening and beginning to soften, the rot will be able to proliferate. If it stays hot and dry—midsummer conditions—the fruit may avoid the rot. Some years are apricot years and some aren't my trees were just having a good year.

SEASONALITY ‣ Apricots are summer fruit, and they ripen best when the season is hot and dry and farmers can let the fruit ripen and develop its sweetness on the tree without fear of rot. The window of opportunity with this fruit is narrow. Don't jump the season by buying early apricots in May or early June. The early varieties have been bred for a market hungry for summer's fresh fruits. But these varieties usually lack flavor and have little real apricot character. The best varieties come in July and August.

WHAT TO LOOK FOR ‣ Keep your eyes peeled for good apricot years. At farmers' markets and roadside stands look for ripe apricots that are beginning to soften but haven't turned to mush. They will be fragrant with an almost citrusy, cinnamony, rich apricot smell, their flesh will be juicy and sweet with a fine texture, and their flavor will match the fragrance. If you take home an unripe apricot it will get softer but not sweeter. When fully ripe, apricots are nearly 10 percent sugar and only then develop their inimitable flavor.

Outside of the prime season, consider buying organic dried apricots. These have been picked at a peak ripeness and have better apricot flavor than most fresh early season apricots. The dried fruit can be chopped and added to couscous or rice or reconstituted by simmering in water.

USES ‣ Apricots have an amazing ability to enhance and blend with other flavors, including many familiar fruits, especially citrus. Apricots and almonds are a natural match. Use the juice or puree to make fascinating sauces with liqueurs, especially citrusy ones such as Grand Marnier and Cointreau. Chefs know that apricot's tangy richness can add zest to many desserts. Add a squeeze of lemon juice to apricot preserves, mix well, strain, and use this syrup to glaze fruit tarts. But don't leave out savory dishes. Apricots' high malic acid content enlivens veal and lamb, chicken and duck. Stew fresh or dried apricots along with braised lamb shanks. Flame your pork chop with brandy exalted with apricot juice.

When the good apricots are in season, make apricot preserves to brighten meals the rest of the year. Or whiz fresh apricots in a blender and spread the puree on nonstick baking sheets (or regular sheets lined with waxed paper). Dry the sheets in the sun, or in a low oven, until the puree turns leathery. Then carefully pull the leather off the sheet, dust it lightly with a little cornstarch, and roll it up and store it in a jar with a lid in a cool, dry place. This fruit leather is great for lunchboxes, quick snacks, and healthful between-meal hunger quenchers.

APRICOT PRESERVES

MAKES 8 HALF-PINT JARS

Wait until the height of the apricot season, around the end of July, and when you find the most delicious apricots, buy a lot, so you'll have plenty to make into preserves. Homemade apricot preserves are an out-of-this-world confection that's perfect to spread on muffins, glaze a ham or a fruit tart, or add a sweet tang to a pork tenderloin.

4 pounds fresh apricots
5 cups sugar
Juice of 2 lemons, strained

1. Pit the apricots and slice them into coarse pieces. Mix them with the sugar in a large bowl and let the mixture stand on the counter, covered, for at least 1 hour or preferably overnight. This allows the juice to run and dissolve the sugar.

2. Chill a dinner plate in the fridge. Transfer the

apricot mixture to a large nonreactive saucepan and bring to a boil over high heat. Stir frequently to prevent sticking, and be careful not to let it foam up and over the sides. Reduce heat to medium and cook, skimming the light foamy material that will rise, until it looks like preserves (around 15 to 20 minutes).

3. While the preserves are cooking, in a separate large saucepan, boil the jars, lids, and bands in water to cover them for 5 to 10 minutes. Keep them in the hot water until you're ready to fill them.

4. You can test the consistency of the preserves by spooning a bit onto the chilled plate. When the preserves obtain the right consistency (as thick or as thin as you like), remove from heat, stir in the lemon juice, spoon the preserves into the jars, leaving 1/2-inch headroom, put on lids and bands and process according to the jar manufacturer's instructions. See page 241 for more information on canning. ■

Asian Pear

PYRUS PYRIFOLIA

ASIAN PEARS are somewhere between an apple and a pear in flavor, with a crisp, even crunchy, texture and a faint sweetness that makes them excellent in salads. Asian pear trees bear russeted, round fruit with a golden bronze color. The crisp white flesh is mild flavored, very juicy, and has a fine texture without many stone cells—those gritty bits that pears can develop. Where you might expect a luscious sweetness like a ripe Bartlett, you get only a light sweetness, and where you might expect an acid tang like an apple, you get only a subdued acidity.

THE ORGANIC FACTOR ► Asian pear trees are fairly delicate, prone to a terrible fungus called fire blight as well as insect infestation, so organic orchardists do spray their trees, but not with toxic chemicals. Instead, they use one of a number of organic sprays. Sulfur, for example, is allowed in organiculture to ward off fungus and mildews. Dormant oil sprays, made from mineral or vegetable oils, are used during the tree's dormant season to kill insects wintering over in bark crevices. *Bacillus thuringiensis* (*Bt*) is a sprayable disease that affects only caterpillars, which emerge in late spring. Liquid seaweed can be sprayed on leaves to feed them—the list of harmless sprays goes on and on.

NUTRITION ► While Asian pears lend an interesting texture and sweetness to salads and fruit compote, they don't pack much nutritional punch. About 4 ounces provides 2.5 milligrams of vitamin C and 4 grams of dietary fiber.

TYPES ► Two species of Asian pear are available in specialty markets. The Japanese Asian pear (*Pyrus pyrifolia*) is shaped like an apple, crisp, crunchy white to yellowish-white flesh, grainy, juicy, mildly sweet. The Chinese white pear (*Pyrus ussuriensis*) is similar to the Japanese varieties of Asian pear but more pear-shaped. Both types ripen on the tree, like apples.

SEASONALITY ► Asian pears ripen in late summer from August into September, depending on variety and where they're grown.

WHAT TO LOOK FOR ► Unlike many other species of pears, such as Bartlett, Asian pears can hang on the tree until fully ripe. So look for fully ripe Asian pears. At farmers' markets, the growers will sometimes have samples for tasting. If not, buy just one Asian pear and try it. If it's juicy, lightly sweet, and crisp-textured but not hard, it's ripe. Now go back for more.

STORAGE ✦ Asian pears are good keepers. You don't need to refrigerate them—they'll keep for a couple of weeks in a bowl on the kitchen counter.

USES ✦ Some people find Asian pears confounding, since we're trained to associate sweetness with a soft texture, but Asian pears simply taste subtle when eaten out of hand. They tend to be less so when used with other foods. Their crisp texture makes them great additions to salads. Slices of fresh Asian pear are excellent splashed with a little lime juice, and a fine accompaniment to a selection of cheeses, especially mild ones such as fresh goat cheese, taleggio, and Swiss. They also pair up beautifully with chocolate. And by combining bite-size pieces—no need to peel them first—with sweet ripe raspberries and acidic bits of peeled and chopped kiwi fruit, you get a wonderfully intriguing medley of textures and flavors. Because crispness is one of their most salient features, Asian pears are generally not cooked.

ASIAN PEAR GRANITA

SERVES 4 TO 6

Asian pears make very delicate and refreshing granita.

1 pound ripe Asian pears (3 or 4 pears), peeled, cored, and roughly chopped
1 cup superfine sugar

In a blender, combine pears and sugar. Puree well, and pour the mixture into a bowl or tray.

Place it in the freezer and give it a stir every 10 minutes or so until it's frozen and grainy. ■

Banana and Plantain

MUSA × PARADISIACA

STRANGELY ENOUGH, although bananas are mostly grown far away in tropical regions of the world, they are one of the most ubiquitous organic fruits available to us. The reason is that while many of our other organic fruits tend to be locally grown by small farms, and therefore of spotty (and seasonal) availability, organic bananas often grow on a huge network of large corporate plantations and reach us through international delivery systems. We may believe our organic bananas come from dedicated, small-scale, organic family farmers, but that's almost never the case.

THE ORGANIC FACTOR ✦ Organic banana culture is light years more eco-friendly than conventional. Farm workers at conventional banana plantations are exposed to harmful chemicals. Conventional growers fertilize the soil with 1.5 tons per acre of a fertilizer called 8:10:8, which refers to the ratio of chemical nitrogen, phosphorus, and potassium in it. And unless organic matter is returned to tropical soils, they soon lose the life in the soil that depends on actively decaying organic matter. Without a rich diversity of soil life, diseases and pests can proliferate.

"Black sigatoka fungus in banana plantations has reached global epidemic proportions," according to Dr. Emile Frison, head of the International Network for the Improvement of Banana and Plantain, as reported in *New Scientist* magazine.

He says the Cavendish banana variety is being attacked around the world by Panama disease, a soil-borne wilt that destroyed the superior Gros Michel banana variety in the 1950s. Fungicides are proving increasingly ineffective, so Dr. Frison is looking to biotechnology and genetic modification to save the world's bananas and plantains, on which half a billion people depend for a staple food. He's looking in the wrong place.

It has been shown that organic soils teeming with life prevent outbreaks of diseases and funguses that wreak wholesale destruction on crops, especially the kind of fusarium wilts of which Panama disease is a type. The problem is that lifeless chemical soils fertilized with nothing but mineral macronutrients have no autoimmunity to diseases. Rich, organic soils do. In addition to fungicides, conventional banana growers also use a host of toxic chemicals against pests. Nematodes (destructive soil worms) are controlled with carbofuran, Dasanit, Ethoprop, and phenamiphos. Yet nematodes can be controlled organically by proper tillage, sun exposure, and crop rotations with nematode-destroying Pangola grass. Black weevil is controlled with dieldrin and heptachlor; banana rust thrips with dieldrin, diazinon, and dursban; and banana scab moth with injections of pesticides into the growing stems. Yet all of these are controlled with nontoxic techniques on organic banana plantations.

Bananas and plantains are heavy feeders. Harvesting five tons of fruit from an acre depletes the soil of twenty-two pounds of nitrogen, four pounds of phosphorus, and fifty-five pounds of potassium. Instead of applying chemical fertilizers, if the old plant stems and leaves from one plantation acre were chopped and incorporated into the soil, 404 pounds of nitrogen, 101 pounds of phosphorus, and 1,513 pounds of potassium would be returned to the soil. If this material is composted with other organic matter, even more is returned. The result? Under organic cultivation, the soil improves in health, amount of soil life, availability of nutrients, resistance to soil pests and diseases, and its ability to produce extra-high-quality bananas and plantains.

That's just what happens on the plantations. After harvest, conventional bananas are floated in tanks of sodium hydrochlorate solution to dissolve the drips of latex sap that can discolor the fruit.

Experiments have shown that fungicide-treated bananas can develop off-flavors. Yet hands of bananas (the small bunches we see in markets) are conventionally treated with fungicides by being placed in polyethylene bags with blocks of vermiculite treated with potassium permanganate to absorb the ethylene ripening gas that bananas give off. This allows the bananas to be stored and shipped over a month before they start ripening.

The point is that organic bananas are well worth seeking out because their production avoids a host of toxic chemicals that affect everything from the health of the plantation soils and surrounding ecosystems, to the health of the workers who grow and handle them, to the health of the bananas and those of us who eat them.

NUTRITION ◆ Bananas are one of our best sources of dietary potassium, which supports cardiovascular health, lowers blood pressure, and prevents muscle cramps. One banana supplies 35 percent of our daily requirement of vitamin B6, 18 percent of our vitamin C, 12 percent of our dietary fiber, and 10 percent of our need for manganese. Bananas stimulate the cells that line the stomach, creating a better barrier against stomach ulcers, and they contain a protease inhibitor that helps prevent the bacteria that cause ulcers. They also stimulate the cells of the intestine that absorb calcium, creating conditions for stronger bones and less osteoporosis.

TYPES ➤ Besides the standard banana variety, the Cavendish, the Red banana (sometimes called Red Cuban or Red Spanish) is becoming more available in our markets. Red bananas are greenish maroon when unripe but turn bronzy-red when ripe, with black flecks and ends when fully ripe. Their flesh is very aromatic, creamy yellowish-orange, and denser than Cavendish. I prefer them for their better flavor and firmer, creamy texture.

PLANTAINS ➤ In Hispanic markets, especially Puerto Rican, you will find 10-inch, green banana-like fruits called plantains. Plantains are a starchy vegetable that is almost always cooked but can be used at any stage of ripeness. They taste like a cross between potato and squash. They're very starchy when green and unripe, and they are usually peeled, sliced on the bias, and added to soups or fried. They become yellow and brown when semiripe, when they're normally boiled or sautéed and served as a side dish. When they turn black and slightly sweet, they're often baked in their skins and served as dessert.

AGRIBIZ GIANT SELLS ORGANIC BANANAS

YOU CAN FIND Dole organic bananas in stores across the United States. Yet Dole is an agribiz giant. Are their bananas really organic? To find out, I contacted Denny Gibson, head buyer for Puget Consumers Co-op (PCC), the largest consumer-owned food co-op in America, with 40,000 members and seven stores. Generally, Denny said, he buys organic bananas from Quinta, a medium-sized grower in southern Ecuador that produces flavorsome and creamy textured bananas, grown in rich, fertile organic soil.

However, when Quintas aren't available, Denny said he gets his organic bananas from Dole—the largest supplier of organic bananas to the United States. Because of Dole's historical record as a chemically oriented agribusiness giant, the co-op members challenged Denny about this. So he and his wife Monica decided to tour several big banana suppliers in South America, including the Dole organic banana plantation in Manabi, Ecuador. Here's what he found:

Overall, we felt the plantation was well organized, the employees had a clean and safe working environment, and the administrators expressed a commitment to organic farming methods, fair treatment of their employees, and protection of the natural environment. Granted, it was a one-day visit, we aren't soil scientists, and we didn't have a chance to interview the employees. Industry insiders claim Dole executives have said publicly they really 'don't believe' in the organic 'fad,' and that Dole imports every [farming] input possible instead of making it locally, which doesn't support sustainable agriculture. But what we saw was quite positive compared to what most people might imagine from a multinational corporation.

SEASONALITY ‣ Bananas are always in season as they produce staggered crops throughout the year in their tropical homelands.

WHAT TO LOOK FOR ‣ Check them over for bruises or tears in the skin. Buy them when there's still a little green showing at the stem ends and eat them when the skins develop a light freckling.

STORAGE ‣ Urban legends to the contrary, bananas can be stored in the refrigerator—but it's not necessary. They ripen slowly on the kitchen counter.

USES ‣ If your bananas are ripening too quickly for you to eat them all, peel them and freeze some in plastic freezer bags. Frozen bananas can be pureed with other, usually fresh, fruits and a splash or three of milk (or use vanilla soy milk) to make a thick milkshake-like smoothie.

Latin Americans make *tostones* using plantains when the skins are still green. They peel them, slice them about ¾ inch thick on the bias, and fry the slices in enough oil to cover until they are light golden and partially cooked. The slices are removed from the oil, drained and cooled, then placed between sheets of waxed paper. The bottom of a glass is used to smash them flat. Then they're returned to the hot oil until they are golden brown and fully cooked. When these are made with fully ripe plantains whose skins are almost entirely black, and only fried once (without smashing), they are called *maduros*.

In the Dominican Republic, casseroles are made from layers of *picadillo* (ground beef fried with tomatoes, onions, and raisins) alternating with layers of boiled, mashed, ripe plantains mixed with eggs, flour, butter, milk, and ground cloves, then topped with cheese and baked until golden brown.

A popular dish in Puerto Rico is *mofongo*. Fried green plantains are mashed with fried pork rind, seasoned with thickened stock, garlic, salt, and pepper, formed into a ball and served hot immediately, before it turns hard. Puerto Ricans also use plantain flour to make a pastry dough, stuff it with meat, and wrap it in plantain leaves to make a sort of tamale that's either boiled or fried.

BANANAS WITH COCONUT CREAM

SERVES 3

This is a wonderful way to make an unusual and delicious dessert of those ripe bananas that you know won't be eaten before they go past the point. I guarantee they'll be eaten when served like this.

3 ripe bananas, peeled
½ cup light brown sugar, mixed with 1 teaspoon
    ground cinnamon
1 tablespoon melted butter
Juice of 2 limes
3 tablespoons coconut cream

Preheat oven to 350°F. Place the bananas in a small baking dish, and sprinkle on the cinnamon sugar. Drizzle with the butter and lime juice, and bake until the bananas are tender, 10 to 15 minutes. Serve each banana on a warmed plate with a tablespoon of coconut cream alongside. ▪

Blackberry

RUBUS, various species

MANY SPECIES of wild brambles of the *Rubus* genus are found in pockets around the country, but the ones that bear the fruits we think of as blackberries are native to the northern temperate regions from the Atlantic to the Great Lakes. Imported blackberries have escaped to the wild in northern California and the Pacific Northwest, where they've lent their fine flavor to many cultivated varieties. Cultivated berries are grown throughout the country, and are the kinds most frequently found in farmers' markets, roadside stands, organic food stores, and as frozen organic blackberries, which are available year around.

THE ORGANIC FACTOR • Blackberries—whether organic or conventional—are subject to rots and mildews in wet weather. Organic growers plant varieties resistant to orange rust, a contagious disease that is otherwise coped with by rooting out infected plants.

NUTRITION • Five ounces of blackberries give us 50 percent of our daily need for vitamin C and 30 percent of fiber. They also have good stores of vitamin K as well as trace elements such as manganese, magnesium, potassium, and copper.

TYPES • Wild Eastern blackberries, called highbush blackberries (*Rubus allegheniensis*), grow in the Northeast and Mid-Atlantic states west to Wisconsin and as far south as Missouri east to North Carolina. The bushes produce small, seedy, but exquisitely flavored berries when ripe.

Dewberries (*Rubus trivialis*) are a trailing form of wild blackberry native to the same area as the highbush blackberry. I first discovered dewberries when I was nine or ten years old, shortly after my family moved to the Poconos. One of my playmates, who had grown up there, pointed them out to me. The berries looked like any other blackberry but grew along stems that nestled down among the moss and wild plants. I found them to be the sweetest blackberries of all.

Now I live in California, where wild Himalayan blackberries (*Rubus procerus*) grow along streams and where there's irrigation, becoming huge, thick, tangled, pestiferous masses of long canes—practically impassable except perhaps to a grizzly bear. Blackberry pickers in Sonoma, Napa, and Mendocino counties pick the berries that proliferate on the outside of the patches, so there's little need to reach deeply into the thorny middle. These western berries are rich and flavorful. Just about everyone looks forward to blackberry season, and most of the berries are wild picked.

In the Pacific Northwest, there is also a wild trailing blackberry (*Rubus ursinus*) similar to the eastern dewberry, supposedly of exquisite flavor, although I've not tasted one. But I have tasted the Marion blackberry, a cultivated variety of the wild species, and I can attest to its remarkable and aromatic blackberry flavor.

BOYSENBERRY AND LOGANBERRY • Boysenberries (or Boysen berries) are named after Ralph Boysen, who discovered them growing on his farm in southern California. They're a cross between a red raspberry and a blackberry, with a purplish color and flavor components of both. The Boysenberry was the basis for the initial development of the Knott's Berry Farm fruit and entertainment complex near Los Angeles. Another delicious crossbreed is the Logan, sometimes called Loganberry, which makes superb jams, jellies, pre-

MY FAVORITE BLACKBERRIES

I'VE ENCOUNTERED wild blackberries on both coasts, and unless you are a lifelong city dweller, you may have picked them wild yourself.

I ritualized blackberry picking on the East Coast by going to a patch of *Rubus allegheniensis* (the native, very seedy blackberry of the Northeast and Great Lakes area) and removing my shirt before proceeding to pick. Blackberries have wicked thorns that point inward along the upright but slightly arching canes. This makes it easy to slip an arm into the patch to gather the fruit, but devilishly difficult to remove the arm without the skin being torn by the thorns. By removing my shirt, I was forced to move as delicately as a ballet dancer, and when my fingers reached the fruit, I gently tickled the clusters of berries with my fingers. Only the ripe berries would separate from the canes. Unripe berries may look entirely black, but they hang stubbornly on the canes.

Exposing my bare flesh to the thorny canes forces me to move with precision and gently fondle the berries to see if any will fall into my palm. This way I'm assured that the berries I gather are dead ripe and perfectly sweet. Blackberries that are even slightly unripe tend to lack flavor and are too tart. Then I slowly and ever so delicately remove my arm. Yet despite my care, returning from a morning's picking, my arms are crosshatched with red scratches. I have found, however, that nature's cure is often found with her ailments and that smearing the scratches with blackberry juice greatly speeds healing.

serves, and pies. It's also a cross between a red raspberry and the wild trailing blackberry (*Rubus ursinus*), which gives it a distinctive and tart flavor. Loganberries were planted on thousands of acres in the west from the late 1800s to the mid-20th century and accounted for millions of dollars of sales but, unfortunately, have fallen out of favor with large commercial growers. Today less than 100 acres are planted with loganberries in Oregon.

Some new varieties of commercial blackberries produce larger berries, greater yields, and ship better, but the standard of quality is still the small-berried wild blackberry with its concentrated, wine-like flavor.

SEASONALITY ◆ Blackberries ripen in most parts of the country in late July, with some varieties continuing to produce berries through September, though most are finished bearing by mid-September.

WHAT TO LOOK FOR ◆ If the berries aren't dead ripe, they'll be sour instead of sweet and lack the full dusky-brambly flavor of the ripe fruit. When they are dead ripe, they lose some of that glistening black brightness in favor of a slightly dull finish.

If at all possible, pick them at peak ripeness yourself from your favorite wild berry patch. Short of that, look for fresh-picked wild berries at the farmers' markets or roadside stands. Commercially grown organic blackberries sometimes appear at pick-your-own patches, more frequently at farmers' markets, roadside stands, and in organic food stores. The Top Varieties listed on page 500 all have an excellent flavor, and if the purveyor is the berry farmer, he or she will definitely know the name of the variety. And when walking along country roadsides in the East in late July, don't forget to keep an eye out for the dewberries.

STORAGE ~ Blackberries are soft and very perishable. They should not be stored fresh, although they can be frozen in a single layer on baking sheets, then transferred to freezer bags and stored for later use.

USES ~ Blackberries make surpassingly good jams and jellies, but squeeze the juice through a jelly bag or your preserves will be very seedy. If very ripe, mash them and pour them over ice cream. Add frozen blackberries to your midwinter freezer-fruit medley (see Putting Up Peaches for the Winter, page 29).

NORA'S SUPERB BLACKBERRY COBBLER

SERVES 4

I received this recipe from Nora Pouillon, one of America's finest organic chefs. She owns two acclaimed restaurants in Washington, D.C., Nora and Asia Nora.

FOR THE BERRY MIXTURE

4 cups blackberries
1 tablespoon Grand Marnier

½ cup sugar
1 tablespoon arrowroot
2 pinches ground cardamom

FOR THE COBBLER DOUGH

1 cup unbleached all-purpose flour
5 tablespoons sugar
1 teaspoon baking powder
½ teaspoon baking soda
½ teaspoon sea salt
3 tablespoons unsalted butter, chilled and cut into
    ¼-inch dice
1 egg yolk
⅓ cup buttermilk, or ⅓ cup milk with 1 tablespoon
    fresh lemon juice
Mint sprigs

1. Preheat the oven to 400°F. Grease a 4- to 6-cup baking dish or ceramic pie plate. Combine the berry mixture ingredients in a large bowl and pour the berry mixture into the dish.

2. Combine the flour, sugar, baking powder, baking soda, and salt in a medium bowl. Add the butter and work the mixture quickly between your fingertips, until it is crumbly and has the consistency of cornmeal. Or use a food processor, pulsing it on and off, to mix the flour and butter. Add the egg yolk and buttermilk and stir to combine. The dough will be soft.

3. Drop the dough in spoonfuls onto the berries with a large spoon. Bake for 30 to 40 minutes, until the topping is browned and cooked through. The berries should be quite liquid. Garnish with mint. ∎

BLACKBERRY AND CHOCOLATE BOMBE

SERVES 10

Bombes are a do-ahead dessert for a special dinner party. They look like domes, and when cut open, reveal several layers of delicious desserts inside. Make this at the height of blackberry season when the berries are perfectly ripe. Underripe blackberries are sour and unappealing, and this bombe is all about lusciousness. You'll need an ice cream maker.

8 cups dead-ripe blackberries
2 cups sugar
2 pints high-quality chocolate ice cream
4 ounces semisweet chocolate, chopped fine
2 tablespoons brandy
Mint sprigs

1. Make the bombe in a 10-cup bowl, preferably stainless-steel, that fits in your freezer. Press two sheets of aluminum foil into the bowl so that they overlap and extend a couple of inches past the edge of the bowl all around. Put the bowl in the freezer.

2. Mash 4 cups of the blackberries with a potato masher, then pour into a sieve set over another bowl. Work the pulp back and forth with the back of a spoon so that as much of the liquid as possible drips into the bowl. Leave the remaining pulp in the sieve. Combine 1$^1/2$ cups of the sugar and 1$^1/2$ cups water in a saucepan and bring to a boil for 2 minutes, until all the sugar is dissolved. Pour the sugar solution through the blackberry pulp remaining in the sieve, and press again to get out as much liquid as possible.

3. Chill the syrup-juice mixture thoroughly, then pour into an ice cream maker and freeze according to the maker's instructions. When it's firm, spoon it into the bowl you've lined with foil and placed in the freezer.

Using the back of a spoon or spatula, smooth the blackberry sorbet over the bottom and up the sides of the bowl, making a layer a generous inch thick and leaving the center hollow. Freeze for 3 hours or more, until very firm.

4. When the blackberry sorbet has frozen firmly, let the ice cream soften slightly. Place it in a medium bowl and mix in the bits of semisweet chocolate. Spoon this into the hollow in the center of the bombe and spread to even the ice cream with the top of the sorbet. Cover with foil and place back in the freezer. Freeze for at least 4 hours more, preferably overnight.

5. While this is freezing, make the sauce. Combine 3 cups of blackberries, the remaining $^1/2$ cup of sugar, and the brandy in a nonreactive saucepan. Bring to a boil, stirring often. When it boils, reduce heat and simmer for 3 minutes. Remove from heat, pour into a covered container, and refrigerate until well chilled, at least 3 hours.

6. To serve, peel off the foil cover from the bombe, then invert the bombe onto a cold platter. Peel off the foil. Sprinkle the last cup of ripe berries on top and around the bombe. You can bring the bombe to the table, where it will elicit oohs and aahs. Place a ladle full of the sauce on each of 10 dessert plates. Cut the bombe into 10 wedges and set each wedge upright on a plate. Garnish each plate with a sprig of mint. ∎

Black Raspberry

RUBUS OCCIDENTALIS

ALTHOUGH THEY GROW WILD all over the northeast and into Canada, black raspberries—or black caps as they're sometimes called—thrive best in a band of territory stretching from New Jersey westward through Pennsylvania and into Ohio. When I lived in Pennsylvania, the Fourth of July meant hanging out the American flag and heading to the wild black raspberry patches to gather a gallon of the shiny berries.

I tried growing cultivated black raspberry varieties in my garden in Pennsylvania, but their flavor lacked the luscious, fruity taste of the wild berries. (If you want to know what wild black raspberries taste like, the raspberry liqueur Chambord gives an overly sweet but fairly accurate approximation.) Finally I stopped trying—why toil to grow inferior berries when the fields and old meadows are full of better berries for free? Now that I live on the West Coast, there are no wild black raspberries and I have to satisfy myself with the cultivated kind.

Almost all frozen cultivated berries come from the Willamette Valley south of Portland, Oregon, where about 1,500 acres are planted. Ohio is another large black raspberry producer, with about 600 acres in production, although that is increasing. You'll have a better chance of the berries having been hand-harvested if they come from Ohio.

THE ORGANIC FACTOR ◆ Black raspberries are still close to the wild state, even the cultivated varieties, and so have good natural disease resistance. Though they may not be certified organic, they most likely haven't been sprayed.

NUTRITION ◆ Black raspberries are super sources of cancer-preventing antioxidants, surpassing other bramble fruits in most categories, including ellagic acid and phenolic compounds like anthocyanins. They are also rich in flavonols like quercetin and catechins.

SEASONALITY ◆ Black raspberry season runs from July 1 to July 15—get them while you can!

WHAT TO LOOK FOR ◆ Around the Fourth of July—the height of black raspberry season—look for ads for pick-your-own operations, especially in the Mid-Atlantic states and New England. The plantings will be cultivated, but cultivated black raspberries are better than none.

You may find them in farmers' markets, but wild black raspberries are so perishable that few make it to big retail outlets. Instead, you may find cultivated black raspberries in season, or bags of frozen organic cultivated berries. Black raspberries freeze well, but almost all will have been mechanically harvested, so you'll probably find some underripe berries in the bag. Look them over carefully and discard any with any significant degree of red drupes (the small seeded knobs that make up the black cap).

STORAGE ◆ Other than freezing or making them into preserves or jellies, they don't store well. Use them right up.

USES ◆ Black raspberries make astoundingly good jam, which is easiest to make if you don't mind seeds. The shiny black berries are beautiful as decorations on tarts, clafoutis, and similar pastries, but the real glory of black raspberries is to pour the plump, juicy berries over vanilla ice cream and dig in.

BLACK RASPBERRY ICE CREAM

SERVES 6

This is an ice cream for high summer. You'll need an ice-cream maker. Because it doesn't use eggs as an emulsifying agent, this ice cream will crystallize if put in the freezer—which means you'd best eat it immediately (as if you'd need any encouragement).

4 cups fresh or frozen black raspberries
1¹/₂ cups sugar
Juice of half a lemon
2 cups heavy cream
1 cup whole milk

1. Thaw frozen berries, if using. Place the berries, sugar, and lemon juice in a medium bowl and toss to incorporate the ingredients. Cover the bowl, leave out at room temperature for 2 hours stirring every half hour.

2. Pour the mixture into a blender and puree until smooth. In a large bowl, combine the cream and milk and stir in the berry puree until thoroughly blended. Pour the mixture into the ice cream maker and freeze according to the manufacturer's instructions. ■

Blueberry

VACCINIUM CORYMBOSUM

BLUEBERRIES, of which several hundred species exist, are native to the circumpolar areas of the world, both north and south of the equator. To the north (starting at about the 38th parallel, from southern New Jersey, west to Mendocino County in California and farther up almost to the Arctic Circle), they are one of the most common plants in the woodlands, growing in millions upon millions of acres.

I remember, as a child in Pennsylvania's Pocono Mountains, I lay in my bed at night and looked at the glowing mountaintops to the south. They were on fire. The fires were nothing exceptional. Everyone knew they were purposely set to burn off the forest canopy so that native blueberries would regrow. The arsonists would then harvest the blueberries and sell them in the big northeastern markets.

Until 1916, when Elizabeth White of the New Jersey Pine Barrens marketed the first cultivated blueberries, they were an entirely wild-harvested crop. Then cultivated varieties began to appear and blueberry farms began to spring up. But the harvesting of wild blueberries continues to this day. In the Poconos and Jersey Pine Barrens, folks with land on which wild blueberry bushes grow thick—around the towns of Long Pond and Tobyhanna in Pennsylvania—often set out pick-your-own signs, sit down on lawn chairs by the sign, and let the public in—for a price. If you find yourself in that area around the third week in July, bring a bucket and gather your fill.

THE ORGANIC FACTOR ◂ There's a blueberry farm not far from in California me where farmer Bruce Goetz has made the transition from conventional to organic blueberry culture. His story is typical of organic blueberry growers. Since blueberries tend to be free of pests and diseases, his conventional cultivation had included only chemical fertilizer and herbicide. Now he's found an organic way to control weeds and fertilize his crop. Blueberries like an acid soil rich in decaying organic matter, and so organic compost, with its acid pH, is perfect for this plant. The cool nights and sunny days of summertime allow Goetz to produce small but highly flavored berries, many of them from his grandfather's original planting of 1942. These were selections from the wild species, still sold today, named Jersey, Rancocas, and Rubel. He says that while most hybrid blueberries are big and watery, with sugar content at about 10 percent (Brix), his smaller but more flavorful berries get to about 15 Brix because of the low pH, organic soil, and local climate.

NUTRITION ◂ Studies show that old varieties closer to the wild species have more nutritional content than modern hybrids, especially the cancer and heart disease-preventing antioxidants that blueberries are noted for. But even the hybrids are nutritional champs. Blueberries contain good amounts of calcium, magnesium, phosphorus, potassium, vitamin C, and folic acid. Researchers at the USDA Human Nutrition Center have found that blueberries rank number one in antioxidant activity when compared to forty other fresh fruits and vegetables. These antioxidants help neutralize harmful by-products of metabolism called free radicals that can lead to cancer and other age-related diseases. Anthocyanin—the phenolic pigment that makes the blueberries blue—is thought to be responsible for this major health benefit, along with vitamin C.

In another USDA lab, neuroscientists discovered that feeding blueberries to lab rats slowed age-related loss in their mental capacity. And according to scientists at UC Davis, blueberries may reduce the buildup of LDL (bad) cholesterol that contributes to cardiovascular disease and stroke. Researchers at Rutgers University in New Jersey have identified a compound in blueberries that promotes urinary tract health and reduces the risk of infection. It appears to work by preventing bacteria from adhering to the cells that line the walls of the urinary tract.

A number of studies in Europe have documented the relationship between bilberries (see Types) and improved eyesight. A Japanese study concluded that blueberries help ease eye fatigue.

TYPES ◂ Cultivated varieties of blueberries from blueberry farms tend to be bigger than wild blueberries, because they are chemically fertilized, while the wildings are suited to nutrient-poor soils and the berries stay small. However, any single blueberry has a set amount of flavor compounds, so the smaller the berry, the more intense the flavor. Really big blueberries tend to be watery and lack that intensity.

The Pocono Plateau, along with southern New Jersey and parts of eastern New England, was the original home of the highbush blueberry (*Vaccinium corymbosum*), the wild species from which most of our modern hybrids have descended. It grows wild in most of the Northeast.

European bilberries (*Vaccinium myrtillus*) are a close wild cousin of the North American highbush blueberry and grow mostly in the northern latitudes in Europe. The bog bilberry (*Vaccinium uliginosum*) is a related species that produces delicious blueberry-like bilberries, and countless acres of this low-growing shrub stretch across the circumboreal regions of the Northern Hemisphere from northern Europe east to Siberia, further east to North America.

Northstar blueberries are bred for cold northern climates but will wither and fail to produce fruit in the Deep South. Rabbiteye blueberries thrive in the hot, humid south but will freeze out in the coldest states, but their flavor is usually inferior to the northern highbush types grown north of the 38th parallel. The variety Summit is recommended in Arkansas.

SEASONALITY ➤ We now have fresh blueberries all year round, "locally" from April to October—in other words, from Florida or southern California to Quebec or British Columbia—and from Chile from November through March. But as far as I can tell, we only get organic blueberries when they are truly in season, which is June through July. They're much cheaper than out-of-season berries, much fresher, and grow closer to home.

WHAT TO LOOK FOR ➤ Check the berries for mold, for squashed berries, and for overly soft berries that are getting too ripe. The bluish bloom on their surface is natural and should be there. Ask your supplier which variety he or she is selling. If at all possible, seek out the nonhybrid, old-fashioned varieties.

STORAGE ➤ Fresh blueberries store well in the fridge for a week or two.

Blueberries freeze beautifully and you can have organic blueberries all year around if you freeze them. No fruit freezes better than blueberries. Their waxy bloom—the whitish coating on the berries—protects them, and they don't stick together. Freeze them in a flash on cookie sheets. When they're frozen hard, put them in freezer bags. When thawed, they're good for winter fruit compotes or baking in muffins rather than eating out of hand, because freezing renders them soft and squishy, not firm, as when they're fresh. If you have a food dehydrator, they can also be dried and used like raisins on cereals and in muffins and pancakes.

USES ➤ They are a choice ingredient in muffins, scones, pies, and pastries. Pour them over your morning cereal. Eat them out of hand. When they're in season and at a reasonable price, keep them on hand daily. Soon they'll be out of season, prohibitively priced, and lower in quality.

BLUEBERRY MUFFINS

MAKES 12 MUFFINS

Here's a recipe for blueberry muffins that goes easy on the satuurated fat but heavy on the nutrition (it's vegan, too). Make lots of these and freeze them. Take them out of the freezer before you go to bed so they'll be ready to go in the morning.

3/4 cup whole-wheat pastry flour
3/4 cup unbleached all-purpose white flour
1/2 cup cornmeal
1 tablespoon baking powder
1/4 teaspoon sea salt
6 tablespoons canola oil
2 ounces soft tofu
1 cup soy or rice milk
1/3 cup maple syrup
1 cup fresh or frozen blueberries

1. Preheat the oven to 375°F. Oil muffin tin cups or line with cupcake papers.

continued

2. In a medium bowl, sift together all the dry ingredients. In a separate bowl, mix all the wet ingredients, including the blueberries. (Using tofu, puree it in a blender with the soy milk, then add to other wet ingredients.) Stir the wet ingredients into the dry ingredients, just enough to mix. Spoon the batter into muffin cups, filling each ²/₃ full. Bake for 20 to 25 minutes, until golden brown. ■

BLUEBERRY PIE

MAKES ONE 9-INCH PIE; SERVES 6 TO 8

This pie is the standard finish to that ultimate Maine feast: a bucket of steamers, a two-pound lobster pulled fresh from the trap and boiled, a basket of french fries, an ear of roasted corn, cole slaw, and a mug of beer. But it's great even without those preliminaries.

FOR THE PASTRY

2 cups pastry flour

10 tablespoons unsalted butter, chilled and diced

2 teaspoons freshly squeezed lemon juice

¹/₃ cup ice water

FOR THE FILLING

1 quart fresh blueberries

1 tablespoon cornstarch

³/₄ cup honey

1 egg, beaten

Whipped cream, optional

1. To make the pie dough: Place the flour and butter in a cold bowl and either cut the butter in with 2 knives or work it quickly with your fingers until it resembles coarse meal. Sprinkle on the 2 teaspoons of lemon juice, then work in the ice water a bit at a time until the dough just forms a ball. Divide this into two balls, a slightly larger ball for the crust and a smaller ball for the lattice. Wrap both and refrigerate for 1 hour.

2. To make the pie: Preheat the oven to 350°F. Roll out the dough to a 12-inch circle and place it in a 9-inch pie pan. Trim most of the excess, then squinch up the edges and press them into the pan with the back of a fork. Pierce the bottom of the dough in several places with a fork. Lay a sheet of waxed paper in the pie shell and fill with pie weights, dry beans, or raw rice. Bake for 20 minutes. Remove from the oven, and remove the weights and waxed paper.

3. While the crust is baking, place the blueberries in a mixing bowl. Mix the cornstarch with 2 tablespoons water and combine it with the honey in a small saucepan. Place over low heat and cook until mixture thickens, 3 to 4 minutes. Remove from the heat and mix with the blueberries.

4. Cut the remaining dough into ¹/₂-inch-wide strips. Fill the pie shell with the blueberry mixture. Make a latticework top for the pie from the dough strips, pressing them onto the partially baked edge where they touch. Brush the latticework with the beaten egg. Lay a sheet of foil on the oven rack to catch drips. Place pie on it and bake for 20 to 30 minutes, until the latticework is lightly browned. Top with whipped cream if desired. ■

Cherimoya

ANNONA CHERIMOLA

CHERIMOYAS (also called custard apples) range from the size of a baseball to a soccer ball. Their inedible light green skin is made up of slightly concave, pentagon-like sections, which give it a scaly look. But inside is an incredibly delicious, pure white flesh that's meltingly soft, juicy, sweet, acidulous, and very fragrant. Its flavor lies somewhere between a strawberry and a bowl of vanilla custard with hints of lemon, kiwifruit, pineapple, banana, papaya, and mango. It's sweet without being cloying; Mark Twain called it "deliciousness itself."

The only places in the United States where cherimoya is grown commercially are in southern Florida, Hawaii, and the coastal regions and foothills of southern California. Since much of that precious land is taken up by developments and state parks, there's not a lot space for cherimoya cultivation. Not only is its growing range severely limited, it must be hand-pollinated because none of the plant's native pollinators of its home region in the cool, tropical inter-Andean valleys of Ecuador and Peru exist in the United States. The fruit has been cultivated in South America since pre-Columbian times, and the name cherimoya comes from the Inca language of Peru. It migrated to North America aboard ships in the 19th century.

THE ORGANIC FACTOR ◆ Cherimoya is likely to be organic, whether there's a USDA Organic seal on it or not. No chemicals are registered for use on cherimoya, so that means it's illegal to use pesticides, herbicides, or fungicides on the tree or fruit. Not only that, cherimoya responds to organic soil amendments with lusher growth and larger harvests of bigger fruits.

NUTRITION ◆ Cherimoyas are good sources of dietary fiber with 7 grams per fruit, vitamin B6, folate, and potassium. They are a very good source of vitamin C, supplying our entire day's requirement in one fruit.

SEASONALITY ◆ If you live in California, you may occasionally see it in specialty fruit markets during its October to May season. Some Florida, Mexican, and Central American cherimoya, which also has a winter to spring season, makes its way to large markets in eastern states—but not much.

WHAT TO LOOK FOR ◆ Very little California cherimoya leaves the state because it is a soft fruit that doesn't travel particularly well, and there's precious little left after Californians take their share. Production is on the increase, however, as plantings are coming on line in Hawaii, Australia, and Spain. If you do find it, it will be expensive. Look for unbruised fruit that has a little give when gently squeezed.

STORAGE AND PREPARATION ◆ This fruit is not for storing. Eat as soon as you can. The flesh is studded with large black seeds come out easily with the tip of a knife or fork.

USES ◆ Cherimoya is commonly eaten raw. You cut it in half, remove the black, inedible seeds, and spoon it from the skin into a bowl or straight into your mouth because it is just so good that way. Each of its segments contains an easily removed seed. The pulp can be seeded and pureed and made into ice cream or sherbet or used to make a cooling fruit drink.

CHERIMOYA AGUA FRESCA

SERVES 4

It seems a shame to do anything to a cherimoya except eat its custard-like flesh with a spoon, yet it makes a fabulous drink.

3 cups seeded cherimoya flesh
4 cups water
1/4 cup sugar, optional
Mint

Scoop out and seed the flesh of the cherimoya, leaving all its integument behind. Add this flesh to a blender and puree to a smooth consistency, adding a bit of the water if necessary to make it blend. Place the remainder of the water in a serving pitcher, mix in the cherimoya, and taste. Add as much of the sugar as you think it needs, if any. Stir until the sugar dissolves, then refrigerate. Serve chilled with a mint sprig atop each glass. ■

Cherry

PRUNUS, various species

THERE COMES a time in late June when the cherries are at their peak of quality, and that alone makes it one of my favorite times of the year. Whoever said "Life is just a bowl of cherries" must have been one happy, well-adjusted person. Whether it's fresh cherries out of hand, cherry-vanilla ice cream, or cherries jubilee, these little fruits brighten our lives.

THE ORGANIC FACTOR ► While sweet cherries are susceptible to rots, sour pie cherries are disease resistant. I have seen sour cherry trees laden with bright red fruit sitting happily in the late spring rains, unsprayed, while a nearby Black Tartarian sweet cherry crop was nearly entirely taken by brown rot. Organic sweet cherry growers aren't entirely at the mercy of the fungi, however. Bordeaux mixture (elemental sulfur mixed with slaked lime) and even a weak alkaline solution of baking soda are allowed in organic culture as fungicides. These compounds do not wreak havoc in the orchard ecosystem.

Another solution is for cherry breeders to make hybrids of sweet and sour cherries—in fact, most modern cherry hybrids (called Royal, Duke, or dual-purpose cherries) are the product of such natural crosses. They are valued for their hardiness, disease resistance, and good cooking qualities.

When buying cherries, it's especially important to find organic sweet cherries because conventional cherries are one of the most heavily sprayed crops.

NUTRITION ► Sweet cherries are high in sugar (about 10 percent), have good stores of potassium, but are relatively low in vitamin C (11 milligrams per 100 grams of fruit). Acerola sour cherries have higher vitamin C levels. Dark-colored cherries are high in antioxidants.

TYPES ➤ All told, there are 900 varieties of sweet cherries and 300 of sour cherries sold in the world's markets. Sweet cherries (*Prunus avium*) are the ones we most often find fresh at our markets. They can contain as much as 20 percent sugar, which makes them perfect for eating out of hand.

Sour cherries (*Prunus cerasus*), also called pie cherries, are sour because they contain an abundance of acid, but when mixed with sugar and used for cherry pie or cobblers, their tartness is one of their features. Their high acidity also makes them more disease and bird-resistant than sweet cherries. There are two categories of sour cherries. Amarelle, such as the Montmorency variety, are light-colored with clear juice. Griotte, such as the Morello and North Star varieties, are dark with colored juice.

SEASONALITY ➤ Sweet cherries are the first stone fruit to ripen; their season runs from May to July. The earliest cherries lack the rich flavor of midseason ones and often show a tendency to split or separate into disfigured twins. Then come the so-called white or yellow cherries, usually Rainier or Royal Ann. The Bings arrive in mid-June and by the end of June are at their peak.

WHAT TO LOOK FOR ➤ Look for whole, fresh cherries with bright, rather than dull, skins without splits or blemishes. They should be firm rather than soft. Cherries grow in pairs and you should find a pair with their stems still joined together.

Organic sweet cherries are mostly sold fresh, but they are also frozen to be sold in supermarkets.

Sour cherries are almost always sold canned. If you want to buy fresh sour cherries, you'll most likely find them at farmers' markets. Dried cherries are also available, usually in bulk, at organic markets.

USES ➤ Sweet cherries are mostly eaten out of hand, but they are also made into ice cream, used in pastries, or dried. If you have a food dehydrator, try drying fresh, pitted sweet cherry halves to use like raisins in ice cream, muffins, or granola.

Sour cherries are typically sweetened and cooked into pies and pastries, but some are also made into cherry soup, and some are dried. These dried sour cherries can add some tang-zing to a wide range of dishes but especially to sweet meats such as pork and duck.

KEEP AN EYE OUT FOR BLACK CHERRIES

A CHERRY THAT GROWS WILD in the east and that is sometimes sold at roadside stands is the black cherry (*Prunus serotina*), also called the bird cherry, or wild cherry.

The dark, reddish-black fruits are small—about the size of a fingernail—and not very sweet, but intensely flavored. They are harvested and a sweetened syrup is made of their juice that's used to flavor soft drinks, ice creams, and candies, as well as rum and brandies. The trees are sturdy-looking and beautiful, and their rich, reddish-brown wood is highly prized for cabinet making.

BRANDIED CHERRIES

ABOUT 8 CUPS OF CHERRIES (½ GALLON)

Cherry season always means for me that it's time to get out the old crock and make brandied cherries. My crock is ceramic, with a lid that snaps closed but any glass container with a tight-fitting lid will do, and a half-gallon size is about the smallest size to make the crock worthwhile. But if the glass is clear, store it in a dark closet while it ages.

1. Fill the container with ripe but firm, unblemished cherries—I'll use either sweet or sour, depending on which look the best. You can pit them, but I think the slight almond flavor of the pits adds a grace note to the cherries, so I don't. If I'm using sweet cherries, I add 1 cup of sugar to the crock for every 2 pounds; if sour, 1½ cups of sugar.

2. Fill the crock with a decent brandy to within an inch of the top, cover with two layers of waxed paper, and snap down the lid. Because my ceramic crock is light-proof, I store the cherries on the kitchen counter, as room temperature allows the cherries to macerate better than in the fridge. Once the cherries have macerated for a month or two, I move them to the fridge to keep the cherries from becoming overly soft and falling apart, and they stay there until the holiday season.

TIP: Brandied cherries over homemade organic vanilla ice cream (using a real vanilla bean) make a fine finish to the Thanksgiving turkey. Or make cherry-vanilla ice cream with them, adding a few tablespoons of the brandy liquid from the crock (don't use too much brandy or the ice cream won't harden). Or, brandied cherries, almonds, chocolate, and a glass of well-aged port (but no cigar) could be the perfect close to a Christmas dinner. ▪

MY FAVORITE CHERRIES

I'M NOT ALONE in thinking that Bing is the best tasting, most satisfying cherry variety. The California Rare Fruit Growers, an organization made up of horticulturists, botanists, hobbyists, farmers, and other fruit-minded folk, occasionally organize fruit tastings. They recently held a cherry tasting, and Bing topped the list. Bings are a purple-skinned variety of sweet cherry with a rich, sweet, wine-like flavor. They originated in Milwaukie, Oregon, in 1875 through the work of an orchardist named Seth Lewelling. He named this exquisite fruit after a Chinese laborer named Bing who worked for him.

One day back in 1973, I visited a friend who had three mature Bing cherry trees on his property, each a good 35 feet tall, with thick trunks and widespread limbs laden with fruit. I climbed up to where a limb forked into two smaller limbs. All around me, burnished burgundy-black cherries hung within reach, and I perched there happy as a bird, gobbling my fill.

It was one of those moments in life that seem so natural and usual when it's happening—just me in a tree with some cherries—but in retrospect becomes an extraordinary pleasure when I realize it is never to be repeated.

CHERRY

DRIED CHERRY, APPLE, AND APRICOT CHUTNEY

MAKES 3 TO 4 HALF-PINT JARS

This recipe was given to me by Chef John Ash, a talented cook and the author of the award-winning *From the Earth to the Table*. Of this chutney, he wrote to me, "This is a versatile, not-too-sweet chutney, a version of which I had years ago in an English pub. There they served it as an accompaniment to a nutty, aged cheddar cheese and wholegrain bread. I also love this with roast turkey, duck, sausages, and game such as venison. It makes a wonderful gift from your kitchen, packed into attractive little hinged glass jars."

2 cups dried tart cherries
1 1/2 cups quartered dried apricots
1 1/4 cups cider vinegar
1 cup dry white wine
1 cup brown sugar
1 teaspoon sea salt
1/2 teaspoon crushed red pepper flakes
2 tablespoons finely chopped crystallized ginger
3 whole star anise
2 teaspoons whole coriander seed
1/2 teaspoon freshly ground black pepper
2 tablespoons slivered garlic
1 1/2 pounds tart-sweet apples such as Braeburn, Fuji, or Gala, peeled, cored, and cut into large dice

Place all ingredients except the apples in a large, nonreactive saucepan and bring to a boil. Reduce the heat and simmer, partially covered, for 10 minutes. Add the apples and return to a boil, then reduce heat again and simmer, partially covered, for 35 minutes or until mixture has thickened. Stir occasionally. Remove and discard star anise. Ladle into hot sterilized jars (see Tips), seal and refrigerate. Keeps up to three months refrigerated, or process and store in a dark, cool place for up to nine months.

TIPS ON CANNING AND PRESERVING: To sterilize jars, check canning jar rims to make sure they have no chips or cracks. Place jars, lids, and rings in a pot of boiling water for 5 minutes. Leave the jars in the hot water until you're ready to fill them.

You can extend the shelf life of this chutney and be able to store it at room temperature by using the water-bath canning method. A water-bath canner is a large covered cooking pot with a rack that fits on the bottom. You can use any large pot as long as it is deep enough for the water to cover the jars by two inches and still have another two inches of headspace for the water to boil. The canner should be no more than four inches wider than the stove burner so that adequate heat reaches all jars. It must have a tight fitting lid and the rack should keep the jars from touching the bottom of the pot.

Sterilize your jars after the chutney is ready to be stored. Next, fill the canner with water and bring it to a full boil. Pour the chutney into the jars immediately after removing them from the sterilizing bath, leaving a 1/2-inch headspace. Wipe any chutney off the rims with a clean, damp cloth and seal using a two-piece canning lid. (Place the flat lid on the jar and then screw the band down tightly.)

With a jar lifter, carefully place the jars on the rack in the canner. Make sure that the boiling water covers the jars by at least 2 inches. If you need to add more water, pour it between the jars and not directly on them, so the jars don't break. Tightly cover the canner and when the water returns to a boil, set a timer for 10 minutes. Check water level occasionally to make sure jars are adequately covered. Using a jar lifter, remove hot jars and place on a rack or dry towel. Let cool at least 12 hours. Check the seal by pressing the center of the lid. If the lid is slightly concave and does not flex up and down, then it is sealed. ∎

FRUITS ▪ 241

CHERRY PIE

MAKES ONE 9-INCH PIE; SERVES 6 TO 8

Best made with fresh, mid-summer pie cherries. During cherry season, you might pit and freeze cherries in one layer on a cookie sheet, then pour the frozen cherries into a freezer bag for year-round pie-making, or make several pies in season to place in sealed plastic bags in the deep freezer to defrost whenever you need to remember the warm days of summer.

Pastry for double-crust 9-inch pie (double the recipe on page 211)
4 cups pitted fresh sour cherries
1 cup sugar
4 tablespoons all-purpose flour
2 teaspoons quick-cooking tapioca
2 tablespoons kirsch, or 1/4 teaspoon almond extract
1 1/2 tablespoons freshly squeezed lemon juice
1 tablespoon butter, diced
Milk, or 1 egg mixed with 1 tablespoon water

1. Cut the dough in half and roll out one half about 1/4 inch thick to line a 9-inch pie pan, keeping the other half refrigerated. Have the cherries in a large bowl. Combine the sugar, flour, tapioca, kirsch, and lemon juice, and gently mix into the cherries. Fill the pie crust with this mixture. Dot the top with the bits of butter.

2. Preheat oven to 450°F. Roll out the remaining dough 1/4 inch thick and cut it into 1/2-inch strips. Weave the strips into a lattice top for the pie, trimming off all but 1/2 inch of the overlap and moistening the ends of the strips where they meet the bottom crust along the edge of the pie plate, squishing them together with the back of a fork. Brush the lattice with the milk. This makes the lattice glossy. Bake for 10 minutes, then reduce heat to 350°F and bake for another 30 minutes, or until the lattice is golden brown. ■

Citrus

CITRUS, various species

WHILE a few of the citrus fruits in commerce are the original wild species, most are hybrids and crosses and further crosses of species and other hybrids. For instance, tangelos are a cross between a Dancy tangerine and a grapefruit. The limequat is a cross between a lime and a kumquat. The oversized pummelo looks like a cross between a grapefruit and a soccer ball, but it is actually its own species and a probable parent of the grapefruit.

THE ORGANIC FACTOR ▸ Buying organic citrus is especially important if you're cooking with citrus peel or zest, because that's where most chemicals reside. But even if you're just eating the inside, it's worth buying organic because the amount of chemicals used to treat citrus fruits is appalling, In 2001, California growers alone used over 3,000 tons (6 million pounds!) of agricultural chemicals on their oranges. Now add more tons of chemicals used on grapefruit, lemons, and other citrus. And add all the chemicals used in citrus-growing states such as Arizona, Texas, and Florida, and you can see the importance of buying organic whenever possible.

NUTRITION ▸ Not only are organic citrus fruits "cleaner" than conventionally grown varieties, they are able to absorb many more nutrients from the rich organic soil. Organic oranges have been found to have up to 30 percent more vitamin C than conventional fruits, even though the conventional oranges tend to be larger and have a deeper color.

Citrus is known to have a cholesterol-lowering effect, and over 20 epidemiological studies have shown that the consumption of citrus is protective against many cancers in humans, including cancers of the oral cavity, larynx, esophagus, pancreas, stomach, lung, colon, and rectum. Citrus is also rich in bioflavonoids and other antioxidants. One cup of fresh orange juice contains 124 milligrams of vitamin C—over four times the recommended daily allowance. Other citrus contains comparable amounts.

TYPES ➤ See citrus Top Varieties, page 501, for a breakdown of the best varieties by type.

SEASONALITY ➤ Citrus are available year-round, but high citrus season is during the late fall and winter.

WHAT TO LOOK FOR ➤ Look for fruit without nicks or cuts, and choose those that feel heavy in the hand.

USES ➤ Citrus fruits are the most widely grown, diverse, and useful fruits in the world. The joy of citrus fruits is their delicious taste and sharp acidity that stimulates the appetite and slakes the thirst so well. Citrus's sweet-sour spectrum ranges from sharply sour in lemons to wonderfully sweet in tangerines and oranges.

Who could predict from the flavor of citrus alone that orange would go so perfectly with chocolate or strawberries, that lime juice would focus the taste of corn and meld with raw fish, that grapefruit and goat cheese are a natural match? And lemons—they make half the celebrated teams of lemon and lime, lemon and honey, and lemon and black currants.

Lemons also have an affinity for olives. The Olive Press in Glen Ellen, California (see Sources, page 517), markets an olive oil they call Limonato made with local Mission olives and Meyer lemons. They give these ingredients for a citrus vinaigrette: 6 tablespoons of Limonato, 2 tablespoons fresh orange juice, and 1 tablespoon of balsamic vinegar. The wide range of citrus fruits have uses far too numerous to mention, but don't forget that you can marinate very fresh seafood such as fillets of sole or catfish in lemon and lime juices in the fridge overnight to make ceviche.

MY FAVORITE CITRUS

FROM DECEMBER THROUGH MARCH, I like to begin the day by eating a Marsh white grapefruit. These fruits make me look forward to the winter. I discovered them when I was in Tampa, Florida, interviewing Bern Laxer, the late owner of Bern's Steak House for a story for *Organic Gardening.* Bern composted all his restaurant's vegetable waste and used it in a large organic garden where he grew the ingredients for his salads. As I left, I noticed a grapefruit had fallen to the ground and I asked Bern if I could have it. He said sure, so I took it to a nearby park and made it my sun-warmed lunch. From that day to this, it was the best grapefruit I ever tasted, juicy, and candy-sweet. When in season, Marsh grapefruit can be found in stores across the country (or order from Cherry Moon Farms—see Sources, page 517).

ASIAN-STYLE ORANGE CHICKEN

SERVES 8

Lemon chicken is the traditional Chinese restaurant kids' favorite, but I think orange chicken is even better. This version of the Chinese-restaurant classic harmonizes sweet citrus with Asian flavors. This is a great dish to make in a large batch to serve to company, or eat it yourself the next day!

2 oranges, such as Valencia or Pineapple
4 scallions, sliced 1/4 inch thick
1/3 cup soy sauce
1/4 cup sugar
1/2 cup freshly squeezed orange juice (1 to 2 oranges)
Canola oil for deep frying, plus 2 tablespoons
3 pounds chicken breasts and thighs, boned, cut into
  bite-size pieces and thoroughly dried on paper towels
1 tablespoon shredded peeled fresh ginger
1/4 teaspoon hot pepper sauce, or to taste

1. Score the peel of 1 orange into quarter sections. Pull off the peel and reserve. Remove the white pith from inside of peel by scraping with the edge of a sharp knife. Cut the peel into long 1/4-inch-thick strips. Repeat with second orange. Section both oranges, and set aside the sections and orange peel strips.

2. In a small bowl, combine the scallions, soy sauce, sugar, and orange juice; set aside. Pour oil to depth of 2 inches into large, heavy saucepan or deep skillet. Heat to 375°F on a deep fat thermometer. Fry the chicken pieces, a large handful at a time, about 4 minutes or until the pieces lose their pink color and are done through. Remove with slotted spoon and drain on paper towels. Heat 2 tablespoons of oil in large skillet or wok. Add the ginger, hot pepper sauce, and strips of orange peel. Stir-fry over high heat 90 seconds. Add the chicken pieces. Stir-fry 3 minutes. Add the orange juice mixture. Stir-fry 3 minutes more. Transfer to a heated serving dish. Garnish with the orange sections. ▪

ORANGE AND ALMOND RICE

SERVES 8

Plain rice can be boring, so here's a way to give it a flavor boost.

6 tablespoons butter
2 cups freshly squeezed Valencia or Pineapple orange
  juice (4 to 5 oranges)
1 teaspoon salt
1 1/2 cups raw long-grain rice
1/2 cup sliced blanched almonds
1/3 cup chopped parsley

Combine the butter, orange juice, salt, and rice with 1 cup water in a 2- to 3-quart saucepan. Bring to a boil, stirring once or twice. Reduce heat to low and cover. Cook, without removing cover or stirring, for 15 to 20 minutes, until the liquid is absorbed and the rice is tender. Meanwhile, toast the almonds in a small dry skillet over medium heat, stirring constantly, until a light golden brown, 3 to 4 minutes. Stir almonds and parsley into rice and serve immediately. ▪

VANILLA-ORANGE VINAIGRETTE

MAKES ABOUT ¾ CUP, ENOUGH TO DRESS 4 SALADS

This recipe was given to me by Ryan Jackson, executive chef of Brix Restaurant in the Napa Valley, California. A little goes a long way to brighten a garden-fresh salad.

¼ cup freshly squeezed orange juice
Juice of ½ lime
½-inch knob of fresh ginger, peeled and sliced
1 whole star anise
1 teaspoon Dijon mustard
½ cup olive oil
2 tablespoons hazelnut oil
½ teaspoon vanilla extract
Salt and freshly ground black pepper

Place the orange juice, lime juice, ginger, and star anise in a small nonreactive pot. Cook over medium heat until half the liquid remains. Strain through a fine sieve (discard the solids) and cool to room temperature. Place the liquid in a blender or food processor. Add the mustard and blend until smooth. While the blender is running, add the olive and hazelnut oils in a slow, steady stream. Add the vanilla. Season the vinaigrette with salt and pepper to taste. ■

KEY LIME TART

MAKES ONE 9-INCH PIE; SERVES 6 TO 8

This sumptuous little tart is from Kimberly Sklar, the pastry chef at Lucques in West Hollywood, California, where Suzanne Goin is executive chef and owner. If you can't find key limes, you may substitute regular limes. But key limes are better because the juice is sweeter and the color is a wonderful yellow.

Key limes are grown year-round in warmer climates all over the world. Indigenous to Malaysia, they were brought to North Africa by Arab traders, to Europe by the crusaders, and to the Caribbean by the Spanish. Around 1835 the first grove was planted in the Florida Keys. Organic key limes are becoming increasingly common.

FOR THE CRUST
15 graham cracker squares
5 tablespoons sugar
10 tablespoons unsalted butter (1¼ sticks)

FOR THE FILLING
3 extra-large eggs, at room temperature
½ cup plus 1 tablespoon sugar
3 tablespoons all-purpose flour
7 tablespoons freshly squeezed key lime juice (2 to 4 limes), strained
1 cup plus 2 tablespoons crème fraîche or sour cream
Whipped heavy cream

1. In a food processor or in a plastic bag using a rolling pin, grind the graham crackers to fine crumbs. (You need 2 cups of crumbs). Mix in the sugar. Melt the butter, add to the graham cracker crumbs, and mix to form a crumbly dough like damp sand. Spray a 9-inch pie pan with nonstick spray and pour in the mixture, pressing it evenly up the sides and across the bottom. Chill in the fridge for 1 hour.

2. Preheat the oven to 350°F. Bake the shell on the middle rack until golden, 18 to 20 minutes. Cool on a rack before adding filling.

3. In a medium bowl, whisk together the eggs, sugar, flour, lime juice, and crème fraîche. Set aside until the pie shell is cool. Whisk one more time before pouring into prebaked shell. Bake until almost set—the center will jiggle slightly when gently shaken—20 to 24 minutes. Chill until ready to serve.

4. Serve with a dollop of whipped cream. ■

GRAPEFRUIT COOLER

SERVES 2

A very simple yet enormously refreshing drink. Use Marsh white grapefruit if you can find it.

4 mint sprigs, plus more for garnish
1 tablespoon superfine sugar
2/3 cup freshly squeezed white grapefruit juice
1 tablespoon freshly squeezed lime juice
3 ounces light rum
Chilled club soda
Dash Angostura bitters
White grapefruit segments for garnish

In a cocktail shaker, crush the mint sprigs with the back of a tablespoon against the inside of the shaker. Add the sugar and fruit juices and stir until the sugar dissolves. Add the rum and about 1 cup of ice cubes, cap the shaker, and shake for 30 seconds. Strain the mixture into two collins glasses filled with ice cubes. Top each glass with club soda and top with a dash of bitters. Stir and garnish with a small mint sprig and a segment of grapefruit. ■

THE ULTIMATE FRENCH TOAST

SERVES 4

You think you've had good French toast before? Wait until you try this. It's partially made the night before the breakfast when you intend to serve it. Make sure all your ingredients are organic for the ultimate experience.

6 eggs
1/2 cup half-and-half
2 cups freshly squeezed orange juice (4 to 6 oranges)

3 tablespoons freshly grated orange zest (well scrubbed if not organic)
1/4 cup sugar
1/4 teaspoon vanilla extract
2 tablespoons Grand Marnier
Pinch of salt
8 slices (1-inch-thick) high quality, densely textured bread
3 tablespoons melted unsalted butter

FOR THE SAUCE

3 tablespoons unsalted butter
2 tablespoons orange marmalade
1 tablespoon Grand Marnier
Maple syrup, warmed

1. In a bowl, whisk together the eggs, half-and-half, orange juice and zest, sugar, vanilla, Grand Marnier, and salt. Place the bread slices in a 9 × 13 × 2–inch pan baking dish and pour the mixture over the bread. Chill overnight, turning after the first half hour to coat the other side.

2. In the morning, preheat the oven to 400°F. Brush the melted butter on a large baking sheet and arrange the bread slices on it, leaving a couple of inches between slices. Bake for 5 minutes on a middle rack, then rotate the pan and bake 5 minutes more. With a spatula, turn the slices over and bake 5 more minutes, then rotate the sheet and bake 5 more minutes.

3. While the bread is baking, make the sauce in a small saucepan by cooking the butter, marmalade, and Grand Marnier over low heat until the butter melts and everything is incorporated smoothly. Place 2 slices of the French toast on each of four plates, drizzle with the sauce, and serve with warmed maple syrup. ■

Cranberry

VACCINIUM MACROCARPON

MEMBERS of the heath family, cranberries grow in the northerly latitudes, in Alaska and Canada, Scandinavia and Russia, and can also be found as far south as North Carolina. I remember gathering them in the woods of Alaska. In all my years tramping through woods and seeking out wonderful wild foods, I never found such a bounty of berries as in Alaska.

The cranberries we're used to, which appear in stores in November in plastic bags, are the American or Large cranberry, botanically named *Vaccinium macrocarpon.* They are the cranberries of commerce, and grow on low bushes across the northern tier of states from the mid-Atlantic west to Oregon. They grow especially well in Wisconsin and Minnesota. They don't necessarily need to grow in boggy, water filled marshes—although they will survive there, too. In fact, they make a vital and interesting part of an evergreen fall home landscape while they produce their fall harvest of berries.

THE ORGANIC FACTOR ◆ Commercial cranberry production goes heavy on the pesticides and on the environment. One of the largest peat bogs in North America—Burns Bog outside Vancouver, British Columbia—is being taken over for conventional cranberry production, displacing the flora and fauna that thrive there. As with many other agricultural products, conventional cranberries have environmental costs that don't show up in the price. But today there are many sources of organic cranberries, sold fresh, as juice, as dried cranberries, and even as canned cranberry relish.

NUTRITION ◆ Cranberries contain good stores of antioxidants, vitamin C (2 ounces—a generous handful—contain the minimum daily requirement), and healthful acids. Especially useful, cranberry acids can increase the acidity of one's urine, which can help relieve urinary tract infections as well as certain kidney stones.

TYPES ◆ The cranberry's genus name, *Vaccinium,* derives from the Latin word for cow, *vacca,* because, it is said, cows will go out of their way to graze upon these plants. One of their common names is cowberry. In addition to the American cranberry, there are two other common species. In northern Europe, Canada, and Alaska, a smaller cranberry species called *Vaccinium oxycoccus* goes by cranberry or, in Scandinavia, lingonberry (see below). Lingonberries have a slightly more acidic taste than American cranberry. However, some Scandinavian fanciers of these fruits reserve the name lingonberry for *Vaccinium vitis-idaea,* a related species.

All three types of *Vaccinium* contain large amounts of benzoic acid, a natural preservative that allows the berries to winter over in plain water without disintegrating due to bacterial action. The benzoic acid also allows the berries to preserve other foods they are mixed with. The Native Americans often made their pemmican—a mixture of meat, grains, and fruit pounded together and dried—with plenty of American cranberries for this reason.

LINGONBERRY ◆ The Swedes are nuts for their lingonberries. In New York City, chef Marcus Samuelsson has made a fine reputation for himself spinning twists on classic Scandinavian cuisine at the restaurant Aquavit, where he often uses both lingonberries and cranberries. Known as the red gold of the Scandinavian forest, the garnet-colored lingonberry that ripens each September is considered indispensable to Scandinavian cooking. Lingonberries are the standard accompaniment to Swedish meatballs, as a garnish or sauce for game dishes, pancakes, and they are often used in Swedish desserts. They're used to make sauces, preserves, candies, jams, syrups, ice creams, wine, liqueurs, and a leaf extract often used to quell stomach disorders. These berries play such a vital role in Swedish cuisine that the right of common law states that all Swedish citizens have access to private land to pick as many wild berries as they wish.

SEASONALITY ◆ Fall is the prime season for fresh cranberries.

WHAT TO LOOK FOR ◆ Look for bright berries that are hard. Soft berries indicate decay.

STORAGE ◆ If not using them right away, they freeze well. They can also be sliced in half and dried.

USES ◆ Although most of us think of cranberries only during the holiday season, these little bites of highly acidic fruit have endless uses—brightening pastries, adding snap to pancakes and waffles, enlivening sweet breads, adding tang to a sour fruit chutney for ham or pork, and otherwise offering their tartness to our culinary creativity. In addition to making for good eating, American cranberry bushes are wonderful plants to use in landscaping (they don't need a bog to grow). The berries, which ripen in the fall, add a lovely color to a fall evergreen landscape.

CRANBERRY RELISH

MAKES ABOUT 2 TO 3 CUPS

This is an old British recipe, sometimes called "cranberry cheese." It is a nice change from plain old cranberry sauce on your turkey. It's thicker and sweeter, with a citrusy tang.

2 cups fresh cranberries
3/4 cup sugar
2 ounces (1/3 cup) seedless raisins, chopped
2 ounces (6 tablespoons) finely chopped walnuts
1 orange (well scrubbed if not organic), peeled and seeded, cut into quarters and thinly sliced crosswise

Combine the cranberries with 1 cup water in a medium nonreactive saucepan. Cook over medium heat until the cranberries are soft. Remove from heat, drain the cranberries and then press them through a sieve back into the saucepan. Add the sugar, raisins, and walnuts. Bring the mixture slowly to a boil, stirring constantly. Add the orange, reduce the heat to a simmer, and cook uncovered for 20 minutes. Pour into a jar, cover, cool to room temperature, and refrigerate. Keeps for 2 weeks in the fridge or for many months in the freezer. ■

Currant and Gooseberry

RIBES, various species

MOST AMERICANS have not eaten an actual currant, because if you look for dried currants in the supermarket, you tend to find small, raisin-like fruits that are in fact dried, seedless Zante grapes. They are labelled currants simply because they look something like dried black currants. (Perhaps currants are not used because they contain seeds, which add a bit of a crunch to the dried fruit.)

THE ORGANIC FACTOR ◆ Currants are very disease resistant and so are almost always grown without the use of chemicals, but that doesn't make them organic. Organic is not just the absence of chemicals but rather a method of enriching the soil, promoting biodiversity, and generally improving the ecosystem as crops are grown and harvested. Nevertheless, fresh currants at farmers' markets and roadside stands will almost surely be free of toxic chemicals, even if the farm isn't certified organic.

NUTRITION ◆ Three and a half ounces of black currants supply about 200 milligrams of vitamin C—seven times our daily requirement—plus good stores of calcium, iron, and vitamin A. Gooseberries and red currants have from a half to a quarter of those amounts, and white currants even less.

TYPES ◆ There are three primary types of true currant—red, black, and white—plus gooseberries, which are of the same genus (*Ribes*) and are something like an oversized currant, about a half-inch in diameter.

BLACK CURRANTS (*RIBES NIGRUM*)—This is my favorite type of currants, prized across the countries of northern Europe, especially Germany. Some people find the musky taste of raw black currants unpleasant, but not me. Yes, they have a strong musky flavor, but it's rich and luscious. I find that processed black currant jams, jellies, fruit juices, and even cassis—black currant liqueur—have lost the musky flavor that makes black currants unique.

RED CURRANTS (*RIBES RUBRUM*)—They are very tart when they first turn a watery light red in early July. If allowed to hang on the bush, they turn a darker, richer red, and that's when they are really good—still tart, but less so, and sweeter. Look for berries that are dark, not bright, red.

KEEP AN EYE OUT FOR CLOVE CURRANTS

A COUPLE OF species of native American currants grow wild across the northern tier of states from Maine to the Rockies, run south to Colorado, and then pass along a southern tier back east to North Carolina. The clove currant (*Ribes odoratum*), so called for the pleasant clove scent to their flowers, and American Black Currants (*Ribes americanum*) produce small red-black currants on medium-sized bushes. Their fruits seldom appear in market, but their genes are found in many of the commercial varieties.

WHITE CURRANTS (RIBES RUBRUM VARIETY ALBUM)—a sort of red currant that lack the red anthocyanin pigment, these are rare to find at the markets, but if you see them, certainly buy them for out-of-hand eating. They are the sweetest and least tart of the currants.

GOOSEBERRIES (RIBES HIRTELLUM) vary in color from translucent green to blushed with red or pink. They have a mild tartness to them with a flavor likened to grapes, kiwis, and even apricots.

Black currants have been crossed with gooseberries to create a hybrid called the Jostaberry. The fruits are black, closer to a gooseberry in size, and lack the musky, resinous flavor of the black currant. They are occasionally found at farmers' markets and roadside stands.

SEASONALITY ◆ Currant season runs June to July.

WHAT TO LOOK FOR ◆ Real currants are almost always sold as fresh fruit, not dried. Look for plump currants that haven't softened or shriveled.

Taste several to make sure they taste fresh. Each fruit is about ¼ inch in diameter and very round; they grow in loose clusters. A gooseberry should spill its juice into your mouth. They should be firm to the touch. Avoid mushy or mealy gooseberries.

It's worth seeking out real fresh members of the *ribes* clan because of their diversity of flavors and uses and, if you have a yard in the northern half of the country, because they make pretty deciduous shrubs that once a year shower you with sweet little fruits. You'll probably never find true currants of any stripe at the supermarket, but look for them in season at the farmers' markets.

STORAGE ◆ Currants and gooseberries freeze well but otherwise aren't for storage except as jams, jellies, and syrups.

USES ◆ Fresh currants—red, black, or white—can be strewn over a summer salad or fruit salad. Decorate fruit tarts and cakes with them. Bake them into scones. Their uses are myriad.

Currants can be cooked into wonderful jams, jellies, and syrups to glaze fruit toppings, cakes, and pastries. Alpine strawberries can be dipped in thinned currant jelly and then dotted over tapioca puddings or cakes. Ricotta-filled blintzes will come alive when currant jelly syrup is poured over them, accompanied by a dab of crème fraîche.

Red currants, probably the most versatile of all currants, make fine syrups and jellies, and the best melba sauces have fresh red currants or red currant jelly mixed into their raspberry base. Stir red currant syrup through a banana smoothie for an ambrosial drink.

The classic gooseberry dish is the gooseberry fool (stewed gooseberries swirled or blended into whipped cream or custard)—a name I love even as I'm tempted to use it as a pejorative. They're also made into jams, preserves, pies, and fruit pastries.

GOOSEBERRY PIE

MAKES ONE 9-INCH PIE

This recipe comes from the 1910 *Hotel St. Francis Cookbook* by Victor Hirtzler, the San Francisco hotel's legendary chef. It may be nearly 100 years old, but it turns out fine for me.

Fill a deep china vegetable dish [pie plate] with gooseberries, add one quarter pound of sugar and two cloves to the dish, wet the edges, cover with pie dough, wash the top with eggs, and bake. When done, dust the top with powdered sugar, allow to cool, and serve cream separate.

Depending on the size and depth of the pie plate, this recipe will take 3 to 4 cups of gooseberries. I might add to pierce the pie dough in several places before baking to let steam escape, set the oven at 375°F, and bake the pie for 45 minutes, or until the top is golden brown and the gooseberry filling yields

an easy clear liquid when a toothpick is inserted. I assume he means to serve the pie completely cooled (which allows it to set since gooseberries and currants have plenty of natural pectin), with heavy cream on the side. ▪

LEMON BAVARIAN WITH BLACK CURRANT SAUCE

SERVES 8

If you can put this dessert together, you will wow whoever tastes it. The tart, soprano note of the lemon flavor harmonizes perfectly with the luscious baritone of the black currant syrup. One of the best things I've ever eaten.

Although this isn't a particularly difficult dessert to make, it does require attention. The Bavarian cream is made the night before and chilled overnight, and the black currant sauce can also be made a day ahead and refrigerated. (The Bavarian can be frozen and defrosted, but it will have a slightly different—although still excellent—consistency.)

Limoncello is the lemon-based liqueur made on the Amalfi coast of Italy.

2 lemons (well scrubbed if not organic)
1 1/2 tablespoons (1 1/2 packets) unflavored gelatin
1 cup plus 3 tablespoons sugar
5 eggs, separated, plus 2 egg yolks
2 teaspoons cornstarch
1 1/2 cups whole milk
2 tablespoons limoncello
Pinch of salt
1/2 cup heavy cream, chilled
Black Currant Sauce (recipe follows)

1. Grate the zest of the lemons, then juice them into a measuring cup through a strainer to catch the

continued

seeds (there should be $^1/_2$ cup juice). Sprinkle the gelatin over the lemon juice, stir, and set aside to soften for about 5 minutes.

2. In a medium bowl, combine the zest with 2 tablespoons of the sugar. Add the 7 egg yolks and beat until smooth with a wooden spoon or whisk. Gradually beat in 1 cup of the remaining sugar until the mixture is very smooth and pale yellow. Beat in the cornstarch.

3. In a medium saucepan heat the milk until almost boiling and dribble it into the egg yolk mixture, beating all the while. Pour back into the saucepan or a double boiler and heat gently, stirring constantly with a wooden spoon, until the mixture thickens just enough to coat the wooden spoon. Be careful not to cook too fast or hard, certainly not to boil, or the egg yolks will curdle. (If they curdle, all is lost.) As soon as the mixture coats the spoon, take it off the heat, add the limoncello and gelatin mixture, and beat for a few moments until the gelatin is completely dissolved and incorporated.

4. In a separate bowl, beat the egg whites with the salt until soft peaks form. Sprinkle on the remaining tablespoon of sugar and beat until stiff peaks form. Fold these egg whites into the hot custard in the mixing bowl. Place it in the fridge to chill, removing it periodically to refold the mixture as it cools, which keeps it from separating, until it's cold but not quite set. Beat the heavy cream until doubled in volume, then fold it into the custard.

5. To prepare the mold, use any 8-cup mold (a ring mold, simple metal bowl, or whatever). Rinse the inside of the mold in cold water and shake out the excess. Turn the cream mixture into the mold, cover with waxed paper and place in the fridge overnight.

6. Before serving, remove the waxed paper, dip the mold in very hot water for one or two seconds, then invert onto a chilled serving plate. To serve, slice the Bavarian into individual servings, place these on chilled serving plates, and drizzle plenty of black currant syrup over each slice. ■

Black Currant Sauce

4 cups black currants
1 cup sugar
Squeeze of lemon juice

In a 2-quart saucepan, over medium heat, heat the black currants and sugar until the berries soften, the juice runs, and the sugar dissolves, about 7 minutes. Continue to cook until the berries are soft and mostly broken (you can use a potato masher to break open any unopened berries). Strain into a bowl, and stir in the lemon juice. Chill and reserve. ■

Date

PHOENIX DACTYLIFERA

THE CULTIVATION of dates began in the region between the Nile and Euphrates rivers in the times of Sumer and ancient Egypt, when wild date palms that had large, palatable fruits were selected from the wild palms with mostly inedible fruits. Eventually, around 4,000 years ago, fruits approximating our modern dates were born. The caravans that wended their way from oasis to oasis across this region planted date palms; the palms flourished with their heads in the furnace heat of the desert and their feet rooted in the high water tables of the oases and brackish marshes. Dates still grow best in this kind of situation, and that's why in the United States certain deserts in Arizona and especially California's Coachella Valley are the center of date production.

There are 600 varieties of cultivated dates in the world, most of them limited to areas of North Africa and the Middle East, with an especially strong presence around the southern Iraqi town of Basra. (California has about 250,000 acres of cultivated dates; Iraq probably has around 22 million acres.)

Before the regime of Saddam Hussein drained the marshes of southern Iraq, the wet soil and fierce heat provided perfect conditions for date growing. It may be that plans are afoot to return the wetlands to their original marshy state, which would allow the reconstitution of date growing on the scale once practiced there by the Marsh Arabs who have inhabited the region for 5,000 years.

THE ORGANIC FACTOR ◆ Growers often say that they use organic methods as much for the quality of the product they reap as for its purity and its light footprint on the environment. One example is the Oasis Date Gardens, in the Coachella Valley in Thermal, California (see Sources, page 517). This relatively small date garden (as date farms are called) has about 9,500 trees on 175 acres and ships just under a million pounds of organic dates a year. The folks at Oasis believe dates obtain the best flavor and fullest sweetness under organic conditions, such as feeding the date palms rich organic compost.

NUTRITION ◆ Dates are energy-packed. Five dates, about 45 grams or a little less than 1½ ounces, contain 115 calories, mostly from the 80 percent sugar content of ripe dates. Dates also contain protein, fat, and plentiful minerals including copper, sulfur, iron, magnesium, and especially potassium. Bedouin Arabs, who eat them on a regular basis, show an extremely low incidence of cancer and heart disease.

TYPES ◆ Dates are classified as soft, semisoft, and dry.

SOFT DATES have been picked from the tree while still moist and fresh. This state is called *tamar,* and soft dates are graded by their tamar, or moisture content. Soft dates, if you can find them, are extremely good. At the tamar stage, they are about 24 percent moisture and so have a juicy, melting quality. If you've had Medjool dates, these are an example of high-quality soft dates. Most soft dates are left on the tree until they become relatively dry, then allowed to cure even further, which shrivels them and concentrates their sugar (these are invert sugars, by the way, which is important for those who can't tolerate sucrose).

SEMISOFT DATES have drier, thicker skins and a sticky, chewy texture. These are the dates

most people are used to seeing sold in markets packed into small boxes. Semisoft dates have a moisture content of around 10 percent and constitute over 90 percent of the market.

DRY DATES, also called bread dates, have been left to dry on the tree and then cured until their moisture content is less than 7 percent. They are dry like pastry and crumble when chewed, and they were a staple of Middle Eastern nomads of the desert because they kept well without refrigeration.

In addition to whole dates, you can find date spreads and pastes, powdered date sugar, jams, jelly, and juice—all utilizing the fruit's intense sweetness—but I have not seen these as organic products.

SEASONALITY ◆ September through December is the harvest season for dates.

WHAT TO LOOK FOR ◆ Dates usually come packaged in boxes. Check to make sure there's no mold, which would indicate they were exposed to moisture.

STORAGE AND PREPRARATION ◆ Dates store perfectly well on the kitchen counter or in the refrigerator. They can be frozen for extensive periods.

USES ◆ Millions of people in the Middle East, especially in Iraq, depend on dates of all kinds as a staple food; they are indigenous, widely available, pleasantly sweet, and nutritious. They're used to sweeten dishes but also in breads and savory recipes such as stews.

For those who haven't cooked with them all their lives, dates can seem so intense that it can be hard to know what to do with those chewy, candy-like, dried fruits other than to eat them plain. Some people stuff them with cream cheese, but that pairs their abundance of sugar with an abundance of fat. If they have to be stuffed, I prefer to stuff them with toasted, ground seeds or nuts such as sesame seeds, pistachios, and pine nuts, held together with a little almond butter.

Besides being eaten out of hand, or stuffed for hors d'oeuvres, chopped dates are used in breakfast cereals, in puddings, breads, cakes, cookies, ice creams, and candy bars.

MEDJOOL DATE NUT LOAF

MAKES ONE 9-INCH LOAF

Soft Medjool dates are best for this recipe as they have the smoothest texture when incorporated into the loaf. Dates and nuts have an affinity for each other, as this sweet, nutty loaf reveals. I like a slice toasted and slathered with butter for breakfast or as a snack with a small glass of port or sherry.

The finer you chop the nuts and the dates for this loaf, the nicer the texture and richer the flavor will be. The recipe comes from the folks at the organic Oasis Date Gardens.

3/4 cup brown sugar
2 tablespoons canola oil
1 large egg
1 1/2 cups whole milk
3 cups sifted all-purpose flour
3 1/2 teaspoons baking powder
1/2 teaspoon salt
1/2 cup chopped walnuts
1 cup pitted and finely chopped Medjool dates or other
   soft date

Preheat the oven to 350°F. Grease a 9 × 5 × 3–inch loaf pan. In a large bowl, combine the sugar, canola oil, and egg, and mix thoroughly. Stir in the milk. In a separate bowl, sift together the flour, baking powder, and salt. Add the dry ingredients to the liquid mixture and stir thoroughly to combine. Add the nuts and dates. Pour the mixture into the pan and let stand for 20 minutes, then bake for 50 to 70 minutes, until a wooden toothpick inserted into the center comes out clean. ■

DATE ENCRUSTED HALIBUT

SERVES 4

Halibut is such a delicate fish that it can easily dry out in a hot oven. The crust helps seal in the natural juices and adds a sweet nuttiness to this nutritious, low-fat, mild-flavored fish.

1 cup pitted dates
1/3 cup butter
3 tablespoons fine bread crumbs or panko
4 (8-ounce) halibut fillets
Salt

1. To prepare the date paste, mash the pitted dates in a food processor or heat them in a saucepan with a little water until they soften and then mash.

2. Preheat the oven to 450°F. In a medium bowl, beat together the butter and date paste; fold in the bread crumbs. Season the halibut pieces with a small pinch of salt and cover the tops with the date mixture. Bake for 10 to 15 minutes, until the fish is opaque all the way through but still juicy, watching that the top coating doesn't blacken or burn. (To prevent this, you can cover the fish with a tent of aluminum foil, removing it for the last 5 minutes.) ■

Fig

FICUS CARICA

THE FIG is native to the Eastern Mediterranean region, where its cultivation has been traced back 4,500 years, almost to the dawn of agriculture. Figs are so rich and delicious, and they dry so well and keep without refrigeration for such long periods that those first farmers would have been crazy not to plant a fig in their dooryard, just as so many who live in the Mediterranean climates around the world do today.

While my own Black Mission fig tree isn't exactly in my dooryard (it's down in the orchard next to the vegetable garden), I'm happy to have it here. Figs came over with the Spanish explorers in the mid-16th century. The Black Mission variety arrived in California in 1769 when Franciscans established the first mission at San Diego. Originally, this fig grew on the Balearic Islands in the Mediterranean off the coast of Spain.

THE ORGANIC FACTOR ◆ While California figs aren't a heavily sprayed crop, nevertheless agricultural chemicals are used annually by conventional farmers, including methyl bromide soil fumigant, glyphosate (Roundup) herbicide, and fungicides. Large scale fig producers may spray ethephon growth regulator on the crop to speed up ripening if rain threatens or it's known that an insect will shortly make its appearance, but this doesn't help the fruit's flavor profile. The best choice is to look for organic figs. They are not hard to find. True Foods Market, an online store (see Sources, page 517) sells dried Calimyrna and Black Mission figs. The San Joaquin Valley Fig Growers' Cooperative includes organic figs in its product line, figs that find their way into several

retail brand names you'll find by searching online for "organic figs." These have all been certified organic.

NUTRITION ◆ Dried figs may reach 50 percent sugar, and they are a good source of dietary fiber, calcium, potassium, and the B vitamins of thiamine, riboflavin, and niacin. While fresh figs have 15 milligrams of vitamin C per 100 grams of fruit, the dried figs have none. Both fresh and dried figs have a mild laxative action.

TYPES ◆ Figs can be blackish purple, green, brownish-bronze, violet, or yellow. However, unlike grapes, where the flavor is concentrated in the skins, fig skin is relatively tasteless and isn't an indicator of their flavor. It's the pulp inside that contributes the taste. The flavor of fresh, tree-ripened figs is sweet, rich, and fruity—very different from the concentrated caramel-nuttiness that dried figs acquire.

SEASONALITY ◆ Most kinds of fig trees produce two crops a year—in the early summer and in the late summer or early fall. The first crop, called the breba crop, grows on older branches that developed over the course of the past year, and they are usually juicy and up to twice as large as the second, main crop, which appears in the late summer and fall and develops on the current year's growth of branches. The breba crop, while larger, is usually not as highly flavored as the second crop—the extra size means it is more diluted with abundant water; the smaller second-crop figs have more concentrated flavor.

WHAT TO LOOK FOR ◆ Only those who have spent time in regions where fig trees grow know the luscious texture and flavor of a fresh tree-

KEEP AN EYE OUT FOR FRESH CALIMYRNA FIGS

THE SMYRNA FIG from Turkey, long ago crowned best-tasting fig of all, was brought to California in the 19th century, where it failed until it was discovered that the plant needed a pollinator wasp to produce fruit. The wasps, from Turkey, were introduced into California fig groves and the trees started producing figs. The name was changed to Calimyrna—a combination of California and Smyrna. These tan-buff figs are mostly found dried but taste exquisite if you can find them tree-ripened and fresh.

Unlike most figs, which don't require pollination, Calimyrna (and Smyrna) figs are pollinated by a rather bizarre method involving a tiny wasp, wild goat figs, and some good luck. The unripe, pear-shaped fig functions like a receptacle with a small hole in the end for the pollinating wasp to crawl in and out. Thousands of little flowers form on the inside walls of the fig receptacle; the wasp pollinates these flowers with pollen from the wild goat figs (which must have coevolved along with the Smyrna figs and wasps on Cyprus and Crete). The pollinated flowers form into tiny drupes, or bits of sweet fig flesh, each enclosing a miniscule, hard-shelled seed. The process makes the figs very seedy; other types of fig are relatively seedless.

ripened fig. That's because tree-ripened figs are supremely perishable as soon as they are picked. In fact, if such a fig is bruised, it will become unmarketable within minutes, as the bruised area begins to break down and disintegrate. Most fresh figs that go the wholesale-retail route are picked unripe, and while they may become a little sweeter within a few days, they never reach their tree-ripened potential. Some may even be picked when the tree's milky latex is evident at the stem end of the fruit—this latex is irritating to the skin and destructive of proteins in the mucus linings of the mouth and should never be eaten.

Luckily, figs dry very easily, and most dried figs are picked tree-ripe, and so something of that appealing fresh flavor appears in the dried fig. With dried figs, look for Black Mission and Calimyrnas first. Kadotas have a rubbery, tough skin when dried.

My wife taught me how to recognize when a fresh fig is, in fact, tree-ripe and ready to pick and

to eat. An immature fig may well be entirely black and look ripe, but it stands out rigidly from the branch held by its strong peduncle—the bit of tissue that attaches the fig to the branch. When the fig is ripe, this peduncle becomes flaccid and the fig hangs limply from the branch. As soon as this happens, it's a race to the fig between the ants and me, for the little black Argentinean ants that have turned California into one giant ant colony love nothing more than sweet, ripe figs.

STORAGE ► Fresh, ripe figs should be eaten as soon as possible. Dried figs store well in a kitchen cabinet for up to four months.

USES ► If you can find fresh figs, by far the best way to eat them is right out of hand. Some people peel them, but unless you have a variety with a tough skin, there's really no need. Figs are excellent with a little cream and sugar. They have an affinity for lavender and rosemary, orange, and lemon flavors. They harmonize beautifully with honey and caramel, combine well with peaches, pears, and raspberries, and marry perfectly with port wine. Figs go with salty foods such as prosciutto and pancetta—an Italian tradition that may hearken to ancient Rome, when figs were used in savory dishes. Sweet meats such as pork and duck can be cooked with fresh figs to enhance their sweetness. Use fresh figs in fruit salads with raspberries, blueberries, melon cubes, and bananas, all given a splash of orange juice. Fresh figs can be preserved in sugar syrup, perhaps with cinnamon to add a spicy note.

With dried figs, poaching softens them and, depending on how they're poached, can form a chord of harmonious flavors. Try poaching them in red wine sweetened with honey and orange juice, a dash of vanilla, and a pinch of cinnamon, and serving them over vanilla ice cream or a fruit sorbet (boil down the poaching liquid to make a sauce).

Dried figs can be stuffed with goat cheese. Or they can be mashed with a fresh juicy fruit such as plums or fresh apricots to make a paste that can be smeared on a butterflied pork roast before it's rolled and tied (see page 428).

FIG AND OATMEAL COOKIES

MAKES ABOUT 24 COOKIES

Make these kid-friendly but nutritious cookies with organic ingredients (especially the citrus zests, because the skins of conventionally farmed citrus may have unacceptable levels of agricultural chemicals) and get none of the chemicals and hydrogenated vegetable oils that food processors feel compelled to put in their cookies and into our children.

1 cup dried figs
1/2 cup unsalted butter
2 eggs
3/4 cup honey
4 tablespoons milk
1 1/2 cups whole-wheat pastry flour
3 teaspoons baking powder
1/4 teaspoon salt
1/2 cup 1-minute rolled oats
1 teaspoon freshly squeezed lemon juice
1 teaspoon freshly grated lemon zest (well scrubbed if not organic)
3 tablespoons freshly grated orange zest (well scrubbed if not organic)

1. Preheat the oven to 350°F. Line 2 cookie sheets with waxed paper and coat the paper with vegetable oil or nonstick spray, or simply grease the sheets. Put the figs in a small saucepan, cover with cold water, cover, and bring to a boil, then turn down heat and simmer for 10 minutes. Drain the figs and chop into small dice.

2. In a medium bowl, heat the butter until it just turns liquid—several 20-second visits to the microwave will do it. Set aside. In another bowl, beat the eggs and honey until well mixed and thick. Combine this with the butter and beat again, then add the milk and beat again until the mixture is smooth. Sift together the flour, baking powder, and salt, and add this to the batter, mixing until fully incorporated. Add the figs, oats, lemon juice, and the zests and mix well. If the batter seems a little stiff, add a splash more milk. Drop heaping tablespoons of batter onto the sheets, about 12 drops to each cookie sheet. Bake 20 minutes or more, depending on the size of the cookies, until golden brown. Check the bottoms of several cookies, being careful not to bake too long or the honey will scorch.

"FIGGY PUDDING"

SERVES 10

This pudding, figgy as all get-out and perfect for the holiday season, is easy to prepare—no worries about over- or understeaming even if you've never made Christmas pudding before. More American than British, as it's flamed with bourbon (rather than brandy), this version is every bit as delicious—spicy, chewy, and sweet. It's a blazing finish to a proper holiday dinner.

For the mold, you can use any a pudding, melon, or charlotte mold with a secure, snap-top lid. A quart to half-gallon size is about right.

FOR THE PUDDING

3 tablespoons butter, plus extra for the mold

2 cups minus 2 tablespoons all-purpose flour

1 teaspoon baking soda

$1/2$ teaspoon salt

$1/2$ teaspoon ground cinnamon

$1/2$ teaspoon ground cloves

$1/2$ teaspoon allspice

$1/2$ teaspoon freshly grated nutmeg

$1/2$ cup molasses

$1/2$ cup honey

$1/2$ cup whole milk

$1/2$ pound dried figs, finely chopped or put through a meat grinder

$1/2$ cup dates, sliced very thin

2 eggs, beaten

Freshly grated zest of 1 lemon (well scrubbed if not organic)

Freshly grated zest of 1 orange (well scrubbed if not organic)

1 cup bourbon (at least 100 proof Wild Turkey is perfect)

FOR THE HARD SAUCE

$3/4$ cup ($1 1/2$ sticks) butter, softened

2 cups sifted confectioners' sugar

3 tablespoons bourbon

1. Butter the inside of the mold.

2. In a large bowl, sift together the flour, baking soda, salt, cinnamon, cloves, allspice, and nutmeg. Set aside. In a medium saucepan, melt the 3 tablespoons of butter, add the molasses, honey, and milk, and whisk to incorporate.

3. Add the figs and dates to the flour mixture, working them in well with your fingers until well incorporated. Add the liquid, then the eggs, then the zests, and mash to incorporate everything as thoroughly as possible, using a potato masher or the paddle attachment of an electric mixer. Pour into the prepared mold, leaving $1 1/2$ inches at the top for expansion, and snap on the lid. Place the mold, lid side up, into a pot large enough to hold it, but not so wide that the mold could fall over. Fill about halfway up the side of the mold (you want there to be enough water, but not so much that when it boils, the water can get inside the lid).

Bring to a boil, reduce the heat, and cook at a low boil for $2 1/2$ hours, adding more water if necessary. Remove from heat and cool the pudding to room temperature.

4. To prepare the hard sauce, cream the butter with the confectioners' sugar until light and fluffy. Stir in bourbon.

5. To serve, unmold the pudding onto a rimmed serving platter, preferably made of heat-proof Pyrex. Slowly pour the cup of bourbon over the pudding so the pudding soaks up as much of the whiskey as possible. Set ablaze and immediately bring blazing to the table. After the flame dies, slice pieces for the guests and place a tablespoon or two of hard sauce alongside the pudding. ▪

Grape

VITIS, various species

GRAPES are the flavor chameleons of the fruit world. Some grapes taste of strawberries, others of black currants, still others of apples, or lemons, or plums. Very few of the top-quality organic table grapes for fresh eating will show up in supermarkets. You will find some of them at farmers' markets and roadside stands in various parts of the country, however.

THE ORGANIC FACTOR ▸ During most of the year, supermarket table grapes usually come from California's Central Valley, where they are subjected to applications of fungicides, pesticides, herbicides, and chemical fertilizers—as well as gibberelic acid, a plant growth hormone that stimulates grapes to grow much larger than their natural size. Unsprayed, they would be about the size of your little fingernail.

It used to be hard to find organic grapes. A grower named Steve Pavich was among the first to supply them in quantity, but today there are many sources of organic grapes. California alone has 66,000 acres of grapes in organic culture—many of them used to make wine.

Grapes are perfectly capable of being grown organically in all the climates of the United States (there are even grapes grown on Mount Haleakala, on the tropical island of Maui). If you're interested in growing some vines organically, perhaps on an arbor over a picnic table, you might look for my book, *From Vines to Wines* (1999), which, although it focuses on growing wine grapes, details all the techniques and materials you'll need to handle table grapes organically.

NUTRITION ▸ Red grapes have good stores of antioxidants, and all grapes supply calcium, potassium, and vitamin C in modest quantities.

TYPES ▸ The best table grapes for eating come from selected varieties of native American grapes, Old World wine grapes called *Vitis vinifera,* or from hybrids the two. Seedless grapes are the best for eating out of hand. Seeded grapes may be delicious, but you have to work those seeds out unless you don't mind crunching the seeds, which then release bitter and astringent flavors.

Red grapes generally have more flavor than white, because the pigments in the skins are also flavor compounds. The darker the skin, the more flavor in the grape. American grape types have that foxy fruitiness, which reduces their value as wine grapes, but also have roots that are resistant to a plant louse called phylloxera, so most vines in Europe and America are planted on American rootstock. European grapes are superb for winemaking, and many crosses have yielded seedless table varieties that we are familiar with at our supermarkets. French-American hybrids, as crosses between American and European grape types are called, have some of the fine flavors of the European varieties but also some of the foxiness of the American parent. And then there are Muscadines and Concord grapes, both derived from native wild grapes and with a flavor all their own (see Wild Grapes and Concord Grapes).

Eastern grape types in general have fruitier flavor than the standard seedless table grapes from California, such as the familiar Thompson Seedless, Perlette, and Ribier. Two seedless varieties in particular are simply outstanding for fresh eating: Einset and Canadice. If you don't mind seeds, Catawba, a reddish-purple grape with a sprightly, slightly foxy, muscat-like flavor, has been a long-time favorite since the early 19th century. It was

WILD GRAPES AND CONCORD GRAPES

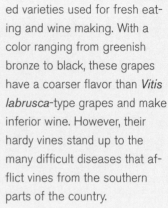

WHEN I WAS eight years old, my family moved from the sheltered suburbs of Long Island, New York, to the wilds of the Pocono Mountains in Pennsylvania. At first I was cautious of this new environment, but within a year I had made so many wonderful discoveries that I was as at home in the woods and fields, along the creeks and swamps, and on the rocky cliffs as I ever was on the shores of Manhas-set Bay. One discovery in particular thrilled me. Walking along a dirt road on a warm and sunny September day, I smelled a strong, fruity scent—sort of like Welch's grape jelly. I followed my nose and soon discovered long vines climbing up the roadside trees; among the branches hung bunches of big black grapes.

Soon I was up among the branches too, tasting them. They had a strong acidic juice, very aromatic, very fruity. The skins slipped easily off the pulp inside, which contained a number of seeds. It wasn't long before my tongue got educated in the art of separating the seeds from the pulp. I'd pop a handful of grapes in my mouth, bite them open, get the skins onto my back teeth on the left side and chew them for their concentrated flavor, spit them out, work the pulp to remove the seeds, spit out the seeds, and chew the pulp like squishy gum, drinking the sweet juice as it came free. These vines were *Vitis labrusca*, the wild grapes of the northeastern states, which announce their presence to your nose many yards before you even see them. If you've ever tasted a Concord grape, you've tasted a choice variation of labrusca that was discovered in Concord, Massachusetts, in 1849. The peculiar flavor of wild labrusca and Concord is sometimes called "foxy."

Down South, you're likely to run into wild grapes, too, but they will be the muscadine grape, *Vitis rotundifolia*, the best-known type of which is called Scuppernong, although there are many named cultivated varieties used for fresh eating and wine making. With a color ranging from greenish bronze to black, these grapes have a coarser flavor than *Vitis labrusca*-type grapes and make inferior wine. However, their hardy vines stand up to the many difficult diseases that afflict vines from the southern parts of the country.

In the northern Midwest, there is a small wild grape, *Vitis riparia*, that grows along streams and in wetlands. And out in California, wild *Vitis californica* grows in the coastal woodlands.

All of these grapes are edible, but only *labrusca* has the ability to project its strong fruity aroma for a hundred yards around itself. Edible is not the same as palatable, however. Among the wild species, *labrusca* comes closest to true palatability.

the chief variety grown along the Ohio River Valley to make sparkling wine in the mid-1800s, until the vines were wiped out by an attack of rot. It's still sometimes juiced for wine or fresh-frozen juice and is a treat as the dessert after a fine meal. The Delaware, another seeded red grape, became the standard of excellence for American grapes after its introduction in 1851 in Delaware, Ohio, and to this day is considered by many to be the best red American grape of them all. It's juicy, with a bright acidity and refreshing quality, a touch of foxiness, and beautiful appearance.

RAISINS ✦ Any grapes can be dried for home-made raisins. I dry mine in a dehydrator, but you can sundry them if you live in a hot, dry climate. Homemade raisins from organic grapes are to ordinary store-bought raisins what a good mattress is to sleeping on the hard ground. They are soft and chewy, sweet and tangy, plump and delicious.

Probably the best white grapes for homemade raisins are the Interlaken, Himrod, and Lakemont seedless varieties (introduced in the 1970s by the New York State Agricultural Experimental Station at Geneva). These green-skinned grapes acquire a light amber or gold color when ripe, and when dried turn a deep amber to brown. On a visit to the Finger Lakes region of New York, I sampled one local grower's homemade Lakemont raisins and they were astoundingly good. He gave me a small bag to take with me, but it never reached my family in Pennsylvania. I couldn't keep my fingers from straying into the bag on the drive home.

The best seedless red grapes for raisins tend to be *Vitis vinifera* types such as Flame Seedless and Ruby Seedless, and among blue-skinned grapes, Black Emerald and Black Monukka.

SEASONALITY ✦ Late summer and early autumn are the peak season for grapes.

WHAT TO LOOK FOR ✦ As grapes age on their bunches, they begin to shrivel. Feel the grapes. They should be plump and turgid, not soft. Hold a bunch up and give it a gentle shake. No grapes should fall off.

STORAGE ✦ They'll hold in the refrigerator for a week or more, but it's best to eat them before they begin to soften. Freeze grapes singly on a cookie sheet then bag them in freezer bags to add to winter compotes.

USES ✦ When white grapes are incorporated in savory meat dishes, the French add the name Veronique to the dish. And, of course, grape leaves are used to make dolmas—the Greek roll-ups—and can be used as festive doilies on plates under slices of dessert. Grapes are essential in fruit compotes, in pies, in jams and jellies, in salads, on open-faced fruit tarts, to make sherbets, or mixed in a tall glass with yogurt and honey.

FRESH (SELF-PRESSED) GRAPE JUICE ✦ Grapes can be juiced and the juice frozen for use during the cold months. Juice is fun and easy to make. Go to a winemaking shop and get a mesh plastic bag of the kind used to press out the new wine from the must (fermented grape mush), or make a bag out of several layers of cheesecloth. Find a tub or large crock made of nonreactive material, such as porcelain, ceramic, or stainless-steel, big enough for you to stand in. Or use the bathtub if you've scrubbed it sparkling clean (using organic cleanser). Figure on 12 to 15 pounds of grapes to yield one gallon of juice. Wash your feet at least as well as you washed the tub, dry them, and slip on a clean pair of socks before your feet touch the floor. Put the grapes in the tub, take off your socks, and get in. You'll find what people through the ages have found—that treading on grapes is the most efficient and gentle way to crush them.

Tread until all the grapes are mashed to a pulp. (You might put on some music and have your spouse do the treading while you sip wine and watch.) Make it an event. When the grapes are crushed, have a clean basin ready and scoop up the crushed grapes and expressed juice into the mesh bag, then twist and squeeze it over the basin to get out as much juice as possible. When you've extracted as much juice as you can, pour the strained juice into containers, leaving 1 to 1½ inch headroom for the liquid to expand when it freezes, and place them in the freezer.

GRAPE AND ALMOND GAZPACHO

MAKES ABOUT 1 QUART; SERVES 4

This recipe is from Cindy Pawlcyn, a legendary chef and restaurateur of San Francisco and the Wine Country to the north. The first time I met Cindy, she was serving this gazpacho at a wine event in the Napa Valley. It was so unusual—creamy, herby, spicy, and sweet-tart—and so good that I begged her for the recipe.

3 cups seedless green grapes (about 1$^1/_2$ pounds)
2 medium cucumbers, peeled and chopped
$^1/_3$ bunch fresh dill
$^3/_4$ cup plain yogurt
1 (8-ounce) package cream cheese
$^2/_3$ cup heavy cream
$^1/_3$ cup unseasoned rice vinegar
2$^1/_2$ tablespoons olive oil
$^1/_2$ teaspoon ground cayenne
$^1/_4$ teaspoon salt
$^1/_4$ teaspoon ground white pepper

FOR THE GARNISH

2 bunches scallions, sliced thin
$^2/_3$ cup almonds, toasted and finely chopped

Whiz the soup ingredients thoroughly in a blender until smooth. Refrigerate until cold. In the meantime, toast the almonds in a dry skillet over medium heat, stirring constantly, until they are fragrant and golden. Let them cool, then finely chop them. Serve the soup garnished with the scallions and almonds. ■

STUFFED GRAPE LEAVES (*DOLMAS*)

MAKES 48 PIECES

Grape leaves can be stuffed with vegetarian fillings—like lentils and rice—or with meat fillings, as here, whereupon they become the centerpiece of the meal.

FOR THE MEAT FILLING

2 tablespoons olive oil
$^3/_4$ cup minced onion
$^1/_2$ cup long-grain rice
$^1/_2$ pound ground lamb
1 clove garlic, minced
$^1/_4$ cup finely chopped fresh dill
$^1/_4$ cup finely chopped fresh parsley
1 teaspoon ground cumin
1 teaspoon dried mint
Salt and freshly ground black pepper
1 egg, slightly beaten

FOR THE LEAVES

$^1/_2$ pound (48 or more leaves) fresh grape leaves
    (see Tip) or canned grape leaves
Juice of 2 to 4 lemons (2 for cooking, plus 2 more
    if you are preparing fresh grape leaves)
Olive oil

1. To make the filling: In a large skillet, heat the olive oil over medium heat, add the onion, and sauté until it's translucent. Add the rice and stir for a minute or two, until the rice turns glossy. Add the lamb and stir until the meat is very lightly browned. Reduce the heat and add the garlic, dill, parsley, cumin, mint, salt and pepper, and 1 cup of water (or more) until the mixture is the consistency of thick oatmeal. Mix thoroughly, cover, and simmer over low heat until the meat is almost cooked and rice is softened but not done, 15 to 20 minutes. Add more water only if necessary to keep the mixture from sticking to the skillet, and continue cooking just

continued

until the meat is done, the rice is al dente, and all the liquid is absorbed. Remove from the heat and allow to cool. When the filling has cooled, mix in the beaten egg.

2. To prepare the fresh grape leaves: If you are using fresh grape leaves, rinse them well. Add the juice of 2 lemons to a large pot of water and bring it to a rolling boil. Drop in the grape leaves. Boil for 3 to 5 minutes to soften, then remove, snip off any hard stems, and drain in a colander. Set aside to cool. If you are using canned grape leaves, drain and rinse well before using.

3. To fill the grape leaves: Spread 2 tablespoons olive oil and 3 tablespoons water in the bottom of a large heavy lidded pot with a cover, such as a Dutch oven, and line the bottom with any torn or unusable grape leaves. Lay a leaf on a cutting board. Place 1 heaping tablespoon of the filling in the center of the leaf. Fold the bottom of the leaf upwards over the filling, then the left side of the leaf over the filling, then the right side of the leaf over the filling, then roll upwards to close; turn the packet seam side down.

4. Place the dolma seam side down in the bottom of the pot, and continue with remaining leaves until all of the filling is used. You may have more than one layer of dolmas. Sprinkle the juice of the remaining 2 lemons over the dolmas, add 2 more cups of water, place a plate on top of the dolmas to prevent them from opening, and put on the lid. Place the pot over medium heat and bring it to a boil, then immediately reduce the heat to low and simmer, covered, for 2 hours, until the rice is cooked and the leaves are tender.

TIP: You can find wild organic grape leaves from wild grapes you might encounter (make sure they grew away from a road or far from field crops that may have been sprayed) or get them from an organic vineyard. You can also use organic leaves from a jar (many organic stores carry them)—in which case they do not need to be processed. ■

Huckleberry

GAYLUSSACIA, various species

TERROIR, the capacity for food and drink to convey the tastes and smells of their place of origin (see the Taste of a Place, page 265), is most noticeable in foodstuffs grown organically. Organic cultivation of any foodstuff is closer to nature than conventional cultivation, resulting in thrifty plants that have every advantage for acquiring some special (and very desirable) characteristic of the local air and soil. On the other hand, the application of chemical fertilizers and pesticides disrupts the naturally occurring mix of organisms found at the spot where the plant grows, destroying any native taste of the place, and resulting in a blander, more generic-tasting food.

With huckleberries, we're invariably dealing with wild plants that are as close to nature as you can get. The berries are small, and, like all wild things, their sweet, tart flavor is less obvious and more complicated, less diluted and more concentrated, than the taste of any of their tame cousins, such as blueberries.

THE ORGANIC FACTOR ▸ Almost all huckleberries are gathered from the wild, so while they're not organic, they are not likely to have been sprayed.

NUTRITION ▸ Huckleberries supply modest amounts of calcium, but their real nutritional benefit is the great amounts of delphinidin—one of the cancer-fighting anthocyanin antioxidants—they contain. They are even more potent than blueberries in that department.

TYPES ▸ As with a number of fruits that grow wild in the United States, huckleberries can be divided into eastern and western species. The eastern huckleberries, which grow east of the Rockies, are a member of the heath family, which also includes the *Vaccinium genus* (blueberries, bilberries, lingonberries, and cranberries), but fall under a separate genus, *Gaylussacia.* The most commonly found species is the black huckleberry, *Gaylussacia baccata,* with a delicious spicy flavor, a focused sweetness, and some crunchy seeds in the interior. The dwarf huckleberry, *Gaylussacia dumosa*, and the dark blue berries of *Gaylussacia frondosa* are less common but just as good to eat.

Western huckleberries, found along the coastal parts of northern California up through the Cascades and east to the Rockies, are really a form of *Vaccinium.* The most common are *Vaccinium membranaceum,* a tall woody shrub that produces fruit more abundantly than the *Gaylussacias,* along with two other species, *Vaccinium ovalifolium* and *Vaccinium deliciosum.* While good, these huckleberries don't have the spiciness of the *Gaylussacias.*

They are ripe toward the end of August and into September.

Huckleberries are rarely (if ever) cultivated and must be gathered from the wild, and again you must harvest them yourself or keep watch for their appearance at roadside stands or perhaps the occasional farmers' market.

SEASONALITY ◆ July and August for the Eastern huckleberries, late August for the Western type.

WHAT TO LOOK FOR ◆ Keep an eye peeled for bears, moose, and snakes while you're tramping around in the woods looking for huckleberries.

Eastern huckleberries are pretty woody shrubs, growing about 3 feet high. The Western types can grow to 8 feet or a little higher or lower. The bushes never seem to make large patches but

THE TASTE OF A PLACE

HIKING THE APPALACHIAN TRAIL brings one in contact with various wonders, among them bushes dotted with ripe, wild huckleberries between June and early July, growing near the trail—a sort of gift from Mother Nature to those who spend some time with her. The huckleberries that grow along the trail that runs along the spine of Blue Mountain, from Delaware Water Gap southwest to Hawk Mountain, possess a distinct, spicy wild flavor that I've not found in huckleberries anywhere else. A couple of years ago, my son sent me a jar of huckleberry jam for Christmas. When I tasted it, I knew right away where those huckleberries had grown. When I looked at the label, sure enough the purveyors were from Palmerton, a town at the foot of Blue Mountain about halfway along that stretch of trail.

The experience reminded me that all sorts of comestibles, not just huckleberries, can acquire a flavor peculiar to the place where they are grown. I've even noticed this effect in oysters. Malpeques from Nova Scotia, Blue Points from Long Island Sound, and Chincoteagues from the Virginia coast are all **Crassostrea virginica,** but they are very different in flavor and texture. And, I'd venture, such variations hold true with every growing thing to a greater or lesser degree.

rather appear in small groups here and there in open woodlands. Each bush produces a handful of huckleberries at most at any one time, so picking a lot of them involves some time searching and more time picking.

STORAGE AND PREPARATION ⚬ Huckleberries are so delicious you probably will eat them the day you pick them.

USES ⚬ These sweet-tart little berries have all the uses of blueberries or currants: in scones, on cereal, in fruit compotes, in muffins, on pastries, in ice cream, stuffed in pork, and of course in luscious pies. But by far the best way to enjoy them is straight off the bush during a nice walk in the woods.

HUCKLEBERRY GAME SAUCE

MAKES ABOUT 1 CUP

Huckleberries have an affinity for game, from roast pheasant or grouse to rabbit and venison.

2 cups huckleberries
2 tablespoons vintage port

Place the huckleberries and port in a nonreactive saucepan and slowly simmer for 15 minutes until the berries soften and the juice flows. If using Eastern huckleberries, you may want to press the mixture through a sieve to remove the seeds. Serve the sauce in a gravy boat. ▪

HUCKLEBERRY PIE

MAKES ONE 9-INCH PIE; SERVES 6 TO 8

Unless you're lucky enough to find huckleberries at a roadside stand, you'll have to work for your huckleberry pie. But the work will be worth it. Nothing tastes richer and fruitier, and it's especially good paired with vanilla ice cream.

Pastry for double-crust 9-inch pie (double the recipe on page 211)
1/2 cup sugar
1 tablespoon freshly squeezed lemon juice
1 tablespoon cornstarch
1 teaspoon ground cinnamon
4 cups fresh wild huckleberries
1 egg, beaten

1. Preheat oven to 350°F. Line a 9-inch pie plate with about two-thirds of the rolled-out pie dough, line the pastry with waxed paper and fill with pie weights, dry beans, or raw rice. Bake for 20 minutes, remove from oven, remove the weights and waxed paper, and let cool.

2. Turn the oven up to 375°F. In a bowl, gently toss the sugar, lemon juice, cornstarch, and cinnamon with the berries, then pour into the partially baked crust. Roll out the remaining dough and cut into 1/2-inch-wide strips; use these to make a latticework top. Trim off any excess crust and seal the edges to the rim with the back of a fork, being careful not to crack the crust underneath. Brush the lattice dough with the egg.

3. Bake about 45 minutes, until the lattice is golden brown and the filling is bubbling with juice. Cool on a rack before serving. ▪

Kiwifruit

ACTINIDIA DELICIOSA

IT'S HARD NOW to remember a time before kiwifruit became widely available in the United States, but that time was before the mid-1970s, when California plantings and large amounts of imported New Zealand fruit came on line. Before that, kiwis could sometimes be found at specialty shops, accompanied by a robust marketing campaign by New Zealand growers, but they were rare indeed, and exotic. They are exotic no more, of course, having taken their place among the wealth of fruits we enjoy.

Kiwifruit is a native of the Yangtze River Valley of northern China, although various species of its large, vigorous, woody vines can be found growing wild in forests around China, Indonesia, and India. Kiwifruit has also found a home very much to its liking in New Zealand, which is the second largest cultivated kiwi-growing nation in the world (Italy, oddly, is first).

The United States ranks seventh, and 95 percent of U.S. kiwifruit is grown in California. Cultivated kiwifruit grows beautifully in the San Francisco Bay Area, although occasionally, unseasonably mild winters may not give the vines enough winter chill for them to flower well. Kiwi vines are either male or female, meaning that all species and cultivated varieties need a male pollinator for fruit to form on the females.

THE ORGANIC FACTOR ◆ You should be able to find organic kiwifruit in most markets that sell organic produce. Most of it will come from New Zealand, which is far ahead of the United States in the production of organic kiwifruit. Zespri International is a worldwide exporter of organic kiwis to the United States and the European Union, among other destinations.

NUTRITION ◆ Kiwis have good stores of vitamin C—3 ounces provide almost twice the daily requirement for an adult.

TYPES ◆ The green-fleshed kiwifruit found in most stores are invariably a variety called Hayward. Another type of kiwi—the golden kiwi (*Actinidia chinensis*)—is becoming more available of late. It's virtually fuzzless, and some cultivars are pure golden yellow inside.

Besides these two, there are more cold-hardy types, notably vines of *Actinidia arguta,* which can withstand continental winters. Recently, this variety has moved from a novelty fruit into an economically important crop. The fruits are small, about the size of large table grapes, and the skins are edible and fuzzless. They were first an enthusiast's crop, planted around North America by backyard fruit growers, until Mark Hurst of Hurst's Berry Farm in Sheridan, Oregon, planted a large acreage and began to market the small fruits as "Baby Kiwi" in the late 1990s.

There's also an ornamental form of baby kiwi, *Actinidia kolomikta,* that has green, pinkish-red, and white leaves. This species, too, has very sweet little fruits. And there's a species called *Actinidia purpurea* that has a few cultivated varieties (Hardy Red, Ken's Red) with sweet, eat-all red-fleshed fruits, but these are not on the market at the present time. See Sources (page 517) for information on growing ornamental kiwis.

SEASONALITY ◆ In America, kiwifruit ripen in late November or December and can be held for months in controlled storage. They are hard and unyielding to finger pressure until they ripen, when they have a slight give under light pressure. If you find only hard ones, a few days to a week on the windowsill should relax and sweeten them, as their starches change to sugar as they ripen.

"Baby kiwis" are in season from September through November.

WHAT TO LOOK FOR ▸ Make sure the kiwis are sound—no cuts or breaks in the skin. And while they can give to slight pressure, they shouldn't feel mushy-soft.

STORAGE ▸ Kiwis store well in the fruit bowl at room temperature, but they can be kept for several weeks in the fridge.

USES ▸ The kiwi's sweet-acidic impression, bright emerald color, and flavor—reminiscent of gooseberries and strawberries—makes them a welcome addition to winter mixed fruit medleys. Their edgy tartness makes them a nice contrast to bananas and a simple and colorful canapé can be made of a slice of banana dipped in lemon juice (to prevent discoloring) under a wedge of peeled, sliced kiwifruit, topped with a halved blueberry or a raspberry and skewered with a toothpick.

Their pretty color makes round slices of peeled kiwifruit perfect for topping tarts and cheesecakes, and chunks of sweet, ripe kiwi can be added to plain organic nonfat yogurt. Although kiwifruit had a major vogue when it first became widely sold in America, I prefer to use it sparingly.

KIWI-LIME-STRAWBERRY SORBET

MAKES ABOUT 1 QUART

This sorbet is immoderately delicious. Serve it in Pecan Lace Tulips for a special treat. You'll need an ice cream maker for this dish. I wouldn't be caught without my Krups "Le Glacière."

2 cups sugar
1 pint fresh strawberries
2 kiwifruit, peeled and coarsely chopped
Juice of 2 limes
Pecan Lace Tulips (recipe follows)

1. Make a simple syrup by bringing 1 cup of water to a boil, adding the sugar, stirring until the sugar is dissolved, and then letting this mixture cool to room temperature.

2. In a blender, whiz 1 cup of the simple syrup with the strawberries, kiwis, and lime juice until they make a smooth puree. Transfer to the ice cream maker and process according to the manufacturer's instructions. I find that mine makes a rather loose sorbet, so I transfer the finished sorbet to a covered plastic container I've cooled in the freezer, and then freeze it overnight so it's firm and very cold for serving. ▪

Pecan Lace Tulips

MAKES 10 TULIPS

4 tablespoons butter
1/4 cup firmly packed brown sugar
1/4 cup light corn syrup
1/3 cup all-purpose flour, plus extra for the cookie sheets

½ cup finely chopped pecans
1 teaspoon vanilla extract

1. Preheat the oven to 350°F. Grease 2 cookie sheets and dust with flour, shaking off any excess.

2. Melt the butter in a 2-quart saucepan over medium heat. Slowly stir in the brown sugar and corn syrup. Turn up the heat until the mixture boils, stirring continually until the brown sugar dissolves. Remove immediately from the heat and stir in the flour and the pecans. Add the vanilla and stir until all is well incorporated.

3. Drop rounded tablespoons of batter onto the cookie sheets at least 6 inches apart until the sheets are full, using the back of a spoon and a circular motion to spread the batter into thin, even circles about 6 inches in diameter. You should have about 10 cookies, 5 per sheet.

4. Bake one sheet at a time for 8 to 10 minutes, until the tulips are browned. Remove from the oven and let stand for 30 to 45 seconds. Then carefully but quickly remove each cookie from the sheet with a spatula and drape it, bumpy side down, over an inverted 3-inch diameter water glass, making the top flat and smoothing the sides so they form a tulip shaped cup that sits upright when removed and turned right side up. If the cookies cool so much they become difficult to shape, return them to the oven for a few moments until they become pliable. Bake the second sheet and repeat until all cups are made. Cool completely. Set the tulips on serving plates and fill with a scoop of the kiwi-lime-strawberry sorbet. ■

Longan and Litchi

DIMOCARPUS LONGAN and
LITCHI CHINENSIS

LONGANS are native to Southeast Asia and are associated most closely with Thailand. They're similar in size and taste to their relative, the litchi, which is native to sourthern China, and, like the litchi, have a thin, tan- to cinnamon-colored shell that peels away from the translucent white flesh underneath. Unlike the freestone litchi, the longan's flesh clings to the single, hard, black seed at the center of the fruit, giving it the common name, Dragon's Eye. Breeders are working on developing a freestone longan.

Longans are planted in Hawaii, California, and Florida, with large-scale production (over 1,000 trees) underway in south Florida. Most litchis are grown in the favorable climate of southern China, but some are grown in Hawaii, Florida, and California.

THE ORGANIC FACTOR ✦ While longans are not yet a well-known fruit, there are organic longans as well as litchis on the market. Saw Mill Farm in Miami, Florida, sells both fruits and will ship (see Sources, page 517).

NUTRITION ✦ The longan is low in calories and a good source of potassium and magnesium, similar to the composition of litchis.

SEASONALITY ✦ The fresh fruit season for longans begins in mid-July and extends through August. Much of the crop is sold fresh, but some is frozen, which extends the season. Litchis tend to ripen a few weeks later.

WHAT TO LOOK FOR ◆ They are usually found in Asian markets in the United States, although that is changing and they are beginning to show up in mainstream markets.

STORAGE ◆ Either eat fresh or freeze. They can also be dried. When litchis are dried within their rinds, they are known as litchi nuts.

USES ◆ Longans are mostly used for fresh eating out of hand. Longans acquire a rich, smoky flavor when dried, and Asian markets sell the dried fruits, mostly imported, for cooking and making teas. Litchis are found fresh, canned, and dried.

Loquat

ERIOBOTRYA JAPONICA

I'D NEVER TASTED a loquat (also called a Japanese plum) until I moved to Sonoma County, California, where their large-leaved, dense trees grow all over the place. That's because the climate there is near perfect for this native of southeastern China. It's not too hot and humid or too cool— conditions under which the tree won't set fruit. But when it does set fruit, what wonderful fruit it sets! Each fruit is about one to two inches in length, round to oval, with yellow to orange skin that sometimes shows a red blush. The skin is smooth or very lightly downy. The flesh inside is succulent, tangy, and apricot- like but juicier. Each fruit has from three to five large brown seeds. I suppose kids who live in coastal California and Florida might have a favorite loquat tree that they visit when the fruits are ripe—the way kids in other parts of the country know where the best apples grow.

Loquat fruits are fragile and need to be hand-harvested by snipping them from the panicles (hanging pyramidal clusters of fruit), leaving a stub of woody tissue attached—if this is pulled off, the fruits tear open and immediately spoil. Loquats must be ripened to a soft stage on the tree, because they don't ripen off the tree and if picked too early will be unpleasantly acidic. When you do find them, it's usually just a few basketsful at farmers' markets or roadside stands. (See Sources, page 517.)

While the loquat seems to especially like northern California, it will grow well where winter minimum temperatures are 12 to 15 degrees Fahrenheit, and it is frequently planted as an ornamental for its big leaves and the dense shade it throws. It will fruit sporadically south of Jacksonville, Florida.

THE ORGANIC FACTOR ◆ Most growers don't spray them, so it's likely loquats will be pesticide-free, if not organic.

NUTRITION ◆ Loquats are a good source of phosphorus, potassium, and beta-carotene, the precursor to vitamin A. The edible peel is five times richer in this nutrient than the pulp.

SEASONALITY ◆ Sweetly—some think intensely—scented flowers appear in late fall or early winter, followed the next spring by panicles of fruits in clusters that range from as few as four to as many as thirty. Depending on the variety, the fruit can ripen as early as February or as late as May.

WHAT TO LOOK FOR ◆ Make sure they are soft and ripe—unripe loquats are sour. Look at the stem end and make sure that it hasn't torn. Blotchy freckles on one side of the fruit usually are simply an indication they've been exposed to strong sun on that side.

STORAGE ► Eat them as soon as possible. Loquats don't store well.

USES ► Loquats make excellent jams, jellies, tarts, and fruit chutneys to accompany sweet meats such as duck and pork. Loquats are high in sugar, acid, and pectin until dead ripe. As they become fully ripe, they lose some of their pectin, so commercial pectin may be needed to firm up jams and jellies.

Most loquats are eaten out of hand, but the peeled and seeded fruit will star with other fruits in a raw compote—especially with orange segments, sliced banana, and shredded coconut—because of the intensity of their flavor. They can be used in pies and tarts and can be poached in a light sugar syrup.

LOQUAT AND STRAWBERRY JAM

MAKES ABOUT 8 TO 10 HALF-PINT JARS

As the loquat season is winding down, the strawberry season is coming on. Happily, the two overlap, and this recipe combines the fruits beautifully.

2 cups strawberries
3 cups peeled and seeded loquats
1 box fruit pectin
7 cups sugar

1. Trim and wash the strawberries. Slice them in half and put them in a large nonreactive saucepan with the loquats. Add $1/2$ cup of water. Cook gently over low heat, and when the fruit begins to soften, mash with a potato masher until the ingredients form a thick paste—this will take about 10 to 15 minutes. Stir occasionally to prevent sticking or burning.

2. Add the pectin and stir it in until it dissolves, stirring from the bottom to prevent sticking. Turn up the heat until it achieves a rolling boil, stirring frequently. Add the sugar and boil until the sugar has dissolved and the mixture has boiled for one minute. Immediately pack into sterilized jelly jars and seal according to jar manufacturer's directions. (See page 241 for more information on canning.) ■

Mango

MANGIFERA INDICA

TAKE A GUESS as to the most-consumed fruit in the world. We in the United States might guess banana or apple, but the answer is mango. The mango is a native of India and Southeast Asia—thus the species name *Indica*. It's a tropical fruit grown only in Hawaii, South Florida, and southern California in the United States, but these plantings are not large. Most of our organic mangoes come from Mexico, with some also coming from Haiti, Jamaica, and Trinidad and Tobago.

On a visit to a fishing village on the island of Tobago, I was pleasantly surprised to find mangoes growing everywhere, not only as dooryard trees but also along streets and at the edges of tropical forests. I discovered just how delicious tree-ripened and unsprayed mangoes can be. Their flesh was meltingly sweet but with a tartness that only added to their succulence. Late in the day, women made mango sauce. Its volatile, piney, floral-sappy aroma and flavor added gustatory color to the delicately fleshed fish that the men of the village catch in purse seines and haul in every afternoon.

THE ORGANIC FACTOR ► Conventionally grown mangoes from other countries, especially Mexico, may have been heavily sprayed with toxic

KEEP AN EYE OUT FOR FAIR TRADE MANGOES

MANY ORGANIC MANGOES are certified as Fair Trade products by Transfair USA, which insures that the workers and growers involved in producing the food have the right to organize and bargain collectively. It's important that the farmers we support with our organic food dollars are not exploited but are able to sell their environmentally sound fruit at a price that assures them dignity and a decent standard of living. People wonder why organic produce costs more than conventional when they imagine that organic simply means using fewer agricultural inputs. The answer, of course, is that organics is not about farming cheaply and maximizing profits for corporations. The organic bottom line supports a system of producing food that's healthy for the environment, fair to the farm workers, profitable for the businesspeople, and safe, wholesome, and tasty for consumers.

chemicals, so it's important to look for organic mangoes. Look for the name of the organic certifying agency on the fruit. If it's not there, ask the produce manager who certified it and ask to see the paperwork. If there is no produce manager and you just have to take someone's word for it, assume they are conventionally grown and being passed off as organic. I always avoid conventional mangoes because I know that they often come from countries that may not have the same kind of pesticide controls that we do.

NUTRITION ▸ A typical 7-ounce mango contains 90 percent of the recommended daily allowance of vitamin C, 75 percent of beta-carotene, 24 percent of vitamin E, and is a good source of fiber and trace minerals.

SEASONALITY ▸ In the northern hemisphere, the season is July through September, but many varieties will produce some mangoes at other seasons.

WHAT TO LOOK FOR ▸ The mangoes we get here in the United States tend to be picked unripe and hard, and they must be allowed to ripen when we get them home. The process can be hastened

by placing the mangoes in a paper bag with an apple, which gives off natural ethylene gas, a ripening agent. When the mango is ripe, it softens and yields to gentle pressure, like the stem end of a ripe pear when pressed with the thumb. Some mango varieties develop a warm yellowish color with a rich red blush as they ripen, while others keep a green cast, so don't go by skin color alone. Don't pass up mangoes that have a few black spots on their skins—that can mean they have a high sugar content. But don't buy any that are squishy-soft, shriveling, or showing signs of decay. I find that a mango ripened at home is a fair approximation of the tree-ripened fruit—but only fair.

STORAGE AND PREPARATION ▸ Mango flesh can be diced and frozen or dried, but fresh mangoes themselves will last for a week or two on the kitchen counter. Don't store in the fridge.

The simplest way I know to prepare a mango for eating, given that its yellow flesh clings to the very large but flat fibrous seed inside, is to stand the fruit upright on its stem end with the narrow side facing you. With a sharp knife, slice off the left and right sides of the fruit, getting as close to the sides of the pit as possible without including the fibers. Lay each slab flat, score it vertically and horizontally, being careful not to cut into the skin. Now turn it inside out so that the fruity part becomes convex. Either get your face in there and have a good and messy time, or slice off the squares with your knife. Trim the remaining skin from the narrow sides of the pit and recover the fruit that clings to it.

USES ▸ Ripe mangoes mix beautifully with other tropical and semitropical fruits like citrus and bananas. Puree ripe mango flesh to make sorbet or to use as a sauce with white-fleshed tropical fish like grouper and escolar. Unripe mangoes are useful, too. They are the main ingredient in mango chutney (see below) and make a tangy pickle. Unripe mangoes are firm to the touch, even on the shoulder of the fruit at the stem end.

MANGO CHUTNEY

MAKES ABOUT 1 QUART

Unripe mangoes give this chutney extra tang and a firm and chunky texture. You can use this chutney to grace crispy duck, with Indian-style curries, as well as many other ways.

FOR THE CHUTNEY BASE

3 firm, unripe mangoes
1/2 cup distilled white vinegar
1/3 cup sugar
1 teaspoon salt
1/4 cup raisins

FOR THE SEASONING

1 knob ginger, about the size of your thumb, peeled
1 fresh jalapeño pepper
5 cloves garlic
1 teaspoon ground cumin
1 teaspoon ground coriander
1/2 teaspoon ground turmeric
2 tablespoons canola oil
1 cinnamon stick (3 to 4 inches)
2 whole star anise

1. To prepare the chutney base: Peel and cube the mangoes. In a medium bowl, mix the mangoes with the vinegar, sugar, salt, and raisins. Reserve.

2. To prepare the seasoning: Cut the ginger into small pieces. Seed and roughly chop the jalapeño. Place the ginger in a food processor or blender and puree, adding a small amount of water if necessary; one at a time, add the jalapeño, garlic, cumin, coriander, and turmeric, and puree, to blend everything into a paste.

3. Heat a large, heavy pot over moderately low heat until hot. Add the oil. Add the seasoning paste, cinnamon stick, and star anise, and cook for 10 minutes, stirring frequently. Stir in the mango mixture, cover, reduce heat to low, and simmer, stirring occasionally, until mango chunks are tender, about 30 minutes. Discard the cinnamon stick and star anise and transfer the chutney to a jar with a lid—a Mason jar is perfect. Allow it to cool, and store covered in the fridge for up to 3 weeks. Or freeze in small freezer bags for a year. ▪

Mangosteen

GARCINIA MANGOSTANA

One of the most praised of tropical fruits. The flesh is slightly acid and mild to distinctly acid in flavor and is acclaimed as exquisitely luscious and delicious.

JULIA F MORTON, *Fruits of Warm Climates*

The texture of the mangosteen pulp much resembles that of a well-ripened plum, only it is so delicate that it melts in the mouth like a bit of ice cream. The flavor is quite indescribably delicious. There is nothing to mar the perfection of this fruit...

DAVID FAIRCHILD, *Exploring for Plants*

THE MANGOSTEEN must be included in this book because of its reputation as the most delicious fruit in the world. It grows primarily in Southeast Asia and the Philippines, and during its summer season it sometimes shows up in Asian markets in Canada and Europe. I found it just once in a Chinatown market in San Francisco, and I tried it with great anticipation. But, alas, it had been frozen and the pulp inside had gone off. I have also found it canned, but it was indistinguishable from canned litchi. Julia Morton, in her survey of the world's tropical fruits, says that the pasteurization needed for canning kills the fruit's delicate flavor. Freezing does, too. The USDA bans the importation of mangosteen from Southeast Asia because they may harbor pests, but the USDA doesn't know which ones. "Better safe than sorry" is the USDA rationale for banning them. They can be imported from the Caribbean, but no one is growing them there for export. Some growers are beginning to experiment with mangosteen culture in Hawaii—so keep your eye out for them.

I keep looking for fresh mangosteen. The season for mangosteen is between June and September, so that's the time to haunt your Asian markets. Keep your eyes peeled for dark purple fruits about the size and shape of a tennis ball or baseball. One cuts off the top half of the fruit's shell with a sharp knife, exposing five, six, or seven white segments loosely held in the bottom half, or cup. These are very sweet with about 15 percent sugar and a lovely flavor (so I hear). It's extremely unlikely you'll find this coveted fruit at a farmers' market.

Although the mangosteen is made into jams and ice creams in Indonesia and other countries where it's plentiful, the fruit is most often eaten out of hand, and that certainly is the way I'll eat it in order to enjoy its full fresh flavor unalloyed. If I ever find it, that is.

Mayapple

PODOPHYLLUM PELTATUM

*And will any poet sing
Of a richer, lusher thing
Than a ripe May-Apple, rolled
Like a pulpy lump of gold
Under thumb and fingertips,
And poured molten through the lips?*

JAMES WHITCOMB RILEY,
Rhymes of Childhood, 1890

MAYAPPLES are herbaceous perennials that grow to 1½ feet tall in the eastern woodlands and produce a round, edible fruit. Some say mayapples taste like lemons, and they do have a lemony, acidic note to them. But more noticeable is their floral fragrance and a sweet flavor that's almost too sweet. The 19th-century botanist Asa Gray described this flavor as "somewhat mawkish, beloved of pigs, raccoons, and small boys." Gray was right about that—when the fruits are ripe, you will have to beat the raccoons to get them. Except for the ripe fruits, every part of the plant, including the unripe fruit and seeds, is very poisonous and was used by Eastern Native Americans as a purgative and emetic.

Although their fruit does not often reach markets, mayapples are fairly ubiquitous, growing in areas that receive decent summer rainfall anywhere east of the Rockies from Canada to Florida. The woods' edges and old fields returning to forest around my boyhood home were lavishly colonized by mayapples, which we boys called "umbrella plants" because each plant's single stem rises about 6 to 10 inches above the ground, then splits into a Y shape, the split stems hoisting two broad leaves another 6 inches or more above the split, which together resemble an umbrella held above the ground. These leaves hold themselves parallel to the ground, and a colony of these wild perennials looks like a group of umbrellas waiting for a rain.

THE ORGANIC FACTOR ✦ There is no commercial culture of mayapples. If you find them, they have been gathered from the wild.

SEASONALITY ✦ Between April and June, depending on latitude, a single white flower with yellow stamens emerges from the split in the stem. After pollination, a small, egg-shaped green fruit grows, and by September reaches the size of a small hen's egg, turning yellow as it ripens and the plant itself begins withering. It's only edible at this stage.

WHAT TO LOOK FOR ✦ I have seen them sold at roadside stands, usually gathered from the woods by farm boys to make pocket money. If you find mayapples at a stand or gather them yourself from the woods, make sure the fruits are yellow, soft, and ripe.

STORAGE ✦ Eat soon after you find them.

USES ✦ Mayapples are mostly eaten fresh out of hand, but they can be seeded and made into jams, jellies, and marmalades. The interior of the very fragrant fruit—it has a sweet, almost cloying aroma—is jelly-like, with seeds that must be spit out.

Medlar

MESPILUS GERMANICA

THE MEDLAR is a rare fruit in the United States, and that's a shame. It was a favorite dessert fruit of 19th-century Britain. A box of moist sawdust or bran would be brought to the table along with a decanter of port. Fully bletted medlars would be fished out of the box, and the pulp inside—something of the consistency of apple butter—would be spooned into a bowl and mixed with sugar and cream. A bite of medlar, a sip of port, and there you have it: a Victorian dessert.

What? You've never heard of medlars? And what's a "fully bletted" anything, let alone a medlar?

The medlar was known to the Greeks and Romans. Around 800 CE, Charlemagne ordered it planted on his lands in the town of Aachen in what is now far western Germany. It was widely cultivated in Tudor England and even today seems somehow associated with medieval and Renaissance banquets.

Medlars grow on a handsome tree that's a member of the rose family, along with the hawthorn, quince, and apple. If you consider the fruits of any of these plants, they have an opening at the blossom end, surrounded by a raised fringe of calyxes. Medlars are no exception, having a very large opening in which you can see the fruit's five seed capsules. Each fruit is about the size of a golf ball.

Mature medlars must undergo a process called bletting; that is, they need to decompose and soften. This is not so strange. We do it to our persimmons in the fall and winter. To prevent spoilage, the medlars are usually bletted in a box of moist sawdust or bran, where the inner pulp turns brown, acidic, and soft, with a brisk flavor of decaying apples and cinnamon that many like, but some don't. The pulp is certainly sweet, with an 11 percent sugar content when ripe.

THE ORGANIC FACTOR ‣ Medlars aren't grown in commerce but may occasionally be found in farmers' markets. Ask the purveyor whether they've been grown organically.

NUTRITION ‣ Medlars are sweet yet low in calories (around 50 calories per 3½ ounces). They have good stores of potassium, calcium, iron, magnesium, and vitamins B and C. Medlars have antioxidants and are high in soluble fiber.

TYPES ‣ There's only one type, but several varieties. Take whichever you can get—there are many, including Royal and Giant Russian. You are most likely to get Nottingham, which is the most widely planted and is reputed to be the most highly flavored and the best in cultivation.

SEASONALITY ‣ When the fruits are mature and ready for picking—usually in late fall after the first hard frost—their skins are green and hard and astringent. They must then undergo bletting over several weeks after being picked. If you're traveling in England in December, you might find medlars in the stores then.

WHAT TO LOOK FOR ‣ Finding medlars at a farmers' market will be sheer serendipity—but they are out there. Just don't eat them until they are fully bletted, a process that will take them to late fall or winter, depending on the temperature where they're stored. They're ready when they've turned brown and yield softly to gentle pressure.

STORAGE ‣ Store them in a cupboard at room temperature until they soften.

USES ‣ Francesca Greensack, in her book, *Forgotten Fruit*, wrote, "The lingering, slightly sweet, slightly winey flavor makes the medlar seem like a natural comfit." And George Saintsbury, in his famous book on wine, *Notes on a Cellar*, wrote: "The one fruit that to me seems to go best with all wine, from hock to sherry and from claret to port, is the medlar—an admirable and distinguished thing in itself, and a worthy mate for the best of liquors." It's that acid briskness and fermented flavor that makes the medlar so natural with rich red wines such as port, cabernet sauvignon, syrah, and perhaps best of all, a glass of inky Charbono. Medlars can be eaten as is, if you are one of those who like its unadulterated flavor. But they can also be roasted with butter and cloves as a traditional English-style winter dessert. The soft pulp can be folded into whipped cream and sugar and chilled for a mousse. Another traditional use is as a jelly to accompany game. And they can be stewed with sugar. But many say that medlars are at their best when beaten with eggs and butter into a curd that's called medlar cheese.

MEDLAR CHEESE

SERVES 4

Serve this as the dessert, along with port, to complete a true English dinner of roast beef, Yorkshire pudding, and mushy peas.

3 eggs
1/2 cup sugar
2/3 cup fully bletted medlar pulp (3 or 4 fruits)
2 tablespoons unsalted butter, diced
Few drops vanilla extract

In a saucepan, whisk the eggs and sugar until smooth and light in color. Add the medlar pulp and butter and set the pan on medium-low heat, continually whisking until the butter is melted and incorporated and the mixture thickens and simmers gently for just a few seconds. Remove from the heat and whisk in the vanilla. Turn the mixture into a serving bowl and let cool. Cover and refrigerate to thicken it further. Use within a week. ■

Melon

CUCUMIS MELO and
CITRULLUS LANATUS

IT TOOK ME YEARS to figure out how to grow really sweet melons. The secret was to keep the vines up off the ground, in full sun, and give them a gentle sulfur spray after each rain—all organic methods designed to keep the leaves free of mildew.

The leaves of melons are the sugar factories, and melons are particularly susceptible to molds and mildews that shut down the leaves' ability to manufacture sugar. With their sugar factories shut down,

the melons, where the sugar is stored, don't get sweet.

THE ORGANIC FACTOR ▸ In California's warm, dry summer climate, melons are less prone to develop mildewed leaves, and so the state produces most of the commercial melons shipped around the United States. Sulfur spray is the chief way melon farmers—both conventional and organic—prevent mildew. However, 1,3-dichloropropene is used by conventional melon farmers to combat nematodes, which are tiny worms that attack plant roots. Animal studies show that this chemical is a carcinogen and the U.S. Department of Health and Human Services says it anticipates that it is a human carcinogen as well. In addition, it can adversely affect the health of farm workers. This is reason enough to search out organic melons, but there are other reasons besides safety.

Organic growers serving local markets are more likely to plant the best-tasting types of melons because they don't have to worry about shipping ability like big conventional growers, who ship across the country. Proximity to market means they can let those melons ripen on their vines. In addition, melons are heavy feeders and rich, organic soil supplies a panoply of nutrients. Such soil holds water like a sponge, keeping the wilt-prone melons supplied with plenty of water. All these factors contribute to the luscious flavor of well-grown organic melons.

NUTRITION ▸ None of the melons is very high in nutrients, since most are mainly water. But more nutritious varieties of melons are being developed. The darker orange-fleshed melons are higher in beta-carotene, the precursor of vitamin A, than green- or white-fleshed types.

TYPES ▸ We usually lump cantaloupes, musk-melons, honeydews, canary, Crenshaw, and water-melons under the heading of melon, but it pays to be a little more categorical. The first five melons in that list are all *Cucumis melo*, while watermelons are *Citrullus lanatus*, another genus and species.

CANTALOUPES (named after the town of Cantalupo near Rome) are generally considered to be the best-tasting melons. Most of the melons that supermarkets label as cantaloupes, however, are actually muskmelons. A true cantaloupe is about the size of a baseball, with a gray-green, hard rind with some bumps or scales, but no netting. Although they have been hard to find in the United States, organic specialty farmers are grow-ing more of them in recent years. A variety called Charentais is the best known, and in France, they serve a particularly ambrosial dish of half a Charentais with a splash of sweet dessert wine, such as a Barsac, in its empty seed cavity (see recipe Charentais Melon Cockaigne, page 279, for a version of this). To be picked vine-ripe, they're cut from the vine when the rind color half-changes from gray-green to buff, so look for that buff color when choosing them. Also, give the blossom end a whiff. It should have a faint aroma of melon.

MUSKMELONS, on the other hand, are so named for the pleasant but definite musky smell they develop when ripe, and a whiff of the blos-som end of a ripe muskmelon will strongly tell you that it's ready to eat. Also, their blossom ends will yield to moderate thumb pressure, telling they're ready or very soon will be. As long as the melons are sound, you can let them ripen a few days more on the kitchen counter, where they'll become even more meltingly delicious, but don't let them go past the point of perfection or they'll only be good

for sorbet. Their flesh can be green, salmon or or-ange, or white. The rinds of the green and white-fleshed types turn golden yellow when ripe.

HONEYDEWS slip when ripe—that is, their fruits separate easily from the stems that attach them to the mother plant. They have cream-colored rinds and green or orange flesh. As with muskmelons, they are ripe when the blossom end softens and yields to moderate thumb pressure. They carry a lovely fragrance.

CRENSHAW melons are a unique sort of *Cucumis melo* with a fine flavor all their own. Their salmon-pink flesh is spicy-sweet and refresh-ing.

CANARY melons are a type of winter melon, which means they keep well into the winter months. Their rinds are bright yellow and their white flesh has an orange lining by the seed cavity. They develop a softening at the blossom end when ripe.

WATERMELONS make summer heat waves fun—or as much fun as they can be. Find Sugar Baby watermelons (or better yet, Seedless Sugar Baby), with their green-black rind, and keep them chilled in the fridge. They're only 6 to 8 inches in diameter and their sweetness and flavor is better than most varieties. Among the full-size watermel-ons, the Charleston Gray is a standard of quality in the East. Flesh colors range from yellow to or-ange to bright red among many varieties. As for quality, I don't think I've ever met a watermelon I didn't like. If your melons are organic, you can have the added pleasure of making pickled water-melon rind to serve with your grilled hamburgers.

SEASONALITY ✦ Melons take the better part of the summer to ripen, and so their season begins in late July and runs until winter, with a peak quality coming in late August and early September.

WHAT TO LOOK FOR ✦ Most melons are ripe when their blossoms ends have a distinct fruity aroma. Watermelons are ripe when the light spot where they rested as they grew turns a yellowish color and they sound hollow when thumped.

STORAGE AND PREPARATION ✦ Melons store well on the kitchen counter or in the fridge for up to three weeks. When the organic melons are at their peak, freeze some for winter and spring consumption. To do this, remove the seeds and rinds from melons and cut the flesh into bite-sized chunks, or make balls with a melon baller. Then, either freeze these chunks in one layer on a cookie sheet and dry pack the frozen chunks into freezer bags, or wet pack them in a sugar syrup (1 cup of water to ⅓ cup of superfine sugar) in freezer bags, leaving a little head space, and freeze. Thaw gently in a bowl of warm water when it comes time to use them, and serve when they still have a little ice in them but have come free of the sugar syrup.

USES ✦ I find that melon slices all by themselves make a perfect dessert, but they do brighten up when I squeeze some lime juice on them. Melon balls make a fine addition to salads, especially paired with pineapple chunks, and to gelatin molds.

Use seedless watermelons or seed 3 cups of watermelon flesh by squishing them through a strainer. Then whiz them in a blender with ½ cup of water, ½ cup of sugar, and 2 teaspoons of freshly squeezed lemon juice. You can make a sorbet with this mixture, or make popsicles for the kids (of all ages).

MELON AND MANGO

SERVES 4

A simple combination, but oh-so-delicious. A vine-ripened muskmelon or watermelon would be the choice for the melon side of this marriage. If using watermelon, finding a seedless, icebox-sized fruit (6 to 8 inches in diameter) makes the job easier.

3 pounds bite-size melon chunks (about 6 cups)
2 mangoes, cut into 1-inch chunks (for cutting instructions, see page 272)
Juice of 1 lime
1 teaspoon freshly grated lime zest (well scrubbed if not organic)
½ teaspoon quick dissolving sugar

Toss all the ingredients in a bowl, then chill in the fridge for at least half an hour. ▪

CHARENTAIS MELON COCKAIGNE

SERVES 4

If you can lay your hands on vine-ripened Charentais, make this. Your dinner guests will be singing your praises as they walk out the door.

2 vine-ripened Charentais cantaloupes
Juice of 1 lemon
½ pint fresh strawberries
1 banana
½ pint fresh red raspberries
½ cup sweet white dessert wine, such as Sauternes, Barsac, or Beaumes-de-Venise
½ teaspoon vanilla extract

continued

1. Scrape out the seeds from the cantaloupes, coat the exposed flesh with lemon juice and reserve.

2. Stem and dice the strawberries; dice the banana. Place them in a bowl with the raspberries, dessert wine, and vanilla. Gently toss, then fill the melon halves with the fruit mixture. Snuggle each half into a bed of crushed ice so it stands upright. ▪

Nectarine

PRUNUS PERSICA variety
NUCIPERSICA

NECTARINES are actually fuzzless peaches, or peaches are fuzzy nectarines. They are both *Prunus persica*, although as breeding carries nectarines farther and farther from peaches, they are classed in the subgroup *nucipersica*. The *New Oxford Book of Food Plants*, however, calls them *Prunus persica* variety *nectarina,* and other sources put them in a separate genus altogether, calling them *Amygdalus persica, Nucipersica* group. The fact remains that peach trees may occasionally produce nectarines and vice versa, the two fruits being that close botanically.

Evidence shows that nectarines were cultivated in their native China as early as 2000 BCE. They arrived in Greece by 300 BCE. From there they were brought to Rome, and then went on to take their place among the world's best fruits.

THE ORGANIC FACTOR ▸ More than 150 varieties are grown in California, which produces most of the country's commercial nectarine crop. It's heavily sprayed. California growers use numerous pesticides, fungicides, and herbicides on the nectarine crop. Organic treatments such as sulfur, dormant oil spray, and treatment with *Bacillus thuringiensis* obviate the need for such chemicals.

This, combined with the fact that the best varieties of nectarine do not ship well, or are shipped unripe, means it's wise to seek out organic fruit sold as close to the source as possible. Here in California it's not hard to find roadside stands or farms selling organic nectarines in season. In other areas of the country, nectarines are grown wherever peaches can be grown and often peach growers will also have some nectarines for sale. That covers most of the United States except for the coldest regions or those prone to early warming and late hard frosts.

NUTRITION ▸ Nectarines have about 8 to 10 percent sugar when ripe, good stores of potassium, and excellent amounts of vitamin C (31 milligrams per 100 grams).

TYPES ▸ Until the mid-1980s, breeders discarded most white-fleshed hybrids in favor of yellow-fleshed varieties because the market demanded yellow, and because whites are more prone to bruising during shipping. It was the Asian markets that were willing to pay for extra sweet, low-acid white varieties. Other ethnicities also shopped Asian markets, and soon the white varieties caught on. Today you'll find both white and yellow kinds in most markets. Like peaches, nectarines have freestone, semifreestone, and cling forms.

SEASONALITY ▸ Nectarine season runs from mid-June to September.

WHAT TO LOOK FOR ▸ When you do find nectarines, whether at a farm, roadside stand, farmers' market, or organic produce section of a

TO PEEL OR NOT TO PEEL

THE SKINS AND PEELS of certain fruits and vegetables contain a wealth of nutrients, but when conventionally grown, they also tend to hold the most concentrated amounts of pesticides. That's why we're accustomed to peeling produce such as carrots. But with organic produce, you can go ahead and leave the carrot skin on—just give it a good washing.

Here is a list of fruits and vegetables that don't have to be peeled, even when eaten raw, as long as they're organic.

FRUITS		VEGETABLES	
Apples	Nectarine	Carrot	Radish
Apricots	Peach	Kohlrabi	Rutabaga
Asian pears	Pear	Parsnip	Salsify
Citrus (zest)	Plum	Potatoes	Turnip

supermarket, make sure there's no green on the skins, and that the fruits aren't hard. Such under-ripe fruit will start to shrivel and never turn sweet before they soften. With white-fleshed varieties, the skins should show a creamy white base color with a pronounced red blush—if you can find the Snow Queen variety (see Sources, page 517), snap them up. For yellow-fleshed varieties, the base color should be yellowish to yellow-orange, with a rosy reddish blush. Gently press the rim of the fruit that surrounds the stem. It should yield a bit to thumb pressure.

STORAGE ◆ Almost-ripe nectarines can finish ripening at home. Sit them on the kitchen counter out of direct sun for a few days. Or place them together in a paper bag. They'll be fully ripe when the raised suture that circles the fruit yields to gentle pressure.

USES ◆ You can't beat nectarines for eating out of hand when they're pulled ripe and sun-warm right off the tree, but otherwise use them as you would peaches. Nectarines mix beautifully with blueberries, blackberries, raspberries, and plums in cobblers, tarts, and pies. They can anchor a fruit salad. Nectarine sherbets and ice creams are delightful. Mix nectarine slices with slices of fresh figs tossed with a little orange juice and given a very light dusting of cinnamon, and garnish with a sprig of mint. Make an easy nectarine jam by cooking peeled, pitted, rough-chopped nectarines with half as much sugar by volume plus fresh lemon juice to taste. Cook over medium-low heat, stirring occasionally, for 30 minutes. Skim the foam off the top, then process as for any jam: Pack the mixture in sterile jelly jars, then place in a boiling water bath for 5 minutes. The jar lids should seal within an hour. If they don't, reprocess. (See page 241 for more information on canning.)

NECTARINE-BLACKBERRY COBBLER

SERVES 4

Nectarines have an affinity for blackberries that makes this summer cobbler a real treat. This recipe calls for a quick cobbler dough. You also can use Nora Pouillon's recipe for cobbler dough (page 230), which is a little more elaborate but also a little more refined.

5 tablespoons cold unsalted butter, plus extra for the pan
1 cup white sugar
2 teaspoons cornstarch
2 large nectarines, pitted and coarsely chopped
2 cups ripe blackberries
1 cup all-purpose flour
1 teaspoon baking powder
1/4 teaspoon salt
1/2 cup milk
1/2 cup brown sugar
1/4 cup crushed almonds

1. Preheat the oven to 350°F. Butter an 8-inch round or square baking dish. In a medium bowl, combine 2/3 cup of the white sugar, cornstarch, nectarines, and blackberries and gently toss to coat evenly.

2. In a separate bowl, mix the flour, the remaining 1/3 cup white sugar, baking powder, and salt. When well combined, cut in the butter with 2 knives until the mixture looks like coarse meal. Add the milk and stir just until well combined. If it seems too stiff, add a tablespoon or two of milk or water but not enough to make the mixture loose and runny.

3. Spread the fruit mixture in the bottom. Drop the dough by spoonfuls onto the fruit to cover. Mix together the brown sugar and crushed almonds and sprinkle evenly over the top. Loosely cover with a piece of aluminum foil and bake for 1 hour, removing the foil during the last 5 minutes of baking so the top is melted and golden. ▪

NECTARINE-VIOGNIER FIZZ

SERVES 6 PEOPLE ONCE OR 3 TWICE

This refreshing summer drink combines the lux qualities of nectarines with the floral-fruity flavor of viognier, made from a white Rhône grape variety now widely grown in California. Start this a day ahead and serve it before an outdoor barbecue. The fizzier the club soda, the better.

1 vanilla bean, split in half lengthwise
1/2 cup sugar
1 cup fresh mint leaves
1 bottle viognier, chilled
2 ripe nectarines, pitted and sliced
2 limes, sliced thin (well scrubbed if not organic)
2 oranges, sliced thin and seeded (well scrubbed if not organic)
2 cups cold, fizzy club soda

1. The day before, in a medium saucepan, combine 1 cup of water, the vanilla bean, and the sugar and bring to a boil, then remove from the heat. Add half the mint leaves. Cover, cool to room temperature, and refrigerate overnight.

2. The next day, remove and discard the vanilla bean and mint. Pour the liquid into a large pitcher. Add the viognier, the nectarine slices, and the lime and orange slices; stir and chill in the fridge for several hours.

3. Just before serving, place ice in tall glasses, pour the club soda into the pitcher, stir once to mix, and fill glasses, allowing a few fruit slices into each glass. Garnish with a couple of fresh mint leaves. Serve immediately. ▪

Olive

OLEA EUROPAEA

MANY ANCIENT CULTURES thought of olives and their oil as the best gift (along with wine) that the gods ever gave to mankind. Given their health benefits and the qualities they give to our cuisines, I concur. But olives need a little coaxing before they yield to our tastebuds. Raw, uncured olives are intolerably bitter due to a glucoside called oleuropein that's contained in the sappy liquid portion of the olive fruits. This liquid was called amurca by the ancient Romans and was used to protect seeds against insects, moles, and weeds; it was also used as a fertilizer.

THE ORGANIC FACTOR ◆ Organic olives, for both oil and eating, are grown in California and are also imported from Peru, Australia, Italy, Greece, and Spain. They make up a small but growing segment of the market. See Sources (page 517) to locate online shippers of olives and olive oil.

As for conventional olives, the insecticide use may be rising because of an infestation of olive fruit fly that was first discovered in the state in 1998 and now infests all the olive growing regions in California. The fly lays its eggs in the olive fruit, rendering it unsuitable to press for oil or eat.

There are many nontoxic and organically approved methods of controlling the fly, however. These include sex pheromone traps, which lure the flies to the traps where they die; sticky yellow cards that attract the flies and hold them fast; and the release of braconid wasps, a natural predator that lays its eggs in the host fly. When the eggs hatch, they devour the host.

TYPES ◆ Oil or salt-cured olives—the kind sold in compartments at the olive bars in supermarkets—are far superior in texture and flavor to

HARVESTING AND PRESSING OLIVES

THE ENTIRE HILLSIDE where I now live was planted with small-fruited olives over a century ago by Italian immigrants who wanted to produce the precious oil that is so lavishly used back in Italy. I suppose they found out that the grape growers down in the valley easily sold their wine, but that Americans of the late 19th century didn't care much about olive oil. The hundreds of olive trees on this hill were abandoned many years ago.

We and our neighbors cut branches laden with olives and strip the fruit off onto tarpaulins every October, when the fruit is half green and half maturing into purplish black. We fill a pickup truck and drive it down to our own *frantoio*, The Olive Press in Glen Ellen, California, where the olives are pressed between crushers set just far enough apart to render the olives into a pulpy paste without cracking the pits, which would leach unpleasant flavors into the oil. The paste separates into pulp and bitter sappy liquid, and the oil floats to the top where it's skimmed off, bottled, and distributed among the neighbors. This happened every year until 2004, when our olives were turned away by The Olive Press due to infestation of the fruit by the olive fly. I'm organizing the neighbors to apply organic control methods to our entire hillside so we can once again press our oil.

canned olives. In fact, canned black olives are simply green olives that have been soaked in lye, which turns them black. Genuine black olives are the ripe fruit, while green olives are unripe.

SEASONALITY ► Fresh olives begin to turn from green to purple, then black, from October to December or January. The Tuscan-type oils—peppery and full of healthful antioxidants—are from olives picked green, then pressed. The more color the fresh olives achieve, the more buttery and mild—and less healthful—their oils.

WHAT TO LOOK FOR ► In terms of cured olives, taste around and choose whichever kind you like best. If you want the most healthful oil, look for oils labeled as "olio nuovo," or "new oil," usually from Tuscany or California.

STORAGE ► Cured olives will last for a month or two in the fridge, but they will soon start to turn rancid at room temperature in the light.

USES ► Olives can be cured in several ways, including in oil, in salt, and in a brine mixture. Some cured olives—especially canned green or black olives—are cured using lye solutions. I prefer the flavor of oil or salt-cured olives, pitted and tossed on a caramelized onion and three-cheese pizza, ground into spreads, simmered with tomato sauce, added to stews, and of course eaten plain. A mixture of several kinds of these olives makes a fine appetizer accompanying bread and olive oil for dipping. Olives can be pitted and tossed in salads, mixed with cream cheese to shmear a bagel, mixed with garlic and olive oil to dress pasta, and plopped into a martini.

CURING FRESH OLIVES ► If you have a source of fresh olives right off the tree, you can try curing your own. When I first moved to my property, I cured a batch of picholine olives I found growing here by cracking open the crisp flesh with a tap from a mallet, then packing the olives in sea salt (I avoided iodized salt that could impart an iodine flavor to the olives). I changed the deliquescent salt every two weeks, and in two months I had cured olives, tangy but not bitter to the taste, which I rolled in oil with some rosemary. They made a great snack with some bread, cheese, and wine. Olives prepared in this way hit almost all the taste buttons: sour, salty, bitter, pungent, and sweet.

ROSEMARY AND LAVENDER MARINATED OLIVES

MAKES ABOUT 1 QUART

This recipe is from Robert Sinskey Vineyards in Napa Valley—most likely from Maria Sinskey, the winemaker's wife, who has a way with food that equals her husband Rob's way with wine.

4 cups cured olives of your choice

1 teaspoon dried lavender

3 or 4 sprigs fresh rosemary

Freshly grated zest of 1 lemon (well scrubbed if not organic)

4 cloves garlic, peeled

¼ cup high quality extra-virgin olive oil

Mix all the ingredients together and marinate in the fridge at least overnight and up to 2 weeks. The longer they marinate, the better they get. They'll last for a month. ■

SALAD NIÇOISE

SERVES 4

This classic salad from the cusp of Italy and France would not have the zing that made it famous without its Niçoise olives. It's at its best at tomato season in late summer.

4 ripe tomatoes
1 green bell pepper
8 radishes
2 (6-ounce) cans olive oil–packed tuna
4 hard-boiled eggs
8 oil-packed anchovy fillets
½ cup chopped chives
½ cup pitted Niçoise olives
Salt and freshly ground black pepper
Peppery extra-virgin olive oil (such as green oils
    from Tuscany, or McEvoy and Lunigiana in the
    United States)

Slice the tomatoes. Stem, seed, and finely chop the bell pepper. Thinly slice the radishes. Drain the cans of tuna. Shell and quarter the hard-boiled eggs. Divide each of the items among four separate salad plates. Garnish each plate with 2 anchovy fillets, a sprinkle of chives, and one quarter of the olives. Season with the salt and pepper and drizzle with olive oil. ■

Papaya

CARICA PAPAYA

PAPAYAS beg to be drizzled with lime juice, so answer their prayers.

THE ORGANIC FACTOR ➤ In the early 1990s, the Hawaiian papaya industry was near collapse because ring-spot virus was attacking the plants. Genetic engineers inserted a foreign gene into two varieties of papaya—Rainbow and SunUp—that conferred resistance to the virus. Organic growers there have since been complaining that pollen from genetically modified (GM) papayas may contaminate their non-GM varieties—mostly Solo, Sunrise, and Washington. To keep the GM pollen from pollinating their papaya flowers, organic growers will have to bag their flowers and get organic seed from elsewhere. The fruit that develops will be GM fruit if the tree is from GM-pollinated seed.

From the consumer's point of view, buying organic papayas insures that you are not ingesting genetically altered food. A problem would arise only if organic growers allowed their trees to be pollinated by nearby GM trees and then planted the seeds and sold the presumable GM fruits as organic.

NUTRITION ➤ Papayas are a nutritious, nonfat, low-calorie, cholesterol-free source of folic acid—so important for pregnant women—and vitamins A and C (even more than apples and oranges).

TYPES ➤ Almost all of the papayas grown in the United States are from Hawaii and are of the small but high-quality Solo type of fruit with sweet golden orange flesh. Our stores also carry jumbo

Mexican papayas that are not as sweet and whose flesh is yellow-orange.

SEASONALITY ‣ Papayas are available year-round, but their peak season runs from April through October.

WHAT TO LOOK FOR ‣ Many of the papayas you find at the store will be green or yellowish green, which means they're not ripe. But unripe papayas are useful, such as in the well-known Thai Green Papaya Salad (see recipe, page 287).

When papayas ripen, they turn a bright yellow all over and soften to the touch. Grab them if you see them in the store, but reject any that have an off aroma or are bruised and moldy. (A few black spots or a tiny bit of mold is usually no problem.) There are companies in Hawaii that ship organic papayas to the mainland (see Sources, page 517).

STORAGE ‣ Once the fruits ripen, they quickly turn to mush if left in a warm kitchen. You can slow this process for a couple of days if you place them in the fridge, but longer than that and they'll lose quality fast. If you want to hasten the ripening of green papayas, place them in a closed paper bag. Papayas don't get sweeter when they're ripened at home, but they will develop that succulent texture that complements their flavor.

USES ‣ If there is a perfect way to eat this fruit, it would have to be luscious slabs of melt-in-your-mouth papaya drizzled with fresh lime juice. I don't care what you do to papaya or how you serve it, you won't beat this simple treatment. The reason is that, texture-wise, papaya is luscious and creamy, but flavor-wise it is mild and slightly musky without much acidity. Lime juice, with its distinct flavor and sharp acidity, exactly fills in the gaps of papaya's flavor profile.

That doesn't mean that you should avoid other ways to use papaya. Pop the peeled, seeded flesh of a couple of ripe papayas in the blender, pour in ½ cup of orange juice and ½ cup of vanilla frozen yogurt and blend for a dreamy smoothie. Papaya contains the meat tenderizing enzyme papain, so the next time you're marinating meat, add mashed ripe papaya to the marinade to give a subtle flavor and tenderize the meat nicely. In fact, the papain in papaya is so strong that you can't use raw papaya in gelatin dishes, as the papain will prevent the gelatin from setting. And if you want to add papaya to a fruit salad, add it at the last moment, because papain will tenderize fruit as well.

Scooped out papaya halves make edible serving containers for mango, passionfruit, kiwifruit, and other tropical fruit macédoines, for berry sherbets, and seafood salads.

PAPAYA SEEDS ‣ Papaya seeds are edible—they have a peppery quality. Try a few out of hand the next time you cut open a papaya. You can make a salad dressing with them by processing ½ cup of sugar, ½ teaspoon of dry mustard, ½ cup of rice vinegar, and a little salt (to taste) until smooth in a blender or food processor, then slowly pouring in ½ cup of olive or canola oil while the blender is running, adding 1 minced small onion and blending again until smooth, and finally, adding 2 or 3 teaspoons of papaya seeds and giving the blender a few bursts to incorporate the seeds and release their peppery quality.

GREEN PAPAYA SALAD

MAKES 4 SALADS

My friend Wai-Ching Lee of the San Francisco Professional Food Society introduced me to this salad in one of the city's Thai restaurants many years ago, and it's been a favorite of mine ever since.

1 green (unripe) papaya (about 1 pound)
1 cup Chinese cabbage, sliced crosswise 1/2 inch thick, then cut into 1/2-inch squares
1/2 pound snap peas, strings removed, julienned
3 cloves garlic, minced
1 red jalapeño pepper, seeded and chopped
1 tablespoon sugar
3 tablespoons soy sauce
3 tablespoons freshly squeezed lime juice
3 small tomatoes, cut into wedges
5 tablespoons peanuts, lightly roasted and coarsely chopped
1/4 cup chopped cilantro leaves

1. Peel, halve, and seed the papaya. Grate it with a coarse grater. You should have about 2 cups. Place cabbage pieces on a serving plate. Layer on the papaya, then the snap peas.

2. In a small bowl, make a dressing by whisking together the garlic, jalapeño, sugar, soy sauce, and lime juice. When ready to serve, drizzle the dressing over the salad and garnish with the tomatoes, peanuts, and cilantro. ▪

Passionfruit

PASSIFLORA EDULIS

O F THE MORE than 450 kinds of *Passiflora* vine, only a handful produce edible passionfruit. Of these, one species, *Passiflora edulis*, stands high above the rest in the quality of its concentrated flavor and tantalizing aroma. Floral, musky, with a spicy tang, the passionfruit seems to define the essence of all tropical fruit—although it's a subtropical rather than a purely tropical plant.

The name of this fruit, incidentally, comes from the composition of the flower, whose elements were used by Spanish missionaries to teach indigenous South American people about the passion of Christ. Three styles for the three nails. Five anthers for the five wounds. The purple corolla for the crown of thorns.

THE ORGANIC FACTOR ► Your best bet for finding organic passionfruit would be from a grower offering them at a farmers' market, most likely in Florida, Texas, California, and Hawaii. There are few, if any, shippers of organic passionfruit, but that can change any time, so you can certainly check with any of the organic produce companies listed in Sources (page 517). Most organic passionfruit in mainland American stores comes from Hawaii or New Zealand.

Organic canned passionfruit juice is sold, but it is pasteurized, which reduces the fruit's lovely aromatics significantly.

Check with the grocer about the fruit's provenance. It may be grown naturally, without chemicals, even if it's not organic. Few pests bother this strong-growing vine.

NUTRITION ‣ Passionfruit is high in carotene and niacin, and contains 23 milligrams of vitamin C per 100 grams of fruit pulp. But you'd need a bowl full of fruit to make 100 grams—a little over 3 ounces—so the amount of vitamin C is negligible.

TYPES ‣ The kind we most frequently find in stores is the purple passionfruit. There is a larger, yellowish kind called *Passiflora edulis* variety *flavicarpa,* but it's more acidic and less aromatic. Both types are native to an area stretching from southern Brazil through Paraguay to northern Argentina. Today they are grown in subtropical climates around the world. Many crosses between the purple and yellow sorts have been made, but the purple kind remains superior.

SEASONALITY ‣ Passionfruit appears in some stores in late summer.

WHAT TO LOOK FOR ‣ At the store, look for fruit whose tough outer purplish-brown rind is wrinkled or dimpled and slightly shriveled. That's when it's at its sweetest. Smooth-skinned fruits aren't quite ripe and will contain enough of a bitter glucoside (a chemical that makes many unripe fruits bitter) to be unpleasant. When the fruits are ripe, the glucoside virtually disappears.

STORAGE ‣ Passionfruit will store on the kitchen counter until they wrinkle and dimple slightly, indicating ripeness. How long depends on the stage at which they were picked.

USES ‣ Most people simply cut the fruit in half and scoop out the seedy pulp inside. Australians, who are passionfruit fanatics, eat this pulp seeds and all, but the juicy pulp can be separated from the seeds by pressing it through a fine-mesh strainer or two layers of cheesecloth. You don't get much of the resulting juice, maybe a tablespoon or less per fruit, and it's very viscous owing to a starch in its makeup.

The pulp, however, is very intensely flavored. It makes an excellent addition to other fruit juices, especially citrus. A drink made from orange juice, passionfruit pulp, a bit of superfine sugar, and a splash of water over ice is ultra delicious and refreshing. And yes, you could add a splash of vodka. Passionfruit pulp goes well with pineapple, too. And though I haven't tried it (yet) I bet an orange-pineapple-passionfruit drink would be a knockout. The Aussies like to add passionfruit juice to yogurt, it makes a wonderful flavor addition to ice creams and sherbets, and it can be used on pastries. But its starring role is reserved for the Australian (and New Zealand) national dessert, the Pavlova.

PAVLOVA

SERVES 8

This dessert appeared in New Zealand and Australia in 1935, nine years after Russian ballerina Anna Pavlova made a triumphal swing, dancing her way across the stages of the Antipodes. Both countries claim ownership, but I'm not getting involved. The dessert is cloud-like, with the aromatic passionfruit giving it a characteristic floral aroma.

The baking technique for making this involves preheating the oven to 400°F, then lowering it to 300°F before adding the meringue. This gives the meringue a blast of heat, but then cooks it more slowly at the lower temperature.

4 egg whites

1 teaspoon vanilla extract

1/4 teaspoon cream of tartar

1/4 teaspoon salt

1 cup plus 1 tablespoon superfine sugar

1 tablespoon cornstarch

1 teaspoon white vinegar

1 cup heavy cream

1/4 cup seeded passionfruit pulp

1. Preheat the oven to 400°F. Line a 9-inch pie pan with waxed paper. Whip the egg whites, vanilla, cream of tartar, and salt until stiff peaks form. Add 1 cup of the sugar by small increments while beating slowly. Add the cornstarch and vinegar and beat on low until incorporated.

2. Turn the oven down to 300°F. Turn the meringue onto the waxed paper. Smooth the top with a spatula to form a rounded mound. Bake for 75 minutes; the outside of the meringue should be crisp but not browned. You can turn the meringue onto a serving plate and remove the waxed paper or serve it still in the pie plate. Either way, let it cool to room temperature.

3. Meanwhile, whip the cream and mix the passionfruit pulp with the remaining 1 tablespoon of sugar. Cover the meringue with whipped cream and dot the surface with the passionfruit pulp. ▪

Peach

PRUNUS PERSICA

THERE ARE over 2,000 cultivated varieties of peach worldwide, in addition to the wild peaches of Tibet and western China, where the peach tree originated. The wild peach bears small, sour, and very fuzzy fruits, but excavations show that indigenous people of that area were selecting for size and taste 4,000 years ago. From China, the tree made its way to Persia, where Alexander the Great supposedly brought it back to Greece in the 4th century BCE, whence it spread around the Mediterranean and into southern Europe. It arrived in the New World with the Spanish.

In the early 19th century, the area around Chesapeake Bay was the peach capital of the United States, and later Georgia and South Carolina.

THE ORGANIC FACTOR ▸ Insects and diseases seem to love this fruit as much as we do. In California, where most of the $1.2 billion U.S. peach crop is grown, over four million pounds of agricultural chemicals are used on it annually. Organic growers, however, have good nontoxic remedies for the common peach problems, of which there are many.

NUTRITION ▸ For all their lusciousness, they aren't nutritional champs, but that shouldn't stop us from eating them. Peaches do have good amounts of potassium, folate, and vitamin A.

TYPES ▸ Peach types are a moving target because the trees are short-lived—10 to 20 years is typical, less if they develop a disease called PTSL (peach tree short life)—and new varieties are introduced every year, so varieties go in and out of fashion quickly.

Despite the constant introduction of new varieties, some old standbys continue to find favor. Red Haven, developed in Michigan, is one of them. Elberta, introduced in the early 1870s, is another. I asked Professor Tom Gradziel, an expert on peaches at UC Davis, about his favorite peaches. He said, "My favorite cling peaches for fresh eating are the old Dixon variety, as well as the newer Dr. Davis and Riegles. For freestones, I'm old-fashioned. I feel the old O'Henry is tops for fresh or culinary use."

Unfortunately, most peaches are sold without variety names attached to them. The easiest way to discover the variety of peach you're buying is to shop at farmers' markets and farmstands. Make sure to ask if the peaches are freestone or cling. Freestone pits are easy to remove while cling peach pits are not and the flesh must be carved off the pits with a knife.

SEASONALITY ‣ High summer is the season for peaches, and this fruit sums up the warm and buttery light in a particularly satisfying way. Peach season runs from mid-June to September in California, depending on the variety, and about the same throughout the Deep South. In the colder states where they can be grown, July is high peach season. Most of the early yellow peaches are cling type, while the mid- to late-season varieties, which are choice, tend to be freestones.

WHAT TO LOOK FOR ‣ Peaches are the sexiest of fruits simply because, when ripened on the tree, their texture, flavor, scent, and lusciousness are incomparably sensuous. But it's not easy finding tree-ripened organic peaches at major markets. Once ripe on the tree, they can quickly fall prey to brown rot, to birds, be blown off by the wind, and be swiped by kids. Not only that, tree-ripened peaches are soft and easily bruised and don't ship well at all. The best place to find them is in your own backyard, but short of that, visit the orchards where they're grown, or roadside stands or farmers' markets. You can also buy tree-ripened organic peaches through online mail-order sources (see Sources, page 517).

STORAGE ‣ Place peaches on your kitchen windowsill if they need to ripen. If ripe, use them right away.

USES ‣ Peaches have so many uses, it's hard to know where to begin: cobblers, compotes, pies, pastries, carved into crescents over your morning breakfast cereal, diced and added to pancake batter. Be creative and try to find ways *not* to use peaches when they're at their peak season.

PUTTING UP PEACHES FOR WINTER

LIVING THE ORGANIC LIFE means that each turn of the seasons brings familiar rituals. For me, warm, sunny, July days announce the height of peach season, when the Red Havens grown by a nearby organic orchardist become just shy of tree ripe—just right for plucking. I drop by my neighbor's barn, where peaches sit in their peck baskets (about 12 pounds) under the overhang, and chat with him about the crop and the weather. At home, I set out a bushel of peaches on newspaper, spacing them so none touch. Within a day or two, they give slightly when I press on their shoulders with my thumb.

Then I get my materials together: A large pot of boiling water on the stove. A sink full of ice water. A jar of honey. Lemons for juicing. A large ladle. Pint-sized freezer bags. And a huge bowl.

I start by pouring a gallon of water in the bowl. To this I add 1 cup of honey and 1 cup of freshly squeezed lemon juice, then stir until the honey is completely dissolved. (To put up fewer peaches, simply divide the quantities.)

I place a half dozen peaches in the boiling water for one minute, then remove them with a slotted spoon and place them in the ice water. This blanching treatment loosens their skins, which slip right off.

Then, knife in one hand and peach in the other, I slice them over the big bowl, letting the slices drop into the syrupy water, where the lemon juice prevents them from oxidizing and turning brown. Then I go back to the sink for the next peach, and do this until my bushel of peaches is processed.

I ladle in a dessert's worth of peach slices along with some liquid into a freezer bag. I set the bag on the table and squeeze out air until the peaches are entirely covered by liquid. I shut each bag securely, and lay them all in the freezer.

Cut to a cold January night. I take a rock-hard bag of peaches from the freezer and place it in a bowl of warm water while I'm making dinner. When I'm ready to serve dinner, I place the just-thawed peaches and some of the honey-lemon-water syrup in which they were frozen (they still have a few ice crystals among the slices) in bowls, then go to the freezer for some of the wild black raspberries, wineberries, blackberries, blueberries, and huckleberries that I picked and froze last summer, and toss them into the bowls, mixing them in with the peaches. By dessert time, all the fruits are thawed but still cold. All organic and fabulously summery in the dead of winter. This has become a ritual. With the radio on, an afternoon's pleasant work becomes a year's worth of ripe organic peaches.

PEACH MELBA

SERVES 4

The great chef Auguste Escoffier himself invented this dessert in 1893 to honor Dame Nellie Melba, the famous Australian opera singer. Her real name was Helen Porter Mitchell, but she took Melba—a shortened version of Melbourne, her hometown—as her stage name. Thank goodness. Peach Mitchell doesn't have nearly the romance.

Escoffier poached his peaches in wine and honey, but if you have good tree-ripened peaches, they'll be just perfect raw, as long as they're juicy and soft enough to eat with a spoon. Make sure to use a freestone rather than cling peaches, because they need to maintain their shape.

2 cups red raspberries
1/4 cup sugar
Freshly squeezed lemon juice
2 tree-ripened freestone peaches
1 pint high quality vanilla ice cream

1. Start by making a sauce from the raspberries. Place the berries and sugar in a medium nonreactive saucepan and heat on low until the raspberries release their juice and the sugar dissolves. Mash the berries and turn the mixture into a fine sieve set over a bowl. With the edge of a spoon, scrape the mixture back and forth against the mesh to express the syrupy juice into the bowl, leaving the dry pulp and seeds behind. Add a little lemon juice to give it just a slight tang.

2. Blanch the peaches in boiling water for a minute, then plunge them into ice water. Before you remove the skins, cut along the suture (the slightly raised line that runs the circumference of the peach) to the pit, all the way around the peach. Twist the halves in opposite directions and remove the pit, and then remove the skins from the halves.

3. Place each peach half in a small bowl, cut side up. Place a scoop of vanilla ice cream in the hollow of the peach half, and drizzle raspberry syrup all over the ice cream and peach. ▪

PEACH PIE

MAKES ONE 9-INCH PIE; SERVES 6 TO 8

Good peaches are quite enough in a pie, although you can mix them with blackberries or blueberries if you wish. Or pair plain peach pie with a scoop of vanilla ice cream for an ultimate summer dessert.

1 1/2 pounds fresh ripe peaches
1 cup sugar
2 tablespoons unsalted butter, at room temperature
2 tablespoons all-purpose flour
2 large eggs
Pinch of freshly grated nutmeg
Single Crust for a 9-Inch Pie (page 211), chilled

1. Preheat the oven to 350°F and position a rack in the center of the oven. Peel the peaches (see page 291) and slice them into a bowl. In another bowl, whisk the sugar, butter, flour, eggs, and nutmeg. Roll out the pastry dough to fit in the pie plate and crimp the edges all around. Spread the peach slices evenly in the pie plate and pour the sugar mixture over them.

2. Bake for 55 minutes until it just sets, then remove from oven and allow to cool completely. ▪

Pear

PYRUS COMMUNIS and
PYRUS PYRIFOLIA

PEARS originated in the same region as apples—the great swath of land in central Asia that runs from the Caucasus Mountains in the west to the Chinese border in the east. There are 20 known wild species, but many cultivated varieties— I've seen estimates of 1,000 to 5,000. Only about twenty of these are of major importance in commerce, however. One of these, the White Doyenne, appears to be a variety known in ancient Rome and described in writing and in wall paintings.

Most of our modern pear varieties came into being due to a great deal of breeding work done in France in the 16th through the 18th centuries, especially in the area around Angers. Anjou and Duchesse d'Angoulême are two popular varieties developed in those years. In the 19th century, Belgium became the center of pear breeding; the so-called butter pears (for their buttery flavor, not their texture), including Bosc, come from that country. Bartlett originated in England around 1770. Comice was bred in Angers in the 19th century, and Clapp's Favorite was bred in Massachusetts in the mid-19th century.

THE ORGANIC FACTOR ‣ In addition to fresh pears, these days one can find canned and dried organic pears in the markets. Make sure that dried organic pears are unsulfured. Sulfuring, usually with sulfur dioxide, inactivates polyphenoloxidase, an enzyme that darkens the fruit

KEEP AN EYE OUT FOR SECKEL AND COMICE PEARS

I'VE LIVED IN A NUMBER OF old Pennsylvania Dutch farmhouses, and each invariably had a Seckel pear growing somewhere near the front of the house. These are small pears, with greenish to yellowish-brown skin, sometimes with a reddish blush, and a spicy, sweet, intensely flavored flesh that remains firm even when ripe. This makes them quite unlike other European pears. I found out later that a man named Dutch Jacob came across this pear as a volunteer seedling (not planted by a person but growing naturally) in a parcel of northern Delaware woodland he bought in 1765. Like apples, pears don't come true to variety from seed, meaning that if you plant one variety, the mature tree won't necessarily produce fruit of the same variety, so it could have been a lucky sport of an existing pear, grown from a seed dropped by a bird. Or maybe, contrary to accepted wisdom, North America did have at least one native pear before the arrival of the Europeans.

Dutch found the Seckel shortly before "pearmania" broke out in New England in the 19th century, when enthusiasm for the fruit reached a fever pitch. And given the novelty and quality of the Seckel, pearmania must have quickly extended its range all over the Northeast.

My dad clued me in to Comice pears. These plump, squat, lop-sided, large pears are less musky and more delightfully aromatic, sweet, and juicy than Bartletts, and without question have the silkiest, most melting texture of any pear. Plus, their flesh has very few sclerenchyma cells: these are the gritty little stone cells that many other varieties of pears display so noticeably in their texture. While these cells detract from a pear's melting texture, they are the source of a pear's food fiber, which includes pectin, gums, cellulose, hemicellulose, and lignins.

during drying, so if the dried pears are light in color, they've most likely been sulfured. This sulfur compound can cause severe allergic reactions in some people. You give up something in appearance but gain in purity with unsulfured organic dried fruit.

Pears are relatively trouble-free to grow, and so lend themselves to organic culture. If you'd like to learn about growing pears organically yourself, visit http://attra.ncat.org/attra-pub/pear.html. This site describes organic solutions to the common pear problems, although I have grown pears on both coasts and have never had to use any controls at all to have fine crops.

NUTRITION ◦ Pears have a good amount of fiber, some vitamin C, and 150 milligrams of potassium per 100 grams of fruit.

TYPES ◦ Pears are grouped into categories by pomologists, or fruit-growing experts. The first category is European pears (as opposed to the very different Asian pears, which get their own entry), which is broken down between pear varieties used only for cooking and pear varieties that can also be eaten, known as dessert pears. All the pears listed in Top Varieties, page 508, are dessert pears. These two subcategories are further divided into sub-subcategories by skin color: green-skinned, yellow-skinned, red-skinned, and purple-skinned. Another type is Southern Cross pears, a hybrid of a cooking pear developed for the southern states where European pears, from more northerly areas, won't grow well. They lack the quality of European pears. A last type of pear, perry pears, are used to make perry—the pear equivalent of hard apple cider.

SEASONALITY ◦ August and early September are the season for pears.

WHAT TO LOOK FOR ◦ Many pears, including the familiar Bartlett, Anjou, Bosc, and Comice varieties, must ripen after harvesting, so you can buy them unripe. Look for pears with no skin breaks, cuts, or scratches.

STORAGE ◦ When I moved to California, my one-acre property contained the remnants of a Bartlett pear orchard. "Oh boy," I thought (not knowing much about Bartletts), "tree-ripened pears!" But when I let the Bartletts turn a ripe yellow on the tree, they were always mushy textured, brown inside, and no fun to eat. I subsequently learned that if Bartletts—and most European pears—are left on the tree to ripen, their pectic enzymes begin dissolving the pectin in their cell walls, turning them brown and mushy. They must be picked green, about three weeks before they ripen, and placed in a cool, shady room with plenty of air circulation around each fruit. In this condition, they slowly turn a fetching yellow, their flesh becomes melting, sweet, juicy, and musky, and they reach a fleeting moment of perfection. It doesn't last long because the pectic enzymes then begin their work—about a day.

So, if you're buying Bartletts (or other European pears that ripen off the tree, such as Bosc, Comice, and Anjou) at the market or farmstand, buy them green and ripen them at home. Don't place them in a plastic bag or in the fridge; pears need fresh air circulation. I place a few layers of newspapers on a cool floor and place the pears on them so none touch each other. Then they ripen fine. You can tell when they're ripe by feeling some "give" when you exert gentle thumb pressure on the top of the neck where the stem protrudes. If I have just a few, they will ripen nicely on the windowsill as long as it's not sunny.

USES ► Pears have a sweet spiciness all their own and are best eaten out of hand.

Softer varieties such as Anjou and Comice also bake well in galettes and tarts, while firmer Seckel and Bosc pears are best for poaching and for putting up as spiced pears.

Pears show a great affinity for a wide range of flavors, including almonds, anise, brandy, chocolate, cloves, cinnamon, figs, honey, ginger, quince, Parmigiano-Reggiano cheese, vanilla, and red wines, especially pinot noir and Beaujolais.

BARTLETT PEAR SALAD

SERVES 4

Stephanie Pearl Kimmel of Restaurant Marché in Eugene, Oregon, kindly shared this recipe.

FOR THE VINAIGRETTE

1 teaspoon minced shallot

2 teaspoons sherry vinegar

Pinch of salt

1 tablespoon walnut or hazelnut oil

1 tablespoon extra-virgin olive oil

Freshly ground black pepper

FOR THE SALAD

1/2 pound mixed greens (3 to 4 cups)

3 ounces hazelnuts (just over 1/2 cup)

1 large, ripe Bartlett pear

4 ounces blue cheese, crumbled (1 cup)

1. Make the vinaigrette. Place the shallot, vinegar and salt in a small bowl and let marinate for up to 1 hour. Whisk in the walnut oil and olive oil until emulsified. Season with freshly ground black pepper.

2. Preheat oven to 325°F. Wash the greens and dry them well. Place the hazelnuts on a cookie sheet and toast them in the oven for 3 or 4 minutes. When hazelnuts are golden and aromatic, remove and allow to cool before chopping them coarsely. Peel, core, and slice the pear.

3. To assemble the salad, toss the greens with half of the vinaigrette. Divide the greens among 4 salad plates, piling them high in the center. Divide the pear slices among the four plates, arranging them around the greens. Sprinkle each salad with the blue cheese and then the chopped hazelnuts, then drizzle with the remaining vinaigrette as needed. ▪

COMICE PEARS WITH PROSCIUTTO AND BABY GREENS

SERVES 4

Here's another recipe from Stephanie Pearl Kimmel of Marché, which she says is a variation of a recipe by Janet Fletcher, which is itself a variation of the classic Italian melon and prosciutto combination. The greens make it a salad.

FOR THE VINAIGRETTE

1 large shallot, minced

1 tablespoon champagne vinegar

1 teaspoon Dijon mustard

1 tablespoon walnut oil

2 tablespoons extra-virgin olive oil

Pinch of salt

Freshly ground black pepper

FOR THE SALAD

8 thin slices prosciutto di Parma

1/4 pound mixed baby greens (about 2 cups)

1 tablespoon chopped chervil

1 Comice pear, peeled, quartered, cored, and sliced lengthwise into many thin wedges

1. Make the vinaigrette by whisking together the shallot, vinegar, and mustard. Gradually whisk in the oils to make an emulsion. Season with the salt and pepper. Let stand for 30 minutes so flavors marry. *continued*

2. Arrange 2 slices of the prosciutto on each of 4 dinner plates, covering each plate's surface. Toss the greens and chervil with just enough vinaigrette to coat them lightly, about 2 tablespoons. Divide the greens among the 4 plates, mounding them in the center. Nestle the pear slices around the edge of each mound of greens and drizzle with a little vinaigrette. ▪

Pepino

SOLANUM MURICATUM

THE WORD *pepino* is Spanish for cucumber, but pepinos are not cucumbers but rather melon-like fruits. They are so named because they resemble a cucumber in shape.

The pepino is native to the Andean foothills of Peru and Chile. It has a mild melon flavor, a juicy sweetness, and a pleasing fragrance. The flesh is soft and creamy white. It mixes well with more highly flavored fruits in a fruit salad or macédoine. The size of a pepino can range from that of a plum to a papaya, and their golden skin is streaked with violet.

Pepinos are ripe when their background color turns to a deep gold, they become fragrant, and they yield slightly to thumb pressure. They're usually peeled and eaten out of hand or served like fresh melon, splashed with a little lime juice.

MEXICAN PEPINO SNACK

MAKES ABOUT ⅔ QUART

Street vendors sell this concoction throughout Mexico.

1 pepino
½ jicama (about ⅔ pound)

½ teaspoon chili powder
Salt
Juice of 2 lemons

Peel, seed, and slice the pepino into a bowl. Peel and slice the jicama and add to the bowl. Sprinkle them with chili powder and salt to taste, then pour lemon juice over them. Chill in the fridge for a half hour before eating. ▪

Persimmon

DIOSPYROS KAKI

WHETHER of the nonastringent or astringent types, persimmons are delicious but underutilized. Once people discover them, they can quickly become their favorite fruit. Because they have few pests of leaves, stems, or fruits, they are favorites with organic orchardists.

THE ORGANIC FACTOR ◆ Although it may be hard to find organically certified persimmons, it's usually not hard to find unsprayed persimmons, because this tree crop is not beset by many pests. Few agricultural chemicals are used on persimmons and most are herbicides used to keep down weeds between the trees. Still, if you can find an organic grower who sells persimmons at a farmers' market, snap them up.

NUTRITION ◆ Persimmons have excellent stores of carotene—one persimmon gives you 50 percent of your daily requirement of vitamin A and 25 percent of your vitamin C. They're also good sources of iron.

TYPES ◆ Persimmons belong to the genus *Diospyros*—meaning "food of the gods." There are dozens of species scattered around the world, including the native American persimmon, *Diospyros virginiana*, whose range spreads from Connecticut to Florida and west to Kansas and Texas. The Algonquin name for the fruit, *putchamin*, gave rise to the word persimmon. The native persimmon tree bears small fruits, from the size of a cherry to a small plum. The unripe fruits are bitterly astringent from tannin, which slowly disappears as the fruits blett (turn soft and ripe), and become candy sweet as they dry still attached to the branches by sturdy stems. A classic American sight would be a native persimmon alive with possums and raccoons feasting on the ripe fruits on a cold fall night.

A second species, *Diospyros kaki*, is the commercial type of persimmon found in stores and markets. It originated in China and Japan and was brought to the United States in the late 1800s. There are two types of this persimmon:

THE HACHIYA TYPE is the familiar deep orange-red heart-shaped kind whose insides must blett until they turn to jelly and the astringent tannins are reduced enough for the fruit to be edible.

THE FUYU TYPE is smaller, round, and flattened and, most important, is nonastringent. It can be sliced and eaten as a crunchy treat before it ripens and softens.

There are many other species. A small black persimmon found in Texas, *Diospyros texana*, is also known as *chapote*. The black *sapote* of Mexico and Central America, *Diospyros digyna*, has sweet, chocolate-brown flesh when soft and ripe. The Chinese date plum, *Diospyros lotus*, has 1-inch dark brown fruits, and the velvet apple, *Diospyros discolor*, is the *mabolo* of Malaysia. Here in America, we're probably only going to encounter the American persimmon, the Asian *kaki* types, and possibly the Texas black persimmon.

SEASONALITY ◆ You'll find persimmons in markets from October through December.

WHAT TO LOOK FOR ◆ Any persimmon should be sound with no cuts or bruises, so that it will blett (soften) evenly. Black spots on the surface of hachiya persimmons are not signs of decay.

STORAGE AND PREPARATION ◆ Ripen hachiya persimmons on the kitchen counter or windowsill. Once they soften and appear to be rotting, they are ready to eat. Fuyu persimmons can be stored on the kitchen counter until you choose to use them. The nonastringent fuyu types have edible but tough skins that are best peeled away with a vegetable peeler or paring knife, or blanched in boiling water for a couple of minutes, the way you peel tomatoes. They are still firm when ripe but develop an even better flavor when allowed to soften a bit.

USES ◆ I like to peel fuyu persimmons and slice them when firm-ripe for use in salads. They will eventually become soft and squishy and are still usable then. But if the flesh turns brown, they have oxidized and have gone past the point of optimum quality.

The same holds true for the astringent hachiya types. When ripe, they theyare like a thin skin filled with thick jelly, but they are past the optimum point if the jelly turns brown. I like to slice them open, spoon out the jelly into a cup, and then spoon on a few tablespoons of organic, nonfat yogurt, stirring

DRYING PERSIMMONS IN THE JAPANESE MANNER

IF YOU GROW or have access to hachiya persimmons growing on a tree, pick some hard but fully colored, and leave a bit of the branch attached. Peel the hard persimmons without breaking off the branch, and tie string to each branch piece. Hang the peeled persimmons from a pole in a warm, dry room. They should be ready to eat in six weeks. In Japan, persimmon lovers watch as they turn brown, then occasionally pinch the flesh gently to break up the pulp and promote even drying. When they are leathery, they're taken down from the pole and placed in a box lined with waxed paper, extra waxed paper is folded over them, and the lid of the box is closed. They turn white as the sweating sugar crystallizes on their surface over the next month or so.

up the jelly with the yogurt. It's a fabulous breakfast. But the jelly is also used to moisten and enrich cakes, pastries, oatmeal bars, and coffee cakes.

DRIED PERSIMMONS ▸ Dried persimmons are a candy-like treat—a perfect addition to kids' lunchboxes, trail mix, cookies, cakes, or oatmeal.

Dried persimmon can also be cut into little pieces and placed in a jar topped with a light rum. Let stand for a day, then drain off the rum and reserve it. Use the pieces in cookies, cakes, or puddings. Serve the persimmon-flavored rum chilled, as you would a fine liqueur—that is, neat in a small liqueur glass.

Nonastringent persimmons (fuyu) can be dried when they are firm and ripe. Cut into thin slices and dry in a food dehydrator overnight, or peel, slice, and rinse the persimmons in lime juice, then set them on a tray in an oven set on low with the door cracked open about 4 inches until they are leathery and no longer sticky, around 3 hours.

Astringent, soft-ripening persimmons (hachiya) are dried while they are still hard and immature. Peel the fully colored but still hard and astringent persimmons and slice them into ¼-inch-thick rounds. You can leave the rounds whole or cut

them into half-rounds. Lay them on the trays of a food dehydrator and dry them for 24 to 36 hours at 115°F. They'll come out sweet and chewy.

Another way to dry hachiya persimmons is to wait until they reach the jelly (ripe) stage, core them, halve them, and cut them into ½-inch-wide slices with skins still attached. Place these in a dehydrator until leathery, or on a cookie sheet in the oven on the lowest setting for 3 hours, then turn off the oven and let them dry some more. Check them and if they need more time, reheat the oven, then turn it off and let them dry some more. Repeat until the strips are leathery, then remove the peel.

You can also make persimmon fruit leather in the dehydrator or oven set on low. In the blender, puree 1 cup of the soft, jelly-like, ripe hachiya pulp with 1 tablespoon of lime juice, then spread on the fruit roll tray of the dehydrator or on a cookie sheet for the oven. The dehydrator will take about 8 hours at 100°F. The oven should be set on low, with the door cracked open about 4 inches, and the persimmon mixture dried until leathery. Take it up with a spatula, dust it lightly with cornstarch, roll it up in waxed paper, and store in a box in a warm, dry place.

SERVES 3

Sometimes simpler is better, as this recipe proves.

3 jelly-soft ripe persimmons
Vanilla ice cream

Place each persimmon in a cup, stem end down. Slice down from the top in an X shape. Remove the cores and fill the centers with vanilla ice cream. ■

SWEET PERSIMMON BREAD

MAKES ONE 9-INCH LOAF

Here's a special sweet bread to serve for the holidays when persimmons are in the stores.

2 eggs
3/4 cup sugar
1/2 cup canola oil
1 teaspoon baking soda
1 cup ripe persimmon pulp (1 or 2 persimmons)
1 1/2 cup all-purpose flour
1 teaspoon ground cinnamon
1/4 teaspoon salt
1/2 cup coarsely chopped walnuts
1/2 cup raisins

1. Preheat oven to 325°F. Grease a 9 × 5 × 3–inch loaf pan. In a large bowl, blend the eggs, sugar, and oil together. Mix the baking soda into the persimmon pulp, then add this to the egg mixture, stirring to incorporate.

2. Place flour in a bowl and add the cinnamon and salt. Add the walnuts and raisins to the dry ingredients and fold in the persimmon mixture. Pour the batter into the pan. Bake for 75 minutes. It's done when a toothpick inserted in the middle of the pan comes out clean. ■

Pineapple

ANANAS COMOSUS

IMAGINE Columbus's delight and astonishment when he landed in Guadeloupe in 1493 and found the natives cultivating pineapples! Here was a new food worthy of the trans-Atlantic exploration. After a couple of months of salt cod and hardtack, a pineapple must have seemed like a gift from heaven.

The pineapple originated in the lowlands of Brazil, where the Tupi Indian word for it was *nana* or *anana,* which meant "excellent fruit." It became pineapple in English because of the fruit's resemblance to a pine cone, and the general use of the term apple for any fruit. Although cultivated in pre-Columbian times in South America, the pineapple didn't make it to Hawaii until Captain Cook brought it in 1777. Native Hawaiians called it *halakahiki,* which meant "foreign fruit." Conditions were so right for pineapple culture on the islands that it soon became a local favorite and eventually a major crop. Hawaiian pineapples have reddish scales covering their segments, while Caribbean pineapples are greenish or yellow-green when ripe.

Botanically speaking, the pineapple is an edible, domesticated bromeliad, a tropical plant with fleshy leaves that form water-catching receptacles. The fruit is composed of from 100 to 200 berry-like fruitlets that fuse together around a central fibrous core. Pineapples contain a protein-digesting enzyme called bromelain (sometimes spelled bromelin), similar in action to the papain enzyme produced in the papaya fruit. Pineapple workers have to wear rubber gloves to prevent the enzyme from digesting the skin of their hands during constant contact. Don't use raw pineapple in gelatin-based dishes because the bromelain will digest the gelatin's protein and prevent jelling. Cooking deactivates the enzyme,

however. Raw pineapple juice used as a marinade will tenderize meat, and if held in long contact, will cause the meat to fall apart. The bromelain in pineapple juice is thought to be a digestive aid.

THE ORGANIC FACTOR ▸ Conventional pineapple growers typically load their soils and plants with fungicides, herbicides, pesticides, and nematocides—the last usually methyl bromide used to kill the root-destroying nematode worms in the soil, but which also destroys most other forms of life, rendering the soil an ecological wasteland. This chemical also contributes to the greenhouse effect in the atmosphere.

Now for the good news: Organic farmers are growing pineapples in Hawaii, Mexico, and the Caribbean, as well as Africa, the Philippines, and Southeast Asia. And pineapples respond to rich, compost-amended soils with better flavor. Look for organic pineapples in organically oriented supermarkets such as Whole Foods.

One organic pineapple farmer, Ronald Cowie on St. Thomas, told a Jamaican news service that the idea to grow pineapples organically came to him in 1999 when a friend offered him a slice of pineapple that was grown without chemicals in his kitchen garden. The fruit, which normally irritates his mouth, posed no such problem on that occasion, according to the report. He makes compost from vegetable waste and manure from his rabbit farm. For pest control, he sprays his crops with the fiery juice he extracts from bird peppers.

Other organic growers report success using mycorrhizal fungi spores in the planting holes. These fungi colonize plant roots in a symbiosis whereby the fungus extends its hair-like filaments far into the soil to gather phosphorus and other nutrients and feed them to the plant. The plant in turn produces root exudates—think sugary

syrup—that the fungus uses for food. Thus both plant and fungus are healthier for the partnership. That certainly can't happen in a soil fumigated with methyl bromide.

NUTRITION ▸ While wonderfully flavorful, pineapples aren't particularly nutritional. They are between 10 and 15 percent sugar and contain 1.3 grams of fiber and 12 to 100 milligrams of vitamin C per 100 grams, depending on the season of harvest. Fall and winter pineapples are less sugary, flavorful, and vitamin rich, whereas spring and summer harvested fruit show better numbers.

SEASONALITY ▸ Conventional growers control flowering and fruit set with plant hormones so that harvests can be staggered throughout the year, but organic growers make most of their untreated harvests in spring and summer.

WHAT TO LOOK FOR ▸ A rich golden yellow color is a chief signal of a pineapple's ripeness—not in the color of the segment scales on the outside of the pineapple, but rather down between the scales, where the yellow-gold color glows as though the fruit is lit from within. The same golden yellow suffuses the base of the fruit when it's ripe. A ripe pineapple softens slightly when it's gently squeezed. A rich fragrance is another sign of its ripeness. Received wisdom has it that a pineapple is ripe when a leaf from the tough greenish leaves on top pulls easily out of the tuft—but sources I consider reliable say it's not true.

STORAGE ▸ Pineapples acquire the bulk of their sugar content right at the end of their development. Once picked, they sweeten no further because they have no starch reserves to change into sugar. That's why you see pineapples marked "jet fresh" in the stores, and why a pineapple that isn't ripe when you buy it isn't going to get much better sitting on your kitchen counter.

USES ✦ Undoubtedly the best way to eat a pineapple is plain and fresh, by itself, savoring the delicious flavors. But of course pineapple makes a fine addition to any fruit salad, especially one that contains tropical fruits such as coconut, bananas, and papayas. They also show a flavor harmony with apricots, raspberries, and strawberries, and spirits such as rum, Kirsch, and Cointreau. Some old-fashioned uses are still valid—they make the perfect garnish for baked ham, but hold off on the tacky maraschino cherries. Pies, cakes, puddings, sauces, and preserves have all been made with pineapple. In Malaysia, it's used in curries and in meat dishes.

PINEAPPLE-OATMEAL COOKIES

MAKES ABOUT 30 COOKIES

Pop a batch of these spicy, tangy, nutritious cookies in the freezer, then put them in the kids' lunchboxes once a week.

1/2 cup butter
1 cup brown sugar
1 egg
1 cup finely chopped fresh pineapple, with juice
1 1/2 cups quick (1-minute) rolled oats
1 cup all-purpose flour
1/2 cup chopped pecans
1/2 teaspoon baking soda
1/4 teaspoons salt
1/2 teaspoon ground cinnamon
1/2 tsp ground allspice
1/2 teaspoon freshly grated nutmeg

Preheat oven to 375°F. Position a rack in the middle of the oven. In a medium bowl, cream the butter and sugar together until light and fluffy. Beat in the egg and pineapple. Mix together the dry ingredients, then add to the pineapple mixture and mix until well blended. Drop rounded teaspoonfuls onto an ungreased cookie sheet, about 3 inches apart in all directions. Bake for 15 minutes, or until cookies are golden brown. ▪

INDONESIAN CHICKEN IN PINEAPPLE SAUCE

SERVES 4

Here's a different way to prepare good old chicken breasts. The flavors marry marvelously.

4 boneless, skinless chicken breasts
4 tablespoons Dijon mustard
1/2 cup crushed gingersnaps
1 tablespoons canola oil
1 medium red onion, chopped
1 clove garlic, minced
1/4 cup unseasoned rice vinegar
1 cup finely chopped fresh pineapple, with juice
1/4 teaspoon ground allspice
1/4 teaspoon crushed red pepper flakes
1/4 cup chopped red bell pepper
2 tablespoons chopped fresh basil

1. Preheat the oven to 350°F. Spray a 9 × 13–inch baking dish with nonstick spray. Place each breast between sheets of waxed paper and flatten to an even thickness with a rolling pin or meat mallet. Brush both sides with mustard, reserving 1 tablespoon for the sauce, then dredge the breasts in the gingersnap crumbs. Place in the baking dish and refrigerate 20 minutes to firm the coating.

continued

2. Heat the oil in a medium skillet over medium heat. Add the onion and garlic and sauté them for 2 minutes. Mix in the vinegar, pineapple, allspice, red pepper flakes, and reserved mustard, and cook, stirring, for 4 minutes or until the mixture bubbles and thickens slightly. Scrape into a blender and whiz until smooth. Pour this sauce back into the skillet and keep it warm—don't overcook.

3. Bake the chicken uncovered about 20 minutes, until it's no longer pink in the center. To serve, mix the bell pepper and basil into the sauce, and put a quarter of the sauce on each of four plates. Top the sauce with the chicken. ■

Plum

PRUNUS DOMESTICA and other species and hybrids

If you violate Nature's laws, you are your own prosecuting attorney, judge, jury, and hangman.

LUTHER BURBANK

OUR MODERN ERA of superior plums really began with an indefatigable plant breeder by the name of Luther Burbank, who lived during the late 19th and early 20th centuries. From his home in Santa Rosa, California, and his 11-acre experimental farm in nearby Sebastopol, he introduced over 700 varieties of fruits, vegetables, and ornamental plants to the world, including the russet potato, the Shasta daisy, the thornless blackberry, and the Santa Rosa plum.

In 1885, Burbank started bringing in Japanese plums to crossbreed with American ones, in the hope of creating new delicious varieties. He made over 30,000 crosses of plums alone, and by the 1920s had released 113 new varieties of hybrid plums, many of which are still with us today. One of the sweetest, most exquisite of these Japanese cross breeds he named the Santa Rosa; it continues to be the gold standard for Japanese-type plums.

When I moved to Sonoma County, one of the first places I visited was Luther Burbank's home and gardens in Santa Rosa. This was a fascinating place, still tenuously in touch with Burbank himself, although he died in 1926. Here were cacti he'd charmed into dropping their needles, the Cedar of Lebanon he planted in the first decade of the 20th century, his original hybrid Paradox walnut tree that grew cabinet-quality wood quickly, and the original Santa Rosa plum tree he'd introduced in 1907—at 78 years it was just a scraggly old stick, but still alive and hanging in there.

THE ORGANIC FACTOR ◆ Most of our country's fresh plums and 99 percent of prunes (dried plums) are grown in California. Conventional growers use agricultural chemicals to deal with a number of difficult pests and diseases, including plum curculios, brown rot, bacterial cankers, aphids, and scale. Organic growers have the same problems to deal with, but the healthier the tree and the more biodiverse the orchard, the less severe the problems tend to be. Still, organic remedies exist for all these problems. I find that organic plums, from trees cared for in an environmentally sensitive way, taste noticeably superior to most conventional types, with a richer, more concentrated flavor. Unsulphured organic prunes (important for people with certain allergies) are widely available at organic supermarkets and online, too (see Sources, page 517).

NUTRITION ▸ All types of plums have good stores of potassium and vitamin C and also contribute selenium, a cancer-fighting antioxidant.

TYPES ▸ Plums most frequently encountered in our markets are hybrids of Japanese and European or American plum varieties. Lesser amounts of pure Japanese, American, and European plums are sold—but they are available.

The Japanese plum (*Prunus salicina*) thrives in California's moderate climate but is problematic at best where late frosts are common. That's because all Japanese plums flower very early—bursting into bloom in February and early March around the San Francisco Bay area. Most years that's late enough to avoid hard frosts, but occasionally those blossoms do get pinched. These plums are juicier than American or European plums and typically larger.

Santa Rosa plums are the best known of the Japanese-type plums and have become the standard of quality for fresh plums across the nation, holding down about a third of the market. One taste of a perfectly ripe Santa Rosa and you'll know why. It's an aromatic, very sweet Japanese-type plum of exquisite flavor, with an evenly red skin, and juicy, yellowish flesh with red overtones. Variations of Santa Rosas have been selected for late blooming, and consequent late ripening, and today we have early to main crop Santa Rosas that appear in mid to late June, a midseason crop that ripens into early July, and a late season crop that matures in late July to mid-August. Many other Japanese-type plums have been introduced over the years, including Beauty, Friar, and Redheart.

The European plum (*Prunus domestica*) is probably a cultivated hybrid of the wild European blackthorn, or sloe (*Prunus spinosa*), and the cherry plum (*Prunus cerasifera*). This type ripens in late August or early September and includes Italian prune plums and varieties such as Coe's Golden Drop and Stanley. The flesh is dense and sweet, greenish to yellow, usually freestone, and the skin varies from yellow to blue-black, usually with a dusty bluish bloom. A very similar species of plum (*Prunus italica*) is the Gage-type plum; it has greenish or yellow skin and a less intense flavor than the European types.

There are also native North American plums. These are small and mostly made into preserves.

KEEP AN EYE OUT FOR DAMSONS AND MIRABELLES

AN ANCIENT PLUM that originated in Damascus, Syria, is the small, oval, blue Damson plum (*Prunus damascena*); its close relative is the yellow Mirabelle from France.

Both are old varieties that were cultivated in Europe before the modern European types were hybridized. They are too sour to make good eating out of hand, but they become wonderful when sugar is added and they are made into preserves, jams (see recipe, page 307) and jellies, or candied to make "sugar plums," visions of which danced in the heads of the children in "A Visit from St. Nicholas." Both types are occasionally grown in the United States and are the kind of plums an interested organic farmer might plant. Look for them at farmers' markets and farmstands. I've never seen them in the organic supermarkets.

They're frequently hybridized with Japanese plums to produce a much hardier and later-blooming plum tree. Native species include the American Plum (*Prunus americana*), a 20- to 30-foot tree with a distorted trunk. Their spring flowers are malodorous, and thumb-sized fruits, with bright red skin and tart yellow flesh, appear in midsummer. Other species include the Chickasaw of the Southeast (*Prunus angustifolia*), the Oregon Plum (*Prunus subcordata*), the black Texan Plum (*Prunus orthosepala*), the American Sloe (*Prunus alleghaniensis*), and the Canadian Plum (*Prunus nigra*). All of these wild plums make interesting and flavorful jams and preserves.

PLUOTS AND OTHER CROSSBREEDS ◦ Luther Burbank (see page 302) had plenty of other *Prunus* family members growing at his farm to cross to make unusual hybrids, including sloes, peaches, apricots, and cherries—all drupes, or stone fruits. And so he came up with the interspecific hybrid he called a plumcot by crossing a plum with an apricot. He even produced a stoneless and seedless plumcot, which, unfortunately, has been lost to us.

Burbank's work has been carried on in recent years by Floyd Zaiger in California's Central Valley, who has bred a great number of hybrids between plums and apricots, called either pluots or apriums. Pluots have predominately plum parentage (¾ plum to ¼ apricot genes) and smooth skins like plums. They tend to show their hybrid vigor in their size—larger than either of their parents. Apriums have more apricot in their heritage and bear more resemblance to apricots in flavor and in the scant fuzz on their skins. The complex, intense flavor of pluots and apriums is like a blend of fruit juices, and they tend to have higher sugar

concentrations than their parents. They have become quite common in markets of all types in the years since their introduction in the late 1980s, with pluots more frequently seen than apriums.

SEASONALITY ◦ Summertime is plum season, with different varieties peaking at different times.

WHAT TO LOOK FOR ◦ When purchasing plums, see if the fruit yields slightly to gentle pressure. If they do, they're perfect. Avoid very hard plums—they'll never sweeten up. And avoid overripe plums, as quality drops off sharply after their peak passes.

STORAGE ◦ When you bring fresh plums home, eat them as soon as possible. They don't keep for very long on the kitchen counter or in the fridge.

USES ◦ Plums, along with pluots and apriums, make wonderful desserts. If they're organic, they are choice eaten out of hand, but they shine just as brightly in galettes, tarts, clafoutis, crisps, and my favorite—cobblers (see recipe, page 306).

Plums are a versatile ingredient, making natural flavor harmonies with citrus such as lemons and orange (serve them sliced and flavored with a little limoncello or Grand Marnier), peaches, rhubarb, walnuts, brown sugar, and cinnamon. The sharp acidity and sweetness of plums ameliorate the fattiness of pork, goose, and duck. Goose with plum stuffing was a well-known dish in centuries past, but it may be that the word plum in those days meant any sort of dried fruit. Thus a plum pudding could be made with raisins as well as prunes. And yes, when Little Jack Horner pulled out a plum, it was most likely a raisin.

Plums are also fermented and distilled into brandy, especially in the Balkans where the fiery drink slivovitz is used to punctuate just about any occasion.

CIDER-GLAZED PORK CHOPS
WITH PRUNE-ARMAGNAC CONFIT

SERVES 4

This is a heavenly way to turn ordinary pork chops into something really delightful. Make the prune confit a day or two ahead. The flavors are intense, at once savory, spicy, and fruity. The dish will win raves.

FOR THE CONFIT

5 ounces pitted prunes (about ¾ cup)

2 cups Armagnac

1 tart apple (Granny Smith or Rhode Island Greening), cored and cut in ½-inch-thick slices

4 shallots, peeled and chopped

2 cups apple cider

2 tablespoons apple cider vinegar

1 tablespoon dark brown sugar

⅛ teaspoon ground cloves

⅛ teaspoon ground mace

FOR THE PORK CHOPS

2 tablespoons all-purpose flour

Salt and freshly ground pepper

4 bone-in pork chops (at least ¾ inch thick)

1 tablespoon canola oil

1 tablespoon unsalted butter

1. To make the confit: Soak the prunes overnight in Armagnac, then drain (reserving the Armagnac) and roughly chop them. Place the prunes, reserved Armagnac, apple, shallots, 1 cup of the cider, the cider vinegar, brown sugar, cloves, and mace in a large, heavy nonreactive saucepan and simmer gently about 1½ hours, stirring occasionally until the liquid reduces to a sticky glaze (about 3 cups).

2. To prepare the pork chops: Preheat the oven to 350°F. Season the flour with salt and pepper. Dip the pork chops in the seasoned flour and shake off any surplus. Heat the oil in a large, ovenproof skillet over medium-high heat until hot but not smoking. Add the butter. When it stops foaming, add the pork chops and brown them on both sides, about 5 minutes per side. When the pork chops are nicely browned, place the skillet in the oven and cook for 8 to 15 minutes, depending on their thickness. Turn them over and continue for another 8 to 15 minutes. (A 2-inch or thicker chop will require 10 to 15 minutes a side, while a ¾-inch chop will take about 8 minutes a side.) Remove the chops to a platter and keep warm, and set the skillet aside.

3. Pour the remaining cup of cider into the skillet, and raise the heat to high until the cider boils briskly, scraping the pan to incorporate any browned bits. Boil 5 minutes, until reduced by about half.

4. Microwave the confit until warm, not hot, or heat in a double boiler or heavy saucepan over low heat, being careful not to scorch it.

5. To serve, place a chop on each of 4 warmed plates and spoon the cider glaze over. Spoon some confit on the side. ■

SUGARPLUMS!

YOU MAY SEE something called "SugarPlums!" in the markets this year (complete with capital *S* and *P,* and exclamation point). California prune growers have discovered a waiting market for "fresh prunes," as they call them. These are European plum varieties, usually dried into prunes but now being sold as fresh plums. They include French Prune, French d'Agen, Tulare Giant, Sierra Sweet, Sugar Prune, and Moyer Prune varieties, among others. Be aware that SugarPlums! is not a cultivated variety but rather a marketing ploy. That doesn't diminish the firm sweetness of the plums themselves, but it does indicate the fruit is most likely conventionally grown.

PLUM AND PEACH COBBLER

SERVES 6 TO 8

The name alone is mouthwatering, but the flavor of this cobbler is even more so. Santa Rosa plums make the best version of this cobbler—the way their sweet flesh and tangy skins mix with the lush peaches is sheer heaven. This is a special-occasion dessert for high summer—perhaps for Midsummer's Eve (June 23) or the Fourth of July. You can bake it in a large casserole or make the cobbler in individual ramekins with little dough tops.

1 pound ripe plums, pitted and sliced

1 pound ripe peaches, peeled, pitted, and sliced

1 cup plus 3 tablespoons granulated sugar, plus more
  for sprinkling

1 tablespoon ground cinnamon

1 tablespoon Grand Marnier

2 cups all-purpose flour

2 teaspoons baking powder

1/4 teaspoon salt

1/2 cup buttermilk

1 1/2 cups heavy cream, chilled

6 tablespoons unsalted butter, chilled and diced small

Melted butter

2 tablespoons confectioners' sugar

1 teaspoon vanilla extract

1. Preheat the oven to 375°F. Place the fruit in a bowl, toss with 1 cup of the sugar, cinnamon, and Grand Marnier, then spoon into a 3- or 4-quart baking dish.

2. In a separate bowl, combine the flour, remaining 3 tablespoons of sugar, baking powder, and salt, and mix well. Add the buttermilk, 1/2 cup of the heavy cream, and cold butter in quick succession. Combine them quickly and coarsely with a spoon or spatula so the mixture is as lumpy as possible.

3. Turn the dough onto a lightly floured board. Use a rolling pin to gently flatten the dough until it's about 1 inch thick and just big enough to cover the fruit in the casserole. Place the dough in the baking dish and pull the edges out so they touch the sides. Brush the dough with melted butter, sprinkle the top with a little sugar, and bake for 20 to 25 minutes, or until the dough is nicely browned.

4. Whip the remaining cup of heavy cream with the confectioners' sugar and vanilla and serve with the cobbler.

TIP: If baking in ramekins, follow the recipe but use a biscuit cutter the size of the ramekin to cut the dough into rounds. (Or set a ramekin on the dough as a template and cut around with a knife.) Bake about 20 minutes. ■

TOMATO • Heirloom • clockwise from top left: **Marvel Striped, Golden Queen, Green Jubilee, Oxheart, Cherokee Purple**

MATO • Sauce and Canning Type • **Roma**

MATILLO • **Giant**

WATERCRESS

TURNIP • **Tokyo Cross**

> *WHEN NO VARIETY NAME APPEARS, FOOD IS THE ORIGINAL SPECIES*

WINTER SQUASH • Clockwise from top: Turk's Turban, Carnival, Delicata, Golden Nugget, Sweet Dumpling

WINTER SQUASH • Pumpkin • Spirit (orange), Lumina (white)

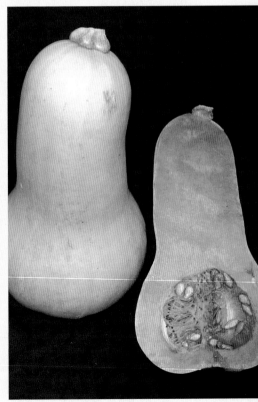

WINTER SQUASH • Butternut • Waltham

Fruit

APPLE • espaliered (trellised)

APPLE • clockwise from top left: Jonathan, Yellow Delicious, Fuji, Gala, Braeburn

APRICOT • Royal, a.k.a. Blenheim

ASIAN PEAR • Hosui

BANANA AND PLANTAIN •
Red Banana

CHERIMOYA • **Bays**

CHERRY • **Rainier (sweet)**

CITRUS • Kumquat • **Meiwa**

CRANBERRY

CITRUS • Lemon • **Eureka, Meyer**

CITRUS • Lime • **Key, Tahitian**

CITRUS • Orange • in back: **Valencia, Washington (naval)**; in front: **Moro (blood)**

CURRANT AND GOOSEBERRY •
Red Currant • **Lake**

FIG • **Mission (black)**

KIWIFRUIT • **Hayward (fuzzy)**

CURRANT AND GOOSEBERRY •
Gooseberry • **Pixwell**

GRAPE • **Redglobe (seeded** *vinifera* **table)**

LOQUAT

DATES • **Barhi (soft)**

GRAPE • **Malbec (seeded** *vinifera* **wine)**

MANGO • **Kent, Ataulfo**

MELON • Watermelon • **Sugar Baby (icebox-size)**

MELON • Watermelon • **Yellow Doll**

NECTARINE • White • **Grand Pearl**

PASSIONFRUIT • **Purple Granadilla**

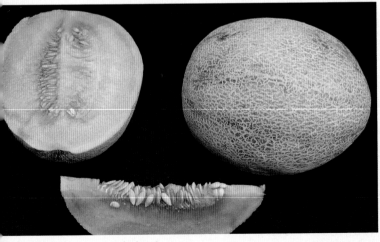

MELON • Muskmelon • **Ambrosia**

PAPAYA • **Mexican**

OLIVE • Picholine, green and unripe

PEACH • Yellow Freestone • Redhaven

PEAR • clockwise from top left: Alexander Lucas, Abate Fetel, d'Anjou, Red Bartlett

PEPINO • Rio Bamba

PERSIMMON • Astringent Type • **Hachiya**

POMEGRANATE • Wonderful, fruit developing and in bloom

PINEAPPLE • Champalla, Extra Sweet

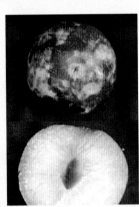

PLUM • Japenese Type • Santa Rosa

QUINCE • Pineapple

RED RASPBERRY AND BLACKBERRY • Heritage, Navaho

STRAWBERRY • Chandler, *frais de bois*, Seascape

DAMSON PLUM JAM

MAKES 6 HALF-PINT JARS

The trick to making the perfect damson plum jam is to get the right consistency—not too thick. It's a tart jam good with cold sweet meats, such as roast pork or ham, and great with breakfast muffins, scones, or on toast.

6 pounds damson plums
3 cups light brown sugar

1. Wash the plums and score each with a sharp knife. Place 1 cup of water and the plums in a non-reactive pot and cover. Cook slowly over medium-low heat for 10 minutes, then cook uncovered for 10 minutes more.

2. Press the plums and liquid through a coarse sieve to remove the pits—you should have about 4 cups of pulp. Return the pulp to the pot and boil over medium heat for 10 minutes, stirring occasionally.

3. Add the sugar, reduce the heat to medium-low, cook for 20 minutes more, stirring occasionally, until thick. Test the jam by placing a small spoonful on an ice cube. It should wrinkle when cold. As it cools, it thickens, and you'll find it's nicer if not too thick. Spoon into sterilized half-pint jelly jars, leaving a 1/2-inch head room. Process in a boiling water bath according to the instructions on page 241. ■

mala punica, or "Carthaginian apple." And punica became the name of the genus to which the pomegranate belongs.

Our name pomegranate comes from the Latin for "grainy fruit." The first recorded instance of the word in English comes from Chaucer's time. In 1320, it was written that "A poumgarnet ther she brak," or as we would say now, "There she broke a pomegranate." Our word garnet comes from the color of the seeds in a "poumgarnet."

In the Dahlem Museum in Berlin, there is a magnificent and dramatic painting by Rembrandt of Pluto, the god of the underworld, dragging Persephone into the Stygian darkness below. The painting illustrates a Greek myth, wherein Persephone vowed never to eat while captured but broke her vow by swallowing six pomegranate seeds, condemning her to life in Hades. Pluto later struck a deal with Ceres, Persephone's mother, that allowed the girl to spend six months above ground and six months below, and this causes our days of summer fruitfulness when Persephone is above ground and our days of barren winter when she is with Pluto.

Today, pomegranates flourish wherever the climate is subtropical or Mediterranean in nature, including the actual Mediterranean, as well as South Africa, Australia, parts of South America, California, Florida, Texas, the Caribbean, and the Middle East.

THE ORGANIC FACTOR ◂ In the markets, organic pomegranates will carry the USDA Organic seal. Organic pomegranates are available through mail order from Diamond Organics or by searching the web site of the Organic Trade Association, where you can find scads of organic comestibles and products (see Sources, page 517).

NUTRITION ◂ Pomegranates have great stores of antioxidants, and 13 milligrams of vitamin C per 100 grams of pulp and juice.

TYPES ◂ Seedless varieties are known, but they are grown mostly in the Middle East. I know of no seedless varieties grown in the United States.

SEASONALITY ◂ Pomegranate season lasts from September into December in the northern hemisphere.

WHAT TO LOOK FOR ◂ When selecting pomegranates, heft the fruits and select those that feel heavy—they'll have more juice. The leathery skin should not be dried out or wrinkled. Pomegranate juice is sold in many stores nationwide.

STORAGE ◂ Pomegranates will keep for several weeks on the kitchen counter, but they do not improve by waiting.

USES ◂ The seeds and juice are the usable part of the fruit, and in its home territories of Iran, Azerbaijan, Armenia, northern Iraq, and India, the juice is boiled to make a sweet-and-sour syrup that's used for flavoring, to color rice, and to add zest to meats such as chicken, duck, and lamb. Persian cooking, especially, makes frequent use of pomegranate juice, both fresh and boiled to syrup.

The French word for pomegranate is *grenade,* hence the pomegranate syrup that's called grenadine. Grenadine is used to add color to drinks and dishes. Commercial and organic pomegranate juices are now available, sweetened and unsweetened. The unsweetened juice can be used in cooking, but it doesn't have the flavor of fresh juice.

Extract the juice by placing a colander in the kitchen sink. Quarter the pomegranate and turn on the cold water. Take each quarter and begin to turn it inside out, letting seeds fall into the colander and removing as much of the whitish-yellow membrane as you can. The membrane contains bitter and astringent tannins, which can negatively affect the juice. When all four segments have been emptied of seeds, turn off the water, drain the colander, and pick out any remaining bits of membrane. There are two easy ways to get the juice out. The best way is to make a bag of a double thickness of cheesecloth, place the bag in a nonreactive saucepan, and mash the bag with a potato masher, then twist and wring the bag until the juice stops flowing. The second way is to place the seeds in a blender and pulse them until they are mostly broken, then dump the contents into a cheesecloth bag or fine strainer and finish mashing. Because some of the seeds in the pulp will be broken open by the blender blades, the juice won't be quite as fine as when using the gentler first method.

Fresh pomegranate juice makes a very refreshing drink if given a little sweetener and splashed with sparkling water and a small squeeze of lime juice. A couple of ice cubes and a shot of vodka in there on a hot day wouldn't hurt either. Use some in the water when cooking white rice to give the rice a pleasant light pink color. Sweeten the juice and mix some in yogurt to eat by itself, or pour over bananas, or make a pomegranate-and-honey-flavored frozen yogurt. Marinate a butterflied leg of lamb in the fridge overnight in fresh pomegranate juice with some fresh lemon juice, lemon zest, and an ounce of Cointreau.

Some people sprinkle pomegranate seeds on salads, rice dishes, or desserts.

DUCK STEW WITH WALNUTS AND POMEGRANATES (FESENJAN)

SERVES 4

This version of the classic Iranian stew originated in the province of Gilan, where the shores of the Caspian Sea teem with wild ducks. Chicken or lamb chunks can be substituted for the duck. If it's not pomegranate season, use unsweetened organic pomegranate juice.

4 tablespoons olive oil
1 large onion, chopped fine
1/2 teaspoon freshly ground black pepper
1/2 teaspoon ground turmeric
1 pound boneless skinless duck breasts, cut into thin strips
1 tablespoon all-purpose flour
1/2 pound walnuts, coarsely chopped (about 1 3/4 cups)
3 cups fresh pomegranate juice
Salt
Juice of 1 lemon, optional
Granulated sugar, optional
1 small eggplant
1 1/2 teaspoons ground cardamom

1. Heat a skillet with 2 tablespoons of the oil over medium heat, and add the onions, pepper, and turmeric, and sauté until translucent, about 5 minutes. Remove onions, keeping oil in skillet.

2. Add the duck and sauté until browned, about 10 minutes, stirring occasionally. Sprinkle the meat with the flour and the chopped walnuts and sauté for 3 more minutes, turning once or twice.

3. Add the pomegranate juice and salt to taste. The taste should be a nice balance of sweet and sour. If it needs more sour to balance the sweetness, add lemon juice. If it needs more sweetness, add a little sugar. Cover the skillet and reduce heat to low. Simmer, stirring occasionally so the nuts don't burn, for 40 minutes. *continued*

4. As soon as this starts to simmer, peel the eggplant and cut lengthwise into 6 or 8 pieces. Sprinkle each piece with salt, stack one on top of the other, and let sit for 5 minutes, then rinse under cold water. Pat dry with paper towels then sauté over medium heat in the remaining 2 tablespoons of olive oil until browned on both sides. When the eggplant is browned, arrange the pieces on top of the meat in the skillet, replace the cover, and finish simmering.

5. Add the cardamom powder and gently mix it into the stew. The sauce should be the consistency of heavy cream. If it's too thick, dilute it with a little warm water. Serve the stew hot with plenty of white rice. ■

POMEGRANATE TAPIOCA

SERVES 4

This makes a glistening, garnet-red pudding that you can serve plain or topped with whipped cream, spread into a crepe and roll, stir into yogurt, or use in any other way you choose.

Juice of 2 pomegranates (about 2 cups)
1 tablespoon grenadine syrup
1/4 cup sugar
3 tablespoons quick-cooking tapioca

1. If the pomegranates don't make 2 cups of liquid, add enough water so you have 2 cups. In a medium saucepan, combine the pomegranate juice, grenadine, and sugar. Sprinkle the tapioca over the surface and let sit for 5 minutes.

2. Heat the mixture over medium heat until it reaches a full boil, stirring all the while. Remove from the heat. Turn into a bowl, cover, cool to room temperature, then refrigerate. Serve cold. ■

Quince

CYDONIA OBLONGA

QUINCES, while still fairly rare, are popping up more and more at farmers' markets and roadside stands. They are much more frequently used in Europe and are common ingredients in the northern range of the Middle East, from Turkey to Iran, where they are autochthonous. Persian cooking, especially, uses them in its meat-and-fruit dishes.

THE ORGANIC FACTOR ▸ Most quinces are someone's backyard fruit and will likely be found only at farmers' markets or roadside stands. They may not be certified organic, but almost assuredly will not have been treated with agricultural chemicals. Ask the purveyor about their provenance just in case, but few insects or diseases attack a small stand of backyard quinces.

NUTRITION ▸ Quinces have some dietary fiber, good stores of vitamin C, and some iron.

SEASONALITY ▸ Quince season runs from October to December.

WHAT TO LOOK FOR ▸ Like apples, quinces will last for weeks until they soften and turn brown and eventually become unuseable.

STORAGE ▸ Store quinces at room temperature until they are fully ripened, yellow all over, and emit a sweet aroma. Then use them quickly before they become mealy, or refrigerate for a couple of weeks. Store them away from apples and pears because their aroma can affect the other fruits.

USES ◂ When cooked and sweetened, quince softens and turns a pinkish color, developing a fine fragrance and a delicious flavor. It's used for jams, preserves, and marmalades, it's stewed with meats, made into pastes. Or throw in a quince the next time you make apple or pear sauce.

Since classical times, quinces have been used to make sweetmeats or candies to be served at the end of a fine meal. The first marmalades were made from quince. Because the fruit has great amounts of pectin, it can be boiled with sugar and then poured into little molds of varying shapes or rounds. These confection-like jellies are called *cotignac* in France, *membrillo* in Spain, *cotognata* in Italy. They're usually coated with sugar for a dessert; plain, they make a perfect accompaniment to cheese and wine.

QUINCE MARMALADE

MAKES 6 TO 8 HALF-PINT JARS

This marmalade is exquisite for its color as well as its flavor.

3 1/2 pounds quinces, quartered and cored
5 lemons, quartered and seeded
6 cups sugar

1. Place five saucers in the fridge to get them cold. Sterilize the jars and lids in boiling water for 5 minutes. Wipe any fuzz from the quinces with a clean, damp cloth.

2. Dice the quince quarters, unpeeled, with a knife or food processor. Place in a large saucepan with 5 cups water. Thinly slice the lemon quarters. Add the slices to the saucepan. Simmer until the fruit is very tender, about 1 hour. Keep your eye on the pan so it doesn't boil over.

3. After the fruit has simmered 1 hour, microwave the sugar for 1 minute in a ceramic bowl so it's warm, then pour the sugar into the saucepan and stir to dissolve. Turn up the heat to medium-high and boil rapidly until a bit of the marmalade placed on a cold saucer quickly forms a skin and, when tilted, runs off the saucer in a lumpy mass. (Try this after 5 minutes and every 3 or 4 minutes thereafter until the consistency is right.)

4. It should be a beautiful pink color. Pour into sterilized jars, leaving 1/2 inch of headspace. Place a lid on each jar and screw it down tightly with the band. Invert the jars for a couple of minutes, then turn right side up to cool. When cool and the lid has become concave and doesn't click when pushed in the center, store in the fridge or process for longer keeping. See page 241 for more information on canning. ▪

Red Raspberry

RUBUS IDAEUS hybrids

MOST AMERICAN red raspberries are grown in the Pacific Northwest and shipped in plastic clamshell packages to all parts of the country. But because raspberries are so delicate, it behooves those interested in top quality to find a source of organic berries close to home—and the berries grow most everywhere in the continental United States.

THE ORGANIC FACTOR ► Berries grown close to your home are most likely to be grown organically and be of higher quality, because Pacific Northwest conventional commercial berries are shipped young to all parts of the country. They will not have the flavor and freshness of berries picked yesterday. However, red raspberries don't need a lot of coddling to produce their crops, so

even conventional berries are not likely to carry a load of toxic chemicals, although organic raspberries are available, too.

NUTRITION ► Red raspberries are nutritious in some interesting ways. Not only are they rich in vitamin C (13 milligrams per 100 grams), but they are rich in ellagitannins, the precursors of ellagic acid. This latter is a phenolic compound that is a potent anticarcinogenic and antimutagenic substance. It also has antibacterial and antiviral properties. Ellagic acid acts as a scavenger to bind cancer-causing chemicals, rendering them inactive. It inhibits the ability of other chemicals to cause mutations in bacteria. Ellagic acid in raspberries also prevents the binding of carcinogens to DNA and reduces the incidence of cancer in cultured human cells exposed to carcinogens.

The Meeker variety of red raspberry is the best source of ellagic acid, followed by Chilliwack and Willamette. In addition, scientific research suggests

KEEP AN EYE OUT FOR WINEBERRIES

THE LOCALLY-GROWN red raspberries we find in the stores and farmers' markets in early summer and again in fall are descendants of the wild European raspberry. But in the northeastern United States there is another red raspberry, commonly called the wineberry (*Rubus phoenicolasius*). Wineberries were brought to the United States from China in the late 19th century and escaped the berry patch to take their place among the wild treasures of the fields.

I have never seen wineberries sold commercially. Those who tramp the eastern meadows will find them growing along east-facing edges of woods and dappled, shady roadsides. When they begin to ripen they are orange or orange-red, but even kids soon learn to be patient and wait until they turn a deep, dark, jewel-like, translucent ruby-red. Then they become sticky, very fragile, and indescribably delicious. More than once I have waited for a precious patch of wineberries to ripen fully, only to find that when I went for them, someone ignorant of their possibility of perfection had taken them all too soon. As you can see, I am tormenting myself with memories of hot, humid, mid-July afternoons in Pennsylvania, gobbling wineberries until I could eat no more.

Unless I decide to visit the Northeast in mid-July, I must now content myself with red raspberries. But that's not so bad, is it?

that the colorants in red raspberries called antho-cyanins play a role in preventing heart disease. Many of its other health benefits depend on the variety as well. The cultivar Caroline, for instance, proved as much as 44 percent higher in beta-carotene, 435 percent higher in vitamin A, 77 percent higher in vitamin E, and 48 percent higher in vitamin C than other raspberry cultivars.

TYPES ◆ Red raspberries are categorized as black, red, purple, and yellow. The black ones are not the same as black raspberries. The differences in taste of the various colors are subtle.

SEASONALITY ◆ High raspberry season is mid-July through mid-September.

WHAT TO LOOK FOR ◆ Proximity of the farm to market is the key to finding perfect berries, because raspberries can develop mold within a few days of being picked during the warm seasons, and mold gives them a strong, unpleasant mustiness. Check them by looking into the recep-tacle—the hollow where they attach to the plant. That's usually where mold starts first. Make sure the berries aren't squished, with juice running out. They should be velvety-looking, plump, and sound. Taste one if you can—it should be notice-ably sweet and aromatic, not sour. Locally-grown, organic berries grown in rich, compost-amended soil will have an exceptionally appealing, bright, sprightly flavor.

If you find a source of perfect, organic berries, buy lots and freeze them in a single layer on cookie sheets. When they're frozen, put them in freezer bags and store for later use.

USES ◆ Red raspberries have an affinity for many other flavors, especially chocolate. Rasp-berry ice cream topped with dark chocolate syrup is perfection. Chocolate and raspberry cake is clas-sic. But chocolate is only one of the foods that pair well with red raspberries. Try them with almonds, cream, lemon, black or red currants, and with red wine. And raspberry vinaigrette (see recipe, page 314) is perfect on summer salads fresh from your own organic garden.

RASPBERRY CLAFOUTIS

SERVES 6

This dish is about as yummy as raspberries get (un-less you just serve them plain, I suppose). It's a French classic. Serve alone, or with raspberry coulis or vanilla ice cream, or both.

2 pints fresh red raspberries
4 1/2 ounces (3/4 to 1 cup) whole raw almonds
3/4 cup all-purpose flour
1 1/4 cups sugar
Juice and freshly grated zest of 1 orange (well scrubbed if not organic)
7 egg whites
2 1/4 sticks butter

1. Puree 1 pint of the raspberries in a blender. Grind the almonds fine in a food processor. In a bowl, combine the raspberry puree, ground al-monds, flour, sugar, orange juice, zest, and egg whites. Whisk together until well blended.

2. Preheat the oven to 350°F. In a saucepan, gently heat the butter until it browns lightly—what the French call *noisette*, or a nut-like color. Pour the butter through a very fine strainer into the raspber-ry mixture, stirring as you pour. When the ingredi-ents are thoroughly mixed, pour the batter into 6 round, fluted ramekins. Drop 6 to 8 raspberries from the remaining pint on top of each ramekin. Bake for 35 minutes until golden brown. ■

RASPBERRY VINAIGRETTE

MAKES ABOUT 2 CUPS

Raspberry vinaigrette could be the ultimate salad dressing because the light raspberry fruitiness adds a sweet note to the greens while the rice vinegar adds tang. Try this recipe and decide for yourself. The long maceration allows the full extraction of the raspberry flavor into the liquid in a way that fresh-made raspberry vinaigrette doesn't. This recipe easily doubles—why not make a good-sized batch?

3 cups fresh red raspberries
2 cups unseasoned rice vinegar
1/4 cup sugar

1. Place the raspberries in a large bowl or heat-proof container with a cover. In a nonreactive saucepan, bring the vinegar and sugar to a boil until the sugar dissolves, then pour it over the berries. Stir and cover loosely. When the mixture has cooled, cover tightly (place the bowl in a plastic bag and seal), and refrigerate for 30 days.

2. At the end of the period, strain the liquid through a piece of cheesecloth into a nonreactive pot. Bring to a boil and simmer for 5 minutes. Remove from the heat and pour into hot, sterilized jars. Seal and process using the water-bath canning method (see page 241). ∎

Strawberry

FRAGARIA, various species

IZAAK WALTON **famously said, "Doubtless God could have made a better berry, but doubtless God never did," referring to the strawberry. One of my earliest memories is the jingle of the Good Humor truck coming up my street, selling vanilla ice cream with frozen strawberry syrup intermingled in it for a nickel a cup. I don't think you need any convincing that strawberries are as heavenly a fruit as there is. Just make sure they're organic.**

THE ORGANIC FACTOR ▪ Perhaps no berry is more delicious than the strawberry, but neither is there a berry more loaded with agricultural chemicals when grown conventionally. Pickers who have to enter the poison-drenched fields call strawberries "the devil's fruit," not just because of the backbreaking labor it takes to harvest them, but also because of the toxic environment of the fields. Millions of pounds of agricultural chemicals have been used on strawberries in recent years in California alone. In a study of 42 fruits and vegetables by the Environmental Working Group, strawberries were found to have the highest concentration of chemical contaminants.

And yet no berry is more beloved by children, who are most susceptible to bodily harm due to these chemicals. That's perhaps the chief reason to seek out organic strawberries—but there are others. Strawberries are delicate things—quick to lose their evanescent esters and other fragrance and flavor compounds, soft and easily crushed in transit, and prone to rapid molding. And so the big, conventional, commercial growers use varieties such as Tioga in California, Surecrop through much of the country, and Blomidon in the northern states and Canada. What these varieties lack in quality they make up in firmness and shipping ability. But how unfortunate are those folks who've only tasted these tough, flavor-challenged commercial varieties.

NUTRITION ◆ Rich June-bearing strawberries allowed to ripen before being picked contain up to 77 mg of vitamin C per 100 grams fruit, as well as folates, potassium, and dietary fiber. Commercial berries have less.

TYPES ◆ Something of the wild strawberry's luxurious flavor persists in our cultivated varieties, because it's one of the parents of our modern hybrids. Wild American strawberry plants were taken to France about 1600, and a century later, another wilding (*Fragaria chiloensis*) from the Chilean coast, was also transported to France. The two species crossed by accident around 1750 and the first modern strawberry hybrid (*Fragaria × ananassa*) appeared. Much work was subsequently done in England to bring about a wide range of cultivars. Eventually the hybrids returned to the Americas to become the basis of the strawberry industry here.

SEASONALITY ◆ Certain varieties of berries produce a big crop in June and then are finished for the season. These June-bearers are usually better flavored than everbearing types, which produce a sprinkling of berries throughout the summer. Something about the intensity of the June sun brings up the sugars and flavors of strawberries, and also their nutritional quality. Commercial berries for shipping—even organic ones—must be picked before they're fully ripe or they get too soft. This means that the best berries are going to be locally grown—the nearer your house the better—so that they can ripen fully on the plant. And they will be from June-bearing types. Then they'll be soft, juicy, and dripping sugar, with a hint of pineapple in their flavor. These are the ones to buy by the flat for freezing.

MY FAVORITE STRAWBERRIES

THE BEST STRAWBERRIES, in my opinion, are the tiny, native wild strawberries of North America that grow east of the Rockies (*Fragaria virginiana*). In the Pocono Mountains, they ripened in the second week of June. The fields around my boyhood home there were carpeted with them—they grew prolifically in the poor shale and clay soils of our hilltop. When the hot June sun baked these fields, great clouds of strawberry fragrance would rise to meet me and I spent many happy, sweaty hours down among the grasses and weeds, eating them straight from the plants. The berries are only the size of your little fingernail, but each packs all the intense strawberry flavor of a full-size hybrid berry—and then some. I was lucky to be back in that vicinity a few Junes ago and drove to that hilltop to see if I could find some wild strawberries. I hadn't tasted them in probably 30 years or more. As I entered an open field near my former home, I was greeted by the familiar smell of strawberries, and looking down, saw them dangling red and ripe from their little plants by the hundreds.

I got a small paper cup from the car and quickly filled it, then drove down to the village diner where I had my first job (washing dishes) and ordered a scoop of vanilla ice cream. When it was set in front of me, I poured the wild strawberries over it and dug in. Though I'm sure time has dulled my senses somewhat, they were still as rich and luxurious a flavor as I remembered.

I'VE BEGUN TO SEE the little European wild strawberries called *fraise des bois*—wood or Alpine strawberries (*Fragaria vesca*)—in farmers' markets, but only occasionally. Like the native American wildings, they have a rich, intense fragrance and flavor that's irresistible. If you're lucky enough to have a good source of these or of native wild strawberries (*Fragaria virginiana*), consider making strawberry wine. A friend of mine went on a picking spree and made several gallons from *virginianas*, and it was a rare, heady, syrupy wine, best taken in small Port glasses or poured over vanilla ice cream.

WHAT TO LOOK FOR ◆ Strawberries are so perishable that you need to make sure they are bright and fresh, not dull, not softening or molding.

STORAGE ◆ They are best eaten as fresh as possible, as soon as you get them home. Strawberries freeze well, although when they come out of the freezer, they are mush and must be used in cooking or sauces.

USES ◆ Fresh strawberries that you have frozen will make wonderful smoothies paired with bananas and other fruits when put through a blender. If you slice them and freeze the slices individually on waxed paper laid on a cookie sheet, then put them in freezer bags when frozen hard, they can be added to winter fruit compotes.

But the glory of strawberries is to get really flavorful June-bearing varieties eaten fresh, maybe with a little cream or red wine and sugar, but at their very best just by themselves. Should you choose to use them in cooking or with other foods, they make some heavenly flavor marriages: classy with Champagne, perfect with crème fraîche or mascarpone, delicious with oranges and tangerines (whose acidic zestiness enhances strawberries' flavor), harmonic with pineapple, and classic with rhubarb—among other flavor pairings. And I don't even have to mention chocolate.

STRAWBERRY AND PEACH SUCCULENCE

SERVES 4

In mid- to late June, strawberries are peaking and peaches are getting there. Time this so that your peaches are perfectly ripe, then buy the best pick-your-own or farm-ripened strawberries you can.

1 pint fresh, ripe strawberries

2 ripe peaches

Freshly grated zest of 1 lemon (well scrubbed if not organic)

2 tablespoons sugar

1 cup Italian Moscato wine or other late-harvest dessert wine (such as a Beaumes de Venise)

1. Stem and slice the strawberries. Peel the peaches by blanching for 1 minute in boiling water, then run under cold water until the skins loosen. Halve, pit, and thinly slice the peaches.

2. In a bowl, toss the fruit with the zest, sugar, and wine. Spoon into individual bowls. ▪

STRAWBERRY CREPES

SERVES 5

I had my first strawberry crepe from a street vendor in Paris and have been a devoted fan ever since. Crepes make a spectacular Sunday breakfast. The crepes should be as thin as possible—practice makes perfect.

2 pints fresh strawberries
Juice and freshly grated zest of 1/2 lemon (well scrubbed if not organic)
1/4 cup maple syrup
2 cups all-purpose flour
1 teaspoon baking soda
1/4 teaspoon salt
3 eggs
13/4 cups milk
Butter or canola oil
Confectioners' sugar

1. Stem and thinly slice the strawberries, then combine them with the lemon juice, lemon zest, and maple syrup. Toss to coat, and set aside.

2. In a separate bowl, combine the flour, baking soda, and salt, and mix well. In a third bowl, beat together the eggs and milk, then slowly pour them into the flour mixture, whisking constantly until the batter is smooth, with no lumps.

3. Preheat the oven on the lowest setting. Heat the butter in a 9-inch cast-iron skillet over moderately high heat until it stops bubbling. Spread enough batter in the bottom of the skillet (while tilting the skillet in a circular motion) so that it thinly and nearly covers the bottom evenly when swirled with the back of a tablespoon. Fill any holes quickly with a bit of batter.

4. When the sides begin to curl and the underside is browned, flip the crepe. When it browns, slide it on a warm plate, spoon on some of the strawberry mixture, and gently roll the crepe. Sift a little powdered sugar on top and place the plate in the warm oven. Repeat with subsequent crepes and plates, apportioning the strawberries to fill about 10 crepes. Everyone will want seconds. ▪

STRAWBERRY-RHUBARB CRISP

SERVES 6

The classic marriage of flavors—strawberries and rhubarb—melt together in this prime summertime dessert.

1 pound fresh strawberries
3 cups chopped rhubarb
1/2 cup white sugar
1 tablespoon cornstarch
1/2 cup all-purpose flour
2/3 cup ground pecans
2/3 cup brown sugar
Freshly grated zest of 1 lemon (well scrubbed first if not organic)
1 teaspoon ground cinnamon
8 tablespoons (1 stick) butter, chilled

1. Preheat over to 350°F. Lightly grease a 11/2-quart baking dish or casserole.

2. Stem and slice the strawberries. In a bowl, thoroughly combine the strawberries, rhubarb, white sugar, and cornstarch, and turn this mixture into the baking dish.

3. Combine the flour, pecans, brown sugar, lemon zest, and cinnamon. Cut in the butter using 2 knives or your fingers until the mixture has the consistency of coarse meal. Sprinkle this over the fruit. Bake for 35 to 40 minutes, until the top is lightly browned. ▪

Chestnuts in Shell

Nuts, Seeds, Beans, and Grains

A SEED—WHETHER CALLED NUT, SEED, BEAN, OR GRAIN—is the life force encapsulated, and so it should be no surprise that it is among the most nutritious and beneficial foods for us to eat. All seeds contain the complete genetic information needed to grow a new plant. An individual plant may die, but it lives on in the genetic template within the seed. As one scientist told me, "Instead of thinking that a seed is a plant's way of reproducing itself, it might be better to think of a plant as a seed's way of reproducing itself." Seeds may live buried in the soil for decades, waiting for the right combination of soil depth, water, and warmth to break dormancy and grow into a new plant. Though seeds are usually small, nature has a lot riding on them. And so she gives them a lot of advantages: high levels of nutritious fat, stores of energy in the form of starches that will be converted to sugar during sprouting, an inchoate version of the plant itself in the germ, vitamins, minerals, fibrous husks that protect the seeds.

Nuts are particularly rich in oils of distinctive flavor, which can add so much to dressings and sauces. Oils from almonds, walnuts, and hazelnuts have fascinating flavors, and toasted walnut and hazelnut oils are also available. Seeds are also rich in oils, and there are organic pumpkin, sunflower, sesame, safflower, grapeseed, corn, and canola oils on the market. Among the beans, soy and peanut oils are available, with peanut oil being a staple of gourmet cooks.

As much as possible, we should try to eat our nuts, seeds, and grains in their whole forms, with everything nature gave them intact. Whole-wheat bread has a lot more flavor than white bread, just as seeded breads have more texture than plain.

Not all nuts, seeds, and grains are created equal, however, particularly not in their denatured forms. It is the intent of this chapter to help you sort out the qualities of each of these foods so you can use them for the health of those you cook for and for the sheer enjoyment of eating these delicious storehouses of energy and nutrients.

Almond

PRUNUS DULCIS

THE ALMOND'S botanical name reveals that it is actually a stone fruit, in the same genus as cherries, peaches, plums, and apricots. In this case, though, it's not sweet, juicy flesh we're after but rather the seed inside the pulpy husk that covers it when it grows on the tree.

Almonds were one of the first plants to be cultivated. According to archeological evidence, almond farming began some time before 3000 BCE. The wild progenitor almond trees are from central and western Asia, as are so many of our familiar tree crops (for example, apple, apricot, and peach; if one draws a line from the Mediterranean basin to the borders of China, roughly following the old Silk Road, many of our most important food crops originated along that line, especially in central Asia).

California is the world champion almond producer today, where it's a billion-dollar-a-year industry. Almost all of America's almonds are grown in California, and 80 percent of the world supply comes from there.

THE ORGANIC FACTOR ► In California, about 10 million pounds of agricultural pesticides, herbicides, and fungicides were used on the 480,000 acres of almonds farmed by 6,000 growers in 2001. And a lot of it found its way into the tributaries that lead into San Francisco Bay, raising pesticide levels above the Environmental Protection Agency's allowable limits—meaning that levels exceeded what is considered safe. Yet an organic almond market is steadily growing, at between 18 and 20 percent a year, depending on crop size.

TYPES OF FATS IN NUTS AND SEEDS

IT'S NOT JUST the amount of fat in your diet that can affect your health but also the type of fat that triggers responses in your cholesterol and triglyceride levels. Nuts and seeds are particularly rich in fats. Here's a breakdown of their fats.

Saturated fats are found primarily in animal foods but also in some vegetable oils. Check out the amount in raw coconut meat below. They tend to raise LDL (bad cholesterol) and triglyceride levels.

Polyunsaturated fats are found in plants and seafood. They consist of Omega-6 and Omega-3 polyunsaturated fatty acids. Omega-6 fatty acids can negatively impact your HDL cholesterol by lowering it. Omega-3 fatty acids may help to beneficially increase your HDL levels. (See page 468 for more discussion of this.)

Monounsaturated fats are found in plant foods such as seeds and nuts. They lower LDL cholesterol and triglycerides in the blood, and if you replace most saturated, trans, and polyunsaturated fats in your diet with monounsaturated fats, they can raise HDL levels. They are the all-around good fats, and they are found in abundance in olive oil, canola oil, peanut, hazelnut, and grapeseed oils, as well as in the seeds and nuts in the chart below. Oleic acid in monounsaturated fats can lower bad cholesterol (LDL) while not affecting levels of good cholesterol (HDL).

The values below are percentages of each type of in the seed or nut.

TYPE OF SEED OR NUT	SATURATED FAT	POLYUNSATURATED FAT	MONOUNSATURATED FAT	OTHER FAT
Almond	6.5	21.1	68.0	4.5
Brazil nut	24.3	36.4	34.8	4.5
Cashew	19.8	16.9	58.8	4.5
Coconut	88.7	1.1	4.3	5.9
Hazelnut	7.3	9.6	78.4	4.7
Macadamia	15.0	1.7	78.9	4.4
Peanut	13.9	31.6	49.6	4.9
Pecan	8.0	24.8	62.3	4.9
Pine nut	15.4	42.1	37.6	4.9
Pistachio	12.7	15.1	67.5	4.7
Pumpkin seeds	18.9	45.6	31.1	4.4
Sesame seeds	14.0	43.8	37.8	4.4
Sunflower seeds	10.5	66.0	19.1	4.4
Walnut	9.0	63.0	23.0	5.0

Source: *USDA Handbook*

Already there are some small almond producers moving away from pesticides and toward a more organic process. (See Sources, page 517.)

NUTRITION ▸ Almonds are nutritious. People think of them as fatty, yet of the 14 grams of fat in 1 ounce of almonds, 9.5 grams are the healthful monounsaturated kind. Studies have shown that almonds lower LDL (bad cholesterol). A 1-ounce handful of almonds delivers 6 grams of protein, which is about the same as one egg or 1 ounce of meat—but without the artery-clogging saturated fat. It also contains 3 grams of dietary fiber, 35 percent of our daily requirement of antioxidant vitamin E, and excellent stores of magnesium, calcium, potassium, phosphorus, and zinc. Almonds make a great snack compared to most items on the snack aisle of the supermarket. For something so small, they're packed with good nutrition.

SEASONALITY ▸ The new crop of almonds comes in at the end of summer.

WHAT TO LOOK FOR ▸ Organic almonds are sold in bulk, and by the bag at many natural food stores. They can be found as almond butter and whole and slivered almonds. Look for whole almonds still in their brown jackets.

USES ▸ Almonds are a multipurpose nut. Add toasted almonds to salads, top muffins with them, stick them to the icing on the sides of a cake, sprinkle on a soup or pasta to add some crunch.

TO TOAST ALMONDS ▸ Place sliced almonds on a baking sheet in a 350°F oven, stirring occasionally, for 8 minutes or until golden.

ALMOND HORCHATA

MAKES 4 SERVINGS

You'll find horchata, an iced drink made with almonds, rice, or melon seeds, in most authentic Mexican restaurants. I like the version made with almonds best because of its nutty flavor and sweet creaminess. Serve horchata with homemade tacos or burritos.

1 cup whole raw almonds
2 cups boiling water
1-inch piece cinnamon stick
1/4 cup sugar
Freshly grated zest of 1 lime (well scrubbed if not organic)
Crushed or cracked ice

GARNISH, OPTIONAL
4 cinnamon sticks
4 twists of lime peel

1. Place the almonds, water, cinnamon, sugar, and lime zest in a blender and blend on low speed for 2 minutes. Blend 1 more minute, working up to high speed, then blend on high speed for 3 minutes. Turn off the blender, add 2 cups of ice, and blend again until the ice is almost entirely melted, 3 to 4 minutes.

2. Pour the horchata through a sieve lined with two layers of moistened cheesecloth, catching the liquid in a bowl. Discard the cheesecloth and solids. Transfer the horchata to a pitcher or bottle. Cover and refrigerate for 1 day—this improves the flavor.

3. Fill tall glasses with ice and fill with horchata. If desired, garnish with a cinnamon stick and a twist of lime peel. ∎

BISCOTTI

MAKES ABOUT 20 BISCOTTI

Kids think they're cookies but adults know they are a superbly nutritious snack (see Nutrition at left).

2 tablespoons canola oil or nonstick spray
1/2 cup roughly chopped almonds
2 cups all-purpose flour
2 teaspoons baking powder
1/4 teaspoon salt
1/2 cup brown sugar
2 tablespoons honey
1/4 cup well-beaten eggs (1 extra-large or 2 small)
1/2 teaspoon vanilla extract
1/2 teaspoon almond extract

1. Preheat the oven to 350°F. Lightly oil or spray a large baking sheet and spread the almonds in a single layer. Toast for 5 to 8 minutes, until golden and fragrant. Set the pan aside to cool.

2. Combine the flour, baking powder, and salt in a small bowl and mix well. In a large bowl, beat together the sugar, honey, eggs, vanilla, and almond extracts until thoroughly mixed. Stir in the toasted almonds. Add the flour mixture and mix until all is well incorporated.

3. Divide the dough into 2 balls. Roll each into a cylinder 10 inches long and 2 inches wide. Lay them on the baking sheet about 6 inches apart and bake for 20 to 25 minutes, until the top is golden brown and slightly cracked.

4. Remove from the oven and let cool until barely warm.

5. Lay the cylinders on a cutting board and cut 3/4-inch-thick slices on the diagonal. Return the slices to the baking sheet and bake 10 to 12 minutes more until firm and lightly golden. Cool on a wire rack. ▪

Brazil Nut

BERTHOLLETIA EXCELSA

ALMOST ALL BRAZIL NUTS are gathered from the wild rain forests of Brazil, with small amounts from Venezuela, Columbia, the Guyanas, Bolivia, and Peru. The trees that bear them are huge—150 feet tall with crowns up to 100 feet in diameter. The fruits, called *ourico,* are spherical pods that weigh from one to five pounds and grow in the tree canopy far out of reach of pickers. So the pickers wait for them to fall. But a five-pound weight dropped from 150 feet can kill a person—and has—so pickers wear large protective wooden hats and avoid gathering the ourico on rainy or windy days.

When hacked open by a machete, each ourico reveals ten to twenty-five nuts packed inside like orange segments. Each nut is covered with the very hard shell we're familiar with. Brazil nuts are related to the *sapucaya* nut, also called the paradise nut, supposedly one of the best-tasting nuts in the world. That treasure is available only in Brazil and the Guyanas, grown locally by property owners.

NUTRITION ▪ Brazil nuts are 17 percent protein and contain 8 grams of fiber per 100 grams of nutmeat. The USDA says that 35 percent of their fat content is monounsaturated.

WHAT TO LOOK FOR ▪ Although Brazil nuts can be bought shelled, they rapidly turn rancid after shelling and so should be purchased in the shell and cracked as needed, despite the difficulty.

USES ▪ When fresh, these oily nuts have a sweet, creamy flavor that's very appealing. The flavor is enhanced by a light toasting in the oven.

They are a familiar addition to mixed nuts, but they can also be used to make a Brazil nut milk by whizzing them in the blender with water until they're thoroughly pulverized, then straining out the liquid.

BRAZIL NUT BARK

MAKES ABOUT 1 POUND

About the only time most of us have chocolate bark is when we buy it at the chocolate shop, but it's easy to make at home. The chocolate must be melted in a double boiler or it will scorch.

12 ounces semisweet chocolate
1 tablespoon butter
1 cup chopped Brazil nuts
$1/2$ cup seedless raisins

Melt the chocolate with the butter in the top of a double boiler, keeping the water beneath at a simmer. When melted, remove from the heat, stir in the Brazil nuts and raisins and spread in a thin layer on a cookie sheet lined with wax paper. Place in the refrigerator until cold and firm. Break into pieces and store in the fridge in a tightly covered container. ▪

BRAZIL NUT AND CASHEW LOAF

SERVES 6

This vegan dish has a rich, nutty flavor and heaps of nutrition. Chestnut puree is available ready-made at gourmet food stores, or make your own (see To Make Chestnut Puree, page 327).

2 tablespoons canola oil, plus extra for the loaf pan
1 medium onion, chopped fine
1 clove garlic, crushed

5 celery stalks, chopped fine
$3/4$ cup finely ground Brazil nuts
$3/4$ cup finely ground cashews
$1/4$ cup flaked millet or quick-cooking (1-minute) rolled oats
$1/4$ cup bread crumbs
$1/2$ cup mashed potatoes
2 teaspoons minced fresh parsley
1 teaspoon crumbled dried sage
$1/2$ teaspoon dried oregano
$1/4$ teaspoon ground ginger
$1/4$ teaspoon crushed red pepper flakes or cayenne
$1/4$ teaspoon curry powder
Salt and freshly ground black pepper
Juice and freshly grated zest of $1/2$ lemon (well scrubbed if not organic)
Vegetable stock
1 cup chestnut puree

1. Preheat the oven to 375°F.
2. Heat the oil in a frying pan over medium heat, add the onion and cook until translucent, about 5 minutes. Add the garlic and celery and cook 1 to 2 minutes longer, until the celery wilts slightly. Turn this mixture into a large bowl and add the Brazil nuts, cashews, millet, bread crumbs, mashed potatoes, parsley, sage, oregano, ginger, red pepper, curry, salt and pepper, and lemon juice and zest. Add enough vegetable stock to moisten the mixture so it holds together, but be careful not to make it soggy and heavy.
3. Put half the mixture into a lightly oiled $8 1/2$ x $4 1/2$-inch loaf pan and spread it evenly. Cover with the chestnut puree, then add the rest of the mixture on top, smoothing it out evenly. Bake for 45 minutes. If desired, serve with Cashew Sauce (page 326). ▪

Cashew

ANACARDIUM OCCIDENTALE

THE CASHEW is a medium size, handsome tree native to northeastern Brazil. It produces pear-shaped fruits called "apples" that have a sour and astringent taste and extremely perishable flesh rich in vitamin C. (Cashew apples are sweetened to make a popular drink in that country.) The cashew nut forms inside a hard shell at the end of the apple. The outer surface of the shell contains urushiol, the substance in poison ivy and poison oak that causes dermatitis, so people who handle the shells have to wear protective gloves. Inside the shell but outside the cashew nut meat is a layer that contains an extremely toxic resin, powerful enough that it's used to burn off warts.

To get truly raw cashews, the shells have to be removed by hand very carefully, because if the toxic elements get on the nuts, they are ruined. There is a company in Indonesia that does this, but it's slow and expensive. Instead of trying to obtain raw cashews, most purveyors steam the shells until they burst open, or roast them until the shells become brittle and crack open—in either case the toxic elements are cooked away. The cashews then can come out safe and clean. By this time the nuts aren't really raw, but since there's no further roasting and salting, they are billed as "raw."

THE ORGANIC FACTOR ◆ While much cashew production is conventional, there are organic suppliers in places like Sri Lanka and Indonesia. Look for organic cashews in markets that specialize in organic products.

NUTRITION ◆ Cashews are rich in protein: about 17 percent. A 1-ounce handful of nuts also contains about 7 grams of monounsaturated fat, 70 to 80 percent of which is oleic acid. One ounce also contains about 5 grams of saturated fat, so folks trying to keep their saturated fat consumption down should have cashews only as an occasional, though nutritionally valuable, treat.

WHAT TO LOOK FOR ◆ In the store, you'll find both organic and conventional cashews sold roasted and salted, and also sold as raw nuts, even though they aren't really raw. I know of only one source of truly raw cashews (www.rawfood.com), but their supply from Indonesia is meager and usually sold out.

USES ◆ Cashews have a wonderful texture, softly crunchy with a light nutty flavor. They are great plain, as a snack all by themselves. Use them, lightly toasted and crushed, in stir-fries with chicken strips and vegetables, and in curries in place of peanuts. They're essential in high-quality trail mixes. Cashew butter is rich and usually made from toasted cashews so it has a nutty flavor. It makes a great topping for veggie burgers.

To toast cashews, place raw cashews on a cookie sheet in a 350°F oven for 5 to 7 minutes; be careful to remove them from the oven when they're just turning a light brown, as they scorch easily.

CASHEW SAUCE

MAKES 1 1/2 CUPS

This easy-to-make sauce is perfect for enhancing stir-fried tofu or grains such as rice or barley.

1/2 cup raw cashews
2 cloves garlic
1/4 medium onion, chopped coarsely
1 tablespoon arrowroot powder
1 tablespoon tamari

Place the cashews, garlic, onion, arrowroot, and 1 cup of water in a blender and blend until smooth. Pour into a small saucepan and add the tamari. Place the pan over medium heat and stir until it thickens, about 5 minutes. Be careful not to overcook, as it thickens further as it cools. ▪

Chestnut

CASTANEA, various species

BEFORE THE CHESTNUT BLIGHT hit the forests of the eastern United States in the late 1800s, an estimated four billion American chestnut trees dominated the woodlands of the Appalachians. The trees were beautiful and could reach 100 feet tall with trunks 6 feet in diameter. The wood was straight-grained, visually beautiful, and exceptionally rot resistant. The annual drop of nutrient-rich chestnuts supported many forms of domestic and wild animals—as well as Native Americans and newly arrived settlers. By 1950, only fifty to 100 American chestnut trees remained in all of North America.

However, European and Asian chestnut varieties that had traveled to North America were resistant to the blight. The remaining American chestnuts were crossbred with these types in order to develop blight resistance, then rebred with American chestnuts again and again in order to yield trees that were almost purely American types but resistant to blight. Today, thousands of these resistant American types have been planted throughout their old range and the lovely American chestnut is making a comeback. Real American chestnuts can again be found in specialty markets. (See Sources, page 517, for suppliers.)

I used to find them occasionally along back roads in Pennsylvania. The giant trees had died, but their roots continued to send up sprouts that reached about 8 to 10 feet in height, whereupon they were taken by the chestnut blight. But sometimes that was tall enough for the sprouts to flower and form a few nuts. I have eaten American chestnuts both raw out of hand and roasted. They are delicious, and their deliciousness only underscores what a tragedy befell the king of the forest.

Chestnut blight continues to be a problem, however, so people all over America are working to grow blight-resistant chestnut trees. You can help the effort by joining the American Chestnut Foundation (www.acf.org).

THE ORGANIC FACTOR ◆ Almost all chestnuts sold in American markets, whether European, Asian, or American, are grown without pesticides. They may not be certified organic, but they are likely to be clean.

NUTRITION ◆ Chestnuts are low in fat and high in complete carbohydrates. They are rich in trace elements and have similar nutritive power to brown rice. Some call them "the grain that grows on a tree."

TYPES ► There are four species of chestnuts grown commercially for food: Chinese (*C. mollissima*), Henry (*C. henry;* also from China), European (*C. sativa*), and Japanese (*C. crenata*). According to Greg Miller, an expert at the Empire Chestnut Company (www.empirechestnut.com), the very best tasting of these are Chinese, because of their rich and nutty flavor. Second best would be American, but it's not yet grown in quantity, and so Henry (which tastes similar to American) takes second place. Third best is European. And last place goes to Japanese, which has an insipid flavor. In Europe and California, many Euro-Japanese hybrid varieties are being grown—Colossal being an example—but its quality isn't as good as Chinese or Henry chestnuts.

SEASONALITY ► The season for fresh chestnuts runs from October to January, although they can be purchased dried or frozen—but of lesser quality—at other times.

WHAT TO LOOK FOR ► When buying them fresh, look for chestnuts with heft and tight shells. They should be plump and fresh-looking, without any cracks. Their condition is determined by how carefully and quickly they were harvested after falling from the trees. Don't buy them peeled, for they surely will have lost quality. Be wary of dried chestnuts. They can turn rancid if stored too long. If you can't find organic chestnuts at the store, they are available online (see Sources, page 517).

STORAGE AND PREPARATION ► The shells must be removed before using, of course, and their bitter inner skin should be peeled away, too.

TO SHELL CHESTNUTS ► Use a paring knife to peel away a strip of shell from each chestnut, then drop them in a saucepan of cold water. Bring to a boil. Boil for 1 minute, then remove from the heat. Lift them out one by one from the hot water, and peel away the shell and inner skin while they're warm. If the inner skin refuses to come loose on a few of them, set those chestnuts aside and reboil for 30 seconds, then try again.

TO ROAST WHOLE CHESTNUTS ► Make a slit in the shell (to prevent bursting), then roast them in a 375°F oven for 30 minutes, until the inside is tender. When our woodstove is going, I just set them on the top of the stove until they're tender (don't forget the slit).

TO MAKE CHESTNUT PUREE ► Boil 2 cups of shelled fresh chestnuts for 10 to 20 minutes until tender, peel them, and whiz them in the blender with a little water.

USES ► Of whatever species, good chestnuts are sweet and flavorful. Given their starchiness, they are culinarily more like potatoes or grains than like other nuts. As such, they are versatile. Shelled chestnuts are excellent as a meat garnish, such as in chestnut stuffing for the Thanksgiving bird. And they have an affinity for game of any sort, sausages, chicken, and pork. (Try adding whole shelled chestnuts to a chicken and vegetable stir-fry.) Whole peeled chestnuts are candied (see recipe on page 328) or preserved in syrup for *marrons glacés.*

Unsweetened chestnut puree (see above) can be served as a savory garnish. It can be added to sauces, or used in poultry and meat stuffings, and is the base for croquettes and chestnut soufflés. Sweetened puree—*purée de marron*—is eaten with yogurt and used in ice creams, candies, cookies, and pastries.

GLAZED CHESTNUTS

MAKES 30 CHESTNUTS

These little sweetmeats are just right for the holidays.

2 cups sugar

Pinch of salt

1 pound shelled fresh chestnuts (see Preparation, page 327)

1. In a 2-quart saucepan, combine 2 cups water with the sugar and salt. Bring to a boil over medium-high heat, then reduce heat to low and cook for 25 minutes, allowing the syrup to thicken.

2. Meanwhile, place the chestnuts in a separate 2-quart saucepan, cover with water and bring to a boil over high heat. Reduce heat to low and cook for 10 minutes, then drain the chestnuts and run under cold water to stop the cooking. Add the drained chestnuts to the sugar syrup, cover, and simmer over low heat for 20 minutes. Remove from heat, let cool to room temperature, then place in the fridge overnight.

3. The next day, bring the chestnuts and syrup to a simmer over low heat and cook for 15 minutes. Cool again to room temperature, then cover and refrigerate overnight for a second time. Remove the chestnuts from the syrup and place in a jar, covered. Store in the refrigerator for up to four weeks. ■

Hazelnut

CORYLUS AVELLANA and
CORYLUS MAXIMA

HAZELNUTS are easy to grow, bear heavy crops of nuts in almost every climate in the United States, and have a mild, delicious flavor after they've cured. If you have the space, I strongly recommend planting a few bushes.

THE ORGANIC FACTOR ► Organic hazelnuts are widely available and can be purchased by mail order (see Sources, page 517). Some are given a mold-prevention treatment with sulfur dioxide and some are not. I never sulfured my homegrown hazelnuts, and they invariably developed a little mold on the more porous part of the shell. But I never noticed that there was any loss of quality in the nuts inside; the small amount of mold was just on the surface of the shell.

NUTRITION ► Hazelnuts are champions among nuts and seeds when it comes to percentage of monounsaturated fat in their oil. Nearly 80 percent of the oil is monounsaturated, the healthiest type of fat for the cardiovascular system.

TYPES ► The commercial hazelnuts (also called filberts, probably after St. Philibert of Burgundy, whose day is August 22, exactly the nutting season) that we find in stores are mostly grown in Oregon and Washington and are usually hybrids of the *Corylus avellana* of western Europe and *Corylus maxima* of southeastern Europe. Besides being more vigorous due to their hybrid nature, these shrubs combine the flavor profiles of both species.

If you're interested in planting a hazelnut bush for ornamental purposes, look for a variety of hazelnut called Harry Lauder's Walking Stick (*Corylus avellana* 'Contorta') with wildly contorted branches.

SEASONALITY ‣ Hazelnuts are ready to pick in late August. They need to dry and cure for a couple of months (November to December) to be at their peak of flavor and texture.

WHAT TO LOOK FOR ‣ The best hazelnuts feel heavy in the hand.

HAZELNUT OIL ‣ Cooks love hazelnut expressed oil for salad dressing. A little goes a long way. The delicate flavor of the oil is quickly ruined by heat, so it's not an oil for cooking. And it tends to go rancid quickly. So buy the oil in small quantities and use it up within a few weeks.

STORAGE AND PREPARATION ‣ Hazelnuts store well at room temperature but slowly lose quality as they dry out.

Sulfured or not, hazelnuts should be eaten within a month of their purchase. They'll store indefinitely in the freezer.

USES ‣ To get the best flavor from hazelnuts, lightly roast the shelled nuts and cool them before crushing or grinding them for breads, pastries, and confections. Their flavor harmonizes well with coffee and chocolate. The brownish skin of the nuts contains fiber and minerals, so there's no need to remove it.

One pound of hazelnuts in the shell equals about 1½ cups of shelled nutmeat, and 1 cup of shelled whole nuts is about 5 ounces.

MY FAVORITE HAZELNUTS

I GREW A TRIO of hazelnut bushes on my property in Pennsylvania and after a few years, they bore magnificently. When they came ripe in late August, I took my young daughter to the tall bushes to gather the nuts, but after looking for a minute, she declared that there were no nuts. I told her we had to sit down and wait and the nuts would appear. After a few more minutes, she saw one—or rather, the fringed, green husk in which the nut resides. Then another. And then another, until finally she saw that the bushes were dripping with nuts.

Imagine my surprise then when I was walking down my driveway and noticed that some bushes along the side looked very much like my hazelnut bushes, only smaller. On closer inspection, there were miniature versions of the husks and nuts. I'd discovered the wild hazelnut, *Corylus americana*, growing right on my own property. There's a version that grows on the West Coast, called *Corylus cornuta*, that ripens about the same time as the wild huckleberries, and a handful of huckleberries and hazelnuts make a delicious snack around Labor Day in these parts. The flavor of wild hazelnuts of either species is incomparably better than the cultivated kinds.

HAZELNUT-CRUSTED PORK LOIN

SERVES 4

This recipe turns an ordinary pork loin into something very special as it combines the sweet meat with toasty nuts, fruity peaches, and tangy lemon. Since you'll be cooking the hazelnuts when you cook the pork loin, don't toast them before grinding.

2 pounds hazelnuts in the shell
1/4 cup flour
1 egg
2 tablespoons milk
2 boneless pork tenderloins, each cut in half crosswise
2 tablespoons canola oil
2 or 3 fresh peaches
1/2 cup half-and-half
2 cups chicken stock
Freshly grated zest of 1/2 lemon (well scrubbed
    if not organic)
Salt and freshly ground black pepper

1. Shell the nuts and pulse in a food processor or blender to grind them fine but not to a pasty meal. You should end up with about 1 1/2 cups of ground nuts.

2. Preheat the oven to 450°F.

3. Set up 3 shallow bowls. Place the flour, egg and milk beaten together, and nuts each in its own bowl. Coat the pork loin pieces in the flour first, then the egg, then the nuts, making sure they're entirely covered, including the cut ends.

4. Heat the oil in a large skillet over medium heat and sauté the loins on all sides until golden brown, about 5 to 8 minutes. Start a pot of water on high heat to be used for peeling the peaches. Transfer the loins to a clean skillet or baking pan and roast them for 20 minutes.

5. While the loins are roasting, drop the peaches in the boiling water for a minute or two, then peel them and cut them into thin slices. (You should have

2 cups.) Mash the slices to a pulp using a potato masher, or whiz them in the blender. Combine them in a 2-quart saucepan with the half-and-half, chicken stock, lemon zest, and a pinch of salt and pepper. Place the pan over low heat and simmer until heated through, about 5 minutes. Be careful not to overcook or scorch the mixture.

6. When the loins are done, cut each piece into 1/2-inch slices and place on a plate, and spoon some of the peach sauce around the slices. ◾

Macadamia Nut

MACADAMIA INTEGRIFOLIA

BEFORE 1880, only Australian Aborigines knew of and feasted on macadamia nuts. But that year, a botanist by the name of Dr. Hill "discovered" them in their native range around Brisbane, Queensland, in northeast Australia, and named them for his friend, Dr. John Macadam. Within a few years, they were brought to Hawaii where they flourished, as the climate was perfect for them. Today, about 90 percent of the world's supply is grown in Hawaii, and the nut joins sugar and pineapples as the top three exports from the islands. Large commercial groves have also been established in Australia and New Zealand. The nut has exceptional qualities—a delicacy of flavor, sweetness, and a wonderfully crunchy (but not hard or brittle) texture—and world demand greatly exceeds supply.

THE ORGANIC FACTOR ➤ On Hawaii, a macadamia nut farmer named Tuddie Purdy and his family is the foremost supplier of naturally grown macadamia nuts. Stinkbugs and tropical nut borers can be a problem for macadamias, but the Purdys remain committed to natural (chemical-free), if not organic, production.

NUTRITION ‣ Given that their oil is almost 80 percent monounsaturated fat, macadamias are very good for you as nuts go—as good as olive oil in lowering cholesterol. Be aware that conventional macadamia nuts may be dressed in coconut oil and salt. Seeking naturally grown nuts is worth the effort.

WHAT TO LOOK FOR ‣ Look for shelled nuts with no blemishes and a light creamy-yellow color. Nuts in the shell are harder to find, but should be without cracks.

STORAGE AND PREPARATION ‣ Store them in the fridge or freezer to prevent rancidity. If you do find unshelled macadamias, you will discover that their shells are tough to crack. The best way is probably to crack—not smash—them on a flat rock or cement with another flat rock or a brick; a nutcracker won't work.

USES ‣ Use macadamias in cookies and as you would any other nut. Freshly shelled, roasted macadamias are probably the premier treat of the nut world.

TO TOAST MACADAMIAS ‣ Place them in a baking pan in a 350°F oven for 10 minutes; lower the heat to 250°F and let the nuts roast to a golden brown, about another 30 minutes, shaking them occasionally. The flavor of the nuts will be concentrated and enriched.

TROUT MACADAMIA

SERVES 4

Instead of the classic French dish of trout with almonds, substitute unsalted, unprocessed macadamia nuts to create a special dinner.

1/2 teaspoon salt
1/2 teaspoon freshly ground black pepper
1 1/4 cups all-purpose flour
4 small trout, cleaned and gutted
4 tablespoons unsalted butter
2 tablespoons canola oil
1 cup chopped raw macadamia nuts
2 tablespoons chopped fresh parsley
Juice of 2 lemons

1. Preheat the oven to 200°F.

2. Mix the salt, pepper, and flour together, then dredge the trout in the mixture, shaking off any excess. Heat the butter and oil together in a large skillet over medium heat and cook the trout for about 7 minutes, turning once or twice, until the flesh is white all the way through. Place the trout on a warm platter and set aside in the oven.

3. Add the macadamia nuts to the pan and stir until they are lightly toasted, about 5 minutes. Add the parsley and lemon juice, and cook them for 1 minute, reducing the pan juices slightly to a glaze. Pour this mixture over the trout and serve. ∎

KEEP AN EYE OUT FOR UNSHELLED MACADAMIAS

MOST MACADAMIA NUTS are sold in vacuum tins already shelled, but if you can find them still in their tough shells, that's the way to go because once shelled, they begin to lose quality. If you're traveling in Hawaii, you can probably find the nuts in their shells at the nut farms or local stores. California plantings in Riverside and San Diego counties are often sold in-shell.

Peanut

ARACHIS HYPOGAEA

PEANUTS have conquered the world since they were brought back from their native Andean lowlands, where the Incas ate them and fashioned gold necklaces and ornaments in their shape.

Peanuts are an unusual kind of little bean. The peanut plant is a little herbaceous bush that produces bright yellow flowers. As the flowers fade, a shoot called a "peg" develops at each flower's base, elongates, and reaches down toward the soil. When it touches the ground, it burrows under the surface, where it grows its seeds—the peanuts. As far as I know, the peanut is the only plant that has this aerial and subterranean reproductive phase. It's certainly the only one I've ever grown that does this.

THE ORGANIC FACTOR ◆ Unlike the commercial brands, organic purveyors don't mix their peanut butter with hydrogenated vegetable oils, which include potentially damaging trans-fatty acids. They also don't put in the kinds of additives and chemicals that make most commercial peanut butters taste like peanut-flavored vegetable shortening. Make sure your peanut butter is from 100 percent organic peanuts and your whole peanuts are certified organic.

Like all legumes, peanuts grow colonies of nitrogen-fixing bacteria on their roots, thus enriching the soil they grow in, and so make excellent additions to any garden.

NUTRITION ◆ About half the oil in peanuts is monounsaturated, the bulk of the rest is polyunsaturated, and there is about 14 percent saturated fat.

TYPES ◆ Red Spanish and Virginia peanuts are the two most common types grown in the United States.

A WORD ON PEANUT SAFETY

ALL PEANUTS, whether grown organically or conventionally, are prone to develop *Aspergillus flavus* mold (which produces a potent carcinogen called aflatoxin) if not stored properly. The mold likes a grain or bean with a high oil content—peanuts and corn, for instance—that has been stored in a poorly constructed bin or silo. Peanuts are especially prone to this if they sit in storage in humid, hot conditions. For that reason, bulk peanuts grown and shipped from China—the peanuts often used to make commercial peanut butters—are to be avoided. But those grown in the United States are just as prone to the mold if stored poorly.

Producers of organic peanuts, peanut butters, and other peanut products must be as vigilant as the conventional producers. A reliable organic producer of peanuts or peanut butter will check aflatoxin levels to make sure it is below government maximum levels.

SOME PEOPLE are violently allergic to peanuts, and even a little bit in their food will cause allergic reactions that send them to the hospital. Such folks need to be extremely careful about what they eat, because there are peanut products used in many foods often without being listed on the labels.

SEASONALITY ▸ Peanuts are harvested in late summer or early fall.

WHAT TO LOOK FOR ▸ The best way to ensure that you get high quality peanuts that haven't sat around in poor conditions (see A Word on Peanut Safety at left) is to order fresh raw organic peanuts when the new crop comes in— August and September—from a reputable mail-order retailer such as Diamond Organics (www .diamond-organics.com), and freeze them as soon as you get them.

STORAGE AND PREPARATION ▸ Peanuts have reddish-brown skins, which I personally like to leave on—even when making peanut butter. If you prefer to remove them, freeze the peanuts overnight: The skins will slip off easily. Peanuts can be eaten raw, but are delicious roasted and lightly salted or made into peanut butter.

TO ROAST AND SALT PEANUTS ▸ Place two cups of shelled raw peanuts on a baking sheet and roast in a 350°F oven for 15 to 20 minutes. Use as much salt as you like, realizing that the more salt you use, the more likely you are to raise your blood pressure.

TO MAKE PEANUT BUTTER ▸ Place 2 cups roasted peanuts in a blender with 1½ teaspoons of peanut oil, salt to taste, and blend them into a smooth paste. This makes about 1 cup of peanut butter, which you should store in the fridge and use within two or three weeks.

Peanuts store indefinitely when frozen in a tightly closed container. Thaw and use them raw or roasted in a wide variety of dishes or to make peanut butter as you need it.

USES ▸ Peanuts have a strong affinity for chocolate. Mix 2 heaping tablespoonfuls of peanut butter into 5 ounces of sweet dark chocolate melted in a double boiler, then use this warm over a hot fudge sundae. If too thick, thin with a little milk.

Peanuts are a staple ingredient in many cuisines, including West African, Indian, Southeast Asian, and Chinese. They go beautifully with chicken (such as Indian curries, Thai satay with peanut sauce, Chinese stir-fried chicken with crushed peanuts) and with beef. Use crushed roasted peanuts to garnish salads.

Peanut oil is mild and used extensively in Chinese stir-frying because it can take high heat without smoking or turning bitter.

THAI PEANUT SAUCE

MAKES ABOUT 1 CUP

Slice raw chicken breasts into long strips, slide them onto bamboo skewers, then dip them in (bottled) plum sauce. Grill until done and serve with this peanut sauce. It's double yummy.

1 cup coconut milk (fresh if possible)
1 tablespoon Thai red curry paste
2 tablespoons smooth peanut butter
1 tablespoon chili paste
2 tablespoons white sugar
1 tablespoon freshly squeezed lime juice
¼ teaspoon salt

Bring the coconut milk to a boil in a small saucepan. Reduce the heat to medium and whisk in the curry and chili pastes. Stir in the peanut butter, sugar, lime juice, and salt. Reduce the heat to simmer and cook for 10 minutes, until thickened. Set aside to cool. It keeps about 3 weeks in the fridge. ▪

PEANUT SALVAGE BARS

MAKES 8 BARS

They're called "salvage" because they'll save you when you need a burst of energy and nutrition. They're as delicious as they are nutritious.

$1/4$ cup raw or toasted wheat germ

$1/4$ cup shelled sunflower seeds

$1/2$ cup shelled peanuts

Salt

$1/2$ cup raisins

2 cups 1-minute rolled oats

2 cups puffed rice cereal

$1/2$ cup crunchy peanut butter

$1/2$ cup brown sugar, firmly packed

$1/2$ cup maple syrup

1 teaspoon vanilla extract

1. Preheat the oven to 350°F.

2. If using raw wheat germ, spread it on a baking sheet and toast for a few minutes until fragrant.

3. Spread the sunflower seeds and the peanuts in an even layer on separate baking sheets and toast in the oven—the sunflower seeds will take about 6 minutes and the peanuts will take 15 to 20 minutes. Remove and let cool; salt the peanuts lightly.

4. Mix the wheat germ, sunflower seeds, peanuts, raisins, oats, and puffed rice in a large bowl. In a separate bowl that fits in your microwave, mix the peanut butter, brown sugar, and maple syrup; microwave on high for 2 minutes. Add the vanilla extract and stir until well blended. Pour over the dry ingredients and fold in until everything is evenly coated.

5. Grease an 8-inch-square baking pan with a nonstick spray and transfer the mixture from the bowl. Cover the surface with wax paper and press it down firmly. Let this stand until completely cool, at least an hour. Cut into eight 2 × 4–inch bars. ∎

Pecan and Hickory Nut

CARYA ILLINOENSIS and CARYA OVATO

PECANS are a species of Carya (*Carya illinoensis*) but grow further to the south than hickories, from the mid-Atlantic states to the Gulf of Mexico. The trees grow to 100 feet and shower the ground with nuts in the fall. The nuts are delicious but not nearly as highly flavored as their cousin the hickory nut (*Carya ovata*). Pecans have some sterling advantages though, especially their thin shells that allow one to crack them and extract whole halves.

NUTRITION ▸ The pecan's oil is about 60 percent monounsaturated fat, with most of the rest polyunsaturated fat, and hickories have similar amounts. Each 1-ounce handful of pecans or hickory nuts contains about 18 grams of fat, thus about 11 grams of monounsaturated fat. No wonder Native Americans laid in great stores of these nuts for winter use. Just as rural people today still do, wherever pecans and hickories grow.

TYPES ▸ If you like pecans but have never tasted a hickory nut—wow, do you have a treat coming. Hickory nuts carry something of the same intense hickory flavor as the wood that's used to smoke meats.

It's rare to find wild hickory nutmeats in markets. They are almost always natural, if not certified organic, because they're gathered from the wild. If shelled out, the essential oils that make them so delicious soon turn rancid. I have seen them at farmers markets in the fall in the East, husks removed but sold in the shell, and a small basket will provide work for several hours because the shells of wild nuts are as hard as bone, and the nutmeats is buried in folds and caverns within. The best way to shell them is to smash them between two bricks, then carefully separate the pieces of nut meat from the pieces of shell. Rare is the nut that shells out a whole half of a wild hickory nut.

In addition to regular pecans and hickory nuts, breeders have crossed the hickory with the pecan to create the hican, of which there are many named varieties. These crosses and selections tend to capture some of the hickory nut's full flavor but have much thinner shells, making it possible to shell out whole halves.

SEASONALITY ► Both pecans and hickory nuts ripen in the fall.

WHAT TO LOOK FOR ► Look for large, plump nuts. Discard any that feel light in the hand. Once shelled out, the nutmeats quickly go rancid and should be frozen if stored.

USES ► Pecans are a healthy snack, great crushed and used to top breakfast cereals, made into pecan pie, marinated in soy sauce then dried, and candied to add to salads. Hickory nutmeat can be substituted in any recipe calling for pecans and will ratchet the flavor up several notches. Add chopped hickory nuts to your chocolate chip cookies—they are out of this world.

SOUTHERN PECAN PIE

SERVES 8

If your mama didn't make pecan pie like this, after one taste you'll wish she did. Using hickory nuts or hicans will make a much more flavorful pie.

1 single crust for a 9-inch pie (see page 211), chilled
2 eggs, separated, plus 1 egg yolk
1 cup sour cream
1 cup sugar
4 tablespoons cornstarch
1/4 teaspoon lemon zest (well scrubbed if not organic)
Pinch salt
1 cup packed brown sugar
1 cup chopped pecans (or hickory nuts, or hicans)

1. Preheat oven to 350°F. Roll out the dough to a circle about 1/8 inch thick and 12 inches in diameter. Transfer to a 9-inch pie pan. Trim the edges 1/2 inch larger than the pan and crimp with the back of a fork. Poke holes here and there with a fork. Fill with pie weights, dry beans, or raw rice. Bake for 20 minutes, remove from oven, remove the weights and waxed paper, and let cool.

2. In the top of a double boiler, mix the egg yolks, sour cream, white sugar, cornstarch, lemon zest, and salt. Cook very gently over low heat (the water beneath should not boil) and stir until the mixture thickens enough to coat a spoon. Don't over cook or heat the mixture too quickly or the yolks will curdle. Pour the thickened mixture into the pie shell.

3. In a large bowl, beat the egg white until soft peaks form. Add the brown sugar slowly and fold it in. Fold in the pecans. Spread this mixture over the pie filling and bake for about 50 minutes or until lightly browned. Cool before serving. ■

Pine Nut

PINUS EDULIS

PINE NUTS are the edible hard-shelled seeds of certain pine trees. They develop in the crevasses between the scales of the pine cones. One reason that pine nuts are so expensive is that they defy cultivation, and most are still gathered from the wild.

Pine nuts are very old foods, both in Europe and the Americas. Pine nuts have been harvested around the Mediterranean since Biblical times; Roman soldiers brought them north on their forays into northern Europe and the British Isles.

Native Americans relied on pine nuts for millennia as a concentrated source of protein-rich food. Then in the 1970s, the Federal Government bulldozed thousands of acres of pinyon pines and ran cattle on the cleared land. This was to give the Native American tribes a source of protein. Ironically, the amount of protein that could be obtained "per acre" from slaughtering and consuming the cattle didn't approach what could previously have been obtained from harvesting nuts from the pinyon pines.

THE ORGANIC FACTOR ► Pine nuts are gathered from the wild, so while they're not organic, they are a natural food.

NUTRITION ► Pine nuts have great amounts of monounsaturated fats, protein, B vitamins, folate, and trace minerals.

TYPES ► In America, most pine nuts come form the pinyon pine (*Pinus edulis*), which grows on the east side of California's great central valley in the Sierra foothills and up on the Sierra Nevada mountains, as well as east to Utah and down to New Mexico. The single-leaf pinyon (*Pinus monophylla*) and the Mexican pinyon (*Pinus cembroides*) also contribute to the pine nut harvest. In Europe, pine nuts are harvested from the Mediterranean stone pine (*Pinus pinea*). Other pine species produce nuts in Asia and South America.

SEASONALITY ► The nuts are gathered in the late fall when the cones open.

WHAT TO LOOK FOR ► Check pine nuts carefully: Pine nuts contain between 48 and 68 percent unsaturated fat (as well as 12 to 30 percent protein) and this oil rather rapidly turns rancid.

FORAGING FOR WILD PINE NUTS

FROM WHERE I LIVE it's just an hour's drive to some nearby mountains where pinyon pines grow, and it's fun to drive there in the fall to gather the big cones and retrieve the small nuts (about half the size of the nail on your little finger—if that). The nuts are fresh-tasting, with a sweet, slightly resinous flavor that makes them unique.

If you are able to forage for your own pine nuts, you will have to shell them. Tap the shells with a hammer: They will break apart fairly easily so you can get to the nutmeat inside.

Rancid pine nuts acquire an unpleasant musty, dirty flavor, while fresh ones have a clean, bright, sweet flavor. Always taste a sample before buying.

STORAGE AND PREPARATION ▸ Store in a freezer bag in the freezer.

USES ▸ Pine nuts are incredibly versatile as well as wholesome. They can be used ground or whole with savory dishes such as meats, fish, and game, with sweet dishes such as cakes, puddings, and all kinds of desserts and sweetmeats, in stuffings, with vegetables, in sauces, and in soups. The classic use for pine nuts, of course, is pesto (see recipe).

With a good supply of pine nuts, you can make your own pesto and keep it in a closed container in the freezer, where it will keep indefinitely. A delicious and quick dinner then becomes as easy as boiling the pasta (try whole-wheat cappellini), thawing a couple of tablespoons of pesto in the microwave just until warm (about 30 seconds), pouring the pesto on the pasta. Other uses for pesto: Spread it on tomato and mozzarella sandwiches, stuff mushroom caps with it before baking, spread it on pizza instead of tomato sauce (using extra diced garlic on the pizza), and dress steamed broccoli with it.

PESTO

MAKES ABOUT 1 ½ CUPS

When made from fresh, sweet pine nuts that you've shelled (I know it's tedious, but once shelled, pine nuts soon lose their resinous charm), pesto sounds a flavor harmony that defines the taste of Liguria in northern Italy. The better the ingredients you use, the finer the pesto.

¼ cup extra-virgin olive oil
½ cup freshly shelled pine nuts
4 ounces Parmigiano-Reggiano cheese
4 large cloves garlic, minced
2 cups fresh basil leaves, loosely packed
1 cup fresh Italian flat-leaf parsley leaves, loosely packed
1 tablespoon fresh oregano leaves
Salt and freshly ground black pepper

1. Place the olive oil in a skillet over medium heat and add the pine nuts. Cook, shaking the skillet occasionally every minute or so, for about 7 minutes, until the pine nuts brown slightly. Don't let them get too dark or burn or they'll become bitter. As the pine nuts are cooking, grate the Parmigiano-Reggiano into a bowl (you should have about 1 cup of cheese).

2. Remove the pine nuts from heat when light brown and set aside to cool slightly. Place the grated cheese, garlic, basil, parsley, and oregano in a blender or food processor. Add the oil, pine nuts, and salt and pepper. Blend or process for about 1 minute, until well mixed but not whipped to a smooth puree. It should have some texture. Use at once or spoon into a freezer container with a tight lid and freeze. ▪

Pistachio

PISTACHIA VERA

PISTACHIO TREES grow wild across the Middle East and Central Asia, where they were eaten since before recorded history, but were brought into cultivation over the last 5,000 years. Pistachios from abroad come mostly from Iran, but the more southerly reaches of California's San Joaquin Valley have a prime climate for these trees and produced 302 million pounds of the nuts in 2002 on 83,000 acres. Most of the pistachios you'll find in the United States come from California.

THE ORGANIC FACTOR ▸ Lots of outlets sell organic pistachios, both grown in California or Nevada and imported. California is the big producer in the United States, and commercial growers use about a million pounds of pesticides of various kinds on the crop, so it's fortunate that organic nuts are widely available.

NUTRITION ▸ The FDA has named pistachios part of a heart-healthy diet (the nuts are 55 percent unsaturated fat). This means that eating a regular portion of tree nuts, including pistachios, may lead to the prevention of heart disease. I've been hearing for years what I shouldn't eat, so it's nice to hear that something so crunchy and satisfying like pistachios is actually good for you.

Additionally, pistachios are 18 percent protein and are very high in potassium and calcium. Besides that, they're addicting. A serving is defined as 49 pistachios, about 1 ounce of shelled nuts. Be aware, though, that the serving supplies over 200 calories. The serving also contains more than 10 percent of the Daily Value for fiber, vitamin B6, thiamine, phosphorus, iron, copper, and other trace elements. The nuts are cholesterol-free and the serving contains 13 grams of fat, all but 1.5 grams of which are monounsaturated. Tree nuts like pistachios are one of the major components of the Mediterranean diet, which is about as tasty and healthy as a cuisine gets.

WHAT TO LOOK FOR ▸ Domestically grown pistachios are usually sold undyed, while imported kinds are often dyed red. Pistachios of an appealing green color are natural and not doctored with dyes. Besides the nuts themselves, you can now buy organic pistachio cream, imported from Italy under the Stramondo label. You can find it online in the gourmet food section of www.amazon.com. It's just pureed pistachios and organic sugar. Use it like any sweet jam or spread—on toasted breads, scones or muffins. Mixed with cream, it's ready to make ice cream.

GRILLED VEGGIE BURGERS

SERVES 6

Yes, you can buy organic veggie burgers at the store, but how wonderful to make your own—and you know exactly what's in them. Make a double batch and freeze the patties you won't use right away. Let them thaw through before cooking. The California Pistachio Commission provided this recipe, and the burgers are delish.

Serve in buns with burger fixings.

1 cup finely chopped pistachios

2 cups coarsely grated zucchini

2 (15-ounce) cans red kidney beans, rinsed, drained, and mashed

1/2 cup freshly grated Romano cheese

1/2 cup dry bread crumbs

1 egg

1 teaspoon freshly ground black pepper

$^{1}/_{2}$ teaspoon dried rosemary

$^{1}/_{2}$ teaspoon dried thyme

$^{1}/_{4}$ teaspoon salt

1 tablespoon extra-virgin olive oil

1 tablespoon unflavored rice vinegar

Combine the pistachios, zucchini, beans, cheese, bread crumbs, egg, pepper, rosemary, thyme, and salt and mix well. Shape into 6 patties. Whisk together the oil and vinegar, and brush both sides of each patty generously with this dressing. Place the patties in a grill basket with a fine grid. Grill in a covered barbecue for about 5 or 6 minutes, until browned, depending on the heat of the coals. Baste with dressing and flip the grill basket, then cook another 5 or 6 minutes. ■

PISTACHIO TURKEY STUFFING

MAKES ABOUT 2 QUARTS, ENOUGH FOR

A 14- TO 17-POUND TURKEY

This recipe makes opulent stuffing—something different for the annual feast, although the nod to tradition is still there in the herb-seasoned stuffing mix.

4 tablespoons butter

$^{3}/_{4}$ cup apricot nectar

1 (16 ounce) package herb-seasoned stuffing mix

1 cup unsalted shelled pistachios

1 cup chopped onion

$^{1}/_{2}$ cup chopped dried apricots

$^{1}/_{2}$ cup chopped dates

1. Preheat the oven to 325°F. Combine the butter, apricot nectar, and 1 cup of water in a saucepan. Heat until the butter melts and stir it into the liquid.

2. Place the stuffing mix in a bowl and add the apricot liquid a little at a time, gently tossing, until well moistened. Add the pistachios, onion, apricots, and dates, and gently toss. Bake in a covered ungreased baking dish for 1 hour. ■

Walnut

JUGLANS REGIA

WE CALL THEM English walnuts and the English call them Persian walnuts. These are cold-tender walnuts—although there is a similar type called Carpathian walnuts that can weather winter temperatures down to 35°F below zero—and so most walnuts grown in the United States are grown in California, especially the Central Valley. There once was a large walnut production in Napa and Sonoma counties during Prohibition, but with the return of legal wine, these regions eventually replaced their walnut acres with wine grapes.

THE ORGANIC FACTOR ◆ Until recently, organic walnut production was held back by the walnut husk fly, which could destroy up to 100 percent of a walnut crop with no organic controls available to stop it. Agricultural researchers have come up with a method of spraying walnut trees with a thin layer of kaolin—a natural clay—that turns trees white. Not only does the clay prevent the husk fly from penetrating the nuts, it prevents intense sun from scalding the skin of the nuts— the white color causes more light to scatter among the leaves—which hastens ripening. This has allowed the development of an organic walnut supply, giving farmers the chance to increase their income by 50 percent over conventional walnuts (Organic nuts bring a 50 percent premium over cheaper conventional nuts.)

NUTRITION ▸ English walnuts are one of the few plant sources of health-promoting Omega-3 essential fatty acids—about 3 grams in a 1-ounce handful of walnuts. That compares to less than ½ gram in other tree nuts. Besides Omega-3, walnuts contain good amounts of vitamin E, thiamine, vitamin B6, folate, magnesium, copper, and zinc.

WHAT TO LOOK FOR ▸ English walnuts are best if bought still in their easily cracked shells. If you find the nutmeats shelled out, it's a good bet they will have lost some quality. Black walnuts (see Keep an Eye Out for Black Walnuts) are most often sold in stores as shelled-out nutmeats sealed in plastic bags. If you see them sold in their hard shells in the fall, they'll most surely be fresh.

KEEP AN EYE OUT FOR BLACK WALNUTS

THERE'S A SAYING among the Pennsylvania Dutch that the trees of the black walnut (*Juglans nigra*) will protect a home from lightning. A 75-foot black walnut tree grew beside our 150-year-old stone farmhouse in Pennsylvania. One June night I took the family to the movies, and when we emerged, a huge flickering thunderstorm was moving away toward the east. When we got home, we saw that the tree had been shattered by a bolt of lightning. The limbs had all fallen, missing the house completely, although the trunk grew only 10 feet from the front porch. The tragedy of losing our sheltering tree—tempered by knowing it had done its job—was compounded when there were no black walnuts in the fall.

We used to gather up the nuts in early fall and lay their green, pebbly husks in the tire ruts of our dirt driveway, driving over them for several days. Black walnuts are so hard that the tires never cracked them. But they did squish open the green husks, after which I could pry out the nuts with a knife. We'd place the nuts in a basket, wash them down with a strong jet from the hose, then leave them in the shed to dry and cure until late fall. Then we'd all sit out on a large rock and smash the nuts open with bricks, picking out the nutmeats and eating our fill on the spot. It was hard work for our young ones, but nevertheless they relished it.

Black walnuts have a very distinct, robust, wild flavor that is to regular English walnuts what hickory nuts are to bland pecans. They have no cholesterol, very little saturated fat, lots of polyunsaturated fat, and some monounsaturated fat. They contain iron and other trace minerals. Black walnuts can be used in any recipe calling for English walnuts, and their unique flavor stands up better to cooking. They are more intensely flavored, with a fresher, more distinct and volatile flavor than English walnuts. Although some black walnuts have been cultivated to produce thinner shells (allowing complete halves to be picked out) most black walnut nutmeats on the market are from wild trees. This means the nutmeat is natural, unprocessed, and not sprayed, even if not strictly organic.

Look for black walnuts sold by the Hammons Products Company of Stockton, Missouri (see Sources, page 517), which purchases millions of wild nuts from 250 locations in 13 eastern states, where people bring the nuts to sell. Or you can find them at www.black-walnuts.com.

When buying walnuts sold out of the shell, make sure they aren't rancid. Because of its large amount of polyunsaturated oil, it goes rancid fairly quickly. If you can find the nutmeats refrigerated or frozen, that's a good sign and an indication of how you should store them at home.

STORAGE AND PREPARATION ◆ Like any oil-rich seed or nut, walnuts can spoil if not stored properly. If you detect a paint-like odor from your walnuts, they have turned rancid and should be discarded. In fact, walnuts have more oil than most nuts. About 70 percent of their weight is oil. So store the shelled nuts in the fridge or freezer so that the oil is protected, and place them in an airtight bag, especially in the fridge, as they can absorb odors from fish, citrus, and other foods. Unshelled walnuts will stay fresh from their fall harvest until late winter or early spring if kept in a cool, dry place.

When chopping walnuts in a blender or food processor, don't overdo it, because the oil in the walnuts will soon reduce the pieces to a paste.

USES ◆ Thin-shelled English walnuts are indispensable in salads, crushed as part of crusty coatings for anything from meats to cheesecake, crushed over ice cream, and used in all sorts of sweet and savory dishes.

One reason English walnuts are so versatile is that they have a mild flavor that seldom interferes with other flavors in a dish. Toasted, they increase in flavor, but not greatly. Candied, they become wonderful additions to salads and desserts. And walnut oil is a superior oil for salads—and for oil painters: Michelangelo used it to thin his paints when working on the Sistine Chapel.

Serve toasted or raw whole walnuts on top of breakfast cereals, tossed into salads or on pastas, in risottos, sprinkled into stir-fries, as a healthy between-meal snack. Chopped, they can be applied to a frosted cake or muffin, used on top of pastries, and added to waffles. Ground walnuts make an excellent coating for fried fish and can be added to bread doughs.

WALNUT GREEN SAUCE

MAKES 3 TO 4 CUPS

This recipe is from Shelley Boris, an organic cook at Bill Brown's Restaurant and Bar at the Garrison Resort in Garrison, New York. This sauce is to be served at room temperature with grilled fish, meats, or vegetables.

2 teaspoons fennel seeds
1¹/₂ cups walnuts
¹/₂ cup bread crumbs
2 tablespoons minced garlic
8 anchovy fillets
2 cups fresh basil leaves, loosely packed
6 cups fresh Italian flat-leaf parsley leaves, loosely packed
¹/₂ cup fresh mint leaves, loosely packed
Salt and freshly ground black pepper
2 tablespoons freshly squeezed lemon juice
1 tablespoon Dijon mustard
1 cup extra-virgin olive oil
1 cup grapeseed oil

1. Toss the fennel seeds in a small dry skillet over medium heat until toasted. Set aside to cool.

2. In a blender or food processor, combine the walnuts, bread crumbs, garlic, anchovies, and fennel seeds, and process until almost smooth. Add the basil, parsley, and mint, salt and pepper, the lemon juice, and mustard, and process until smooth. With the motor running, slowly add the oils, one at a time. Store in the fridge. ■

HOT CANDIED WALNUTS

MAKES ABOUT 2 DOZEN CANDIED WALNUT HALVES

Candied walnuts are best when they have a little spicy heat to them, which this recipe provides. They're great in salads.

1 cup walnut halves
$1/4$ cup sugar
$1/4$ teaspoon cayenne
$1/8$ teaspoon salt

Place a large skillet over medium heat and when it's hot, add the walnuts, sugar, cayenne, and salt. Shake the skillet constantly until the sugar melts and the walnuts are thoroughly coated, 3 to 5 minutes. Pour the mixture onto a greased cookie sheet and set it aside to cool. When the mixture has cooled completely, store in a tightly covered jar. ▪

BLACK WALNUT AND OATMEAL COOKIES

MAKES ABOUT 40 COOKIES

These are extra yummy cookies because of the strong, tangy flavor of the black walnuts. The flavor of black walnuts is about five times stronger than that of the English or Carpathian walnuts you purchase at the supermarket. One teaspoonful of these nutmeats can usually flavor an entire cake.

$1^{3}/4$ cups all-purpose flour
$3/4$ teaspoon baking soda
$3/4$ teaspoon baking powder

$1/2$ teaspoon salt
$1/2$ teaspoon ground cinnamon
$1/2$ teaspoon freshly grated nutmeg
$1/2$ pound unsalted butter, at room temperature
$1^{1}/2$ cups brown sugar, firmly packed
$1/4$ cup white sugar
2 large eggs
$2^{1}/2$ teaspoons vanilla extract
$3^{1}/2$ cups old-fashioned rolled oats
$1^{1}/2$ cups chopped black walnuts

1. Preheat the oven to 350°F. Place a rack in the upper third of the oven. Grease two cookie sheets.

2. Mix together the flour, baking soda, baking powder, salt, cinnamon, and nutmeg. In another, larger bowl, beat the butter with the sugars until light and fluffy, then mix in the eggs and vanilla extract. When it's well blended, mix in the dry ingredients. Stir in the oats and black walnuts.

3. Drop the dough by the teaspoonful onto the cookie sheets, spaced about 3 inches apart in all directions. Using the greased bottom of a glass, press each lump of dough down until it's an even $1/2$ inch thick. (Regrease the glass bottom as necessary to prevent sticking.) Bake 1 sheet at a time for 7 to 8 minutes, or until lightly browned and nearly firm when pressed in the center of the cookie. Rotate the sheet 180 degrees halfway through the baking. Remove each sheet from oven when done and set aside to cool for 2 minutes, then remove the cookies to a wire rack to finish cooling. ▪

Flaxseed

LINUM USITATISSIMUM

FLAXSEED is more of a food supplement than a tummy-filling food.

A tablespoon of flaxseed daily, either well-chewed or ground in a coffee grinder—to break open the hard seed coat that would otherwise prevent the grains from being digested—provides the daily requirement of alpha-linolenic acid, one of the essential Omega-3 fatty acids that help reduce LDL (bad) cholesterol. Its soluble fiber levels have been shown to reduce triglyceride levels and blood pressure. Flaxseed is of special benefit to women. It provides lignan, a plant source of the female hormone estrogen, which is thought to inhibit the onset of estrogen-stimulated breast cancer. Flaxseed oil is used by menopausal women to help balance hormone levels. One teaspoon a day is enough. Tasty ways to incorporate flaxseed into your diet include mixing ground flaxseed into fruit smoothies, or sprinkling it on top of cold cereals. Cooking destroys some of the benefits of flaxseed oil.

Pumpkin Seed

CUCURBITA PEPO and CUCURBITA MAXIMA

THE REASON for the two botanical names is that there are two common species of pumpkin and therefore pumpkin seeds. But no matter which species they are, they are very similar in flavor and appearance. Most commercially available pumpkin seeds in this country (and in Spain and Mexico where they are most popular) are from *Cucurbita pepo;* however, the seeds you get from Halloween pumpkins are *Cucurbita maxima.*

THE ORGANIC FACTOR ► Pumpkins, being members of the squash family, are beset with the mildew and insect problems common to other squash. Conventional growers use chemicals to counteract the squash bugs, stem borers, cucumber beetles, and mildews that attack the plants. Organic growers have nontoxic, nonchemical methods of foiling all of the diseases and pests of pumpkins.

NUTRITION ► Pumpkin seeds are a storehouse of B vitamins, macronutrients such as calcium and potassium, and per ounce contain more than 2 milligrams of zinc and 4 milligrams of iron, among other important trace elements. Zinc is essential for the body's growth and development.

WHAT TO LOOK FOR ► Organic pumpkin seeds are easy to find, sold loose at most organic food stores. Pumpkin seeds can be purchased raw from organic purveyors. Organic seeds can also be found roasted or fried, sometimes drenched first with some kind of salty flavoring such as tamari. I like to buy raw, hulled, unflavored, organic pumpkin seeds and roast them myself.

Besides the seeds, you can find raw, organic pumpkin seed oil made in France on the market. It has a lightly nutty taste and is rich in Omega-3 and Omega-6 essential fatty acids, along with zinc and other vitamins and minerals.

STORAGE AND PREPARATION ▸ Store pump- kin seeds in the freezer and use them raw, or roast and salt them as needed.

USES ▸ Raw pumpkin seeds have a chewy texture and a slightly vegetal flavor. They are good to grind to add to soups or stews as a nutritious thickener and to breads and sweet rolls to boost their nutrition. Roasted, they become rich and nutty, with a crunchier texture that works well in savory dishes and soups, in a trail mix, or simply by themselves as a snack. You can also toast them. They take only about 5 to 7 minutes in a single layer on a cookie sheet in a 350°F oven to darken slightly and develop an irresistibly nutty flavor. If you want them salted, rub a pinch of kosher salt between your thumb and forefinger over the roasted seeds, allowing them to pick up just a smidgen, which is all you really need.

Make a nutritious salad dressing by whisking together 4 tablespoons of pumpkin seed oil and 2 tablespoons of freshly squeezed lemon juice, then add 1 teaspoon (or less, to taste) of *fleur de sel*, ½ teaspoon of dried basil, ½ teaspoon of dried oregano, 1 clove of garlic mashed through a garlic press, and a few grinds of black pepper. Whisk until everything is well blended. Store in the fridge for a week.

Make a great coating for fried fish by placing 2 tablespoons of toasted sesame seeds, ½ cup of toasted pumpkin seeds, 1½ cups of fresh bread crumbs made from crustless bread, and salt to taste in a blender or food processor, and whiz until the pumpkin seeds are coarsely chopped. Ocean fish such as Pacific halibut or Dover sole and farmed fresh-water fish such as catfish and tilapia fillets have mild flavors that won't interfere with the flavor of the coating. Dredge the fish in flour, then dip it in beaten eggs, then coat with the pumpkin seed mixture. Fry in canola or olive oil for a few minutes on each side, until the coating is golden and the fish is just done. Serve the fish with lemon wedges.

If you like peanut butter and jelly sandwiches, vary your routine with fresh, raw, organic pumpkin seed butter (available at www.rejuvenative.com; see Sources, page 517).

WINTER SQUASH SOUP WITH PUMPKIN SEEDS

SERVES 8

This is a fine, warming, and nutritious late fall or winter soup just brimming with flavor. Butternut squash makes the richest, most texturally velvety soup, but any other hard winter squash—such as acorn or kabocha—will do.

1 large winter squash (about 4 pounds)
1 cup raw hulled pumpkin seeds
2 yellow onions, peeled and diced
1 jalapeño pepper, seeded and diced
2 tablespoons extra-virgin olive oil
3 cloves garlic, crushed
2 quarts chicken or vegetable stock
2 teaspoons yellow miso paste
1½ tablespoon curry powder
3 tablespoons dry sherry
Salt and freshly ground black pepper

1. Preheat oven to 350°F. Halve the squash, remove the seeds and strings, and bake for 45 minutes, or until tender. While the squash is baking, lay the pumpkin seeds in a single layer on a baking sheet and bake for 10 minutes, until fragrant.

2. In a skillet, sauté the onions and chile over medium heat in the olive oil for 2 to 3 minutes, add the garlic, and continue cooking for 1 to 2 minutes more, until the vegetables are soft but not browned.

3. When the squash is done, remove from the oven, let it sit until cool enough to handle, then scoop out the flesh. Use a blender or food processor to puree the squash, onions, garlic, and chile together. Grind 1/2 cup of the pumpkin seeds with 1/2 cup water in the blender to make a cream.

4. In a large pot, bring the stock to a boil. Dissolve the miso in a small bowl with 2 tablespoons of hot water. Add the pureed vegetables, miso, and curry powder to the soup pot, reduce the heat, and simmer for 15 minutes, stirring occasionally. Add the pumpkin seed cream. This will thicken the soup. Stir in the sherry. Season with salt and pepper to taste. Serve with remaining pumpkin seeds sprinkled on top. ▪

Sunflower Seed

HELIANTHUS ANNUUS

SUNFLOWERS are native to many temperate zones around the world. In North America, their seeds have formed a significant part of the diet of Native Americans for about the last 3,000 years. Who eats these seeds eats well. And the top sunflower seed munchers, oil pressers, and growers in the world are the Russians. In fact, sunflower seed oil is the cooking oil of choice in that country. More importantly for Americans, they have thankfully replaced chewing tobacco among most baseball players.

THE ORGANIC FACTOR ▸ Few insects attack sunflowers, which are native to North America and which coevolved with the native pests, and so they are relatively easy to grow organically. A rich, organic soil helps, and these plants can grow to giant sizes with seed heads more than a foot across.

NUTRITION ▸ A 1-ounce handful of sunflower seed packs a whopping 76 percent of your daily requirement of vitamin E—the antioxidant vitamin that helps prevent the build-up of arterial plaque. It also contains 25 percent of the copper you need, 20 percent of the pantothenic acid, plus good stores of folate (especially important during pregnancy), vitamin B6, iron, and zinc.

TYPES ▸ Many of the open pollinated types— that is, the kinds that come true to type when their seeds are planted—are used for hulled seed (seed with their hulls removed) and for birdseed. The seeds of hybrid varieties, on the other hand, produce plants with a grab bag of genetic traits pulled from the hybrid's parents, and therefore aren't true to the type of plant that produced them. Most sunflowers develop a single large head atop a tall stalk, but there are multiheaded and short-stature varieties. Oilseed sunflowers have small black seeds that can be up to almost 50 percent oil.

Seeds sold in their hulls and used for snacking are called confectionery sunflower seed. Sunflowers are rarely sold by variety name, but you could ask growers if they have any of the following high quality varieties. Hybrid types include SIGCO SL70, Sunseed, Sunbred 254, and the popular Sun 891. Open-pollinated types of high quality include Giganteus, Grey Stripe, Mammoth Russian, and Sunspot.

SUNFLOWER OIL ► Sunflower seeds are about 20 percent high quality protein and 20 to nearly 50 percent oil, mostly polyunsaturated linoleic acid, although monounsaturated oleic acid—the kind that makes olive oil so beneficial— is also present; in some new varieties, such as SIGCO SL70, oleic acid is predominant, up to 70 percent of the total oil. This extends shelf life of such seeds tremendously, as oleic acid is much more stable than linoleic. Oilseed types include the high-oil varieties called Peredovik and Rostov.

WHAT TO LOOK FOR ► Organic sunflower seeds are sold, hulled and loose in bins, at most organic food stores. They're inexpensive and full of nutrition. Look for snack seeds that indicate high oleic acid content on the package, because oleic acid is the type of monounsaturated fat that improves the blood cholesterol and triglyceride levels, leading to improved cardiovascular health. Unfortunately, sellers don't ordinarily label seeds with their variety names.

USES ► In addition to eating them out of hand, lightly toasted sunflower seeds can be used in breads, pastries, muffins, and cookies to give a chewy texture and nutty flavor.

TO TOAST SUNFLOWER SEEDS ► Place the seeds in a single layer on a cookie sheet in a 350°F oven for 5 to 7 minutes, until they brown slightly and acquire a fine toasty, nutty flavor.

Sprinkle them on salads, on vegetables such as cauliflower, or coat cheese balls with them.

SPROUTING YOUR SEEDS AND BEANS

THE CHEMICAL CHANGES that occur during sprouting change starch to complex sugars and activate powerful enzymes. Some vitamins increase fivefold. Vitamin B12 in wheat berries quadruples, other B vitamins increase three to twelve times, and vitamin E content triples. Sprouting seeds, grains, and legumes (with the exception of soybeans and kidney beans) greatly increases their vitamin content. For example, the vitamin A content of sprouted mung beans is two and a half times higher than the dried bean, and some beans have more than eight times as much vitamin A after being sprouted.

Dried seeds, grains, and legumes, while rich in protein and complex carbohydrates, contain no vitamin C. But after sprouting, they contain around 20 milligrams per 3.5 ounces. Also, if grown in decent soil or taken from your own garden, seeds, grains, and legumes will be high in minerals—so your sprouts will be an excellent source of minerals as well as vitamins.

SUPER DELICIOUS SUNFLOWER SEED GRANOLA

MAKES ABOUT 10 TO 12 CUPS

You will never find granola this delicious at the store. It would be cost prohibitive to make commercially and the honey would make it too prone to stickiness. This recipe is from my son Shane and his friend Miriam. How they invented this stuff is unknown to me, but please give it a try—it's the best granola I've ever had.

1½ cups whole almonds

4 cups plain puffed wheat

3¾ cups raw rolled (1-minute) oats

1 cup minus 2 tablespoons raw sunflower seeds

¾ cup raw unsweetened flaked coconut (not shredded)

¼ cup raw sesame seeds

¾ cup good quality honey

¼ cup canola oil

1. Preheat the oven to 200°F. Roughly chop the almonds so that a few are still almost whole, most are little chunks, and some almost powdery. Place the almonds, wheat, oats, sunflower seeds, coconut, and sesame seeds in a large bowl and mix thoroughly. Heat the honey and oil in a saucepan over medium heat just until hot and runny. Drizzle this over the dry ingredients, and immediately stir until everything is coated evenly.

2. Spread the granola on 2 large baking sheets and place on the top rack of the oven. Bake for 1½ to 2½ hours, stirring every 20 minutes or so, until golden brown. Once evenly browned, turn off the oven and let the granola sit inside with the door closed until the oven and the granola are completely cooled. This will insure perfect crunchiness. Immediately store in airtight containers, or the granola will absorb moisture and become sticky and chewy. ∎

Sunflower seeds make wonderful sprouts. The oilseed types are preferred for sprouting, but any sunflower can be used as long as the seed is organic. Best results are obtained by using seeds still in their hulls, submerging them in water for about 12 hours, then sprinkling them on the surface of moist soil in a tray in a sunny location at a temperature that ranges from 60 at night to 80 in the day, but not more extreme than that. Room temperature is perfect. Make sure the soil never dries out or the sprouts will die. When the seedlings are about 4 to 5 inches tall, harvest them with a scissors by cutting ½ inch or so above the soil. The sprouts are tender and delicious, full of vitamins and enzymes.

Dried Beans and Other Legumes

PHASEOLUS VULGARIS

THE CATEGORY of dried beans covers a lot of ground. *Phaseolus vulgaris*, or the common field bean, includes cannellini, kidney beans, French beans, navy beans, black beans, pinto beans, and more. And each of these categories carries many different cultivated varieties. For instance, some of the more popular varieties of kidney beans include Black Turtle, Swedish Brown, Hutterite Soup, Anasazi, Jacob's Cattle, Soldier, Yellow Eye, Red Mexican, Great Northern, White Kidney, and White Marrow, among many dozens of others.

But besides *Phaseolus vulgaris*, there exist three other common species that include the tepary bean, runner bean, and lima (or butter) bean. Another whole group of beans falls into the separate genus of *Vigna*, with seven common species, including azuki bean, fava bean, moth bean, mung bean, rice bean, black-eyed peas, and yard-long beans. Finally, there are 10 other genera that include jack beans, broad beans, chick peas, soybeans, lentils, velvet beans, and winged beans, among others.

Which of the different varieties within each species is best? Take your pick. I once attended a tasting of many different kidney beans and I liked Jacob's Cattle, but others in the group liked Swedish Brown, or Soldier—the differences were subtle and I doubt if blindfolded we could tell which was which. This would be especially true if the beans were given a flavorful sauce, as most are.

THE ORGANIC FACTOR ▸ A field or patch of beans not only provides food for humans (or any critters such as rabbits who get into the field), but also improves the soil in which they're grown. That's because, as legumes, bean roots are colonized by nitrogen-fixing bacteria. After the beans are harvested, organic farmers turn the bean plants into the soil, where they add organic matter along with the nitrogen and other nutrients in their tissues. Bean plants are also choice additions to any compost pile and stimulate the thermophilic bacteria that turn plant detritus into valuable fertilizer. Beans are subject to a wide variety of pests and diseases, but organic farmers have nontoxic solutions for them.

NUTRITION ▸ The protein of beans is considerable. Soybeans are the champion, containing about 35 percent protein by weight, then French green lentils with 24 percent, but most other dried beans contain nearly that much. Black-eyed peas, for instance, are 23 percent protein and have five times more folate—so important for pregnant women because it insures proper fetal growth—than any other bean. Unlike meat, however,

legumes do not contain all the necessary proteins and must be supplemented with foods containing the other proteins, notably cereals, to make them complete and fully nourishing to humans. Mexicans mix corn and beans in their cooking, and many tribes of the pre-Columbian Native Americans had their Three Sisters—corn, beans, and squash—as their staple food. Many dishes combine beans and rice, such as New Orleans' red beans and rice. Dried beans also have good stores of soluble fiber, potassium, and calcium.

Be aware that it's not safe to eat raw or uncooked kidney and soybeans, even in their dried state. Hemagglutinin is a substance in raw beans that causes red blood cells to clump together and prevents the transport of oxygen to the body's tissues. As few as four raw beans have caused serious hemagglutinin poisoning. Hemagglutinin is completely destroyed by high heat cooking—hence the 10 minutes of rapid boiling required before simmering. Slow cookers do not reach high enough temperatures, so kidney and soybeans should be boiled for 10 minutes before being added to these appliances. Kidney beans must never be sprouted. Azuki, chickpeas, whole lentils, marrowfat peas, and mung beans are all safe to sprout, and sprouting increases their nutritive value.

STORAGE AND PREPARATION ▸ Dried beans are the dried seeds that grow within the bean pods. When dried to just a few percent moisture, they keep for up to a year in closed containers in a cool, dark place.

Canned beans and other legumes are already cooked and immersed in a salty liquid in the can. Drain them in a colander and rinse them with cold tap water to remove the salt. While canned beans are convenient, they don't taste as good as beans you soak and cook yourself.

SOAKING BEANS ◂ Most dried beans need an overnight soak before cooking. The exceptions are lentils, which need no soaking, and mung beans, which require just four hours of soaking. Soak beans in water to cover.

COOKING DRIED BEANS ◂ After soaking beans, discard the soaking water and replace it with fresh water at a ratio of three parts water to one part beans. Avoid any temptation to salt the water. Salting the water toughens the beans. If you want to add salt, add it after the beans have finished cooking. Bring the water to a full boil and boil for 10 minutes uncovered, then reduce the heat and simmer covered for 1½ to 2 hours, skimming off any scummy foam that appears on the surface. Be careful the beans don't boil dry and scorch. Add more water if necessary. The exceptions to this procedure:

*Boil dry soybeans for 1 hour, then simmer
    for 2 hours
Simmer fava beans for 2 to 2½ hours
Simmer black beans and lima beans for just
    1 to 1½ hours
Bring lentils to a boil, then cover, reduce the
    heat and simmer for 25 minutes
Bring mung beans to a boil, then cover,
    reduce the heat and simmer for 1 hour*

USES ◂ Different beans are favored in different regions of the world. Lentils are a staple in India, soybeans in China and Japan, black beans and pigeon peas in the Caribbean, kidney beans in North America, and so on.

Add cooked beans to soups and stews; make chili con (or without) carne; sprinkle a few in a salad; use chickpeas (garbanzos) to make hummus; use white beans for minestrone or cassoulet, or mix them with leftover rice, some minced garlic and tomato paste, then microwave to make a quick side dish. Germans like the flavor of beans cooked with winter savory so much that the herb's name in German is *bohnenkraut*, meaning bean-herb. The aroma of a pot of beans simmering on the stove is evocative of home for many of us. And if flatulence is a worry for you, add a pinch of aniseed, caraway, dill, or fennel seeds to the pot.

MEXICAN REFRIED BEANS

MAKES ABOUT A QUART

Refried beans are a tasty way to start putting together a burrito. Smear some of the bean paste on the tortilla. Or serve them as a side dish along with rice and salad with grilled meat.

1 pound dried pinto beans
1 medium onion, minced
2 cloves garlic, minced
¼ teaspoon salt
¼ teaspoon crushed red pepper flakes
3 tablespoons lard
3 tablespoons bacon fat (or substitute 6 tablespoons canola oil for these two fats)
4 ounces grated Jack cheese (about 1 cup)

1. Soak the beans overnight, then place in a large pot along with 2 quarts fresh water, the onion, garlic, and red pepper flakes. Bring to a boil, boil for 10 minutes, reduce the heat, and simmer for 1½ hours. Drain the cooked beans and reserve the cooking liquid. Add the salt. Mash the beans with a potato masher—do not use a blender or food processor.

2. In a large skillet, heat the lard and bacon fat (or oil) over medium-high heat until the fat just

continued

begins to smoke, or the oil sizzles if a small drop of water touches it. Add the mashed beans, being careful not to let any spatter on you. Reduce the heat to medium-low and cook, stirring constantly, until the fat or oil is absorbed. Add the reserved cooking liquid a little at a time to thin the beans until a moist but not too liquid consistency is reached.

3. Add the cheese and cook 15 minutes longer until the cheese has melted and been incorporated completely. ■

BRAZILIAN FEIJOADA

SERVES 4 WITH PLENTY OF LEFTOVERS

Brazil's national dish is based on black beans and is a mouthful of rich, hearty flavor. This is a pared-down version of the classic.

The classic accompaniments to this dish can all be prepared while the beans are cooking.

4 cups dried black beans

1 pound dried beef

1 pound sweet sausage (see Tip)

1 pound baby back ribs

1 bay leaf

1 medium onion

1 clove garlic

1 tablespoons olive oil

ACCOMPANIMENTS

Cooked white rice (see page 368)

Peeled, sliced oranges

Sautéed kale or collard greens (see page 135)

1. The night before you're going to make the feijoada, soak the beans, covered 3 or 4 inches deep. Soak the dried beef separately in water to cover. (Dried beef is cured with salt and the soaking removes much of the saltiness.) The next morning, drain the beans and place them in a large,

heavy cooking pot (such as a Dutch oven) and cover with fresh water to a depth of 3 inches. Turn the heat to medium and bring the beans to a boil.

2. While the beans are coming to a boil, prick the sausage and simmer it separately for 10 minutes, then cut into 1-inch pieces. Drain, rinse, and cut the dried beef into wide strips a couple of inches long; add to the beans. Cut the ribs into 2-rib sections. Add the sausage, ribs, and bay leaf to the beans (it's all right to add them either before or after the beans reach a boil).

3. When the beans reach a boil, boil for 10 minutes, reduce to a simmer and cook covered for 1 1/2 hours, until the beans are soft. Stir occasionally to keep the beans on the bottom from burning. Add water if necessary to keep the feijoada from becoming too dry and scorching.

4. Chop the onion and garlic. Heat the olive oil in a skillet over medium heat. Sauté the onions and garlic until golden, about 5 minutes. Add 2 large spoonfuls of beans to the skillet and mash them with a spoon. Put the contents of the skillet back into the pot. This will thicken and season the beans. Continue to simmer for 1 hour more, adding water if necessary. The consistency should be creamy when done. Remove the bay leaf.

5. To serve feijoada, make a base of the rice on each plate. The feijoada goes on top of this, and the orange slices and kale go around the outside.

TIP: Linguiça is a Portuguese sausage that will be familiar to residents of southeast Massachusetts, where there's a large Portuguese community. Otherwise use any sweet—not spicy—sausage. Dried beef will be familiar to folks in the Pennsylvania Dutch country, where it's a staple. Dried beef can also be found in Portuguese markets in cities with large Brazilian communities, such as New York, Los Angeles, Miami, Boston, Chicago, Anaheim, and Washington, D.C. Otherwise use the kind of dried beef that comes in a jar at the supermarket. ■

TUSCAN WHITE BEANS

SERVES 3 TO 4

This standard side dish across northern Italy goes well with roasted or rotisseried meats and a green vegetable such as broccoli.

1 cup dried cannellini or Great Northern beans
1 stalk celery, cut in half lengthwise
1 onion, cut in half crosswise and studded with
   two whole cloves
1 carrot, cut in half lengthwise
1 bay leaf
Salt

Soak the beans in cold water overnight. Drain, place in a heavy 2-quart pot and cover with fresh water to a depth of 3 inches. Add the celery, onion, carrot, and bay leaf. Bring to a boil and boil for 10 minutes, then reduce the heat, and simmer, covered, for 1 1/2 hours. Drain the beans. Discard the bay leaf and the vegetables. Add salt to taste. ▪

THE BEST HUMMUS YOU'VE EVER TASTED

MAKES ABOUT 2 CUPS

Hummus is the thick, addictive spread you scoop up with torn bits of pita bread and eat along with tab-bouleh salad. Organic chickpeas—also called gar-banzo beans—are available both as dried beans and canned in water. Several sources also sell organic tahini, which is raw sesame seeds ground to an oily paste.

Chickpeas contain low glycemic carbohydrates, which means that instead of spiking your body's insulin levels, they slowly release sustained energy to the body and keep insulin levels steady, which keeps your blood sugar levels moderated instead of jumping all over the place.

When soaked chickpeas and tahini get together, a synergy of flavor makes the result irresistible. The following recipe is from Chef Mark Stark of Monti's Rotisserie and Bar in Santa Rosa, California. His additions of spices and harissa to the basic recipe give this hummus a flavor surge. Serve with pita bread.

1 cup dried chickpeas, or 2 cups cooked or canned
   chickpeas, drained
2 teaspoons cumin seeds
5 cloves garlic, chopped coarsely
3 tablespoons freshly squeezed lemon juice
3 tablespoons tahini
1/2 teaspoon Harissa (page 107)
Pinch of salt
3 tablespoons extra-virgin olive oil
1/2 teaspoon minced fresh parsley

1. If you're starting with dried beans, soak them in cold water overnight. Drain, place in a heavy pot, and cover with fresh water to a depth of 3 inches. Bring to a full boil and boil for 10 minutes, then reduce the heat, and simmer, covered, 1 to 2 hours, until they are uniformly tender. Cool and drain. If using canned chickpeas, rinse them in fresh water.

2. Toast the cumin seeds in a small dry skillet over medium heat until fragrant, just a minute or two. Set aside to cool, then grind in a spice or coffee grinder, or with a mortar and pestle.

3. Place the chickpeas, garlic, lemon juice, and 1/4 cup water in a blender and puree until smooth. Add the cumin, tahini, harissa, and salt, and blend until incorporated. Place the hummus in an oval shallow bowl and with the back of a tablespoon, make a depression down the center. Fill the depression with the olive oil. Sprinkle the parsley over the top. ▪

Soybean

GLYCINE MAX

SOYBEANS have been cultivated in China for at least 5,000 years, but in America they've been grown in quantity only since World War II, when they were used as a meat extender during wartime rationing. About that time, margarine (which is frequently made with soybean oil) also came on the scene as a supposedly healthy butter substitute.

Nowadays, soybeans are used in all sorts of food products to add nutrition and texture, and as extenders. They're grown across the United States as part of a typical corn-and-beans crop rotation that supports dairy and meat production farms, concentrated mainly in the Midwest.

THE ORGANIC FACTOR ‣ Most American soybeans are produced using a wide range of agricultural chemicals, and genetic engineers have been working on them, too. Under organic production, they are usually grown as part of a crop rotation that includes grains like wheat or oats, corn, and forage legumes like alfalfa. By only growing soybeans every third or fourth season, the life cycles of many soybean pests are interrupted.

NUTRITION ‣ Soybeans are fabulously nutritious, containing 30 to 50 percent protein, more than any other plant product and more than most meat. But because they are legumes, the protein is not complete (that is, it doesn't contain all the essential amino acids). Eating soybeans with rice or whole grain pasta will make a complete protein, however. Good amounts of the B vitamins and minerals complete the nutritional package.

Higher intake of soy foods has been linked with reduced incidence of heart disease and some forms of cancer. Studies on humans have established that soy consumption is significantly associated with reduced levels of blood cholesterol.

Epidemiological data show that consumption of soy is particularly associated with reduced risk of breast, lung, and prostate cancers, as well as leukemia. Menopausal problems, including osteoporosis, are favorably affected by consumption of soy isoflavones, making soybeans especially beneficial for women. Hot flashes are significantly reduced in some women who consume soy isoflavones either as soy products or supplements. Studies show that the isoflavone daidzein has demonstrated a significant ability to prevent osteoporosis in both animals and humans.

In addition to these very significant health benefits, soybeans lack the glycosides that can be so harmful when raw common beans (*Phaseolus*) are eaten (see Nutrition, page 348). They do, however, contain a trypsin inhibitor. To inhibit the enzyme trypsin is to inhibit the body's ability to utilize proteins. But there's conflicting medical opinion on whether this is significant, especially at the level of soybean ingestion in the American diet. The trypsin inhibitor is destroyed by one hour of boiling before simmering. Anyway, there's no quarrel about soybeans' anticancer properties, which have been shown in many tests on lab animals.

USES ‣ In their whole form, soybeans remain tough even after long cooking. They have a bitter, beany flavor that's not very appealing, and they're not very digestible due to the trypsin inhibitor, which prevents much of their nutritional value from being absorbed by the body.

So in areas of the world where soybeans are a staple—Indonesia, China, Korea, Japan—people have learned ways of processing the beans to render them tasty and digestible. They are processed into nutritious milk, which can be used as a milk substitute or processed further into cheese-like tofu. The whole beans can be inoculated with a mold that predigests them, producing tempeh.

Tempeh is a fermented food made by the controlled fermentation of cooked soybeans with a starter of *Rhizopus* mold. The fermentation binds the soybeans into a compact white cake. Tempeh fermentation also produces natural antibiotic agents, which are thought to increase the body's resistance to intestinal infections. Fermentation leaves the desirable soy isoflavones intact. It also increases the flavor of the beans, giving them a mushroom-like taste.

Soybeans can also be fermented into tamari (soy sauce), Chinese black beans, or a paste called miso, which dissolves in hot broth to give miso soup.

Soybeans are the world's chief source of cooking oil. Fourteen to 20 percent of the bean is oil, mostly unsaturated, containing good amounts of healthful linoleic and oleic acids.

SOY MILK

MAKES ABOUT 1 QUART

1 pound dried soybeans

1. Cover the soybeans with cold water and let stand 8 hours, changing the water twice. At the end of the soak, boil the beans rapidly for 10 minutes. Drain the soybeans.

2. Place 1 cup of soaked, boiled soybeans and 3 cups of fresh water in a blender. Run the blender on top speed for 3 minutes, until you have a milky-looking slurry. Pour this into a large cooking pot. Repeat with as many batches as you need to use up all the soybeans, always using the same ratio of beans to fresh water. When the beans are used up, place over low heat, slowly bring to a simmer, and cook for 10 minutes. Line a colander completely with a clean cotton dishtowel and place the colander in a second large pot so the ends of the dishtowel hang over the edge of the pot.

3. Pour the hot soybean mixture into the towel. Some milk will run through, but most will not. Let the mixture cool until it's just warm. Gather up the edges of the towel and twist them to make a sealed ball of the mixture. Tighten the ball by twisting the gathered edges, scraping the outside of the towel to encourage the milk to flow. Don't let any of the solids get into the milk. Continue tightening and scraping until most of the milk has been expressed. Cover and refrigerate for up to 3 days before you need to make the tofu. ▪

BARBECUED TEMPEH

SERVES 4

Tempeh is a very nutritious soy product made by the predigestion of soybeans by a beneficial mold. If you've never tried tempeh, this barbecued version is an excellent, delicious introduction. Most of the flavor comes from the barbecue sauce.

1 pound tempeh
2 cups barbecue sauce

1. Cut the tempeh into 4 equal chunks. Put these in a steamer, cover, and steam over boiling water for 15 minutes. Place the steamed tempeh pieces in a bowl and cover with the barbecue sauce. Marinate in the fridge for 1 hour.

2. While the tempeh is marinating, start a fire in the outdoor grill so that the coals will be ash gray and the heat moderate when the tempeh is ready to cook. Or turn your gas grill to medium hot. Place the tempeh on the grill and brush on some of the barbecue sauce. Turn frequently and cook thoroughly until heated through and the barbecue sauce is baked on. ▪

HOMEMADE TOFU

MAKES ABOUT 2 PINTS

It's fun and easy to make tofu at home. If you want to make a firm rectangular block such as you find at the store, you'll need to make a tofu press from 3/4-inch lumber (pine is best because it doesn't have tannins or flavors to impart). This is simply a rectangular box with no top or bottom, usually 6 inches wide by 8 inches long and 4 inches deep. It needs a pressing board that's 1/2 inch shorter and narrower than the 6 × 8 opening. Or simply fold the curds into cheesecloth in a colander placed in the sink, place a plate to cover on top, and weight the plate with a pot full of water. Otherwise, you can wash the loose tofu and let it drip dry before using it in a form that resembles cottage cheese.

2 quarts Soy Milk (recipe page 353)
4 teaspoons coagulant (see Tip)

1. In a 3- or 4-quart stainless-steel pot, heat the soymilk over low heat to 180°F (steaming but not boiling), stirring frequently. Remove it from the heat and let it cool until you can put a finger into it without discomfort. In a cup, mix the coagulant with 1/4 cup of hot tap water to dissolve. Pour it a little at a time into the soy milk, stirring constantly. The milk will begin to thicken and curdle. If you want a soft curd, stop adding coagulant while the curd is still easy to stir. If you want to make a firm tofu, add coagulant until the curd becomes thicker and harder to stir.

2. To make tofu with the texture of cottage cheese (using the soft curd tofu), fold a large piece of cheesecloth over twice to make four layers. Place the tofu curd in the middle, then draw up the opposite corners of the cheesecloth and tie together to form a bag. Hang this bag from the kitchen sink faucet and slowly pour the curdled soymilk into the bag. Let it drain for 1 hour, then gently rinse with cold water and let drip dry another hour.

3. If you want to press tofu in a mold, place the mold (using either the soft or hard curd prepared above) in the sink, then place several folds of rinsed cheesecloth in the mold so the edges overlap the sides of the mold all around. Carefully pour the curdled soy milk into the mold and fold the extra cheesecloth flaps back over the curd, then insert the pressing board. For soft tofu, press with about 3 to 5 pounds of pressure (a container with 2 quarts of water will work) for 5 minutes. For firm tofu, increase the weight to 10 pounds (1 1/2 gallons of water) and press for 10 to 15 minutes. Remove the cheesecloth and place the tofu in a container and submerge in clean cold water. Cover and refrigerate. If not using right away, change the water every day, for up to a week.

TIP: Several compounds can be used to coagulate soy milk and make a curd. Epsom salts is one, magnesium chloride is another. I find that Epsom salts (magnesium sulfate) is the easiest to find, but magnesium chloride gives the best results. Check your drugstore to see which they have. ■

Barley

HORDEUM VULGARE

BARLEY is the foundation grain of western culture. It was likely the first grain to be cultivated, even earlier than rice in the Far East. From its initial cultivation in 6000 BCE, barley reigned from North Africa through pharaonic Egypt, ancient Greece, the Levant, and eastward to Afghanistan. And it was the chief bread grain of Europe and the Near East until the 16th century, although wheat was the favored grain of the wealthier classes since the times of classical Rome. (Unlike wheat, barley has no gluten and makes a thick, dense bread that will not rise, which relegated it to being a staple of the poor.)

There are several reasons for this. Foremost, barley is tolerant of all kinds of climates, from the far north to the semitropical, and grows well even in harsh soils, including those containing salt residues. Because it could be grown just about anywhere, it was. Even today, the staple food of Tibetans is *tsampa,* a kind of dense bread made from barley grown at high elevations.

The second reason is that when barley sprouts, enzymes develop that change its stores of starch to sugar, and sugar can be fermented to make beer. In fact, the Old English word for barley was *baere,* pronounced BEE-rah; hence our word beer. Much later, the Scots learned to make barley wine, which they then distilled over peat fires to produce rich, smoky, delicious Scotch whisky.

Yet another reason for barley's ubiquity is that before the Industrial Revolution, most people lived on farms, and barley (then as now) is a superb fodder for domestic animals. Its grains are nutritious and its straw makes an excellent bedding.

THE ORGANIC FACTOR ▸ The better the soil it's grown in, the better the barley—a benefit of organic barley that grows in rich soil.

NUTRITION ▸ Barley—especially hulled barley—is the richest of all the cereals in cholesterol-lowering fiber, very high in potassium and calcium, and rich in iron and folate.

WHAT TO LOOK FOR ▸ The barley grain is covered with a fiber and nutrient-rich layer of bran. In most countries, including the United States, this layer is ground away during milling, producing a form known as pearled barley. This has about half the nutrients of hulled barley, which still has its bran layer intact. Hulled barley is worth seeking out for its full complement of nutritive substances, although it takes longer to cook than pearled barley, about an hour and 40 minutes compared to 45 minutes.

Barley is also sold as flakes; toasted and cracked into grits, as quick barley (which is pearled barley,

WHAT IS A "WHOLE" FOOD?

WE HEAR a lot about whole foods these days—and there's even a supermarket chain that uses the term for its name. But what exactly is a "whole food"? Simply put, it's an unprocessed food that includes all the nutritive elements Nature gave it when it grew. The more that's stripped away by milling, processing, and manipulating, the less nutrition the foodstuff provides. Study after study shows that a whole grain, for example, with everything intact, gives us all its nutritional advantages.

precooked by steaming); and Scotch barley, which is simply husked then coarsely ground barley with its nutritive bran layer still attached. Some people sprout hulled barley and harvest the barley grass to juice like wheatgrass because there's some evidence the grass juice can lower blood cholesterol.

USES ➤ While pearled barley may be used to give bulk to delicate, refined soups and stews, hulled barley that retains its bran is much to be preferred when used for cereals, as an addition to breads, and as an ingredient in soups, stews, and meat-based dishes.

SCOTCH LAMB AND BARLEY SOUP

SERVES 6

There are any number of recipes for this classic Highland soup, but this is my favorite. It freezes well—and on cold nights, it warms us well, too.

1 cup hulled barley
1/2 pound ground lamb
1 tablespoon all-purpose flour
2 teaspoons olive oil
1 cup diced leek, white parts only
1 cup chopped onion
5 cloves garlic, minced
2 medium carrots, diced
2 medium parsnips, diced
1 small turnip, diced
2 cups chicken stock
1/2 teaspoon dried oregano
1/2 teaspoon freshly ground black pepper
1 tablespoon freshly squeezed lemon juice
Salt

1. Cook the barley in 2 cups boiling water for about an hour and 40 minutes, until the liquid is almost gone and the barley is tender. Reserve.

2. Meanwhile, brown the lamb in a dry skillet over medium heat, breaking up the meat as it cooks to prevent clumping. When the meat is fully browned, sprinkle it with the flour to absorb the fat and reserve. Later, this will thicken the soup.

3. In a Dutch oven or soup pot, heat the oil over medium heat. Add the leeks, onion, and garlic and cook until the onions are translucent, about 7 minutes. Add the carrots, parsnips, and turnips, and stir them to coat. Stir in the chicken stock, 3 cups of water, the oregano, and pepper, and raise the heat to high. When it reaches a rapid boil, reduce to a simmer, cover, and cook until the vegetables are tender, 15 to 20 minutes. Stir in the lamb and the barley, cover, and simmer for an additional 10 minutes. Add a bit more water if necessary to keep the consistency of a soup rather than a stew. Remove from the heat and stir in the lemon juice and salt to taste. ■

Buckwheat

FAGOPYRUM ESCULENTUM

ALTHOUGH treated like a grass-family grain (wheat, oats, barley, etc.), buckwheat is not a grass. The seeds are actually the fruits of an annual herbaceous plant that's related to the Japanese knotweed and Silver Lace Vine.

The seeds consist of an outer layer or hull, an inner layer that is the seed coat (or middling), and a starchy endosperm and germ in the center. In milling, the hull—about 20 percent of the weight of the grain—is removed. A second milling removes the seed coat, comprising 4 to 18 percent of the weight, depending on how much is milled away. Most buckwheat flour has some seed coat remaining, making the flour a light greyish brown. Further milling yields a whitish flour.

THE ORGANIC FACTOR ► Buckwheat is one of the chief "green manures" used by organic farmers and gardeners. It is sown thickly on a plot of tired ground previously used for a crop that takes up a lot of nutrients from the soil. When it flowers, bees love it and make buckwheat honey. If allowed to go to seed, we get the nutritious buckwheat seeds. But most farmers plow it into the soil just after it flowers for its strong fertilizing and soil rejuvenating powers.

NUTRITION ► Buckwheat is high in calcium and protein, especially lysine, an essential amino acid that corn lacks, making any corn-and-kasha dish a source of complete protein (see recipe at right).

USES ► Most of the buckwheat sold in the United States is ground into flour and used as an addition to enrich wheat flour for use in pancake batter, breads, and other baked goods. Some whole buckwheat is roasted, after which it is called groats or kasha. Whole buckwheat is also used in chicken scratch. Middlings are often fed to livestock, because they're high in protein.

KASHA, BEAN, AND CORN TACOS

MAKES 8 TACOS

This recipe comes from Birkett Mills in Penn Yan, in the Finger Lakes region of upstate New York. Birkett is the world's largest processor of buckwheat products. In this dish, the combination of buckwheat, beans, and corn yields a complete protein and has a delicious earthy flavor.

Serve with toppings such as grated cheese, salsa, pico de gallo, hot sauce, chopped cilantro, shredded lettuce, diced tomato, sour cream—the usual Mexican garnishes.

1/2 cup whole kasha
1 tablespoon extra-virgin olive oil
1 1/2 cups diced onion
1 cup diced green bell pepper
2 tablespoons chili powder
1 tablespoon minced garlic
2 cups boiling water
8 taco shells or small corn tortillas
1 (15-ounce) can black beans, drained and rinsed
1 cup fresh corn kernels (see page 108)
Salt

1. Choose a skillet with a lid. Place the skillet, uncovered, on high heat, add the kasha, and stir until kasha is hot and slightly toasted, 2 minutes at most. Pour the kasha into a bowl and reserve. Reduce the heat to medium-hot and add the oil. When hot, add the onion and pepper, and cook and stir until tender, about 5 minutes. Add the chili

continued

powder and garlic, and cook until fragrant, 1 minute longer. Add the reserved kasha and boiling water. Reduce the heat to a simmer. Cover and simmer until the kasha is almost tender, about 7 minutes.

2. Meanwhile, heat the taco shells or tortillas in a dry hot frying pan; cover with a dry clean towel to keep warm. When kasha is almost tender, stir in the beans, corn, and salt to taste. Cover and cook until the kasha is tender, about 3 minutes. Spoon into the warm taco shells or if using soft tortillas, spoon onto one side of each tortilla and fold over for a soft taco. Serve immediately. ◾

Millet

PANICUM MILIACEUM

A MERICANS in general don't eat a lot of millet, unlike many cultures around the world for whom it's a staple food. Aficionados of multigrain breads, however, get their share because millet is often one of the grains.

THE ORGANIC FACTOR ◂ Organic millet flour is a mild-tasting addition to breads and a thickener for soups and baby food. Millet is typically grown as part of a crop rotation on organic farms as one of the cereal grasses.

NUTRITION ◂ Millet's protein content is on a par with other cereal grasses such as wheat. Its chief virtues are good amounts of vitamins B1 and B2, and an alkaline pH that increases its digestibility and can help turn an acidic system—linked by some practitioners to health problems from the flu to arthritis—alkaline.

TYPES ◂ Millet is the seed of a grass, but there are many different genera and species. When shopping for millet, one can easily find the light yellowish-brown bulrush or pearl millet (*Pennisetum americanum,* also known by the species name *typhoideum*) here in the United States. Red or White Proso millet (*Panicum miliaceum*) is also available. Other types, mostly found in Africa, India, and Japan (all great consumers of the grain), include finger millet (*Eleusine coracana*), which has several small upright seed heads that resemble little fingers; teff (*Eragrostis tef*), a staple in parts of Africa; Japanese barnyard millet (*Echinocloa frumentacea*), which is eaten as a porridge in India and Japan, or mixed with rice; "hungry rice" (*Digitaria exilis*), which is really a kind of millet and a common food in Nigeria; kodo millet (*Paspalum scrobiculatum*), a staple in parts of India; and brown-top millet (*Bracharia ramosa*), another common millet in India.

All these grains are classed as millet, and biologically they share a drought tolerance and an ability to grow in difficult situations. This agricultural heartiness makes them an important grain in dry, tropical areas such as sub-Saharan Africa and parts of India. Proso millet has been cultivated in the Near East since prehistoric times. By 5000 BCE, it had spread east to China. Bulrush millet is thought to have originated in West Africa about 3000 BCE, selected from wild plants. By the time of the Romans, it had reached East Africa and India. Where it's the exclusive grain, a substance in it called thioamide can promote the development of goiter as it binds iodine. Iodine supplementation is encouraged where millet is the chief grain.

USES ◂ Millet is a useful grain that we should get to know better. It gives texture to stews, casseroles, and stuffings. Its flavor is accepting of other ingredients such as cheese, tomatoes, or spices. It can also be cooked as a porridgey breakfast cereal much the way we use oats and barley for cereal. It can be ground into a coarse flour to make flatbreads such as pita. When lightly toasted in a pan or in the oven, its flavor improves considerably. It can be sprouted like any grain and popped like popcorn or amaranth.

Besides its use as human food, millet is used as animal feed, especially for poultry. And "organic pillows" made of hypoallergenic materials and stuffed with organic millet hulls are sold as a head-and neck-supporting substitute for feather pillows.

MILLET AND CAULIFLOWER MEDLEY

SERVES 4

If people in your house don't applaud when you serve cauliflower, try this recipe. The flavors tumble one into the other and spark up cauliflower's natural mildness.

1 cup millet
1/2 medium head cauliflower
3 cloves garlic, chopped
1 tablespoon olive oil
3 tablespoons freshly squeezed lemon juice
1/4 teaspoon salt
1/4 teaspoon freshly ground black pepper
1 tablespoon minced fresh parsley

Rinse and drain the millet. Slice the cauliflower into thin slices so it will cook quickly. Put 2 1/2 cups water, the millet, cauliflower, and garlic into a heavy saucepan and bring to a boil over medium heat. Cook 7 minutes, then cover the pan and let it sit for 20 minutes. Mash the contents with a potato masher until well mashed and mixed. In a small bowl, whisk together the olive oil, lemon juice, salt, and pepper and add to the millet mixture, combining it thoroughly. Turn into a serving bowl and sprinkle the top with the parsley. ∎

Oat

AVENA SATIVA

AMONG GRAINS, oats came late to the table. The earliest evidence of their cultivation dates from about 1000 BCE. Wild oats have the bad habit of dropping their seeds as soon as the husks open, making those first harvests chancy at best because as soon as they got ripe, the darn things would drop on the ground. Early farmers kept seeds of those wild oat plants that held their seeds in the seedheads longer than most, and eventually had strains of oats that they could reliably harvest before the seeds shattered to the ground.

Most oats are grown in northerly climates such as the upper tier of states in the United States, lower Canada, Scandinavia, Germany, Poland, and especially Russia, because they are a cool-season, moisture-loving crop. Often oats are planted in the fall as a cover crop to hold the soil together during fierce winters, after which they awake early in the spring to produce a crop before the heat of summer.

THE ORGANIC FACTOR ⊱ Like the other cereal grains, oats are part of a good, organic crop rotation, along with corn and a legume. They are a relatively trouble-free crop to grow.

NUTRITION ⊱ It's become a cliché that childhood mornings used to begin with a bowl of steaming hot oatmeal and mothers told their children that the porridge would "stick to their ribs." But for me it was true: My dad made the oatmeal from old-fashioned Quaker oats (he called them "Dr. Cox's Cream Oats" because he'd stir them while cooking into a thick, hot, gluey mass) while my mom delivered the admonishment to eat them because of their rib-sticking qualities. In my imagination, I pictured my thorax plastered all over inside with sticky oatmeal and wondered how that could possibly benefit my health.

Now that I've grown up (an arguable proposition, if you talk to my wife), I know why oats are just the thing to start a school kid's—or anyone's—day. They have the largest percentage of protein of any grain: 12 to 20 percent. Their fat content (5 to 9 percent) is the highest among the cereal grains, and it's almost entirely unsaturated fat. It contains the most calories of any grain. Only rye and whole wheat among whole grains have more soluble fiber—and then not by much. Oat bran, where the fiber is concentrated, is the richest source of soluble dietary fiber. To top it off, oats are high in folate.

TYPES ► Besides the familiar oats we use as breakfast porridge, in granolas, in cookies, in breads, and pastries, there's another species called red oats (*Avena byzantina*)—but it's seldom found in American markets.

By the way, those steel-cut oats from Ireland and Scotland don't have to take 40 minutes to cook. Soak them in water overnight and you'll be able to cook them in 10 minutes after draining them the following morning.

USES ► Oats have always had a split personality, appreciated by some as a useful food staple, and shunned by others. The Greeks made a sweet called *plakous* from oat flour, honey, and cheese, but the Romans considered oats barbarian food until they conquered Celtic Britain, where they found oats to be an easy-to-grow and nutritious grain. Oats have been identified with the British Isles ever since, but only in Wales, Ireland, and Scotland. The English consider oats to be fodder for horses.

Oats are also used to make a number of drinks. The Japanese sometimes use oats instead of rice to make a sweet kind of sake called *amazake*. Oatmeal stout, a dark, delicious, viscous beer, is made with 5 to 10 percent oats in the grist (the grains used to brew the stout). It doesn't impart a taste of oats to the brew, but it does add a creamy texture that's quite appealing. There is also "oat milk," which should probably be renamed an "oat smoothie." It consists of 4 cups of cold water, 1 ripe banana, 2 cups of cooked oatmeal, 1 teaspoon of vanilla, a pinch of salt, and 1 tablespoon of maple syrup, all whizzed together in a blender until entirely smooth, and then refrigerated. Shake it before drinking. It is delicious.

QUAKER OATS

IF YOU ARE an aficionado of oats, or just curious, travel to Akron, Ohio, and stay in the Crowne Plaza Quaker Square Hotel. The hotel is built into the original grain silos of the Quaker Oats Company, which invented rolled oats in the 1870s. The lobby is full of rolled oat memorabilia. This was an extraordinary advance for the consumption of oats. The folks at Quaker took steel-cut oats—the chunks of the whole oat grains that take 40 minutes to cook—steamed them to stabilize the fats and oils so they wouldn't turn rancid, then sent them through roller mills that flattened them into oat flakes, which cooked up in just five minutes. The company still sells tons of them, and they're still just as good for you now as they were 130 years ago.

CHEWY OATMEAL-COCONUT COOKIES

MAKES ABOUT 48 COOKIES

These delicious cookies have a caramel flavor and a chewy consistency that makes them irresistible.

1¼ cups old-fashioned (5-minute) rolled oats
½ cup brown sugar, firmly packed
¼ cup shredded coconut
1 tablespoon all-purpose flour
½ teaspoon freshly grated nutmeg
¼ teaspoon salt
4 tablespoons unsalted butter, melted
1 large egg, beaten
¾ teaspoon vanilla extract

1. Preheat the oven to 350°F. Grease two baking sheets.

2. In a large bowl, combine the oats, brown sugar, coconut, flour, nutmeg, and salt. In a separate bowl, whisk together the butter, egg, and vanilla, then mix this into the dry ingredients. Drop teaspoonfuls onto the baking sheets about 3 inches apart in all directions and flatten with the back of a fork. Bake about 8 minutes, until nicely browned. Remove the baking sheets to the countertop and let the cookies cool for a couple of minutes, then transfer them to a wire rack to cool completely before stacking. ■

DR. COX'S CREAM OATS

SERVES 2

This bowl of oatmeal will make you feel good all over. Serve with milk and brown sugar or maple syrup.

1 cup milk, plus extra for serving
Pinch of salt
1 cup old-fashioned (5-minute) rolled oats

Place the milk, 1 cup of water, and the salt in a saucepan and set over high heat until it boils. Add the oats in a stream, stirring as you add them, then reduce the heat to medium. Stir constantly for 5 minutes. Turn into bowls and serve immediately. At the table, add some more milk and stir to make it loose and creamy. ■

Quinoa and Amaranth

CHENOPODIUM QUINOA and
AMARANTHUS EDULIS

QUINOA (pronounced KEEN-wah) and amaranth are two modern-day superfoods.

They're called superfoods because, unlike most grains such as wheat, corn, and barley, quinoa and amaranth are not missing the key amino acid lysine in their proteins, and so they contain all the amino acids needed for building muscle, tendons, and other tissue. That's why I've grouped them together here. The World Health Organization has rated the quality of their proteins as at least equivalent to that of milk, which makes them invaluable for people on vegan and vegetarian diets, who are seeking alternate sources of protein.

Quinoa grows under harsh conditions of soil and climate and has been cultivated in the Peruvian Andes for more than 5,000 years. Because of its high nutritional value, the Incas called quinoa the "mother grain." Their armies could march for days eating "war balls" made from quinoa mixed with fat. Today, most quinoa is imported from South America, although some is grown in high altitudes of the Colorado Rockies. Amaranth is widely distributed around the world in temperate and tropical climates (see The Food of the Gods, page 363).

THE ORGANIC FACTOR ▸ It was the organic community that popularized these two grains in the United States, mostly because of their great nutritional content. They are easy to find in organic markets, both as grains and in breakfast flakes.

NUTRITION ▸ In addition to protein, quinoa contains high levels of iron, potassium, riboflavin, vitamin B6, niacin, and thiamine. It's also a good source of magnesium, zinc, copper, and manganese, and supplies some folic acid. Amaranth is nutritionally on a par with quinoa. It has rich stores of complete, lysine-rich protein, iron, zinc, and copper, and it is high in folic acid, calcium, and vitamin E. It even contains a bit of vitamin C. Both of these foods are far more nutrient-rich than the grass-family grains.

Like quinoa, amaranth is the seed of an annual herbaceous plant. It contains between 15 and 18 percent protein. Combining it with wheat, corn, or rice produces a protein that's as nutritious as fish, red meat, or poultry. It has three times the fiber of wheat and five times more iron. It contains twice the calcium of milk. It also contains good amounts of vitamins A, C, and E. The E is contained mostly in the oil, which makes up about 8 percent of the grain and is mostly polyunsaturated and high in linoleic acid.

WHAT TO LOOK FOR ▸ Today, one can go to the supermarket and see not only amaranth and quinoa in their grain forms but also as cereal on the shelves along with the cornflakes, as well as amaranth and quinoa flour, and even a butter substitute made with amaranth oil.

STORAGE AND PREPARATION ▸ Harvested quinoa grains have a bitter, resinous coating of saponin, which must be removed before eating, as it interferes with digestion and the body's ability to absorb nutrients. For quinoa grown in South America, this removal is usually accomplished by washing the grains in an alkaline solution. The saponin can also be milled off. Before using, rinse the grains under cold water until the water runs clear to remove any remaining saponin.

USES ▸ Quinoa is a small grain with a light and delicate flavor. It cooks up to a light, fluffy texture, with a little crunch provided by the germ, which forms a tiny tail when cooked. The grain will develop a rich, toasted flavor if placed into a dry skillet over medium heat and stirred for about 5 minutes. Use quinoa as you would rice: two parts water to 1 part quinoa. Use a large enough pot, because quinoa expands to about three or four times its uncooked size when it's finished. Bring the quinoa and water to a boil, then reduce the heat to simmer, cover the pan, and simmer about 15 minutes, until the grains become translucent and the tails have emerged from each grain.

Amaranth can either be cooked like rice or popped like popcorn. (See recipe on page 364 for popping instructions.) The popped grains are tiny, but delicious as a snack, and can be added to pancakes to make Popcakes (page 364).

When cooking amaranth, use 2½ times as much liquid as grain, put the grain and liquid on high heat until it boils, then reduce to simmer, cover, and cook about 20 minutes, until most of the liquid has been absorbed and the texture is slightly crunchy—not hard or gritty and not overcooked and gummy.

Amaranth and quinoa can be used as a thickener. Quinoa and amaranth flour can be combined with all-purpose flour to make a nutritious addition to breads, muffins, pastas, cookies, gravies, sauces, pancakes, flatbreads, and dumplings. To use: if making a yeast bread, use ½ cup of amaranth flour to each 2 cups of wheat flour. You can use up to twice that in flatbreads and pancakes.

QUINOA PILAF

SERVES 4

You'll be surprised at the delicacy of the texture and intensity of flavor that quinoa lends to this Moroccan-style pilaf. Serve it as the side dish for roast chicken—or better yet, cut a whole roast chicken into quarters and serve on top of the pilaf so some of the chicken juices percolate down.

1 cup quinoa grain

2 tablespoons extra-virgin olive oil, plus extra for the casserole

⅓ cup blanched whole almonds

1 cup minced onion

½ cup minced carrot

½ teaspoon ground cinnamon

3 cups chicken stock

⅓ cup golden raisins

2 teaspoons freshly grated orange zest (well scrubbed if not organic)

¼ teaspoon cayenne

1. Rinse the quinoa thoroughly until the water runs clear. Preheat the oven to 375°F.

2. Lightly oil a 1½-quart covered casserole. Place the olive oil in a skillet on medium-high heat. When hot, add the almonds and sauté for about 2 minutes, until they become golden and fragrant. Add the onions, carrots, and cinnamon and cook for about 3 minutes, stirring occasionally. Add the quinoa and stir thoroughly so that all the little grains are coated with oil; cook 1 minute. Add the chicken stock, raisins, orange zest, and cayenne and bring the mixture to a boil. Pour this hot mixture into the casserole, cover, and bake for 45 minutes. When done, turn the pilaf onto a platter. ■

THE FOOD OF THE GODS

I FIRST HEARD about amaranth when *Organic Gardening* publisher Bob Rodale, J. I. Rodale's son, returned to the office one day in the mid-1970s and said he'd been to Mexico and discovered a new grain that the Aztecs called the "food of the gods." It was amaranth. What made the grain special was first that—like quinoa—amaranth is easy to grow just about anywhere and, second, that amaranth's seeds contain a lot of high lysine protein.

Bob thought it could make a dent in world hunger and be useful for farmers in difficult climates. Rodale Press had recently purchased a 300-acre farm in the Pennsylvania Dutch country and Bob hired scientists to search the world for varieties of amaranth to start a center for the plant's cultivation and dispersal to farmers worldwide. We soon had the world's largest collection of amaranth varieties. The research center staff distributed amaranth seeds to farmers around the world and published many scientific papers on its cultivation. Today amaranth has taken its place among the world's important grains.

AMARANTH POPCAKES

SERVES 4

These pancakes awaken the taste buds and satisfy that craving for a little crunchiness as it boosts the protein power of the pancakes. Let the kids watch you pop the amaranth.

$1/2$ cup whole amaranth grain

1 cup all-purpose flour

$1/2$ teaspoon salt

1 tablespoon baking powder

1 large egg

1 cup milk

$1/4$ cup canola oil

1. To pop the amaranth: Heat a large dry skillet over medium-high heat, then pour in the amaranth grain in a single layer. Shake the skillet so the grains don't burn. They'll soon start to pop. When the popping slows and is nearly finished, immediately remove from heat and pour the popped amaranth into a bowl and reserve.

2. Combine the flour, salt, and baking powder and mix until well blended. In a separate bowl, beat the egg into the milk, then pour this into the dry ingredients and lightly fold them together, drizzling the oil into the batter as you do so. Fold in the popped amaranth. You don't have to beat the batter smooth—a little lumpiness is fine. If too thick, add a little more milk or water.

3. Heat a well-oiled skillet over medium heat. When hot, ladle in $1/2$ cup of batter and turn once when the bubbles that arise consistently form holes that retain their shape. There's an old saying, "The first child is like the first pancake," so don't worry if the first one is a learning experience. ∎

Rice

ORYZA SATIVA

RICE covers about 10 percent of the world's arable land, an area second only to wheat in size. It grows in semitropical and tropical areas around the world and is the subject of intense research because it is the staple food of so many people. It's a member of the grass family.

THE ORGANIC FACTOR ◦ While organic growers like the Rauns and the Lundbergs (see Keep an Eye Out for These Special United States-Grown Rices, page 366) are developing new and better ways to produce high quality organic rice in efficient, environmentally sound ways, conventional rice agriculture is plowing ahead with genetic modification and engineering of rice strains. Studies are underway to develop nonconventional rice varieties through genetic engineering and mutation breeding, looking for increased herbicide tolerance, among other things. Syngenta, one of the world's leading genetic engineering companies, has engineered a so-called golden rice, which has about 8 percent more pro-vitamin A than ordinary rice. However, an adult would have to eat 20 pounds a day to satisfy his or her need for vitamin A from golden rice alone.

NUTRITION ◦ In many countries, especially tropical lands of high rainfall, rice is the chief source of calories, carbohydrates, and protein. Although its protein content is not particularly high (6 to 7 percent), it is a good, complete protein except for lysine, and the content of B vitamins, at least in brown rice, is excellent. When the bran and germ are milled away to produce white rice, much of the fiber and many of the minerals and B vitamins are lost. In many places such as India, where the populations depend on rice for the bulk of their calories, brown rice is parboiled—steeped in hot water, then steamed and dried, then milled into white rice. During the heating, some of the B vitamins and minerals move into the interior of the rice grains, improving them nutritionally compared to ordinary white rice.

TYPES ▸ Worldwide there are 40,000 different varieties of rice. They include unmilled brown rice in long, medium, and short-grain varieties, plus aromatic rices such as basmati and jasmine. Here are some of the most commonly found varieties in the United States, along with cooking instructions for each:

Arborio rice—A plump, medium-grain rice with a characteristic white dot in its center. It has an enormous capacity to soak up liquids as it's cooking, making it perfect for risottos. It's also used in paellas. Cook like medium-grain brown rice, page 368, or make risotto.

Basmati rice—Its long, slender grains don't swell much when cooked, but the grains elongate. This is an aromatic rice with a beautiful, nutty smell. Great for side dishes or as a base for light vegetable stir-fries and medleys. To cook, place rice grains in twice their volume of water, bring to a boil, reduce the heat, cover, and cook for 15 minutes. Brown basmati rice will take about 20 to 25 minutes to finish.

Converted or Parboiled rice—Parboiling or steaming rice is a technique, first developed in India, to improve its nutritional content (historically this prevented the thiamine—vitamin B1—deficiency disease called beriberi). The process gelatinizes the starch, rendering the grains extra fluffy and separate. Do not rinse this rice. To cook, place the rice in twice its volume of water, bring to a boil, reduce the heat, cover, and cook for 15 minutes.

Enriched rice—White rice that has had vitamins or minerals added back after they've been milled away with the bran and germ. Do not rinse for that reason. To cook, add rice to twice its volume of water, bring to a boil, reduce the heat, cover, and cook for 15 minutes.

Glutinous (or Sticky) rice—Sticky rice comes as long-, medium-, and short-grain. When cooked, the grains stick together, making the rice easy to eat with chopsticks. It's great for making sushi and for the basic rice that goes under Asian stews and stir-fried dishes. Soak overnight and cook in an equal volume of water for 12 minutes.

Instant rice—Instant rice has been completely precooked, then dehydrated. Don't rinse as nutritive elements have usually been added back. Rehydrate according to the package directions.

Jasmine rice—Jasmine rice is the perfect base for Thai food. Its aromatic steam, lovely texture, and fluffiness make it ideal under curries. To cook, place it in twice its volume of water, bring to a boil, reduce the heat, cover, and cook for 15 minutes. Brown jasmine rice takes 30 minutes.

Long-grain brown rice—The rice looks pleasantly golden brown after it's cooked, and the grains are fluffy. It's chewy, with a firm texture and nutty flavor. It can be used in pilafs, fried rice dishes, salads, as a side dish, and as a base for meat or vegetable stews. Soak overnight, then cook with an equal volume of water for 20 minutes.

Long-grain white rice—Same uses as long-grain brown rice, and it yields a fluffy rice good for fried rice

OCCASIONALLY, my wife and I sneak away to Victorian Gardens, an isolated and beautiful inn on the Mendocino coast operated by Luciano and Pauline Zamboni. Luciano, who's Italian, cooks authentic Italian dinners for his guests, and these sometimes include risotto. He told me that he considers the organic Arborio rice from Lundberg Family Farms in the Sacramento River Delta superior to any Italian Arborio he's tasted.

The Lundbergs have been growing rice since 1937. Over the years, they have sunk a lot of money into their operation to make sure their product is as clean as can be. For example, organic standards require that rice silos be refrigerated to suppress insects rather than fumigated with chemicals, so a large capital investment is required. In addition, it costs about $22 an acre more to produce organic rice than conventional, due to added costs for extra tractor and hand work pulling weeds, among other requirements.

That is, unless you follow the method of Japanese rice farmer Masanobu Fukuoka. This man, the author of *The One Straw Revolution*, a book about his experiences growing rice, told me that he achieved enlightenment when he stopped asking himself, "What can I do next to grow rice better?" and started asking himself, "What can I stop doing to grow rice better?" After a number of years wrestling with the question, he decided to scatter rice seed amid the clover that was growing in his paddy. When the rice grew to a foot tall, he would flood his paddy, killing the clover, which would then decay and fertilize the paddy. When the rice was ripe and ready to harvest, he'd scatter clover seed among the rice plants, harvest the rice, and cut the stalks—the stalk clippings would then decay themselves and give the clover plants a good source of fertilizer. When the clover was lush, he'd scatter rice seed then flood the paddy again, and another yearly cycle would begin. Today he's got it down to three operations a year—most rice farmers are out in the paddies working all year long. And his yields are as good as if not better than his conventional neighbors. His rice is sold only in Japan, but his Zen way of thinking is applicable to our hustle-bustle way of doing things.

Another grower, Lowell Farms, produces organic jasmine rice on a farm in El Campo, Texas. Linda Raun and her husband Lowell G. operate the business and sell a long-grain jasmine rice called Jasmine 85 (the year it was developed from Thai jasmine rice) from coast to coast through retail, and even more through mail order. Their rice is grown under USDA organic rules. The Texas Department of Agriculture oversees the certification. The rice is very aromatic and very high quality.

Meanwhile, Glenn Roberts at Anson Mills, a certified organic rice grower and processor in South Carolina, is reviving an old heirloom variety of American rice that dates back to the antebellum south, called Carolina Golden Rice. "It was the most

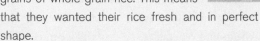

popular rice on earth from 1720 until the Civil War," he says. "So much so, that Carolina Golden Rice allocations to royals in Asia became the reason for battles there. Also, until 1930, most rice produced in the United States for retail was labeled 'Carolina Rice,' whether it was grown in the Carolinas or not." Once he mentioned that, I remembered the Carolina Rice jingle on the radio during my childhood: "serve it in a dozen ways, take my advice, nothin' could be finer than some Carolina Rice."

Carolina Golden Rice is softer than normal longgrain rice and cooks to independent grains. Roberts says that "this heirloom rice was named Carolina Gold for its beauty at harvest and the fortunes made from it by the antebellum Carolina and Georgia plantation aristocracy. It became the foundation for America's first internationally recognized antebellum cuisine named 'The Carolina Rice Kitchen,' where French, German, Italian, and English colonial cooking merged with Native American and African foodways. It can be argued that the greatest cooks in America before 1800 were south of Virginia and they were almost all African."

The real cause for the rise of this special rice in bygone days was the Gullah community on the sea islands of Georgia and the Carolinas. In the late 17th century, Carolina plantation owners tried growing rice by old European methods but they didn't work well here. The African method of rice growing worked fine, though. The Gullah community only bought what they needed that day, and they would only eat unbroken grains of whole grain rice. This means that they wanted their rice fresh and in perfect shape.

"Carolina Golden Rice is lightly milled, but it's still viable seed," Roberts said. "The germ is still in there. That means the rice doesn't dry out." With the germ intact, the seed is a living organism. When the germ is removed, only the starch is left, the grain is dead, and it gives up its moisture. The germ is gone in all the other milled rice in the United States today and the grains dry out, he added. "So with the germ in place, it can go rancid or even mold. To protect it, we cold-mill the rice and keep it in an envelope of carbon dioxide as we process it."

Roberts waxed ecstatic as he described the smell of the cooked Carolina Golden Rice: "The aromas are like those you experience out in the rice fields—hay, alfalfa, caramel, lemon blossoms, floral; a high nuttiness, from sesame to pecan with walnut in between; beyond that, almost herb-like aromas, green, then into lilac, violet, jasmine—seductive, deep, floaty stuff; finally: mushroom. This rice gives a sense of well being, a sense of comfort. I suspect there's melatonin in this rice."

Lundberg, Lowell, and Anson Mills sell their products by mail order as well as through retail outlets. See Sources, page 517, for details.

dishes. Place rice in twice its volume of water, bring to a boil, reduce the heat, cover, and cook for 15 minutes.

Medium-grain brown rice—These plump grains aren't as dense and sticky as short-grain brown rice, but they have a moist, tender texture. Use this rice in soups, and as the starch dish along with meats and vegetables. To cook, place in twice its volume of water, bring to a boil, reduce the heat, cover, and cook for 25 minutes.

Medium-grain white rice—Same uses as the medium-grain brown, but a stickier texture. Soak the grains overnight, then cook with an equal volume of water for 12 minutes.

Short-grain brown rice—This whole grain type becomes somewhat sticky when cooked, and is chewy in texture. It's good for rice pudding, croquettes, veggie burgers, and sweet desserts. Soak it overnight and then cook it for 20 minutes in twice its volume of water.

Short-grain white rice—Removing the bran and germ to make white rice results in a stickier and softer grain. Use for sushi, rice balls, and sweet desserts. Soak the rice for 20 minutes, then cook, covered, in 1⅛ times its volume of water for 10 minutes or until it's done.

USES ◄ Rice is a starch to use as a base for a wide variety of cuisines. Indian tikka masala and vindaloos beg to be served on rice. It soaks up all kinds of sauces. Whole-grain brown rice is most nutritious.

In addition to its almost endless uses as a grain, rice is also made into beverages, many of them organic. There's Rice Dream, a milk substitute, and the ice creams and other "dairy" foods based on rice milk. There's sake, the Japanese rice wine of significant alcohol content, and many other products.

PAELLA

SERVES 6

This version of the classic Spanish rice dish comes from my friend Max Cohen, who served it at a party for his neighbors in Minisink Hills, Pennsylvania, in 1964. I never forgot that wonderful party—or the incredible paella he served. When the time came to serve the paella, Max produced a huge pan about 1½ feet in diameter heaped with mounds of steaming, fluffy yellow rice redolent of saffron. The rice was studded with grilled chicken, shrimp, clams in their shells, lobster chunks, peas, bits of sausage, onions, and tomatoes. I thought it was the best plate of food I'd ever had. The recipe is updated—sugar snap peas hadn't been developed in 1964.

1 live 1½-pound lobster
½ pound medium shrimp, shelled and deveined, shells reserved
1 tablespoon tomato paste
3 tablespoons brandy
1 pound smoked ham hock
2 bone-in chicken breasts
3 chicken thighs
3 chicken legs
1 medium onion, minced
1 large clove garlic, minced
1 tablespoon extra-virgin olive oil
1 cup peeled, seeded, and chopped tomatoes
1½ cups Arborio rice
1 teaspoon paprika
¼ teaspoon saffron threads, crumbled
Salt and freshly ground black pepper
8 little neck clams
8 black mussels, debearded
¼ cup shelled fresh peas
4 ounces sugar snap peas

1. Get a large pot of water boiling. Plunge the lobster's head into it, holding the beast upside down after removing the rubber bands on its claws. The lobster will die peacefully without tensing up, as it would if the whole body was dropped into the boil. Once the lobster has stopped moving, drop it into the pot and cook for 2 minutes. Drain and let cool slightly. Then remove the meat from the tail and claws. Reserve the shells. Cut the tail meat into 4 equal pieces.

2. Heat 1 cup of water in a very large saucepan. Add the lobster and shrimp shells and cook over high heat, stirring occasionally, for 5 minutes. If it appears that the water will boil away, add another half cup. Add the tomato paste, stir it in, and cook for another 2 minutes. Add the brandy, ignite it, and cook until the flames go out. Remove from heat, strain out the shells, and return the liquid to the pot. Add the ham hock and 8 cups of water and bring it to a boil. Reduce the heat to medium and cook for 45 minutes, or until the stock is reduced by half. Remove the ham hock and cut half of the lean meat off the bone and reserve. Strain the broth and skim off any fat; keep the broth warm.

3. On a grill (or under the broiler), cook the chicken breasts, legs, and thighs until fully cooked. When done, remove the skin.

4. In a large covered skillet, cook the onion and garlic in the olive oil until translucent, about 4 minutes, then add the tomatoes, rice, paprika, and saffron. Cook until the liquid is absorbed, about 4 minutes. Stir in the warm broth, reserved ham hock meat, chicken, and salt and pepper to taste. Cover the pan and bring to a boil over high heat, then reduce the heat to simmer. Cook for 10 minutes, shaking the pan occasionally. Add the clams, mussels, and lobster meat; cover and cook at a simmer until the clams and mussels open, about 7 or 8 minutes. Add the shrimp, peas, and sugar snap peas and cook until the shrimp are cooked through, about 5 minutes. Make sure the rice is finished. If not, continue cooking until a test grain is tender. If the rice is done, remove from the heat, let rest about 10 minutes, then serve. ▪

CHEESE AND RICE FRITTATA

SERVES 4

I used to make a breakfast dish called "pizza eggs," so named because of the cheese and pizza spices I used. I eventually created this Mexican-style frittata; it's much nicer than pizza eggs and has the advantage of marrying eggs, cheese, and rice. But it's the same idea.

8 large eggs
Pinch of ground cumin
2 tablespoons chopped fresh cilantro
1/4 teaspoon salt
1 cup shredded Jack cheese (about 4 ounces)
1 tablespoon unsalted butter
2 scallions, white part only, minced
1 teaspoon minced garlic
1 1/2 cups cooked Arborio rice (1/2 cup rice cooked for 25 minutes with 1 cup water–see page 365)

Preheat the oven to 350°F. Whisk together the eggs, cumin, cilantro, and salt in a large bowl, then stir in the shredded cheese. Melt the butter in a large ovenproof skillet over medium heat, making sure the butter coats the bottom of the pan. Add the scallions and garlic and cook for 30 seconds. Add the rice and cook until hot, about 1 minute. Pour the egg mixture over the rice mixture. Reduce the heat to low and cook without disturbing for 5 minutes. Put the skillet in the oven and cook until the eggs are set, about 15 minutes. ▪

Wheat

TRITICUM, various species

LIKE MANY PEOPLE who grew up in the mid-20th century, I grew up on Wonder Bread—or its ilk—and knew little about other kinds of wheat breads. Yes, there was something called cracked wheat bread, which seemed to be white bread with some cracked grains and bran added. And there was rye bread. And that was it.

Oh, how far we've come since then. Within a few miles of my home, I can find several sources of rich loaves made of organic whole-wheat flour, leavened with starter cultures of native yeasts and bacteria that float through the air just looking for warm, wet pools of spring water and wheat flour to colonize and exalt. These loaves are baked in ovens fired with dried splits of native oak. The smell of the bread! The look of it! The taste! The texture! If bread is the staff of life, then these loaves make it worth living.

Wheat is a grass, as are many other of our common grains such as oats, barley, and corn. We use the seeds of this grass to make our flour. The seeds—or wheatberries, as they're called—grow in heads inside dry husks called chaff. (Chaff is itchy stuff, as I found out when the teenage sons of my farmer neighbor threw me in the chaff bin in their barn when I was 10.) The wheatberries themselves are covered with a fibrous coat of bran. Under the bran is the white starchy grain and its germ, the living part of the grain. When a wheatberry sprouts, the germ sends out a small root. The starchy part of the grain is food for this growing seedling.

During milling, if the whole wheatberry—bran, germ, and starch—is all ground into flour, you have very nutritious whole-wheat flour. If the germ and bran are removed, the white starchy part of the berry makes unbleached white flour, which is far less nutri-tious. If the flour is bleached to make bleached white flour, avoid it. It's just too far removed from the natural grain and too devoid of its nutritional potential.

THE ORGANIC FACTOR ‣ Tests at the Danish Research Center for Organic Farming show that organic wheat fertilized with green manure or cow manure has better baking characteristics than conventional wheat grown with chemical nitrogen fertilizers. The gluten in the organically fertilized wheat, researchers found, has more elasticity and holds carbon dioxide better than that in conventional wheat. Chemical fertilizers are shown to promote quick, lush, but ultimately weak plant tissue.

NUTRITION ‣ Whole-wheat flour is a nutritious protein, although one lacking in the amino acid lysine. (By combining wheat with legumes—lentils or beans—you have a meal complete in necessary protein, with no need for meat.) Whole-wheat flour also has good stores of iron, fiber, potassium, calcium, the B vitamins, and especially folate. Processed white flours show reduced amounts of nutrients; for example, white flour has half the folate of whole wheat.

TYPES ‣ About 90 percent of the wheat grown in the world is bread wheat (*Triticum aestivum*), mainly adapted to temperate climates. Various strains of this wheat are planted in the spring for harvest in late summer (spring wheat) or planted in the fall to overwinter and ripen in early summer (winter wheat). Kernels of bread wheat vary in color from yellow (called white) to reddish-brown (called red). Cultivars tend to have either a hard kernel that shatters into tiny bits when ground, or a kernel that is more mealy in texture—these are

THE NEED FOR VITAMIN B12

IN THE 1970S, Frances Moore Lappé wrote a seminal book called *Diet for a Small Planet*, in which she said that world hunger could be erased if cultures stopped farming meat animals and got their complete protein from grains, seeds, beans, and vegetables. Much of the book is an extended discussion of how mixing various vegetable protein sources produces proteins with as much or more nutritional value as meat.

In this book, I've mentioned many times how mixing legumes, grains, and vegetables produces a combination of proteins that have all 20 amino acids in good supply. Our bodies disassemble the proteins in our food into their constituent amino acids, then reassemble them into the proteins that make up our tissues. But protein isn't all that wheat, other grains and seeds, and legumes provide. They provide the B vitamins so necessary to our health. But here, too, there's a limiting factor and that's vitamin B12. The only reliable, unfortified sources of B12 are meat, eggs, and dairy products, such as milk or cheese. Boiled milk and yogurt have had their B12 destroyed.

Researchers have investigated plant foods to see if any contain B12, including fermented soy products such as tempeh, tofu, and miso but haven't found any B12. Spirulina algae and seaweeds have been suggested as sources of B12, but while they have substances called B12 analogs, they contain no B12. Researchers have suggested that spirulina may actually increase the risk of B12 deficiency as the B12 analogs can compete with B12 and inhibit its metabolism.

Vitamin B12 plays an important role in DNA synthesis and neurologic function. Deficiency can lead to a wide spectrum of blood, cardiovascular, and neuropsychiatric disorders, such as anemia and atherosclerosis.

It's been said that bacteria in our digestive tracts can synthesize B12, and indeed they do, but it happens too far down the colon for absorption to occur.

The current view among nutritionists is that no plant foods contain a reliable and safe source of B12. Vegetarians, therefore, should make sure that eggs and dairy products are a regular part of their diets, and vegans should absolutely include B12-fortified foods (many are available as yeast extracts, breakfast cereals, textured vegetable protein, and veggie burger mixes) in their diets.

---

known as hard and soft wheats, respectively, in miller's parlance. So, for example, you may find a flour or bread labeled "Hard Red Winter Wheat."

Flour can also be—and this is important for home bakers to know—strong or weak; these designations refer to the amount of protein in the grains. Strong flour (sometimes also called hard, just to confuse us) contains 10 to 16 percent protein. The more of the proteins called glutenin and gliadin in the overall protein profile of the wheat, the stronger it is. These proteins are the building blocks of gluten, and it is elastic, gluey gluten that captures the bubbles of carbon dioxide given off by yeast fermentation, causing the loaf to rise. When baked, the bubbles in the dough cook and stabilize, and bread emerges porous and spongy.

Soft wheats contain less protein, usually 7 to 9 percent, and thus less gluten; the weak flour made from them is generally called pastry flour and is used for pie doughs, cakes, cookies, biscuits, pancakes, and nonyeast-risen pastries. These are usually leavened by baking powder or steam, because the soft wheat isn't as elastic as hard wheat and won't hold the bubbles produced by the yeast. Hard wheat would make stiff pastries, but soft wheat makes tender and cakey pastries.

The hard, high-protein winter wheats grow best across the colder northern regions of the world, and so yeast-leavened loaves of high-gluten breads were the staples of cultures in northern Europe, Russia, Canada, and the northern part of the United States. All-purpose and bread flours are made from hard wheat. Soft wheats are typically grown in warmer climates, such as the southeastern United States, giving us southern biscuits, pancakes, and such.

Most of the rest of the world's wheat is durum (*Triticum durum*), well suited to the warm, dry climate of the Mediterranean region, where it's used to make pasta, couscous, and bulgur. The word semolina refers to the coarse flour made from the starchy part of durum's kernel after the bran and germ are milled away. Semolina is high in protein and is used to make pastas.

There are some other wheat-like grains. Spelt (*Triticum spelta*) was one of the earliest forms of wheat to be cultivated, preceded only by einkorn and emmer, two wild precursors of modern wheat. Spelt has a high protein level, lots of B vitamins, and a tough outer husk that protects the grains from insects and makes spelt very suitable for organic culture. It tends to have more flavor than

regular bread wheat. Triticale is another wheat-like grain available today—it's a cross between bread wheat and rye.

Many organic bakeries include sprouted wheat in their bread. This addition makes a slightly sturdier and denser loaf than one made with flour alone. Wheat germ and bran, removed in milling all-purpose flour, are often added back by bakeries interested in boosting the nutritional content of their breads. Wheat germ is a rich source of vitamin E, iron, folic acid, and thiamine. Bran is a good source of insoluble fiber, which studies show lowers the risk of heart disease. Despite what many people think, insoluble fiber doesn't protect against colon cancer. But it is a healthy addition to every diet.

USES ➤ Wheat is often mixed with other flours to make more nutritionally diverse and flavorful bread. Quinoa or amaranth flour (see page 361) will improve the amino acid profile of wheat flour. Crushed walnuts are often mixed into whole-wheat flour. But don't stop there—oat, barley, rice, and other grain flours, ground-up seeds such as flaxseed (page 343), rye, or pumpkin seeds (add a tablespoon of tahini, which is ground sesame seed, to your bread dough when making a loaf from scratch), crushed nuts such as macadamias, black walnuts, hickory nuts, filberts, and cashews will enrich your breads. Just remember that the dough must be at least three-quarters wheat to have enough gluten to rise properly. The rule of thumb is that the more variety, the better the nutrition and flavor, but the more of these variety additions to the dough, the denser the final product.

CINNAMON ROLLS

MAKES 24 ROLLS

These rolls perfume the house with the wonderful scent of fresh-baked bread and cinnamon, and they will disappear very rapidly after you make them.

FOR THE CINNAMON FILLING

1 cup brown sugar, lightly packed

1 cup white sugar

$1/2$ cup unsalted butter, at room temperature

$1/2$ cup chopped walnuts or black walnuts (see page 339)

$1/2$ cup dried currants

$1/4$ cup all-purpose flour

$1^1/2$ tablespoons ground cinnamon

FOR THE DOUGH

3 cups whole-wheat flour

3 cups all-purpose flour

$3/4$ cup whole milk

$1/2$ cup sucanat or white sugar

1 teaspoon salt

$1/2$ cup unsalted butter, at room temperature

2 packages active dry yeast (about 2 tablespoons)

$1/3$ cup warm (105°F) water

3 eggs

Olive oil for brushing

FOR THE CARAMEL TOPPING

$1/3$ cup heavy cream

2 tablespoons brown sugar

$1^1/2$ cups confectioners' sugar

1 teaspoon vanilla extract

1. To make the cinnamon filling: Place all ingredients in a bowl and mix until crumbly. Set aside.

2. To make the dough: In a bowl, sift together the whole-wheat and all-purpose flours. In a small saucepan, combine the milk, sucanat, salt, and butter. Heat on low until the sugar dissolves and the butter melts, then remove from the heat and let it cool to lukewarm. Dissolve the yeast in the warm water (water should feel comfortably warm, not hot; hot water will kill the yeast).

3. Warm a mixing bowl. Pour in the lukewarm milk mixture and add the yeast mixture, eggs, and 3 cups of the sifted flours. With an electric mixer on low speed, mix everything together for 1 minute, occasionally scraping down the sides of the bowl. Stir in enough of the remaining flour to make the dough easy to handle and no longer sticky. Turn the dough onto a lightly floured board and knead for 8 minutes, until smooth and elastic. Warm a second large mixing bowl, wipe the inside with olive oil and put in the kneaded dough, turning the greased side up. Cover with a damp kitchen towel and let rise in a warm place until it about doubles in size, about $1^1/2$ hours.

4. Grease a $15^1/2 \times 10^1/2$–inch baking sheet. Punch down the dough and transfer to a lightly floured board. Roll it out to a rectangle about 10 inches wide by 30 inches long and $1/4$ inch thick. Spread the cinnamon filling evenly over the surface of the dough. Roll it up tightly, starting along the long edge, to make a 30-inch roll. Pinch the seam together. Cut the roll into 24 rounds, each $1^1/4$ inches wide. Space them evenly apart on the baking sheet. Cover and let rise in a warm place for 1 hour, or until doubled in size.

5. While the rolls are rising, make the caramel topping. Place the cream and brown sugar in a small saucepan and place over medium heat, stirring constantly, until mixture becomes hot and the sugar dissolves. Don't let it boil. Pour it into a mixing bowl, add the powdered sugar and vanilla and beat with a spoon until the mixture becomes smooth and creamy.

5. Bake the rolls at 350°F for 20 minutes. As soon as you take them from the oven, remove them to a cooling rack to cool. Don't stack them. Spread the caramel topping over the tops of the still-warm rolls. Let cool completely. ∎

PITA BREAD

MAKES 8 PITAS

Fresh, golden pita bread hot from the oven is a revelation. Sauté summer squash and tomatoes in a little olive oil, give the vegetables a sprinkle of fresh oregano and a topping of grated Asiago cheese, and slip the mixture into the pocket for a quick, superb lunch. These pitas puff up beautifully.

3 cups all-purpose flour, or 2 cups all-purpose and 1 cup whole-wheat, plus extra for kneading

2 teaspoons white sugar

2 teaspoons active dry yeast (about ²/₃ of a package)

2 tablespoons extra-virgin olive oil, plus extra for the bowl and baking sheet

1 teaspoon salt

1. Combine all of the ingredients in a warm mixing bowl and mix until they form a loose, somewhat dry dough. Place the dough on a lightly floured board and knead for 10 minutes, until smooth and elastic. Clean and lightly oil the mixing bowl, place the dough in it, cover with a damp kitchen towel, and let rise in a warm place for 1 hour. It will become puffy.

2. Preheat oven to 500°F. Place one rack on the lowest position and another at the upper-middle position. Punch down the dough and place it onto a lightly oiled, nonporous surface, such as a plastic cutting board or clean countertop. Cut it into 8 equal pieces. Lightly oil a baking sheet. Roll several dough pieces into 6-inch circles, depending on how many fit on your baking sheet (usually 2 to 4 circles; don't have them touch). When the sheet is full, place it on the lower rack and bake for 5 minutes. Roll out the next batch of dough while the first batch bakes. If the first batch hasn't puffed up after 5 minutes, bake another minute. If still not puffed, your oven isn't hot enough—raise the heat to 550°F for the

next batch. As soon as the bread is puffed, place the baking sheet with the first batch on the top rack for 2 minutes, or until the pitas have browned. Remove from the oven and cover the baking sheet in a clean dish towel to keep the bread soft.

3. Bake the next (and subsequent) batch. Store the cooled pitas in a plastic bag. ∎

Wild Rice

ZIZANIA AQUATICA

WILD RICE is not actually rice. It's an aquatic grass that grows wild in the thousands of lakes and ponds of the upper Midwest region of America. Early French explorers saw it growing in the water and called it rice.

Traditionally, the grain—called *manomi*—was harvested as a staple food by Native Americans of the Ojibway tribe and other nearby tribes of what are now Minnesota, Wisconsin, and Michigan. It sustained them over the long winters.

Harvesting the grain from the wild traditionally is done by two people in a canoe. One guides and propels the canoe through the stand of rice plants, the other has two sticks, one in each hand. One stick is used to sweep the seedheads over the canoe, the other to rap the seedheads so the grains fall into the canoe. Commercially grown wild rice uses modern harvesting equipment. California is now the world's production leader of the grain, where it's grown in the waters of the Sacramento River delta.

Until the 1970s, wild rice was expensive because it was all harvested wild from the Great Lakes regions. Then commercial growing began in order to satisfy the huge demand. That makes wild rice the only grass grain domesticated in historical (rather than prehistoric) times.

THE ORGANIC FACTOR ▸ Even commercial growers plant wild rice in natural settings, and so it's almost natural, if not certified organic.

NUTRITION ▸ Nutritionally, wild rice is a champion, with 12 to 15 percent protein that's high in lysine and methionine. It contains more of the B vitamins of thiamine, niacin, riboflavin, and folate than other cereals. It's high in complex carbohydrates, fiber, and potassium. And its fat is unsaturated. Because it's heat-treated to loosen its tight hulls so they can be removed, the grains develop a nutty flavor and chewy texture in processing that has given it a reputation as "the caviar of grains." Even the Ojibway parched the grains to remove the hulls, and undoubtedly to improve the flavor.

WILD RICE AND CORNBREAD STUFFING

MAKES ABOUT 2 QUARTS, ENOUGH FOR A 14- TO 17-POUND TURKEY

Here's one of the traditional Thanksgiving turkey stuffings we make at our house. My wife and I rotate through several different stuffings because we grew up in different families with different ideas of what constitutes the best stuffing, plus we've added a couple of our own favorites over the years. We both agree that this one is the winner.

1 cup uncooked wild rice

6 cups chicken stock

1/2 pound pork sausage, casing removed

2 medium onions, diced

4 stalks celery, diced

4 cups crumbled cornbread

3 cups toasted bread cubes (or Sage Turkey stuffing, page 409)

2 teaspoons ground dried sage

1 teaspoon freshly ground black pepper

2 large eggs

1. Cook the wild rice in 3 cups of the chicken stock over medium heat for 40 minutes, until the grains pop open and are soft.

2. In a large skillet over medium heat, cook the sausage, onions, and celery until the sausage is cooked through and the onions are translucent, about 7 to 8 minutes. In a large bowl, combine the cornbread, bread cubes, sage, and pepper. Add the sausage mixture and the wild rice and combine thoroughly. Lightly beat the eggs, whisk them into the remaining chicken stock, and add to the stuffing, a little at a time, until the stuffing is moist but not soggy. Correct the seasoning. Use to stuff the turkey loosely. Cook the remaining stuffing (or all the stuffing, if you prefer) in a covered baking dish at 350°F for 45 minutes. ▪

Genovese Basil

Herbs
and Spices

WITHOUT HERBS AND SPICES, eating would simply satisfy a need rather than fulfill a desire. In herbs and spices lie the joy of food, the nuances, the sensual pleasures, the art and the fun of cooking. They complete flavors, as when cumin rounds out the taste of hummus. In some cases, herbs and spices transform, as when a little mint is added to fresh garden peas, the combination different from either of the ingredients.

The good cook uses herbs and spices the way a painter uses touches of pure, intense color. Less is often more. They're usually best when they're an accent rather than a feature. Of course, exceptions abound for every rule, and some dishes, such as firehouse chili, pumpkin pie, Moroccan-spiced flank steak, or Indian curry, are all about the spices.

A note on nomenclature: Herbs are usually the leaves of an aromatic plant used fresh or dried (horseradish is an exception—it is an herb). Spices are usually fresh or dried nonleafy parts of a plant such as the seeds or roots.

Most herbs and spices quickly lose their aromatics when ground or crushed. This means that it's important to get your fresh herbs in particular picked as close to the time you'll use them as possible and to grind or crush your dried herbs and spices just before you use them. Avoid the cabinet full of years-old plastic boxes of dead seasonings. My kitchen equipment includes a peppermill, a nutmeg grater, a mortar and pestle, and an electric spice mill dedicated to reducing whole spices such as cardamom, anise, cumin seed, and caraway, among others, to flavorful bits.

Fresh herbs carry the purest flavors, with all their aromatic essential oils and nuances intact. If you have the outdoor space, put in a little culinary herb garden. A small area (5 by 9 feet) is plenty big enough. Or if you have a sunny deck but no land, most herbs do well in containers. Some of the leafy herbs such as basil, chervil, cilantro, and parsley like a rich soil, but Mediterranean herbs such as thyme and oregano prefer dry, well-drained soils that intensify their essential oils. Some, such as rosemary and lavender, thrive in poor, sandy, dry soil.

Herbs are easy to grow for several reasons. Most of our common culinary herbs come from areas of the world with poor, dry soil and can take a lot of neglect because of it. Their essential oils tend to keep insects at bay (except nectar-gathering honeybees, which just love the flowers of thyme, oregano, and rosemary).

THE ORGANIC FACTOR ▸ The strong essential oils in some herbs and spices that act as natural insect repellents obviate the need for chemical insecticides. However, mildews, fungi, and weed competition are often controlled chemically. The only way you can be sure that your herbs and spices will not be contaminated is to seek out their organic versions.

All the herbs and spices listed in this chapter can be found grown organically. Large supermarkets with organic sections will carry many of them. Others can easily be found by searching online. The best solution for many of the herbs, of course, is to grow your own.

Anise and Star Anise

PIMPINELLA ANISUM and
ILLICIUM VERUM

THE ANISE PLANT is a biennial with flowering umbels, umbrella-shaped flower and seed heads familiar from Queen Anne's lace, dill, and fennel. After the flowers come the familiar seeds; they sometimes are sold with a small bit of the stems clinging to them. Star anise is the seedpod and seeds of a Chinese evergreen magnolia in the shape of an eight-pointed star.

Anise is traditionally used in cakes, breads, and cookies. It has a mild licorice-like flavor and sweet, spicy scent. Because aniseed doesn't have the strong flavor of licorice (*Glycyrrhiza glabra*), fennel, or star anise, you can use the spice creatively. Anise seeds are small and oval, while pretty star anise takes the form of an eight-rayed pod with a seed in each ray. These pods are more aromatic than the seeds and have a strong anise or licorice-like aroma.

STORAGE AND PREPARATION ► Aniseed will stay fresh for a couple of years, but it quickly loses its savor when ground, so only grind it as needed.

USES ► Both aniseed and star anise may be used whole or ground into a powder. Use the ground spices to season flour to coat a rolled pork roast before roasting. Flavor beets or carrots with them. Toss some seeds in the poaching water with fish, or stuff some inside the fish before cooking. Dip fresh figs in the ground seed powder or add to baked goods—it's a classic flavor in Italian biscotti and in the German *pfeffernüsse* (see recipe at right). Use anise-flavored liqueur such as pastis or anisette in water for cooking rice. If you grow anise in your herb garden, use the young leaves in salads and in a bouquet of herbs placed in a seafood stew.

PFEFFERNÜSSE

MAKES ABOUT 65 TO 70 COOKIES

The German holiday cookie called *pfeffernüsse* includes anise. The name is German for "pepper nuts." Black pepper enhances the spices without adding heat to the cookies. Citron is the cured and candied peel of a citrus sold in most supermarkets.

2 cups sugar
4 cups all-purpose flour
1 teaspoon crushed aniseed
1/4 teaspoon freshly grated nutmeg
1/2 teaspoon ground cloves
1/2 teaspoon freshly ground black pepper
1 1/2 teaspoons baking powder
1/2 cup grated or minced citron
Finely grated zest of 1 lemon (well scrubbed
    if not organic)
4 large eggs, beaten slightly

1. Preheat the oven to 375°F. Grease two 13 × 9 cookie sheets.

2. In a large bowl, mix together the sugar, flour, aniseed, nutmeg, cloves, pepper, and baking powder. Add the citron and zest. Add the eggs. With buttered hands, shape the mixture into small balls about the size of a whole nutmeg (the size of the outermost joint of your index finger), place on cookie sheets 1 inch apart in all directions, and bake for 10 minutes or until they're a light golden brown. Let cool completely before storing in closed tins lined with waxed paper. ■

Basil

OCIMUM, various species

BASIL is an indispensable herb for any cook, especially the organic cook who looks to p-reserve and enhance the garden-fresh flavors of organically grown vegetables. Basil is easy to grow in compost-enriched soil, which puts its refreshing, sweet, spicy pungency at your fingertips during the growing season.

Yes, you can find fresh basil at almost any time of year in the supermarket, but off-season, it's usually tired and has lost some of its oomph. Better to put up some of your own, or buy fresh basil at the farmers' market during the height of its summer season.

TYPES ✦ Basil has more species and varieties than most other herbs, and they vary by flavor, color, texture, size, and aroma. These types loosely fall into one of five categories: regular (cinnamon or clove-scented), anise-scented, dwarf, lemon-scented, and purple-leaved.

Here is a cook's take on the commonly available top basil varieties:

Cinnamon Basil (*Ocimum basilicum* 'Cinnamon')— Distinct cinnamon scent with a hint of cloves.

Genovese (*Ocimum basilicum* 'Genovese')—Also called perfume basil because of its intense basil fragrance. Best for pesto.

Holy Basil (*Ocimum sanctum*)—Very pungent, with the aroma of black walnuts and exotic spices. This is one basil that takes to cooking methods like stir fries, soups, and curries, but add the leaves toward the end of cooking.

Lemon Basil (*Ocimum basilicum variety citriodorum*) —Has a distinct lemon scent. A new cultivar,

Sweet Dani, is an improved variety with a strong lemon character.

Lime Basil (*Ocimum americanum*)—Has a distinct lime scent.

Purple Basil (*Ocimum basilicum variety purpurascens*)—Also called opal basil. This is the one to use to make infused vinegar because of the pretty pink color it imparts.

Purple Ruffles Basil (*Ocimum basilicum* 'Purple Ruffles')—Ruffly, highly-colored leaves carry an anise scent with a hint of mint.

Sweet Basil (*Ocimum basilicum*)—A strong clove and anise scent rises from the leaves; perfect for pesto, tomato and mozzarella salads, and pizza.

Thai Basil (*Ocimum basilicum horapa*)—Small, slender, but highly aromatic leaves used in many Thai dishes, soups, and curries. Siam Queen is a prized new variety with a strong licorice character.

SEASONALITY ✦ Basil is at its best from high summer through fall.

STORAGE ✦ Drying the leaves doesn't work—it drives off the delicate essential oils that give the herb its aroma. There are four ways to preserve basil's freshness for the winter months.

The first way is to make pesto. Use the freshest, most aromatic leaves of regular or Genovese basil. Follow the Pesto recipe on page 337.

The second way is to freeze cubes of basil puree: Get the freshest, most aromatic leaves of sweet or Genovese basil and put them in a blender along with just enough water to blend them into a thick slurry. Pour the slurry into ice cube trays and freeze them solid. When frozen, transfer the basil cubes to a freezer bag and store in the freezer. One cube will flavor two cups of spaghetti sauce or a sautéed mixture of fresh tomatoes, onions, garlic, and oregano.

The third way is to make basil oil: Place fresh, pungent basil leaves of any variety loosely in a jar with a tight-fitting lid and fill the jar with good-quality olive oil and a tablespoon of red wine vinegar. Shake the jar daily and store it in a warm place, such as the top of the fridge or a sunny windowsill. After three or four weeks, fish out the leaves and pour off the oil into a nice-looking jar (discard the vinegar at the bottom). Store in a cool, dark place and use the oil to drizzle on pizzas, salad, or baked fish. Don't use it as cooking oil, as the heat will disrupt some of the flavor.

Fourth, you can make basil vinegar: Take a tightly packed cup of purple basil and place it in a quart Mason jar. Cover the basil with a mild vinegar. I like unseasoned rice vinegar for this purpose. Its light acidity allows the spiciness of the basil to come through, and its light color shows off the pretty pink-ruby color the basil imparts. Place waxed paper over the top of the jar and then screw on the lid with a ring band. Keep it on a shelf out of direct sunlight for a month, then pour the vinegar through a strainer into a pitcher, then into pretty glass jars. You'll love the color and the pungency. Combine this vinegar with some of the basil-infused olive oil to make an all-basil salad dressing.

USES ► Tear up bits of leaves to add color and aroma to salads. Use whole leaves as a bed for baked or poached fish. All basils marry beautifully with tomatoes and with Italian-oriented foods like eggplant, lemons, olives, pastas, pizza, cannellini beans, summer squash, and Italian cheeses. Chop it finely and mix with bread crumbs and pine nuts to stuff light meats like pork and veal. Thai basil merges beautifully with Southeast Asian condiments like garlic, ginger, galangal, kaffir lime leaves, and lemongrass.

Borage

BORAGO OFFICINALIS

BORAGE is a relative of blue-flowered comfrey, pulmonaria, and hound's tongue, and one of the first wildflowers to bloom around northern California in late winter, where it continues to flower well into the summer. Like comfrey, it has fuzzy leaves, and pretty pendant flowers that nod and hang downward, with sky blue petals surrounding a cone of dark anthers. This herb looks beautiful in a garden and every herb garden should have a plant or two. (Borage is an annual plant that will reseed; it grows most anywhere.) Borage is more a decoration than a source of flavor.

The herb's name, incidentally, comes from the Latin *borra,* meaning "rough hair, short wool," or the late Latin, *burra,* a shaggy garment—either way a reference to the bristly hairs on the leaves and stems of the borage plant. In the famous medieval children's book on manners, *Babee's Book* circa 1500, the entry under "To Serve a Lord" says, "Sawse hym with mustard, burage, and suger."

USES ► Borage is grown mostly for its blue flowers, which are edible and carry a distinct cucumber flavor. They're perfect for adding color to salads and cooling drinks such as lemonade. They can also be crystallized and used as decorations on cake icing (see recipe, page 382). The succulent stems can also be added to salads but first must be shorn of their hairy bristles with a vegetable peeler.

CRYSTALLIZED BORAGE FLOWERS

Crystallizing your own flowers is fun and easy and bound to be a hit when used to stud your grandmom's birthday cake. In addition to borage, try crystallizing other small, edible flowers, such as Johnny-Jump-Ups, apple blossoms, and lilac florets.

You will need a small, unused artist's paintbrush and a baking rack covered with waxed paper.

Fresh borage flowers
1 large egg white, at room temperature
1 cup superfine sugar

1. In a small bowl, lightly whisk together the egg white with a few drops of water until the white just shows a few bubbles. Place the sugar in a shallow dish. Holding a flower in one hand, dip the paint brush into the egg white with the other and gently paint the flower with it. Cover the flower completely but not excessively. Holding the flower over the sugar dish, gently sprinkle sugar evenly over all sides. Place the flower on waxed paper to dry.

2. Continue with the rest of the flowers. Let the flowers dry until they are completely free of moisture. This may take between 12 and 36 hours, depending on the humidity. To hasten drying, place the candied flowers in an oven with a pilot light overnight, or in a warmed electric oven with the heat off and the door ajar for several hours. Make sure they are completely dry, then store the dried, candied flowers in an airtight, moisture-proof container until ready to use. If thoroughly dried and properly stored, they'll keep indefinitely. ∎

Caraway

CARUM CARVI

CARAWAY is a spice native to Europe, where it grows wild from north to south and into the Middle East and North Africa. It has naturalized in parts of New England.

The first condiment in recorded history was caraway—it appears in the medical papyrus of Thebes in 1552 BCE. Since then, the small, striped seeds of the biennial *carum* plant have never gone out of style. In Elizabethan times, the seeds were part of the tea service, eaten plain to sweeten the breath. Today we associate them most familiarly with rye bread and German or Austrian cheese. But there are plenty of other uses.

Caraway is easy to grow in good, organic soil in full sun. Sow the seeds from spring to midsummer. The plant is a biennial and will make a low mound of ferny leaves the first year, then send up an umbel of flowers, followed by seeds, the next. If you're buying seed, look for the variety called Karzo, which yields plentiful seeds with a high content of carvone, the essential oil that gives caraway its distinctive aroma.

STORAGE ◆ Caraway seeds keep their flavoring power for up to a year when kept whole, but the essential oils evaporate quickly after the seeds are crushed or ground. So use a spice mill or mortar and pestle to grind just what you need.

USES ◆ Although the taste of caraway is familiar to many, it's nevertheless hard to describe and totally unique. Some describe it as a cross between anise and cumin with a bitter finish. To me it tastes like good rye bread.

Boiling cabbage with caraway seeds reduces the heavy mustard smell of the cooked cabbage.

Whole caraway seeds flavor sausages, pumpernickel, soups, stews, roast pork, and Moroccan Harissa (page 107). Caraway makes a fine partnership with sauerkraut and goes well with turnips, carrots, and potatoes. The spice is used in cookies, cakes, breads, and biscuits; it flavors the German liqueur called Kümmel, makes the caraway-flavored liquor aquavit, and is a part of most pickling spice blends.

CARAWAY-INFUSED PORK WITH SAUERKRAUT AND APPLES

SERVES 5

This recipe came straight from the Black Forest and crossed the Atlantic with the Schwabian immigrants who became the Pennsylvania Dutch. A dish very similar to this was a yearly feature at The West End Harvest Fair in Gilbert, Pennsylvania, where locals would wash down heaping platefuls with cold beer.

You'll need a slow cooker to make this old-fashioned dish correctly. Put it on the low setting in the morning and come home to a ready-made dinner. Serve it with slabs of good whole-wheat or rye bread to soak up the liquid. If you want to go all the way, make your own sauerkraut following the recipe on page 84.

1 pound red potatoes, unpeeled, cut into 1-inch chunks

2 pounds sauerkraut, drained and lightly rinsed

1 green apple, unpeeled, cored and coarsely chopped

1/2 cup chopped onion

1 1/2 pounds lean, boneless, country-style pork ribs

1/2 pound Polish sausage, cut into 1 1/2-inch chunks

3/4 cup apple cider

3 tablespoons brown sugar

1 teaspoon whole caraway seeds

1 teaspoon ground mustard

1/2 teaspoon ground allspice

1. Place the potatoes in the slow cooker. In a large bowl, combine the sauerkraut, apple, and onion. Spoon half this mixture over the potatoes. Place the pork and Polish sausage on top of the potato mixture. Spoon the remaining sauerkraut mixture over the top.

2. In a small bowl, mix together the apple cider, brown sugar, caraway seeds, mustard, and allspice. Lightly stir the mixture into the contents of the slow cooker. Cover and turn on low. Cook for 8 to 10 hours. ■

CARAWAY FARMER CHEESE

MAKES 2 CUPS

Here's a simple recipe for a tasty farmer-type cheese that's easy to make and spreads beautifully on toast for breakfast. It keeps for a week in the fridge.

1/2 gallon milk, any type

Juice of 2 lemons, strained

1 tablespoon crushed caraway seeds

1/4 teaspoon salt

1. In a large heavy saucepan over low heat, warm the milk to 165°F, stirring often and being careful not to scorch the milk. Stir in the lemon juice, remove from the heat, and allow it to set for 15 minutes. The curds that form will be stringy and the whey will be a greenish fluid.

2. Line a colander with 2 layers of wet cheesecloth and set it into a large pan to capture the whey. Pour the curds and whey into the colander. (You can save the whey and use it in place of water to make bread. If not, don't pour it down the drain; give it to a plant outside. Plants love whey's nutritional boost.)

3. Tie up the four corners of the cheesecloth into a knot and lightly rinse the bag of curds with

continued

cold tap water. Hang the cheesecloth bag from the kitchen sink faucet for 1 hour, or until the dripping stops. Untie the cheesecloth and turn the cheese into a bowl.

4. Crush the caraway seeds with a mortar and pestle or spice grinder. Add the seeds and salt to the cheese and work them in thoroughly. Place it in a covered container and refrigerate for up to one week. ▪

Cardamom

ELETTARIA CARDAMOMUM

THIS LARGE, PERENNIAL HERB—a native of southern India—now is cultivated in Guatemala, Sri Lanka, Southeast Asia, and Papua New Guinea. Most of the cardamom that we import in the United States comes from Guatemala.

WHAT TO LOOK FOR ◆ The useful part of cardamom are the seeds inside the oval pod. Cardamom with white pods has been bleached. Look for unbleached pods that are green to yellowish green. If you can, pry open a hull to see if the 15 to 20 seeds inside are plump and sticky or if they are dry. If they are sticky, that's a sign of freshness. Don't accept pods that have already broken open, because the seeds soon dry out and their aromatic oils are lost. For that reason, never buy hulled seeds or ground cardamom. Fresh cardamom seeds have a strong aroma and a pungent taste like camphor overlain with notes of lemon that give it a clean, refreshing flavor.

STORAGE ◆ Store cardamom pods in an airtight jar for up to a year, because exposure to air quickly saps the seeds of their essential oil, as does grinding. Grind what you need with a mortar and pestle or spice grinder as you use it.

USES ◆ Because it was originally brought west along the caravan routes from India, cardamom is a part of the cooking of cultures along those routes. At home in India, it's used there in both sweet and savory dishes, where its penetrating, camphor-citrus-eucalyptus flavor adds intensity to curries and to pastries and sugared sweets. A couple of lightly crushed whole pods added to the cooking pot will nicely flavor rice. It's a part of the classic Indian garam masala spice mixture (see recipe, page 91), where its lemony-camphorous note blends with cloves, mace, cinnamon, cumin, coriander, fennel, black pepper, and fenugreek seeds. In Turkey and in some Arab nations, it's used to flavor thick black coffee. When cardamom was taken south to Ethiopia, it became a key component of the country's spicy-hot Berbere Sauce (see recipe at right). Taken to northern Europe and Russia, it became a popular addition to sweet rolls, breads, and pastries.

I've used cardamom successfully with oranges to flavor roast duck—just follow a recipe for duck à l'orange but add the ground seeds from three cardamom pods to the finished orange sauce. This spice also has an affinity for yellow-fleshed vegetables such as winter squashes and sweet potatoes, but it's best used sparingly.

Cardamom is a pickling spice, contributing a smokiness to dill's fruitiness. It likes sweet dishes, giving a warm and mellow flavor to spiced peaches, poached pears, and applesauce as well as to slow-cooked savory meats such as brisket, lamb shanks, and pulled pork. It marries with the Middle Eastern and North African spice blends of cumin, coriander, black pepper, and saffron, and with the aromatic pie spices, such as cinnamon, cloves, and nutmeg.

BERBERE SAUCE

MAKES ABOUT 2 CUPS

This spicy sauce is a staple of Ethiopian cooking. Slow cooked, saucy stews of lamb and potatoes are typically eaten by swiping some up on a piece of Ethiopian flatbread that's been dabbed with it. I like to eat the sauce with a cold beer near at hand to quell the flames. The Ethiopians use small, fiery-hot bird peppers, or piquins. Mexican chipotle chiles have less heat but are more widely available.

24 dried bird peppers, Thai chile peppers or piquins,
    or substitute 4 seeded dried chipotle chiles
2 teaspoons cumin seeds
4 whole cloves
$1/2$ teaspoon cardamom seeds removed from pods
$1/4$ teaspoon ground allspice
$1/2$ teaspoon fennel seeds
$1/2$ cup chopped onion
1 teaspoon salt
1 teaspoon ground ginger
2 cloves garlic, chopped
1 teaspoon turmeric
$1/2$ cup extra-virgin olive oil
$1/2$ cup red wine

1. Put the chiles, cumin, cloves, cardamom, allspice, and fennel in a dry skillet and toast over medium heat for 2 minutes, or until they start to release their fragrance.

2. Remove the skillet from the heat and coarsely chop the chiles. Put the chopped chiles and the skillet contents into a blender, and blend on high speed until the ingredients are coarsely ground. Add the onion, salt, ginger, garlic, turmeric, oil, and wine.

3. Blend until the mixture forms a thick, brownish paste. Store covered in the freezer indefinitely. Spoon out and warm to room temperature as needed. ■

Chervil

ANTHRISCUS CEREFOLIUM

IN THE EARLY SPRING in southeastern Europe, the Caucasus, and western Asia, the air is cool, the ground moist with winter rains and snowmelt, and in dappled shady copses, the native chervil appears, looking like a delicate form of parsley.

When it's young, its green leaves are sweet and aromatic and carry a scent and flavor of anise with a touch of parsley. Within a couple of months, the weather turns hot and it flowers and goes to seed. Then its leaves turn a greenish purple or yellow and its flavor is lost.

SEASONALITY ‣ For millennia, Europeans have broken the long winter dependence on stored root vegetables, dried fruits, and meats by making a refreshing spring tonic out of new leaves of chervil, dandelion, and watercress. Their vitality-restoring vitamins and minerals, and just the taste of breath-cleansing chlorophyll, was a sign of the new season—chervil even became associated with Easter rituals. Because it's a hardy annual, chervil can be planted in late summer or early fall, and it will last through the winter for new growth early in the spring, or it can be planted in the spring as soon as the ground thaws out and can be worked. It goes to seed quickly in hot weather and baking sun, so plant subsequent sowing in a cool, partially shaded part of the garden. Keep weed competition away and the herb is easy to grow.

WHAT TO LOOK FOR ‣ When buying chervil, choose fresh-looking plants with no sign of seed stalks.

STORING ‣ Fresh chervil will last for a week in the fridge. To preserve the taste of fresh chervil year-round, whiz some in the blender with just enough water to make a thick slurry, then pour into ice cube trays and freeze. Place the frozen cubes in a freezer bag and mark its contents. You can also make minced *fines herbes* (see Uses), and freeze them as cubes or in a small container for use in the winter. Freezing the herbs will dry them out but will still preserve much of their fresh flavor and aroma.

USES ‣ Chervil is a quintessentially French herb. It must always be used fresh and raw or frozen as described above. Drying it destroys its character, as does the heat of cooking. It's best added after the cooking is completed.

Chervil has myriad uses: in salad dressings; as a component of sauce béarnaise; in omelets; as chervil butter (work 3 tablespoons of minced chervil into ½ pound of room-temperature butter and spread it over hot baked fish or on toast or biscuits); or sprinkle it liberally on springtime's wonderful fava beans. It enhances light meats such as chicken and veal. It goes with peas, carrots, and potatoes. Little sprigs of chervil make a lovely addition to green salads.

Chervil is the most delicate partner in the French herb combination *fines herbes,* a marriage of finely chopped chervil, parsley, chives, and French tarragon, which is added to season dishes just before serving, as its flavor is lost in cooking. Because chervil is a spring herb, it has a natural affinity for other spring vegetables, such as asparagus, baby carrots, and salads of new spring greens.

CHERVIL SAUCE BÉARNAISE

MAKES 1½ CUPS

You must make sauce béarnaise carefully, for overheating the egg yolks will cause them to cook and adding too much butter will cause the sauce to turn. I've used the following recipe many times with success. Use it on grilled or baked fish or chicken. The chervil adds a delicate anise flavor and aroma to what is otherwise just a tangy, fluffy butter sauce for meat, fish, egg dishes, and vegetables.

¼ cup white wine vinegar
¼ cup dry white wine
1 tablespoon minced shallots
⅛ teaspoon freshly ground black pepper
Pinch of salt

3 egg yolks
2 tablespoons cold butter
8 tablespoons (1 stick) butter, melted
3 tablespoons minced fresh chervil

1. In a 1-quart nonreactive saucepan boil the vinegar, wine, shallots, salt, and pepper over medium heat until the liquid reduces to 2 tablespoons. Let it cool, then strain and reserve the liquid.

2. In a small heat-proof bowl, whisk the egg yolks until thick and creamy. Add the reduced liquid. Place this mixture in the top of a double boiler and cook slowly, keeping the heat low, and whisking constantly until the mixture thickens. Add 1 tablespoon of the cold butter, and whisk until it's melted and incorporated. Beat in the other tablespoon of cold butter. (The cold butter prevents the egg yolks from overcooking.) Add the melted butter ¼ teaspoon at a time, until it thickens nicely, using a whisk to make sure each addition is incorporated before the next addition. Once the sauce thickens to a thick creamy consistency, you can add the butter a tablespoon or two at a time. Keep the heat low.

When the butter is all incorporated and the béarnaise sauce is light and fluffy, whisk in the chervil. Use immediately or refrigerate for a day or two.

TIP: To use, let it come back to room temperature, but don't heat or cook. If the sauce has separated or curdled, whizzing it in the blender will restore some of its proper texture. If your béarnaise turns, all is not lost. Let it cool for a few minutes, then pour it a little at a time into a blender. If it still doesn't fluff up, it's still too warm. Pour it out and try again. ■

Chive

ALLIUM SCHOENOPRASUM

CHIVES—as you might guess by their taste—are members of the onion genus (*Allium*) that includes garlic, onions, ramps, scallions, leeks, and many other forms.

Because chives should be used fresh and raw, having a container full or a small patch in the herb garden for them is essential. They're easy to grow. They can be grown all year in a pot if brought into a protected place such as a sunroom or under a skylight where they won't be subject to hard freezes and will get adequate sunlight. They need watering, as they don't tolerate drought.

Think of chives as small onions—which they are—and never cut them off wholesale at ground level, which removes their source of energy and damages the plant, sometimes irreparably. Rather select a few good-looking leaves from the outside of the clump and snip them off 2 inches above ground level. This encourages new bulblets to form under the soil. A pot of chives can last and proliferate for years, until they get so crowded they give up. To prevent this, gently divide the bulbs after four or five years and replant some in a new pot.

Let them flower, which they will do in late spring. Tear the light fuchsia blossoms into florets and sprinkle them in salads. Or infuse unseasoned rice vinegar with the flower heads for three weeks, then strain off the vinegar into a fancy clear glass

KEEP AN EYE OUT FOR RAMPS

WHILE we're talking about chives, this is a good place to mention a much-sought-after relative called ramps (*Allium tricoccum*), a kind of leek that grows wild in open woodlands and fields from Appalachia across to the Great Lakes states and from eastern Canada to the Carolinas. In Appalachia they're called ramps; in the Midwest, wild leeks. When I was a kid growing up in Pennsylvania, where we bought milk from a local dairy, it was not uncommon to be confronted with onion-flavored milk in the spring. The cows, turned out to early pasture, ate the ramps that grew among the shrubs on a slope near our house. While onion milk doesn't have much to recommend it, the ramps that imparts the flavor do: It's a strong oniony aroma and flavor.

Ramps are best from March to May, before the flower stalks appear. Their leaves can be used to wrap delicate fish for poaching or braising, and to flavor egg dishes, soups, or sauces. The bulbs can be used like shallots to impart a strong onion flavor to omelets and other dishes. Three tablespoons of minced leaves can be whisked together with 1/2 cup each of mayonnaise and yogurt, 1 tablespoon of fresh lemon juice, and 1 tablespoon of Dijon mustard to make a sauce for spring asparagus.

container. This will give the vinegar a light onion aroma and a pretty pinkish color.

TYPES ➤ Ordinary, hollow-leaved chives have a subspecies called Siberian chives. They have a stronger, garlicky flavor.

Garlic chives (*Allium tuberosum*), with flatter green leaves that contain a mild garlic flavor and aroma, flower later in the summer with white florets that carry a sweet smell. Let them flower, then go to seed: If left to proliferate by themselves, garlic chives will usually self-sow, slowly enlarging their territory and making a pretty ground cover.

SEASONALITY ➤ There's a variety of ordinary chives called Windowsill Chives that will produce all winter in a sunny window. Other cultivars may turn yellow and die back in winter. When completely yellow, cut off the dead spears and new spears will soon return.

USES ➤ Chives are a natural on baked potatoes topped with sour cream or butter. For a healthier alternative, potatoes can be stuffed with soft tofu that's been mashed with a little canola oil and lemon juice, seasoned with salt and pepper, then topped with minced chives.

Garlic chives will add a mild garlic flavor to foods. Toss a few leaves into the soup pot, then remove them when the soup is done. Or chop them into small bits to use in soups, stews, or any time a garlic flavor is called for. The flowers can be torn up and used to garnish a salad, but they won't impart much garlic flavor.

CAPONATA WITH CHIVES

MAKES ABOUT 2 CUPS

Caponata is an intensely flavorful sweet-and-sour Sicilian eggplant relish that benefits from the texture, appearance, and light onion flavor given by the chives. Serve this on bruschetta or as a side dish to accompany chicken, broiled fish, or veal.

4 cups peeled and chopped eggplant (1 large
   or 2 smaller eggplants)
Kosher salt
1 medium onion, chopped
2 tablespoons olive oil
2 cloves garlic, chopped
2 stalks celery, chopped
3 tablespoons toasted, crushed pine nuts
2 tablespoons pitted, chopped black oil-cured olives
1/2 teaspoon capers
2 plum tomatoes, chopped
1 tablespoon balsamic vinegar
1/2 cup chopped chives

1. Place the chopped eggplant in a colander, set in the sink, and toss liberally with kosher salt. Let sit 1 hour, then drain, rinse off the salt, and squeeze to extract the excess moisture.

2. In a skillet over high heat, sauté the onion in the oil until it is translucent and golden, about 8 minutes. Add the garlic and celery and cook 2 minutes longer. Add the chopped eggplant to the skillet. Cook for 5 minutes. Add the pine nuts, olives, and capers and cook 5 more minutes, until the eggplant is tender. Remove the skillet from the heat, turn into a serving bowl, and let cool to room temperature. Stir in the tomatoes, vinegar, and chives. Serve at room temperature. ■

Cilantro and Coriander

CORIANDRUM SATIVUM

CILANTRO refers to the fresh, frilly leaves of the coriander plant, whose seeds are the spice we know as coriander. And while most people, including myself, find coriander seed's sweet, spicy, lightly lemony flavor very agreeable, opinion is strongly divided on the flavor of cilantro's leaves and similar tasting roots. Those who like it use it enthusiastically, while others find it offputting, almost soapy tasting.

Coriander is a cool weather crop best suited to spring and fall cultivation. In hot climates, it loses its peculiar aroma and taste. In the garden, it dislikes weed competition, so young plants should be mulched. It likes rich, humusy, constantly moist soil and reaches leaf-harvest stage after a couple of months; it will flower within a month after that.

USES ◆ Cilantro is a chief flavoring in many Mexican salsas, in guacamole, and appears extensively in South American and Southeast Asian cooking, usually as a garnish or in a raw sauce, as cooking destroys its unique aroma and flavor. The herb has an affinity for chicken and fish, coconut, corn, lamb and lentils, shellfish, tomatoes, parsnips, and citrus.

Coriander is a mainstay in chutneys, curries, and Garam Masala (see Tip, page 91). It pairs nicely with lamb, lentils, pork, and potatoes, and many cooks use both the herb and the seed form of the plant to flavor these staples. It makes a natural partnership with cumin and sweet spices such as allspice, cinnamon, cloves, and nutmeg. It also enhances ginger, soy, and garlic marinades. In the United States, whole coriander seed is a principal component in pickling spice blends. Coriander is one of the spices whose essential oils dissipate rapidly after grinding, so buy the seeds whole and grind them as needed in a spice mill.

FRESH, HOT SALSA

MAKES 4 CUPS

Serve with tacos or burritos, spoon some over roast chicken, or add some to your morning omelet to wake up your taste buds.

10 fresh serrano chiles, stemmed
5 cups chopped ripe tomatoes
1/2 cup chopped white onion
1 cup chopped cilantro leaves (from 1 bunch)
4 cloves garlic, chopped
2 teaspoons fresh oregano leaves, chopped
1 teaspoon salt

1. Preheat the oven to 350°F. Roast the chiles until tender, about 5 to 7 minutes or until a fork easily penetrates a chile.

2. Transfer them to a blender with 1 cup of tomatoes and blend to a chunky texture. Add the remaining ingredients and blend to a coarse consistency. ∎

CORIANDER PORK

SERVES 4

This is a simple and delicious way to prepare pork tenderloin that shows how well coriander's delicate seasoning blends with the sweetness of the pork. Note that the meat marinates for a day before you cook it.

1 tablespoon coriander seeds
1 cup apple cider
2 tablespoons freshly squeezed lemon juice
1/2 cup olive oil
1/2 teaspoon freshly ground black pepper
1/4 teaspoon salt
1 to 2 pounds of pork tenderloin (1 large or 2 small loins), sliced into 1/2-inch rounds
2 tablespoons heavy cream

1. Crush the coriander seeds with a mortar and pestle or spice mill. Mix together the cider, lemon juice, 6 tablespoons of the oil, coriander, pepper, and salt. Lay the pork rounds in a deep, nonreactive dish and pour the marinade over them. Cover and refrigerate.

2. The next day remove the meat from the marinade and pat dry on paper towels. Reserve the marinade. Heat the remaining 2 tablespoons olive oil over medium heat in a skillet large enough to accommodate the meat in a single layer. Brown the meat on both sides, about 2 minutes per side. Add the marinade, bring to a boil, reduce the heat to simmer, cover, and cook until the meat is tender, about 20 minutes. Remove the meat to a serving dish and keep warm. Add the cream to the liquid in the pan, and stir until well mixed and heated through. Pour over the pork and serve. ■

Cumin

CUMINUM CYMINUM

CUMIN SEED forms a part of nearly every cuisine from the Mediterranean Sea to China—including Greek, North African, Middle Eastern, Iranian, Indian, and other cuisines across the entire swath of land we call Central Asia—imparting its characteristic strong aroma and flavor to chili powder, curry powder, sauces, and chutneys.

Cumin is one of those slender umbelliferous (ferny) annuals like dill that grows quickly up to 2 feet tall and sets seed readily. Both its genus and species names refer to the Arabic word *kamun*, which means cumin. It has been cultivated in the Mediterranean basin for at least the last 4,000 years. It's native to North Africa and the western Middle East.

STORAGE ► I keep cumin seed whole and grind it as needed because, like many spices containing volatile oils as their flavoring, cumin loses its potency if kept as ground powder. Before grinding, I usually toast it in a hot skillet for a minute or two, which releases its oils and intensifies its flavor and aroma. Whole cumin seed will keep for a year or two, but loses its essential oils if kept much longer than that. Freezing it preserves it indefinitely.

USES ► This small, oily seed carries a warm, earthy, instantly recognizable flavor that conjures up Moroccan tagines, the sharp pungency of Northwest African harissa, Indian curries, and the spice bazaars of the steppes of Central Asia. But you'll also find cumin in Mexican dishes mixed with chiles and sweet peppers, and in South America with onions and cilantro.

Cumin's strong flavor lends itself to inclusion in other strongly flavored food such as cheeses, sausages, chili, sauerkraut, and meat stews. Additionally—and despite its potency—it also combines well with a wide range of other strong flavors, including allspice, cardamom, cinnamon, cloves, coriander, fennel seed, garlic, and oregano; meats such as chicken, lamb, and pork; and cereals, seeds, and vegetables such as couscous, rice, beans, peas, lentils, and potatoes. Because of its potency, a little goes a long way, and cumin is usually best where it plays a supporting role.

garlic scorch. Remove from heat and transfer the onions and garlic to a large bowl. Add beef, egg, serrano chile, tomato paste, chili powder, cumin, salt, thyme, parsley, bread crumbs, and milk, and mix thoroughly. (Use two forks so as not to compact and mash the beef, or it will become dense and tough.)

2. Oil an ovenproof glass loaf pan and spread 3 tablespoons of the chili sauce in the bottom. Add the meat-loaf mixture and smooth it out evenly. Spread the remaining chili sauce over the top. Bake for 1 to 1¼ hours or until the top layer of chili sauce begins to brown. ∎

ROCK 'EM SOCK 'EM MEAT LOAF

SERVES 4

No wimp, this meat loaf has flavors and savors way beyond grandmom's bland meat loaves from the past. Especially when the beef is grass-fed and organic.

1 teaspoon olive oil, plus extra for the pan
1 medium onion, minced
2 cloves garlic, crushed
1 pound lean ground beef
1 large egg
1 serrano chile, seeded and minced
2 tablespoons tomato paste
1 teaspoon chili powder
$^1\!/_2$ teaspoon freshly ground cumin seed
$^1\!/_2$ teaspoon salt
$^1\!/_2$ teaspoon dried thyme
$^1\!/_4$ cup minced fresh parsley
$^1\!/_4$ cup dry bread crumbs
$^1\!/_4$ cup skim milk
6 tablespoons chili sauce

1. Preheat the oven to 350°F. Heat the oil in a skillet over medium heat. Add the onions and garlic and sauté until soft, about 5 minutes. Don't let the

CHICKEN WITH CITRUS AND CUMIN

SERVES 4

When the barbecue grill is just at a medium heat (when the coals have all turned gray and the fierce heat has subsided), it's time to grab this chicken out of the marinade and start cooking. The combination of citrus and cumin gives a North African accent to the chicken.

4 boneless, skinless chicken breast halves
1 teaspoon freshly ground cumin
2 tablespoons fresh oregano leaves
2 cloves garlic, minced
Grated zest and juice of 1 lime (well scrubbed
    if not organic)
Grated zest and juice of 1 orange (well scrubbed
    if not organic)
1 tablespoon olive oil
$^1\!/_2$ teaspoon salt
$^1\!/_2$ teaspoon freshly ground black pepper

1. Place the chicken breasts, cumin, oregano, garlic, citrus zests and juices, and olive oil in a shallow bowl and cover, then place in the fridge for 1 hour. *continued*

2. Remove the chicken and discard the marinade. Sprinkle the breasts with the salt and pepper. Grill over medium heat for 5 to 7 minutes on each side, until the breasts are browned and cooked through. ∎

Dill

ANETHUM GRAVEOLENS

EVEN IF you only use dill once in a while, it's still a blessing to have this herb in one's garden because, like most umbelliferous plants, such as fennel, carrots, and caraway, it attracts and supports beneficial insects. I've planted it under my apple trees, where it helps bring in beneficial insects to control apple pests.

Dill is an annual plant that will self-sow in the garden, so once you start a patch, it will continue year after year on its own if the soil is rich and moist. The leaves, flower heads, and seeds are all used in cooking, and all carry the distinctive dill flavor. By the way, dill and fennel can cross-pollinate and make intergeneric hybrids, so keep them far apart in the garden.

DILL WEED ‣ The ferny, feathery leaves of dill are called dill weed and are widely used in poaching liquids for fish and shellfish. Creamy dill sauce is standard with gravlax. Dill is commonly paired with cole crops—cabbage and cauliflower—across the northern tier of states and in Europe, and with sour cream as a sauce for cucumbers, as folks of Polish descent will know. And Germans like horseradish and dill with their beef.

DILL SEED ‣ Dill seed is a chief ingredient of dill pickles—and for most Americans, pickles don't taste like pickles without dill seed in the

pickling mix. The seeds can also be infused in vinegar to make an interesting vinaigrette: Simply add ½ cup of dill seeds to 1 quart of white vinegar and let it infuse for a month, then pour off the vinegar, rinse the spent seeds from the bottle, pour the vinegar back into the bottle, and use as you would other vinegars in a vinaigrette recipe.

SEASONALITY ‣ Dill seed is available all year, but dill weed is usually only available in the summer through early fall.

DILLED SALMON

SERVES 4

This is my favorite way to cook salmon—so much so that I hardly ever cook it any other way. I find that salmon done this way is incomparable.

Ask your fishmonger to remove the skin from a salmon fillet of whatever size you prefer.

4 bunches fresh dill weed
1- to 2-pound salmon fillet, skin removed

1. Arrange the oven racks so that the distance between the bottom rack and the one above it will accommodate an uncovered Dutch oven. Preheat the oven to 300°F. Fill a Dutch oven half-full with water and bring to a boil over high heat on the stovetop.

2. Line the bottom of a baking pan with the dill weed in approximately the same shape as the salmon fillet, and then lay the fillet on top of the dill, with what was the skin side down.

3. When the pot is boiling well, set it on the bottom rack of the oven and place the salmon on the rack above. Bake exactly 30 minutes. Lift the salmon off the dill, using two spatulas if necessary, and transfer it to a warmed serving platter. Discard the dill. ∎

Epazote

CHENOPODIUM AMBROSIOIDES

EPAZOTE is a member of the goosefoot family, the same genus as lamb's-quarters, the common garden weed. Like lamb's-quarters, it is a tough herb that will become a pest in the garden if allowed to grow there. Better to grow a few plants in a pot on a sunny deck. It will grow even in hot, dry conditions but tastes best if given adequate water.

SEASONALITY ◂ Epazote is found in Mexican markets from late spring into summer. Choose fresh, young-looking sprigs.

USES ◂ Epazote is native to Central America and Mexico, where it was a staple herb in Mayan and Aztec dishes; its name comes from the Nahuatl words for an off-odor.

Off-odor or not, it's used in mole verde sauce, a Oaxacan preparation made with epazote, tomatillos, *hoja santa* (aka root beer plant, and a relative of black pepper), parsley, pumpkin seeds (pepitas), and green chiles.

To my taste, epazote has a strong tarry, resinous flavor that's not particularly appealing. But if just a few leaves are added to Mexican black beans, it can add a subtle minty note and—supposedly—reduce the flatulence associated with beans.

MEXICAN BLACK BEANS WITH EPAZOTE

SERVES 4

In Mexico, this recipe uses both epazote and avocado leaves. If the avocado leaves are unobtainable, French tarragon can be substituted.

1 large onion, chopped
3 cloves garlic, minced
1 tablespoon canola oil
2¹/₂ cups dry black beans
1 tablespoon fresh or dried epazote
1 quart beef stock
1 tablespoon young avocado leaves or fresh
   French tarragon
Salt

In a large heavy covered pot, sauté the onion and garlic in the oil until the onion is translucent and tender. Add the beans, epazote, beef broth, and 5 cups water to the pot. Bring the pot to a rolling boil, reduce to a simmer and cook, covered, until beans are tender, about 2¹/₂ hours. If the beans are too watery, raise the heat to medium-high and boil, stirring frequently, until the proper thickness is reached. Add the avocado leaves during the last 10 minutes—you don't want them to cook too long. Season with salt. ▪

Ginger

ZINGIBER OFFICINALE

I HAVE FOUND many processed organic ginger products, from ginger beer to ginger snaps to food supplements, but the only fresh organic ginger I have found has been at a local farmers' market.

One solution is to grow your own. If you live in a warm climate (where the ground doesn't freeze), you can plant pieces of store-bought ginger root with well developed growth buds in a pot of rich soil or in the garden in the spring. It will sprout bamboo-like shoots. Keep it well watered and the root will sprout new root extensions. Harvest pieces of young, nonfibrous roots beginning after three months. The ginger will naturally die back in the fall, even if in a pot, and may rot in cold, wet, winter earth, and so digging it up and planting it in a pot stored in a warm place over the winter is a good idea. Or just use it up and start again with a new root next spring.

TYPES ◆ Besides the familiar *Zingiber officinale,* there is another species called *mioga* or Japanese ginger (*Zingiber mioga*); it's a native of Japan with good but not snappy ginger flavor. In this case it's the swollen flower buds at the base of the leaves that you use, rather than the root (you can grow this ginger as well, in a humusy, moist soil, where winter minimums don't get below 12 to 15 degrees Fahrenheit). You may also find Chinese Yellow Ginger root, a variety of *Zingiber officinale* with yellowish flesh and a strong flavor.

STORAGE ◆ Most people put their ginger root in the butter compartment of the fridge, but it will last for several weeks longer if you moisten a paper towel, wrap the root in it, and store it in a plastic bag in the crisper.

USES ◆ You can make your own ginger juice by coarsely grating ginger into a few folds of cheesecloth and then wringing it out firmly. You can add the juice to chocolate or vanilla ice cream, use it to baste a pork roast, or mix with mashed garlic to flavor chicken. Ginger juice also softens the fishy odors of bluefish and freshwater bass. A knob of ginger will give you a scant ½ teaspoon of juice.

Grated ginger adds a crisp bite when just a little bit is tossed with salad. Ginger, lime juice, garlic, tamari, and white wine make a perfect marinade for fish or chicken.

A sauce of grated ginger, minced garlic or scallions, and soy sauce is a classic accompaniment for many Asian foods. Much can be added to this triumvirate: toasted sesame oil, lemongrass, kaffir lime leaves, lime juice, coconut, galangal, onions, chiles, tamarind. But why stop at Asian food? Now that all these condiments and spices are eas-

ily available in our markets, it's time to apply these flavors to more all-American types of dishes.

CHICKEN, ASIAN-ITALIAN STYLE

SERVES 4

The fusion of Asian with European influences makes for interesting combinations. This one, a creation of Chef Hubert Keller at Restaurant Fleur de Lys in San Francisco, exemplifies the idea perfectly. This dinner takes only about 45 minutes to reproduce at home.

1 cup Arborio rice
2 tablespoons olive oil
1 (2- to 3-pound) chicken, cut into 8 pieces
Salt and freshly ground black pepper
¼ cup Marsala wine
2 tablespoons grated peeled ginger root
1 teaspoon tamari
1 large ripe tomato, peeled, seeded, and roughly chopped
1 tablespoon minced Italian flat-leaf parsley
1 tablespoon minced purple basil

1. Cook the rice in lightly salted water (see page 365). Set aside and keep warm.

2. Place the olive oil in a large covered skillet and heat over medium-high heat. Dust the chicken pieces with salt and pepper, add them to the skillet, and brown all over, then cover and reduce the heat to medium-low. Cook for 30 minutes, turning twice. Preheat the oven to 200°F.

3. Transfer the chicken to a serving platter and place in the warm oven. Add the Marsala, ¼ cup water, the ginger, and the tamari to the juices in the skillet. Raise the heat to high and cook rapidly for 2 minutes, scraping up the browned bits. Add the tomato and cook for another 2 minutes.

4. Pour some of the sauce over the chicken, then garnish with the chopped parsley and basil. Any extra sauce can be poured over the rice. ■

GADO GADO SAUCE

MAKES ABOUT 2 CUPS

This is a traditional mildly spicy Indonesian sauce dominated by the flavors of toasted sesame oil, ginger, and peanuts. Use it to dress a platter of steamed or stir-fried Asian vegetables such as baby bok choy and bean sprouts, as well as carrots, fresh cucumbers, and fried tofu. It's used as a dipping sauce but also can be drizzled over tofu or added to a stir-fry during the last minute in the wok. Crush the toasted peanuts well in a plastic bag with blows from a rolling pin, or pulse in a blender. Five-spice powder is found at most Asian markets, or can be ground fresh from equal parts cloves, cassia (or cinnamon), fennel seed, star anise, and Sichuan pepper.

2 tablespoons canola oil

$1/2$ teaspoon toasted sesame oil

1 (1-inch) piece of fresh ginger root, peeled and minced

2 fresh red jalapeño peppers, seeded and minced

$11/2$ cups of thoroughly crushed, lightly toasted unsalted peanuts

Juice of 1 lime

1 teaspoon five-spice powder

Salt and freshly ground black pepper

Heat the oils in a skillet over medium heat. Add the ginger and jalapeños and sauté for about 2 minutes. Add $2/3$ cup water and the peanuts, and cook for another 4 minutes. Add the lime juice, five-spice powder, and salt and pepper to taste, and stir together. Remove from heat and transfer to a serving dish. ◼

Horseradish

ARMORACIA RUSTICANA

HORSERADISH is in the cabbage family. It's a perennial herb native to southern Russia or eastern Ukraine. Today it's cultivated widely throughout Europe and North America for its uniquely pungent roots (while horseradish is used for its roots rather than its leaves culinarily, it is still considered an herb). The aboveground parts of the plant are large, wavy-edged, strap-like leaves that die back when winter's hard freezes hit.

It's one of the bitter herbs of the Jewish Seder supper at Passover. One would think that its Seder use is a tradition that started in the diaspora when many Jews found their way to eastern Europe, western Russia, and the Ukraine, where the plant is native and still grows wild. But it was known to the ancient Greeks (the story is told that the Oracle at Delphi told Apollo that the radish was worth its weight in lead, the beet in silver, but the horseradish in gold) and horseradish is reported to have been cultivated in Egypt before the Exodus, around 1500 BCE.

IF YOU LIKE TO GARDEN

SOME PEOPLE are content to use prepared horseradish from the jar, but I'm not one of them. Quite the contrary, I love an excuse to go to the garden and dig out a chunk of root. Horseradish is one of the more persistent garden denizens and once you plant it, you'll always have plenty. Be aware, though, that water stress produces bitter roots: The more you water it, the better the horseradish's taste—but the more quickly the plant will spread beyond its boundaries.

WHAT TO LOOK FOR ‣ Fresh horseradish is often found in organic supermarkets and farmers' markets. Ask the grower if it's organic. Examine the cut ends of the roots—the cuts should be fresh-looking, not dried or shriveled.

STORAGE ‣ If you have a fresh root, it will keep for several weeks in the fridge, even when cut. Another way to keep the fresh root's pungency is to grate it and pack the gratings with a bit of water into ice cube trays and freeze them: Store them tightly wrapped in a plastic bag in the freezer and thaw as needed.

USES ‣ Horseradish is at home with salty meats, such as ham, pastrami, corned beef, Polish sausage, and gravlax. Its pungency adds verve to bland dishes such as potatoes. It pairs well with sweet vegetables, such as beets, and fatty fish, such as salmon. It turns sour cream into an incredible sauce. It combines with chili sauce to make a cocktail sauce for shellfish, and it's essential as part of the traditional Austrian spread called *Apfelkren* that goes with the Viennese boiled beef dish, *Tafelspitz. Apfelkren* is an apple-horseradish sauce made by combining 1 peeled, cored, grated green apple with 1 tablespoon of wine vinegar, 1 tablespoon of lemon juice, and 3 tablespoons of freshly grated horseradish. Serve with roast or boiled beef.

Cooking diminishes horseradish's strong pungency. When you grate it fresh, mix in a little lemon juice to prevent browning. And you might want to wear protective gear.

SALMON FILLETS WITH HORSERADISH CRUST

SERVES 4

Roasting salmon at high heat helps maintain a moist interior. However, it helps to have a crust to keep the outside from burning or drying out. This light, crisp horseradish breading turns beautifully golden brown and cuts the oiliness of this fish.

1 cup panko (Japanese breadcrumbs)
2 tablespoons fresh grated or prepared horseradish
1½ tablespoons chopped fresh thyme leaves
2 tablespoons Dijon mustard
Salt and freshly ground black pepper
1½ to 2 pounds of salmon fillets, skin removed

Preheat the oven to 475°F. Mix the panko, horseradish, thyme, mustard, and salt and pepper to taste. Spread evenly on the salmon fillets. Bake about 8 minutes, or until just cooked through. ∎

Lavender

LAVANDULA ANGUSTIFOLIA

LAVENDER is one of the most drought-tolerant of herbs. It likes a poor, sandy, dry soil and in that situation makes more of the aromatic, clean-scented essential oil we grow it for.

TYPES ▸ The best lavender for culinary use is English lavender. It's used in classic sachets and potpourris, to make perfume, and in the kitchen. French lavender (*Lavandula dentata*) and Spanish lavender (*Lavandula stoechas*) have more pungency and less of the prettiness that makes lavender so attractive.

SEASONALITY ▸ Lavender blooms from mid- to late-June or early July through much of its range.

WHAT TO LOOK FOR ▸ Although sometimes sold as fresh bunches in areas where it grows well (where winter minimums don't get below 10 degrees Fahrenheit), it's usually sold as dried bunches in farmers' markets. Even dried, it retains its clean, refreshing aroma. If the dried flower heads have little scent, pass them by.

USES ▸ Lavender is not much used in American kitchens, and it can be hard to find in the colder zones. And even where it grows well, such as in the Mediterranean climate of Sonoma County, it's not often used. That's because when it is used, it's usually overused. Lavender has a pretty, fresh, clean smell that's best left as a grace note, just a hint, rather than a featured aroma or flavor in cuisines. In quantity it smells camphorous, but as a touch it can be delightful. I've run across lavender ice creams and sorbets, and lavender crème brûlées (see recipe below) at restaurants here, and they are best when the lavender is just barely detectable.

One of my favorite uses is as an addition to sauvignon blanc. Add one small lavender flower head, fresh or dried, to a cold glass of sauvignon blanc and see what happens.

In France, lavender flower heads are stored with sugar to impart a fresh scent to the sugar (to do this, store 1 cup of dried flower heads in a canister of sugar for at least 4 weeks, as you would a vanilla bean). It also makes a volatile herb medley when combined with equal parts fresh thyme and rosemary that can be used to flavor lamb or rabbit.

LAVENDER CRÈME BRÛLÉE

SERVES 2

The trick here is to just scent the cream with lavender. The final custard will have the merest hint of lavender in its aroma and taste.

1½ cups heavy cream
4 fresh lavender flower heads or 2 dried
2 egg yolks
4 tablespoons plus 2 teaspoons sugar

1. Place the cream and lavender in a saucepan and bring to a boil. Remove from the heat and allow to steep for 5 minutes (no longer), then remove the lavender.

2. Meanwhile, preheat the oven to 300°F. In a bowl, beat the egg yolks and the 4 tablespoons of sugar together until light yellow and smooth. Strain the lavender out of the cream and slowly pour the cream into the bowl as you keep stirring to blend everything together. When well blended, divide the mixture into 2 ramekins. Set these in a baking dish

continued

and carefully add enough warm water to reach halfway up the sides of the ramekins.

3. Place the baking dish on a middle rack of the oven and bake for 45 minutes. The edges will be set and the middles loose.

4. Remove the baking dish from the oven, but leave the ramekins in the water. Let the dish cool completely. When cool, the custards should be set. Remove them from the water and chill them in the fridge for a couple of hours at least.

5. Before serving, sprinkle the top of each custard with 1 teaspoon of sugar in an even layer. Restaurants use a propane torch to melt the sugar until it turns a crinkly golden brown, but you can also pass them under a broiler. ∎

Lovage

LEVISTICUM OFFICINALE

Lovage is an extremely hardy, easy-to-grow perennial herb, and—with its strong celery flavor—useful to have on hand when you want to capture celery's herbal qualities without the bulk of celery stalks. When I worked at *Organic Gardening* magazine, we were always encouraging people to grow lovage. Despite our best efforts, it's still not popular in America, although in Europe it has been a staple herb since Roman days. Its name, in fact, comes from the ancient Latin adjective for Liguria, *ligusticum.* By the time of the Norman conquest of England in 1066 CE, this had become *lufestice* in Old English, and love-ache in the Middle English of Geoffrey Chaucer's day—which meant "love parsley," due to its use in love potions. From there it's a short linguistic step to modern English lovage. Lovage is easy to grow in good garden soil with adequate moisture.

SEASONALITY ▸ It peaks in midsummer.

STORAGE ▸ Lovage leaves can be frozen, and their flavoring power actually increases when they're dried. Its seeds are sometimes found in herb shops and have a similar celery flavor.

USE ▸ Lovage is used as you would use celery as a flavoring, except in smaller quantities, as it's much stronger. Figure that lovage is twice as strong in flavor as celery—three times as strong when dried. Use it cautiously at first, until you know its strength. Cooking will diminish its volatility. As you might imagine, it's good in soups and stews, especially seafood chowders (added near the end, as you would almost every other fresh herb). Substitute it for celery in tuna salad. It can wake up potatoes, and it works like celery in stuffings. It can help flavor lighter meats such as chicken, pork, and veal. A little goes a long way when flavoring haricots verts. Use dried lovage or its seeds to flavor potato salad and poultry stuffing.

POTATO-LOVAGE SOUP

SERVES 4

A simple soup that would have been enjoyed by forebears from the British Isles back to medieval times. Serve this with rustic bread and butter.

1 medium onion, chopped
2 tablespoons extra-virgin olive oil
3 cups peeled and diced red potatoes, about
    4 to 5 medium tubers
1 cup milk
2 tablespoons minced fresh lovage
Salt and freshly ground black pepper

In a large saucepan, sauté the onion in the oil over medium heat until tender and golden, about 5 minutes. Add the potatoes and 3 cups of water, reduce heat to medium-low and simmer until the potatoes are tender, about 20 minutes. Remove from the heat and let the pan cool slightly. Puree the mixture in a blender or food processor. Return the puree to the pan, add the milk, lovage, and salt and pepper to taste, and heat the soup, stirring occasionally. Serve hot. ◾

Mint

MENTHA, various species

MINT'S sweet menthol aroma and flavor, its calming effect, and its digestive properties make it perfect for the organic herb garden —except that if the soil is rich and constantly moist (such as around a leaky garden hose), it will spread invasively. So it's best to grow it in a large pot where it can be kept moist and get morning sun, but remain confined. If you are a lover of mojitos, plant two pots. It will grow all summer until fall frosts cut it down.

TYPES ◂ While spearmint (*Mentha spicata*) is the most useful and prevalent of the culinary mints, there are other mints to be aware of. The entire mint family of many plants has one feature in common: The stems are square.

Apple mint (*Mentha sauveolens*) withstands full sun and dry soil better than most other mints. Its big fuzzy leaves carry an apple flavor. They are the best for making candied mint leaves—the tiny hairs on the leaves hold the sugar mixture better than smooth-leaved varieties. To candy them, whisk 1 egg white with a few drops of water and paint this on leaves of apple mint. Then coat the leaves with superfine sugar by shaking it onto the leaves from a spoon and set them aside on a sheet of waxed paper until they dry completely. This could take a day or two. When crisp and absolutely dry, store them in a closed jar in a cool, dark cupboard for up to 6 months. A variegated mint called pineapple mint (*Mentha sauveolens*, variety *variegata*) is actually a variety of apple mint and can also be candied.

Peppermint (*Mentha × piperita*) smells like candy canes. It has a pungency and a sharp, biting sensation that can overwhelm, and so should be used judiciously, especially in peppermint tea, as too much of the volatile oil is not good for you. Pour boiling water over a teaspoon of the fresh leaves to make a light peppermint tea.

The variety of peppermint called chocolate mint (*Mentha × piperita citrata* 'Chocolate') has a bit of the aroma of a peppermint patty.

SEASONALITY ◂ Mint grows between the last frost of spring and the first frost of fall.

USE ◂ Spearmint is what's usually meant when a recipe simply calls for mint. It is wonderfully versatile; used fresh and roughly chopped, it merges seamlessly with chocolate desserts, punctuates the sweetness of fruit salads, and blends nicely with yogurt and peeled, sliced cucumbers on a hot summer's evening. Added during the last minutes of cooking to carrots, black beans, and lentils.

Spearmint is used as a jelly or a sauce for lamb, but also try that sauce with other light meats, such as veal. Its use with peas is classic, but try simmering snipped mint leaves with tomatoes, summer squashes, or eggplant.

Or take a tip from the Vietnamese, who use it to make refreshing, uncooked spring rolls, by combining the fresh leaves with bean sprouts, shredded lettuce and chopped shrimp, served with a peanut sauce for dipping (or try the Gado Gado Sauce on page 395). Middle Eastern Tabbouleh (page 203) depends on mint for its refreshing kick. Sprigs belong in iced tea and, of course, in the mint julep, where the aroma of fresh mint disguises the drink's potent kick.

MOJITO

SERVES 1

Few drinks are as refreshing as a mojito on a hot day—but be careful; they can sneak up on you. Feel free to try other flavor mint leaves, like chocolate mint.

2 sprigs mint
2 ounces silver rum
2 tablespoons simple syrup (see Tips)
Juice of 1 lime
Mint ice cubes (see Tips)
Club soda
Lime wedge

Muddle the mint sprigs with the back of a tablespoon in the bottom of a tall glass. Crush them well. Add the rum, simple syrup, lime juice, mint ice cubes, and top with club soda (Schweppes has a good, strong fizz). Stir once with a long spoon, add lime wedge, and serve.

TIP: To make simple syrup, combine equal parts water and superfine or regular sugar, heat to dissolve, then cool.

The key to keep a mojito from diluting is to use ice cubes made from spearmint tea. Brew a light spearmint tea and freeze the tea in ice cube trays. ▪

MOROCCAN MINT TEA

MAKES 6 CUPS

Sweetened mint tea has long been the libation over which social interaction occurs in North Africa.

2 cups fresh spearmint leaves, loosely packed,
    plus more for garnish
2 tablespoons green tea leaves
1/4 cup sugar

In a tea kettle, bring 6 cups water to a boil. Place the mint, tea, and sugar in a teapot and add the boiling water. Let it steep for 10 minutes. Strain the tea through a fine-mesh sieve into cups, then garnish the cups with fresh mint sprigs. ▪

Red Orach

ATRIPLEX HORTENSIS.
variety RUBRA

RED ORACH is a burgundy-colored herb with a wavy-edge leaf and a rather firm texture. Like epazote, orach is a member of the goosefoot family. In times past, orach, which is native to Europe and Asia, was gathered as an addition to the soup pot. Orach has both red and green forms, but the green form isn't much seen today. Red orach is grown to make a colorful but mild addition to the salad bowl. A few leaves of red orach torn up and tossed with lettuce, frisée, tatsoi, and baby spinach makes for a visually stunning salad.

Plant red orach in your herb garden; it is even more worthwhile for how gorgeous it will look in the ground than for what it will add to the salad bowl. Its purplish-red leaves make a striking edging to separate areas of other herbs or vegetables. Orach does best in rich garden soil. Just keep it pinched back, because left to its own devices, it will grow into a tall, straggly plant. For strictly culinary purposes, a few plants will keep you in good supply of orach all summer if you keep the young leaves picked and nip off any flower buds that begin to form.

SEASONALITY ◂ Successive sowings of annual orach produce young leaves from late spring through fall.

WHAT TO LOOK FOR ◂ At the farmers' market, where you're most likely to find orach, look for tender young leaves. Hold one up to the sun, and it should glow a translucent ruby red.

Oregano and Marjoram

ORIGANUM, various species

THE DIFFERENCE between these two members of the genus *Origanum* is instantly recognizable when you taste them side by side. Oregano (*Origanum vulgare*) is more bitter, with a strong, sharp quality. Sweet marjoram (*Origanum majorana*) shares a similar aroma with oregano, but on the palate has a sweet pungency, with a spicy note. In appearance, oregano has a more open habit, with slender but tough, almost woody, stems. Sweet marjoram has twisty, almost knotted-looking leaves on more herbaceous stems. Oregano is a hardy perennial that grows in cold winter areas, while sweet marjoram is tender, but it is easily grown as an annual in cold winter states.

Having several plants of oregano and sweet marjoram is an absolute must in any complete herb garden. If you have a sunny windowsill, sweet marjo-

ram will overwinter nicely there in a generous pot.

If you're an apartment dweller with not enough sunlight, a nice alternative is to pick up bunches of the herbs at farmers' markets in midsummer when the essential oils are strongest, and hang them in a warm, dry spot out of direct sunlight. The thin, woody branches and stems will dry. Rub the leaves, which will crumble off the stems, and store the dried leaves in an airtight container. They'll keep for up to a year, at which point you can repeat the process. Both oregano and sweet marjoram are more intensely aromatic dried than fresh.

TYPES ◂ You may find started plants of Greek oregano (*Origanum heracleoticum*) sold at nurseries or in racks of herbs in spring. The leaves have a dark gray-green appearance, and the flavor is stronger, with a resinous note, than other oreganos.

Another oregano that I've grown for years is the delightful Dittany of Crete (*Origanum dictamnus*), but not for culinary use. When planted in a hanging basket, its long stems and gray-green, woolly leaves arch gracefully up and over the edges of the basket, and the flower heads, resembling those of hops, hang pendant and show little lavender pink petals between the bracts. It's as charming a plant as there is.

Another visual beauty, with arching stems and pendant flowers, that does do double duty as a culinary herb, is Pot Marjoram (*Origanum onites*). It grows wild in Greece and on Crete, where it is called *rigani*, and is used liberally on grilled meat and baked fish, tomatoes, eggplant, and summer squashes.

SEASONALITY ◂ Oregano and marjoram's highest quality is achieved in July.

WHAT TO LOOK FOR • When buying them fresh, make sure the leaves are perky and fresh and the stems aren't browned and shriveling.

USES • Oregano is a natural with fava beans, eggplant, tomatoes, and most all tomato-saucy Italian dishes—such as pastas with marinara sauce, pizzas, calzones, Italian hoagies, sausage sandwiches—and with Greek dishes such as souvlaki. Unlike many herbs, its flavor persists during cooking so you can add it at the beginning.

Sweet marjoram is good for flavoring vegetables such as carrots, summer squashes, and potatoes. Its sweet spiciness adds a brisk note to salads. It's good in omelets. Use it on light meats such as chicken, pork, and veal. Like oregano, it marries well with tomatoes, beans, and eggplant. But cooking reduces its flavor, so add it at the end.

SWEET MARJORAM POTATO PATTIES

MAKES 8 PATTIES

Sweet marjoram was the plant of Aphrodite, the Greek goddess of love, so you might be able to kindle a flame by serving these yummy potato cakes to a special someone.

2 pounds red or russet potatoes

3 egg yolks

2 tablespoons minced fresh sweet marjoram

2 tablespoons butter

1 tablespoon half-and-half

Pinch of freshly ground nutmeg

Salt and freshly ground black pepper

All-purpose flour

1 whole egg, beaten

1. Bring a large pot of water to a boil. Peel and halve the potatoes, then boil them until almost tender, about 15 minutes. Preheat oven to 400°F.

2. Drain the potatoes, pat dry with paper towels, and place them on a baking sheet in the oven for a few minutes to dry off excess moisture. Remove from the oven and use a ricer or potato masher to mash the potatoes into a bowl. Beat in the egg yolks, marjoram, butter, half-and-half, nutmeg, and salt and pepper to taste. Mix together well. Flour a board and turn the potato mixture onto it. Separate the mass into 8 equal pieces, and shape each into a round patty about 1 inch thick.

3. Grease 1 or 2 baking sheets as needed. Use a spatula to lift the patties onto the baking sheets. Brush the tops of the patties with the beaten egg. Bake about 20 minutes, until well browned. ▪

Parsley

PETROSELINUM CRISPUM

THE SUREST WAY to have a supply of healthful, organic parsley is to grow a few pots on the deck or plants in the garden. It's a biennial, but leaf stem production is much reduced in its second year, when the plant rushes to produce flowers, after which the leaves turn bitter. So it should be treated like an annual.

NUTRITION • Parsley is one of the healthiest foods for you. Just one ounce supplies over 60 percent of our daily need for vitamin C, 30 percent of vitamin A, excellent stores of folate and iron, and many trace elements. Its volatile oils have been shown to have anticancer, antioxidant, and cardio-protective potency.

TYPES • Italian flat-leaf parsley seems to be gaining favor with cooks for its rich, straightforward parsley flavor and the way it makes little

Nuts, Seeds, Beans, and Grains

ALMOND • **Nonpareil**

CHESTNUT • European Type • **Nevada, on the tree**

BRAZIL NUT

CASHEW

CHESTNUT • European Type • **Nevada, on the tree ready to harvest**

CHESTNUT • American chestnuts

➤ *WHEN NO VARIETY NAME APPEARS, FOOD IS THE ORIGINAL SPECIES*

HAZELNUT

MACADAMIA NUT

PEANUT • **Virginia type**

HAZELNUT •
**Barcelona,
on the tree**

PECAN AND HICKORY NUT • **pecan**

PISTACHIO • **Kerman**

PINE NUT • **from pinyon pines**

WALNUT • **English type**

WALNUT • **Black**

PUMPKIN SEED

FLAXSEED

SUNFLOWER SEED ·
confectionary type

BUCKWHEAT · **raw and toasted**

DRIED BEANS · **Anasazi, Tepary, Good Mother Stallard**

MILLET · **on the stalk and pearled with husks removed**

BARLEY · **hulled and pearled**

OATS · **hulled and rolled**

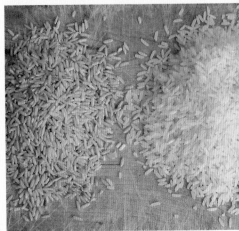
RICE · Jasmine · **brown and white**

RICE · **long-, medium-, and short-grain**

QUINOA AND AMARANTH · Amaranth · **pendant seedheads**

WHEAT · **hard (red)**

QUINOA AND AMARANTH · Quinoa · **white and red**

WHEAT · **soft (pastry)**

Herbs and Spices

BASIL • Genovese

BASIL • Thai

BASIL • Holly's Painted

ANISE AND STAR ANISE • Anise • whole and ground

CUMIN • whole and ground

BORAGE

CARAWAY

DILL • seed

DILL • weed

CARDAMOM • **whole pods and ground seeds**

EPAZOTE

CHERVIL

CHIVES

CILANTRO AND CORIANDER • **cilantro**

NGER

ORSERADISH • **Maliner Kren**

LAVENDER • French

VAGE

OREGANO AND MARJORAM • **Greek oregano**

OREGANO AND MARJORAM • **Italian oregano**

NT • **catmint**

MINT • **spearmint**

PARSLEY • Italian Flatleaf   PERILLA • red and green   SAVORY • winter

TARRAGON • French

ROSEMARY • Upright • Tuscan Blue

THYME • lemon

SAGE • purple   SAGE • variegated

flakes when minced. The curly-leaved types are similar in flavor, if a little milder, and make little twisty shapes when minced. Either can substitute for the other in a pinch.

If you grow your own parsley, you have many cultivars to choose from. Among the curly-leaved type, I prefer Champion Moss Curled, an older type with great production. Among the Italian flat-leaf types, Giant Italian (*Petroselinum crispum*, variety *neapolitanum*) is the one to look for. It has much thicker stems than the curly type, and these can be used like celery. When a recipe calls for only chopped parsley leaves, reserve the flat-leaf stems, tie them in a bundle with butcher's string and add them to stocks, broths, soups, and stews. Remove them when cooking is finished.

You may occasionally find a parsnip-like vegetable labeled as parsley root or Hamburg parsley. It's a parsley subspecies grown for its large whitish-beige root. The flavor is somewhere between a carrot and a celery root. You're most likely to find it in a farmers' market in fall, when the best parsnips come in, because frosts improve both vegetables' sweetness and flavor.

SEASONALITY ✦ Parsley produces leaves from mid-June to late fall. It's ubiquitous at plant and herb sales in the spring, and it takes easily to pot culture as long as your potting soil is rich and kept moist but not sopping wet.

WHAT TO LOOK FOR ✦ Buy fresh parsley that is turgid, not limp, and looks just-picked.

STORAGE ✦ To store it, shake off any excess moisture, wrap it in paper toweling, and put it in a plastic bag in the crisper. You will also find dried parsley flakes in the spice racks in the markets, but avoid them. When parsley dries, it gives up most of its flavor.

USES ✦ Eating an ounce of parsley (about ½ cup loosely packed) is a lot, and it's hard to eat that much every day. So I run a handful of parsley through the juicer along with carrots, kale, a beet, and chard leaves. A pint of this juice daily is my super-energizer. You could also mix it with spinach, collards, and other foods that juice well with parsley.

If juicing isn't your thing, use parsley liberally with just about any cooked or raw vegetable, in omelets, with fish, with lemony sauces, and in risottos and other rice dishes. Use it in pastas, with tomato sauces or slices, and in the classic dish mussels in white wine, garlic, and parsley. Italian salsa verde relies heavily on parsley. No stuffed, baked mushroom cap would be complete without minced parsley mixed with butter.

While we in America tend to use parsley as a garnish or as a finishing sprinkle over fish and other dishes, other cultures use a lot more of it. It's one of the chief components of Tabbouleh (page 203). It can be paired with basil to make Pesto (page 337)—or even be used in place of basil. The French include parsley in fines herbes, bouquets garnis, and the mixture of minced parsley and garlic they call *persillade*, a flavor enhancer that can be tossed into most anything—sauces, eggs, salad dressings, cheese fillings—or mixed with bread crumbs to make a flavorful breading for meats. To retain the fresh flavor, the persillade is ordinarily used just before the end of cooking. The Italians have a similar garnish they call *gremolata*. It's the same as a persillade with the addition of a spoonful of grated lemon zest. An osso buco positively demands a sprinkling of gremolata over the top to cut through the richness and add a lively flavor.

CHIMICHURRI SAUCE

MAKES ABOUT 1 1/2 CUPS

In Argentina, they brush this tangy, spicy sauce over the top of their grilled meats, which they consume in great quantity along with their good red wines. This recipe is from the winery Bodega Catena Zapata of Agrelo, Argentina, maker of excellent malbecs and other varietals grown on the slopes of the Andes.

4 cloves garlic
2 teaspoons dried oregano or 1 tablespoon fresh
1 coarsely chopped shallot
1 jalapeño pepper, stemmed and seeded
1/4 cup Champagne vinegar
Salt and freshly ground black pepper
1 cup minced Italian flat-leaf parsley, loosely packed
1 cup extra-virgin olive oil

Place the garlic, oregano, shallot, jalapeño, vinegar, salt, and pepper in a blender or food processor and whiz to a smooth paste. Transfer to a bowl and stir in the parsley and oil. Store the excess in the freezer, and spoon out and let warm to room temperature as needed. ■

GREEN GODDESS DRESSING

MAKES ABOUT 1 1/2 CUPS

It was San Francisco in the 1920s. The famous actor George Arliss was visiting the Palace Hotel while he was in town, starring in the play *The Green Goddess* at a local theater. The chef cooking for him became inspired, and here's the now-famous result. Store in the fridge and use within a week. Some versions of this salad dressing call for mayonnaise, but this eggless recipe works just fine.

1 cup half-and-half
1/3 cup canola oil

4 anchovy fillets
1 scallion, chopped
1 tablespoon chopped fresh parsley
1 tablespoon chopped fresh chives
1 teaspoon chopped fresh tarragon
1 tablespoon tarragon vinegar
2 tablespoons tahini

Place all ingredients in a blender and whiz until smooth. ■

Perilla

PERILLA FRUTESCENS

PERILLA, an herb called *shiso* in Japan, is a member of the mint family. You may not recognize the name, but you've seen its spade-shaped, light green or wine-red leaves with the crimped edges on your plates of sushi and tasted its fruity spiciness in mesclun mixes.

TYPES ◆ Many types of perilla are grown around the world. The leafy vegetable perillas include both green and red types, with both pinked edges and smooth edges. In Korea, they add green perilla to soups, while the Japanese use green types for garnish and fry them as tempura. The Japanese also use the pink flower buds in salads and as garnish. Purple-red perilla is used in Japan to color pickled *umeboshi* plums, and other types are used in Thailand. They have specific fragrances from their aromatic oils (much like the different mints do).

SEASONALITY ◆ Its season runs from June to the first frost.

PERILLA is very easy to grow, whether in the herb garden or in a pot. Just press seeds into the top of the soil and water, but don't bury them, as perilla needs light in order to germinate. The plants reach about 3 feet tall. Actually, if you want to grow perilla organically, just type "organic perilla seed" in your Internet search engine to get a raft of places to purchase it. If you have an herb garden, red perilla will make a charming color contrast with all that green. It's a tender annual. The seeds of red and green perilla make fine sprouts for salads, as well.

WHAT TO LOOK FOR ➤ Red and green perilla is most easily found in Japanese markets, although it is becoming easier to find in better food stores. You may also find it in farmers' markets, sometimes even sold as a pot herb—it's easy to grow.

USES ➤ Green perilla, or green shiso as it's now often called, has been discovered by chefs for its delicate aroma and refreshing flavor, which combines mint and anise with overtones of cinnamon and citrus. With increasing popularity, Americans are coming to know this useful herb and to use it in salads, tempura, ceviche, as a flavoring for poached and baked fish, white radishes, even beef and chicken. Chopped green perilla adds a lovely note to cooked rice.

Red perilla is often found torn up in salad mixes these days. It isn't as aromatic as the green sort, but it is prettier. The leaves are deep burgundy, which has prompted the sobriquet "beefsteak plant." The flavor has something of basil, but much milder.

Perilla oil is being sold as a food supplement because the seeds are a rich source of Omega-3 essential fatty acids. Omega-3 is usually provided by fish oil, so here's a good source of this heart-protective substance for vegetarians.

GREEN PERILLA SALAD

SERVES 3

This is a refreshingly different salad with the unique aroma and flavor given by the green perilla.

1 cup fresh green perilla leaves
1 1/2 cups peeled and thinly sliced cucumbers
1/4 cup seasoned rice vinegar
1/2 cup peeled, cored, thinly sliced tart green apple
Salt

Make a chiffonade of half the perilla leaves by rolling them up and slicing them into 1/8-inch-wide strips. Place the chiffonade, the cucumbers, vinegar, apple slices, and salt to taste in a bowl and toss to mix. Place servings on plates and top with the remaining whole perilla leaves. ▪

Rosemary

ROSMARINUS OFFICINALIS

I AM AMAZED at this herb's tenacity. This lovely plant sails through California's natural summer drought (May or June to October or November) without irrigation, and greets the height of the hot, dry season not with exhaustion but with scads of pale lavender blue flowers that call in every honeybee in the neighborhood.

Rosemary has a place in every herb garden. If you live in an area where it grows (where winter minimums don't get below 12 to 15 degrees Fahrenheit), and you have a garden, you could further use it to hold in banks and trail over rock walls. Originally from the Mediterranean region, it's now grown all over the world, wherever the climate is supportive. You can take cuttings for the kitchen at any time of year—its aromatic properties never diminish.

It has a strong, resinous smell and imparts a wonderful, volatile note to whatever it's cooked with. I like to lay tough, woody stems of rosemary under meats such as chicken, steak, or butterflied leg of lamb on the gas grill.

The rosemary smoke adds a pleasing, smoky-rich note, rather than the harsher flavor of the fresh leaves.

TYPES ◆ Here on my dry hillside in Sonoma County, California, I grow dwarf rosemary (*Rosmarinus officinalis* 'Prostratus') in a small walled garden. It spills over the wall like a foamy ocean wave. And I have another type, Miss Jessup's Upright, which grows to 4 feet tall with violet blue flowers. As long as the plants are in poor, dry, well-drained soil, they seem to love it there. I use Miss Jessup's leaves to flavor my racks of lamb, and Prostratus's curvy, flowery sprigs as a garnish on the plate.

These are the top varieties of rosemary to look out for:

Collingwood Ingram—Upright type with arching branches, blue-violet flowers.

Corsican Prostrate—Arching, spreading plant to about a foot tall.

Huntington Blue—Makes dense, 20-inch shrubby mat; pale blue flowers.

Majorca Pink—Upright type to 4 feet with lavender-pink flowers.

Miss Jessup's Upright—Stiff branches reach 4 feet; violet-blue flowers.

Prostratus—Dwarf rosemary cascades over walls, grows to 20 inches.

Tuscan Blue—Strong upright branches can reach 6 feet or taller.

USES ◆ My favorite use for rosemary is to slip pinches of the needle-like leaves into shallow slits cut in the thin layer of fat remaining on a frenched rack of lamb, slip garlic slices into other slits, and roast the rack at 425°F for exactly 25 minutes—it comes out smelling like a dream, perfectly done (see recipe, page 424).

Use rosemary sprigs as a brush to spread marinades such as Chimichurri Sauce (page 404) on your grilled beef or barbecue sauce on your baby back ribs. I have had pieces of chicken thigh skewered on rosemary sticks and grilled to a juicy perfection.

Chopped rosemary leaves can be added to or sprinkled on top of breads, focaccia, and crackers. If you grow your own rosemary, the flowers make pretty little light blue stars sprinkled on a salad. Chopped rosemary, sage, parsley, thyme, sweet marjoram, and summer savory make a Provençal herb blend to add to braising liquids for slow-cooked meats such as lamb shanks—but go easy on the rosemary, because its strong flavor doesn't diminish much during cooking and can dominate.

Add a pinch of rosemary to fava beans, or a tad to mushrooms, roast pork, and oven-roasted potatoes. Italians use it to flavor veal, and it has a strange but likable affinity for spinach.

ROSEMARY PESTO

MAKES ABOUT 1 1/2 CUPS

Who says pesto has to be made with basil? You can make it with parsley. Or you can make a robust and highly flavored version with rosemary that will carry you back to that night in Tuscany. Place a big spoonful on a plate of hot, organic, whole-wheat pasta, stir, shake on some red pepper flakes, and you've got a meal.

3 tablespoons pine nuts
2 cups lightly packed chopped Italian flat-leaf parsley
1 cup lightly packed fresh rosemary leaves
2 cloves garlic
1/2 cup extra-virgin olive oil, plus extra for storage
1/4 cup grated Parmigiano-Reggiano cheese
Salt and freshly ground black pepper

1. Toss the pine nuts in a small dry skillet over medium heat until toasted light brown. Set aside.

2. Place the parsley, rosemary, pine nuts, and garlic in a blender. Whiz to make a smooth paste. Add the oil in a very slow, steady stream until the paste is creamy. Pour the mixture into a bowl and add the grated cheese, then salt and pepper to taste. Transfer the pesto to a jar and cover the surface with a thin layer of olive oil. Seal the jar with a tight-fitting lid and refrigerate for up to 2 months, or freeze indefinitely. ▪

ROSEMARY CHICKEN TOSCANA

SERVES 4

Not just in Tuscany but all over northern Italy you can find versions of this delicacy. I found the inspiration for this dish in Verona.

4 bone-in, skin-on chicken breasts
1 1/2 tablespoons minced rosemary leaves
Salt and freshly ground black pepper
24 peeled cloves garlic (1 1/2 to 2 heads)
2 tablespoons extra-virgin olive oil
1 cup chicken stock
2/3 cup dry Italian white wine, such as Orvieto

1. Preheat the oven to 475°F.

2. Loosen the skin on the breasts by running your fingers under it, then insert 1/2 teaspoon of the rosemary leaves under each skin. Sprinkle each breast with a little salt and pepper. Place the breasts in an ovenproof skillet or flameproof baking dish, skin side up.

3. Mix the garlic, oil, and one teaspoon of the remaining rosemary together in a small bowl. With a spoon, lift out the garlic cloves and arrange them evenly around the chicken. Drizzle the remaining oil and rosemary over the chicken. Put the skillet in the oven and roast for 15 minutes.

4. Add the chicken broth to the skillet, being careful not to spatter the hot oil. Continue to roast until the chicken is cooked through, another 5 to 7 minutes.

5. Remove the skillet from the oven and transfer the chicken to individual plates; keep warm. Place the skillet over high heat, bring the liquid to a boil, and add the wine. Boil for 1 to 2 minutes to reduce the pan juices and evaporate the alcohol, scraping the bottom to loosen any clinging bits. Spoon the reduced liquid over the breasts and serve. ▪

Sage

SALVIA OFFICINALIS

THE SALVIAS (of which our culinary herb is one) have become ornamental superstars in the past couple of decades, and breeders have introduced dozens of varieties. There are at least four dozen species of salvia now commonly sold in the United States and most of the species have a number of cultivated varieties.

Sage is as pretty in the organic garden as it is useful in the kitchen. It's one of the aromatic herbs of Provence and the Mediterranean basin, and, like thyme, rosemary, and oregano, likes poor, dry soil if it's going to produce the most flavorful leaves. It's easy to grow in the herb garden, and perfectly hardy even in areas with cold winters. The culinary sages are perennials, returning each year from their roots.

TYPES ► Besides common green garden sage, with its nubbly texture, there are plenty of attractive varieties you could mix and match in an herb garden: purple sage (*Salvia officinalis* 'Purpurascens'), which sports dark greenish-purple leaves; three-colored sage (*Salvia officinalis* 'Tricolor'), which has leaves with green, white, and pink variegations; and golden sage (*Salvia officinalis* 'Icterina') with green and gold markings. Other species of salvia have culinary uses, too, such as pineapple sage (*Salvia elegans*), whose bright red flowers add dots of pure color to salads.

But for cooking and that appealing sage flavor, no cultivar beats the plain old green variety. The fresh leaves have a friendly spiciness and a musky, even medicinal scent.

SEASONALITY ► Spring through fall.

WHAT TO LOOK FOR ► The leaves should be blemish-free and the cut ends should be freshly cut.

STORAGE ► Whether home-grown or purchased as fresh sprigs at a farmers' market, sage is easy to dry, and its flavors and aromas intensify when the leaves are dried. Just tie the stem ends of the sprigs together and hang the bundle from the ceiling in a warm, dry place out of direct sun. When the leaves are crisply dry, you can rub them vigorously between your palms or mash them in a mortar with a pestle and watch them turn into a fluffy mass. Store in an airtight jar.

USES ► The most common culinary use for the herb in America is for flavoring the Thanksgiving turkey's stuffing—but that's just the most obvious use. Sage tea has been used as a sovereign remedy for colds, sore throat, and tonsillitis and as a digestive aid. Its genus name, meaning "to save," reflects its medicinal history. In ancient times, it was thought to promote wisdom.

Ordinary green sage is quite potent, especially when dried, so use it judiciously. It pairs well with other strongly flavored herbs such as rosemary and oregano, as well as the lemon herbs such as lemon balm and lemon verbena. Sage exalts fatty meats such as pork, sausages, veal, and poultry. Stuff a rolled pork roast with a mixture of chopped sage and apples. It also makes a warm partnership with liver and onions. And speaking of onions, mix minced sage and parsley and add it to the batter you use to make fried onion rings. Tie fresh sage in a bouquet with parsley and thyme and add it to soups and stews, removing it before serving.

Sage has an affinity for Italian dishes such as pizzas, focaccia, pastas, and gnocchi. It adds a pleasant herbal note when used in small quantities with mild cheeses. Chop it fine and use it in your cornbreads and biscuits. Use it to flavor bean, lentil, and pea soups.

Add a fresh sage leaf to other herb teas when you brew them to augment and enhance their flavor. Add a pinch to tuna salad, to seared ahi, and to baked or poached ocean fish.

SALTIMBOCCA

SERVES 4

This classic Italian dish jumps into your mouth, if the name is true, for that's what saltimbocca means. If you have an aversion to veal, use chicken breasts pounded to $^1/_2$-inch thickness. However, organic veal is humanely raised—by law.

4 organic veal cutlets, pounded $^1/_2$ inch thick
8 thin slices of prosciutto
4 slices of Fontina cheese
2 tablespoons butter
$^1/_4$ cup dry white wine
$^1/_2$ teaspoon fresh minced sage
$^1/_4$ teaspoon Dijon mustard

1. Top each of the veal cutlets with two slices of prosciutto and a slice of Fontina. Roll them up, turning in the sides so the filling is completely enclosed. Secure them with toothpicks, but don't let the ends of the toothpicks stick out too far, as it will make it impossible to brown the rolls all over.

2. Preheat the oven to its lowest setting. Place a skillet over high heat for 1 to 2 minutes, then add the butter. When the butter is sizzling, add the rolls. Cook for about 5 minutes, turning them frequently, until well browned all over. Remove the skillet from the heat and place the rolls in a serving dish; keep warm in the oven. Put the pan back on the heat; add the wine and cook until the alcohol is evaporated,

scraping up any browned bits. Add the sage and mustard and mix well. Pour this sauce over the rolls. ■

SAGE TURKEY STUFFING

MAKES ABOUT 10 CUPS

Yes, store-bought stuffing mix is traditional, but you can make a far more tasty stuffing using fresh, organic ingredients. Notice that the recipe starts well before the big day.

2 (1-pound) loaves sliced white country bread, crusts on
Giblets from 1 turkey
$^1/_2$ pound loose pork sausage
1 large onion, minced
3 tablespoons butter
2 stalks celery, chopped
1 large egg, slightly beaten
1 teaspoon dried sage
$^1/_4$ teaspoon salt
$^1/_4$ teaspoon freshly ground black pepper

1. Cut the bread slices into $^1/_2$-inch cubes, then place them in a large bowl, well exposed to air, and let dry for 4 or 5 days, tossing frequently as they dry.

2. On Turkey Day, simmer the giblets in water to cover for about $1^1/_2$ hours. Remove and chop them fine, reserve the cooking stock. Cook the sausage in a skillet over medium-high heat until just cooked through, about 7 minutes, turning and separating it into little pieces as it cooks. Remove the sausage from the skillet, reduce heat to medium-low, add the butter and onions, and cook until golden.

3. Combine the bread cubes, chopped giblets, sausage, cooked onions, and fat from the pan, celery, egg, sage, salt, and pepper and toss to mix thoroughly. Use the giblet stock to moisten the stuffing,

continued

but be careful. A little too much moisture renders the stuffing clumpy and dense. Keep the stuffing just lightly moist and fluffy. Stuff the turkey loosely, both in the body cavity and under the neck skin. Don't pack it tightly.

4. The rest of the stuffing can be cooked in a lightly greased Dutch oven on the stovetop over low heat. Stir from the bottom occasionally and add a little water by pulling the stuffing aside and dribbling a little water onto a bare spot on the bottom if the stuffing appears to be drying out. It's done when it's all hot and steamy and the celery is tender—about 1 to 1¹/2 hours. Correct the seasoning and serve hot in a separate bowl from the prized stuffing that comes from the bird. ∎

Savory

SATUREJA HORTENSIS and SATUREJA MONTANA

THERE ARE two kinds of savory, summer and winter. Both are low growing herbs for the herb or rock garden. Summer savory (*Satureja hortensis*) is an annual, while winter savory (*Satureja montana*) is a perennial. Both are native to southern Europe, from Spain to Turkey.

Both savories have a place in the herb garden and are easy to grow in good garden soil. Summer savory, being an annual, will need replanting each spring, but winter savory will return from its roots.

Both savories have wiry stems and small, needle-like leaves, similar to rosemary. The name—savory—indicates how useful they are in a wide variety of recipes. They have many of the same, spicy-pungent characteristics and can be used mostly interchangeably in the kitchen. The differences are these:

- Summer savory has a more subtle aroma and flavor than its perennial cousin—a slight hint of dill, a

bit of mint, with some of the resinous qualities of Greek oregano and thyme. It has reddish stems and tender green leaves.
- Winter savory has a more intense version of summer savory's aroma and resinous flavor. Here in coastal California it's an evergreen that needs cutting back to keep it fresh. In cold winter areas it will provide its strong pungency in all but the coldest months. It has thicker, almost woody stems and tough leaves.

In Germany, winter savory is called *bohnenkraut*, which means "bean herb," and a pot of beans in Deutschland isn't complete without a sprig of winter savory in the pot. Savory's pungency—on a par with rosemary's and thyme's—adds a spicy tartness to the bland flavor of long-cooked beans.

SEASONALITY ‣ Both savories are available from midspring to fall.

WHAT TO LOOK FOR ‣ If buying fresh, just make sure the leaves are fresh-looking and aromatic when a leaf is crushed.

STORAGE ‣ Both savories dry well and keep their character. Whole sprigs can also be frozen, although the thawed leaves will be better for cooking than used in raw salads. You can whiz the leaves in the blender with a little water until they make a thick slurry; freeze in ice cube trays; and when frozen, transfer to a freezer bag.

USES ‣ The useful part of the savories is their leaves, which can easily be stripped off the stems. If kept on the stem, either savory can be tied up in a bouquet of herbes de Provence along with sprigs of rosemary, thyme, oregano, and sage—summer savory is my choice because winter savory can be too dominant. Such bouquets garnis are good for long, slow cooking of braised lamb shanks, coq au vin, or osso buco. They're then removed at the end of cooking. For salads, chop fresh summer savory leaves fine and sprinkle a little on mild flavored greens. Both savories complement German potato salad for the same reason they flavor beans so nicely: They fill out the mild flavor of the potato. They also augment the tartness of the vinegar used in the German potato salad. Savory of either type goes well with cooked vegetables that need a lift, in tomato dishes, and with fish, especially salmon. But use winter savory more sparingly.

Both savories work equally well when cooked slowly with beans, but be more cautious in your use of winter savory because of its greater potency. Savory enhances green beans as well. Cook and drain a pound of snap beans. Chop fresh summer savory to make 1 tablespoon or winter savory to make 1 teaspoon fresh. Melt 1 tablespoon of unsalted butter in a saucepan and add the beans and savory. Stir to heat through, 2 to 3 minutes. Season with salt and pepper to taste.

SAVORY ROASTED POTATOES

SERVES 6

Roasted potatoes are so good plain, it seems that giving them an herb boost would be gilding the lily. But no—savory and its herb friends work wonders.

2 tablespoons extra-virgin olive oil
2 pounds red potatoes, peeled and halved if small, or quartered if large
Salt and freshly ground black pepper
1 teaspoon fresh summer savory leaves
1 teaspoon fresh thyme leaves
1 teaspoon fresh oregano leaves

1. Preheat oven to 450°F. Place 1 tablespoon of the oil in a heavy, flameproof baking pan over medium-high heat and add the potatoes. Brown on all sides (well, most of the sides), turning every few minutes until most surfaces are sealed, about 10 minutes total. Add the rest of the oil, toss with the potatoes, and season with the salt and pepper.

2. Place the pan in the oven and roast for 15 minutes, turning several times. Add the herbs and toss. Roast another 15 minutes, turning several times, until the potatoes are golden brown. Test for doneness, roasting a bit longer if necessary. ▪

GERMAN POTATO SALAD

SERVES 6

German potato salad gets a spicy kick from the savory to go with its piquant flavor.

6 medium red potatoes, peeled, about 2 pounds
4 slices bacon
1/4 cup extra-virgin olive oil
1/2 cup chopped scallions
1/4 cup white wine vinegar
1 tablespoon chopped fresh summer savory
2 tablespoons chopped fresh Italian flat-leaf parsley
Salt and freshly ground black pepper

1. Boil the peeled potatoes for 15 minutes, until cooked but still firm. Chop them into the desired size (1/2-inch dice works for me) and place in a serving bowl. cook the bacon in a sauté pan over medium heat, until crisp. Drain and pat the bacon dry on paper towels, then crumble it into the bowl of potatoes.

2. In a skillet over medium heat, place the olive oil and scallions and cook the scallions lightly until they soften. Remove the pan from the heat and let cool a minute, then add the vinegar, summer savory, and parsley, being careful that the vinegar doesn't cause the hot olive oil to spatter. Return to the

continued

stovetop just long enough to heat through, and add to the potatoes. Stir to combine thoroughly, then season with salt and pepper to taste. Serve warm. ■

Tarragon

ARTEMISIA DRACUNCULUS,
variety SATIVA

SOMEWHERE, at some time—nobody knows for sure when, except that it was a long time ago—a native Siberian perennial form of tarragon produced a sterile subspecies with a sweet anise aroma and a pronounced anise flavor. Because it produced no viable seed, the only way for its owner to grow more was to take stem cuttings and root them or to divide the plant's brittle white roots and replant the separated pieces.

The owner must have done one or the other, because the plant spread, and moved south to the Arab lands (probably in classical times), whence it was carried west to North Africa and then up to Spain during the Moorish invasion. Finally it reached France, and the French adopted it with such enthusiasm it came to be called French tarragon and was made an indispensable part of their national cuisine. Despite the fact that it had been divided or stem-rooted thousands of time, it was still the same seedless plant that Mariana found by good fortune back in Siberia.

Other plants of *Artemisia dracunculus* have also continued to develop. They grow taller than Mariana's French tarragon plant, and do set seed; but they have dull rather than shiny leaves, with a bitter taste and little of the sweet anise flavor that made French tarragon so cherished. This weedy plant has come to be known as just plain tarragon, or sometimes, Russian tarragon.

WHAT TO LOOK FOR ▸ If you buy a plant of tarragon for your herb garden, be cautious: Make sure it's true French tarragon and not the inferior Russian species that is almost tasteless by comparison. Nick off a piece of leaf and crush it. It should smell like anise, with a resinous note. It should taste like spicy anise. The leaves should be glossy and pointed or, if they are young leaves, rounded at the tips. Being a native of Siberia, French tarragon needs a winter dormancy, and it doesn't do well where good hard freezes don't knock it back.

USES ▸ Loosely pack a Mason jar with French tarragon, then fill it with a white vinegar (I like the mild, unseasoned rice vinegar), screw the cap on, and let it sit in a cabinet for 3 months. Pour off the vinegar into a fancy bottle and add a fresh sprig of tarragon. Use it in homemade tartar sauce, in marinades, and to baste chicken or fish. Tarragon vinegar has a special relationship with mushrooms, adding a light, high note to the mushrooms' bass earthiness. In a vinaigrette, it has an anise assertiveness that combines well with tomatoes and basil.

French tarragon is a featured player—along with parsley, chervil, and chives—in the fresh blend called fines herbes that may flavor the poaching liquid for fish or be added at the end of cooking to brighten a dish. A few fresh leaves torn into a salad add a touch of licorice. Adding a little to other herbs will augment their flavor, but, because of its assertiveness, less is more. It's excellent for flavoring shellfish, light fish such as sole and salmon, and white meats. Spinach becomes a whole new vegetable when a little tarragon is sprinkled among its leaves before steaming.

TARRAGON CHICKEN

SERVES 4

Seek out a fresh-killed organic chicken for this classic. It will be worth it. This is a simple dish and the tarragon flavor is not lost in the cooking.

This recipe uses chicken breasts, legs, and thighs. Use the rest to make Chicken Stock (page 454).

1 (2 to 3 pound) chicken
1/2 cup all-purpose flour
1/4 cup minced fresh tarragon
1 teaspoon salt
1/2 teaspoon freshly ground black pepper
6 tablespoons tarragon vinegar
4 tablespoons extra-virgin olive oil

1. Cut the chicken into 2 legs, 2 breasts, and 2 thighs. Reserve the wings, giblets, and backs for stock.

2. Combine the flour, tarragon, salt, and pepper in a plastic bag. Put the vinegar in a shallow bowl. Dip the chicken pieces in the vinegar until entirely wet, then place them in the bag. Shake until the pieces are coated. Shake off any excess.

3. In a large skillet, heat the olive oil over medium heat. When hot, add the chicken pieces and cook on both sides until nicely browned, 15 minutes total. Pour any remaining vinegar over the chicken, reduce heat to medium-low and continue to cook and turn the pieces about 25 minutes, until chicken is done and a fork can be easily inserted into a piece. ∎

TARRAGON PRAWNS

SERVES 8 AS AN APPETIZER

These make a delightful opening for a dinner party. Serve them on toothpicks and accompany with a white Rhône wine, such as a Condrieu.

1 1/2 tablespoons minced fresh tarragon
1 scallion, minced
1/4 cup Dijon mustard
3 tablespoons extra-virgin olive oil
3 dozen large prawns or shrimp, peeled and deveined

1. Mix together the tarragon, scallion, mustard, and olive oil in a bowl. Add the prawns and toss to coat. Refrigerate for at least 1 hour.

2. Preheat the broiler. Line a baking tray with aluminum foil and spray with nonstick spray. Arrange the prawns in one layer. Broil 2 minutes. Turn the prawns and broil 2 minutes on the other side. Place a toothpick in each prawn and arrange on a serving platter. ∎

Thyme

THYMUS, various species

FOR ME, thyme is the central herb—the one around which all others revolve. Its spicy, peppery aroma, its slightly resinous taste that leaves the mouth refreshed, its ability to hold its essential oils when dried, and its perfumed smoke are the very essence of goodness.

If you have an herb garden (even just a pot) that contains nothing else, it should be planted with as much thyme as will fit the space. Like the other Provençal herbs, thyme likes a dry, sandy, poor soil—it makes more of its aromatic oils than if it's in rich, moist soil. Grow thyme in sandy, well-drained soil in full sun. The more heat it gets, the more aromatic it gets.

TYPES ◦ *Thymus vulgaris* is garden or common thyme. It's a low-growing, upright, shrubby, and woody plant that reaches about 1 foot tall. This is the basic thyme for most recipes.

Lemon thyme (*Thymus × citriodorus*) is another thyme easily found at herb stands, farmers' markets, and nurseries, where you can find the hybrid and also a cultivar called Lemon Mist. It's a perfect flavoring agent for fish, light stocks, pastries, salads—anywhere a light and lemony herbal touch is needed. You can make a tea from it as well by pouring a cup of boiling water over 4 or 5 sprigs.

Other thymes you may encounter (there are dozens upon dozens) are caraway thyme (*Thymus herba-barona*), which got its species name when the English decided it was the precise herb to flavor a baron of beef—a huge cut that included both sirloins. This thyme is native to the islands of Corsica and Sardinia, and it has an overtone of caraway in its thymol scent (thymol being the name of thyme's essential oil).

You might also encounter mother-of-thyme (*Thymus serpyllum*), a highly scented but very low-growing, creeping form of thyme with very tiny leaves, whose little lavender flowers are beloved of honeybees. Many people plant it between flagstones in a pathway, but be careful of the bees when it's flowering.

A variegated form of thyme with green centered leaves edged with yellow is fairly common, but it's not highly scented. I understand there's an orange-scented thyme, but I have never encountered it.

SEASONALITY ▸ Fresh thyme is available from midspring through fall.

WHAT TO LOOK FOR ▸ When buying the herb fresh, either for planting or to dry for your spice cabinet, brush your hand across the leaves. It should lightly scent your hand. If it doesn't, look for a pot or bunch that does. To dry, tie bundles at the base of the stems and hang them in a warm, dry place out of direct sun until the leaves crumble easily off the stems. Store the crumbled leaves in a closed container in a dark cabinet. Save the empty stems to brush marinades onto most anything, or barbecue sauce on baby back ribs.

USES ▸ Thyme does so much in so many ways. It goes with almost all meats—fish and chicken, beef, lamb, and pork, and game such as rabbit and venison. It goes with sweet vegetables, such as carrots, and cooked onions and tomatoes, and even sweet fruits such as figs. It's wonderful with beans and other legumes and with tangy cheeses such as chevre and Cheddar. It flavors soups and stews and ragouts, and there are times when you can use it by the bushel, such as in the Italian classic, *Pollo Schiacciata*, below.

GRILLED CHICKEN WITH THYME (*POLLO SCHIACCIATA*)

SERVES 4

I discovered *pollo schiacciata* while traveling in the Veneto region of Italy, visiting wineries where the celebrated Amarone wine is made. For lunch one day, the woman taking me around brought me to a sunny roadside restaurant. As I walked inside, I could see sheets of flame in the kitchen. A grease fire, I thought. "Pollo schiacciata," explained my companion. The somewhat unhelpful translation is crushed chicken. Likewise, calling this dish "chicken under a brick," as we sometimes do here in the United States, doesn't do it justice. There are just two ingredients—split chicken halves and about an armload of fresh thyme—the result is incomparable.

This recipe works better on a charcoal grill than a gas grill, because you need to get the heat really cranking.

Here's the perfect recipe for those with space to grow a 20-foot-long row of thyme.

2 chickens (3 pounds each), split in half
1 peck (8 quarts) freshly cut thyme

1. Start a charcoal grill using a lot of briquettes, and when they have just turned white and the heat is most intense, put a large griddle that will accommodate the four chicken halves on top. Wait until the griddle is really hot. Then cover the whole griddle with half the fresh thyme in a layer about 3 to 4 inches thick, and place the chicken halves, bone side down, on top of the thyme. Completely cover the chicken with a second griddle or heavy iron skillets and weigh this down with 4 or 5 bricks or other very heavy weights so that the chicken is forced into the thyme and the thyme is forced against the very hot griddle.

2. Shortly, the thyme will send out a great deal of perfumed smoke. (For fun, set a match to the smoke. Any thyme protruding from under the top griddle will burn away.) After 5 minutes, remove the weights and the top griddle, lift the chicken off the spent thyme onto a plate, and remove any residue of thyme from the bottom griddle.

3. Now load on another 3 to 4 inches of thyme and place the chicken on top, this time laying it skin side down. Replace the top griddle with its weights and let it cook for 4 or 5 more minutes, again setting the smoke ablaze. If your griddle has been really sizzling hot and the thyme nice and thick, the chicken will be thoroughly cooked. Remove the weight and test for doneness by wiggling a leg. The joint should be easily moved. Or prick the thick part of a thigh with a knife; the juices should run clear, not bloody. If it needs more time, remove the thyme

residue from the griddle and give the chicken 2 more minutes on each side, this time right on the metal under the weight.

4. Brush off any burnt bits of thyme from the chicken and serve. You'll find that during the cooking process the thyme vaporized and the essence of thyme was forced into the chicken meat so deeply that every bite is deliciously smoky and thyme-flavored. ∎

THYME PIZZA

SERVES 2

Pizza has a thousand variations, but this one tastes truly Italian from the garlic and the herbs. You can make pizza dough from organic flour or buy one of those ready-made, organic, sprouted-wheat pizza shells available at many organic grocery stores.

1 (12-inch) pizza shell, or any pizza dough rolled into a 12-inch circle
2 tablespoons extra-virgin olive oil
6 tablespoons marinara sauce, preferably homemade
1/2 cup chopped fresh garlic
2 tablespoons chopped fresh thyme
1 tablespoon chopped fresh oregano
1/2 cup shredded mozzarella (about 2 ounces)
1/2 cup freshly grated Parmigiano-Reggiano cheese (about 2 ounces)

Preheat oven to 500°F and position a rack at the top of the oven. Brush the pizza shell with the olive oil, then spread on the marinara sauce. Sprinkle on the garlic, thyme and oregano, and cheeses, in that order. Bake for 12 minutes until the cheeses are bubbling and browning. ∎

Eggs

Meat, Dairy, and Eggs

MEAT AND DAIRY ANIMALS live at or near the top of the food chain. That means that any contaminants on plants or soil farther down the chain are concentrated in their tissues, especially their fatty tissues, or in their milk or eggs. As one moves up the food chain from plants to herbivorous animals, and finally to carnivorous animals or omnivores like humans, toxic substances are concentrated—"bioaccumulation" is the term of art.

All this makes it ever more important for human beings—who are at the very top of the food chain—to find organic meat, dairy, and eggs. If the toxins aren't in the food to begin with, they can't bioaccumulate in us.

THE CERTIFIED HUMANE LABEL

WHEN YOU SEE the "Certified Humane Raised & Handled" label on eggs, dairy, meat, or poultry products, it means they were produced with the welfare of the farm animal in mind. Food products that carry the label are certified to have come from facilities that meet precise, objective standards for farm animal treatment.

A team of veterinarians and animal scientists developed animal care standards to allow animals to engage in their natural behaviors; to give them sufficient space, adequate shelter, and gentle handling to limit stress; and to make sure they have ample fresh water and a healthy diet without antibiotics or hormones. So, while such products may or may not be certified organic, they are produced in a reassuring way.

To acquire the label, meat processors must comply with the American Meat Institute Standards for slaughter, a higher standard for slaughtering farm animals than that set by the Federal Humane Slaughter Act, the base standard for all USDA-inspected meat.

Humane Farm Animal Care is the independent, nonprofit organization that conducts regular inspections and administers the Certified Humane Raised & Handled program. Participating businesses must pass an initial inspection as well as annual re-inspection to remain part of the program.

Inspectors are educated and trained in animal science, veterinary medicine, or other relevant backgrounds. To further assure fairness, the USDA's Agricultural Marketing Service verifies the inspection process.

MEAT

Most of the early organic farms of the 1980s were a more pragmatic sort: They abstained from giving their animals routine antibiotics and they fed them organically grown feed, but they still felt that pens and cages were a practical necessity to get the meat to market in an affordable way. Over the past few decades, organic farmers have begun to understand more clearly that they must do more to care for their animals in humane and compassionate ways. The National Organic Program emphasizes the humane treatment of animals, which gives them a chance to at least savor most, if not all, of the pleasures their natures may offer. Ducks kept for meat may not be able to fly, but at least they can have a pen with water to play in. Veal calves may not be able to run totally free, but they can have pasture and the pleasure of suckling their mothers rather than living in a cage and being fed milk substitutes.

The animals raised by organic certified farmers are never given antibiotics, hormones, or doused with pesticides. For chickens, this is true from the moment they crack out of their eggs. For beef cattle and hogs, this is true for pregnant mothers from the last trimester of gestation on. During their entire lives, the animals receive only 100 percent organic feed or pasture. This certified feed or pasture has not been treated with chemicals for a minimum of three years and is grown without chemical fertilizers, pesticides, fungicides, nematocides, or herbicides. The finished product does not contain preservatives or artificial colorants. If an animal falls sick and must receive antibiotics, it is removed from the organic herd or flock, treated, and, after a suitable time, possibly reinstated.

Conventional feedlot cattle not only wallow in their own manure but when they are slaughtered, the meat is often irradiated using radioactive isotopes to kill any bacteria. But filthy slaughter-houses are still filthy, even if the meat is irradiated. And while the feeding of cattle parts to cattle is now banned due to the danger of mad cow disease, beef parts may still be fed to chickens and hogs, and parts of those animals may be fed to cattle. In addition, conventional beef cattle can be fed

KEEP AN EYE OUT FOR HERITAGE FOODS

A GREAT VARIETY of different domestic animal breeds characterized the agriculture of the 19th century and earlier, but modern agribusiness focuses its attention on the most productive and profitable—if not the best tasting—breeds of meat animals to maximize profits. Organic-minded folks are changing that, however. Many are returning to raising and selling breed-specific meat animals, especially those rare and endangered breeds that offer superior flavor even at the expense of sheer quantity of meat.

Heritage foods are defined as foods derived from rare breeds of American livestock (and crops) with strong genetic authenticity and well-defined production methods. They include humanely raised farm animals, such as the naturally mating American bronze turkey, and place-dependent foods that can only be raised in a certain area of the country, such as hand-harvested wild rice from the upper Midwest's lakes and marshes. These foods are part of the identity of this country, yet risk extinction if demand for them does not increase soon.

A group called Heritage Foods USA is devoted to preserving rare breeds of animals and place-specific foods by working with farmers and communities where these foods are still produced and helping to bring them to a wider audience of consumers. The organization is committed to paying farmers a fair price for their products, to selling breed-specific foods that excel in quality and flavor, to the ethical treatment of livestock, to sustainable (and organic where possible) agriculture, and to maintaining genetic diversity in the food supply. An array of other products, such as heritage chickens, lamb, and pork, are coming on line.

One of Heritage's biggest strides, and the reason it first formed (as an offshoot of the Slow Food movement—although it is independent), was to help double the population of heritage breeds of turkey across the United States. Due to its efforts, one breed of turkey, the Bourbon Red, moved up from "rare" to "watch" status on conservations lists. Other efforts include working with a group of Native American communities, including the Anishinaabeg, Tohono O'odham, and Seri tribes, to increase production of place-dependent wild rice, tepary beans, wild oregano, and mesquite flour. Heritage has introduced a traceable label on its products. The label allows consumers to track their food on the Heritage Foods USA's web site (www.heritagefoodsusa.com), where these foods can also be ordered.

genetically modified grains, growth hormones, and antibiotics, and be chemically wormed to kill parasites. Under organic rules, none of these practices is allowed. Organic beef producers are also required to manage manure so that it doesn't contaminate crops, soil, or water and that it optimizes the recycling of nutrients. Though the organic rules don't prohibit finishing cattle on corn and soybeans in feedlots, it would be almost impossible to do so while following the other rules, according to the Organic Trade Association.

This not only makes farming more pleasant but raises the quality of the meat products they yield.

A leader in this kind of meat production is Niman Ranch (www.nimanranch.com), which was started in California about 25 years ago. Niman Ranch began as a physical ranch in Marin County, California, but the founder of the ranch, Bill Niman, ultimately created a system for involving farmers around the country to raising animals using humane and sustainable methods approved by the Animal Welfare Institute (see www .awionline.org) and distributing their meat under the label of Niman Ranch, Inc. In the Niman Ranch system, livestock are fed the purest natural feeds and never given hormones or routine doses of antibiotics, and they are raised on land that is cared for as a sustainable resource. Many conventional livestock farmers routinely feed their stock antibiotics to ward off disease resulting from the animals being kept in confinement, either in feedlots for cattle or metal-barred crates for hogs.

Animals raised according to organic principles of animal welfare are allowed space to express their nature, and that greatly reduces stress. Stress creates imbalances, disease, and results in meat of lesser quality. If you've ever raised chickens, or if you buy eggs from chickens raised in a healthy environment—with a yard where they can scratch and peck bugs or worms—you know that these eggs barely resemble factory farm eggs.

Without human husbandry, we would have none of the meat-, milk-, or egg-producing breeds of animals we're familiar with today. These animals are the product of thousands of years of selective breeding—much like our modern breeds of dogs are the result of the selective breeding of wolves. There's not much resemblance between a wolf and a shar-pei, and not much resemblance between an aurochs—the original wild cow—and a Holstein dairy cow, but the former are the forebears of the latter. Livestock animals could not survive without farmers to breed them. If left on their own, within a few generations, pigs would revert to the wild boars from which they descended. Because our farm animals are dependent on human beings for their welfare, it is thus incumbent on human beings to provide for their welfare.

Beef

ORGANIC BEEF follows one of two ways to market. One way, beef is 100 percent grass-fed, meaning that the animals are pastured until slaughter. The other way takes the animals to feedlots for the last months of their lives, where they're fed a diet rich in grains, which fattens them up for slaughter. Grass-fed is a much more natural way for cattle to finish their days. (Cows are ruminants, whose four stomach compartments are designed to digest grass, not grains; and feedlots, even organic feedlots, can be smelly, messy places.)

Between these two kinds of organic beef, 100 percent grass-fed carries a premium (it is ordinarily labelled grass-fed at the the store). In both cases organically raised beef is free from hormones and antibiotics. A Michigan State study of conventional beef cattle in twelve states in the early 1990s showed that about 3,000 animals a year had antibiotic residues (mostly neomycin and tetracycline) above allowable limits in conventionally raised veal calves and culled cows. That's the tip of the iceberg,

however, as many more animals had antibiotic residues within the government's allowable limits. According to the Canadian Food Safety Inspection System, residues from environmental pollutants, pesticides, and veterinary drugs can all be present in the tissues of agricultural animals, and these chemicals have been associated with risks to humans including allergic reactions and toxic or carcinogenic effects.

All organic producers, on the other hand, have zero tolerance for antibiotic residues in beef animals.

TREATING SICK ANIMALS

ALTHOUGH the use of antibiotics or drugs isn't allowed in animals that are sold as organic, this is not to suggest that the animals' health problems are ignored if they become sick. In fact, the National Standards on Organic Agricultural Production and Handling establish that a producer of organic livestock must administer vaccines and other veterinary biologics as needed to protect the well-being of farm animals. When, despite the use of prevention and veterinary biologics, an animal falls sick, the producer can administer certain medications. The rule states that the producer must not withhold treatment from a sick animal in order to maintain its organic status. All appropriate medications and treatments must be used to restore an animal to health when methods acceptable to organic standards fail. Livestock treated with prohibited substances, however, must be clearly identified and cannot be sold, labeled, or represented as organic until a suitable period of time has elapsed following treatment.

What is on the list of synthetic substances allowed for use in organic production systems? They include:

- **Electrolytes without antibiotics**—used to treat dehydration, especially in young pigs.
- **Magnesium sulfate (Epsom salts)**—used as a laxative for gestating and lactating sows.
- **Milk replacers without antibiotics**—powdered milk used for disadvantaged and starving young animals, but it must not contain nonmilk products or milk products from bovine growth hormone–treated cows.
- **Copper sulfate**—A copper source used for trace mineral supplementation.
- **Vitamins**—FDA-approved synthetic vitamins used for enrichment or diet fortification. (However, natural sources of vitamins, such as seaweed, kelp meal, natural rock powders, molasses, sprouted grains, and brewer's yeast, may be required by some certifying agencies.)

A PROFILE OF AN "UNCERTIFIED" GRASS-FED BEEF FARMER

THE HUDSON VALLEY Farmers Coop in Dutchess County, New York, is a small-scale beef producer that supplies some of the best restaurants in New York City. They were once certified organic by NOFA (the Northeast Organic Farmers Association, a regional certifying organization). But they dropped organic certification when the USDA took over the National Organic Program. The director Steve Kay explained to me, "For the organic rules to be successful, we had to get the government out of the process. But that didn't happen. The rules were written for the big growers—it's all about the label, not small farmers like us."

Although not certified organic, some small farmers can be even more careful about their husbandry than large certified producers—you need to know the producer and his or her product.

The Hudson Valley Farmers Coop follows the grass-fed-is-best philosophy and is constantly testing its meat for Omega-3 and the cancer-fighting conjugated linoleic acid (CLA) (see page 423)—to see how feed affects their content in the tissues of the animals.

"I used to grow potatoes," Kay says. "I cared for them like they were my pets. Now I grow beef—Angus and short-horns. I used to finish the animals on grain, but now that I've seen the health benefits for the animals and for humans from grass-fed only, I finish them on pasture." He says the meat is more intensely flavored but denser: Muscle is leaner and the fat cooks away more quickly, so the meat must be cooked more carefully.

"The reason I farm," Kay added, "is to produce the best possible product, not to follow rules for farming set up by the government, of all people. Under the USDA organic rules, you can finish beef animals on grain in a feedlot, where they are wallowing in their own manure, and still call it organic. My animals never see a feedlot." A big problem with beef finished on grain is that their digestive systems simply aren't meant to digest corn. It renders their digestive tracts acidic and hospitable to *E. coli* and other pathogenic bacteria. Hence there's a need in conventional beef production for more antibiotics and the risk (and reality) of promoting the evolution of antibiotic-resistant bacteria.

"I avoid the word 'organic,' " he said. "It's a regulated word now. The rulemakers don't understand meat production. If I'm driving and see a farm with fabulous hay, I'll stop and buy it right off the fields. I insist on giving my animals the best possible feed." His animals are raised in a chemical-free environment. Steve Kay represents the kind of independent, stiff-necked Yankee farmer who isn't going to be told what to do or how to do it by the government. He may not be certified, but he farms with the organic spirit. His clients include top-flight places like Blue Hill, Compass, Il Buco, and Savoy. "They know me," he said. "I supply them with well-grown beef that tastes better and is clean." That's the organic ideal.

NUTRITION ► Among organically raised cows, grass-fed cattle contain less artery-clogging saturated fat in their muscle tissue than cattle finished on grains. Grass-fed beef also contains more of the essential fatty acid Omega-3, as well as CLA (conjugated linoleic acid), a substance that helps regulate the way our bodies deal with other fats, boosts the immune system, fights cancer, and has other health benefits.

WHAT TO LOOK FOR ► Ask your butcher for organic beef and look for 100 percent grass-fed beef when possible.

Grass-fed beef is less tender than the meat from animals finished on grain, but if the meat is aged by hanging for a period of time in a cooler, the aging process will tenderize it. Ask your butcher about aging. For more information about what the various labels for beef mean, visit the web site: www.eco-labels.org.

PREPARATION ► Cook grass-fed ground beef lightly and cover the pan. For steaks, the best way to cook them is to sear both sides, then finish the steaks in a 350°F oven for 10 or 15 minutes, depending on the thickness of the steak and the degree of doneness you want. But grass-fed beef is best rare.

SLOPPY JOES

SERVES 4

You can get the prepared Sloppy Joes mix and ordinary hamburger and white bread buns—or you can make this simple dinner the organic way.

1 pound lean ground grass-fed beef
1/2 cup chopped onion
1 cup chili sauce
1 tablespoon white vinegar
1 tablespoon freshly squeezed lemon juice
1 tablespoon Worcestershire sauce
1 teaspoon Dijon mustard
1 teaspoon paprika
1 tablespoon dark brown sugar
Salt and freshly ground black pepper
4 whole-wheat hamburger buns

In a heavy skillet over medium-high heat, sauté the ground beef and onion until the meat is no longer pink, about 7 minutes, stirring frequently to break up clumps. Stir in the chili sauce, vinegar, lemon juice, Worcestershire sauce, mustard, paprika, brown sugar, and salt and pepper to taste, and cook over low heat, stirring occasionally, until thickened, about 15 minutes. Fill hamburger buns with Sloppy Joe mixture and serve. ▪

Veal

VEAL, the meat from calves, is shunned by many people because they believe the calves are raised inhumanely, confined to crates, unable to nurse, fed "milk replacer" instead of their mother's milk, and become close to anemic because they get no hay to chew. In conventional farms, this malnourished condition is the point, because there's a market for the pallid white veal that results. This kind of veal is called "special fed" by the industry. It is to be shunned by people who care about animal welfare. Not all conventional veal is raised by such cruel methods, however.

But organic veal is being raised humanely. The calves are turned out to pasture with their mothers so they can suckle her and nibble a little grass, too. This produces a pinker meat, but a meat that still has the qualities of good veal: a subtle flavor, and lots of juicy gelatin that results from the collagen in the meat dissolving in liquid during cooking, which makes veal perfect for creating the sauce bases of classic French cuisine.

Producers of humanely raised veal are generally small scale, and many are associated with dairy farming, running what's called a cow-calf operation. To continue lactating, a dairy cow must calve once a year. Much veal comes from male calves born from dairy cow mothers.

WHAT TO LOOK FOR ◆ Organic veal is pink, not white, from calves raised naturally and humanely. (Milk-fed calves, whether conventional or organic, are not anemic, therefore their flesh is pink, not white.) Organic veal will most likely be labeled as such—but ask your butcher. If the veal is organic, the calf is guaranteed by law to be raised in a humane way.

If you can't find organic veal, some suppliers ship. See Sources (page 517) for a list.

Lamb

THE HILLS of western Sonoma County turn green with the first significant winter rains and by early spring lambing, the birthing of lambs, begins. The lambs stay with their mothers, suckling them and beginning to eat the grasses and wildflowers. If the production is organic, these lambs are born from mothers fed only organic feed during their last trimester of pregnancy, and the lambs themselves are given no antibiotics, hormones, genetically modified feeds, chemical parasite dips, or chemical worming agents.

Therein lies a problem for organic sheep and lamb producers, as intestinal worms need to be dealt with. Studies have shown that "safe" worming agents that would be allowed in organic lamb culture, such as garlic, herbs, and diatomaceous earth (containing the sharp-edged skeletons of minute sea plants and animals), simply don't work.

So ingenious organic farmers have developed methods of dealing with the parasites by understanding their life cycles. The parasites tend to move toward the tips of grass blades when they're wet with morning dew, so lambs are turned onto new pasture in the afternoon when the grass is dry. They are also rotated more frequently through new pastures to head off trouble. And far fewer animals occupy any given acre of organic pasture than under conventional systems, lessening the population density and making infections less likely. In addition, certain breeds of sheep seem to be less prone to infection by intestinal parasites than others, and organic farmers are taking note of that phenomenon. As for parasites of the wool or skin, there are organic insecticides made from plants such as rotenone, sabadilla, and pyrethrum that can be dusted on the animals.

All these measures add to the cost of producing organic lamb, but the cost is worth it for health-minded people who know that humanely-raised organic lamb is clean and flavorful.

SEASONALITY ◆ Yes, there is a season when lambs arrive. Spring (late February through June) is lambing time in North America, with an abundance of organic lamb available in both the United States and Canada. During the other half of the year, some fresh organic lamb is shipped in from New Zealand, so that fresh lamb is available pretty much year-round.

WHAT TO LOOK FOR ▸ Look for organically certified lamb. During spring lambing season, American organic lamb is widely available. Look for young lamb—legs less than 5 pounds, racks with small bones, with rich red meat and white, not yellow, fat. New Zealand lamb, which arrives six months later, may also be organic. Ask your butcher. See Sources (page 517) to locate producers of naturally raised, grass-fed organic lamb near you.

GARLIC AND ROSEMARY RACK OF LAMB

SERVES 2 TO 3

There's a scrumptious synthesis of flavors, resulting from the combination of the lamb, the garlic, and the rosemary, that's incomparably savory and mouthwatering. Serve it with creamed spinach and potato chunks browned in the fat you remove from the rack.

1 rack of lamb (1½ to 2 pounds), chine bone removed, frenched (see Tip)

3 cloves garlic, sliced into thin rounds
1 sprig fresh rosemary
Salt and freshly ground black pepper

You will need a roasting pan with a slotted top rack. Preheat the oven to 425°F. Using the point of a sharp knife, make horizontal slits in the fat covering the "eye," or solid meat portion, of the rack, about 2 inches apart in all directions. Alternately, insert slices of garlic and pinches of rosemary leaves into the slits. Place the lamb fat side up on the slotted top of the roasting pan. Roast for exactly 25 minutes. Carve the rack into chops at the table.

TIP: You can ask your butcher to french a rack of lamb for roasting, but you can also do this yourself. Cut away the layers of fat from the bones, back to where the eye of the rack begins. Slice the connecting tissue between the bones, removing the fat and tissue back to but not into the eye. Remove the layer of fat and the thin bit of meat from the top of the eye, leaving a covering of white fat on the eye. ▪

KEEP AN EYE OUT FOR NAVAJO-CHURRO LAMB

ONE OF THE BEST BREEDS for producing tasty lamb is the Navajo-Churro sheep, descended from sheep brought to America from Spain in the 16th century. They are hardy, small, fine-wooled sheep with a distinctive flavor. Slow Food U.S.A. has taken these sheep under its Ark of Taste program, designed to preserve breeds and types of food that might go extinct. Once numbering two million, the breed was dissipated by a federally imposed interbreeding initiative and a government-mandated livestock reduction program. By the 1970s, only 450 of these valuable sheep were left in the United States. Protection in the Ark program means that their numbers will be increased, especially good news for Navajos, who not only partake of the excellent meat but also use their wool to make their traditional rugs.

Pork

PIGS are not naturally filthy animals. In fact, given proper care, they are rather clean. They like to wallow in mud on a hot day because they have no sweat glands and because evaporating water from the mud cools them down. They like to hunt for roots, corms, and tubers. A field infested with yellow nutsedge—an invasive, tough weed with small, juicy tubers (called nutlets)—can be cleaned up by running hogs in the field and letting them root out the nutlets, which they naturally love to do.

In the fall when wild apples, acorns, and mast (beech seeds) are dropping in meadows and forests, hogs that have access to this kind of land will eat massive quantities of them. On this kind of natural diet, pork becomes wildly flavorful. The last time I ate at the French Laundry restaurant in California's Napa Valley, I had such a piece of pork: Its flavor and tenderness were exquisite. Chef Thomas Keller said the animal had been fed apples on the Pennsylvania farm where it was raised. Before 1950, turning pigs out to forage was generally considered a part of good animal husbandry. It provided vitamins and minerals, but that practice ended as hog farming became more technological and focused on mass production.

Pigs are tough on pasture, tearing up the soil to get at roots, especially if too many animals are put out on an acre. Organic culture keeps the forage pressure low. Conventional farmers who pasture pigs may clamp a ring through their noses. This hurts the pigs if they try to root. Organic hog producers consider this mutilation and consequently inhumane. Conventional pigs for the most part get a steady diet of corn and soybeans.

Organic pigs are given access to pasture when it's available, meaning the spring, summer, and fall. They're also supplied with feed, which must be organic.

There are other rules contributing to healthy living conditions for the pigs. They can't be housed on 100 percent slatted floors, where manure and urine fall through holes into a holding pit, as pigs are in conventional operations; instead the pigs are given the chance to have some flooring that's not above manure, and that floor is cleaned daily. They also can get outside in the fresh air. All their feed and bedding has to be certified organic. Early weaning at less than four weeks is not allowed, meaning that for a longer time, they get the benefit of mother's milk— and closeness to mom—leading to less stress and

COOKING PORK TODAY

YOU MAY REMEMBER that years ago it was advised to cook pork to well-done to prevent trichinosis, a painful parasitic disease. That advice is obsolete. Scientists have discovered that the trichina parasite is killed at 137 degrees Fahrenheit, well below the 160 degrees Fahrenheit reached when pork is cooked to medium. And hogs today—both organic and conventional—are raised under conditions and fed foods that decrease the possibility of trichina infection.

Also, today's pork products are leaner than they used to be. If cooked to well done, they would be very chewy. Years ago, when pork meat had more fat, they would have been juicier when well done. So cooking pork to medium is perfectly safe. To be safe, medium rare to raw pork should still be avoided, though.

TWO PROFILES OF ORGANIC PIG FARMERS

IN PAULLINA, IOWA, Dan and Colin Wilson raise hogs on 800 acres but not in typical confinement pens, where pigs only have room enough to eat, drink, sleep, and get bored. In the late 1980s, seeking a way to bring in more money, the Wilsons tried using confinement pens, but they didn't like confining their animals and hated the smell in the confinement houses, which clung to them when they went home.

Their outlook of using pens changed in 1994, when Dan and his wife, Lorna, toured swine farms in Sweden. The Swedish pork industry is known for its focus on the protection of the natural environment, quality of the meat, and quality of life for the animals.

Following the Swedish model, all of the Wilsons' swine buildings now give pigs room to move freely, build nests, and root in bedding. In a story in *New Farm* online, Dan Wilson said, "We joke that it takes us too long to do chores because it's so fun to stay in the barns and watch the pigs play."

It's telling that the Wilsons, who spend a lot of time with pigs, get a kick out of watching them. Piglets are cute when they're little and will hop about and play like naked pink babies. That affection for the animals is very important in any farmer. The story's author, Wendell Berry, the poet of organic farming and the closest person we have to a Ralph Waldo Emerson these days, characterized the farmer-animal relationship, saying, "I have never known a good stockman who didn't like animals and take the trouble to know them. Good stockmen know that a cow is a cow, not a four-legged human. They know what a cow is, and what to require and what to expect. They know their animals individually and are known by them."

more hog happiness, and that means better meat. At least 55 percent of their feed has to come from their own farm, or an arrangement has to be in place with another organic grower. Routine confinement in crates or boxes—a cruel but common practice in conventional hog operations—is prohibited. Fresh air and daylight have to be provided. Spacious lying and resting area with adequate bedding must be provided. There has to be land enough to handle the incorporation of composted pig manure as fertilizer (pig manure is exceptionally good manure for this purpose) where crops can be rotated. Manure management has to minimize soil and water degradation and optimize the recycling of nutrients back to the land where hog feed is grown. And all this is in addition to the usual prohibitions on genetically modified feed, routine antibiotics, drugs, pesticides, animal by-products, chemically extracted feeds such as solvent-extracted soybean meal, synthetic amino acids, and other agricultural chemicals.

Will pork raised organically be more expensive than conventional? Of course, but the cost of conventional pork doesn't include the hidden costs associated with it: erosion of depleted and chemically-treated soils, fouling of waterways with runoff from manure piles, and chemicals in the meat that cause illness in human beings.

WHAT TO LOOK FOR ◆ Ask your butcher to source organic pork for you. Look for a pleasing pink color. Avoid gray-looking meat. Pork tenderloins should be pinkish-red. The fat layer covering roasts and chops should be thin and even, not thick. Organic hams—fresh or smoked—should not have a water content over 10 percent. (Water content often appears on the label, or ask the butcher.)

Besides fresh cuts of pork and cured hams, cured organic Italian-style pork products, such as prosciutto, pancetta, mortadella, and coppa, are available, made by domestic producers such as Applegate Farms (carried in most stores with organic sections). You may find imported Italian prosciutto that's organically produced, as Italy is one of the leaders in the European organic movement.

PORK LOIN ROAST WITH DRIED FRUIT AND SWEET SPICES

SERVES 5

Pork is a sweet meat, and its flavor blends beautifully with dried fruit and spices. Try this for a special occasion dinner.

You'll need butcher's string and a sharp knife.

4 cups finely chopped dried fruits such as raisins, cherries, figs, pitted prunes, and mango
1 (3-pound) rolled pork loin roast
Freshly grated nutmeg
1 cup canola oil
3 tablespoons butter
1 tablespoon ground cinnamon
2 cups apple cider
1 tart apple, peeled, cored, and roughly chopped
Salt and freshly ground black pepper

1. When you buy the roast it will be tied with butcher's string. Cut these strings away. The cylindrical roast will spread open into two connected halves. With a sharp knife, slice into each half at a shallow angle, but not all the way through, so that the roast opens out into a rectangle of pork.

2. Lightly dust the interior surfaces with nutmeg (don't overdo this). Spread 1 1/2 cups of the chopped fruit over the surface of one half and another 1 1/2 cups over the surface of the other half. Close the two halves up, spreading the final cup of fruit between them. If any fruit is sticking out the ends or the seam, stuff it back in. Retie the roast with butcher's string where it was tied before so that it's a secure cylinder.

3. Preheat the oven to 400°F. Heat the oil in a heavy ovenproof skillet or flameproof baking dish. When it's hot but not smoking, put in the roast and brown it all around, but not on the ends. Remove the meat to a plate, pour off the oil from the skillet, return the roast to the skillet, place in the oven and roast for 1 hour and 20 minutes.

4. After you've put the roast in the oven, combine the butter, cinnamon, apple cider, and chopped apple in a saucepan and bring to a gentle boil. Reduce the heat and simmer for 30 minutes, until the apple chunks are soft.

5. When the roast has been in the oven for 50 minutes, pour all of the cider mixture over it. Push any apple chunks off the surface of the roast into the liquid in the skillet. Sprinkle the roast with a little salt and pepper. Roast the meat for the final 30 minutes. Let rest for a few minutes out of the oven, and serve with the apple cider sauce. ■

Poultry

ACCORDING TO the USDA guidelines, poultry may be labeled "natural" if it doesn't contain any additions to its natural state, such as artificial flavoring, coloring, chemical preservatives, growth hormones, or stimulants. Organic goes well beyond those restrictions.

Organic chickens must be fed a diet of organically grown and nongenetically modified feed, free of any animal by-products or fat, and be raised without antibiotics. These birds must not be permanently confined and must have access to sunlight, fresh air, and a scratch yard. In addition, they must have eight hours of darkness at night. They are also slaughtered at a somewhat older age than conventional broilers.

Contrast this with the common conventional situation where chickens are raised two birds to the square foot, up to 40,000 birds in an intensive chicken house. The building often is windowless, with almost constant lighting to speed growth. Stress levels are high, and antibiotics are used to keep the birds alive.

Growth-promoting drugs and stimulants force such a rapid rate of growth that their legs often can't support their bodies. Fans exhaust the ammonia-laden air. At six weeks of age, they are slaughtered—and inhumane practices at conventional slaughterhouses don't bear repeating.

Ducks and geese are waterfowl, of course, and become depressed and dirty if they can't swim and play in the water every day. So organic duck and goose production, which requires a water source, is an expensive method of raising these animals. Organic waterfowl farming is still in its infancy, or it is being done in small scale on mixed organic farms. Slow Food U.S.A. is involved in preserving two rare breeds of heritage geese—the American Buff Goose and the Pilgrim Goose.

Of the 400 million turkeys consumed in the United States each year, all but 10,000 are one variety, the Broad Breasted White. Raised conventionally, these birds are overbred for white breast meat and have lost the ability to run, fly, or breed naturally. According to Slow Food U.S.A., many are unhealthy, never see natural sunlight, and have their beaks shaved off so they don't injure one another in their cramped and stressed environment. Organic turkeys, by contrast, have the same rights to fresh air, sunlight, and pasture as chickens.

Other small scale organic poultry operations include the farming of Coturnix quail for eggs and meat. These quail are very efficient producers of eggs, requiring only two pounds of feed to make a pound of eggs, as contrasted with chickens, which require three pounds.

Pheasant, squab, and guinea fowl are available, but their organic provenance is usually from a local rather than national organic farmer.

TYPES • The most efficient meat-producing chickens are crosses between the Plymouth Rocks and Cornish breeds, known as Rock-Cornish. Small Rock-Cornish chickens are sometimes sold as "Rock Cornish Game Hens," which is a marketing ploy, since most meat chickens are Rock Cornish crosses. White Jersey Giants are also raised for meat. Organic farmers, on the other hand, may take advantage of niche markets by raising some of the less well-known breeds (there are many out there), but even organic farmers will generally raise the standard meat crosses.

Some ducks, such as Khaki Campbell and Indian Runner, are kept primarily for their eggs. Ducks for meat are usually Rouen, White Pekins, Aylesburys, or Muscovys for regular sized ducks, or Calls for smaller ones. For geese, the meat varieties include all-white Emdens, gray and white

COMING TO A SUPERMARKET NEAR YOU

SOME YEARS AGO, I started noticing "Rocky the Free-Range Chicken" showing up in my local supermarkets. These were locally raised birds, and judging from the words "free-range," I assumed they were given plenty of access to scratch pens without crowding.

That summer I was hosting a television show about growing organic vegetables and interviewed a fellow who had several organic acres near a "Rocky" facility. I noticed that the birds had a scratch pen all right, but they were almost as tightly packed into the space as if they were caged birds. Watch out for labels like "free range" or "naturally raised" because those terms have no specific regulated meaning the way "organic" does.

It wasn't long before "Rosie, the Organic Chicken®" started showing up. These were certified organic by Oregon Tilth—a very reputable organization, and they carried the USDA Organic seal as well. The birds seemed to be a cut above anything else available: fat, plump, delicious, and seemingly made to order for an organic guy like me.

Both Rocky and Rosie, it turns out, are brands owned by Petaluma Poultry Processors, Inc., the second-largest processor of poultry in California. This fast-growing company has also acquired B3R Country Meats and Coleman Natural Products, two major natural beef processors. (B3R started in Texas in 1986 and Coleman in 1979 in Colorado.) Both sell "natural" beef nationwide. The company is heading in the direction of becoming the major supplier of organic meats, but right now, Rosie is the first of the meat animals to move from natural to organic. Over a million Rosies were sold in 2004.

The bottom line is that while chickens marketed as "free range" may be better than birds raised crammed together in cages, only the Organic seal and certification guarantee that they're given proper access of fresh air and are raised without agricultural chemicals, hormones, and medicines.

Toulouse, and the noisy and belligerent African and Chinese geese.

Slow Food is working with 45 heritage breed farmers in 17 states to help sustain diversity in turkey breeds such as the Bourbon Red, Narragansett, Jersey Buff, American Bronze, and Blue Slate. Willie Benedetti, in Sonoma County, California, raises 90,000 free-range, natural or organic turkeys annually and sells them around the Bay Area, and he's also started raising Bourbon Reds. "Heritage birds are a lot more flighty and much more independent than regular turkeys. I can tell these birds will want to roost. They are very pretty birds," Benedetti says. They are also infinitely better tasting than their industrial cousins. Their meat is dark, rich, and succulent.

WHAT TO LOOK FOR ➤ Look for organic chickens. The fat should be yellow, not white, and the bird should appear plump. Pass over any birds that look scrawny or have broken breast skin. The skin helps seal in juices, and if broken, the breast meat can dry out before the rest of the bird is done. If you're buying ground chicken meat, be aware that ground thigh and leg meat—the dark meat—cooks up juicier than ground white meat.

You should be able to find local organic poultry farmers, and there are some brands, such as Shelton's Poultry, that are sold nationally.

For turkeys, if at all possible, look for a source of organically raised heritage turkeys (see Sources, page 517). If you are limited to the standard broad-breasted white turkeys, make sure your butcher has a source of organic birds. The turkey should look plump and the skin should not have serious tears, especially over the breast. As with ground chicken, ground turkey dark meat has more flavor and substance and cooks juicier than ground breast meat.

SEARED DUCK BREAST WITH SPICY SQUASH-MANGO CHUTNEY

SERVES 4

This recipe is from Gordon Hamersley, chef and owner of Hamersley's Bistro in Boston. The dish is a crowd pleaser at his restaurant and, he says, makes a fabulous dinner at home for guests. The chutney is best prepared a day or more ahead.

FOR THE CHUTNEY

1 tablespoon canola oil
$1^1/2$ cups peeled, seeded, and diced butternut squash (one medium squash)
$1/2$ small onion, finely diced
1 jalapeño pepper, stemmed, seeded, and sliced thin
2 cloves garlic, peeled and sliced
Pinch of crushed red pepper flakes
1 teaspoon coriander seeds
1 cinnamon stick
1 bay leaf
$3/4$ cup red wine vinegar
$1/4$ cup sugar
1 ripe mango, peeled and roughly chopped
8 fresh spearmint leaves, chopped

FOR THE DUCK

4 boneless duck breast halves (magrets)
1 teaspoon canola oil

1. To make the chutney: Heat the oil in a large skillet over medium-high heat. Add the squash and onion and cook for 5 minutes, stirring occasionally.

The squash should be cooked about halfway. Reduce the heat to medium and add the jalapeño, garlic, red pepper, coriander, cinnamon, and bay leaf. Stir to combine. Add the vinegar and sugar, and stir to combine. Cook over medium heat until the squash is tender, about 10 minutes, stirring occasionally. (Much of the liquid will evaporate during this time, so watch that the pan doesn't become completely dry. Reduce the heat if that seems to be happening.) Remove from heat and let it cool. Add the mango and mint leaves. Remove the cinnamon stick and bay leaf. Let the chutney mellow for at least 30 minutes before serving. It will hold in the fridge for 3 days.

2. To prepare the duck for cooking: With a sharp knife trim away the silver skin—the silvery, shiny layer that cooks up tough—from the meat side of the duck breasts (not the skin side) and trim away any excess skin and fat from along the edges. Score the skin side by making diagonal cuts at $1/8$-inch intervals.

3. Heat the oil in a large skillet over medium heat, coating the bottom. When the oil is hot, add the duck, skin side down. As the meat cooks, the fat under the duck's skin will render. Pour off this fat at intervals, using a large spatula or plate to hold the duck breasts in place. Keep cooking the duck and pouring off the fat, adjusting the heat if the skin begins to burn, until almost all of the fat under the skin has melted away and the skin is dark and crispy, about 12 minutes. Turn the duck over and cook an additional 2 minutes. Take the pan off the heat and let the duck rest in the pan for at least 5 minutes before slicing it.

4. To serve: Place each breast on a cutting board and slice the breasts across the grain, about six slices per breast. Place 1 breast's worth of duck slices on each plate and dress on the side with a generous amount of the chutney. ■

SOUTHERN-FRIED CHICKEN

SERVES 4

My mom was from Kentucky and claimed that down South, the women were beautiful but the men so-so; up North, the women were so-so but the men were handsome. She would impart these pearls of knowledge while setting a plate full of fried chicken on the table. To me, the chicken was beautiful.

1 cup buttermilk
1 large egg
1 cup all-purpose flour
1 cup finely crushed herbed crackers
1 tablespoon minced fresh parsley
1/2 tablespoon dried thyme
2 teaspoons salt
2 teaspoons freshly ground black pepper
2 cups canola oil
3 tablespoons bacon fat
1 frying chicken (about 3 pounds), cut into 8 pieces

1. Preheat the oven to 350°F. In a medium bowl, whip together the buttermilk and egg. In a separate bowl, mix the flour, crushed crackers, parsley, thyme, salt, and pepper.

2. Select a heavy frying pan deep enough to hold the oil and bacon fat, and large enough to hold all the chicken pieces. Add the oil and bacon fat to the pan and heat over medium heat. When the oil is hot, starting with the dark meat pieces, dip each piece of chicken in the buttermilk mixture, coat it well in the dry ingredients, and carefully add to the frying pan using tongs, to avoid having the hot fat spatter on you. Don't let the pieces touch each other.

3. Fry the chicken for 5 minutes on each side, then reduce the heat to medium-low and continue frying for 15 more minutes, turning once, until nicely browned. Drain the chicken on paper towels.

Check for doneness by slicing into the thickest part of the chicken: There should be no pink and the juices should run clear. Check the white meat first. If more time is needed, place the chicken pieces on a baking sheet in a 350°F oven and check every 5 minutes. ◾

CHICKEN MARVELS ON RICE

SERVES 4

The flavor of these meatballs goes best with a sunny white wine like chardonnay.

1 cup brown jasmine rice
1 cup white wine
6 ounces herbed crackers,
1 medium onion, minced
1/4 teaspoon salt
2 tablespoons freshly ground black pepper
1 1/4 pounds ground dark chicken meat
2 cups panko (Japanese bread crumbs)
1/2 cup extra-virgin olive oil
1 1/4 cups roasted garlic and tomato spaghetti sauce
1 cup freshly grated Parmigiano-Reggiano (about 4 ounces)
2 tablespoons minced fresh Italian flat-leaf parsley

1. Preheat the oven to 350°F. In a small, heavy saucepan, combine the rice, 1 cup water, and the white wine. Bring to a boil and cook for 10 minutes at full boil, then reduce heat, cover, and simmer for 20 minutes.

2. In a medium bowl, combine the cracker crumbs, onion, salt, and pepper; add the ground chicken and work the mixture into the chicken, first using two knives, and then with wet fingers. Place the panko in a second bowl. Form the chicken into 1-inch balls and roll in panko.

3. Heat the olive oil in a skillet over medium-low heat. When the oil is hot, add the chicken meatballs and brown, turning once or twice. When brown all over, remove onto paper towels, then place into a clean baking pan. Bake for 18 minutes, shaking the pan twice during that time.

4. Turn the rice into large skillet and add the sauce; heat on low and stir to incorporate sauce into rice. Place the chicken meatballs on top. Sprinkle with the cheese and the parsley. Serve immediately. ▪

Rabbit

WHILE MOST PEOPLE don't cook rabbit at home, it is frequently found on the menus of high-end restaurants. As a boy, I went hunting rabbits with my buddies every fall, and we came home with plenty. They were gamier than domestic rabbits, but delicious. We had to check them carefully for parasites, but no one to my knowledge ever got sick from eating wild cottontails.

Most store-bought rabbits today are raised by specialty growers using specific meat breeds. To get the organic seal, they can't be raised in permanent cages; they must be allowed the company of other animals; they must get a minimum of eight hours of daylight each day; if given access to pasture each rabbit must have five square meters of room;

breeding does (moms) must not have more than six litters per year (they breed like rabbits); and the kits (babies) must be allowed at least thirty-five days with their mothers before being weaned.

Rabbit ranchers will often use the manure as fodder for red wiggler worms. The resulting worm-enriched castings are a fabulously nutrient-rich fertilizer for crops. Rabbit manure, like the meat itself, is rich in zinc.

Buck rabbits are either screamers or fainters. That is, after they mate with a doe, they either scream or faint. Just a point of interest.

Other Meat Animals

FOR WHAT IT'S WORTH, the best tasting red meat I've ever eaten is reindeer, prepared by Philippe Jeanty, who was then chef at Domaine Chandon in the Napa Valley. Antelope living naturally on huge expanses of acreage in New Mexico comes in second. Organic bison meat, often labeled as "buffalo," is becoming more available in supermarkets. Tiensvold Farms in Nebraska is one such purveyor. Bison are raised on pasture, and their meat is very flavorful, low in fat, without any gamey taste. Elk, caribou, wild boar, and other specialty meats are available, and most probably natural but not certifiably organic.

Seafood and Freshwater Fish

FISH SUPPLIES are dying out. It doesn't seem so long ago that the Grand Banks southeast of Newfoundland were considered an inexhaustible source of cod as well as other species of fish—numbers beyond imagining.

Yet by 1995, all major cod fisheries on the Grand Banks were closed. Fished out. Canada imposed a 200-mile no-fishing limit along its Maritimes coast to allow fish stocks to recuperate. And then oil was found beneath the underwater plateaus that make up the Grand Banks. Oil development is now proceeding. So much for the Grand Banks as a resource for fish. And around the world, stocks of certain ocean fish are similarly threatened.

It's imperative, then, that organic-minded folks choose their seafood wisely, with an eye on sustainability—that is, fishing at levels that don't deplete stocks but sustain or even increase current fish stocks.

A second concern having to do with seafood is the presence of mercury in fish. Mercury levels in certain fish are dangerously high, caused by industrial pollution. It's especially important for young women of childbearing age, pregnant women, and young children to avoid fish species with high levels of mercury because of that element's role in developmental abnormalities. Among the most contaminated fish are king mackerel, shark, swordfish, and tilefish from the Gulf of Mexico. While light tuna is acceptable, white tuna (albacore) has levels of mercury elevated enough to warrant limiting intake. You can find a complete listing of commercial fish and shellfish mercury levels at: www.vm.sfsan.fda.gov/~frf/sea-mehq.html or at www.epa.gov/ost.fish.

As of this writing, thirty-five projects to produce genetically engineered (GE) fish are underway, and the Food and Drug Administration has also received an application to allow the marketing of a salmon engineered to grow 30 times faster than a wild salmon, according to the Center for Food Safety. Slow Food Researchers at Purdue University have found that GE fish, due to their larger size, have a mating advantage over native fish, meaning that GE fish will be more successful fertilizing the eggs of native females. But the offspring of GE fish have a one-third greater mortality rate than native fish, due to the impact of the added genetic material. Some scientists predict that the introduction of GE fish could cause the extinction of native species, such as Atlantic salmon (already endangered) within only a few generations. Remember that the government so far refuses to permit labeling of genetically modified organisms (GMOs, meaning the same thing as GE)—plant or animal foodstuffs—and therefore is actively blocking consumers' ability to identify GE foods. If these Frankenfish find their way into supermarkets, the average consumer won't know about it.

For more information, visit www.gefish.org.

THE ORGANIC FACTOR ◆ Because of the stress put on the world's wild fish stocks, fish farming is becoming more and more prevalent. As of this writing, there is no organic fish farming in the United States because the Department of Agriculture Organic Rules don't cover farmed fish, although a Florida firm has achieved organic certification for its farmed shellfish. You may find farmed fish labeled "Organic Certification Pending," as USDA is being pressured to adopt rules for organic farmed fish. Canada and Scotland are working to achieve organic certification, too.

While wild Pacific salmon can't be labeled organic because there is no way to certify where the fish have been or what they've been eating, these cold-water salmon eat their natural diet and swim the cold, clean waters of the North Pacific, and are natural, even if they can't earn certification. The same holds true for halibut, petrale sole, and other Pacific fish, and for wild Atlantic fish as well.

We are now beginning to see certified organic shrimp in our markets, some even available by mail order (see Sources, page 517). Organic certification for shrimp means that the company breeds its own pathogen-free, post-larvae shrimp until they are big enough to move to the grow-out ponds. There they're nurtured with organic feed processed from organically-raised tilapia. Certification also means that the shrimp are grown without antibiotics, hormones, dyes, or chemicals—which tells us something about the way nonorganic shrimp and fish are raised. Organic shrimp production discharges no waste water into the environment. Water is bio-filtered through a series of vegetation filters and reused.

NUTRITION ► Seafood is generally rich in Omega-3 essential fatty acids. Salmon is the champion in this department, with almost 2 grams of Omega-3 per 100 grams of fish. Anchovies, of all things, are right behind. Also look for West Coast fresh or canned sardines with 1.5 grams per 100 grams of fish. Pickled herring is good, and among freshwater fish, farmed rainbow trout are rich in this essential nutrient.

WHAT TO LOOK FOR ► The Audubon Society and the Monterey Bay Aquarium in California issue cards that tell you at a glance which fish are caught in an environmentally sound manner and which stocks aren't depleted, which are questionable, and which should be avoided because of their mercury content, endangered status, or because the way they're caught depletes or injures other species, including cetaceans. You can download these cards at www.seafood.audubon.org and at www.montereybayaquarium.org.

The fish are ranked according to three categories: Best Choices, Proceed with Caution, and Avoid. Among Best Choices are farmed catfish, farmed caviar, farmed crawfish, stone crab, wild-caught Alaskan salmon, tilapia, and Pacific halibut. The Avoid list includes Atlantic and Icelandic cod, Chilean sea bass, grouper, Caribbean lobster, orange roughy, queen conch, swordfish, imported shrimp, red snapper, shark, and Gulf of Mexico tilefish. When buying any type of fish, it pays to know your fishmonger. Don't be afraid to ask when the fish was delivered. With fish, fresher is always better. It's hard to tell how old fish filets or salmon steaks are, but if you can see a whole fish, look it in the eye. It should be bright and clear and well defined. You might speak with the manager of the fish department about when deliveries are scheduled so that you can pick up your seafood or fresh fish the day it's brought in. Oysters, mussels, scallops, and clams should be as fresh as possible—you'll have to rely on your merchant to give you accurate information.

SHRIMP RISOTTO SUPREME

SERVES 4

This risotto combines an interesting mix of flavors that has real synergy. My wife Susanna asks for her "fix" of this dish about every six to eight weeks.

1 pound medium shrimp
1 bunch asparagus
2 ears fresh corn, shucked
1 1/2 quarts chicken stock
1/4 cup extra-virgin olive oil
1 1/3 cups arborio rice
1/2 cup white wine
1 jalapeño pepper, stemmed, seeded, and minced
1/2 teaspoon freshly ground black pepper
2 limes
1/2 cup grated Parmigiano-Reggiano
2 tablespoons chopped fresh flat-leaf parsley

1. Shell and devein the shrimp, then steam them in a basket over boiling water until they are just cooked through, about 3 to 5 minutes. Remove and coarsely chop. Chop off the top 2 inches of the asparagus tips and reserve. Save remaining asparagus for another use. Add the tips to the steamer and gently steam until just tender, about 5 to 7 minutes. Boil the corn for about 3 minutes just until the kernels are tender; when cool enough to handle, cut the kernels off the cob and reserve.

2. In a 2-quart saucepan, bring the chicken broth to a simmer, then reduce the heat to low and keep warm.

3. Heat the olive oil in a large, deep, heavy skillet over medium heat. When the oil is fragrant, add the rice and stir for 2 minutes until it turns opaque. (This prepares the rice for its task of absorbing the chicken stock.) Add the white wine and stir until the liquid is fully absorbed.

4. Add chicken stock, a half cup at a time, stirring constantly, adding another half cup as all the liquid is absorbed. After about 15 minutes of cooking (the rice grains will still have a chalky center), add the corn, jalapeño, and black pepper. When the rice is almost cooked through (about 20 minutes of cooking total), add the shrimp and asparagus tips. When the rice grains are just al dente, tender with perhaps the slightest bite in the center, juice the limes straight into the skillet, add the cheese, stir thoroughly and remove from the heat.

5. Sprinkle with the chopped parsley; serve immediately. ■

Milk

COWS ARE RUMINANTS, natural grazers, and their four stomachs are exquisitely designed to metabolize grass. In nature, grains are a minimal part of a grazer's diet. Feeding them grain throws their metabolism into high gear—thus they produce more milk, with more milkfat in the milk, just as feeding steers grain in the confinement pens called feedlots fattens them up for slaughter. Grass-fed cows don't produce as much milk, but it's better milk, with more CLA (conjugated linoleic acid, a beneficial fatty acid) and vitamins, and a richer flavor—as nature intended.

CLA protects against cancer in lab animals and shows promise against breast and prostate cancer in humans. Studies show that the more CLA in the milk, the less the risk of breast cancer in those who drink it. Milk from grass-fed cows has been found to contain five times higher levels of CLA than milk from cows fed supplements of corn kernels and corn silage.

The difference between conventional milk and organic milk from grass-fed cows is striking. I used to buy milk from a lady who ran a very small dairy in the hills of eastern Pennsylvania. You brought your own bottles and she filled them from five-gallon milk cans. Her cows were pastured except for the twice-daily milking. The milk was raw, unpasteurized, and not homogenized. I could skim the cream from the top of each bottle. But most of us do not have access to such a dairy, and I have not seen organic milk labeled "from grass-fed cows." Until organic dairies start labeling their milk as grass-fed, about all we can do as consumers is to call our local organic dairies and ask them if their cows are pastured or confined and fed grains.

While the ideal of the happy cow grazing her lush green pasture is a pretty picture, it too often is an idealized one. When the National Organic Program was established, access to pasture for organic cows

MILK NUTRITION CHART

Here's an interesting chart comparing the nutrients in several milks. The fat, protein, and carbohydrates are given as percentages, the calcium, phosphorus, and vitamin C as milligrams per 100 grams (about three and a half ounces).

MILK	FAT %	PROTEIN %	CARBOHYDRATE %	CALCIUM mg	PHOSPHORUS mg	VITAMIN C mg
Cow	3.5	3.5	4.9	118	93	1.0
Goat	4.0	3.2	4.6	129	106	1.0
Sheep	7.0	6.0	5.3	193	N/A	2.5
Human	4.0	1.1	9.5	33	14	5.0

You can see at a glance that sheep's milk is richer in fat and higher in protein and minerals than the others. Interestingly, human milk has a quarter of the protein and twice the carbohydrate of the others, plus much greater vitamin C. That stands to reason because the other animals have the ability to manufacture vitamin C within their bodies, while humans don't. Nature has compensated by giving human mammary glands the ability to synthesize vitamin C.

POTENTIAL DANGERS IN CONVENTIONAL MILK

MANY IN THE MEDICAL PROFESSION believe that one reason that illnesses caused by new strains of antibiotic-resistant bacteria are cropping up is because the routine use of antibiotics in farm animals, including milk cows, is accelerating mutations among bacteria. It's the same old story as with pesticides—whether applying pesticides to the fields or antibiotics to the farm animals, only the resistant microorganisms survive, to breed new strains of resistant organisms. So an organic cow is treated homeopathically, without antibiotics. If a cow is sick enough to require an antibiotic to save her life, she has to temporarily leave the organic program. For a calf to be organic, its mother must have been placed on organic pasture after her first trimester.

Organic milk comes from cows that are not given rBGH, which stands for recombinant bovine growth hormone. The U.S. Food and Drug Administration says this genetically engineered invention, created by Monsanto corporation, is okay to give to milk cows, even though it's banned in Canada and Europe. (And so McDonald's serves organic milk at all its outlets in England.) This synthetic hormone, also sometimes called rBST, increases milk production in cows about 20 percent, but at the cost of adverse effects on the animals, including reproductive difficulties and mastitis, an infection of the udder.

The synthetic hormone works to increase milk production by increasing cows' blood levels of IGF-1 (insulin-like growth factor). A study of U.S. women published in *The Lancet*, a British medical journal, showed a seven-fold increase in breast cancer among premenopausal women who had the highest levels of IGF-1 in their bodies.

Elevated levels of IGF-1 have also been associated with higher risks of colon and prostate cancers. The IGF-1 found in rBGH milk is not destroyed by human digestion. Instead, IGF-1 is readily absorbed through the intestinal wall. Research has shown that it can be absorbed into the bloodstream where it can affect other hormones. Some scientists studying IGF-1 believe it's likely that IGF-1 promotes the transformation of normal breast cells to breast cancers and that IGF-1 maintains the malignancy of human breast cancer cells, including their invasiveness and ability to spread to distant organs. IGF-1 is found in organic milk—and human breast milk—because it's a growth factor that helps babies grow. But it's not found at nearly the concentrations found in milk from rBGH cows. Cows that get rBGH show as much as a 44 percent increase in IGF-1 levels over cows that don't receive the hormone. Adults have stopped growing, so excess growth hormones floating in adult blood streams may find cancer cells and encourage their growth.

IGF-1 in milk is not destroyed by processing or pasteurization, and therefore it will be found in elevated amounts in yogurt, butter, ice cream, cheese, and other milk products made from the milk of cows that receive doses of rBGH.

was written into the rules. This was to protect small dairy farmers and prevent large confinement dairies from taking over the organic milk business. It was also to promote the health of the dairy animals and increase the quality of organic milk and milk products. But the USDA, which has responsibility for enforcing the organic rules, is not enforcing the access to pasture rule because, it says, the word "pasture" is not defined in the rules—therefore they can't enforce it. Whether the USDA is enforcing the access to pasture rule or not, most organic dairy farmers allow their cows to graze pasture anyway, at least in spring through fall. In winter the cows are in the barn and fed corn, silage, or hay.

Organic milk, especially milk from cows fed solely on pasture or hay, is a true success story. And not just because of 25 percent jumps in sales each year for several recent years, to about $300 million in 2004, while conventional milk consumption fell 10 percent in 2003.

A debate is ongoing in the organic farming community about the subject of grass-fed versus grain-fed dairy cows. You can keep up to date on this and other organic farming issues by visiting www.newfarm.org.

NUTRITION ▸ The composition of milk varies with the breed of animal, the feed it gets, and the health of the animal. A healthy cow fed on pasture will give the highest quality milk. The milk of Jersey and Guernsey cows is higher in butterfat than that of the black-and-white-splotched Holsteins, but Holsteins give more milk.

On average, whole milk has 3.5 percent butterfat, low-fat milk either 1 or 2 percent, and nonfat or skim milk, less than .5 percent. Heavy cream has a minimum butterfat of 36 percent, while half-and-half must have between 10.5 and 18 percent butterfat.

Milk is usually homogenized, meaning it's forced through tiny openings under pressure, which breaks apart the fat globules and disperses them evenly through the milk so they don't rise as cream to the top. Pasteurization heats milk to inhibit bacteria, while ultra-pasteurization completely sterilizes milk.

WHAT TO LOOK FOR ▸ Look for milk labeled "organic." That assures you that the milk is not from cows given bovine growth hormone or routine antibiotics. It's up to you whether you want whole milk, low-fat milk, or nonfat milk.

You may notice the letters UHT on a milk carton. The letters stand for ultra-high-temperature pasteruization (the same thing as ultra-pasteurization), in which the milk is sterilized so it can be stored at room temperature for extended periods and shipped around the country without worrying about spoilage. Although practitioners of ultra-high-temperature processing contend that heating milk to 230°F for several seconds doesn't alter the milk in any way, the issue remains open. Enzymes, for one thing, don't survive those temperatures.

Though I have not found them in markets as yet, organic powdered milk, condensed milk (sweetened to 40 percent sugar), and evaporated milk (unsweetened) may some day be offered.

USES ▸ We use organic nonfat milk around my house, but I've found that it has different cooking qualities than milk with more fat, and especially cream. The more fat, the less likely the milk or cream is to curdle at high heat. This is true of organic as well as conventional—or even evaporated—milk.

Nondairy milks can be made from nuts and seeds. Whiz almonds, hazelnuts, Brazil nuts, or other nuts or seeds in the blender until powdered, then whiz with water and strain through a cheese-cloth-lined colander. Don't use these milks to cook at high heat, or they will separate. Use them, for instance, on your morning granola.

J. I. Rodale used to say that cows' milk was made to raise calves, not kids. For kids, he said, the ideal is mother's milk. Next to that, goat's milk has a smaller and much more easily digested curd than cows' milk, and it is much gentler to a baby's young digestive system than cows' milk. For those who are lactose intolerant, organic soy and rice milks are widely available. I have not cooked with them, but I have made ice cream from rice milk and it tasted sweet, pure, and good.

CITRUS PANNA COTTA

SERVES 6

After I tasted the best panna cotta of my life, I prevailed on Christopher Herrera, then the talented pastry chef at Jardinière in San Francisco, to give me his recipe, and here it is. Serve this with fresh seasonal fruits.

2 teaspoons powdered gelatin (²/₃ of a packet)
1 cup heavy cream
1 cup sugar
Grated zest of 1 orange (well scrubbed if not organic)
Grated zest of 1 lemon (well scrubbed if not organic)
Grated zest of 1 lime (well scrubbed if not organic)
2 cups (1 pint) sour cream

1. In a small bowl, combine the gelatin with ¹/₂ cup of cold water to soften; let sit 5 minutes.

2. In a medium saucepan, combine the heavy cream, sugar, and zests, and bring to a boil. When the cream begins to boil and the sugar is entirely dissolved, remove from the heat and allow it to

stand for 2 minutes, then strain through a very fine sieve into a bowl to remove the citrus zest.

3. When the gelatin is entirely dissolved, whisk it into the cream. Whisk in the sour cream until well combined. Pour the mixture into six 6-ounce custard cups, ramekins, or other small molds. Chill at least 6 hours. To unmold, set the molds in a shallow pan of hot water for a few seconds so the panna cotta releases. Invert onto plates. ▪

Cheese and Dairy Products

CHEESE is one of life's exquisite bounties. And like wine and bread, cheese is a fermented feast. At the dawn of agriculture, when wild cattle, sheep, and goats were first domesticated, milk was a perishable product. Left sitting around for a few days, it turned naturally into curds and whey, and when the first farmers drained off the whey and pressed the curds, they had cheese. It's still made that way, except that the curdling agents are rennet and specific strains of bacteria. In other words, it's still a natural product, a collaboration between animal, human, and bacteria. Conventional cheesemakers have developed a slew of additives to preserve and texturize their processed cheese food. But as you might suspect, organic cheese is not only additive-free but is made with milk from organically raised animals that are fed organic feed of the kind nature intends for ruminants.

It's not hard to find organic cheese from grass-fed cows. I typed "organic cheese from grass-fed cows" into my Internet search engine and got pages of sources. So if you can't find it at the store, many of these sources will ship.

A PROFILE OF AN ORGANIC DAIRY FARMER

ONE MIGHT THINK that milk is just milk, and that organic milk can't be that different from ordinary milk. But then, you probably haven't heard of Mark McAfee, a third-generation dairy farmer, and his Organic Pastures Dairy in Fresno, California. Thousands of people have visited this dairy because it is so unusual. Instead of using confinement sheds, where cows wallow in their own manure, necessitating washing before milking (a practice Mark tells me only washes bacteria down to the udder and into the milk), Mark puts his cows out to permanent pasture. Instead of building a milking barn, where the cows are concentrated together, Mark devised a milking parlor on wheels that he drives out to the pastures. He can milk a cow in 10 minutes and turn it back to pasture. He rotates the cows from pasture to pasture on a regular basis, but they are never confined. This means that manure doesn't build up and he doesn't have to have holding tanks to hold the manure-water slurry. Visiting his dairy farm, one detects very little of that cow-country smell that arises from cows in close quarters.

McAfee raises Jersey cows, whose milk is richer in butterfat than milk from Holsteins, which are favored by conventional dairy farmers because they produce copious amounts of milk. And his milk is unpasteurized and raw. While the idea of raw milk sounds scary, it's not. Most of the fine cheese of America and Europe is made from raw milk. McAfee told me he tests each batch of his milk for disease-causing salmonella, *E. coli*, and listeria, and that in more than six years of doing his organic pastures program, he's never found a human pathogen in the milk. He has even had researchers introduce such bacteria to test samples, and the pathogens have been unable to reproduce. In the varied ecosystem within Mark's milk, the competition from healthy bacteria stifles them. He explained that a healthy balance of bacteria in the milk comes from a healthy cow, and a healthy cow comes from a healthy farm. And so he has designed what he calls a "pro-cow environment." As cows dry up at the end of their lactating cycle, they are taken out of rotation for fifty days before they are impregnated again. As they dry up for good, they are put out to pasture but never slaughtered.

Most dairies would say all of this is uneconomical, and it is if you think of animals as production units. Organic farmers think of them as animals that are part of the ecosystem of the farm. Mark's attention is on the cows' welfare. He wants them to have strong joints and good hooves. To keep them strong, he feeds them organic alfalfa hay to supplement the hay he grows on his own pastures. Because the cows rotate among several pastures, they naturally fertilize the fields that grow this hay.

Conventional wisdom would say that he'd have a tough time making a decent bottom line, but just the opposite is true. Although his production per cow is low (40 pounds of milk a day per cow compared to 100 at the big commercial dairies) and he has to care for old, dry cows, people are willing to pay more for his milk and he's doing fine. His cows are doing fine. And his customers are happy to get raw, organic milk with all its nutrients and enzymes in place.

SLOW FOOD U.S.A. HONORS RAW MILK FARMSTEAD CHEESES

SLOW FOOD U.S.A. has inaugurated the American Raw Milk Farmstead Cheese Consortium to raise awareness of the quality of these cheeses and to defend the right for them to be produced. The federal government has in the past threatened to prevent any raw milk cheese from being made in the United States. Slow Food expects that as America's cheesemakers continue to refine their craft and place increasing trust on the quality of farmstead milk, their cheeses will rank in excellence with the world's best.

NUTRITION ◆ Just as with milk (see page 437), cheese from grass-fed cows is five times higher in conjugated linoleic acid (CLA), a potent cancer fighter, than from dairy cows fed grains. Nutritionists encourage people to get more Omega-3 into their diet, and pasture grass with some weeds present contains more Omega-3 than Omega-6 essential fatty acids, while corn and soybeans (the grains usually fed to cows) contain far more Omega-6 than Omega-3. That's why cheese from grass-fed cows has an excellent ratio of these two essential nutrients. Finding a source of grass-fed organic cheese is a way to do that.

And there's more: Organic cheese from grass-fed cows has higher levels of beta-carotene and other vitamins than cheese from grain-fed animals. The reason goes back to the concept that naturally fed organisms grow into thrifty plants and animals (see page 24). Cows are meant to eat fresh grass or hay in the winter. Fed the diet nature intends for them, they give less milk but better milk. Better milk makes better cheese.

TYPES ◆ Cows' milk cheese is only part of the picture. Sheep, goat, and water buffalo cheeses are also produced organically.

We're all familiar with goat cheese—both chevre from France, feta from Greece, and American goat cheese, among others. Of all the American goat cheese I've tasted, the most amazingly delicious is Hubbardston Blue, produced in Hubbardston, Massachusetts.

Sheep milk cheeses are made in France, Italy, the United States, and many other places. In Italy, the word for sheep is *pecora*—hence, pecorino. They are full-flavored, rich, and made in many styles.

The original mozzarella cheese is made from water buffalo milk in Campania, the region around Naples, and also in Apulia and Basilicata. After the rennet is added to the buffalo milk, the curds are allowed to sit in the whey for some time before the whey is drained off. The curds then are transferred to a tub of boiling water where they are stirred with a paddle. This gives mozzarella its plasticity and melting quality. Using the paddle, the cheesemakers pull and stretch the curd until it's smooth and elastic. Next they cut the mozzarella into individual portions (*mozzare* is Italian for cut, hence mozzarella), stretch and pull them taut, and form them into balls or braids and plunge them into cold water, which firms them. Once firm, the cheese is soaked in brine until it's sent to market.

Real buffalo-milk mozzarella should be as fresh as possible. It should have the color of white porcelain. The texture should be elastic and the surface tight and smooth. Press it with your finger—it shouldn't be gooey soft or hard-rubbery, but should slowly regain its shape. When you cut the mozzarella, you should be able to see its layers, like an onion sliced open. After about half a day, these layers dissolve and the mozzarella loses some elasticity. That's why it's hard to get good fresh buffalo mozzarella here in the states. When you taste good mozzarella, you'll notice some milky liquid exuding from the cheese. And the mozzarella should melt in your mouth. The "mozzarella" they use on pizza in the United States? That's cows' milk and bears little resemblance to the real thing.

Be aware that low-fat or nonfat cheeses are strange creatures. They don't taste like much. Their texture is weird. And nonfat cheese doesn't melt, so don't try using it in cooking. Nonfat cream cheese produces dips and cake frostings that are very runny. Not only that, heating nonfat cheeses of any type turns them sweet. I don't know the chemistry behind that, but I've given up on nonfat cheese entirely. If you are watching your intake of fats, cut back on your consumption of cheese, but when you do eat some, whether by itself or incorporated in a dish, make it a real cheese.

WHAT TO LOOK FOR ► Artisanal cheeses—made in small batches by local artisan cheesemakers—have the most flavor and character. When they use raw milk, even more flavor characteristics are preserved. When the milk is organic, that's a big bonus. And when the milk is raw, organic, and from grass-fed cows, it doesn't get any better than that.

If you find that you are becoming more and more enamored of fine cheeses, check out the American Cheese Society's web site at www.cheesesociety.org. This small group of artisan cheesemakers, purveyors, and others who love good cheese has played a large part in getting the FDA to back off its proposed rule to ban raw milk cheeses in the United States—which would have effectively banned the best cheeses in Europe, since almost all of them are raw milk cheeses. With Slow Food U.S.A., the American Cheese Society cofounded

HOW TO TELL IF A CHEESE IS ORGANIC

ORGANIC CHEESES (made from certified organic milk) are being produced both here in the United States and in Europe. As more and more dairy farmers are switching to organic production to capitalize on the premiums paid for organic milk, finding such cheeses is becoming easier. The Organic Valley Co-Op, for example, has introduced a line of organic cheeses.

In Europe, myriad farmstead cheeses have been made naturally for thousands of years, so the imported cheese you buy—especially the artisanal ones—may be naturally organic. But more and more, European cheesemakers are seeing the value in obtaining organic certification, which reassures buyers that the milk does not contain growth hormones or cause mad cow disease.

Virtually any kind of cheese—from cow, goat, sheep, or even buffalo—can be organic, as long as the milk is organic and no artificial flavorings, texturizers, or other such ingredients are added.

To find organic cheese, shop in the cheese section of better stores and look for the USDA Organic seal on domestic cheeses. European cheeses may be labeled as "biologique" or by other terms, depending on the country. Visit www.organic-europe.net for access to the organic certifiers and movements in the various European countries.

the Farmstead Cheese Consortium, which seeks to preserve the heritage and production of cheeses by cheesemakers who raise and milk their own animals and produce cheeses on the farms where the animals live. At present, 53 of the American Cheese Society's 200 cheesemaker members are classified as farmstead cheesemakers.

USES ◆ Cheese, like wine, is a huge subject. Have fun exploring it. One way to do that, especially at dinner parties, is to insert a cheese course between the main course and dessert—a noble tradition in France but not much seen in American homes, where the tradition has been to serve cheese and crackers as hors d'oeuvres before dinner. We now have a huge selection of artisanal and farmstead cheeses available in our markets from which to choose items for a cheese course. Serving it after the main course allows the dinner party to refresh their glasses of wine or start a different bottle.

Besides cheese, other forms of dairy products made from organic milk are butter, yogurt, cottage cheese, buttermilk, sour cream, cream cheese, ice cream, gelato, ricotta, crème fraîche, quark, and the list goes on. All of these provide the cook with chances to be creative.

For instance, Spring Hill Farms in Petaluma, California, sells a lemon quark, a very soft-curd cheese with a light hint of lemon. David Frakes, the chef at Beringer Winery in St. Helena, California, uses it as an ice cream base. It can also be used like a crème anglaise. Crème fraîche can be bought at the store nowadays, but you can make your own by stirring 2 tablespoons of buttermilk into 1 cup of heavy cream and letting it stand at room temperature for 8 to 12 hours, or until it thickens. Spoon some over fresh fruit. Or use it to make creamy soups.

Sometimes sheep's milk ricotta is available in our area. After the curds are drained, the whey is cooked (ricotta is Italian for recooked, just as panna cotta is Italian for cooked cream) until ricotta forms. I find sheep's milk ricotta to be enormously superior to most cow's milk ricotta on the market. Blintzes stuffed with sheep's milk ricotta filling and served with strawberry jam and sour cream are a dream come true. If cows' milk ricotta is all you can find, blintzes are still a dream.

Traditionally in the classic *insalata caprese*, slices of mozzarella are paired with vine-ripened tomatoes and basil and drizzled with a little extra-virgin olive oil (but please, no balsamic vinegar or lemon juice). If you are lucky enough to have a source of fresh, organic water buffalo mozzarella, you will find it indispensable in all sorts of Italian dishes—spaghetti, gnocchi, eggplant parmigiana, calzone, and pizza. It will melt into tomato sauce and give whatever it touches a rich, delicious texture and taste.

GOUGÈRES (TRADITIONAL FRENCH CHEESE PUFFS)

MAKES 36 PIECES

This recipe was given to me by chef Terrance Brennan of Artisanal Fromagerie and Bistro in Manhattan. Chef Brennan has been a leading force in exposing America to the world of fine cheeses by presenting the best varieties from abroad as well as world-class cheeses being made here in the United States and Canada.

"*Gougère* is the classic French name for the hors d'oeuvres known to most Americans as cheese puffs," Brennan told me. "I prefer the classic name because it hints at the elegance they possess when properly made. These are the most popular hors d'oeuvres at Artisanal. One of the most appealing things about them is convenience; they require very little work and, once made, they can be gently reheated in the oven in a matter of minutes." Brennan says that "gougères can be adapted to include your favorite cheese. Think about making them with Roquefort or Parmigiano-Reggiano in place of Gruyère. You can also add 1 to 2 tablespoons of minced herbs or chives to the mix."

4 tablespoons (1/2 stick) unsalted butter
1/4 cup plus 2 tablespoons milk
11/4 teaspoons sea salt
6 grinds of black pepper
3/4 cup all-purpose flour, sifted
1/4 teaspoon baking powder
3 eggs, at room temperature
1 cup plus 2 tablespoons coarsely grated Gruyère cheese
(a little over 4 ounces)

1. Preheat the oven to 375°F. In a 2-quart saucepan, combine the butter, 1/4 cup of the milk, 1/2 cup of water, 1/4 teaspoon of the salt, and the pepper, and set over medium heat. Bring to a boil, then remove from heat and add the flour and baking powder all at once. Stir well with a wooden spoon and return to the heat. Cook until the dough pulls away from the side of the pan and forms a ball, approximately 5 minutes.

2. Transfer the dough to the bowl of an electric mixer fitted with the paddle attachment and beat on low until just warm, approximately 2 minutes. (Or stir with a wooden spoon for about 4 minutes.) Add the eggs one at a time, beating well with each addition, then add 1/2 cup of the cheese. Beat the mixture until uniformly smooth and shiny, approximately 12 minutes.

3. Line 2 baking sheets with parchment paper. Place the dough into a pastry bag fitted with a #3 tip. Use the pastry bag to pipe small mounds ap-proximately 1 inch in diameter on the baking sheets. Or, if you don't have a pastry bag and tip, use a tablespoon to make the mounds. Make sure that the gougères are evenly spaced, leaving 1/2 inch between them. Make 18 gougères on each baking sheet.

4. Brush the tops of the gougères with the remaining 2 tablespoons of milk and sprinkle with the remaining cheese and salt. Bake for 7 to 10 minutes, until the gougères take on a deep, golden-brown color. Serve warm. ▪

Eggs

THE AVERAGE AMERICAN eats about 175 "shell eggs"—the kind you buy by the dozen at the market—a year, or about one every two days. Most of these are produced in egg factories by hens crammed into cages. But those of us who buy organic get eggs that are qualitatively different from the factory sort.

Because of the abundant minerals and natural foods in the organic hen's diet, organic eggs' shells are thick and smooth. When you crack them open, the yolk is a richly colored dark orange due to an abundance of beta-carotene and stands up tall above the white. Again, because of the hen's natural diet, the white is gelatinous, with substance—it doesn't just spill out across the pan or bowl. It has a light greenish-yellow tint that indicates it's high in riboflavin. It has prominent chalazae, the thick white place in albumin strings that center the yolk in the shell.

The first time I used fresh organic eggs from free-range hens I had to separate four eggs. I remember that the whites were not runny, but clear and viscous, holding together in a thick, jelly-like mass. The yolks

MY FAVORITE EGGS

THE BEST WAY to ensure a supply of farm-fresh organic eggs is to keep a coop of chickens yourself. It doesn't take much room: A 10 × 12-foot henhouse with nesting boxes keeps the hens safe at night from marauding foxes, possums, raccoons, and other critters who cherish eggs even more than we do. A 20 × 20-foot, fenced-in scratch yard will afford enough room for a dozen laying hens. Feed them organic grain and mineral supplements, but also vegetable kitchen scraps. In the fall, empty bushel baskets of leaves in there. As the chickens scratch and tear apart the leaves looking for insects, they layer their manure into the shredded leaves. Save this precious, fertile mulch for your spring garden.

If a backyard chicken house and yard sounds like something you'd like to try, pick up a copy of *Keep Chickens* by Barbara Kilarski.

were deep orange and gave the batter of the cake I was making a rich, warm color. The yolks were also plump, standing up in the bowl before I beat them into the batter with a fork. They were thick and clung to the tines of the fork, so I had to squeeze the tines with my fingers to get the last of the yolks off the fork. They clung to my fingers, they were that thick and sticky. There is no substitute for eggs like these.

Compare these against eggs from a factory farm, where hens spend their lives cooped up in tiny cages under 24-hour-a-day lighting, fed genetically modified and pesticide-sprayed corn, and routinely treated with antibiotics to prevent the diseases that would otherwise flourish in these smelly, noisy, inhumane conditions. I've been in such egg factories, and they are a vision of chicken hell. Forced to lay too many eggs, fed as cheaply as possible, and living in unnatural conditions, factory hens lay eggs that may have rough and ridged shells, loose light yellow yolks, and watery whites. In the kitchen, this translates into poor performance in what eggs are supposed to do: bind ingredients, add body, and support light, well-risen cakes, among other functions.

The organic farm, however, is much closer to chicken heaven. According to the standards for the National Organic Program, "All organically raised animals must have access to the outdoors. ... They may be temporarily confined only for reasons of health, safety, the animal's stage of production, or to protect soil or water quality."

This means that organic eggs come from hens with a scratch yard. Notice it says they can be shut in the henhouse only temporarily—in other words, they are truly free-range birds. That doesn't mean they can fly out of the scratch yard and start living under the hydrangea. Laying hens and roosters usually have their flight feathers clipped so they can't fly. Humane treatment, healthy diet, and lack of stress translate into organic eggs that perform beautifully in the kitchen, including functions such as coagulation, foaming, emulsification, and browning.

THE ORGANIC FACTOR ▸ Organic hens eat only organic feed, so the danger of the bioaccumulation of pesticides and other toxins in their eggs is minimal. In years past, unsanitary conditions led to fecal contamination of some eggs with salmonella bacteria, a pathogen that causes food poisoning. Today, salmonella contamination of eggshells is very rare, according to the USDA. Most salmonella today comes from sick hens whose ovaries and ovarian tracts are infected with salmonella and whose eggs are infected before the shell is formed. Healthy hens are unlikely to become sick with salmonella. Even so, it's wise to cook eggs, which destroys salmonella, rather than eat them raw.

A new trend among some organic farmers is to raise chickens on pasture under large wire enclosures, moving the enclosures daily so that the chickens have a fresh supply of green matter, insects, and seeds to eat every day, and pasture that's not littered with their droppings from previous days. This will afford such chickens added protection against disease.

NUTRITION ‣ For many years, the high cholesterol content of egg yolks made them anathema to health-conscious people who wanted to cut their cholesterol levels. But it's now known that there is little if any connection between dietary cholesterol and blood cholesterol levels. Nutrition experts have concluded that people on a low-fat diet can eat one or two eggs a day without measurable changes in their blood cholesterol levels. In fact, investigators found that intake of saturated fat—not of cholesterol—influences blood cholesterol levels the most.

Eggs are a great source of low-cost, high-quality protein, providing 5.5 grams of protein (about 12 percent of our daily requirement) in one egg at only 68 calories. One egg yolk also provides 300 micrograms of the vitamin-like compound choline, a precursor of acetylcholine—the substance that allows our muscles to obey our brains. Eggs are also an excellent source of vitamin K, selenium, biotin, tryptophan, vitamins B2 and B12, iodine, pantothenic acid, vitamin D, phosphorus, and vitamin A (in the form of lutein and zeaxanthin, which are carotenoids and have a central role in protecting the eyes).

Not only that: Eggs also protect us against stroke and heart attack–causing blood clots; against macular degeneration of the eyes and cataracts in advancing age; against Alzheimer's disease and age-related cognitive decline. A chemical in eggs called biotin boosts our energy and promotes skin health and nervous system function.

WHAT TO LOOK FOR ‣ You'll see eggs at the store labeled "cage free." That means the chickens live in a room somewhere—they're not confined to cages—but most likely still have no access

KEEP AN EYE OUT FOR PULLET EGGS

IF YOU BUY your eggs at a farmers' market or directly from farmers, ask if they have any pullet eggs—eggs laid by a hen in her youth. Hens start laying around their 18th week of life. By their 31st week they are termed adults and will lay for about two more years. But in those 13 weeks between 18 and 31, they produce small, extra high quality pullet eggs. Although smaller than ordinary large eggs, pullet eggs get all the advantages of the hen's youth—vigor, a fresh reproductive tract, a healthy metabolism running at full tilt. Pullet eggs have a luscious quality and superior flavor, in my experience. Chefs and pastry chefs know about this and use pullet eggs to make their soufflés rise higher and puffier, to add lusciousness to their ice creams, to give their omelets lightness, to give their cakes better texture. With eggs, bigger is not better. Large, extra-large, and jumbo eggs come from older hens.

to the great outdoors. These shenanigans aren't allowed with hens laying organic eggs. You may also see "vegetarian" eggs. That means the chickens are not fed any animal by-products. They could still be raised in cages. And you may see eggs labeled as "Omega-3." That simply means that flaxseed has been added to their feed to boost the amount of Omega-3 essential fatty acid in the egg. That's a good thing, but unless they're organic, they could still be raised in either cages or confinement rooms.

If you see eggs labeled "fertile," that means that a rooster is allowed to run with the hens. Farmers chiefly do this to get eggs to incubate and make chicks to replace their older hens. Fertile eggs were once thought to be superior to nonfertile eggs in nutritional terms, but I can find no evidence of that. In fact, fertile eggs have a shorter shelf life and are more expensive to produce (you have to feed the roosters). By the way, that little blood spot you sometimes find in eggs is not evidence that they're fertile. It's caused by a blood vessel rupturing on the yolk's surface during egg formation. As the laid egg ages, water moves from the white into the yolk, and dilutes away that blood spot. So the presence of the blood spot actually indicates a fresh egg. You can determine whether an egg is fertile or not by looking at the germ spot, which is the white spot on the yolk. A nonfertile germ spot is opaque white. A fertilized germ spot appears as a donut-like ring with a clear center.

Some people think brown eggs are better or more nutritious in some way than white eggs, but it's a myth. Egg shell color is determined strictly by the breed of hen. Araucana chickens, incidentally, produce gorgeous light blue eggs. When crossed with other breeds, they may produce eggs in a variety of light pastel colors.

USES ► You'll find the use of eggs in recipes scattered throughout this book. I will only say, for your own sake, for the sake of the birds who give them to us, for the sake of the organic farmers who are striving to do things correctly, and for the sake of the earth, find a source of organic eggs.

A FINE OMELET

SERVES 1

I learned to make an omelet from the late Julia Child. Not personally—but from one of her television programs. Over the years I've added a fillip here, subtracted a fillip there, but now turn out omelets that my wife says are the best she's ever had. Maybe that's because of Julia, or because I've had a lot of practice, or because I'm being buttered up, but I think it's because I use fresh, organic eggs. When all I have on hand is factory eggs, my omelets tend to be thin and dense, but from organic eggs they're thick and richly flavored.

With omelets, the pan is all-important. Ideally, you need a dedicated omelet pan, one with sloping sides and a slick or nonstick finish so the eggs won't stick. When you wash it, don't scratch it. Treat it gently and it will reward you with excellent omelets.

Omelets should be made quickly—but not too quickly. This is a delicate dish that needs a delicate touch.

2 eggs
1 teaspoon olive oil
2 tablespoons diced yellow onion
1 tablespoon chopped red sweet pepper
1 teaspoon minced garlic
1 tablespoon unsalted butter
1 tablespoon peeled, seeded, chopped fresh tomato
2 tablespoons shredded Gruyère cheese
Freshly ground black pepper

1. Crack the eggs into a shallow bowl and add 1 tablespoon of water. Use a fork to combine the eggs and the water without whipping, beating, or folding. Just swirl the fork, avoiding incorporating any air bubbles into the eggs. They don't need to be homogenized, just well mixed.

2. In a small skillet, heat the olive oil over medium heat, then add the onion, red pepper, and garlic, and cook until the onions are translucent, 3 or 4 minutes. Turn them into a small bowl.

3. Heat an omelet pan on medium-high heat. The pan should be just hot enough that the butter sizzles when added but not turn brown. As soon as the pan is hot, add the butter and let the water in the butter foam and fizz. When it stops, lift the pan off the heat, swirl the butter in the bottom of the pan to coat the bottom. Return the pan to the heat and pour in the egg mixture. Sprinkle on the cheese. Sprinkle on the onion, pepper, and garlic. Sprinkle on the tomato.

4. Work quickly. When the bottom of the egg has set to the edges and the cheese has melted, 1 to 2 minutes, run a spatula under the omelet so it's loose in the pan. Shake it back and forth to insure that it slides. Using two spatulas, fold the omelet into a half-moon. Slip it out of the pan onto a warmed plate. Grind one or two turns of black pepper over the top and serve immediately.

TIP: If you like spicy heat, finely dice a jalapeño, serrano, or—if you dare!—a habanero pepper and add a sprinkle to the omelet along with the tomato. ■

POACHED EGGS

SERVES 1 TO 2

When poaching organic eggs, you'll notice that the thicker viscosity of the whites and greater density of the yolks keep the eggs together much better than conventional eggs whose whites tend to disperse in thin, ragged layers.

2 eggs

Break the eggs into a small bowl, being careful not to break the yolks (using the freshest possible eggs insures this). Bring 3 inches of water to a boil in a skillet, then reduce heat and keep it to a slow simmer before adding eggs. Swirl the poaching water to create a whirlpool well in the center. Hold the bowl close to the water and when the well has formed, slip the eggs into it. Poach the eggs for 4 minutes. Remove them from the water gently with a slotted spoon. Let them drain thoroughly. Place them on warmed plates. You can trim off any strands of white at the edges if you want to improve their looks. ■

HARD-BOILED EGGS

SERVES 1

You'd be surprised how many people don't know how to hard-boil an egg. This method guarantees success, with no breakage, every time. It also prevents overcooking, which can lead to greenish yolks. The fresher the egg, the easier it will be to peel when hard-boiled. Harold McGee, the expert on food chemistry, says the peelability of a hard-boiled egg depends on pH of the egg white, which rises over time, so fresh eggs have a lower pH and peel more easily.

1 egg

Place egg in a saucepan and add water to cover by 1 inch. Turn on the heat and bring to a full boil. Remove the pan from the heat. Cover and let stand for 15 minutes. Cool under running cold water. ■

Malbec Wine Grapes

Kitchen Staples

I N THIS CHAPTER, we take a look at foods that most small farmers and backyard gardeners can't or don't grow or make themselves. Here are the staple ingredients we cook with: stock, coffee, chocolate, flours and meals, oils, wine, and more—all available in organic forms.

Not that long ago it was all but impossible to have this panoply of organic ingredients accessible either from a nearby store or by mail order. Today it's no problem. The next time someone complains about how the world is going to hell in a hand basket, respond that when it comes to eating, we live in the best of times.

Bouillons and Broths

READ THE LABELS carefully when you buy bouillon, bouillon cubes, broths, canned soups, or dry soup mixes. If you're using commercial stock, check those salt levels on the label. Most contain a superabundance of salt, which is a great argument for making your own. I look for "no salt added" stocks when I'm buying commercial stock.

And, unless they are organic, these handy bases could contain substances dubbed "excitotoxins." (see at right). These substances, added to many processed foods, especially to savory flavor enhancers such as bouillon, may cause damage to nerve cells, which would be of particular concern to parents of growing children. Apart from their potential danger to nerve tissue, there a number of other problems linked with many additives to soup mixes. Yeast extract, for example, which is the base for most dry soup mixes, bouillons, and other conventional products, may be made with genetically manipulated starters. Other additives common to these mixes include monosodium glutamate (MSG) and aspartame (NutraSweet).

Some additives can have natural-enough-sounding names, although their makeup is far from natural. If hydrolyzed vegetable protein sounds like it might be allowed in organic products, one only has to look at its manufacturing process to see why it's not. According to Dr. Russell Blaylock, a professor of medicine at the University of Mississippi, this substance is made from junk vegetables that have been deemed unfit for sale. The protein is extracted by hydrolysis, which involves boiling the vegetables in acid; the acid is then neutralized by treating the vegetables with a caustic basic soda. The resulting product, a brown sludge that collects on the top, is scraped off and allowed to dry into a brown powder high in three known excitotoxins: glutamate, aspartame, and cystoic acid. The powder appears in many types of bouillon, as well as food products ranging from canned tuna to baby food.

Will eating excitotoxins hurt you? At the very least, it pays to be educated about what we are eating and feeding our children, to read food labels carefully, and to understand what we are reading. Buying organic products avoids these problems altogether, because they can contain no genetically modified ingredients or chemical additives. Anyone interested in learning more about excitotoxins should read Blaylock's book *Excitotoxins: The Taste That Kills*.

The list below includes a set of highly vague ingredient terms that make frequent appearances on processed food labels. These may be perfectly natural and safe; or they may have been created through questionable processes and contain excitotoxins. There is no way of knowing just from reading the label:

Autolyzed yeast
Calcium caseinate
Enzymes
Glutamate
Hydrolyzed oat flour
Hydrolyzed plant protein
Hydrolyzed protein
Hydrolyzed vegetable protein
Malt extract
Malt flavoring
Monosodium glutamate
Natural beef or chicken flavoring
Natural flavoring
Seasoning
Sodium caseinate
Soy protein concentrate
Soy protein isolate

Spices
Textured protein
Whey protein concentrate
Yeast extract

DEMI-GLACE

MAKES ABOUT 12 CUBES

This all-purpose savory flavor enhancer forms the base for rich soups, stews, and any dish that needs a flavor kick. It is like a dark, stiff jelly, condensed from beef bones and marrow and sometimes flavored with sherry or Madeira. Look for it at an organic supermarket or directly from an organic cattle farmer.

5 pounds beef or veal soup bones
1/4 cup dry sherry or Madeira, optional

1. Preheat the oven to 350°F. Place the bones in a roasting pan and roast for 2 hours or until they are browned darkly, checking periodically and turning them to ensure they don't burn.

2. Place the bones in a large pot with water to cover. Make sure there's plenty of room above the water so it won't boil up and over the sides. Bring to a boil, then lower the heat to medium. Simmer the stock, covered, for 2 hours, being careful the liquid doesn't boil away.

3. After 2 hours, remove the bones and continue gently boiling, uncovered, to reduce. When the liquid is reduced to about 4 cups, transfer to a smaller saucepan and continue to boil. During the boiling, occasionally skim off the scum and fat with a skimmer. Add the sherry at this point, if using, but it's not necessary. Continue to reduce the liquid, lowering the heat as it turns darker and thicker.

4. Eventually it will be just 1 or 2 cups at most and will thickly coat a spoon. Prevent burning by

lowering the heat as it thickens. Pour into ice cube trays and freeze. When frozen, turn the cubes into a freezer bag. They will have the consistency of rubber and be a dark brown. But a tiny bit placed in the mouth will melt invitingly and release a burst of rich, beefy flavor. Seal tightly and store in the freezer. Label the bag with contents and date put up. Keeps in the freezer for 1 year. ▪

VEGETABLE STOCK

MAKES 4 TO 6 CUPS

This vegetarian stock forms the base for soups and vegetable or even meat stews. Since this is a stock and the vegetables will ultimately be discarded, the exact size of the vegetables isn't important.

2 onions, peeled and quartered
1 celery root, trimmed and quartered
4 stalks celery, cut into 3-inch pieces
4 large carrots, cut into chunks
3 medium potatoes, skins on, quartered
1 large tomato, quartered
2 turnips, quartered
1 rutabaga, quartered
1 bunch Italian flat-leaf parsley, tied tightly with string
2 green bell peppers, seeded and quartered
1 head bok choy, quartered
5 cloves garlic, peeled
10 whole black peppercorns

Combine all ingredients in a large pot and cover with water. Cover the pot and bring to a boil over medium-high heat. Boil the vegetables for 2 hours. Strain the liquid, return to the pot, and boil to reduce by half. Place in freezable plastic containers, leaving 3/4-inch headroom for expansion, and freeze. Label containers with contents and date put up. Keeps in the freezer for 1 year. ▪

CHICKEN STOCK

MAKES ABOUT 2 CUPS

This can be made with any poultry—chicken, turkey, duck, goose, or guinea fowl. It's a great way to make use of the leftover carcass of a roasted bird after you've eaten the meat, and the wings, backs, and giblets you've saved from cutting up chickens for other dishes.

Carcass of 1 chicken (or any poultry)
1 large onion, peeled
2 stalks celery
5 to 7 whole peppercorns
1 bunch Italian flat-leaf parsley, tied with string

Place all skin, bones, clinging meat, wing tips, back, neck, and giblets in a large pot with the onion, celery, peppercorns, and parsley, and cover with water. Boil gently for 2 hours. Strain the liquid, return to the pot, and boil to reduce by half. Allow to cool, then refrigerate. When chilled, remove the fat from surface of liquid (save the fat for cooking, especially duck or goose fat for confits) and store the stock in freezable plastic containers. Mark container lids with contents and date put in freezer. Keeps in the freezer for 6 months. ■

Coffee

COFFEA ARABICA and
COFFEA CANEPHORA

COFFEE is the world's most popular beverage—after water—with an estimated 400 billion cups consumed worldwide every year. Over $10 billion in coffee was traded worldwide in 2000—an amount of trade surpassed only by petroleum. I don't know about you, but I start my day with a freshly brewed cup—organic, of course.

THE ORGANIC FACTOR ▸ It's often said that when we buy organic products, we are voting for a clean, environmentally safe agriculture with our dollars. A great example of this is coffee. When we elect to buy organic coffee, we help the impoverished families who grow this beverage in some of the most economically deprived places on earth.

When organically grown within the shade of a rain forest, coffee trees don't need the chemical fertilizers and insecticides required when coffee is grown conventionally as the single crop on sprawling plantations. The reason is that mammals, insects, fungus, and the many other life forms that inhabit the rain forest create a healthy biodiversity that eliminates or keeps pestiferous insects and fungus at bay—the coffee plants are simply part of the ecosystem, and pesticides and other agricultural chemicals aren't necessary.

But there's more. The great diversity of life in the rain forest includes migratory birds that summer in the United States and Canada, and winter in the American tropics. Populations of migratory birds that use the Central and South American rain forests as winter grounds are being seriously depleted by clear-cutting for, among other things, full-sun coffee plantations. This has caused the

National Zoo and Smithsonian Migratory Bird Center to encourage us to drink "bird-friendly coffee," or coffee grown on environmentally sustainable farms.

A healthy, biodiverse ecosystem that includes coffee trees protects not only migratory birds but the entire ecosystem of plants, animals, and even the fertility of the soil and integrity of water supplies. In the tropics, nutrients don't build up in the soil the way they do in cold winter regions. If a leaf falls to the ground, it does fertilize the soil but the tropical vegetation is so dense that, after decomposing, the nutrients are sucked up by plant roots and used to build trees, vines, and other life forms. In a rainforest, nutrients tend to be stored "upstairs" in plant and animal life rather then in the soil. So, when a rain forest is clear-cut, almost all the nutrients stored in its ecosystem are thus removed. If the land is replanted entirely with coffee trees, it becomes a monoculture of one plant species, and nutrients must be supplied in the form of chemical fertilizers. Because the natural enemies of the coffee pests will have been destroyed along with the rain forest canopy, the pests are free to multiply in plantations consisting entirely of their favorite food, and so pesticides need to be applied and reapplied. Because the shading, sheltering canopy has been removed, groundwater supplies dry up. Nutritionless soil with hardly any organic matter becomes exposed to tropical sunlight and laterizes—a soil scientist's term for "turns to stone." When you choose triple certified shade-grown coffee, you're protecting a valuable ecosystem, including the human beings who live in it and from it.

The world coffee market is now being flooded with cheap, inferior coffee grown in such full-sun plantations around the world, especially Vietnam. This coffee drives prices so low that many small coffee farmers receive less than the cost of production for their beans, which drives them off the land. The land may then be bought by corporations that clear-cut in order to plant full-sun coffee plantations. Transfair, a nongovernmental organization that attempts to provide growers with a fair price for their products, (www.transfairusa.org or www.fairtradecoffee.org), attempts to pay enough to keep indigenous coffee farmers on the land so they can grow their coffee under the rain forest canopy. While this helps, too many coffee farmers are seeing their incomes shrink and life becoming untenable. Even during the good years, when crops do well and prices are high, growing coffee provides barely enough income to sustain a family. In bad years, things grow desperate.

More and more organically minded coffee businesses in the United States are trying to help desperately poor coffee farmers. For example, Sustainable Harvest Coffee Importers of Portland, Oregon, works directly with family-owned coffee farms in Central America to insure they can uphold stringent standards to produce premium-quality coffees for which they are paid premium prices. Allegro Coffee Company of Thornton, Colorado, a subsidiary of Whole Foods Market, forges relationships with its growers, assuring them of a fair price, requiring that they use sustainable and traditional coffee growing techniques, and bringing members of coffee co-op farms and family farms to Denver from Guatemala, El Salvador, Mexico, even India, so they can see how their coffees are roasted and marketed. The JBR Coffee Company of San Leandro, California, has developed a program called Source Aid to help organic coffee growers in Central America through the efforts of its green bean buyer, Pete Rogers. (To find out more, visit www.naturefriendly.org.) For more general information on about specialty coffee and some of the important issues today, visit the Specialty Coffee Association of America web site (www.scaa.org). I guarantee that a trip through these web sites will be an eye-opener regarding our daily cup of joe.

WHAT TO LOOK FOR ✦ The highest grade of coffee is *Coffea arabica*, usually called just arabica in stores. It's a bean that thrives in shaded mountain regions. Today the market is being flooded with lower quality robusta (*Coffea canephora*), which comes mostly from Vietnam and Brazil. Don't buy it; in addition to being of poorer quality, it's causing immense social disruption in coffee-growing countries.

Truly good coffee should meet certain requirements. It should be grown at high elevations (mountain grown) and be specialty grade arabica. However, as with wine, you can have an award winning coffee from a plantation one year, and the next year it will be unremarkable. The best bet is to find a company whose product you know, like, and trust as truly organic, shade-grown, and high-grade arabica, and stick with it until you find something even more to your taste. Look for coffees that are certified by all three organizations listed below. With triple-certified coffee, the consumer makes a direct connection with the people and places where the coffee is grown.

These certifications represent a landmark standard for the food industry (or any industry). See Sources, page 523, for a list of companies that sell triple-certified coffees, both by mail and in major retail outlets.

1. **Certified Organically Grown and Processed by QAI.** Quality Assurance International is a worldwide organic certification agency.

2. **Certified Fair Trade by Transfair USA.** Fair Trade helps to support 550,000 of the world's top coffee-growing farms belonging to the Fair Trade co-op. Keep in mind that the average Third World family farmer supporting a family of five lives on the equivalent of $500 to $600 a year! The premium put on organic-certified coffee alone is about 15 cents more per pound. In a market that pays only 30 to 50 cents a pound, that premium will not go very far toward improving farmers' lives. Fair Trade currently guarantees to the farmer a minimum of $1.26 per pound, regardless of the market price.

3. **Certified Shade Grown by the Smithsonian Institution.** Coffee has a symbiotic relationship with canopy trees: Coffee trees do better when grown under a canopy of shade (ideally with 50 to 60 percent shading). While shade-grown coffee is not as productive in terms of the amount of fruit, it ripens more completely, with more nutrients going to each fruit, creating a richer, fuller flavor. There is only one meaningful certification for shade-grown trees, and that is Smithsonian. A Smithsonian certification means that the coffee plantation has been inspected annually for optimal biodiversity. It requires that everyone from farmer to roaster be independently audited. Most shade-grown coffee, however, is broker or roaster certified, using loose standards or no standards at all.

STORAGE AND PREPARATION ✦ Coffee should be stored away from light or in a light barrier bag in a cool dry place (not the refrigerator). It should be frozen only if you are going to store it for longer than a month. Freezing will change the cell structure of the coffee bean (subtly affecting the flavor) and also change the way it grinds. Many coffee grinders have a mechanism to change the grind from coarse to extra fine, allowing you to grind your coffee to the grind recommended for your type of coffee maker. The longer coffee is brewed (steeped), the coarser the grind can be. The more it's a drip or percolator extracted coffee, the more medium to fine the grind can be, depending on how you like your coffee. Espresso machines require a grind about halfway between fine and medium.

TIRAMISÙ

SERVES 6

Good tiramisù (meaning "pick me up") starts with good espresso. If you don't have an espresso machine, buy a half-cup (about four shots) of espresso at a coffee shop, but bring your own ceramic or glass jar or the espresso will taste like cardboard.

$1/2$ cup freshly brewed espresso

$1/2$ cup sugar

2 tablespoons brandy

12 ladyfingers

3 large egg yolks

$1/4$ cup freshly squeezed orange juice

1 cup (8 ounces) mascarpone cheese

1 tablespoon orange liqueur, such as Grand Marnier

1 teaspoon freshly grated orange zest (well scrubbed if not organic)

$1/2$ cup heavy cream

$1/4$ cup grated semisweet chocolate (2 ounces)

1 teaspoon ground cinnamon

1. In a large bowl, combine the espresso, $1/4$ cup of the sugar, and the brandy, and mix well.

2. Grease a 9 × 9–inch glass baking dish. Quickly dip 8 of the ladyfingers in the coffee mixture and lay them in the bottom of the dish. Don't let them soak up too much or they will turn mushy. Reserve the remaining espresso mixture.

3. In the top of a double boiler, whisk the egg yolks until smooth. Add the remaining $1/4$ cup of sugar and the orange juice. Fill the bottom of the double boiler with water (don't let the water touch the top part of the double boiler) and bring to a boil. When it boils, reduce the heat down to simmer. Place the top over the simmering water. Cook, whisking the mixture evenly and lightly, for 4 minutes, until the egg yolks are thickened and light yellow in color. Don't let the yolks curdle. Remove the top of the double boiler from the heat and continue whisking until the mixture is just warm.

4. Beat the mascarpone until it's light and airy and add it to the egg yolk mixture along with the orange liqueur and orange zest, mixing thoroughly. In a separate bowl, whip the cream to soft peaks and gently fold this into the egg-mascarpone-orange mixture until well incorporated. During the last few turns of your rubber spatula, fold in the grated chocolate.

5. Spread two-thirds of this mixture over the ladyfingers in the baking dish, smoothing it flat. Break each of the remaining ladyfingers in half and soak them in the remaining espresso mixture until all the liquid is soaked up. Lay them on top of the baking dish, then cover them with the remaining mascarpone mixture. Place the dish in the refrigerator and chill for at least 2 hours, then dust the top with cinnamon. ▪

Chocolate

SUDDENLY organic chocolate is everywhere. And if you think we've got a good selection here, you should see what they have in the United Kingdom. But what's so good about organic chocolate?

The monoculture setup of conventional chocolate plantations encourages the spread of disease. As with coffee plantations, clearing away swaths of rainforest to grow cacao trees kills off the naturally occurring organisms that fight off pests, fungi, and diseases (which forces the farmers to use chemical pesticides and fungicides in their place). This means that if a disease manages to get a toehold, it has the potential to devastate the entire plantation, which is exactly what happened in South America in the 1990s, when a virulent fungus wiped out whole plantations of cacao trees and the incomes of workers who labored on the plantations.

The way organic chocolate is grown presents a more diversified ecosystem, less prone to epidemics of pathogenic organisms. Jupara, a local nongovernmental organization in Bahia, Brazil, taught the landless workers how to grow cacao in its natural habitat of lowland rainforest, under the canopy of taller trees, using organic techniques. This helps preserve the native canopy trees as well as the livelihood of the workers. The midges—small gnat-like insects—that pollinate cacao require the humid shade of the rainforest with a wide range of plant species and decaying matter on the ground. These insects have no reason to leave their natural habitat and venture into the sunny, dry, cultivated groves of conventional cacao. That's why big cacao plantations have a very low rate of pollination of the tree's flowers. Grown organically in its natural habitat, the pollination rates are much higher. This means more

pods per tree, and therefore fewer trees—and environmental disruption—needed for the same amount of cocoa bean crop.

Naturally grown cacao has over 400 distinct smells (compared to fourteen in roses and seven in onions). Cultivated conventional cacao has only a small percentage of those smells, making it even harder for the pollinating midges to find the flowers. So, what's so great about organic chocolate? Richer flavor expression from beans, and cacao trees grown in ways that protect, not threaten, the fragile tropical ecosystem.

After learning how to enrich the soil naturally and use other nature-friendly practices, the farmers—who now call themselves "agroecologists"—sell their cacao to green markets around the world. The organic cacao, certified by the Brazilian Instituto Biodinamico de Desenvolvimento, brings a price 40 percent higher than conventional chocolate. This kind of success is being repeated in the Caribbean, Central America, and other parts of South America where cacao is grown. On the Caribbean island of Grenada, for example, the Grenada Chocolate Company gained organic certification in 2004. The cacao is grown in the island's tropical rainforest and the chocolate is roasted and ground on site in a solar energy-powered facility.

Once this organic cocoa gets to the manufacturers, it is turned into what we think of as chocolate through a process known as *conching*—a constant sloshing and stirring that triggers an oxidation process that reduces the natural bitterness of cacao beans. Many conventional chocolate manufacturers conch for 3 or 4 hours. The highest quality chocolate makers, by contrast, will conch their chocolate for up to 72 hours, producing an extra silky texture and premium flavor. Instead of white sugar, organic producers will often use organic whole cane sugar, which layers in another subtle flavor of cane syrup.

Soy lecithin is used in conventional chocolate making as an emulsifier, and much soy lecithin comes from genetically modified soybeans. But none of that can be used in organic chocolate. Where soy lecithin is used as an emulsifier in organic chocolate, it must come from soybeans that have not been genetically modified. And organic cocoa isn't treated with potassium carbonate to alkalize it, as is done in the manufacture of Dutch-processed chocolate. The alkalizing makes the chocolate easier to dissolve in liquids, but it does nothing for the flavor.

NUTRITION ◂ Chocolate has some nutritional pluses. Flavonoids that are found in cacao (and the darker and more concentrated the chocolate, the more the flavonoids) have several positive health effects. First, flavonoids are antioxidants that block arterial damage caused by free radicals. Second, cacao flavonoids inhibit platelet aggregations—clumps of blood cells—that can block blood vessels, causing heart attack or stroke. And there are studies that suggest cacao flavonoids relax the blood vessels, which inhibits an enzyme that causes vessel wall inflammation. (The body responds to such inflammation by covering the surface with plaque. Plaque clogs the blood vessels. As its opening shrinks, blockage by blood clots becomes ever more possible.)

WHAT TO LOOK FOR ◂ As with conventional chocolate, organic chocolate ranges in quality from mediocre to excellent. It's a lot like coffee in that it grows best under the canopy of a rainforest (see page 454), so look for chocolate that is certified rainforest grown, fair traded, and organic.

Chocosphere (www.chocosphere.com) is an excellent Internet site devoted to listing sources of organic chocolate from around the world, both for eating and for baking and other culinary uses.

FUDGE

MAKES 1¼ POUNDS OF FUDGE

When I was a small child, my mom and older sister both made fudge. I mean the real stuff—melt-in-your-mouth delicious inside, crusty and shiny on the outside. When I started my own family, I missed fudge, so I tried making it myself. After 30 years of trying, I finally perfected it. Be forewarned: It's a delicate process that depends on good timing. Cook it too little and it will never become fudgey, cook it too long and it will become a hard, gritty mass.

Decide beforehand which child goes first in scraping the saucepan clean. You get to lick the wooden spoon.

2 cups sugar
2 ounces unsweetened chocolate
³/₄ cup whole milk
¹/₈ teaspoon salt
¹/₄ teaspoon cream of tartar
3 tablespoons unsalted butter, plus more for greasing the pan
1 teaspoon vanilla extract

1. In a nonreactive saucepan, place the sugar, chocolate, milk, salt, and cream of tartar, and place over medium heat. Stir gently until the sugar is all dissolved, without splashing ingredients up on the sides of the pan. Reduce the heat to medium-low and cook, stirring occasionally (again without splashing).

2. As it nears the soft ball stage (238°F on a candy thermometer), it will begin to show a quilted appearance. If you don't have a thermometer, take some of the syrup and drip a drop or two into a glass of cold water. If it forms a thread, it's not done. When it forms a soft ball (a slightly flattened ball), immediately remove it from the heat. (Knowing

continued

exactly when to remove it from the heat is the secret to good fudge. All I can tell you is that when the droplet forms a ball that holds its round shape, it's overdone.)

3. Drop the butter into the center of the fudge, but don't stir it in. Let the fudge cool for 5 minutes. During this time, grease a glass pie plate with butter. Add the vanilla to the fudge and beat the butter and vanilla vigorously into the fudge with a wooden spoon until the mass loses its sheen and begins to thicken. Immediately turn it into the prepared pie plate. Cut it into squares before it hardens. ∎

DARK CHOCOLATE–PEANUT BUTTER SAUCE

MAKES 1 1/2 CUPS

Mart Buck ran a soda shop near my high school and his signature topping for ice cream was this chocolate–peanut butter sauce. A generation or two of kids grew up on this delicious stuff. It's best on vanilla.

1 cup dark brown sugar, firmly packed
2/3 cup heavy cream
2 ounces unsweetened chocolate, chopped coarsely
1/2 cup peanut butter
1 1/2 teaspoons vanilla extract
1/8 teaspoon salt

Stir the sugar and cream in a saucepan over medium heat until the sugar dissolves. Add the chocolate and continue to stir until the chocolate melts and the mixture is smooth. Allow it to come to a boil, still over medium heat, and cook for 8 minutes, stirring occasionally to prevent scorching. Remove from the heat, allow it to cool for 2 minutes, then stir in the peanut butter, vanilla, and salt until smooth. Let the sauce cool completely before covering or it will turn grainy. ∎

Dried Fruit

IN TIMES PAST, fruits were dried to the point where they were inedible unless rehydrated by soaking in water. That was so they could last over a long winter. Today most dried fruits retain about 20 percent moisture, so they can be eaten right from the package—or bin, if you buy in bulk. To test a piece of fruit for its proper dryness, cut a piece in half. There should be no moisture visible, and you shouldn't be able to squeeze any moisture from the fruit. It can be pliable, but not sticky or tacky. If a piece is folded in half, it shouldn't stick to itself.

THE ORGANIC FACTOR ◆ Because drying concentrates fruit, including any pesticides it may contain, it's doubly important to use organic dried fruits.

Conventional dried fruit is usually sulfured to retain a light color and retard spoilage. This used to be done by burning sublimed sulfur in a closed space with the fruit intended for drying. Today it's usually a dip in a sodium or potassium metabisulfite solution. Some people have adverse reactions to the sulfites in sulfured fruits; those who suffer from asthma are particularly at risk. Better to avoid the potential problems by buying unsulfured dried fruits. Organic dried fruit is not sulfured. A dip in lemon juice or vitamin C will keep the fruit from darkening too much, although most organic dried fruit is darker than the conventional sorts.

NUTRITION ◆ Drying fruit removes water, which concentrates what remains—the sugar, acids, and nutrients. That sugar may pose a problem, especially for men. The sugar in fruit is fructose, which may raise triglyceride levels in the blood of middle-aged and older men. It doesn't seem to have this effect on women. (Triglycerides are a type of fat, and are they implicated in clogging of the arteries as much as cholesterol.)

So the advice for older men is to limit your intake of dried fruit. Studies have shown that a high dried-fruit diet can raise plasma triglycerides by as much as one-third. That doesn't mean you can never eat a raisin. But it does mean that dried fruit is one of those dietary items to be eaten in moderation, especially if you're overweight.

By the way, check labels for high fructose corn syrup, widely added to sweet snacks such as ice cream and processed snack foods. That fructose raises triglyceride levels, too. And be aware that sucrose—table sugar—is converted in the body into glucose and fructose.

STORAGE ◂ Once you open a package of dried fruit or if you bring it home in bulk, store it in glass jars with tight lids in a cool, dark place. Check from time to time to make sure it hasn't re-absorbed moisture and gone moldy. Discard moldy fruit.

USES ◂ Dried fruits, along with seeds and nuts, are part of a high-energy trail mix. I also like to chop various kinds of dried fruit and slivered almonds into a small handful of bits that I toss into couscous as I make it. Dried apricots are frequently a part of Moroccan tagines. All sorts of dried fruits enliven the flavors of Indian curries. Dried cherries can make a clafoutis come to life and can substitute for raisins in rice pudding or tapioca. Dried cranberries add zing to sweet breads. Fruit leathers are a favorite for kids' lunchboxes.

SWEET-AND-SOUR RAISIN SAUCE

MAKES ABOUT 2 CUPS; SERVES 8

Wherever there's a baked ham, there's a need for this enticing sauce. It's old-fashioned, but then so is Shakespeare.

1 cup dark brown sugar
1 cup raisins
1/2 cup red currant jelly
1/4 cup white wine vinegar
2 tablespoons butter
1 tablespoon freshly squeezed lemon juice
1/4 teaspoon ground cloves
1/4 teaspoon freshly grated nutmeg
Salt and freshly ground black pepper

In a medium saucepan, combine 1/2 cup water and the brown sugar and heat over medium heat, stirring until the sugar dissolves. Add the raisins, jelly, vinegar, butter, lemon juice, cloves, spices, and salt and pepper to taste. Reduce the heat to low and cook, stirring occasionally, for 15 to 20 minutes, until the sauce reduces to about 2 cups. Serve warm with baked ham. Refrigerate the leftover sauce for tomorrow's leftover ham feast. ■

DRIED FRUITS EASILY AVAILABLE

MOST OF THESE dried fruits can be obtained by mail order (see Sources, page 517) and at organic supermarkets in bulk and in packages.

Apples—Toss some in the slow cooker when you're doing pork and sauerkraut.

Apricots—Royal Blenheims are soft and chewy. Westleys are full flavored and chewy. Turkish are good for chopping and adding to North African dishes.

Bananas—Chips are sometimes lightly sweetened and can be part of a high-energy trail mix. Or top your oatmeal with a few.

Blueberries—Usually sweetened, they go in muffins and on cereals.

Cherries—Great for desserts. Rehydrate in fruit juice and top ice cream. You can find dried Bing and Rainier varieties.

Coconut—Available shredded for use in Asian and Indian dishes, as well as many desserts.

Cranberries—Usually sweetened; great for breads, muffins, stuffings.

Currants—These are usually dried, seedless Zante grapes. But they look like currants. Use them in scones, in pancake batter.

Dates—Get Barhi dates if you can find them. Good in North African and Middle Eastern dishes.

Figs—Usually available as dried Mission or lighter-colored Calimyrna varieties. I use the black Missions chopped and mixed with fresh chopped apples and plums to stuff pork loin.

Ginger—Usually crystallized and set out as candy—as the Brits do.

Mango—Rehydrate and chop these delicious morsels, and use them in desserts and in vegetarian curry; use them chopped and dry in chutneys.

Papaya—Use with dried pineapple, coconut, and crushed macadamia nuts to make a Hawaiian snack.

Peaches—Stew them like prunes, or make a peach chutney.

Pears—Make a dried pear and fig compote, or stuff a bird with chopped dried pears, bread crumbs, and crushed hazelnuts.

Persimmons—Use in cookies, scones, cakes, breads, and chutneys.

Pineapple—Chop fine and add to pancake batter; use as base for Tarte Tatin; add chopped to ice cream.

Prunes—You could do worse than the prune-Armagnac confit with glazed pork chops on page 305. Toss some pitted prunes into coq au vin.

Raisins—You can get big, sweet monukkas or biodynamic Thompson seedless, or sultanas. But the best raisins are those you dry yourself in a food dehydrator from fresh, organic seedless grapes. It takes anywhere from 12 to 20 hours, depending on the grape.

Strawberries—Add to your breakfast cereal, to ice cream, to muffins, to anything that needs a sweet light lift.

Flours and Meals

NOT ONLY do organic flours and meals offer the kind of full flavor that comes from grains grown in soils rich in organic matter, but they are often used in whole grain form, which increases their flavor and nutrition even more.

Kathleen Weber, who runs Della Fattoria, one of the best organic bakeries in California's wine country, describes why organic bread is so good:

Commercially grown wheat sends out shallow roots that only absorb the chemical fertilizers given to it. Organic wheat roots have to go deep, where they get what they need to add richness and flavor to the grain. It makes better flour.

Over-processed flours from chemically grown grain are gray, not gold and warm and beautiful like organic flour.

The gold color Kathleen praised comes from an abundance of carotene—the precursor of vitamin A—in the organic wheat. Great taste and great nutrition is the winning combination that careful bakers like Weber achieve by using organic flours and meals.

NUTRITION • Whole-grain flours and meals contain complex carbohydrates that contribute to good health. They comprise bran, the fibrous covering of the grain; the germ, the seed's embryo; and the endosperm, the protein-rich starchy part. Refining removes the bran and the germ, where most of the trace elements and vitamins lie. Most often the endosperm is ground to flour by hammer mills or roller mills that create quite a lot of heat. The heat destroys enzymes and further reduces nutrients. Bleaching to turn the flour white further reduces nutrients. Refining removes 80 percent of wheat's magnesium, 70 to 80 percent of its zinc, nearly 90 percent of its chromium and manganese, and 50 percent of its cobalt—trace elements the body uses to function properly. It also removes most of the thiamine, riboflavin, and niacin, which the government mandates be put back—but is invariably added back chemically.

Organic stone-ground whole-wheat flour, on the other hand, contains all the bran and germ. It is not bleached. The stone milling creates much lower temperatures than the high speed mills, preserving nutrients. There's a great deal of evidence of the benefits of whole-wheat flour. One study, called the Nurses' Health Study, surveyed 65,173 women's diets. Among the results are lower rates of heart disease, less obesity, less diabetes, and healthier digestion and regularity.

WHAT TO LOOK FOR • Some good sources of organic flours are Champlain Valley Mills, Community Mill and Bean, Cooks Natural Products, Giusto's, and Arrowhead Mills, all available on the East Coast; Cooks, Giusto's, and Arrowhead are available on the West Coast. In the center of the country you may be able to find flours from all these sources. If not, check Sources for mail-order suppliers of organic flours (page 522).

STORAGE • Whole-grain flour or meal should be stored in the freezer. It contains the oil-rich germ that can go rancid if left at room temperature. Whether wheat, corn, rice, quinoa, spelt, barley, millet, or any other flour or meal, make it whole-grain as well as organic. That doesn't mean you have to go without your all-purpose flour or pastry flour for making delicate baked goods. But it does mean that for regular consumption, whole grains have such proven and obvious health benefits that it's only smart to use them as much as possible.

AN UNADDRESSED PROBLEM WITH GRAINS AND FLOUR

IT MAY BE A GOOD IDEA to slice your bread and store it in the freezer. Baked goods, especially moist breads such as cakes, pastries, and cornbread, turn moldy if allowed to sit out for more than a few days. In fact, the mold is growing in the bread before it becomes visible to the naked eye. Freezing bread delays the growth of mold, and frozen slices or portions can be quickly thawed in the toaster or a warm oven—but not the microwave. Microwaving bread turns it gummy.

Is a little bread mold a problem? Wasn't penicillin derived from bread mold?

As it turns out, mold on wheat, corn, and other food grains—and on subsequent products made from their flours and meals—may be a huge problem, or it may not be, because the problem is unaddressed. Yes, penicillin is derived from a certain species of bread mold, but it's just one of an array of molds and funguses that produce substances called mycotoxins—that is, toxic compounds produced by fungus or mold. Think of the toxic—even lethal —effects of poisonous mushrooms, which are also caused by mycotoxins.

In a study published in the *Canadian Journal of Physiology and Pharmacology*, researchers at the University of Manitoba wrote:

Ochratoxin A (OA) is a mycotoxin produced by certain species of storage fungi of the Penicillium and Aspergillus genera.... OA has been shown to occur in various grains, cereals, animal feeds, meats, and human tissues in countries throughout the world.... OA is acutely toxic to many different animals (including human beings) and in addition to being a nephrotoxin (toxic to the kidneys), it is a hepatotoxin (toxic to the liver), a teratogen (causes birth defects), a very potent carcinogen (potent cancer causing agent), possibly a mutagen (causes mutations) and an immunosuppressive agent.

OA is rapidly absorbed throughout the entire gastrointestinal tract.... It would appear that this compound presents a true potential hazard for humans as its occurrence is widespread and it is highly carcinogenic.

OA is some nasty, nasty stuff. The mean dietary intake of OA in countries of the European Union was 1 to 2 nanograms of OA per kilogram of body weight per day. But "the estimated tolerable daily intake in humans ranges from .2 to 4.2 nanograms of OA per kilogram of body weight," according to the Bureau of Chemical Safety, Health and Welfare Canada, in Ottawa.

The Institute of Health at the University of Science in Rome collected samples of milk

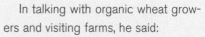

from four lactating Italian mothers and samples of their food for a week. "The obtained results," the Institute's concluding report said, "revealed a significant exposure of sucklings and mothers to OA levels higher than the tolerable daily intake as estimated from animal models.

"On the basis of these data, a major effort in planning surveillance and research programs to control OA contamination in food, feed, and biological fluids should be pursued."

OA is just one type of mycotoxin, albeit one produced by 18 different species of fungus. Aflatoxin is another highly carcinogenic mycotoxin that is found on grains, corn, and peanuts, among other foodstuffs. And there are many others. Most of them are not destroyed by processing grains into flour, nor by the heat of baking.

I called Brendan McEntee, owner of Cooks Natural Products, an organic flour supplier in San Francisco, and asked him if the grain used to make his flours is tested for the presence of mycotoxins, or if his flour is tested. "Organic grains are tested the same as conventional grains," he said. "When the grain is delivered from a farmer to the grain elevator, the receiving agent takes a sample and checks it by sight, feel, and smell and tests it

for percentage of protein—but detailed toxicology? No."

In talking with organic wheat growers and visiting farms, he said:

Organic growers are aware that fungal contamination can ruin their crop, and so they traditionally install aerators to keep the grain dry. And when we get our grain, it's from a specific farmer at a specific protein test weight, and we keep these lots separate, moving them by blowing the grain through the mill. So when a customer orders flour at a certain protein percentage from a certain cultivar, or even grown by a specific farmer, we can give it to him. But we don't have occasion to test for mycotoxins.

This traceability at least is reassuring, knowing that should an outbreak of mycotoxicosis occur in organic flour, the product can be traced back to a specific mill, grain elevator, and farm, and the problem area pinpointed. Nothing like this happens with conventional grain, where everything tends to get mixed together.

What's not reassuring is that no testing is done for mycotoxins such as OA or aflatoxin in our food supply, whether conventional or organic. Support for this testing needs to be encouraged.

USES ► When baking bread, look for organic flour ground from whole wheatberries—that way you get the maximum nutritional content. When I bake bread, I use some whole-wheat and some all-purpose organic flour, which produces a lighter loaf than if the dough is entirely whole wheat; the proportions depend on the kind of loaf I'm after. For a light loaf, I use perhaps a 7:1 ratio of all-purpose to whole-wheat flours; for a whole-wheat loaf, a ratio of 5:2 makes an acceptable loaf. And I usually toss in a little rye flour for the flavor—but rye doesn't have the gluten needed for a good rise, so I use it sparingly.

Some folks allow the naturally occurring yeast and bacteria in the air to colonize a mixture of rye flour and water, creating what's often called a sourdough culture. Depending on where you live, these starter cultures (a more accurate term) might indeed be sour, but they also might yield bread that's tangy, tart, vinegary, milky, mellow, or complex. In the San Francisco Bay Area, naturally occurring bacteria called *Lactobacillus sanfrancisco* and yeast called *Candida milleri* work together to produce a starter culture with a strong sour taste that really can't be duplicated in other regions of the country where these microorganisms don't exist together.

Wherever bread is baked, however, the loaves that the French call *pain levain*—made with an indigenous starter culture—have something of the taste of the place they are made, along with the quality of the flour they're made from. That's why organic breads are so superb. From the wheat fields through the milling process to the bakery with its homegrown starter culture, someone cares deeply enough about the product and the customer to add quality at every step. That gives this kind of bread *terroir*—the term for the idea that the product has the signature taste of the place it's from.

WHOLE-WHEAT AND BLACK WALNUT QUICK ROLLS

MAKES 6 ROLLS

These little rolls are quick and delicious. Warm from the oven, they make an ordinary dinner into something special.

1 cup chopped black walnuts (see page 340),
    or regular walnuts
2 cups whole-wheat flour
1 cup all-purpose flour
1/4 cup dark brown sugar, packed
1 teaspoon baking soda
1/2 teaspoon salt
4 tablespoons (1/2 stick) unsalted butter, chilled
1 cup chilled buttermilk
1 large egg
2 tablespoons maple syrup

1. Preheat the oven to 375°F. Lightly toast the walnuts in the oven until just aromatic. Lightly flour a 10 × 15-inch baking sheet.

2. In a large bowl, stir together the flours, brown sugar, baking soda, and salt. Using two knives, cut the butter into the dry ingredients until it's reduced to small bits and the mixture resembles coarse meal. Add the walnuts and mix to incorporate.

3. In a separate bowl, whisk together the buttermilk, egg, and maple syrup until well blended. Gradually add the wet ingredients to the dry, stirring until a dough forms and everything is well incorporated.

4. Lightly flour a board and turn the dough onto it. Knead the dough for 1 minute, giving it a quarter turn after every push. Cut the dough into 6 equal pieces and form each into a ball. Space them on the baking sheet and flatten each into a 3-inch round. Using a sharp blade, cut an X into the top of each round. Bake them for about 30 minutes, until golden brown and a toothpick inserted into the center of one comes out clean. Let them cool on a rack until just warm. ∎

CORNBREAD MUFFINS

MAKES 12 MUFFINS

Who doesn't relish a basket of fresh, hot cornbread muffins? You should let them cool a bit, but serve them warm enough that the butter in the bread is still liquid.

1 cup finely ground corn meal
3/4 cup all-purpose flour
1 tablespoon baking powder
1/2 teaspoon salt
6 tablespoons unsalted butter, chilled
2 large eggs
1 cup whole milk
1 tablespoon honey
1 1/2 teaspoons blackstrap molasses

1. Preheat the oven to 350°F. Grease 12 muffin cups.

2. In a large bowl, mix together the corn meal, flour, baking powder, and salt. Using 2 knives, cut in the butter until the mixture resembles coarse meal.

3. In a separate bowl, whisk together the eggs, milk, honey, and molasses until blended. Add the wet ingredients and stir until well blended.

4. Add equal amounts of the batter to each muffin mold and bake for 10 minutes, or until a toothpick inserted in the center of one comes out clean. Let cool for 5 minutes then remove from muffin tin, wrap in a clean kitchen towel in a basket, and serve. ∎

Cooking Oils and Fats

DESPITE the low-fat, no-fat craze that persists in our culture, judicious amounts of the right kind of fats are health promoting.

Toss out your polyunsaturated fats such as safflower oil and corn oil. And especially avoid any products that contain hydrogenated or partially hydrogenated vegetable oils—the notorious trans-fatty acids—such as margarine and vegetable shortening. Stick with monounsaturated fats such as extra-virgin olive oil for low-heat cooking or cold use; almond oil, canola oil, and peanut oil for high-heat cooking, such as frying.

Beyond this, finding a good source of organic oils for culinary use is essential for several reasons:

1. Many mass-produced cooking oils such as canola, soy, corn, and cottonseed are from plants that have been genetically engineered to resist damage by herbicides or to incorporate the gene that expresses the toxin produced by *Bacillus thuringiensis*—a self-defeating practice described on page 46. Cottonseed, especially, unless organic, is from plants given heavy doses of pesticides.
2. Sewage sludge containing heavy metals may have been used on the fields where the conventional oil-producing crops were grown and been taken up by the plants. Or, if the fields were fertilized with chemical fertilizers, they may be depleted of trace minerals and organic matter, which can affect the quality of the oil-producing crops grown on them.
3. Agricultural chemicals such as pesticides have a tendency to accumulate in plant fats and so may be concentrated in the resulting oils. (The chemicals also accumulate in fatty tissues in our bodies, female breast tissue, for instance.)

4. Bulk oils are usually extracted by a process that utilizes hexane, a petroleum by-product and nervous system toxin. While the hexane evaporates at the end of the extraction process and is said to be completely gone from the oil it extracts, it poses a risk to workers. And while the FDA vouches for the safety of chemically extracted oils, their assurances are not reassuring to everyone.

All these worries are void if I buy organic, cold-pressed, sinolea knife extracted (see page 471), or expeller pressed oil. It's not hard to find organic oils these days. Spectrum Naturals, the nation's largest supplier of a variety of organic culinary oils, reports that its business is growing about 25 percent a year, and grossed about $50 million in 2004.

NUTRITION ► Olive, canola, peanut, sesame, almond, and avocado oils have more than 50 percent monounsaturated fat—the kind that helps lower bad cholesterol.

Canola, corn, safflower, sunflower, walnut, sesame, hemp seed, and soy oils are rich in polyunsaturated fats that contain the important Omega-3 and Omega-6 essential fatty acids, necessary for proper growth in children and the maintenance of cardiovascular health, brain and visual function, and cell replacement in adults. But there's a catch.

Recent studies suggest that the *ratio* of Omega-6 to Omega-3 fatty acids may be the most important factor to consider in oils regarding their health benefits, such as lowering the risk of cardiovascular disease, lowering blood pressure, preventing irregular heartbeats, and promoting cardiovascular health. For example, if your intake of Omega-6 fats is too high, it competes with the Omega-3 fats and prevents them from doing their beneficial work, which may lead to an Omega-3 deficiency. For a healthy balance, it is recom-

mended that the ratio of Omega-6 to Omega-3 in the diet should be 3 or 4 parts Omega-6 to 1 part Omega-3. The typical Western diet has a ratio estimated at 20:1.

The following table shows the ratios of Omega-6 to Omega-3 in various vegetable oils.

OIL RATIO (OMEGA-6 TO OMEGA-3)

Canola	3:1
Corn	8:0
Flaxseed	2:7
Hemp seed	3:1
Olive	1:0
Peanut	4:0
Safflower	8:0
Sesame	6:0
Soy	7:1
Sunflower	8:0
Walnut	5:1
Wheat germ	7:1

Source: Spectrum Naturals

Unfortunately, corn, safflower, walnut, sesame, soy, and sunflower oils, while they are rich sources of Omega-6, don't have much Omega-3, if they have any at all.

FISH OIL ► Fish such as cod, sardines, anchovies, mackerel, and salmon are excellent sources of Omega-3, and if you choose to use a lot of Omega-6–rich oils in your cooking or on your salads, you might want to consider fish oil for Omega-3 supplementation. That's why mom made sure you got your cod liver oil. In the old days, you got your daily dose from a spoon. Today fish oil supplements are sold in convenient gel capsules.

FLAXSEED OIL ◆ Flaxseed oil is especially good because of its greater amounts of Omega-3 than Omega-6, which will balance some of the excess Omega-6 we get in our Western diet. It should not be heated, however, but rather used cold as you would use any unheated oil—on salads, as a dip, in homemade mayonnaise, in smoothies, shakes, or straight up.

CANOLA OIL ◆ Some folks are leery of canola oil because they may have heard it contains erucic acid, which studies show causes heart lesions in lab animals. It's an old finding. Canadians began a series of hybridizations of the rape plant—the source of canola oil—after World War II that led to varieties with less than two percent erucic acid. Today's canola (for Canadian oil) has acceptable levels of erucic acid.

OLIVE OIL ◆ There's no denying the benefits of extra-virgin olive oil. The essential fatty acid in olive oil is Omega-9, so consuming olive oil won't upset the balance of Omega-6 and Omega-3 in the rest of your diet. Omega-9 fatty acids are important monounsaturated fats and one of the chief reasons why the olive oil–rich Mediterranean diet contributes so splendidly to cardiovascular health. Olive oil has been proven to lower bad cholesterol and raise good cholesterol, and it has more antioxidants than any other oil.

At the store, you'll find many olive oils labeled extra-virgin. Why "extra?" Because there is a classification called simply "virgin olive oil," although it's rarely seen on the market. Virgin oil can contain up to 3.3 percent acidity, which means the oil is becoming rancid. (As olive oil turns rancid, its acidity goes up.) Extra-virgin means low acidity, which in turn means that the oil is fresh. Most extra-virgin oils state a percentage of acidity on the label. By law it must be less than 1 percent, and is usually less than ½ a percent. To be labeled extra-virgin, the oil also has to score at least 6.5 out of a possible nine quality points by the International Olive Oil Council Tasting Panel in Madrid for European oil, or by the recently formed California Olive Oil Council Tasting Panel for California oil. The oil must show no defects such as mustiness. It also means the oil hasn't been messed with. No additives, no heat treatments to get extra oil from the pulp.

If you're looking for the highest quality olive oil, first make sure it's organic, then that it's labeled extra-virgin. Another thing to look for is an oil with a fruity, peppery, almost bitter flavor. When olives are picked green, they are intensely fruity and peppery—though maybe a bit throat-gripping for most Americans. Those peppery, aggressive oils have the most antioxidants—polyphenols and tocopherols—that help keep bad cholesterol from clogging the arteries.

According to *Science News* for April 15, 2000, biochemist Hiroshi Maeda of Kumamoto University School of Medicine in Japan and his colleagues surveyed a range of cooking oils and discovered that "unprocessed olive oils were especially effective in scavenging the free radicals" and "quashing their destructive abilities."

Olive oil that has reached its smoke point loses flavor, loses nutrition, loses many of its health benefits, and can transition into trans-fatty acids.

Here's a quick rundown of some other health benefits of extra-virgin olive oil.

- The monounsaturated fat in olive oil may help lower LDL (bad) cholesterol while raising levels of HDL cholesterol (the good kind).
- Eat more fat, lose more weight! Studies have shown that a diet containing a moderate

CHOOSE THE RIGHT OIL FOR KITCHEN USE

WHEN OIL USED FOR FRYING or sautéing gives off smoke, it not only emits an acrid smell, but healthy fats in the oil can be transformed into unhealthy trans fats. In addition, free radicals form that can oxidize cholesterol in the blood to create artery-clogging plaque. Discard any oil that has reached its smoking point. Use this table to determine which oil is the best to use for your purposes.

HIGH HEAT OILS

For high heat applications such as frying and sautéing.

OIL	SMOKING POINT (°F)
Avocado	510
Almond	495
Apricot kernel	495
Sesame	445

MEDIUM-HIGH HEAT OILS

For lower-heat sautéing and baking.

OIL	SMOKING POINT (°F)
Canola	425
Grapeseed	425
Walnut	400
Coconut	365
Soy	360
Peanut	355

MEDIUM HEAT OILS

Full flavored, unrefined oils for sauces and salad dressings, and for medium heat sautéing where the oil's flavor is integral to the dish.

OIL	SMOKING POINT (°F)
Sesame, unrefined	350
Toasted sesame	350
Olive, extra-virgin	325
Corn, unrefined	320
Coconut, unrefined	280

NO HEAT OILS

Unrefined oils with a robust flavor and a fragile structure for use on a finished dish or blended into a dressing or sauce without heating.

OIL	SMOKING POINT (°F)
Borage	225
Flaxseed	225
Wheat germ	225
Evening Primrose	225

Courtesy of Spectrum Organic Products, Inc.

amount of olive oil is as effective as a very low-fat diet in promoting weight loss over a six-month period. On top of that, an olive oil diet is easier to stick with after the weight is gone.

- Swigs of olive oil help curb hunger pangs: According to Thomas Jefferson University Medical College professor and endocrinologist Marshall Goldberg, taking two teaspoons of extra-virgin olive oil 20 to 30 minutes before a meal helps people feel full and eat less. He also found that taking olive oil can help people who've just quit smoking manage the hunger attacks that often come with giving up nicotine.
- Olive oil appears to have a protective effect against cancer of the colon and rectum.
- Olive oil preserves a youthful skin. Australian researchers have found that a diet rich in olive oil, fish, and vegetables was associated with less skin wrinkling due to sun damage, and a diet high in butter, margarine, and sugar was associated with more skin wrinkling. The study appeared in the February, 2001, issue of the *Journal of the American College of Nutrition*.
- Olive oil may help fight off infections. Certain immune functions have displayed increased activity in people who eat a diet rich in olive oil, according to the report published in the January 1998 issue of the *American Journal of Clinical Nutrition*.

Some olive oils are labeled first cold press, but the term is meaningless today. Years ago, oil was actually pressed, and the first pressing yielded the best oil. Today most oil—at least oil made in quantity—is separated from the pulp using centrifuges, or the sinolea knife process in which metal blades are dipped into the pulp; oil clings to the metal and is then collected.

Extra-virgin olive oil should be stored at a cool temperature in a dark cupboard or closet. Storing it in the fridge makes it start to solidify and actually hastens rancidity. When it's taken out and warms up, moisture in the air condenses inside the bottle, the fatty acids in the oil separate, and it starts turning rancid. Unopened in proper storage, extra-virgin oil will stay fresh for from 18 to 24 months because of its antioxidants. Once opened, oil will last from six weeks to two or three months, depending on storage conditions. For a list of good organic olive oils to look for, see Sources (page 517).

BUTTER SUBSTITUTES AND SHORTENINGS ◆ Use saturated fats such as butter in moderation. Such conflicting claims about butter and margarine leave people understandably confused about which fats to eat and which to avoid. I agree with Dr. Joan Gussow, the well-known nutritionist, who, when asked about butter versus margarine, said, "I trust cows more than chemists." For some purposes, such as making a flaky piecrust, butter is essential. And it sure tastes better than any margarine. Use organic butter when possible, because the cows will not have been given antibiotics or growth hormones. Pesticides used on conventional dairy farms concentrate in fatty tissues of cows and in the butterfat in their milk, so using organic butter helps to avoid the danger of ingesting them.

When using a solid fat is necessary for culinary reasons, those trying to keep saturated fat to a minimum or who do not eat dairy products have a wide range of organic nondairy butter substitutes to choose from. Here's what you should look for:

Certified organic. The package will have the USDA Organic seal.

Non-GMO. Because it's organic, it will contain no oils from genetically modified plants.

Nonhydrogenated. A hydrogenated fat such as regular margarine will contain harmful trans fats created when hydrogen is bubbled through liquid oil to render it semisolid at room temperature.

At least 80 percent fat content. This makes the product good for cooking and baking as well as spreading. One tablespoon of spread (one serving) is 11 grams. Nine of those grams should be from fats. A lower percentage of fat means that too much water or filler has been added, which will affect your baked goods.

Balanced fats. Check the ratio of fats: The spread should have approximately a third each of saturated fat, polyunsaturated fat, and monounsaturated fat.

Oil content. You'll usually find a mix of palm, soybean, canola, and olive oils, plus soybean powder and lecithin.

There is also a new kind of organic margarine (such as Earth Balance) that remains firm at room temperature yet claims to contain no hydrogenated or trans fats. Instead, what gives this margarine its soft but solid consistency is palm fruit oil, which is also called just palm oil. It is a semi-solid, nonhydrogenated oil. Note that this is different from palm kernel oil or coconut oil, both of which are significantly higher in saturated fat. Palm fruit oil is used worldwide as a cooking oil. Studies on human health have shown that it helps reduce LDL (bad) and increase HDL (good) cholesterol and its antioxidants scavenge free radicals that can cause a number of diseases.

USES ◆ Generally in baking, a liquid oil will render a different taste and texture than a solid fat. A good rule of thumb is to substitute a solid fat for another solid fat—say, butter for vegetable shortening (which is a hydrogenated fat and should be avoided), and a liquid oil for another liquid oil, such as olive oil for corn oil.

Lard is 100 percent fat, rendered from hogs. There are many sources of organic lard, easily found through an Internet search. Look out for leaf lard—it's the internal fat lining a pig's stomach and kidneys and is said to make the most tender, flakiest pastries. It's not usually sold in markets, but you might be able to buy some from a butcher, or contact an organic pig farmer.

Sweeteners

MY TAKE on sweeteners is that we should use them sparingly, and the most natural ones take preference over the refined sorts. I long ago swore off soft drinks, although I do think longingly of a cold Coke on a hot day—and occasionally indulge. I've found that a container of unsweetened tea brewed from green tea and mint tea in the fridge is completely thirst quenching after work in the garden, or to sip while working or relaxing.

Here are the eight kinds of organic sweeteners, a list of their benefits, and suggestions for how I use them.

Honey. Since it's the product of bees, honey is a natural substance, if not organic. Look for raw, unprocessed honey, which will contain all the enzymes, pollen, and other nutrients that the bees gave it. As a liquid, honey dissolves more readily in cold drinks than granulated sugar. Some people mix honey, lemon juice, and cider vinegar in water as a cold remedy. In baking, honey adds its flavor to breads, cakes, and pastries and keeps them moist. Figure that honey has about 35 percent more sweetening power than an equivalent quantity of granulated sugar.

Maple Syrup is our regular sweetener. I use it in my morning coffee, on breakfast cereals, on pancakes, French toast, and waffles, and anywhere the sweetener doesn't have to be in hard, crystal form. Some people prefer Grade B because it is the darkest and most strongly maple-flavored. We prefer the lighter Grade A Medium or Grade A Fancy because we don't want everything tasting like maple. About 250 years ago when sugar from the Caribbean was a scarce commodity in New England and maple syrup was the sweetener of necessity, the lighter grades were most prized for the same reason.

Molasses is what's left over from sugar cane juice when the white sugar is refined out. It's high in iron and other minerals. Organic molasses will have been produced without the use of chemicals and will be unsulphured.

Stevia Rebaudiana and Stevioside. This sweet herb of Paraguay is used extremely sparingly because of its intense sweetening power and odd flavor. It has few calories and can be used by diabetics because it's not a sugar. The dried leaves are 10 times sweeter than sugar, while extracts made from it called steviosides are 300 times sweeter. You can find it in the vitamin departments of natural and organic food stores. You can also grow it in your backyard unless you live in the very coldest zones.

Sucanat is a brand name for organically grown sugar cane juice that has been dried so it contains all the natural substances in the juice. There are no additives. Brown sugar contains half a percent of naturally occurring mineral salts, while Sucanat (a contraction of SUgar- CAne NATural) contains 3 percent mineral salts, including calcium, iron, magnesium, zinc, copper, and chromium. It has traces of B vitamins. It can be substituted for refined white sugar, or light or dark brown sugars, on a 1:1 basis.

White, Dark, and Confectioners' Sugar. Whether refined or unrefiined, all sugar can be organic, meaning it comes from organically grown sugar cane and no synthetic chemicals are used in its processing. Even the popular Domino brand of sugar sells an organic version these days.

SUGARLESS VANILLA ICE CREAM

MAKES 1 QUART

Yes, there's butterfat in this ice cream but no sugar. You could substitute good organic, additive-free yogurt for the half-and-half, but it will have slight tanginess—perfect with fresh berries and a drizzle of maple syrup or sweet fruit sauce.

1 cup whole milk
1 vanilla bean, sliced open lengthwise
1/2 teaspoon stevioside (see page 473)
3 cups half-and-half
1 1/2 teaspoon vanilla extract
Pinch of salt

1. Place the milk in a saucepan. Scrape the inside of the vanilla bean halves with the back of a knife and add the scrapings to the milk, then add the bean halves.

2. Heat the milk to just shy of boiling, and when it's hot, add the stevioside and stir until dissolved. Remove from heat, add the half-and-half, vanilla extract, and salt, and let cool. Remove the bean halves but not the scrapings. Freeze according to your ice cream maker's instructions. ∎

Wine

And much as wine has played the infidel,
And robb'd me of my robe of honor—well,
I wonder often what the vintners buy
One half so precious as the stuff they sell.

The Rubaiyat OF OMAR KHAYYAM

WINE completes a meal. It is the finishing touch for everyday dinners and essential for special occasions. If the wine is particularly good and properly aged, it can steal the show.

But must it be organic?

Behind that question lies a story. Years ago, some producers who were more focused on the political implications of organic wines than the sensuous aspects of the beverage itself made some pretty poor wines with the word "organic" loudly displayed on the label. Organic wine became synonymous with mediocrity. Meanwhile, many fine wineries wanted their grapes grown organically because they knew that a biologically active soil would produce better tasting grapes; they didn't want themselves and their vineyard workers exposed to harmful chemicals; and they wanted to preserve the purity of the beautiful country where fine wine grapes flourished. But they didn't want to put "organic" on their label, because that would hurt sales.

Do you like Frog's Leap Zinfandel? It's organically grown. Kenwood Cabernet? Organically grown. Phelps, Lolonis, Fetzer, Bonterra, Coturri, Niebaum-Coppola, ZD wines, Morgan—all organically grown. And the list goes on and on. But you wouldn't necessarily know it from their labels.

That reluctance to use the word "organic" may finally be changing. The demand for organic wine has resulted in a boom in organic viticulture in California, where total organic acreage has zoomed from 178 acres in 1989 to approximately 15,000 fifteen years later. It's becoming easier and easier to find organic and organically grown wines in supermarkets.

One of the world's largest wineries is Boisset of France, with sales of $330 million in 2003 and exports to eighty countries. Bill Arbios, one of Boisset's winemakers, says, "Around the world, Boisset has numerous ventures and they are taking all of their projects biodynamic or organic. It is all predicated on maximizing quality in the vineyard rather than in the winery, when it's too late" to do much to improve the quality of the grapes.

Biodynamic agriculture follows theories laid down by Rudolf Steiner, founder of the Waldorf School system, in the 1920s. His metaphysical approach involves connecting agriculture to a higher, spiritual wisdom through the preparation of certain soil- and plant-enhancing natural sprays, the use of auspicious and inauspicious days for farm activities, and the degree of understanding of life processes exhibited by the farmer. Although it sounds fetishistic to some, biodynamics can show good results, and satisfy a longing in many individuals for a deeper connection to the earth. All biodynamic farms are organic.

Many top wineries worldwide are increasingly using organic or biodynamic techniques in the vineyards.

THE ORGANIC FACTOR ◂ Grapevines are sturdy plants that don't need to be drenched in chemicals to perform their task. With wine grapes, soils shouldn't be too rich or too moist or the plant will respond with big berries. Since almost all the flavor components of wine are in the skins, small berries mean a higher ratio of skin to juice—and consequently more flavor in the wine. Small berries result when vines are forced to struggle for water and nutrients. A little compost, a meager sip of water from irrigation lines—that's about all they get. If mildew threatens early in the year when rains are occurring, organic culture allows vineyardists to spray with naturally occurring sulfur.

Insects are dealt with organically, which means without lethal pesticides. Rows are planted with clover and other cover crops that harbor beneficial insects as they add nutrients to the soil. Gophers and other rodents are kept down by owl and raptor boxes placed about the vineyards. Bats are encouraged by the placement of bat houses and these creatures help keep mosquitoes and other insects under control. All the pressed skins and seeds are composted and returned to the soil, creating a closed system that promotes the establishment of a site-specific mix of microorganisms in the soil and in the air. This in turn promotes terroir—the term for the unique flavor of a specific place that emerges in wine and other food products produced from that place.

Many wineries that are not certified organic practice a form of sustainable grape growing that is organic in just about everything but name. The Mondavi winery is one of them. "We've learned over the years," Tim Mondavi, Robert's son, told me, "that every time we had a choice between a repressive technology (such as the use of pesticides) or an inspired technology (such as the use of cover crops to help establish beneficial insects that control pests naturally), the inspired technology proved to be a better method. It addresses the fundamental vineyard and winemaking problems and not just the symptoms. Technology should help you look into life, to see how and why it works as it does, not to just slaughter it."

WHAT TO LOOK FOR ◂ Stores like Whole Foods have a special section just for organic wines. But snooping around a regular wine shop for "organic wines" can be confusing. Here's how to tell what's what.

An American wine labeled "organically grown" or "made from organically grown grapes" means that the vineyards have been handled in accordance with the National Organic Program administered by the USDA and additionally in accordance with the organic certifying agency of the state in which they were grown. Such wines may have sulfur dioxide added to preserve the wine.

"Organically grown" wines include Lolonis and the Bonterra label from Fetzer, which produces close to 100,000 cases per year through a full range of *Vitis vinifera* varieties. New York State has Silver Thread Vineyards, Four Chimneys, and Swedish Hill. In Oregon, there are Amity, Archery Summit, Brick House, Cameron, Cattrall Brothers, Cooper Mountain, and St. Innocent. And in Washington State, China Bend. And more organic vineyards and wineries are coming on line all the time.

Wines from France and other countries labeled "organic" or "organically grown" are probably what they purport to be, and the name of a certifying agency, such as Eco-Cert or other bodies affiliated with the International Federation of Organic Agriculture Movements (IFOAM), may sometimes be found on the labels. But many long-time organic producers, either through tradition or obstinacy, do not get certification.

If wines are labeled "transitional," that means that the vineyards are handled organically, but the necessary three years since conventional culture ceased have not yet passed.

Wines labeled "organic wine" means the fruit is certified organic and no sulfites have been added.

Biodynamic farms must meet not only the USDA and state certification standards but also be certified by the Demeter organization, an internationally recognized certification agency for biodynamic agriculture.

Wines labeled "no sulfites added" are not necessarily free of sulfites. The fermentation process creates sulfites in small amounts. What's more, the daily process of digestion in the human body produces about the same amount of sulfites as can be found in 100 bottles of wine, according to wine consultants at Motto, Kryla & Fischer. White wines contain about twice the sulfites of reds, although in almost all cases less than 80 parts per million of sulfur dioxide. So, if you're sensitive to red wines, it's probably not the sulfites that are causing the reaction. European winemakers, especially the French, tend to use significantly more sulfites in their wine than American producers.

At least eight wineries in California and Washington produce what most would consider "organic wine," that is, made with certified fruit and no added sulfites. These labels are Frey, H. Coturri & Sons, La Rocca Vineyards, Orleans Hill, Nevada County, Wine Guild, Organic Wine Works, and Badger Mountain.

See Sources, page 517, for a list of resources for organic wines (and beer, too).

COQ AU VIN

SERVES 4

This dish is easy to make and wonderfully delicious. I've tried it with several kinds of red wine and with whites, and I prefer it made with a good bottle of pinot noir. Ideally it should be served with the same wine used in the pot.

2 slices thick-cut bacon (4 ounces)

1 (3¹/₂ pound) chicken, cut into 8 pieces

1 medium onion, diced

¹/₂ carrot, peeled and diced

3 tablespoons all-purpose flour

Salt and fresh ground black pepper

3 cups pinot noir

1 frozen "ice cube" (or 2 teaspoons) Demi-Glace
    (see page 453), optional

1 cup chicken stock

2 tablespoons tomato paste

¹/₂ pound sliced mushrooms

2 bay leaves

¹/₂ teaspoon dried thyme

¹/₂ teaspoon dried oregano

1. In a large Dutch oven over medium heat, fry the bacon until most of its fat has been rendered.

Remove the strips and reserve. Add the chicken pieces and brown them on both sides, about 4 minutes on a side. Remove the chicken to a plate and reserve.

2. Pour off most of the fat and add the onions and carrots and cook, stirring occasionally, until the carrots are tender, about 10 minutes. Stir in the flour and the salt and pepper to taste. Reduce the heat to low and stir until the mixture turns light brown, about 5 minutes (do not allow to burn).

3. Add the wine (the mixture will bubble up), whisking constantly until combined, then add the demi-glace, chicken stock, tomato paste, mushrooms, bay leaves, thyme, and oregano, and stir thoroughly. Bring up the heat to medium, stirring well, until the mixture boils. Add the chicken and bacon back to the pot and let the liquid return to a boil, then reduce heat to low, cover, and simmer for 30 minutes until the chicken is cooked through to the deepest bone. Preheat the oven to 200°F.

4. Remove the chicken and bacon to a platter and put in the warm oven. Bring the sauce to a full boil and reduce it until it's syrupy, stirring constantly, 5 to 8 minutes. Pour the sauce over the chicken and serve. ▪

Sweet Peppers

Top Varieties
of Organic Produce

ONE OF THE JOYS of buying or growing organic produce is being able to try new varieties and experience the huge range of flavors and textures in something as simple as an apple or a potato. (For more discussion on varieties, see Variety Name Makes a Difference, page 6.) Below are hundreds of my favorite varieties of vegetables and fruits. While many of these are grown predominantly by small-scale organic farmers and sold from the farm or at farmers' markets, more and more varieties are appearing in supermarkets every year. Even if their names seem unfamiliar, many of these may be varieties you've seen before—you just didn't know what they were called.

If you don't see produce labeled by variety at your market, ask whoever is selling them to label by variety name. The more we start requesting foods by their variety name, the more these labels will start turning up.

Indicates photo in insert, throughout listings.

Vegetables

ARTICHOKE

An earthy, nutty flavor, sweetness, and meatiness are all pluses in a globe artichoke. The green, heady, aromatic quality of good organic chokes leaves the mouth and breath feeling fresh and stimulated. Most of the prized, distinctly flavored European varieties have a purplish cast, or at least combine burgundy and green colors on their globes.

KISS OF BURGUNDY—Considered by some the best-tasting full-sized artichoke. Entering commerce in California. A two-tone burgundy and green choke.

PURPLE DE JESI—Produces lots of small heads of fine quality. Reddish-purple in color. Sweet enough to be eaten raw if sliced thin.

PURPLE ROMANESCO—Greenish violet and spineless, makes many small buds on lower nodes of this herbaceous perennial. Excellent for marinating.

PURPLE SICILIAN—A spineless artichoke that makes buds with a dark purplish color and a refreshing flavor.

➤ **GREEN GLOBE, GREEN GLOBE IMPROVED, DESERT GLOBE, BIG HEART, AND IMPERIAL STAR**—Examples of standard market varieties.

VIOLETTA DI CHIOGGIA—More conical than globe shaped, and another of the flavorful Italian varieties.

ARUGULA

You're most likely to find true arugula at the farmers market or store, but keep watch for the wild types if you like a seriously peppery leaf for cooking. Pepperiness is only one of the qualities of this leafy green. It has a succulent texture and an earthy, musky flavor that puts an appealing bottom note under the brighter, crisper, sweeter flavors of its salad companions like lettuce and endive. Arugula responds to rich organic soil by expressing more of its earthy quality.

ASTRO—A cultivated variety of true arugula with a mild, nutty flavor, and leaves that aren't as toothed as the common form.

GREEK—Another selection of true arugula, this one from Greece. It has a spicy, nutty flavor.

TURKISH ARUGULA—Very slender, deeply toothed leaves with a strong peppery characteristic.

WILD ARUGULA—Usually one or another species of *diplotaxis*, more peppery than "regular arugula," with more slender and deeply cut leaves. Also found as *selvatica arugula*, *rucola selvatica*, or *sylvetta*.

ASIAN VEGETABLES

It's very possible that the Asian merchants who stock these vegetables in their markets will have their own variant names for them, so it may be hard to identify some. Remember that flowering bok choy types have yellow flowers while Chinese kale has white flowers (well, there is a yellow-flowered Chinese kale, but it's relatively rare).

American-type mustard greens, hybrids made in the United States with names like Florida Broadleaf, Southern Giant Curled, and Magma can often be found at farmers' markets in the southeast United States.

BOK CHOY

➤ **CHINESE FLAT CABBAGE**—A foot-round rosette of tatsoi leaves.

➤ **MEI QING CHOY**—A baby bok choy with thick base; very tender and sweet.

MING CHOI—Tall leaf stems are tender and succulent; mild cabbage flavor.

TSOI SUM—Aka Flowering White Cabbage, whole plant great for stir-fry.

VITAMIN GREEN—Leaves only three or four inches long, stems juicy.

CHINESE CABBAGE

NAPA TYPE

➤ **BURPEE'S TWO SEASONS**—Finely textured leaves and tangy flavor.

NERVA—Thick, juicy leaves; good for kim chee.

ORANGE QUEEN—Has a nutritious, orange heart, sweet flavor.

MICHIHLI TYPE

GREEN ROCKET—Hybrid with tight head and sweet cabbage flavor.

MICHIHLI—Dark green leaves with white midribs, fine mild flavor.

CHINESE KALE

➤ **ASPARATION**—A cross with broccoli, very fine flavored.

BLUE STAR—A popular variety with white flowers, crisp flesh.

GREEN DELIGHT—Tender leaves and stems, late spring type.

CHINESE SPINACH

FOTE TE—A leafy amaranth originally from Africa; fine herby flavor.

PERFECTA—Narrow leaves of red, yellow, green are eaten raw.

RED STRIPE—Big oval leaves carry red pattern; tangy flavor.

MUSTARD GREENS

FLORIDA BROADLEAF—Popular in the South as a potherb.

MAGMA—Peppery, savoy-type leaves that are purple on top.

RED BROAD-LEAF MUSTARD—Purplish red, very pungent leaves.

RED GIANT—Often sold when leaves are just 5 to 6 inches, for salads.

SOUTHERN GIANT CURLED—Big leaves for stews, small ones for salads.

ASPARAGUS

There aren't a great many varieties of this vegetable on the market, but some new developments are very promising.

APOLLO, ATLAS, AND GRANDE—Three cultivated varieties that have just entered commerce have been bred for superior quality and large spear size.

ASPARAGUS ACUTIFOLIUS—Wild asparagus native to the Mediterranean region that has escaped and naturalized in the United States. Sometimes found at farmers' markets.

JERSEY KNIGHT AND JERSEY GIANT—These varieties are red for natural disease resistance and may therefore be the choice of many organic market gardeners.

➤ **MARTHA, MARY, AND WALTHAM WASHINGTON**—The Washington strains are usually the standard asparagus sold around the country. They are fine-flavored variety, familiar to all. All three are resistant to asparagus rust, making them another good choice for organic growers.

PURPLE PASSION—The spears have a purplish cast to them given by their Italian heritage and the flavor is sweet and rich. They're extra juicy and virtually fiber free. Steaming them lightly will preserve most of the appealing color.

AVOCADO

While Florida avocados of the West Indian race have a mildly fruity flavor and a juicy rather than buttery texture, Mexican-Guatemalan hybrids are all smooth as butter. The flavor is mildly nutty and rather bland, which is why avocado needs that jolt of lemon or lime juice.

MEXICAN-GUATEMALAN HYBRIDS

FUERTE—Green skin dotted yellow, found January to June in most markets.

➤ **HASS**—Small, almost black, pebbled skin; high-quality flesh, buttery.

SHARWIL—From Australia, pear-shaped, high-quality flesh.

MEXICAN RACE

GOTTFRIED—Pear-shaped fruits with 13 percent oil, excellent flavor.

MEXICOLA—Small fruits. Black skin, creamy texture, and good flavor.

WEST INDIAN RACE

POLLOCK—Large, pear-shaped fruit, low in oil, but superior quality.

RUSSELL—A long-necked variety often planted in home gardens in Florida.

TRAPP—An excellent variety that originated in Miami.

GUATEMALAN RACE

EDRANOL—Pear-shaped, olive-green skin, with a nutty flavor.

LYON—Rough, bright green skin with yellow dots and high-quality flesh.

NABAL—The smooth, high-quality flesh is green near the skin.

REED—Flesh cream-colored with rich, faintly nutty flavor.

SHARPLESS—Flesh of superior texture and flavor. A winter fruit.

GUATEMALAN-WEST INDIAN HYBRIDS

COLLINSON—Large, elliptical fruits have excellent flavor.

FUCHS-20—Large, elliptical fruits have yellow speckles, excellent flavor.

BEET

BULLS BLOOD—The beet root is good, but it's the purplish, red-bronze leaves that are the star of this show.

BURPEE'S GOLDEN—Sometimes found at markets as simply Golden. A rich orange-gold-yellow color and a mild sweet flavor.

CHIOGGIA—An Italian heirloom variety with alternating white and ruby rings; mild flavor that livens up when cooked.

DETROIT DARK RED—My personal favorite for a red beet, when young. Stays tender until it reaches baseball size, then tends to toughen up.

EARLY WONDER—A fast-maturing beet often found at farmers markets, grown by farmers who want to be first on the scene with the new season's beets. But it's exquisitely flavored nevertheless.

FORMANOVA—These beets are about 8 inches long and 2 inches in diameter. They make lots of same-size slices as you cut down the cylinder. Best used for pickled beets.

LITTLE BALL—A gourmet beet for its sweetness, tender texture, and small size.

LUTZ GREENLEAF—If you find Lutz at the market, you can be sure that the beet will be tender through and through, even if it's the size of a football.

PRONTO—A beet that stays small and tender, hence one of the best for baby beets.

RED ACE—A very sugary Detroit Dark Red type beet, great for roasting, canning, pickling.

RUBY QUEEN—This dark red beet won an All-America Selections award in 1957 and it has justifiably become a standard variety for red beets.

BROCCOLI

If you have a chance to "talk broccoli" with a grower at a farmers' market or want to grow your own, these are some varieties to look for. However, broccoli feeds so heavily from the soil that its quality and flavor tend to be more affected by the soil and other growing conditions than by the variety. All well-grown, fresh broccoli will be wonderful.

DECICCO—An old variety that has stayed in commerce because of its rich flavor and all-around high quality.

EARLY PURPLE CAPE—Aka Purple Sicilian, this is an excellent variety with a sweet, mild flavor. The purple color disappears during cooking.

GREEN COMET—A standard market broccoli, winner of an All-America Selections award.

GREEN VALIANT—Sweetness and tenderness are the hallmarks of this standard market variety.

PREMIUM CROP—Another All-America Selections winner. Fine flavor and tenderness.

PURPLE SPROUTING—Another specialty broccoli with a purple color and high-quality flavor.

SMALL MIRACLE—A diminutive broccoli that grows only 1 foot or so tall and produces tender, sweet, 6-inch heads—just the right amount for one person.

UMPQUA—A top-quality variety developed for the cool, coastal regions of the Pacific Northwest. Likely to be found at farmers markets there and in northern California.

BRUSSELS SPROUT

The best sprouts are tender but not mushy, sweet rather than herbaceous or vegetal; they can have a nutty note and taste mildly of cabbage rather than having a heavy, sulfurous cabbage flavor. They should never be leathery or tough. Here are some that fit this bill.

ENERGY—Earthy, nutty, luscious, tiny sprouts ½ to ¾ inches in diameter.

FALSTAFF—Droplet-shaped sprouts the color of red cabbage.

IGOR—A certified organic hybrid for gardeners.

JADE CROSS—The standard brussels sprout, blue-green color, large size.

LONG ISLAND IMPROVED—Tender and sweet if between ¾ and 1½ inches.

PEER GYNT—Another Dutch variety, dark green, 1-inch sprouts.

PRINCE MARVEL—Grown primarily for the fresh market; high quality.

RUBINE RED—Purple sprouts retain color when cooked.

VALIANT—A Dutch introduction of mild flavor, cylindrical heads.

CABBAGE

GREEN TYPES

DARKRI—Small, sweet heads are often the right size for meals.

EARLY FLAT DUTCH—Mild flavor makes it one of the best for sauerkraut.

EARLY JERSEY WAKEFIELD—Highest-quality summer crop, conical heads.

GOLDEN ACRE—Gray-green leaves cover tightly wrapped heads.

STONEHEAD—Tight, firm heads with extra-high quality.

VERY EARLY PARIS MARKET—19th-century heirloom noted for sweet flavor.

RED TYPES

LASSO RED—Small, compact heads excellent raw in salads.

RUBY BALL—Reddish purple head, All-America Selections winner in 1972.

SAVOY TYPES

LISBOA SAVOY—Produces 6-inch heads with excellent buttery-sweet flavor.

SAVOY ACE—Finely savoyed leaves with a sweet, delicate flavor.

SAVOY KING—A large version of Savoy Ace with darker green color.

CARDOON

You would think that with a vegetable as rarely seen as the cardoon, there wouldn't be a great many varieties in commerce, but there are about a dozen. These are considered the finest.

GIGANTE D'INGEGNOLI—An Italian fall variety found on the East Coast.

GIGANTE DI ROMAGNA—Italian variety found in specialty markets in December.

LARGE SMOOTH—Extra-thick, meaty stalks; plant grows 6 feet tall.

PLEIN BLANC INERME—A small French variety with spineless stalks.

CARROT

Carrots, like many others of the umbelliferae group (dill, fennel, parsley, celery, celery root, parsnips, chervil—any plant that has an umbrella-like seedhead), are highly aromatic, a trait that is preserved through even intense cooking.

LONG TAPERED (7 TO 10 INCHES)

DANVERS—Full-flavored, rich orange color.

GOLD PAK 28—An All-America Selections winner for taste and texture.

IMPERATOR—Standard supermarket carrot; much better when very fresh.

MEDIUM LONG (5 TO 6 INCHES)

NANTES HALF LONG—One of the finest-flavored carrots available.

SCARLET NANTES—A Nantes type with a reddish orange color.

TOUCHON—A French type of Nantes; exquisite taste, texture.

YELLOW CARROT

YELLOWSTONE—Mild flavor; makes contrast with richer types.

RED CARROT

ROTHILD—High in beta-carotene, with good flavor and red color.

BABY OR GOURMET CARROTS

AMSTERDAM FORCING—A purple carrot with a succulent flavor.

KUNDULUS—A standard for baby carrots that still have full flavor.

PARMEX—A spherical carrot the size of a golf ball with good flavor.

ELEVATED VITAMIN A

A-PLUS—Two and a half times the beta-carotene of ordinary carrots.

BETA-SWEET—A release from the Texas Vegetable Improvement Center with 40 percent more beta-carotene than ordinary carrots, a maroon color from cancer-preventing anthocyanins, high sugar content to attract children, and an improved texture.

CAULIFLOWER

Many of the varieties of cauliflower grown by organic farmers are weather tolerant and disease resistant. Fortunately for us cooks and folks who eat the crop, these are also fine-tasting varieties, with a clean, creamy, nutty flavor and just a light hint of cabbage-family herbaceousness.

CANDID CHARM—Exceptionally delicate flavor and texture. Good fresh market cauliflower.

MARMALADE—Creamy orange, high beta-carotene head with fine flavor.

➤ ROMANESCO—Beautiful, whorled heads have nutty, sweet, delicate flavor.

➤ SELF-BLANCHE—A snowball type whose leaves curl up over the head.

➤ SNOW CROWN—Another All-America Selections winner with exceptionally delicate flavor.

SNOW KING—An All-America Selections winner; large heads of pure white curd.

SNOWBALL—A late cauliflower good in November and December.

CELERY

GIANT PASCAL—Standard fall celery; requires no blanching.

GOLDEN-SELF-BLANCHING—An excellent market garden variety with a rich celery flavor.

MATADOR—Disease resistance makes it popular with organic growers.

TALL UTAH 52-70—Tender texture, high quality; large, self-blanching heads.

TENDERCRISP—Favorite on the East Coast.

➤ VICTORIA—A vigorous hybrid celery with mild flavor and lots of crunch.

CELERY ROOT

ALABASTER—Produces large, mildly sweet, aromatic roots.

DIAMANT—Great celery flavor and a reliably high-quality root.

DOLVI—Excellent herby flavor and fine texture; one of the best varieties.

➤ LARGE SMOOTH PRAGUE—Widely grown and a standard of quality.

MARBLE BALL—A market garden favorite for its ease of growth, fine flavor.

MENTOR—Becomes sweeter after a few frosts.

PRESIDENT—A modern innovation for its large size and fine texture.

SNOW WHITE—As the name implies, a pure white, fine-textured root.

CHARD

ARGENTATA—Italian heirloom with wide, white stems, yellow-green leaves.

➤ BRIGHT LIGHTS—A rainbow of colored stems plus top quality tangy flavor.

CHARLOTTE—Scarlet midribs, reddish-green leaves, very sweet flavor.

FORDHOOK GIANT—A standard for top yields and tangy flavor.

LUCULLUS—White midribs, bright green leaves, and gourmet-quality taste.

MONSTRUOSO—Large chard, grown for its extra wide stems.

PAROS—Bred in France for mild, sweet flavor; savoyed-type leaves.

VIRGO—Another strain of chard bred for its wide leaf stems.

CHICORY AND ENDIVE

BROAD-LEAVED ESCAROLE TYPE
(*CICHORIUM ENDIVIA*)

BATAVIAN FULL HEART ESCAROLE—Broad, twisted, creamy-yellow leaves.

GROSSE BOUCLEE—Hard-to-find, choice French variety of escarole.

CURLY-LEAVED FRISÉE TYPE
(*CICHORIUM ENDIVIA*)

GALIA—Slender, finely-cut leaves with white midribs.

PANCALIERE—Very fine frisée with pinkish midribs.

RUFFEC—A green, bitter frisée often used as a garnish.

BELGIAN ENDIVE OR WITLOOF TYPE
(*CICHORIMUM INTYBUS*)

MONROE—Red leaves and pale yellow midribs.

➤ **RED**—Red Belgian endive with superb flavor.

WITLOOF IMPROVED—Produces 5- to 6-inch chicons; good for braising.

ZOOM—Growers like it because it needs no sand for forcing.

HEADING CHICORY TYPE
(*CICHORIMUM INTYBUS*)

CRYSTAL HAT—Similar in appearance to romaine; sweet flavor.

SUGARLOAF—Forms self-blanched, crisp, sweet, tender heart.

LOOSE-LEAF CHICORY TYPE
(*CICHORIMUM INTYBUS*)

DENTARELLA (*ITALICO ROSSO*)—Red-stemmed dandelion-like leaves in spring.

PUNTARELLA—The stems (puntarelle) are used in a salad.

SWEET TRIESTE (*BIONDISSIMA DI TRIESTE*)—Small green heads in winter.

RADICCHIO; ROUND HEAD TYPE
(*CICHORIMUM INTYBUS*)

INDIGO—A new variety; fine bittersweet flavor; red and white heads.

➤ **ROSSO DI VERONA**—Traditional round-headed, red and white type.

VARIEGATA CHIOGGIA—Speckled leaves form tight ball-like heads.

RADICCHIO; LOOSE HEAD TYPE
(*CICHORIMUM INTYBUS*)

EARLY TREVISO—Like a small romaine with deep red leaves, white veins.

VARIEGATA CASTELFRANCO—Inner leaves speckled red and yellow-white.

CORN

Thousands of corn varieties are cultivated around the world. The best corn mixes sweetness with rich, buttery corn flavors in about equal proportions.

Colors of the following corn are indicated thus: white (W), yellow (Y), bi-color (BC), ornamental (O).

STANDARD SUGARY TYPES (SU)

GOLDEN CROSS BANTAM (Y)—Small but flavorful ears with rich corn taste.

HONEY AND CREAM (BC)—Buttery flavor; often seen at roadside stands.

SILVER QUEEN (W)—Very common at farmers markets; good corn flavor.

SUGARY-ENHANCED TYPES (SE)

AMBROSIA (BC)—Very tender, holds sweetness two weeks after picking.

HOW SWEET IT IS (W)—All-America Selections winner, very tender.

INCREDIBLE (Y)—Honey sweet, with rich corn flavor. Seek this one out.

SILVERADO (W)—One of the best white, sugary-enhanced varieties.

SUGAR BUNS—Tender, retains sweetness for two weeks.

XTRA SWEET (SH2)

EARLY XTRA SWEET (Y)—All-America Selections winner for superior flavor, sweetness.

HONEY & PEARL (BC)—Superior in tenderness, flavor, sweetness.

INDIAN SUMMER (O)—All-America Selections winner; yellow, white, red, purple kernels.

➤ SUPERSWEET JUBILEE (Y)—Like popular Jubilee, but with super sweetness.

SWEET BREED™

These varieties, with all-white kernels, include standard sugary, sugary-enhanced, and extra sweet kernels on each ear. Varieties include Sweet Chorus, Sweet Ice, Sweet Rhythm, Sweet Riser, and Sweet Symphony.

TRIPLE SWEET

HONEY SELECT (Y)—All-America Selections winner in 2001 with sweet honeyed corn flavor.

OPEN-POLLINATED AND HEIRLOOM

COUNTRY GENTLEMAN (W)—Long a favorite late summer corn for roasting.

GOLDEN BANTAM (Y)—Sweet, tender, with rich corn flavor.

LUTHER HILL (W)—A roadside stand favorite in New Jersey, where corn is king.

STOWELL'S EVERGREEN (W)—Old-fashioned shoepeg corn, originated in 1848.

TRUE GOLD (Y)—Large, fat ears with golden kernels of superior flavor.

CUCUMBER

The following varieties are noted for their refreshingly vegetal, almost floral flavor, and their fine texture.

SLICING

BURPLESS—Doesn't need peeling; crisp.

MARKETMORE 70—An American heirloom variety; dark green skin.

SWEET SUCCESS—All-America Selections winner; sweet, mild flesh.

➤ SWEET SLICE—Very sweet flavor and thin, easy-to-eat skin.

PICKLING

ANKA—Popular German variety. Small seeds, sweet crunchy flesh.

COUNTY FAIR 83—Fruits seedless if kept away from other cukes with male blossoms.

HOMEMADE PICKLES—Crisp and crunchy flesh is extra high quality.

LIBERTY HYBRID—All-America Selections winner; juicy, with black spines.

PICKLEBUSH—High quality; can be grown at home in a container.

CORNICHONS

COOL BREEZE—Fruits picked at 2-inch lengths for French-style pickles.

VERT PETIT DE PARIS—Dense French variety still widely grown in France.

MIDDLE EASTERN

AMIRA—Look for slender, 4- to 5-inch fruits; refreshing flavor, fine texture.

KIDMA—Tender, nonbitter, sweet-fleshed variety can be eaten as a snack.

ASIAN

ORIENT EXPRESS—Used in sushi for crisp texture and rich flavor.

PALACE KING—Thin skin, fine flavor, 12-inch fruits only 1 inch in diameter.

EUROPEAN GREENHOUSE

➤ HOLLAND—Very high quality; standard "hothouse" variety from Holland.

PETITA—Shorter than other hothouse types but with same high quality.

EGGPLANT

BLACK-PURPLE

BABY BELL—Golf ball–sized fruits with glossy black skins.

DUSKY—Has firm, fine-textured flesh, earthy flavor.

KURUME LONG—Long, slender, purple-black eggplant is standard of quality in Japan.

PINGTUNG LONG IMPROVED—Popular in Chinese markets; excellent flavor.

VIOLETTA LUNGA—Popular in Provence; fine old cultivar.

PINK-LAVENDER (ITALIAN)

NEON—Bulbous, rich pink fruits with few seeds. Popular in Caribbean.

ROSA BIANCO—Premium quality, fine-textured, pretty eggplant.

VIOLETTA DI FIRENZE—Lavender striped with white; good for stuffing.

WHITE

CASPER—Ivory skin; 3 by 6 inches long; pure white, earthy flesh.

ITALIAN WHITE—Fruits round, 3 or 4 inches wide; mild, sweet taste.

SNOWY—Cylindrical 7-inch fruits with glossy white skin, firm texture.

GREEN

LOUISIANA LONG GREEN—Yields fruits 3 by 8 inches long, pale green, fine mild taste.

THAI LONG GREEN—Slender, foot-long heirloom; mild flavor.

FENNEL

Because it's a relatively new crop in America, there aren't a lot of varieties in agriculture. Most farmers simply plant the species. There is one superior variety called Zefa Fino that's mentioned by Shepherd Ogden in his seed catalog, *The Cook's Garden*. "The Zefa Fino is a cultivar," Ogden says. "It's the best in most university and European trials, and by far the highest yielding and most bolt resistant. The results were just head and shoulders above everything else." While fennel is a perennial, it's easily grown like an annual in most parts of the country.

GARLIC

SOFT-NECK TYPE

CALIFORNIA EARLY—White-skinned type first on the market in early summer.

CALIFORNIA LATE—Similar to Early; standard through much of the country.

CREOLE—A red-skinned type grown in the South, especially Louisiana.

SUSANVILLE—Large bulbs of good garlicky flavor, grown in western United States.

HARD-NECK TYPE

CARPATHIAN—Good all-purpose garlic from Poland and Eastern Europe.

ITALIAN PURPLE—Small, firm bulbs with a strong, spicy flavor and bite.

SPANISH ROJA—A large-bulbed, brown-skinned garlic of gourmet quality.

GARLIC-TYPE BULBS

ELEPHANT GARLIC (*ALLIUM AMPELOPRASUM*)—A super-large bulb with a mild garlic flavor, and can be cooked and eaten as a vegetable.

GARLIC CHIVES (*ALLIUM TUBEROSUM*)—Makes a fine ornamental but is culinarily useful, too—they're flat-leaved chives with a mild garlic flavor. Mince them and sprinkle on omelets and scrambled eggs. (See Chives, page 387.)

RAMPS (*ALLIUM URSINUM*)—Gathered wild in the spring in the Midwest and eastern United States and imparts a strong garlic flavor to dishes. This plant also grows in Europe, where it's known as *ramsons*. (See Chives, page 387.)

ROCAMBOLE (*ALLIUM OPHIOSCORODON*)—Looks more like a leek than garlic but has a distinct garlic flavor. It resembles the wild garlic from which our modern type descended.

SOCIETY GARLIC (*TULBAGHIA VIOLACEA*)—Unrelated to true garlic and is grown as an ornamental in mild winter areas. The flowers and leaves have a strong garlic odor when cut or crushed. If used to flavor salads, a very little goes a very long way.

GREEN BEAN

Slender filet beans are probably the best flavored and have the meatiest texture, even though they are smaller than regular snap beans.

BUSH SNAP BEANS

- **BLUE LAKE**—A standard of solid quality, with a fresh, green flavor.

REGAL SALAD—Curved, bronzy pods with smooth texture, superior flavor.

- **ROMANO**—Flat-podded; rich, unique flavor; for frenching.

POLE SNAP BEANS

BLUE LAKE STRINGLESS—Free of fiber, with a sweet, green-bean flavor.

KENTUCKY BLUE—Combines flavors of Blue Lake and Kentucky Wonder.

- **SCARLET RUNNER**—Red flowers for decorating salads; stringy but tasty pods.

SUNSET RUNNER—Flowers are salmon-pink, beans mild in flavor.

BUSH FILET BEANS (HARICOTS VERT)

- **FIN DE BAGNOLS**—Slender French bean with rich, bean flavor.

FINAUD—High-quality taste and texture; developed in Holland.

MASAI—Very slender filet bean; rich, herby flavor.

TRIOMPHE DE FARCY—Long and very slender; meaty; rich in flavor.

POLE FILET BEANS (HARICOTS VERT)

EMERITE—Fiberless, grows to 7 inches long, with a rich, sweet flavor.

FORTEX—Completely stringless, best at 7 inches long or less.

BUSH WAX BEANS

DRAGON TONGUE—Long, light yellow flat pod streaked with purple-red.

GOLD CROP—Fiberless yellow-gold pods, 6 inches long, mild flavor.

ROC D'OR—Slender, bright yellow pods with excellent flavor and texture.

POLE WAX BEAN

- **KENTUCKY WONDER WAX**—Tall-growing variety is a standard of wax bean quality.

YELLOW ANNELINO—Slender, pale yellow, crescent-shaped pods. Heirloom.

SHELL BEANS

BORLOTTO—Italian bean, classic in *pasta e fagioli, fagioli in brodo*.

CANNELLINI—White kidney-type bean for hearty soups and stews.

FLAGEOLET—Quintessential French bean for cassoulets. Superior flavor.

FRENCH HORTICULTURAL BEAN—Seeds, pods speckled red; beany flavor.

KWINTUS—Eat flat pods or shell fresh beans, tender, flavorful.

LOW'S CHAMPION—Large oval seeds with smooth texture, fine flavor.

FAVA BEAN

VICIA FABA OR FABA VULGARIS—The common fava or broad bean, used so many ways around the world.

APROVECHO SELECT—A particularly great variety.

SOY BEAN

GLYCINE MAX—Used around the world for fresh beans, dried beans, tofu, soybean paste, tempeh, soy milk, and a hundred and one other uses.

LIMA BEANS (*PHASEOLUS LUNATUS*)

(See Lima Bean varieties, page 490.)

KALE

KONSERVA—High-quality, hardy Danish strain.

LACINIATO—Very dark, blue-green Italian heirloom; very fine flavor. Good for long cooking. Also known as dinosaur kale and Tuscan Black.

- **REDBOR**—Finely curled leaves, deep red-purple color, and top flavor.

RED RUSSIAN—This is *Brassica napus* variety *pabularia*, a very pretty species with red stems and a fine, mild flavor.

SALAD SAVOY—Better as ornamental than for food; use as garnish.

VATES DWARF BLUE CURLED—Finely curled little leaves with fine flavor.

WINTERBOR—Hardiest kale with finely curled blue-green leaves. Sweet.

KOHLRABI

It's a good bet you'll at least run into Early White and Early Purple Viennas, but hopefully organic farmers will be planting more of the large-globed types in the future.

EARLY PURPLE VIENNA—Deep rose-purple skin; gets woody larger than 3 inches.

➤ **EARLY WHITE VIENNA**—Green skin and high-quality flesh; best at 2 to 3 inches.

GIGANTE—Grows to 8 to 10 inches and stays crisp and nonwoody. Rare in the United States.

GRAND DUKE—An All-America Selections winner that is still tender at 4 inches diameter.

KOLIBRI—Flattened dark purple globes of superior flavor; best at 3 inches.

SUPERSCHMELZ—Grows to a nonwoody 6 to 10 inches with mild, sweet flavor.

LEEK

BLEU DE SOLAISE—Fine French heirloom with violet shading on stalk.

➤ **ELECTRA**—Thick stems, delicate flavor; French import for market gardeners.

GIANT MUSSELBURGH—Thick stems, fine flavor; favored by organic growers.

KING ALFRED—Variety with extra-long stems, often to 12 inches of the white part.

KURRAT—Middle Eastern species of leek with narrow, edible leaves.

LARGE AMERICAN FLAG—Thick-stemmed, often found at farmers markets.

TITAN—Thin-stemmed, usually grown for summer markets.

VARNA—Stays slender so often sold as "baby leeks" in summer.

LETTUCE

BUTTERHEAD

BIBB—Small rosettes of paddle-shaped leaves of delicate flavor.

BUTTER KING—Excellent texture, taste in an easy-to-grow plant.

➤ **BUTTERCRUNCH**—Creamy yellow centers, buttery texture, superb flavor.

LIMESTONE—Miniature heads of crispy butterhead lettuce; each serves one.

MERVEILLE DES QUATRE SAISONS—Creamy center and red tips; excellent.

RED PERELLA—An heirloom Italian red butterhead; gourmet quality.

TOM THUMB—A true miniature butterhead to 3 inches across.

BATAVIAN

NEVADA—Improved Sierra with all-green leaves; very sweet and crisp.

SIERRA—Standard market garden cultivar has a slight red tinge to leaves.

CRISPHEAD

GREAT LAKES—Winner of All-America Selections; best of iceberg types.

LOOSELEAF

BLACK-SEEDED SIMPSON—Old variety with still-unequalled flavor.

FORELLENSCHLUSS—Speckled variety with delicate texture, mild flavor.

RED OAK LEAF—Much like the old oak-leaf lettuce, but with red tips.

RED SAILS—Another All-America Selections winner with curvy leaves, delicate flavor.

RED SALAD BOWL—Oak leaf–type leaves with red tips.

ROYAL OAK LEAF—Improved green oak leaf–type; delicate, delicious.

RUBY—Frilly leaves have red coloring at tips.

SALAD BOWL—All-America Selections winner; standard of quality for looseleaf lettuces.

ROMAINE

PARRIS ISLAND—Standard market variety romaine of fine quality.

ROUGE D'HIVER—Deep red leaves and loose, open habit.

◆ **VERTE MARAICHERE**—Crisp green romaine with top flavor profile.

LIMA BEAN

BUSH LIMAS

BABY FORDHOOK—Small beans of delicate flavor; often grown for freezing.

DIXIE WHITE BUTTERPEA—A favorite in hot-weather areas of the Deep South.

FORDHOOK 242—All-America Selections winner, tender and buttery.

HENDERSON—Cream-white seeds have delicate flavor; an old standard.

JACKSON WONDER—Calico-speckled bean favored in the South.

KING OF THE GARDEN—A bush butterbean that sets the standard for quality.

POLE LIMAS

BURPEE'S BEST—A favorite with market gardeners; high quality.

CHRISTMAS—Large creamy seeds with red splotches taste like chestnuts.

FLORIDA BUTTERBEAN—Does well in Florida; grown for fresh market.

KING OF THE GARDEN—Same excellent quality in a climbing version.

MÂCHE

COQUILLE—A pretty, diminutive rosette of fine-flavored leaves.

GALA—The most widely grown variety in France; cold-tolerant.

◆ **VERT D'CAMBRAI**—Popular variety with a strong, herbal flavor.

VIT—"Baby mâche" stays small and crisp, with a mild, fresh taste.

MUSHROOM

This is not a guide to finding or identifying wild mushrooms but rather an indication of what you might find at a farmers' market at certain times of the year. If you are going to pick wild mushrooms, you need a thorough field guide and preferably a mushroom expert to educate you.

MUSHROOMS FOUND ON THE FOREST FLOOR

BLACK TRUMPET (*CRATERELLUS CORNICOPIOIDES* OR *CRATELLERUS FALLAX*)—One of my favorite wildings. I'd find them in pine and hardwood forests in the East, but they grow across North America. They are black to grayish black, carry a delightful fruity aroma, have a satisfying, chewy texture, and are best slow cooked with lamb shank or pot roast.

CANDY CAPS (*LACTARIUS FRAGILIS*)—These small orange mushrooms have the distinct aroma and flavor of maple syrup, and a little goes a long way. The maple property is intensified by cooking or drying. Chef John Ash, the culinary director at Fetzer Vineyards, uses them to make a candy cap gelato. Good in sweet custards, soufflés, cookies.

CHANTERELLES (*CANTHARELLUS*, various species)—These egg yolk–colored mushrooms are plentiful across the United States, especially on northeast slopes where hemlocks abound, or in oak forests in the West. They have a mild flavor and a slight apricot aroma. They are delicious sautéed or baked into casseroles.

HEDGEHOG MUSHROOM OR SWEET POLYPORE (*HYDNUM* OR *DENTIUM REPANDUM*)—A popular mushroom in Europe and gaining more popularity in the United States. Vaguely chanterelle-like, it has soft spines under its cap. Usually marketed fresh, it has a sweetness that enhances stir-fries.

◆ **HEN OF THE WOODS (*GRIFOLA FRONDOSA*)**—Also known as maitake, this is a frilly mushroom that can reach several pounds. Best when young and the caps are tender. Delicious when stir-fried.

KING BOLETE (*BOLETUS EDULIS*)—Known as king bolete in the United States, as *cèpes* in France, as *porcini* in Italy, *steinpilz* (stone mushroom) in Germany, and prized everywhere for its intense flavor that is richer when dried than fresh. Perfect in any dish that calls for mushrooms. Excellent as a flavoring with rice, especially risotto.

MATSUTAKE OR PINE MUSHROOM (*TRICHOLOMA MAGNIVELARE*)—Prized in Japan and becoming more popular in the United States, it has a spicy cinnamon-like aroma and a rich taste when grilled or sautéed. Can be steamed as well. This is the American species.

MILK CAP (*LACTARIUS VOLEMUS*)—A common mushroom in the eastern United States, it shows a milky sap when the stem is broken. Mild flavored and best when grilled or sautéed.

OREGON WHITE TRUFFLE (*TUBER GIBBOSUM*)—European truffles need no introduction, mostly because at $1,000 a pound, who can afford them? Our native truffles are from Oregon and have that divine earthy flavor, but the tubers quickly lose their flavor and aromatics if allowed to sit around after they're cut—so cut them immediately before use. Use in any recipe calling for white or black truffles.

➤ **YELLOW MOREL (*MORCHELLA ESCULENTA*)**—Several species of morels are found in commerce, but especially this one. Delicious, distinct, and earthy mushroom flavor marries well with roasted meats, gravies, sauces, stews, and cheese. Found in burned over forest, abandoned orchards.

MUSHROOMS FOUND IN FIELDS, ON COMPOST, AND ON DECAYING WOOD

BUTTON MUSHROOM (*AGARICUS BISPORUS*)—The common mushroom sold whole or sliced in stores. Its mature heads are sold as portobellos. Some call this mushroom the champignon of France, but the French would argue that name is reserved for *Agaricus campestris*. Used raw in salads, sautéed to pour over steak and veal scaloppini, ubiquitous, fine-flavored, and nicely priced.

CORN SMUT OR *HUITLACOCHE* (*USTILAGO MAYDIS*)—It doesn't look very appetizing, but this common corn fungus was a favorite food of the Aztecs and is still prized in Mexico, where it's often sliced and fried with onions. Its grayish, purplish black, lumpy appearance belies its refined flavor.

CREMINI (*AGARICUS BISPORUS*)—Flavor and use very much like the common button mushroom, but creminis have an attractive brown cap.

ENOKI (*FLAMMULINA VELUTIPES*)—Long, filamentous stems and tiny caps make this a favorite in Asian dishes. Commonly cultivated and sold in supermarkets.

FIELD MUSHROOM (*AGARICUS CAMPESTRIS*)—This is the champignon of France, and it is widely used in the United States for the same purposes as the commercially grown button mushroom, which is another species of agaricus.

GIANT PUFFBALL (*CALVATIA GIGANTEA*)—When young and pure white inside and about the size of a softball, it can be sliced or cubed, fried, and sauced, or used like tofu, which it resembles. Will grow much larger but loses best quality. Easily spotted in fields and sunny, open places.

OYSTER MUSHROOM (*PLEUROTUS OSTREATUS*)—Found wild on decaying wood and easily cultivated on straw or sawdust. Has a mild flavor and may be seen in shades of black, gray, white, tan, or very light blue. Adds body to soups and stews.

➤ **SHIITAKE (*LENTINULA EDODES*)**—Grows on decaying logs, stumps, and is grown commercially worldwide. Has rich, meaty flavor and meaty texture. Excellent sliced and added to stews and soups or sautéed and served with grilled meats. Research suggests it supports the immune system.

OKRA

Except for Annie Oakley, all these varieties have won All-America Selections awards.

GREEN OKRA

ANNIE OAKLEY—Slender pods, an early bearer, high quality.

CAJUN DELIGHT—Ornamental leaves and flowers, good production.

CLEMSON SPINELESS—The standard green variety for quality and yields.

PALE OKRA

BLONDY—Compact plants with very tender pale green pods.

RED OKRA

BURGUNDY—Keeps color when cooked; ornamental, with a mildly herbaceous flavor.

ONION

MILD BULBING VARIETIES

BURGERMASTER—Excellent red onion for topping that burger.

COPRA—Sweetest onion of them all, with mild white flesh.

MAUI—Maui's volcanic soil produces a sweet, mild onion.

RED GRANEX—Mild red flesh and thin skin.

RED TORPEDO—Elongated bulb with red-purple, mildly pungent flesh.

SUPER STAR—Large, sweet onion; an All-America Selections winner.

SWEET SANDWICH—Pungent at harvest but mellows in 2 months.

TEXAS 1015Y—Mild, sweet flesh and good storage capability.

VIDALIA—Grown around Vidalia, Georgia, as a choice sweet onion.

WALLA WALLA SWEET—A Corsican variety now at home in Washington.

WHITE GRANEX—Popular mild white onion of the Southeast.

WHITE LISBON—Harvested young as a superior bunching onion.

YELLOW GRANEX—Yellow version of the sweet Granex type.

PUNGENT BULBING VARIETIES

BLANCO DURO—Very pungent white fleshed and thin-necked bulbs.

NEW YORK EARLY—Standard yellow onion grown in Orange County, New York.

NORTHERN OAK—Very pungent, small necked, superior keeper.

PRINCE—Champion keeper up to 7 months; very pungent.

SOUTHPORT RED GLOBE—Strongly pungent red onion is a good keeper.

SOUTHPORT WHITE GLOBE—White version of Southport Red Globe.

YELLOW GLOBE DANVERS—Good keeper, copper-yellow skin, good flavor.

BUNCHING ONIONS

BELTSVILLE BUNCHING—Crisp, sweet flavor; seen in summer markets.

EVERGREEN WHITE BUNCHING—Good-quality scallion-type onion.

KINCHO—Winter hardy scallion shows up early in spring markets.

RED WELSH—Coppery red perennial bunching onion.

TOKYO NEGI—Very long, white stalk, and excellent flavor.

PEARL ONIONS

BORETTANO—*Cippolini*-type with rose-copper color and superb flavor.

PACIFIC PEARL—All-season pearl onion; great in salads or pickled.

PURPLETTE—Red-purple skinned baby onion; good pickled.

WHITE PORTUGAL—Mild flesh is firm and flavorful; silvery skin.

YELLOW BORETTANO—Fine-textured flesh of excellent, gourmet flavor.

EGYPTIAN TOPSET ONION

CATAWISSA—Good flavor and a plethora of bulbils to have fun with.

PARSNIP

ALL-AMERICA—Very sweet, tender root with good keeping quality.

COBHAM IMPROVED MARROW—Extra sweet with smooth, white skin.

GLADIATOR—The first hybrid parsnip; large, with high-quality flesh.

HARRIS' MODEL—Ivory-white skin and fine texture; very sweet.

HOLLOW CROWN—An heirloom with an indented crown; choice.

THE STUDENT—Root grows to 30 inches long; flavor said to be best of any parsnip.

PEA

Pea pods, whether from sugar snap or snow peas, have a mild flavor and crunchy texture. Freshly shelled peas have an unequalled and delightful sweetness, an herbaceous and clean flavor, and a wholesome, refreshing aftertaste. The following varieties excel in all these qualities.

ENGLISH OR GARDEN PEAS

FREEZONIAN—A full-sized vine with superbly flavored peas.

GREATER PROGRESS—Improved Laxton's Progress variety.

GREEN ARROW—A favorite with market gardeners for many years.

LAXTON'S PROGRESS—Among the top-yielding peas; excellent, sweet flavor.

LINCOLN—Probably the best tasting of all the garden peas.

LITTLE MARVEL—Dwarf vines with full-sized peas of excellent flavor.

MR. BIG—Large, easy-to-shell pods and extra sweet peas.

WAVEREX—French petits pois type with rich, herbal flavor.

SNOW PEAS

CAROUBY DE MAUSSANE—French heirloom variety of superb flavor.

DWARF GRAY SUGAR—Bush-type vines with thin, flat, sweet pods.

MAMMOTH MELTING SUGAR—Standard snow pea variety of high quality.

SNAP PEAS

SUGAR ANN—Dwarf vine but full-sized flavor in an eat-all pod.

SUGAR SNAP—High-yielding 8-foot vines with stringless pods.

SUGAR SPRINT—Bred for even less fibrous material in the sweet pods.

SUPER SUGAR MEL—Superior flavor and extra sweet peas.

POTATO

Not all potatoes are created equal. I find the flavor of French or German Fingerlings to be exquisitely rich and clean, with subtle aromas of warm bread, earth tones, and even baked pie crust. And no matter the variety, fried potatoes acquire a heavenly flavor that's caramelized and savory. Here is a rather long list of potatoes, any one of which is worth picking up.

WAXY

ALL RED—Waxy-textured potato is perfect for mashed potato dishes.

ANNA CHEEKA'S OZETTE—An excellent fingerling type originally from Peru.

BINTJE—Waxy yellow flesh best for baking or boiling.

CHIEFTAIN—Canada's favorite red potato, great for boiling.

DESIREE—Yellow fleshed, unique fine flavor, best steamed.

GERMAN FINGERLING—My personal favorite potato with dense, waxy flesh.

RED CLOUD—Satiny textured flesh can be cooked all ways.

RED LASODA—Bright red skin and pure white flesh, great for mashed.

ROSE FINN APPLE—Rosy buff colored fingerling type of excellent flavor.

RUBY CRESCENT—Long fingerling type of superior texture and flavor.

STARCHY

BUTTE—Russeted Idaho type best for baking.

ISLAND SUNSHINE—Superior yellow spud developed by organic farmers.

KENNEBEC—Excellent for boiling, baking, and making french fries.

NORGOLD RUSSET—A russeted potato that's superior for french fries.

RUSSET NUGGET—Rated first in taste tests at Colorado State.

WHITE ROSE—Thin skinned, with white flesh, and a fine flavor.

YELLOW FINN—Some say it makes the best mashed potatoes.

YUKON GOLD—A sweet, yellow potato easy enough to find in stores.

RADISH

The joy of small radishes is that they are the first crop of the new growing season, when they'll be crunchy and mildly pungent, with a clean, refreshing taste that quickly expunges the boring flavors of winter vegetables and prepares the palate for the marvels to come.

SMALL OR WESTERN RADISHES

CHAMPION—All-America Selections winner, scarlet-skinned and globe-shaped.

CHERRY BELLE—Another All-America Selections winner; bright cherry-red skin and white interior.

D'AVIGNON—Gourmet radish, red and white, with medium pungency.

EASTER EGG—Roots may be pink, scarlet, purple, violet, or white.

FRENCH BREAKFAST—Roots are cylindrical, red above, white at tips.

PLUM PURPLE—Bright purple skin and white flesh is pretty in salads.

SPARKLER—Round roots scarlet above, white at root end; holds crispness.

WHITE ICICLE—Yields 5-inch cylindrical roots that are white, mild, and never turn woody.

ASIAN RADISHES

APRIL CROSS—Daikon type to 18 inches long with mild pungency.

MISATO ROSE—Size of a hardball; good raw or cooked; rose-red flesh.

XIN LI MEI—White and green skin with pink-red flesh and sweet flavor. Also known as Beauty Heart.

BLACK RADISHES

LONG BLACK SPANISH—Pungent roots are seven inches long, skin very black.

ROUND BLACK SPANISH—Very pungent, keeps well, black skin with white flesh.

RHUBARB

CANADA RED—Holds color after cooking, needs no peeling; red flesh.

CHERRY RED—Red surface with greenish flesh inside. Very tart yet sweet.

CRIMSON CHERRY—Red throughout, fiber free, with sweet-tart flavor.

GLASKIN'S PERPETUAL—Low in oxalic acid, can be harvested all season.

MACDONALD—Rich red color throughout, needs no peeling.

VALENTINE—Very sweet deep red flesh, holds color after cooking.

RUTABAGA

ACME—Very high-quality root, small size with purple top, yellow flesh.

AMERICAN PURPLE TOP—Most often grown in United States, very good quality.

LAURENTIAN—Very popular, mild-flavored root; the standard in Canada.

SHALLOT

More and more organic growers are adding shallots to their list of available vegetables. Chefs are anxious to find locally grown young shallots, and regular customers of organic suppliers at farmers' markets can get dibs on the new crop in summer.

DRITTLER WHITE—An heirloom variety from Arkansas since 1885. Whitish papery skin.

DUTCH YELLOW—A high-quality, yellow-fleshed type sold in clusters.

FRENCH GRAY—Gray shallots are considered the finest flavored of all. Grayish-brown skin.

FRENCH RED—A gourmet type of fat clove with reddish skin.

SHALLOT—A variety name as well as the common name for the plant; it has brown skin with a pinkish cast; a market favorite.

SPINACH

SAVOY TYPE

AMERICA—If any variety has superior flavor, it's this one. All-America Selections winner.

BLOOMSDALE LONG STANDING—Good flavor, most commonly grown variety.

INDIAN SUMMER—Often grown as a fall crop; dark green leaves.

WHALE—Slow-bolting type for summer production; organic seed available.

BABY

CORRENTA—Oval, Asian type sold as single leaves by weight.

MELODY HYBRID—Semisavoy-type leaves and good flavor. All-America Selections winner.

MONNOPA—Low in oxalic acid, good raw and used for baby food.

TETON—Crisp, very dark green leaves.

WOLTER—A flat-leaved variety known for its tenderness and tangy flavor.

SUMMER SQUASH

PATTY PAN (SCALLOP) TYPE

EARLY WHITE BUSH—Pale green, exceptionally flavorful patty pan type.

PETER PAN HYBRID—An All-America Selections winner with scalloped edges, sweet flavor.

STARSHIP—Dark green, with a nutty taste that consistently wins contests.

SUNBURST—A yellow patty pan type with a green starburst pattern.

OTHER SCALLOP TYPE

TROMBONCINO—Curlique shape, dense flesh, fine flavor; harvest at 10 inches.

YELLOW CROOKNECK

DIXIE—Old-fashioned crookneck style squash; a Southern favorite.

EARLY GOLDEN SUMMER CROOKNECK—Thin neck, bulbous base.

EARLY PROLIFIC STRAIGHTNECK—An All-America Selections winner, with bulbous base.

SUNDANCE—True crookneck type with warty surface, great flavor.

SUNDROP—Egg-shaped squash, bright gold, with scrumptious flavor.

ZEPHYR—The top portion is yellow, the blossom end is green.

ZUCCHINI

AMBASSADOR—Similar to Burpee Fordhook with prolific production.

ARISTOCRAT—All-America Selections winner, standard for market gardeners, gourmets.

BLACK BEAUTY—Almost black skin; harvest when young and tender.

BURPEE FORDHOOK—All-America Selections winner; the standard garden variety zucchini.

CASERTA—All-America Selections champ in 1949; very productive.

GOLD RUSH—Like a regular zucchini, only a bright gold color.

GREYZINI—Differs primarily in the gray-green color of its skin.

ITALIAN LARGO—Delicious, ribbed zucchini found in Italian markets.

TATUME—A zucchini, but egg-shaped; harvest when golf ball sized.

ROUND

EIGHT BALL—All-America Selections winner; dark green, harvest when the size of golf ball.

ELITE—Very flavorful, early producer of medium green fruits.

RONDE DE NICE—French heirloom variety best when one inch in diameter.

MIDDLE EASTERN TYPE

GRISE DE ALGIERS—Excellent flavor, bulbous on blossom end, pale green.

SWEET PEPPER

BLUSHING BEAUTY—Flat pepper changes from ivory to pink to red; All-America Selections winner.

CHERVENA CHUJSKI—Bright red Bulgarian heirloom is extremely sweet.

CHOCOLATE BEAUTY—Brown pepper, very sweet and highest in vitamin C.

GIANT MARCONI—7-inch tapered pepper rated best for grilling; All-America Selections winner.

GOLDEN SUMMER—Gold pepper that won an *Organic Gardening* taste test.

LIPSTICK—Slender, tapering, 4-inch red peppers of high quality.

NARDELLO—A superior sweet, red Italian frying pepper.

QUADRATO D'ORO—Rated sweetest pepper in a taste test at *Organic Gardening*.

RED HEART—Pimento-type pepper highly rated in taste tests.

VIDI—European gourmet red pepper perfect for grilling.

SWEET POTATO

The orange-colored, moist-flesh sweet potatoes commonly sold in the United States have a rich honeyed flavor and smooth texture. Asian and Caribbean dry-flesh types are less sweet, more starchy, firmer, and perform more like regular white potatoes or other starchy roots, but still have a lovely mild sweetness to them.

MOIST FLESH (ORANGE)

GARNET—Red-purplish skin and very flavorful, orange, creamy flesh.

JEWEL—Most common U.S. type, and a worthy root with good flavor.

VARDAMAN—One of the choicest gourmet types with dark orange flesh.

YELLOW YAM—aka Nancy Hall; old type with fine, honeyed flavor.

DRY FLESH (WHITE)

BONIATO—Cuban type with edible skin that bakes up crunchy.

WHITE TRIUMPH—White skin and flesh; mildly sweet and smooth textured.

TOMATILLO

GIANT—Guatemalan tomatillo with superb flavor.

INDIAN—For salsa when green, preserves when ripe.

LARGE GREEN—Produces fruits up to 3 inches in diameter.

PURPLE—Small purple fruits with a sharp acid tang.

RENDIDORA—Greenish yellow fruits ripen early; top yielder.

TOMA VERDE—New strain but already most popular; top quality.

TOMATO

There are dozens of heirloom tomato varieties being grown today, and most have interesting flavors. Be sure to try some that you run across at farmers' markets and roadside stands.

CHERRY TOMATOES

JULIET—Each fruit is about 1 ounce, sweet, with an elongated shape.

MS-5—A superior red cherry tomato perfect for gourmet salads.

SUN GOLD—Great fruity, tropical, sweet flavor in an orange fruit.

SWEET 100—Sweet, red cherry tomatoes in abundance; high in vitamin C.

CONTAINER PLANTING

BETTER BUSH—Takes well to container on a sunny deck; quality fruit.

STANDARD VARIETIES

AUNT GINNY'S PURPLE—Slight purplish cast.

BEEFSTEAK—A large tomato with focused tomato flavor.

BIG BEEF—An early Beefsteak type with true tomato flavor.

BLACK FROM TULA—Heirloom introduction with luscious flavor.

BRANDYWINE—Amish heirloom with gourmet-quality fruit.

CARMELLO—Gourmet French tomato with perfect acid-sweet balance.

CARO-RICH—Ten times the provitamin A content of other tomatoes.

CASPIAN PINK—A Russian variety deemed best in taste trials.

CHEROKEE PURPLE—Excellent purple-pink flesh; a Cherokee heirloom.

COSTOLUTO FIORENTINO—Italian heirloom with excellent flavor.

DOUBLERICH—Five times the vitamin C content of other tomatoes.

DR. WYCHEE'S YELLOW—Mild, sweet, sub-acid; best out of hand.

EARLY GIRL—Small to medium red fruits of extra-high quality.

GARDEN PEACH—Yellow-orange skin, red flesh, good keeper.

GOLDEN QUEEN—Old yellow heirloom; has sweet, mild flavor.

GREEN JUBILEE—High-quality Jubilee type that holds green color.

MARVEL STRIPED—Brightly colored with luscious flavor; comes from Mexico.

OREGON SPRING—Excellent for cool summer climates.

OXHEART—Very large, heart-shaped, pink tomato of fine flavor.

PERSIMMON—Looks like a ripe persimmon; rich, acid flavor.

SIBERIA—For short-season regions; sets fruit at 38 degrees Fahrenheit.

VARIETIES FOR SAUCE AND CANNING

ROMA—Excellent flavor for marinara and homemade sauces; meaty.

SAN MARZANO LAMPADINA—Improved San Marzano type with rich flavor.

TURNIP

There are a surprisingly large number of turnip varieties, both root and foliage types. Here is a list of the best.

ROOT CROP

AMBER GLOBE—Yellow skin, flesh; good sweet flavor and fine texture.

GOLDEN PERFECTION—Yellow-fleshed, resistant to certain insects, so a favorite with organic growers.

LONG DES VERTUS MARTEAU—Parisian market favorite; sweet, tender, mild. Sometimes sold as Jersey Navet.

PURPLE TOP MILAN—White flesh is fine-grained, choice quality.

PURPLE TOP WHITE GLOBE—Standard of quality for home gardens, markets.

ROYAL CROWN—Globes have purple tops with white below, tender flesh.

TOKYO CROSS—Look for 2-inch white roots; like sweet, crisp radishes.

TURNIP GREENS

ALL TOP—Very high-quality greens grown in Southeast as winter annual.

SEVEN TOP—Cool season crop of very tender, dark green, large leaves.

WINTER SQUASH

The best varieties of winter squash have fine-grained, nonstringy (except for spaghetti squash), sweet, nutty flesh that acquires a savory caramelized taste from baking in the hot oven. Here are some to look for at the organic markets.

BLUE BALLET—Smaller Blue Hubbard type with bright orange flesh.

BLUE HUBBARD—Blue-gray, warty surface; fine-grained yellow flesh.

BUSH DELICATA—Sweet potato-like quality flesh on a bush plant.

CARNIVAL—Gaily colored acorn-type squash with good flavor.

DELICATA—Richly colored orange flesh is sweet; finely textured.

GOLD NUGGET—One-pound, deep golden fruits; an heirloom variety.

GOLDEN HUBBARD—Big, 10- to 12-pound fruits with high-quality flesh.

RED KURI—Also called Orange Hokkaido; yellow-orange flesh.

ROUGE VIF D'ETAMPES—Decorative French heirloom pumpkin.

SPAGHETTI SQUASH—Buff-colored fruits yield long, tender strands.

SUNSHINE—All-America Selections winner has improved flavor and garden growth habit.

SWEET DUMPLING—Small fruits can be hollowed and used as soup bowls.

SWEET MEAT—Extra large, round fruits; Northwest favorite for pies.

TABLE ACE—Best of the acorn-type squashes; fine flavor, texture.

TURK'S TURBAN—Ornamental winter squash rather than culinary.

WALTHAM BUTTERNUT—Very fine texture, flavor, rich color. Superb.

Fruit

APPLE

An apple fresh from the tree on a cold autumn morning—what could be better? Well, it could be a Northern Spy, one of the best-tasting apples there is. Or look for the following varieties:

ARKANSAS BLACK—Fine textured fruit with old-fashioned apple flavor.

ASHMEAD'S KERNEL—Russeted skin, aromatic flesh, great fresh or for cider.

BRAEBURN—A New Zealand introduction; very crisp, sweet flesh.

COX'S ORANGE PIPPIN—Floral winey flavor, crisp flesh, juicy.

EMPIRE—Dark red color, good keeper, high quality for fresh eating.

ESOPUS SPITZENBURG—Tom Jefferson's favorite apple; superior quality.

FUJI—A very sweet, juicy and crisp apple originated in Japan.

GALA—Fine-textured apple with very sweet, juicy flesh.

GOLDEN RUSSET—Russeted skin; excellent for cooking, fresh eating, cider.

GRAVENSTEIN—Ripens very early; best when slightly underripe.

HONEY CRISP—Considered the standard of quality for very hardy apples.

JONAGOLD—Consistent taste test winner; keeps quality for months.

JONATHAN—Old variety with small but sweet flesh and a definite apple fragrance.

NEWTOWN PIPPIN—An old favorite with coarse texture, superb flavor.

NORTHERN SPY—Lively flavor and highly aromatic; New England favorite.

PINK PEARL—Pink flesh shows through thin skin; very aromatic, flavorful.

POUND SWEET—Has a unique flavor; often stewed with quinces.

RHODE ISLAND GREENING—Another fine apple with a unique flavor.

SMOKEHOUSE—Best when slightly underripe; turns mealy when fully ripe.

SPARTAN—Dark red skin, white flesh, very crisp and sweet.

STAYMAN WINESAP—Dark red skin, yellow flesh of rich, winey flavor.

WEALTHY—Flesh white, crisp, sweet; skin green and yellow streaked red.

➤ YELLOW DELICIOUS—An excellent green-to-yellow apple with sprightly flavor.

APRICOT

GOLDBAR OR GOLDSTRIKE—Golden fruit is highly aromatic with choice flavor.

MOORPARK—A very high-quality apricot with juicy, sweet, rich flesh.

PATTERSON—Very firm fruit great for canning, cooking, or fresh eating.

RIVAL—Sweet, juicy, firm flesh is deep orange, skin is light orange.

➤ ROYAL BLENHEIM—Delicately perfumed fruit; rich, sweet flesh. They can be recognized by the purplish-red dotting that appears on the pale yellow skin where the fruit has been exposed to the afternoon sun.

ASIAN PEAR

It wasn't that long ago that Asian pears were found only in specialty stores serving the Japanese or Chinese communities. Now there are dozens of varieties. The best have a delicate perfume about them and a fine-grained texture.

HAMESE—Rated high in taste tests; very sweet and juicy.

➤ HOSUI—Especially firm, sweet flesh with excellent flavor.

KOSUI—The Japanese consider this the highest-quality Asian pear, and that in a country that adores Asian pears.

SHINKO—Rated best tasting by a *Sunset* magazine tasting panel. Sweet, rich flavor.

SHINSEIKI—aka New Century, has firm, crisp texture, fine flavor.

TWENTIETH CENTURY—Greenish-yellow skin; flesh white, slightly tart, juicy.

BANANA

The standard yellow bananas we find in our markets are forms of Cavendish. They are an acceptable banana, but there are other types that offer more flavor and better texture.

BANANAS

ENANO NAUTIA—Grown in Mexico; very high-quality fruits.

GROS MICHEL—Once the standard of quality but fell from commerce due to disease. Still occasionally found in markets.

ICE CREAM—7- to 9-inch, aromatic, creamy, melt-in-mouth fruits.

LADY FINGER—Small, 4-inch fruits of excellent quality.

MANZANA—4- to 6-inch fruits with apple flavor; aka Apple and Silk.

POPOULU—Hawaiian variety with salmon-pink flesh; cook or eat fresh.

➤ RED—Also called Cuban Red; red skin, aromatic fruit with creamy texture.

SUCRIER—Dark brown skins, small fruits, very sweet flesh.

PLANTAINS

HARTON—High culinary quality; cook at any stage of ripeness.

HORN—Very popular plantain; similar qualities to Harton.

MARICONGO—Popular for cooking throughout Latin America.

BLACKBERRY

STANDARD BLACKBERRIES

APACHE—A thornless blackberry with an extra sweet flavor.

ARAPAHO—Another thornless type, sweet with extra small seeds.

BLACK BUTTE—Berries are twice the size of normal blackberries.

BLACK SATIN—Fine flavor in a popular cultivated eastern blackberry.

NAVAHO—Thornless canes; small berries packed with dark fruit flavor.

SISKIYOU—Extra-large berries with exceptional sweetness.

TRIPLE CROWN—Large, flavorful berries bred by USDA's fruit lab.

HYBRID BLACKBERRY-RASPBERRY CROSSES

BOYSENBERRY—A raspberry-blackberry hybrid with sweet-tart flavor.

LOGANBERRY—Tart and juicy; great for pies and preserves.

MARIONBERRY—Renowned flavor and aroma, true blackberry taste.

OLALLIEBERRY—Black hybrid berries with true blackberry flavor.

BLACK RASPBERRY

Look for wild black raspberries, of course, but among the cultivated varieties, these are the best, with flavor closest to the wild.

ALLEN—Outstanding variety for making jam; large, sweet berries.

BLACK HAWK—Very large berries; nice balance of sweetness and acidity.

BRISTOL—A nearly seedless variety of excellent quality, good flavor.

HAUT—A favorite in mid-Atlantic states; sweet, high-quality fruit.

JEWEL—Similar to Bristol, except more productive. Intense flavor.

BLUEBERRY

Blueberries are seldom sold by variety name, which is a pity. Blueberry growers, however, will know the names of their cultivars, so don't hesitate to ask variety names at farmers' markets and roadside stands whose berries purport to be farmer-grown. At the very least, you should find out if the berries are wild harvested because they'll usually be sweeter, more highly flavored, and richer in nutrients and antioxidants.

BLUECROP—The most popular blueberry in New Jersey plantings.

BLUERAY—Sweeter than Bluecrop, aromatic, much planted in Michigan.

BRIGITTA—Excellent flavor in firm fruit; an Australian introduction.

NORTHBLUE—Very good flavor in a berry suited to northern areas.

NORTHLAND—Small berries approximate flavor of wild berries.

PATRIOT—Planted in the northern tier of states; excellent flavor.

SIERRA—Quality is excellent; relatively new, vigorous variety.

SPARTAN—Early, high-quality blueberry; pick-your-own favorite.

TORO—Medium size fruit with firm flesh, excellent quality.

CHERIMOYA

There are fifteen cultivated varieties of cherimoya, but the names are rarely given on any label that might attach to the fruit. Still, if you can ask the grower, do, because the following four are worth seeking out.

EL BUMPO—Not much in commerce, but flavor among the finest grown in California.

LIBBY—Originated in California in 1986; sweet, strong flavor.

NATA—Grown from Ecuadorian seed; good sweet-acid balance.

SABOR—Fruits vary in size; among the very best in flavor.

CHERRY

Cherries are on the list of the twelve fruits and vegetables most highly contaminated with pesticides, so buying only organic (or wild) cherries is a wise choice. Here are excellent varieties to look for at farmers' markets and roadside stands, and even certain supermarkets.

SWEET

BING—Consistently rated best cherry in taste.

BLACK TARTARIAN—Firm, meaty flesh of exceptional flavor; black skin.

GIANT—Dark red fruit with fine rich flavor, bred by Luther Burbank (see page 302).

MERTON HEART—Mahogany-black skin with juicy flesh, sweet flavor.

MERTON LATE—Orange-yellow skin flushed red; flavor exceptional.

MONA—Pretty heart-shaped red cherries with a sweet, mild flavor.

RAINIER—Yellow skin with a reddish blush, excellent flavor.

STARKRIMSON—Excellent quality in a medium-red cherry.

UTAH GIANT—Some consider more flavorful than Bing; purple-black skin.

YELLOW SPANISH—An ancient variety of yellow skin cherry, exquisite flavor.

SOUR

MARASCA DI OSTHEIM—Rare in the United States, but a superior Morello type.

MONTMORENCY—The standard pie cherry in the United States, for good reason.

NORTH STAR—Beautiful semidwarf trees become laden with bright red fruit.

CITRUS

The following are the cream of the citrus crop. Common names change from place to place. Tangors, for instance, are called orangelos in some parts of the country. I've included kumquats, as they're commonly considered a citrus fruit, although they actually have their own genus, *Fortunella*.

GRAPEFRUIT (*CITRUS \ PARADISI*)

WHITE

DUNCAN—An old variety with sharply acidic, crisp flavor; seedy.

MARSH—Today's standard of quality, juicy, sweet, mildly acid.

PINK

RIO RED—Deep red flesh with sprightly flavor.

SHAMBAR—Pink flesh, very juicy, with same flavor as Marsh, of which it is a mutation.

THOMPSON—Also known as Pink Marsh; colorless juice, sweet, sub-acid flavor.

KUMQUAT (*FORTUNELLA CRASSIFOLIA*)

MEIWA—A superior kumquat, sometimes seedless, very tart, for eating out of hand or for making marmalade.

LEMON (*CITRUS × LIMON*)

EUREKA—The standard, very acidic, high-quality lemon.

LISBON—Very acidic, juicy, tender, nearly seedless fruit.

MEYER—Sweeter and less acidic than Eureka; unique aroma and taste.

LIME (*CITRUS AURANTIFOLIA*)

BEARSS—These small, yellowish-green fruits have a lemon-lime flavor.

EVERGLADE—The best of the yellowish key lime or Mexican lime; its low acidity makes it great for cooking.

TAHITIAN—*Citrus latifolia;* seedless, green rind and flesh, acidic lime flavor

MANDARIN ORANGE AND TANGERINE (*CITRUS RETICULATA*)

BROWN'S SELECT—Satsuma type; flesh sweet, melting.

CLEMENTINE—Excellent small tangerine with rich flavor. Often seedless.

DANCY—America's favorite tangerine—the most common variety; rich tangerine flavor, but seedy.

FINA—Spain's favorite tangerine; a type of Clementine.

HONEY—Superbly rich in flavor and aromatics.

KINNOW—Large tangerine with distinct, pleasant aroma, extra sweet juice.

OWARI—Old Japanese satsuma with rich, sweet flavor and tender flesh.

SATSUMA—Easy to peel, seedless, very juicy, with sweet-tart flavor.

SILVERHILL—Much like Owari, but even sweeter.

ORANGE (*CITRUS × SINENSIS*)

BLOOD ORANGE—This is a type of orange whose flesh has red splotches, sprightly flavor with hints of raspberry. Many varieties are grown; the best for lovely, fruity flavor is probably Sanguinello Moscato from Italy.

The Moro is the most highly red-colored while Tarocco has outstanding flavor.

CADENERA—Nearly seedless flesh is juicy with true orange flavor; the favorite orange of Spain.

CARA CARA—A pink-fleshed navel much sought after for its sweetness and mild acidity.

HOMOSASSA—Seedy, rare, but excellent concentrated orange flavor.

JAFFA—Oblong, seedless, easy to peel, with a fragrant, rich juice.

LANE LATE—Excellent late-maturing, seedless navel from Australia.

NEWHALL—Small navel with good aroma and excellent flavor.

PINEAPPLE—Florida's best midseason orange with pineapple aroma; for juice, fresh eating.

REPUBLIC OF TEXAS—Old-fashioned orange with excellent "true orange" flavor.

VALENCIA—The standard late juice orange of Florida, California. A sub-acid orange with copious juice.

WASHINGTON NAVEL—The big, nearly seedless, rich-tasting navel.

SOUR ORANGE (*CITRUS × AURANTIUM*)

Also called Seville orange, its high acidity and bitter taste make it not much of an eating orange, but wonderful in marmalade.

PUMMELO (*CITRUS GRANDIS*)

CARTERS RED—Large pummelo with dry-textured red flesh.

CHOY—Flavor similar to sweet grapefruit; grown in Hawaii.

RED SHADDOCK—Rich, red flesh is very sweet and low in acid.

TANGELO (*CITRUS × TANGELO*)

MINNEOLA—Deep red-orange peel; melting, sweet-acid flavor.

UGLI—Tangerine-grapefruit cross with orange flesh of sweet, sub-acid flavor.

WEKIWA—aka Lavender Gem; irresistibly delicious cross between Duncan grapefruit and tangelo.

TANGOR (*CITRUS × NOBILIS*)

MURCOTT—Also called Honey Murcott; flavor is remarkably sweet and rich.

TEMPLE—Orange flesh, very juicy, rich and sprightly flavor.

CRANBERRY

Typically, you will not find cranberries sold by variety name, but rather (if you see any name at all) by one of the three botanical names. But you might ask for the names listed below, as they are some of the superior cultivars.

PEARL—A lingonberry (*Vaccinium vitis-idaea*), native to Eurasia and North America with a sharply acidic taste.

STEPHENS—An American cranberry that makes a fine landscape plant. Check web site at: www.ediblelandscaping.com.

THUNDERLAKE—An American cranberry that doesn't need a bog to thrive. Standard American cranberry flavor.

CURRENT

I love true currants and gooseberries. If you decide to grow your own currants or gooseberries (something that's very easy to do, see page 250), you can use this list as a starting point.

BLACK CURRANTS

BEN SAREK—A compact bush that bears large quantities of black berries.

CONSORT—Black, strong-flavored; four times more vitamin C than oranges.

CRUSADER—Black currant–Asian currant cross with vitamin C–rich berries.

WHITE CURRANT

PRIMUS—The sweetest of the white currants, and highest in vitamin C.

WHITE IMPERIAL—The richest flavor of any white currant; pink blush color.

WHITE PEARL—A heavy fruiting plant—lots of berries.

RED CURRANT

JONKEER VAN TETS—Extra-large, red, tart berries; ripens early.

RED LAKE—The most popular red currant; juicy little red berries.

GOOSEBERRIES

CAPTIVATOR—A thornless variety with large green berries.

GLENDALE—Known to produce well in warm climates. These are probably the gooseberries you'll find at markets in more southern regions.

HINNOMAKI RED—Skin is tangy while the flesh is sweet; rich red color.

INVICTA—So named for its hurtful thorns, but the fruits are huge and tasty.

PINK GOOSEBERRY—Similar to Pixwell, but has slightly better flavor.

PIXWELL—Standard greenish gooseberry; makes great jams and preserves.

POORMAN—Originated in Utah in 1888; survives because of great flavor.

CURRANT HYBRIDS

JOSTABERRY—Cross between black currants and gooseberries; fine flavor.

NATIVE AMERICAN WILD CURRANTS

CLOVE CURRANT—*Ribes odoratum* has small but highly flavored berries.

RIBES AMERICANUM—Wild native species, not found in commerce.

DATE

The flavor of dates ranges from lightly sweet to caramel-nutty. Soft dates are more choice than most semidry or dry dates.

SOFT

BARHI—Thick flesh of rich flavor and superb quality.

HALAWY—Small to medium date with extremely sweet flesh.

HAYANI—Dark red to nearly black fruit.

KHADRAWI—One of the highest quality soft dates, favored by Arabs.

MEDJOOL—Large and luscious, caramel-flavored, best for making date pastes for pastries.

SEMIDRY

DEGLET NOOR—The main crop date in California and Arizona, with dark amber brown skin and very sweet, translucent flesh.

KHASTAWI—Leading dessert date in Iraq; syrupy, small sized.

DRY

THOORY—The dry date most commonly found, less sweet than the Zahidi.

ZAHIDI—Very sugary date sold fresh, most often sold dried hard and used as a dry date.

FIG

BLACK

- **BLACK MISSION**—Plump fig with strawberry-colored pulp. Flavor juicy, rich.
- **NERO**—Purplish-black fig with a mild, sweet flavor adapted to grow in the Southeast and Southwest.

GREEN

- **KADOTA**—Thick-skinned, greenish-white fig, delicious fresh or dried. Often canned.

BROWN-BRONZE

- **HUNT**—A small brown fig, excellent caramel flavor (make sure to buy the second crop of this variety, around late summer or early fall, as the first crop tends to be relatively tasteless); adapted to grow in the Southeast.

VIOLET

- **HARDY CHICAGO**—Violet skin and strawberry-pink flesh; hardy, and so can be grown in the North if protected during winter.

YELLOW

- **CALIMYRNA**—Yellow fig; amber pulp with sweet, rich, nutty flavor.
- **EXCEL**—Superb flavor in a yellow fig; aka Kadota Hybrid but sweeter than Kadota.
- **LSU GOLD**—Yellow with red blush. Outstanding flavor. Sweetest of the figs for the southeast.

GRAPE

American grapes are very fruity, fragrant, with the familiar grapey flavor. Muscadines are larger and have a coarser, more vinous flavor. *Vinifera* grapes are European grapes; whether strongly or subtly flavored, they tend to have a purer, superior flavor to the other types.

SEEDLESS AMERICAN

- **CANDICE**—Spicy, saucy flavor in a firm, juicy, red-purple grape.
- **EINSET**—Flavor reminiscent of strawberry; hardy northern red grape.
- **HIMROD**—Loose clusters of crispy sweet grapes are golden when fully ripe.

- **INTERLAKEN**—Delightful grapey aroma with refreshing tangy flavor.
- **LAKEMONT**—Crisp, juicy green berries are honey-sweet; roadside stands.
- **MARQUIS**—Exquisitely rich and fruity white grapes.
- **VANESSA**—Blushing red skin with zesty, tangy, sweet flavor.

SEEDED AMERICAN

- **ALDEN**—Large dark red berries have sweet, wine-like quality.
- **CATAWBA**—Red grape; almost like a muscat in its aromatic fruitiness.
- **DELAWARE**—Best flavor of any American red grape; sprightly, sweet, and rich.
- **DIAMOND**—Clean, foxy, refreshing white grape makes superb juice.

MUSCADINE

- **BLACK BEAUTY**—The top-rated black muscadine for its sweet, vinous flavor.
- **DARLENE**—Large, bronze-colored berries, very sweet, intense flavor.
- **DIXIELAND**—Bronze skin, high sugar content, superior flavor.
- **SWEET JENNY**—Very large bronze berries with tart, juicy flavor.

■ ■ ■

The following muscadines are grown in the Southeast, where it's too humid and hot for most other grapes. In taste tests, these varieties scored near or at the top for their sweet-tart muscadine flavor.

- **FRY**—Very large bronze berries.
- **JANET**—Large bronze berries.
- **SUGARGATE**—Very large black-purple skins.
- **SUMMIT**—Thin, tender red skins.
- **SUPREME**—Black muscadine rated just below Black Beauty for taste.

SEEDLESS *VINIFERA*

- **BLACK MONUKKA**—Large, oblong red-purple fruits; very sweet.
- **CRIMSON SEEDLESS**—Bright red skin and translucent yellow flesh.

FLAME SEEDLESS—Familiar pink-red variety has high-quality sweet flavor.

PERLETTE—Firm textured green seedless grape with a mild, vinous flavor.

RUBY SEEDLESS—Dark red, crisp, meaty flesh is sweet, juicy, luscious.

SEEDED *VINIFERA*

GOLD—Large, greenish-gold berries with light muscat flavor.

MUSCAT HAMBURG—Large, oval, black berries with sweet, floral flavor.

MUSCAT OF ALEXANDRIA—Berries have musky, sweetly aromatic flavor.

KIWIFRUIT

Kiwifruit has a wide variety of flavors, depending on the species and cultivar.

FUZZY KIWIFRUIT

CHICO HAYWARD—Quality like Hayward, widely planted in California.

➤ **HAYWARD**—Spicy, tangy, and crisply acidic taste. The standard of excellence for green-fleshed, fuzzy kiwis.

KORYOKU—New, extra-sweet variety from Japan; as sweet as wine grapes.

COLD-HARDY KIWIFRUIT (BABY KIWIFRUIT)

ANANASNAYA—Has the aroma and flavor of pineapple; hardy to minus 38 degrees Fahrenheit.

DUMBARTON OAKS—Found growing in a Georgetown garden; sweet flavor.

MICHIGAN STATE—Large fruits with excellent flavor; developed at Michigan State University.

ROSY—Red-green skin and very sweet flesh; from Italy.

ACTINIDIA KOLOMIKTA

MICHURIN'S LARGE—Large, smooth fruits; very sweet, high in vitamin C.

GOLDEN KIWIFRUIT (*ACTINIDIA CHINENSIS*)

CANTON—Flesh is golden yellow when ripe, skin lacks fuzz.

FIRST EMPEROR—Very sweet, yellow-fleshed.

MANDARIN—One of the sweetest varieties of *Actinidia chinensis*.

LONGAN AND LITCHI

The longan, like the litchi, has something of a honeydew melon in its flavor, with a floral note of gardenia. It's sweeter than a litchi, but not as juicy. Although there are thirty to forty named cultivars of this fruit, only a few are commercially important in the United States.

DIAMOND RIVER—A late-season variety that bears less erratically than Kohala.

KOHALA—Most U.S. plantings are of this variety, which yields fruits about 1 inch in diameter with a very good, sweet flavor.

➤ **TAI TSO**—Popular litchi with firm, juicy flesh surrounding large seeds.

LOQUAT

There are two types of loquats—those with orange flesh and those with white flesh. Most of the cultivars you'll find in California have yellow to orange flesh, with broad leaves and round to oval fruits. White-fleshed fruits, though more rare, are grown.

BENLEHR—White flesh; juicy, sweet, high quality; peels easily.

BIG JIM—Yellow-orange flesh, very sweet, excellent apricot-like flavor.

EARLY RED—Skin red-orange, flesh orange, with superior tangy flavor.

TANAKA—Flesh firm, orange, aromatic, with sweet, excellent flavor.

VISTA WHITE—Flesh is pure white with a very high sugar content.

MANGO

There are about 800 named varieties of mango world-wide. We see but a few due to their fragility in shipping. The most common variety in our stores and farmers' markets early in the spring season is Tommy Atkins, a fair-tasting type. The really good mangoes come later. Here are the varieties to hold out for.

- **ATAULFO**—Excellent Mexican variety with rich, tangy, sweet flavor and yellow-orange skin.
- **CARRIE**—Greenish-yellow skin, with extra rich, aromatic, fiberless flesh.
- **EDWARD**—Yellow skin with red blush; flesh melting, floral aroma, quality excellent.
- **JULIE**—Excellent cropper in Trinidad and Tobago, exported to Europe.
- **KENT**—Superior sweet, melting, piney, juicy flesh; ripens into September. Greenish-yellow skin with red blush and a grayish bloom on the skin.

MELON

Although Europeans have been enjoying great varieties of melons, such as the French Charentais, for decades, these varieties are just beginning to be grown commercially here. Keep an eye out for them, as they have exquisite flavor.

CANTALOUPES

- **ALIENOR**—Aromatic, dark orange flesh of superior quality.
- **CHARENTAIS**—Very fragrant and sweet, with dark orange flesh.
- **SWEETHEART**—A favorite in England with salmon-red flesh.

HONEYDEWS

- **EARLI-DEW**—Extra-sweet and juicy melon with lime-green flesh.
- **GREEN-FLESH HONEYDEW**—Hard rind is white; flesh is bright green, spicy.
- **ORANGE BLOSSOM**—Inside cream-colored rind is fragrant, orange flesh.

MUSKMELONS

GREEN FLESH

- **PASSPORT**—Yellow, netted rind with greenish white flesh.
- **ROCKY SWEET**—Very sweet, lime-green flesh.

SALMON/ORANGE FLESH

- **AMBROSIA**—Strong musky fragrance and unique flavor.
- **BURPEE HYBRID**—Orange flesh, very sweet and melting.
- **IROQUOIS**—Ribbed and netted; superior deep orange flesh.

WHITE FLESH

- **ANGEL**—All-America Selections winner; mouth-watering aroma, delicious.
- **GOLDEN CRISPY**—Rind is golden yellow, thin, and edible. Sweet, fragrant, firm white flesh.

OTHER MELONS

- **AMY**—Canary type melon; very sweet flavor and crispy texture.
- **CANARY**—Bright yellow rind, crisp white flesh, very sweet and juicy.
- **CASABA**—A nonfragrant melon with greenish-white, juicy flesh.
- **CRANE**—A superb melon developed in Sonoma County, California.
- **CRENSHAW**—Yellow rind; salmon-pink flesh, sprightly, unique flavor.

WATERMELON

- **BLACK DIAMOND**—Fruits weigh 40 to 50 pounds; excellent quality, crisp flesh.
- **CHARLESTON GRAY**—Gray-green rind; perfect red color and sweet flavor.
- **NEW QUEEN**—Unique orange flesh is crisp and sweet; icebox size.
- **SUGAR BABY**—Icebox-size watermelon with full-sized flavor, red flesh.
- **SWEET BEAUTY**—All-America Selections winner; icebox size; exceptional quality.
- **YELLOW DOLL**—Icebox-size melons with sweet yellow flesh, black seeds.

NECTARINE

YELLOW FLESHED

FLAVORTOP—Rich yellow flesh with red streaks, superior flavor.

MERICREST—One of the best nectarines for the Northeast markets.

RED GOLD—Skin yellow with much red; flavor excellent; freestone.

SUNRED—Developed for Florida; bright red, gourmet quality flesh.

WHITE FLESHED

ARCTIC GLO—Good tart-sweet balance, rich flavor, fine texture.

GRAND PEARL—Midseason white-fleshed nectarine; flavor like white peaches.

HEAVENLY WHITE—Creamy skin with deep red blush, super quality.

SNOW QUEEN—Melting white flesh and superior flavor, texture.

OLIVE

If handled properly, almost any olive is good, but some varieties are artisanal olives rather than high-production commodities and thus are more likely than others to have been handled with low-tech curing methods. The following usually offer exquisite flavor.

ARBEQUINAS—Small Spanish variety with a sharp, biting flavor.

CERIGNOLA—Large, green and meaty Italian olives; can be stuffed.

HONDROELIA—A large Greek olive, fruity taste, with a reddish blush.

KALAMATA—A Greek olive, large, purple, and almond-shaped; tangy.

LUCQUES—From Provence, France; small, with very crisp green flesh.

MANZANILLA—Large black olive usually brine cured; tangy, smoky flavor.

NAPHLION—A Greek olive, dark green, brine cured, and meaty.

NIÇOISE—Small olives, usually cured purple-black, with intense flavor.

PICHOLINE—Very small, tangy olives, usually cured at the green stage.

SARACENE—Small and brownish-purple in color, with a rich olive flavor.

PAPAYA

The smaller Hawaiian papayas are sweeter than the Mexican variety. All share a mild flavor that's slightly apricoty and a little musky.

MEXICAN—Large hybrid fruits with yellowish-orange flesh.

SOLO—Very high quality, sweet Hawaiian with golden-orange flesh.

SUNRISE—Also called Strawberry Papaya; sweet red-orange flesh.

WASHINGTON—Medium-sized, sweet oval fruits of aromatic, fruity quality.

PASSIONFRUIT

Passionfruit takes well to pot culture, so you could try growing your own. A variety called Black Knight was developed in Massachusetts. It produces dark purple-black fruit the size of an egg with excellent flavor, according to the California Rare Fruit Growers (see Sources, page 517).

AUSTRALIAN PURPLE—Mild, sweet flavor; grown in Hawaii, Australia.

COMMON PURPLE–aka Purple Granadilla, naturalized in Hawaii; small, but fine flavor and big aromatics.

EDGEHILL—Best grown in southern California; large fragrant fruit.

KAHUNA—Favored in Hawaii; vigorous vine with sweet fruit.

PURPLE GIANT—Very large fruit with dark purple rind and a tangy flavor.

PEACH

ELBERTA—Freestone, with tender, juicy yellow flesh.

FLAVORCREST—Excellent quality; semifreestone peach; firm, yellow flesh.

BABCOCK—White flesh, tender, juicy, and sweet with fine flavor and aroma.

HALEHAVEN—Exceptional quality; one of the best for roadside markets.

J. H. HALE—An old, fine-grained variety with a sprightly flavor.

O'HENRY—Large, freestone peach with delicious yellow flesh streaked red.

RED HAVEN—Becomes freestone when ripe; fine texture, excellent flavor.

SPRINGCREST—Small fruit with delightful aroma, juicy and melting flesh.

WHITE LADY—Freestone white-fleshed peach with sweet, rich flavor.

PEAR

ABATE—Also known as Abbe Fetel; large, sweet, melts in the mouth.

ALEXANDER LUCAS—European pear similar to d'Anjou, but denser fleshed.

BARTLETT—Delicious at its peak; aromatic, musky.

BOSC—Firm, thoroughly russeted pear with a fine, light flavor.

COMICE—Melting, sweet, juicy, silky texture and tantalizing fragrance.

D'ANJOU—Good winter pear that's slow to ripen; sweet, juicy.

DUCHESSE D'ANGOULÈME—Very sweet and juicy pear for fresh eating.

MADELEINE—Small, round, and delicious, with green and russet skin.

RED BARTLETT—Excellent flavor, similar to Bartlett and deep red skin.

SECKEL—Firm, succulent, sweet, spicy, and small pear; good for poaching.

WHITE DOYENNE—Rich flavor, aromatic; known to the ancient Romans.

WINTER NELIS—Spicy-flavored, small pear from Belgium; ripens for winter.

PERSIMMON

AMERICAN PERSIMMONS (ASTRINGENT, OR SOFT-RIPE, TYPE)

EARLY GOLDEN—Top-quality American cultivar selected in 1880.

GARRETSON—Very like Early Golden, with same sweet flesh.

YATES—Flavor like a fine apricot; ripens early; prize-winning quality.

FUYU (NONASTRINGENT, OR FIRM-RIPE, TYPE)

CALIFORNIA FUYU—Often seedy, orange to red-orange fruits.

COFFEECAKE—Nishimura type with rich, spicy, cinnamon-like flavor.

FUYU—Medium-sized, flattened, red-colored, high-quality, spicy fruit.

GIANT FUYU—Large, more rounded type; flavor similar to Fuyu.

IZU—Very sweet, tasty, medium size.

JIRO—Flat shape, still hard when ripe, called the apple persimmon.

NISHIMURA—Almost round, chocolate-colored, sweet, juicy flesh.

HACHIYA (ASTRINGENT, OR SOFT-RIPE, TYPE)

CHOCOLATE—Small fruits; red-orange flesh is streaked with brown.

EUREKA—Very high-quality, though seedy, type favored in Texas.

HACHIYA—Large, acorn-shaped persimmon with red-orange skin.

MARU—Glossy, orange-red skin; flesh cinnamon-colored; sweet and rich.

TAMOPAN—Large, irregularly globed, rounded, deep orange-red color.

TANENASHI—Cone-shaped, yellow-orange type grown in southeast United States.

PINEAPPLE

ABACAXI—Called the most delicious pineapple for its rich, succulent flesh; often found in Florida.

CHAMPALLA—Top-quality pineapple flavor; organically grown on Maui.

ESMERALDA—A Cayenne type grown in Mexico; sweet, acidic flesh.

EXTRA SWEET—Twice as sweet as other pineapples; high in vitamin C.

QUEEN—Sometimes imported from the Philippines; excellent sweet-tangy flavor.

RED SPANISH—Top-rated variety in Puerto Rico; orange-red outside.

SMOOTH CAYENNE—The most popular, familiar variety found in the United States.

SUGARLOAF—Very sweet, juicy, white to yellowish flesh; high quality.

PLUM

"Plums" here include not only pure plums but also interspecific hybrids like pluots and apriums—all of which can be used in the same ways as plums. (In case you're wondering about *umeboshi*, those salty Japanese plums, they're really a kind of preserved apricot.)

JAPANESE TYPES

CATHERINE BUNNELL—Extraordinary flavor, but rare; Luther Burbank hybrid (see page 302).

ELEPHANT HEART—Red skin and flesh; excellent flavor; a Burbank hybrid.

PTITSIN #5—Yellow skin with sweet, juicy, aromatic, flavorful flesh.

RED ACE—Crimson skin with sweet, delicious red flesh; a Burbank hybrid.

SANTA ROSA—Burbank's standard of excellence in a Japanese type plum.

EUROPEAN TYPES

COE'S GOLDEN DROP—A very sweet plum with an apricot-like flavor.

GOLDEN TRANSPARENT—A yellow gage-type plum with translucent flesh.

ITALIAN PRUNE—Blue skin, firm yellow flesh is very sweet; good for drying to make prunes.

REINE CLAUDE VIOLETTE—Purple gage type; excellent dessert quality plum.

STANLEY—Blue-black skin, freestone, excellent quality and very sweet.

DAMSON TYPES

BLUE DAMSON—A small, tart, damson-type plum perfect for jams, jellies.

MIRABELLE TYPES

MIRABELLE—French favorite for preserves and pastries; yellow skin, sweet flesh.

MIRABELLE DE NANCY—Small, oval, yellow-green fruits are juicier than Mirabelle.

NATIVE AMERICAN TYPES

ACME—*Prunus nigra* hybrid from Canada; dark red skin, excellent quality.

INTERSPECIFICS

DAPPLE DANDY—Dappled skin with sweet, subacid, mild flavor; pluot.

FLAVOR DELIGHT—Resembles apricot; unique texture, flavor; aprium.

FLAVOR KING—Plummy, with tangy skin, rich apricot-like flavor; pluot.

FLAVOR QUEEN—Candy-like sweetness with amber-orange flesh; pluot.

FLAVOR SUPREME—Taste test winner; mottled skin; sweet red flesh; pluot.

FLAVORICH—Large black fruit with sweet orange flesh; pluot.

GEO PRIDE—Ranked near top at taste tests; plum-apricot flavor; pluot.

POMEGRANATE

There aren't a large number of pomegranate varieties sold in the United States, but most of what we find in the markets is a high-quality variety called Wonderful, so lack of many cultivars is no big problem. The juice of the Wonderful is bright wine-red with a fine balance of sweet and sour.

AMBROSIA—Large, tasty fruits with yellowish skin and garnet seeds.

GRANADA—Early ripening variety with mild, sweet juice; dark red skin.

SWEET—Pink juice is very sweet, just mildly acidic; best for beverages.

WONDERFUL—The standard variety in commerce; excellent quality.

QUINCE

It's hard enough just finding quince these days, but they are experiencing a resurgence of interest. If you know a grower, see if you can find one of these choice varieties.

AROMATNAYA—Recent import from Russia; excellent quality; fragrant.

ORANGE—Variety for cold regions that turns red when cooked.

PINEAPPLE—A Luther Burbank introduction (see page 302) with hint of pineapple.

RED RASPBERRY

BABA—An everbearing type with sweet; almost wild flavor.

CAROLINE—New cultivar packed with nutritional substances.

CHIEF—Summer-bearing type of exceptionally fine flavor.

CHILLIWACK—Northwest cultivar with glossy, extra sweet berries.

HERITAGE—A standard of quality among everbearing raspberries.

MAMMOTH RED THORNLESS—Big, very flavorful, aromatic berries.

MEEKER—Excellent quality in a bright red berry. Good for home gardens.

SEPTEMBER—Bright red fruit of superior flavor; an everbearing raspberry.

SUMMIT—Dark red everbearer with high quality; firm fleshed fruits.

TAYLOR—Very large, bright red berries with exceptionally good flavor.

STRAWBERRY

ALPINE TYPE

ALPINE YELLOW—Long, conical berries are highly aromatic; great flavor.

BARON SOLEMACHER IMPROVED—Berries are 1 inch long; "wild" flavor.

RUEGEN—Small fruits with the intense flavor of wild strawberries.

EVERBEARING TYPE

CHANDLER—Bright red berries of very good flavor, from UC Davis.

MARA DES BOIS—Wild woodland type ripens late summer, early fall.

SELVA—Produces good-flavored fruit summer through fall.

TRISTAR—Deep red flesh, skin with excellent flavor for an everbearer.

JUNE-BEARING TYPE

CAVENDISH—A Nova Scotia introduction with an excellent, sweet flavor.

DELMARVEL—A standard of quality in the Mid-Atlantic states; large fruits.

FAIRFAX—Early season bearer; dark red when ripe; aromatic and flavorful.

ROYAL SOVEREIGN—An old English variety with a distinct, delicious flavor.

SEQUOIA—Frequently planted in U-Pick farms; excellent quality.

SPARKLE—Wins my personal taste test as best-flavored hybrid strawberry.

SUWANNEE—Large berries that are also frequent taste-test winners.

Recipes by Category

Starters

Caraway Farmer Cheese – *Caraway*   383
Extra Good Guacamole – *Avocado*   70
Gougères – *Cheese and Dairy Products*   444
Rosemary and Lavender Marinated Olives –
   Olive   284
Stuffed Grape Leaves – *Grape*   263
Tarragon Prawns – *Tarragon*   413
The Best Hummus You've Ever Tasted –
   Dried Beans and Other Legumes   351

Salads and Salad Dressings

GREEN SALADS

Arugula and Mesclun with Grapefruit and
   Avocado – *Arugula*   60
Bartlett Pear Salad – *Pear*   295
Comice Pears with Prosciutto and
   Baby Greens – *Pear*   295
Green Perilla Salad – *Perilla*   405
Looseleaf Lettuce and Roasted Beet Salad –
   Lettuce   144
Red and White Salad – *Chicory and
   Endive*   103

Red and Yellow Beet Salad with Orange
   Vinaigrette – *Beet*   75
Salad Niçoise – *Olive*   285
"Spring Tonic" Salad with Sweet Dressing –
   Mâche   147
The True Caesar Salad – *Lettuce*   143
Watercress, Beet, and Orange Salad –
   Watercress   207

VEGETABLE AND GRAIN SALADS

Crosnes, Pear, and Hazelnut Salad –
   Crosnes   114
Fennel and Tomato Salad – *Fennel*   126
German Potato Salad – *Savory*   411
Greek Salad – *Cucumber*   116
Green Papaya Salad – *Papaya*   287
Tabbouleh – *Tomato*   203
Wakame Orange Salad – *Seaweed*   182

DRESSINGS

Blue Cheese Dressing – 144
Carrot-Juice Salad Dressing – *Carrot*   88
Green Goddess Dressing – *Parsley*   404
Raspberry Vinaigrette – *Red Raspberry*   314
Vanilla-Orange Vinaigrette – *Citrus*   245

Soups

Carrot Soup with Rice – *Carrot*   88
Celery and Seafood Consomme – *Celery*   93
Crab and Squash Soup – *Winter Squash*   212
Grape and Almond Gazpacho – *Grape*   263
Green Gazpacho with Shellfish –
    Tomatillo   199
Portugese Kale Soup – *Kale*   137
Potato-Lovage Soup – *Lovage*   398
Scandinavian Pea Soup – *Pea*   166
Scotch Lamb and Barley Soup – *Barley*   356
Untraditional Gazpacho – *Tomato*   202
Watercress Soup – *Watercress*   208
Winter Squash Soup with Pumpkin Seeds –
    Pumpkin Seed   344

Main Dishes

FISH

Brussels Sprouts and Sherry Shrimp –
    Brussels Sprout   81
Date Encrusted Halibut – *Date*   255
Dilled Salmon – *Dill*   392
Halibut Wrapped in Chinese Cabbage
    Leaves – *Asian Vegetables*   63
Paella – *Rice*   368
Salmon Fillets with Horseradish Crust –
    Horseradish   396
Shrimp Risotto Supreme – *Seafood and
    Freshwater Fish*   436
Trout Macadamia – *Macadamia Nut*   331

POULTRY

Asian-Style Orange Chicken – *Citrus*   244
Chicken, Asian-Italian Style – *Ginger*   394
Chicken Filé Gumbo – *Okra*   153
Chicken Marvels on Rice – *Poultry*   432
Chicken with Citrus and Cumin – *Cumin*   391
Coq Au Vin – *Wine*   477
Duck Stew with Walnuts and Pomegranates –
    Pomegranate   309
Grilled Chicken with Thyme – *Thyme*   414
Moroccan Chicken – *Chile Pepper*   108
Rosemary Chicken Toscana – *Rosemary*   407
Seared Duck Breast with Spicy Squash-Mango
    Chutney – *Poultry*   431
Southern-Fried Chicken – *Poultry*   432
Tarragon Chicken – *Tarragon*   413

MEAT

Beef Stew with Porcini – *Mushroom*   150
Brazilian Feijoada – *Dried Beans and Other
    Legumes*   350
Caraway-Infused Pork with Sauerkraut and
    Apples – *Caraway*   383
Cider-Glazed Pork Chops with Prune-Armagnac
    Confit – *Plum*   305
Coriander Pork – *Cilantro and Coriander*   390
Garlic and Rosemary Rack of Lamb –
    Lamb   425
Hazelnut-Crusted Pork Loin – *Hazelnut*   330
Lamb and Cauliflower Stew – *Cauliflower*   91
New England Boiled Dinner – *Cabbage*   83
Roast Pork Loin with Dried Fruit and Sweet
    Spices – *Pork*   428
Rock 'Em, Sock 'Em Meat Loaf – *Cumin*   391
Saltimbocca – *Sage*   409
Sausage and Turnips in their Shells –
    Turnip   205

Sloppy Joes – *Meat*   423
Sukiyaki – *Asian Vegetables*   64
Veal Scallops with Sherry-Shallot Sauce –
   Shallot   185

VEGETARIAN

Angel Hair Pasta with Summer Squash –
   Summer Squash and Zucchini   190
Artichokes Siciliano – *Artichoke*   58
Barbecued Tempeh – *Soybean*   353
Battered and Fried Summer Squash – *Summer*
   Squash and Zucchini   191
Cheese and Rice Frittata – *Rice*   369
Cheesy Corn Soufflé – *Corn*   112
Fingerling Potato and Chanterelle Gratin –
   Potato   169
Grilled Veggie Burgers – *Pistachio*   338
Homemade Tofu – *Soybean*   354
Humita Casserole with Corn Husks –
   Corn   111
Indian Eggplant and Potato Stew –
   Eggplant   122
Kasha, Bean, and Corn Tacos –
   Buckwheat   357
Middle Eastern Stuffed Eggplant –
   Eggplant   122
Moroccan-Style Artichoke Stew –
   Artichoke   57
Pasta with Hunter's Sauce – *Sweet Pepper*   194
Penne with Broccoli and Fava Beans –
   Broccoli   77
Potato Soufflé – *Potato*   169
Ratatouille – *Eggplant*   123
Salsify Gnocchi – *Salsify*   179
Spaghetti Squash with Tomato and Basil –
   Winter Squash   213
Stuffed Squash Blossoms – *Summer Squash*
   and Zucchini   191

Sweet Potato and Spinach Flan –
   Sweet Potato   197
Savory Chard No-Crust Quiche – *Chard*   99
Tacos of Creamy Braised Chard – *Chard*   98
Thyme Pizza – *Thyme*   415

Side Dishes

FRESH "GREEN" VEGETABLES

Baked Sugar Snap Peas – *Pea*   165
Braised Belgian Endive – *Chicory and*
   Endive   103
Braised Hiziki with Vegetables – *Seaweed*   183
Broccoli in Excelsis – *Broccoli*   77
Butterbeans and Collards – *Green Bean*   133
Caponata with Chives – *Chive*   388
Cardoons, Spanish Style – *Cardoon*   186
Creamed Spinach – *Spinach*   188
Indian Pudding – *Corn*   112
Leeks à la Grecque – *Leek*   141
Lima Bean Succotash – *Lima Bean*   146
Okra, North African Style – *Okra*   153
Peas Braised with Lettuce and Onions –
   Pea   165
Spicy Roast Cauliflower – *Cauliflower*   91
Stewed Rhubarb – *Rhubarb*   174

ROOT VEGETABLES

Austrian-Style Kohlrabi – *Kohlrabi*   139
Bashed Neeps, Sonoma Style – *Rutabaga*   176
Celery Root and Rice, Bulgarian Style –
   Celery Root   95
Daikon Stir-Fry – *Radish*   172
Garlic Mashed Potatoes and Celery Root –
   Celery Root   96

Sauté of Parsnips, Chestnuts, and Brussels
Sprouts – *Parsnip*   161
Savory Roasted Potatoes – *Savory*   411
Scandinavian Potato Pancakes – *Potato*   170
Sweet Marjoram Potato Patties – *Oregano
and Marjoram*   402
Tempura Roots in Ohsawa Sauce –
Parsnip   160

SLAWS AND PICKLES

Homemade Sauerkraut – *Cabbage*   84
Kim Chee – *Asian Vegetables*   63
Mexican Pepino Snack – *Pepino*   296
Midwestern Sweet-and-Sour Coleslaw –
Cabbage   83
Okra-Merliton Slaw – *Okra*   154
Pickled Beets – *Beet*   74
Winter Green Slaw with Warm Bacon
Dressing – *Chard*   99

BEAN, GRAIN, AND NUT SIDES

Glazed Chestnuts – *Chestnut*   328
Mexican Black Beans with Epazote –
Epazote   393
Mexican Refried Beans – *Dried Beans and
Other Legumes*   349
Millet and Cauliflower Medley – *Millet*   359
Orange and Almond Rice – *Citrus*   244
Quinoa Pilaf – *Quinoa and Amaranth*   363
Tuscan White Beans – *Dried Beans and
Other Legumes*   351

Baked Goods and Desserts

BREADS

Cinnamon Rolls – *Wheat*   373
Pecan Lace Tulips – *Kiwifruit*   268
Pita Bread – *Wheat*   374
Sweet Persimmon Bread – *Persimmon*   299
Whole-Wheat and Black Walnut Quick Rolls –
Flours and Meals   466

COOKIES

Biscotti – *Almond*   323
Black Walnut and Oatmeal Cookies –
Walnut   342
Chewy Oatmeal-Coconut Cookies – *Oats*   361
Fig and Oatmeal Cookies – *Fig*   258
Pfeffernüsse – *Anise and Star Anise*   379
Pineapple-Oatmeal Cookies – *Pineapple*   301

PIES, TARTS, COBBLERS, AND CRISPS

American Apple Pie – *Apple*   220
Blueberry Pie – *Blueberry*   236
Cherry Pie – *Cherry*   242
Gooseberry Pie – *Currant and
Gooseberry*   251
Ground Cherry Pie – *Ground Cherry*   134
Huckleberry Pie – *Huckleberry*   266
Key Lime Tart – *Citrus*   245
Nectarine-Blackberry Cobbler – *Nectarine*   282
Nora's Superb Blackberry Cobbler –
Blackberry   230
Peach Pie – *Peach*   292

Plum and Peach Cobbler – *Plum*   306

"Pumpkin" Pie Made with Butternut Squash –
Winter Squash   211

Rhubarb-Huckleberry Pie – *Rhubarb*   174

Single Crust for a 9-Inch Pie – *Winter
Squash*   211

Southern Pecan Pie – *Pecan and Hickory
Nut*   335

Strawberry-Rhubarb Crisp – *Strawberry*   317

Tarte Tatin – *Apple*   219

FROZEN DESSERTS

Asian Pear Granita – *Asian Pear*   224

Blackberry and Chocolate Bombe –
Blackberry   233

Black Raspberry Ice Cream – *Black
Raspberry*   231

Kiwi-Lime-Strawberry Sorbet – *Kiwifruit*   268

Sugarless Vanilla Ice Cream – *Sweeteners*   474

CUSTARDS

Citrus Panna Cotta – *Milk*   440

Figgy Pudding – *Fig*   259

Fudge – *Chocolate*   459

Lavender Crème Brûlée – *Lavender*   397

Lemon Bavarian with Black Currant Spice –
Currant and Gooseberry   251

Pomegranate Tapioca – *Pomegranate*   310

Raspberry Clafoutis – *Red Raspberry*   313

Tiramisù – *Coffee*   457

FRUIT DESSERTS

Bananas with Coconut Cream – *Banana*   227

Charentais Melon Cockaigne – *Melon*   279

Medlar Cheese – *Medlar*   277

Melon and Mango – *Melon*   279

Pavlova – *Passionfruit*   288

Peach Melba – *Peach*   292

Persimmon Sundae – *Persimmon*   299

Strawberry and Peach Succulence –
Strawberry   316

NUT DESSERTS

Brazil Nut and Cashew Loaf – *Brazil Nut*   324

Brazil Nut Bark – *Brazil Nut*   324

Hot Candied Walnuts – *Walnut*   342

Medjool Date Nut Loaf – *Date*   255

Peanut Salvage Bars – *Peanut*   334

Breakfast

A Fine Omelet – *Eggs*   448

Amaranth Popcakes – *Quinoa and
Amaranth*   364

Blueberry Muffins – *Blueberry*   235

Cornbread Muffins – *Flours and Meals*   467

Dr. Cox's Cream Oats – *Oat*   361

Hard-Boiled Eggs – *Eggs*   449

Poached Eggs – *Eggs*   449

Scallion Frittata – *Onion*   159

Strawberry Crepes – *Strawberry*   317

Super Delicious Sunflower Seed Granola –
Sunflower Seed   347

Sweet Pepper and Sausage Frittata –
Sweet Pepper   195

The Ultimate French Toast – *Citrus*   246

Sauces, Stocks, Stuffings, and Preserves

SAUCES

Ancient Greek Garlic Sauce – *Garlic*   130

Berbere Sauce – *Cardamom*   385

Black Currant Sauce – *Currant and Gooseberry*   252

Cashew Sauce – *Cashew*   326

Chervil Sauce Béarnaise – *Chervil*   386

Chimichurri Sauce – *Parsley*   404

Dark Chocolate–Peanut Butter Sauce – *Chocolate*   460

Fresh, Hot Salsa – *Cilantro and Coriander*   389

Gado Gado Sauce – *Ginger*   395

Garlic Rub for Meat – *Garlic*   130

Harissa – *Chile Pepper*   107

Huckleberry Game Sauce – *Huckleberry*   266

Pesto – *Pine Nut*   337

Pico De Gallo – *Onion*   158

Radish Salsa – *Radish*   172

Rosemary Pesto – *Rosemary*   407

Salsa Molcajete – *Chile Pepper*   107

Salsa Verde – *Tomatillo*   107, 199

Sweet-and-Sour Raisin Sauce – *Dried Fruit*   461

Thai Peanut Sauce – *Peanut*   333

Tzatziki – *Cucumber*   116

Walnut Green Sauce – *Walnut*   341

STOCKS

Chicken Stock – *Bouillons and Broths*   454

Demi-Glace – *Bouillons and Broths*   453

Vegetable Stock – *Bouillons and Broths*   453

STUFFINGS

Pistachio Turkey Stuffing – *Pistachio*   339

Sage Turkey Stuffing – *Sage*   409

Wild Rice and Cornbread Stuffing – *Wild Rice*   375

PRESERVES

Apricot Preserves – *Apricot*   222

Brandied Cherries – *Cherry*   240

Cranberry Relish – *Cranberry*   248

Crystallized Borage Flowers – *Borage*   382

Damson Plum Jam – *Plum*   307

Dried Cherry, Apple, and Apricot Chutney – *Cherry*   247

Loquat and Strawberry Jam – *Loquat*   271

Spicy Squash–Mango Chutney – *Mango*   431

Quince Marmalade – *Quince*   311

Violet Jelly – *Edible Flowers*   120

Beverages

Almond Horchata – *Almond*   322

Cherimoya Agua Fresca – *Cherimoya*   238

Grapefruit Cooler – *Citrus*   246

Mojito – *Mint*   400

Moroccan Mint Tea – *Mint*   400

Nectarine-Viognier Fizz – *Melons*   282

Soy Milk – *Soybean*   353

Sources

For More Information about Organic Foods

Learn about organic foods and their production, about the environmental consequences of conventional farming methods and related topics at these web sites.

WWW.NEWFARM.ORG

THE NEW FARM

A great resource with up-to-date info on organic farming, from the Rodale Institute.

WWW.ORGANICCONSUMERS.ORG

ORGANIC CONSUMERS ASSOCIATION

A public-interest organization dedicated to environmentally safe and sustainable food production. It posts news reports covering issues of food safety, chemical and biotech agriculture, corporate accountability, and environmental sustainability.

(888) 403-1007

WWW.SLOWFOODUSA.ORG

SLOW FOOD

The U.S. arm of a worldwide nonprofit educational organization dedicated to supporting food traditions and finding viable alternatives to the globalization and homogenization of the world's tastes. Slow Food supports local, farm-fresh produce, and keeps you in touch with the practitioners thereof.

WWW.FACTORYFARM.ORG

GRACE FACTORY FARM PROJECT

(GLOBAL RESOURCE ACTION CENTER FOR THE ENVIRONMENT)

A New York nonprofit organization that works to oppose factory farming and to promote a sustainable food production system that is healthful, humane, economically viable, and environmentally sound.

WWW.IATP.ORG

INSTITUTE FOR AGRICULTURE AND TRADE POLICY

A Minneapolis nonprofit organization that supports sustainable family farms, farm communities, and ecosystems around the world. A good site to visit if you want to support organic agriculture.

WWW.IFG.ORG

INTERNATIONAL FORUM ON GLOBALIZATION

Learn more about the role of globalization on the production of foodstuffs.

WWW.NATURALHUB.COM/SITE_CONTENTS.HTM

An interesting web site about natural foods in the strictest sense of that term—that is, foods our Paleolithic hunter-gatherer ancestors might have eaten. Not everything listed is organic but much is.

WWW.VIVIDPICTURE.NET

ENVISIONING A SUSTAINABLE FOOD SYSTEM IN CALIFORNIA

This site is devoted to nothing less than the transformation of the entire state of California's food industry toward a sustainable system. It's a project of the Roots of Change Fund (www.rocfund.org), a collaborative of foundations and experts that supports the transition to a healthier food system and healthier environment in California, and Ecotrust Food & Farms (www.ecotrust.org).

WWW.CAVIAREMPTOR.ORG
CAVIAR EMPTOR
Deals with environmentally sound alternatives to fishing Caspian Sea sturgeon, which are growing increasingly endangered.

Locating Organic Food near You

Learn about farmers' markets and farmers who sell from their farms located near you by investigating these web sites. Here are also large retailers that sell organic food. The list is far from exhaustive.

WWW.NAL.USDA.GOV/AFSIC/CSA
ALTERNATIVE FARMING SYSTEMS INFORMATION CENTER
This is the place to start if you're looking to buy organic produce through *Community Supported Agriculture,* a system that links buyers to local organic farmers for regular purchases of seasonal produce (see page 13). Other sites that can connect you with participating local farms are the Biodynamic Farming and Gardening Association (www.biodynamics.com/csa.html), and the Rodale Institute's New Farm farm locator (newfarm.org/farmlocator/index.php).

WWW.LOCALHARVEST.ORG
LOCAL HARVEST
Links to farms, farmers participating in Community Supported Agriculture, farm markets, food co-ops, and organic restaurants all over the United States.

Online ordering of organic foods from their member farms, too.

WWW.AMS.USDA.GOV/DIRECTMARKETING
USDA FARMER DIRECT MARKETING
The USDA's Agricultural Marketing Service has created the National Farmers Market and Direct Marketing Association Directory, which lists farmers' markets and farmers' market associations across the country. The site also lists which markets accept WIC coupons (see page 12).

WWW.OMRI.ORG
THE ORGANIC MATERIALS REVIEW INSTITUTE
This organization posts its list of subscribers, which include regional organic farmers' associations, organic certifiers, and state departments of agriculture that you can turn to to find sources of local organic foods.

WWW.EATWELLGUIDE.ORG
EAT WELL GUIDE, WHOLESOME FOOD FROM HEALTHY ANIMALS
Enter your zip code and up comes a list of suppliers of organic and natural meat products in your area. There's also a list of national mail-order meat suppliers.

WWW.GOURMETSLEUTH.COM
GOURMETSLEUTH.COM
A portal to great sources of information on high-quality food, including online ordering.

WWW.EATWILD.COM
THE CLEARINGHOUSE FOR INFORMATION ABOUT PASTURE-BASED FARMING
One of the best sources of information and access to grass-fed, organic meats (including bison and lamb) and dairy.

FANCY MEATS FROM VERMONT

Fancy Meats from Vermont is a co-op of fifty farmers producing lambs, pigs, humanely raised veal, venison, goats, rabbits, eggs, and specialty cheeses. Individuals must pick up the meat at the slaughterhouse.

2604 East Hill Road, Andover, Vermont 05143
(802) 875-3159; fax (802) 875-3159

WWW.ECOFISH.COM
ECOFISH

Track down sustainable, low-mercury fish and organic shellfish. EcoFish distributes seafood from environmentally sustainable fisheries to over 1,000 natural and organic food stores.

WWW.SEASONALCHEF.COM
SEASONAL CHEF, CELEBRATING
LOCALLY GROWN PRODUCE

A listing of what's in season and when in California, with links to farmers' market listings nationwide.

WWW.VERMONTFRESH.NET
THE VERMONT FRESH NETWORK

Lists farms, food producers, restaurants, and distributors in Vermont.

WWW.WHOLEFOODSMARKET.COM
WHOLE FOODS

A supermarket chain emphasizing organic products, plans to expand to 400 stores by 2010.

WWW.WILDOATS.COM
WILD OATS

Another organically oriented supermarket chain, not far behind Whole Foods in size.

Mail Order Sources: General

Mail-order shippers of a range of organic foods can be found at these web sites.

WWW.DIAMONDORGANICS.COM
DIAMOND ORGANICS

Carries an array of organic products.

1272 Highway 1, Moss Landing, California, 95039
(888) ORGANIC or (888) 674-2642

WWW.EARTHYDELIGHTS.COM
EARTHY DELIGHTS

Carries many organic gourmet products; started as a service to professional chefs, shipping produce overnight to anywhere in the country. It's a sort of natural-foods Dean & Deluca, offering fiddlehead ferns, fresh morel and chanterelle mushrooms, caviar, foie gras, artisanal cheeses, pastas, grains, beans, truffles, fruits, nuts, fresh seasonal produce and more.

1161 East Clark Road, Suite 260, DeWitt, Michigan 48820
(800) 367-4709 or (517) 668-2402; fax (517) 668-1213

WWW.THEORGANICPAGES.COM
THE ORGANIC TRADE ASSOCIATION'S
ORGANIC PAGES

The Organic Trade Association's web site, containing a huge amount of information on mail order suppliers of all kinds of organic products, plus info on organic restaurants, farmers, retailers, and more.

60 Wells Street, P.O. Box 547, Greenfield, Massachusetts 01302
(413) 774-7511, ext. 13; fax (413) 774-6432

WWW.ROCKCREEKORGANICS.COM
ROCK CREEK ORGANICS,
NATURAL AND ORGANIC FOODS

Carries everything you need for organic baking, including whole wheat flour, golden wheat flour, wheat bran, almond butter, almonds, walnuts, pecans, pistachios, fruit spreads, pancake mix, muffin mix, and more.

P.O. Box 255, 215 Kennaday Lane, Idleyld Park, Oregon 97447
(866) 571-NUTS (6887) or (541) 496-4705;
fax (541) 496-4266

WWW.SHOPNATURAL.COM
SHOP NATURAL
Based in Arizona, this site carries a wide variety of foods, personal care, and pet items, with many links to information on organics.

WWW.SUNORGANIC.COM
SUN ORGANIC FARM
Packaged organic food products, dried fruits, and vegetables, even wines.

411 South Las Posas Road, San Marcos, California 92078
(888) 269-9888 or (760) 510-8077; fax (760) 510-9996

WWW.TRUEFOODSMARKET.COM
TRUE FOODS MARKET
Online retailer of natural and organic foods, beverages, and cleaning supplies.

WWW.FORESTFARM.COM
FOREST FARM
Thousands of ornamental and edible plants available.

990 Tetherow Road, Williams, Oregon 97544-9599
(541)846-7269; fax (541)846-6963

Mail Order Sources: Specific Foods

Mail-order shippers of specific or hard-to-find organic foods are listed under this heading. Note: A wide variety of organic dried fruits are available online. Type "organic dried fruits" in your search engine. In fact, there are so many online mail-order sources that a simple online search may turn up just what you're looking for.

VEGETABLES
WWW.AUXDELICES.COM
MARCHÉ AUX DELICES OF NEW YORK
A great source for *crosnes*; also carries fresh and dried wild mushrooms.

(888) 547-5471; fax (413)604-2789

WWW.SEAWEED.NET
MENDOCINO SEA VEGETABLE CO.
Recipe books and a catalog of seaweed products, harvested from clean coastlines.

P.O. Box 1265, Mendocino, California 95460
(707) 895-2996

FRUIT
WWW.MELISSAS.COM
MELISSA'S WORLD VARIETY PRODUCE, INC.
Specializes in a wide range of organic fruits and vegetables, including specialty items like loquats.

P.O. Box 21127, Los Angeles, California 90021
(800) 588-0151

WWW.FROGHOLLOW.COM
FROG HOLLOW FARM
An excellent source of tree-ripened organic peaches, nectarines, pluots, asian pears, and other fruit, as well as peach conserves, chutneys, marmalades, and more.

P.O. Box 2110, Brentwood, California 94513
(888) 779-4511

WWW.PROFLOWERS.COM/CHERRYMOONFARMS

CHERRY MOON FARMS

A source for organic fruits, including pineapples.

   5005 Waterridge Vista Drive, Suite 200, San Diego,
California 92121

   (800) 862-9958

WWW.VIVATIERRA.COM

VIVA TIERRA ORGANIC

Carries a number of organic apple varieties that
tend not to be found in most store–but only as long
as the harvest lasts!

   922 Third Street, Sedro-Woolley, Washington 98284

CITRUS

Many mail-order sources for organic citrus can be
found by plugging any of the following firms into
your search engine. The ones below are some of the
best. Surely there will be many more by the time
you read this.

   South Tex Organics, Mission, Texas
   Beck Grove, Fallbrook, California
   Kelly Hall Groves, Port St. Lucie, Florida
   Ladera Fruit Company, Fillmore, California
   Uncle Matt's Organic, Clermont, Florida
   New Harvest Organics, Patagonia, Arizona
   Purepak, Inc., Oxnard, California
   Sutherland Produce Sales, Inc., El Cajon,
     California

WWW.OASISDATEGARDENS.COM

OASIS DATE GARDENS

Carries several varieties of organic dates, as well as
other dried fruits and nuts.

   59-111 Highway 111, P.O. Box 757, Thermal, California 92274

   (800) 827-8017

WWW.REDLANDORGANICS.COM/SAW_MILL_
FARM.HTM

SAW MILL FARM

While longans are not yet a well-known fruit, this
farm near Miami sells them, as well as lychees, and
will ship.

   (305) 252-2357

NUTS

WWW.MAISIEJANES.COM

**MAISIE JANE'S CALIFORNIA SUNSHINE
PRODUCTS**

Soft-shelled almonds, plain and processed.

   1324 Dayton Road, Chico, California 95928

   (530) 899-7909

WWW.BLACK-WALNUTS.COM

HAMMONS PRODUCTS COMPANY

A great source of deliriously delicious eastern
black walnuts.

   105 Hammons Drive, P.O. Box 140, Stockton, Missouri 65785

   (888)-4BWNUTS; fax (417) 276-5187

WALNUTS

Some companies that sell organic walnuts. You can
look for these names on packages in the stores or
search for their web sites online and order directly
from the nut farms.

   Baker Walnut, Modesto, California
   Dixon Ridge Farms, Winters, California
   Ferrari Farms, Linden, California
   Gibson Farms, Hollister, California
   John Potter Specialty Foods, Patterson, California
   Poindexter Nut Company, Selma, California
   Sierra Orchards, Winters, California
   Tufts Ranch, Winters, California

WWW.MOLOKAI-ALOHA.COM/MACNUTS

PURDY'S NATURAL MACADAMIA NUTS

A source for organic macadamia nuts.

   P.O. Box 84, Ho'olehua, HI 96729

   (808) 567-6601

WWW.REJUVENATIVE.COM

REJUVENATIVE FOODS

Sells many kinds of organic nut and seed butters, including a really delicious pumpkin seed butter.

P.O. Box 8464, Santa Cruz, California 95061

(800) 805-7957; fax (888) 363-8310

WWW.ECO-NATURAL.COM

SPIRIT BEAR BODYCARE

Numerous organic products, but in particular it's a source for pumpkin seed oil.

P.O. Box 585, Kaslo, British Columbia, V0G1M0 Canada

(250) 353-7680; fax (250) 353-7677

GRAINS

WWW.LUNDBERG.COM

LUNDBERG FAMILY FARMS

One of the largest purveyors of organic rice. Sixty percent of Lundberg products are certified organic; the company also offers "eco-farmed" products, which use innovative environmental practices to sustain and preserve the ecosystem

5370 Church Street, P.O. Box 369, Richvale, California 95974-0369

(530) 882-4551; fax (530) 882-4500

WWW.ANSONMILLS.COM

ANSON MILLS

A source for Carolina Golden Rice, as well as organic corn products and whole-wheat flours.

1922-C Gervais Street, Columbia, South Carolina 29201

(803) 467-4122; fax (803) 256-2463

WWW.LOWELLFARMS.COM

LOWELL FARMS

A source for organic jasmine rice.

4 North Washington, El Campo, Texas 77437

(888) 484-9213

WWW.MCFADDENFARM.COM

MCFADDEN FARM

Organic wild rice.

Potter Valley, California

(800) 544-8230

WWW.NORTHERNNATURALS.COM

NORTHERN NATURALS

Quinoa and amaranth, as well as almonds, dried shiitakes, pumpkin seeds, millet, and spices.

Box 1182 Main Street, Middletown Springs, Vermont 05757

(888) 293-3985

MEATS

WWW.NIMANRANCH.COM

NIMAN RANCH

Niman Ranch started business nearly thirty years ago in Marin County, California. They still raise cattle on the original ranch but have expanded to sell pork and lamb, too. They now work with over 300 independent family farmers nationwide who raise livestock according to their strict protocols. Niman Ranch products are available through the web site as well as in retail stores.

WWW.HILLSFOODS.COM HILLS FOODS LTD.

Suppliers of certified organic meats, game meats, and specialty poultry. Custom smoking and sausage making. Cash & carry.

1-130 Glacier Street, Coquitlam, British Columbia, Canada

(604) 472-1500

WWW.LASATERGRASSLANDSBEEF.COM

LASATER GRASSLANDS BEEF

Grass-fed beef from one of America's pioneers of eco-minded cattle farming.

(866)-4LG-BEEF or (719) 541-2855

MEADOW RAISED MEATS

Shipping their meat frozen to New York, Vermont, New Hampshire, northeast Pennsylvania, and the western half of Massachusetts.

P.O. Box 103, East Meredith, New York 13757
(315) 829-5437

HUDSON VALLEY FARMERS CO-OP

A farmers cooperative of producer-members who are committed to a "grass-based," ecological agriculture, humane animal management, and high-quality, clean meats.

P.O. Box 38, Stanfordville, New York 12581
(845) 868-1826

VERMONT QUALITY MEATS

A cooperative representing thirty-eight small family farms, predominantly in Vermont, that raise premium-quality lamb, goat, pork, veal, venison, rabbit, chicken, free-range turkey, and gamebirds.

P.O. Box 116, Rupert, Vermont 05768
476 Route 7B North, North Clarendon, Vermont 05759
(802) 394-2558 or (802) 747-5950; fax (802) 747-5994

OLIVE OIL

THE OLIVE PRESS

High-quality California organic olive oils and Limonato lemon olive oil. They carry Lunigiana Estate, a small-production Tuscan-style (very peppery and bitter) oil made from olives grown in Sonoma County, California.

14301 Arnold Drive, Glen Ellen, California 95442
(800) 965-4839

DAVERO SONOMA, INC.

Stone ground and pressed the old-fashioned way at a ranch in the Dry Creek Valley near Healdsburg in Sonoma County. Fruity, peppery tasting oil won a gold medal at the Sonoma County Harvest Fair.

1195 Westside Road, Healdsburg, California 95448
(888) 431-8008 or (707) 431-8000; fax (707) 433-5780

MCEVOY RANCH

A very peppery and bitter, green-gold, certified organic, extra-virgin oil in the Tuscan style.

(866) 617-6779, (707) 769-4122, or (707) 778-2307

SPECTRUM NATURALS

The Arbequina olives used to make this organic oil are grown in Spain and Argentina. It's a mild oil, good for cooking. It's relatively inexpensive for a good extra-virgin oil. Many other organic cooking oils also available.

(800) 995-2705 or (707) 778-8900

STELLA CADENTE

Although they are not certified organic, the olives are pesticide free and hand picked at Stella Cadente ("shooting star" in Italian), Sue Ellery and Tom Hunter's ranch in Mendocino County. Their oil has won numerous awards, including "Best Domestic Olive Oil" at the Los Angeles County Fair.

Shooting Star Ranch, Boonville, California 95415
(707) 895-2848; fax (707) 895-9556

CHOCOLATE AND COFFEE

CHOCOSPHERE

An Internet-only chocolate shop based in Portland, Oregon. Many organic and sustainable brands among the thirty-two carried.

(877) 99-CHOCO (992-4626)

WWW.GRENADACHOCOLATE.COM

GRENADA CHOCOLATE COMPANY LTD.

One of the best organic chocolates on the market.

WWW.RAPUNZEL.COM

RAPUNZEL PURE ORGANICS

An eco-friendly and farmer-supportive company that sells 100 percent shade-grown, organic Arabica coffee, delicious organic chocolate, baking yeast, yeast extracts, bouillon, and broths.

ORGANIC WINE (AND BEER, TOO)

Access these web sites or call their phone numbers to discover the world of organic wines and beers.

WWW.CHARTRANDIMPORTS.COM

CHARTRAND IMPORTS

Paul Chartrand imports and distributes organic and organically grown wines from Australia, Europe, New Zealand, and the United States.
P.O. Box 1319, Rockland, Maine 04841
(800) 473-7307 or (207) 594-7300

WWW.ECOWINE.COM

ORGANIC WINE COMPANY

Imports organic French wines to the United States.
888-ECO-WINE (326-9463)

WWW.ORGANICVINTAGES.COM

ORGANIC VINTAGES

Certified organic wines, sparkling wines, and beers.
(877) ORGANIC

WWW.ORGANICWINEPRESS.COM

THE ORGANIC WINE PRESS

Organic wines from around the world.
175 Second Street, Bandon, Oregon 97411
(541) 347-3326

WWW.BEERTOWN.ORG

THE BREWERS ASSOCIATION

Here's a web site that can help you find small-scale beer producers.
736 Pearl Street, Boulder, Colorado 80302
(888) 822-6273 or (303) 447-0816; fax (303) 447-2825

WWW.BREWORGANIC.COM

SEVEN BRIDGES COOPERATIVE

Organic ingredients and supplies for home brewing. Also certified organic green coffee.
325A River Street, Santa Cruz, California 95060
(800) 768-4409

Major Organic Producers and Distributors to Look Out for

These are some of the most prominent wholesale producers of reliable organic foods. Distributors are companies that buy their raw materials (like produce and milk) from independent farmers and then distribute them to stores under their own label. They can usually be found in the organic sections of supermarkets. This list is not comprehensive—a perusal of your organic supermarket will turn up many more wonderful brands.

WWW.ANNIESNATURALS.COM

ANNIE'S NATURALS

Carries one of the widest arrays of organic condiments, such as mustards and organic salad dressings, and other pantry items.

WWW.ALBERTSORGANICS.COM

ALBERT'S ORGANICS

A full-service, wholesale distributor of a year round line of certified organically grown fruits and vegetables, along with regional lines of organic dairy products. Albert's distributes to 5,000 natural stores nationwide.

WWW.CFARM.COM
SMALL PLANET FOODS

The pinnacle of organic big business. The company includes Cascadian Farms, an organic food processor in Washington State, as well as Muir Glen, a line of nationally distributed tomato and marinara sauces. In 1999, Small Planet was bought by the multibillion dollar food giant General Mills.

WWW.EBFARM.COM
EARTHBOUND FARM

Started by husband and wife Drew and Myra Goodman as a roadside stand selling raspberries and lettuces, Earthbound Farm now farms over 13,000 acres of organic land, and sells over 100 different organic fruits and vegetables year round, shipped across the country in refrigerated trucks.

WWW.EDENFOODS.COM
EDEN FOODS, INC.

This company has been around since 1968, when it was founded in Ann Arbor, Michigan, to supply the macrobiotic community. You've undoubtedly seen its Edensoy soy milk boxes, but its catalog holds about 200 products from pastas to fruit juices to condiments to sea vegetables.

WWW.GREATSPICE.COM
THE GREAT SPICE COMPANY

If your devotion to organic food extends to your spice cabinet, you probably are well stocked up on the products of the Great Spice Company. The spices come from seven continents and are certified organic.

WWW.HORIZONORGANIC.COM
HORIZON ORGANIC DAIRY

A nationwide distributor of organic milk, other dairy, egg, and juice products.

WWW.KINGBLOSSOMNATURAL.COM
KING BLOSSOM NATURAL MARKETING, LLC

Organic growers with their own Controlled Atmosphere storage facility to ensure year-round availability of their apples and pears.
P.O. Box 2952, Wenatchee, Washington 98807
(888) 959-5464 or (509) 664-8855

WWW.OCEANBOYFARMS.COM
OCEAN BOY FARMS, INC.

Ships fresh (never frozen) shrimp in July through December and individually quick frozen shrimp year-round. Their products are available through distributors and retail stores
2954 Airglades Boulevard, Clewiston, Florida 33440
(863) 983-9941; fax (863) 983-9943

WWW.ORGANIC-PLANET.COM
ORGANIC PLANET

A wholesaler who imports and sells organic ingredients from around the world to retail stores in the United States. Products are certified by Quality Assurance International and include many types of seeds and nuts, spices, oils, and other kitchen staples. It's definitely a wholesale operation, with a one-ton minimum order, but there are undoubtedly many products on your kitchen shelves that have come through Organic Planet.
231 Sansome Street, Suite 300, San Francisco, California 94104-2304
(415) 765-5590; fax (415) 765-5922

WWW.ORGANICVALLEY.COOP
ORGANIC VALLEY COOPERATIVE

A source of organic meat, dairy, produce, and other products. Formed in 1988 by George Siemon and a few other organic farmers in the Midwest, the cooperative now encompasses 450 organic farms in 17 states from California to Maine and from Florida to Oregon. One of the largest organic brands in the nation, Organic Valley is the only one to be solely owned and operated by organic farmers. These farmers today are at the heart of the organic revolution in agriculture. The web site can help you find a local store that sells Organic Valley products, but it is not a mail-order site.

WWW.PROORGANICS.COM
PRO ORGANICS

Canada's leading distributor of fresh organic produce for the last fifteen years. It offers a complete line of certified organic products year round, with distribution points in Burnaby, British Columbia; Toronto, Ontario; and Montreal, Quebec.

WWW.SHELTONS.COM
SHELTON'S POULTRY, INC.

Processed organic poultry products; sold through retail stores (directory of stores on the site).

204 North Loranne, Pomona, California 91767
(800) 541-1833 or (909) 623-4361

WWW.SUMMERFIELDFARM.COM
SUMMERFIELD FARM PRODUCTS, LTD.

Raising free-range milk- and grass-fed veal and lamb, and dry-aging beef. Not currently selling retail; wholesale only.

10044 James Monroe Highway, Culpeper, Virginia 22701
(800) 898-3276; fax (540) 547-9628

WWW.TRADE-ORGANIC-WINE.COM
TRADE-ORGANIC-WINE

A business to business site that has a large variety of organic wine.

WWW.UNFI.COM
UNITED NATURAL FOODS, INC.

UNFI is an umbrella organization that procures organic foodstuffs from thousands of vendors around the world and sells them to 7,000 conventional supermarkets, natural and organic food stores, and independent retail stores. It's a huge operation and the first coast-to-coast certified organic distributor.

WWW.WALNUTACRES.COM
WALNUT ACRES

Located in Penns Creek, Pennsylvania, this is the granddaddy of all organic mail-order services, but it recently dropped its mail order business in favor of sales through retail outlets. From its humble beginning selling homemade apple butter, Walnut Acres has grown into one of the largest and most trusted purveyors of organic foods in the country.

Bibliography

Aaron, Chester. *Garlic is Life: A Memoir with Recipes.* Berkeley, CA: Ten Speed Press, 1996.

—*The Great Garlic Book: A Guide with Recipes.* Berkeley, CA: Ten Speed Press, 1997.

Arora, David. *All That Rain Promises and More ... : A Hip Pocket Guide to Western Mushrooms.* Berkeley, CA: Ten Speed Press, 1991.

Ash, John, with Sid Goldstein. *From the Earth to the Table.* New York: Dutton, 1995.

Bailey, Liberty Hyde, and Ethel Zoe Bailey. *Hortus III.* New York: Macmillan, 1976.

Blaylock, Russell L. *Excitotoxins: The Taste that Kills.* Santa Fe, NM: Health Press, [1998], c1997.

Bomhard, Gloria M., *Simply Irresistible.* Kearney, NE: Morris Press Cookbooks, 2002.

Brissenden, Rosemary. *Asia's Undiscovered Cuisine.* New York: Pantheon, 1982.

California Master Gardener Handbook. Davis, CA: University of California Division of Agriculture and Natural Resources, 2002.

Child, Julia, Simone Beck, and Louisette Bertholle, *Mastering the Art of French Cooking.* New York: Alfred A. Knopf, 1964.

Corum, Vance, Marcie Rosenzweig, and Eric Gibson, *The New Farmers' Market.* Auburn, CA: New World Publishing, 2001.

Cox, Jeff. *From Vines to Wines: The Complete Guide to Growing Grapes and Making Your Own Wine.* Pownal, VT: Storey Books, 1999; Harper & Row, orig. 1985.

Davidson, Alan. *The Oxford Companion to Food.* New York: Oxford University Press, 1999.

Dornenburg, Andrew, and Karen Page. *Culinary Artistry.* New York: John Wiley & Sons, Inc., 1996.

Dr. Richter's Fresh Produce Guide. Apopka, FL: Try-Foods International, Inc., 2000.

Facciola, Stephen. *Cornucopia II.* Vista, CA: Kampong Publications, 1998.

Fairchild, David. *Exploring for Plants.* New York: Macmillan, 1930.

Fallon, Sally. *Nourishing Traditions.* Washington, DC: New Trends Publishing, Inc., 2001.

Foster, Gertrude B., and Rosemary F. Louden. *Park's Success with Herbs.* Greenwood, SC: Geo. W. Park Seed Co., Inc., 1980.

Fruit Facts, Vols. 1 & 2. Fullerton, CA: California Rare Fruit Growers, Inc., undated.

Gorman, Marion. *Cooking with Fruit.* Emmaus, PA: Rodale Press, 1983.

Greenoak, Francesca. *Forgotten Fruit: The English Orchard and Fruit Garden.* London: A. Deutsch, 1983.

Griffiths, Sally. *Hot & Spicy Sauces & Salsas.* New York: Rizzoli, 1995.

Hamersley, Gordon. *Bistro Cooking at Home.* New York: Broadway Books, 2003.

Hamilton, Cherie Y. *Cuisines of Portuguese Encounters.* New York: Hippocrene Books, Inc., 2001.

Hazan, Marcella. *Essentials of Classic Italian Cooking.* New York: Alfred A. Knopf, 1998.

Herbst, Sharon Tyler. *The New Food Lover's Companion,* 3rd ed. Hauppauge, NY: Barron's Educational Series, 2001.

Horn, Jane, ed. *Cooking A to Z.* Santa Rosa, CA: The Cole Group, 1992.

Kander, Mrs. Simon, compiler. *The Settlement Cook Book.* Milwaukee, WI: The Settlement Cook Book Co., 1934.

Kilarski, Barbara. *Keep Chickens!: Tending Small Flocks in Cities, Suburbs, and Other Small Spaces.* North Adams, MA: Storey Pub., 2003.

Kochilas, Diane. *The Food and Wine of Greece.* New York: St. Martin's Press, 1993.

Lappe, Frances Moore. *Diet for a Small Planet.* New York: Ballantine Books, 1975.

Lauck, Joanne Elizabeth. *The Voice of the Infinite in the Small: Revisioning the Human-Insect Connection.* Berkeley, CA: Shambala, 2001.

Lorenz, Oscar A., and Donald N. Maynard, *Knott's Handbook for Vegetable Growers,* 3rd ed. New York: John Wiley & Sons, 1988.

Madison, Deborah. *Local Flavors.* New York: Broadway Books, 2002.

Martinez, Zarela. *Foods from My Heart.* New York: Macmillan, 1992.

Morash, Marion. *The Victory Garden Cookbook.* New York: Alfred A. Knopf, 1982.

Morse, Kitty. *Cooking at the Kasbah.* San Francisco: Chronicle Books, 1998.

Morton, Julia F. *Fruits of Warm Climates.* Miami: Florida Flair Books, 1987.

Norman, Jill. *Herbs & Spices.* New York: DK Publishing, Inc., 2002.

Patraker, Joel, and Joan Schwartz. *The Greenmarket Cookbook.* New York: Viking, 2000.

Pellaprat, Henri-Paul. *Modern French Culinary Art.* Cleveland, OH: The World Publishing Co., 1966.

Robinson, Jancis, ed. *The Oxford Companion to Wine.* New York: Oxford University Press, 1994.

Rombauer, Irma S., and Marion Rombauer Becker. *The Joy of Cooking.* New York: The Bobbs-Merrill Company, Inc., 1953.

Schneider, Elizabeth. *Vegetables from Amaranth to Zucchini.* New York: William Morrow, 2001.

Specialty and Minor Crops Handbook, 2nd ed. Davis, CA: University of California Division of Agriculture and Natural Resources, 1998.

Stearn, William T. *Botanical Latin,* 4th ed. Portland, OR: Timber Press, 1992.

Torres, Marimar. *The Catalan Country Kitchen.* London: Addison-Wesley, 1992.

Tucker, Arthur O., and Thomas DeBaggio. *The Big Book of Herbs.* Loveland, CO: Interweave Press, 2000.

Vaughan, J.G., and C.A. Geissler. *The New Oxford Book of Food Plants.* New York: Oxford University Press, 1998.

Waldin, Monty. *Organic Wine Guide.* London: Thorsons, 1999.

Waters, Alice. *Chez Panisse Fruit.* New York: HarperCollins Publishers, 2002.

Waters, Alice. *Chez Panisse Vegetables.* New York: HarperCollins Publishers, 1996.

Weiner, Hal, and Marilyn Weiner. *World of Cooking.* New York: Macmillan Publishing Company, 1983.

Wernert, Susan J., ed. *Reader's Digest North American Wildlife.* Pleasantville, NY: The Reader's Digest Association, Inc., 1982.

Index

A

Aaron, Chester, 127
Adams, Jane, 10
Additives, in processed food, 452–453
Aflatoxin, 40, 332
Agricultural Experiment Stations, 17–18
Agricultural Marketing Service (AMS), 34
  contact information for, 518
Agriculture
  Community Supported, 13–14, 518
  corporate, 2–3
  decline of family farm, 9
  direct-to-consumer marketing, 6, 8–14, 518
  factory farms, 6, 9, 35, 446
  herbicide use in, 24, 25, 27
  irradiation in, 29–31
  nutritious cultivar development, 16–17
  pesticide use in, 24, 26, 28–29
  sustainable, 10, 16, 33, 41
  See also Animal husbandry; Genetically modified crops; Organic farming; U.S. Department of Agriculture
Agua Fresca, Cherimoya, 238
Allicin, 127
Alliums, 117
Almond(s)
  about, 320, 322
  Biscotti, 323
  fats in, 321
  Granola, Sunflower Seed, Super Delicious, 347
  and Grape Gazpacho, 263
  Horchata, 322
  and Orange Rice, 244
  Quinoa Pilaf, 363
Amaranth
  about, 361–362

flour, 362–363, 372
  leaves, 62, 187
  Popcakes, 364
American Cheese Society, 443
American Meat Institute Standards, 418
American Outlook, 42
American Raw Milk Farmstead Cheese Consortium, 442, 444
Anaheim chile, 105
Ancho chile, 105
Anchovies
  Artichokes, Siciliano, 58
  Broccoli in Excelsis, 77
  Green Goddess Dressing, 404
  Green Sauce, Walnut, 341–342
  nutrients in, 435
  Salad Niçoise, 285
Angel Hair Pasta with Summer Squash, 190–191
Angelica, 117
Animal husbandry
  antibiotic use in, 24, 27–28, 30, 34, 418–422, 424, 427–429, 435, 438–439, 446
  dairy farming, 437, 439, 441
  E. coli, 40, 422, 441
  feedlot cattle, 419–420
  grass-fed cattle, 40, 50, 420–423, 437–439, 442
  grass-fed lamb, 424–425
  growth hormone use in, 26, 29
  heritage breeds, 419, 429, 430
  humane care in, 418, 420
  mad cow disease, 30, 419, 443
  manure management, 420, 427, 441
  Niman Ranch system, 420, 522
  organic production system, 24, 27–28, 30, 50, 418–421, 424, 427
  rabbit ranchers, 433
  salmonella and, 27–28, 42, 441, 446–447

Animal Welfare Institute, 420
Anise, 379
  Pfeffernüsse, 379
Anise hyssop, 117
Anson Mills, 366–367
Antelope meat, 433
Antibiotic-resistant bacteria, 27, 422, 438
Antibiotic use, in animal husbandry, 24, 27–28, 30, 34, 418–422, 424, 427–429, 435, 438–439, 446
Apple(s)
  about, 217–219
  blossoms, 117
  Chutney, Dried Cherry, Apricot and, 241
  commercial standardization of, 2
  dried, 462
  -horseradish sauce (*apfelkren*), 396
  pest control, nontoxic, 217
  pesticide levels in, 20
  Pie, American, 220
  Pork, Caraway-Infused, with Sauerkraut and, 383
  Pork Loin Roast with Dried Fruit and Sweet Spices, 428
  Tarte Tatin, 219–220
  unpeeled, 281
  varieties, 1–2, 218–219, 498–499
Apple mint, 399
Apricot(s)
  about, 221–222
  Chutney, Dried Cherry, Apple and, 241
  dried, 462
  Preserves, 222–223
  unpeeled, 281
  varieties, 221, 499
Apriums, 304
Aprotinin, 26
Arame, 182
Arborio rice, 365, 366
  Paella, 368
  Risotto Supreme, Shrimp, 436

Ark of Taste Project, 3, 425
Arora, David, 149
Artichoke(s)
  about, 54–56
  baby, 55
  locally grown, 17
  Siciliano, 58
  Stew, Moroccan-Style, 57
  varieties, 55, 56, 480
Artisanal producers, 16, 443
Arugula
  about, 58–60
  and Mesclun Salad with Grapefruit
    and Avocado, 60
  varieties, 59, 480
Asian-Italian Style, Chicken, 394
Asian pear(s)
  about, 223–224
  Granita, 224
  unpeeled, 281
  varieties, 223, 499
Asian-Style Orange Chicken, 244
Asian vegetables
  about, 61
  Chinese Cabbage Leaves, Halibut
    Wrapped in, 63–64
  Gado Gado Sauce, 395
  Kim Chee, 63
  Sukiyaki, 64–65
  varieties, 61–63, 480–481
  See also Bok Choy; Chinese Cabbage;
    Chinese Kale; Chinese Spinach;
    Mustard Greens
Asparagus
  about, 65–67
  to grill, 67
  pesticide levels in, 40
  to roast, 66–67
  Shrimp Risotto Supreme, 436
  Steamed, with Hollandaise Sauce,
    67–68
  varieties, 65, 481
  wild, foraging for, 66
Asparagus bean, 132
Asparation, 62, 76
Audubon Society, 435
Austrian-Style Kohlrabi, 139
Avery, Dennis, 42
Avocado
  about, 68–70
  Arugula and Mesclun Salad with
    Grapefruit and, 60
  Guacamole, Extra Good, 70–71

"Hollandaise" Sauce, Healthy, 68
oil, 69
pesticide levels in, 40
Pico de Gallo, 158
varieties, 69–70, 481–482

B

B12 deficiency, 371
Bacillus thuringiensis (Bt), 46–47, 82,
  121, 467
Bacon
  Dressing, Warm, Winter Green Slaw
    with, 99
  Potato Salad, German, 411–412
Baker, Linda, 33
Banana(s)
  about, 224–227
  chips, 462
  with Coconut Cream, 227
  Dole organic, 226
  pesticide levels in, 40
  varieties, 226, 499
Barbecued Tempeh, 353
Bark, Brazil Nut, 324
Barley, 355–356
  and Lamb Soup, Scotch, 356
Bars, Peanut Salvage, 334
Basil
  about, 380–381
  flowers, edible, 117
  Green Sauce, Walnut, 341–342
  insalata caprese, 444
  oil, 381
  Pesto, 337
  vinegar, 381
Basmati rice, 365
Bavarian, Lemon, with Black Currant
  Sauce, 251–252
Bean(s), dried
  about, 347–349
  Black, with Epazote, Mexican, 393
  Feijoada, Brazilian, 350
  Kale Soup, Portuguese, 137
  Kasha, and Corn Tacos, 357–358
  Refried, Mexican, 349–350
  to soak and cook, 348–349
  to sprout, 346
  Veggie Burgers, Grilled, 338–339
  White, Tuscan, 351
  See also Green beans; Soybeans
Bearg, Larry, 13
Béarnaise Sauce, Chervil, 386–387
Beebalm, 117

Beef
  about, 423
  certified organic, 422
  Demi-Glace, 453
  Feijoada, Brazilian, 350
  Garlic Rub for, 130
  grass-fed, 40, 50, 420–423
  hormone-treated, 29
  humanely treated, 418–419
  irradiated, 419
  mad cow disease, 30, 419, 443
  Meat Loaf, Rock 'Em Sock 'Em, 391
  New England Boiled Dinner, 83
  organic, 30, 418–419, 420
  Sloppy Joes, 423
  Stew with Porcini, 150–151
  Sukiyaki, 64–65
  See also Animal Husbandry
Beet(s)
  about, 71–74
  juice, 18, 73
  New England Boiled Dinner, 83
  Pickled, 73, 74
  to roast, 72–73
  Roasted, and Looseleaf Lettuce Salad,
    144
  Salad, Red and Yellow, with Orange
    Vinaigrette, 75
  varieties, 72, 482
  Watercress, and Orange Salad, 207
Beet greens
  to braise, 73–74
  Slaw, Winter Green, with Warm
    Bacon Dressing, 99
Belcastro, Tricia, 218
Belgian endive
  about, 101
  Braised, 103
  varieties, 485
Bell pepper(s). See Sweet pepper(s)
Benbrook, Charles M., 26
Benedetti, Willie, 430
Beneficial insects, 25, 131, 392, 475
Benepe, Barry, 11
Benziger, Mike, 43
Berbere Sauce, 385
Berry, Wendell, 427
Best, Renae and Don, 10
Betaoestradiol, 29
Beverages
  Agua Fresca, Cherimoya, 238
  Grapefruit Cooler, 246
  Horchata, Almond, 322

Mojito, 400
Nectarine-Viognier Fizz, 282
oats in, 360
passionfruit, 288
rice in, 368
Soy Milk, 353
Tea, Moroccan Mint, 400
wine, organic, 474–476
See also Juice
Bilberries, 234
Biodynamic farming, 475, 476
Biscotti, 323
Bison meat, 433
Black bean(s)
    to cook, 349
    with Epazote, Mexican, 393
    Feijoada, Brazilian, 350
    Kasha, and Corn Tacos, 357–358
Blackberry(ies)
    about, 228–229
    and Chocolate Bombe, 231
    Cobbler, Nectarine-, 282
    Cobbler, Nora's, 230
    varieties, 228–229, 500
    wild, 229
Black currant(s), 249, 250, 503
    Sauce, Lemon Bavarian with,
        251–252
Black-eyed peas, 348
Black raspberry(ies)
    about, 232–233
    Ice Cream, 233
    varieties, 500
Black trumpet mushrooms, 490
Bladderwrack, 182
Blaylock, Russell, 452
Blueberry(ies)
    about, 233–235
    dried, 462
    Muffins, 235–236
    Pie, 236
    varieties, 234–235, 500
Blue cheese
    Bartlett Pear Salad, 295
    Dressing, 144–145
    Fingerling Potato and Chanterelle
        Gratin, 169
Boisset winery, 475
Bok choy, 61–62, 480
Bolete mushroom, king, 490–491
Bombe, Blackberry and Chocolate, 231
Borage
    about, 381

Crystallized Flowers, 382
flowers, 117, 381
Bouillon/bouillon cubes, 452
Bouquets garnis, 410–411
Bovine growth hormone, 26, 29, 438
Bovine spongiform encephalopathy
    (mad cow disease), 30
Boysenberry, 228
Bran, 372
Brandied Cherries, 240
Brassica oleracea, 8
Brazilian Feijoada, 350
Brazil nut(s)
    about, 323–324
    Bark, 324
    and Cashew Loaf, 324
    fats in, 321
Bread(s)
    Date Nut Loaf, Medjool, 255
    French Toast, The Ultimate, 246
    Muffins, Blueberry, 235–236
    Muffins, Cornbread, 467
    Persimmon, Sweet, 299
    Pita, 374
    Rolls, Cinnamon, 373
    Rolls, Whole-Wheat and Black
        Walnut Quick, 466–467
    starter culture, 466
    to store, 464
    See also Flour
Bread stuffing
    Pistachio Turkey, 339
    Sage Turkey, 409–410
Breast cancer, 26, 28, 438
Broccoflower, 89
Broccoletti (romanesco), 76
Broccoli
    about, 75–77
    Chinese, 62
    in Excelsis, 77
    nutrients in, 17, 76
    Penne with Fava Beans and, 77–78
    pesticide levels in, 40
    varieties, 8, 76, 482
Broccolini, 76
Broccoli raab, 76
Brown rice, 365, 368
Brussels sprouts
    about, 78–80
    Sauté of Parsnips, Chestnuts and,
        161
    and Sherry Shrimp, 81
    varieties, 483

B12 deficiency, 371
Buckwheat, 357
    Kasha, Bean, and Corn Tacos,
        357–358
Bulgarian Style, Celery Root and Rice,
    95
Bulgur, Tabbouleh, 203
Burbank, Luther, 304
Burdock root, Tempura Roots in
    Ohsawa Sauce, 160–161
Burgers, Veggie, Grilled, 338–339
Butter, 471
Butterbeans and Collards, 133
Butternut squash, 209, 210
    "Pumpkin" Pie Made with, 211

C
Cabbage
    about, 81–83
    Coleslaw, Midwestern Sweet-and-
        Sour, 83–84
    New England Boiled Dinner, 83
    odor problem, 82–83
    Sauerkraut, Homemade, 84
    varieties, 82, 483
    See also Chinese Cabbage
Caesar Salad, The True, 143–144
Calendula, 117
California Organic Food Production
    Act of 1990, 31
Calimyrna Figs, 257
"Campaign to Label Genetically
    Engineered Foods," 32
Campylobacter bacteria, 27–28
Canary melons, 278
Cancer risk
    agricultural chemicals in, 24, 28
    bovine growth hormone in, 29, 438
    genetically modified plants in, 25–26
    pesticide exposure in, 28
Candy cap mushrooms, 490
Canning and preserving, 241, 281
    See also Preserves
Canola oil, 468, 469
Cantaloupe(s)
    about, 278
    Charentais Melon Cockaigne,
        279–280
    varieties, 506
Caponata with Chives, 388
Caraway
    about, 382–383
    Farmer Cheese, 383–384

Pork, -Infused, with Sauerkraut and
    Apples, 383
Cardamom, 384
    Berbere Sauce, 385
Cardoons
    about, 85–86
    Spanish-Style, 86
    varieties, 483
Caribe chile, 105
Carolina Golden Rice, 366–367
Carrot(s)
    about, 86–88
    juice, 18
    -Juice Salad Dressing, 88
    Kim Chee, 63
    New England Boiled Dinner, 83
    Soup with Rice, 88
    Tempura Roots in Ohsawa Sauce,
        160–161
    unpeeled, 281
    varieties, 87, 483–484
Cascabel chile, 105
Cascadian Farms, 14
Cashew(s)
    about, 325
    and Brazil Nut Loaf, 324
    fats in, 321
    Sauce, 326
Cattle. See Animal husbandry
Cauliflower
    about, 89–90
    cheese sauce with, 90
    and Lamb Stew, 91
    and Millet Medley, 359
    pesticide levels in, 40
    Spicy Roast, 91
    varieties, 89, 484
Caviar, 518
Cayenne chile, 105
Celery
    about, 92–93
    juice, 18
    pesticide levels in, 40
    and Seafood Consomme, 93–94
    varieties, 92–93, 484
Celery root
    about, 94–95
    and Mashed Potatoes, Garlic, 96
    and Rice, Bulgarian Style, 95
    varieties, 484
Celtuse, 143
Centers for Disease Control (CDC), 42
Center for Urban Education about

Sustainable Agriculture (CUESA),
    10–11
Certification, 10, 39
    beef, 422
    coffee, 456
    fish, 434–435
    of humane treatment, 418
    small farmers' avoidance of, 33, 35,
        47, 50, 422
    wine, 476
Certification agencies, 33
Chamomile, 118
Chanterelle, 490
    and Fingerling Potato Gratin, 169
Chard
    about, 96–98
    juice, 18
    Quiche, Savory No-Crust, 99–100
    Slaw, Winter Green, with Warm
        Bacon Dressing, 99
    Tacos of Creamy Braised Chard,
        98–99
    varieties, 97, 484–485
Charleston hot chile, 105
Chavez Plaza Certified Farmers' Market,
    Sacramento, 10
Cheese
    artisanal, 16, 443
    cauliflower with, 90
    Farmer Cheese, Caraway, 383–384
    low-fat/nonfat, 443
    Omelet, A Fine, 448–449
    organic, about, 440–444
    Puffs, Traditional French, 444–445
    Quiche, Chard, Savory, No-Crust,
        99–100
    raw milk farmstead, 442
    and Rice Frittata, 369
    Saltimbocca, 409
    site-specific flavor in, 4
    Soufflé, Corn, Cheesy, 112
    See also Blue cheese; Mozzarella
Chefs, organic cooking and, 15, 16
Chefs Collaborative, 16, 35, 53
Cherimoya(s)
    about, 237
    Agua Fresca, 238
    varieties, 500
Cherry(ies)
    about, 238–240
    black, 239
    Brandied, 240
    dried, 462

Dried, Apple, and Apricot
    Chutney, 241
    pesticide levels in, 40
    Pie, 242
    varieties, 239, 240, 501
    See also Ground cherry
Cherry pepper chile, 105
Cherry tomatoes, 496–497
Chervil
    about, 385–386
    flowers, 118
    Sauce Béarnaise, 386–387
Chestnut(s)
    about, 326–327
    Glazed, 328
    puree, 327
    to roast, 327
    Sauté of Parsnips, Brussels Sprouts
        and, 161
Chicken
    about, 429–430
    antibiotic-resistant bacteria in, 27
    Asian-Italian Style, 394
    with Citrus and Cumin, 391–392
    Coq au Vin, 477
    free range, labeling, 14, 16
    Grilled, with Thyme, 414–415
    Gumbo, Filé, 153–154
    heritage, 419
    Marvels on Rice, 432–433
    Moroccan, 108
    Orange, Asian-Style, 244
    Paella, 368–369
    Rock Cornish, 429
    Rosemary, Toscana, 407
    Southern-Fried, 432
    Stock, 454
    Tarragon, 413
Chickpeas, in Hummus, The Best
    You've Ever Tasted, 351
Chicory
    about, 100–103
    flowers, 118
    puntarella, 102
    varieties, 101, 485
    See also Belgian Endive; Endive;
        Escarole; Frisée; Radicchio;
        Sugarloaf Endive
Chilaca chile, 105
Children, pesticide exposure in, 28–29
Chile(s)
    about, 104–106
    Berbere Sauce, 385

Gazpacho, Green, with Shellfish, 199–200
Harissa, 107
Harissa, in Chicken, Moroccan, 108
Pico de Gallo, 158
Salsa, Extra Hot, 107
Salsa, Fresh, Hot, 389
Salsa Molcajete, 107
Salsa Verde, 107
Tacos of Creamy Braised Chard, 98–99
varieties, 105–106
Chimichurri Sauce, 404
Chinese cabbage
Green Papaya Salad, 287
Kim Chee, 63
Leaves, Halibut Wrapped in, 63–64
varieties, 62, 480–481
Chinese celery, 92
Chinese kale, 62, 481
in Sukiyaki, 64–65
Chinese spinach, 62, 481
Chipotle chile, 105
Chives
about, 387–388
Caponata with, 388
garlic, 388, 487
Green Goddess Dressing, 404
Chlorpyrifos, 29
Chocolate
Bark, Brazil Nut, 324
and Blackberry Bombe, 231
Fudge, 459–460
mail order sources, 523
nutrients in, 459
organic, 458–459
Sauce, Dark Chocolate-Peanut Butter, 460
Chrysanthemum, 118
Chutney
Cherry, Dried, Apple, and Apricot, 241
Mango, 273
Squash-Mango, Spicy, Seared Duck Breast with, 431
Cilantro
about, 389
flowers, 118
Gazpacho, Green, with Shellfish, 199–200
See also Salsa
Cinnamon Rolls, 373
Cippolini, 157

Citrus
about, 242–243
avocado with, 70
Chicken with Cumin and, 391–392
flowers, 118
mail order sources for, 521
Panna Cotta, 440
varieties, 501–502
See also specific fruits
Clafoutis, Raspberry, 313
Clams, Paella, 368–369
Clark, Theo, 41–42
Cleaning supplies, organic, 524
Clover, 118
Cobbler
Blackberry, Nora's, 230
Nectarine-Blackberry, 282
Plum and Peach, 306
Coconut, 321, 462
-Oatmeal Cookies, Chewy, 361
Coconut Cream, Bananas with, 227
Coffee
certified, 456
to grind, 456–457
mail order sources, 523
organic, 454–456
Tiramisù, 457
Cohen, Mitchell, 42
Coleman, Eliot, 35–36
Coleslaw, Midwestern Sweet-and-Sour, 83–84
Colicchio, Tom, 202
Collards and Butterbeans, 133
Colon cancer, 25–26, 438
Comice pears, 293
with Prosciutto and Baby Greens, 295–296
Community Supported Agriculture, 13–14, 48–49, 158–159
resources for, 518
Composting, 4, 22–24, 33, 46, 225
Concord grapes, 260, 261
Confit, Prune-Armagnac, Cider-Glazed Pork Chops with, 305
Congressional Organic Agriculture Caucus, 31
Consoli, Lorenzo, 32
Consomme, Celery and Seafood, 93–94
Consumer Product Safety Commission, 34
Consumer Reports, 27
Consumers Union, 41
Consumers Union Guide to

Environmental Labels, 14, 16
Cookies
Biscotti, 323
Black Walnut and Oatmeal, 342
Fig and Oatmeal, 258
Oatmeal-Coconut, Chewy, 361
Pecan Lace Tulips, 268–269
Pfeffernüsse, 379
Pineapple-Oatmeal, 301
Coq au Vin, 477
Coriander, 389
Pork, 390
Corn
about, 108–111
baby, 110
earworms in, 109
fungal disease in, 18, 111
genetically modified, 26, 32, 47
Humita Casserole with Corn Husks, 111–112
Indian Pudding, 112
pesticide levels in, 40
Soufflé, Cheesy, 112
Succotash, Lima Bean, 146
varieties, 109–110, 485–486
Cornbread
Muffins, 467
and Wild Rice Stuffing, 375
Corned beef, in New England Boiled Dinner, 83
Cornell University, organic research at, 37–38
Cornflower, 118
Cornichons, 115, 486
Corn oil, 468
Corn smut, 491
Corporate agriculture, 2–3
Couscous, Steamed, 57
Cowie, Ronald, 300
Cox's Orange Pippin apple, 218
Crab(meat)
Consomme, Celery and Seafood, 93–94
Gazpacho, Green, with Shellfish, 199–200
and Squash Soup, 212
Cranberry(ies)
about, 247–248
dried, 462
Relish, 248
varieties, 247, 502
Cream. See Milk and cream
Crème Brûlée, Lavender, 397–398

Crème fraîche., 444
Cremini mushroom, 491
Crenshaw melons, 278
Crepes, Strawberry, 317
Crisp, Strawberry-Rhubarb, 317
CropLife America, 32
Crosby, Kevin, 106
Crosnes
  about, 113–114
  Pear, and Hazelnut Salad, 114
CSA farms, 13, 518
Cucumber
  about, 114–116
  Gazpacho, Green, with Shellfish,
    199–200
  Gazpacho, Untraditional, 202–203
  Greek Salad, 116–117
  pickles, 116
  Tzatziki, 116
  varieties, 115, 486
  Wakame Orange Salad, 182–183
Cumin
  about, 390–391
  Berbere Sauce, 385
  Chicken with Citrus and, 391–392
  Meat Loaf, Rock 'Em Sock 'Em, 391
Currant(s)
  about, 249–251, 462
  Black Currant Sauce, Lemon
    Bavarian with, 251–252
  varieties, 249, 503
Custard
  Bavarian, Lemon, with Black Currant
    Sauce, 251–252
  Crème Brûlée, Lavender, 397–398
  Panna Cotta, Citrus, 440
  Tiramisù, 457

D

Daikon, 171, 172
  Stir-Fry, 172–173
Dainello, Frank, 186
Dairy farming, organic, 437, 439, 441
Dairy products
  butter *versus* margarine, 471
  humane treatment of animals, certifi-
    cation of, 418
  organic co-ops, 36
  organic products, 444
  See also Animal husbandry; Cheese;
    Milk and cream
Dandelions, 118
Date(s)

about, 253–254, 462
  Halibut, Encrusted, 255
  Nut Loaf, Medjool, 255
  varieties, 253–254, 503
Daylilies, 118
DDT, 28
Delicata squash, 209, 498
Demi-Glace, 453
Dianthus, 117–118
Dierkhising, Mark, 36–37
Dietary guidelines, U.S., 3
Dietary pyramids, 3
Dill(ed)
  about, 392
  flowers, 118
  Salmon, 392
DiMatteo, Katherine, 30
Dips and spreads
  Farmer Cheese, Caraway, 383–384
  garlic, 129
  Guacamole, Extra Good, 70–71
  Hummus, The Best You've Ever
    Tasted, 351
  Tzatziki, 116
Direct-to-consumer marketing, 6, 8–14,
  518
Distributors of organic food, 525–526
Drinks. *See* Beverages
Duck
  Breast, Seared, with Spicy Squash-
    Mango Chutney, 431
  humanely treated, 418
  Stew with Walnuts and
    Pomegranates, 309–310
  varieties, 429
Duesing, Bill, 34
Dulse, 181
Dumplings, Gnocchi, Salsify, 179

E

Eco-Cert, 33
E. coli, presence of, 42
  in grain-fed cattle, 40, 422
  in raw milk, 441
Egg(s)
  about, 445–448
  Flan, Sweet Potato and Spinach,
    197–198
  French Toast, The Ultimate, 246
  Hard-Boiled, 449
  keeping chickens, 446
  Omelet, A Fine, 448–449
  Poached, 449

pullet, 447
  quail, 429
  See also Frittata; Soufflé
Eggplant
  about, 120–122
  Caponata with Chives, 388
  and Potato Stew, Indian, 122–123
  Ratatouille, 123–124
  Stuffed, Middle Eastern, 122
  varieties, 121, 487
Elderberry, 118
Endive
  about, 100–103
  Braised Belgian Endive, 103
  varieties, 101–102, 485
  See also Belgian Endive; Chicory;
    Escarole; Frisée; Radicchio;
    Sugarloaf Endive
England, organic standards in, 34–35
Enoki mushroom, 491
Environmental benefits of organic farm-
  ing, 5–6, 41
Environmental Protection Agency
  (EPA), 24, 29
Environmental Working Group, 28, 40
Enzymes, flavor and, 6
Epazote, 393
  Black Beans with, Mexican, 393
Epstein, Samuel, 29
Escarole, 101–103, 485
Ethnic market, for fruits and vegetables,
  17–18
European Union (EU), 29
  labeling law in, 26, 31
  organic farming policy of, 41
Excitotoxins, 452

F

Factory farms, 6, 9, 35
Fair Trade
  coffee, 456
  mangoes, 272
Farmer Cheese, Caraway, 383–384
Farmers of Forty Centuries, 33
Farmers' markets, 9–12, 6, 45, 158–159
  locating, 518
Farming. *See* Agriculture; Organic farm-
  ing
Farr, Sam, 31
Fats
  butter substitutes/shortenings,
    471–472
  health promoting, 467, 468–489, 471

in nuts and seeds, 321
See also Oils
Fava beans
dried, to cook, 349
fresh, to cook, 132–133
Penne with Broccoli and, 77–78
to remove seed coat, 132
varieties, 488
Fayter, Cher and Tom, 56
Federal Humane Slaughter Act, 418
Fennel
about, 124–126
fish stuffed with, roasted, 125–126
flowers, 118
pesto, 126
and Tomato Salad, 126
varieties, 124–125, 487
Fennel seed(s), 125
in Berbere Sauce, 385
Ferry Plaza Farmers' Market, San
Francisco, 10–11
Fertilizer
chemical, 24
compost, 4, 22–24
Feta, in Greek Salad, 116–117
Fig(s)
about, 256–258, 462
dried, to poach, 258
and Oatmeal Cookies, 258
Pudding, Figgy, 259
varieties, 256, 257, 504
Fines herbes, 386, 403, 412
Fingerling potato(es), 168
and Chanterelle Gratin, 169
Fish
about, 434
fennel stuffed and roasted, 125–126
genetically engineered, 434
mercury in, 434
oil, 468
organic certified, 434–435
seed coating for, 344
sustainable fishing, 16
Trout, Macadamia, 331
Tuna, in Salad Niçoise, 285
See also Anchovies; Halibut; Salmon;
Shellfish
Flan, Sweet Potato and Spinach,
197–198
Flavor
freshness and, 6
organic growing practices and, 4, 15
site-specific, 3–4, 265

variety name and, 7
Flaxseed, 343
Flaxseed oil, 468, 469
Flour
all-purpose to whole-wheat ratio, 466
mycotoxins in, 464–465
quinoa and amaranth, 372, 462–463
whole-grain, 463
whole-wheat, 370–372, 463
Flowers, edible
about, 120
Borage, Crystallized, 382
organic, 117
Summer Squash Blossoms, Stuffed,
191–192
types of, 117–119
Violet Jelly, 120
Food and Agriculture Organization
(FAO), 40, 41
Food and Drug Administration (FDA),
434, 438
Food irradiation, 29
Food labels. *See* Labels and labeling
Food processing companies, 2–3
Food stamps, 12
Foraging
for asparagus, 66
for blackberries, 229
for huckleberries, 264–266
for mayapples, 275
for mushrooms, 149
for pine nuts, 336
for ramps, 387
for salsify, 177
for strawberries, 315
for wineberries, 312
for watercress, 206
Fraise de bois, 316
Frakes, David, 444
Free range label, 14, 16, 430
French Cheese Puffs, Traditional,
444–445
French Toast, The Ultimate, 246
Fresno chile, 105
Frisée
about, 102
Salad, Red and White, 103
varieties, 485
Frison, Emile, 224–225
Frittata
Cheese and Rice, 369
Scallion, 159
Sweet Pepper and Sausage, 195

Fromer, John, 35
Fruit(s)
antioxidants in, 215–216, 234
dietary recommendations, 216
dried
about, 460–461
Pork Loin Roast with, and Sweet
Spices, 428
varieties, 462
genetic diversity in, 18–19
mail order sources for, 520–521
nutritious cultivar development,
16–17
pest control, 217
pesticide levels in, 40
ripe-picked, 6, 48
by season, 216
unpeeled, to eat, 281
variety names, 7–8, 45, 479
See also Organic food; *specific fruits*
Fuchsia, 118
Fudge, 459–460
Fukuoka, Masanobu, 366
Fungal disease, 18, 111, 224–225
Fungicides, 24, 25, 54
Fuyu persimmons, 297, 298, 508

G

Gado Gado Sauce, 395
Gardenia, 118
Garlic
about, 127–129
Broccoli in Excelsis, 77
Chicken, Rosemary, Toscana, 407
Chimichurri Sauce, 404
Lamb, Rack of, Rosemary and, 425
Mashed Potatoes and Celery Root, 96
pasta with, 129
persillade, 403
to roast, 128
Rub for Meat, 130
Sauce, Ancient Greek, 130
varieties, 127–128, 487–488
Garlic chives, 388, 487
Gazpacho
Grape and Almond, 263
Green, with Shellfish, 199–200
Untraditional, 202–203
General Mills Corporation, 14
Genetically diverse crops, 18–19, 39, 41
Genetically engineered fish, 434
Genetically modified crops
ban on, 32

labeling of, 26–27, 31–32
pest resistant, 47
problems with, 25–26, 467
Geranium, 118
German Potato Salad, 411–412
Germany, organic certification in, 33
Gibbons, Euell, 66
Ginger
    about, 393–394, 462
    Chicken, Asian-Italian Style, 394
    Gado Gado Sauce, 395
Gladiolus, 118
Gnocchi, Salsify, 179
Goat cheese, 442
Goetz, Bruce, 233–234
Goldberg, Marshall, 471
Goodyear, Dana, 21–22
Goose, 429
Gooseberry(ies)
    about, 250
    Pie, 251
    varieties, 503
Gosling, Doug, 85
Gougère, 444–445
Grains. *See specific grains*
Granita, Asian Pear, 224
Granola, Sunflower Seed, Super
    Delicious, 347
Grape(s)
    about, 260–262
    Gazpacho, and Almond, 263
    juice, fresh, 262–263
    nutrients in, 216, 260
    pesticide levels in, 40
    varieties, 260–262, 504–505
Grapefruit
    about citrus fruit, 242–243
    Arugula and Mesclun Salad with, 60
    Cooler, 246
    varieties, 243, 501
Grape Leaves, Stuffed, 263–264
Grapestone, 182
Gratin, Fingerling Potato and
    Chanterelle, 169
Greek
    Garlic Sauce, Ancient, 130
    Leeks à la Grecque, 141
    Salad, 116–117
Green beans
    about, 130–133
    Butterbeans and Collards, 133
    varieties, 131, 488
    See also Fava beans; Lima beans

Green Goddess Dressing, 404
Green manure, 46
Greens. *See* Lettuce; *specific greens*
Greensack, Francesca, 276
Gremolata, 129, 187, 403
Ground cherry, 133–134
    Pie, 134
Guacamole, Extra Good, 70–71
Guajillo chile, 105
Gussow, Joan, 17, 471

H

Habanero chile, 105
Hachiya persimmons, 297, 298, 508
Halibut
    Chinese Cabbage Leaves, Wrapped
        in, 63–64
    Date Encrusted, 255
Ham
    New England Boiled Dinner, 83
    Quiche, Chard, Savory No-Crust,
        99–100
Hamm, Ulrich, 43
Haricots verts, 132
Harissa, 107
    Chicken, Moroccan, 108
Haumann, Barbara, 36
Hazelnut(s)
    about, 328–329
    Crosnes, and Pear Salad, 114
    -Crusted Pork Loin, 330
    fats in, 321
    oil, 329
Heaton, Shane, 41
Hedgehog mushroom, 490
Hemagglutinin, 348
Hemp seed oil, 468
Henderson, Elizabeth, 13
Hen of the woods, 490
Herbicides, 24, 25, 27, 50
Herbs
    about, 377–378
    bouquets garnis, 410–411
    fines herbes, 386, 403, 412
    flowers, edible, 117–119
    See also specific herbs
Heritage foods, 419, 425, 429, 430
Heritage Foods USA, 419
Hibiscus, 118
Hickory nuts, 334–335
Hill, David, 17
Hiziki, 182
    with Vegetables, Braised, 183

Hollandaise Sauce
    Healthy, 68
    Steamed Asparagus with, 67–68
Hollyhock, 118
Honey, 473
Honeydews, 278, 506
Honeysuckle, 118
Horchata, Almond, 322
Hormonal disrupters, 28
Horseradish
    about, 395–396
    -apple sauce (*apfelkren*), 396
    Crust, Salmon Fillets with, 396
Hoskins, Sharon, 42
Huckleberry(ies)
    about, 264–265
    Game Sauce, 266
    Pie, 266
    Pie, -Rhubarb, 174–175
Hudson Institute, 35, 42
Huitlacoche, 491
Humane Farm Animal Care, 418
Humita Casserole with Corn Husks,
    111–112
Hummus, The Best You've Ever Tasted,
    351
Hungarian wax chile, 105
Hunter's Sauce, Pasta with, 194–195
Hybrids, 8

I

Ice Cream
    avocado, 70
    Black Raspberry, 233
    Bombe, Blackberry and Chocolate,
        231
    Peach Melba, 292
    Persimmon Sundae, 299
    Vanilla, Sugarless, 474
Impatiens, 118
Indian Eggplant and Potato Stew,
    122–123
Indian Pudding, 112
Indonesian Chicken in Pineapple Sauce,
    301–302
Insect control. *See* Pest control, nontox-
    ic; Pesticides
Institute for Agricultural Trade Policy,
    27, 517
Institute of Science in Society, 26
International Federation of Organic
    Agriculture Movements (IFOAM),
    43, 476

Irradiated foods, 29, 419

J

Jacobowitz, Jay, 14
Jalapeño, 105
 Salsa Molcajete, 107
Jam
 Damson Plum, 307
 Loquat and Strawberry, 271
 nectarine, 281
Jamaican hot chile, 105
Jasmine, 118
Jasmine rice, 365, 366
Jelly, Violet, 120
Jilo, locally grown, 17–18
Johnny-jump-up, 118
Juice
 grape, 262–263
 pomegranate, 306–307
 vegetable, 18, 73

K

Kale
 about, 135–137
 Chinese, 62, 481
 Chinese, in Sukiyaki, 64–65
 juice, 18
 nutrients in, 17, 135
 Slaw, Winter Green, with Warm
  Bacon Dressing, 99
 Soup, Portuguese, 137
 varieties, 135, 488–489
Kasha, Bean, and Corn Tacos, 357–358
Kay, Steve, 422
Keller, Thomas, 426
Kelp, 180, 181
Key Lime Tart, 245
Kidney beans, 347, 348
Kim Chee, 63
Kiwi(fruit)
 about, 267–268
 -Lime-Strawberry Sorbet, 268–269
 pesticide levels in, 40
 varieties, 267, 505
Koenig, Rose, 35
Kohlrabi
 about, 138–139
 Austrian-Style, 139
 unpeeled, 281
 varieties, 138, 489
Kraus, Sibella, 49, 141–142
Kumquat, 501

L

Labels and labeling
 of eggs, 447–448
 of free range poultry, 14, 16, 430
 of genetically modified foods, 26–27,
  31–32
 by Hudson Institute, 35
 of processed food, 452–453
 by variety name, 479
 of wine, 476
Lamb
 Artichoke Stew, Moroccan-Style, 57
 and Barley Soup, Scotch, 356
 and Cauliflower Stew, 91
 Garlic Rub for, 130
 Grape Leaves, Stuffed, 263–264
 heritage breed of, 419, 425
 organic, 424–425
 Rack of, Garlic and Rosemary, 425
Lamborn, Calvin, 163
Lappé, Frances Moore, 371
Lard, 472
Lavender
 about, 397
 Crème Brûlée, 397–398
 flowers, 118
 and Rosemary Marinated Olives, 284
Leahy, Patrick, 32
Leek(s)
 about, 140–141
 à la Grecque, 141
 locally grown, 17–18
 ramps, 387, 487
 varieties, 489
Lemon(s)
 about citrus fruit, 242–243
 Bavarian with Black Currant Sauce,
  251–252
 Marmalade, Quince, 311
 Panna Cotta, Citrus, 440
 varieties, 501
Lemon verbena, 119
Lentils, 348, 349
Lettuce
 about, 141–143
 Arugula and Mesclun Salad with
  Grapefruit, 60
 Baby Greens, Comice Pear with
  Prosciutto and, 295–296
 Bartlett Pear Salad, 295
 Caesar Salad, The True, 143–144
 celtuse, 143
 genetically modified, 27

Looseleaf, and Roasted Beet Salad,
 144
 Peas, Braised with Onions and,
  165–166
 varieties, 142, 489–490
 See also specific lettuces
Lilac, 119
Lima beans
 about, 131, 145–146
 and Collards (variation), 133
 dried, to cook, 349
 Succotash, 146
 varieties, 490
Lime(s)
 about citrus fruit, 242–243
 Chicken, with Citrus and Cumin,
  391–392
 Key Lime Tart, 245
 -Kiwi-Strawberry Sorbet, 268–269
 Mojito, 400
 Nectarine-Viognier Fizz, 282
 Panna Cotta, Citrus, 440
 varieties, 501
Lingonberries, 247–248
Litchis, 269–270, 505
Livestock. *See* Animal husbandry
Lobster
 Celery and Seafood Consomme,
  93–94
 Paella, 368–369
Loganberries, 228–229
Longans, 269–270, 505
Loquat(s)
 about, 270–271
 and Strawberry Jam, 271
 varieties, 505
Lovage, 398
 -Potato Soup, 398–399
Lowell Farms, 366, 367
Lundberg Family Farms, 366, 367

M

Macadamia nut(s)
 about, 330–331
 fats in, 321
 to toast, 331
 Trout, Macadamia, 331
Mâche
 about, 147
 Salad, "Spring Tonic," with Sweet
  Dressing, 147–148
 varieties, 490
Mad cow disease, 30, 419, 443

Maeda, Hiroshi, 469
Mail order organic foods, 519–524
Mango(es)
    about, 271–272
    Chutney, 273
    Chutney, Spicy Squash-, Seared Duck
        Breast with, 431
    dried, 462
    and Melon, 279
    pesticide levels in, 40
    varieties, 506
Mangosteens, 274
Manure management, 420, 427, 441
Maple syrup, 473
Margarine, 471–472
Marjoram
    about, 401–402
    flowers, 119
    Potato Patties, 402
Marmalade, Quince, 311
Martins, Patrick, 35
Mayapples, 274–275
McAfee, Mark, 441
McEntee, Brendan, 465
Mead, Paul, 42
Meat
    about, 418–420
    antibiotic-resistant bacteria in, 27,
        422
    hormone-treated, 29
    humanely raised certification, 418
    irradiated, 419
    mail order sources, 522–523
    organic, 30, 50, 418–419, 420
    See also Animal husbandry; Beef;
        Lamb; Pork; Veal
Meatballs, Chicken Marvels on Rice,
    432–433
Meat Loaf, Rock 'Em Sock 'Em, 391
Medlar(s), 275–276
    Cheese, 277
Melon(s)
    about, 277–279
    Charentais Melon Cockaigne,
        279–280
    and Mango, 279
    varieties, 278, 506
Meringue, Pavlova, 288–289
Mesclun
    about, 142
    and Arugula Salad with Grapefruit
        and Avocado, 60
    "Spring Tonic" Salad with Sweet

Dressing, 147–148
Mexican
    Black Beans with Epazote, 393
    Pepino Snack, 296
    Refried Beans, 349–350
Michigan State University, organic re-
    search at, 37
Microorganisms, beneficial, 25
Middle Eastern Stuffed Eggplant, 122
Midwestern Sweet-and-Sour Coleslaw,
    83–84
Militello, Mark, 15
Milk cap mushroom, 491
Milk and cream
    about, 437–439
    bovine growth hormone and, 26, 438
    contaminated, 40–41
    marketing of organic products, 36, 37
    nutrients in, 437, 439
    organic, 40–41, 437, 439–440, 441
    Soy, 353
    Spinach, Creamed, 60, 188
    ultra-pasteurization, 36, 439
    See also Custard
Millet, 358–359
    and Cauliflower Medley, 359
Mint
    about, 399–400
    flowers, 119
    Mojito, 400
    Tabbouleh, 203
    Tea, Moroccan, 400
Mirliton-Okra Slaw, 154–155
Mojito, 400
Molasses, organic, 473
Mondavi winery, 475
Monounsaturated fats, 321, 467, 468
Monsanto corporation, 26, 27, 438
Monterey Bay Aquarium, 435
Morel mushroom, yellow, 491
Moroccan (-Style)
    Artichoke Stew, 57
    Chicken, 108
    Tea, Mint, 400
Morton, Julia, 274
Mozzarella
    buffalo, 442–443, 444
    insalata caprese, 444
    Pizza, Thyme, 415
    Summer Squash Blossoms, Stuffed,
        191–192
    Sweet Pepper and Sausage Frittata,
        195

Muffins
    Blueberry, 235–236
    Cornbread, 467
Mulatto chile, 105
Mung beans, 349
Mushrooms
    about, 148–149
    Beef Stew with Porcini, 150–151
    Chanterelle and Fingerling Potato
        Gratin, 169
    foraging for, 149
    Hunter's Sauce, Pasta with, 194–195
    Sukiyaki, 64–65
    varieties, 149–150, 490–491
Muskmelons, 278, 506
Mussels, in Paella, 368–369
Mustard flowers, 119
Mustard greens, 63, 481
Mycotoxins, 464–465

N

Napa cabbage, 62, 480
    Halibut Wrapped in Chinese
        Cabbage Leaves, 63–64
    Kim Chee, 63
Nasturtiums, 119
National Academy of Sciences, 216
National Institute of Environmental
    Health Sciences, 27
National Organic Program (NOP), 34,
    36, 38, 418, 422, 437, 439
National Organic Standards, 30, 32,
    33–35, 421
National Soil Fertility Program, 33
Navajo-Churro lamb, 425
Nectarine(s)
    about, 280–281
    -Blackberry Cobbler, 282
    jam, 281
    pesticide levels in, 40
    varieties, 7, 280, 507
    -Viognier Fizz, 282
Neeps, Bashed, Sonoma Style, 176–177
New Crops Program, Connecticut, 17
New England Boiled Dinner, 83
New Farm Organic Price Index, 49, 517
Niman, Bill, 420
Niman Ranch, 420, 522
Nitrogen-fixing bacteria, in soil, 24
Nori, 181
North African Style, Okra, 153
North Carolina State University, organic
    research at, 38

Northeast Organic Farmers Association (NOFA), 34, 422
Nurses' Health Study, 463
Nut(s)
    fats in, 321
    genetic diversity in, 18–19
    mail order sources for, 521
    Medjool Date Loaf, 255
    milk, 439–440
    oils, 319
    See also specific nuts

Oatmeal
    about, 359–360
    Cream Oats, Dr. Cox's, 361
    Granola, Sunflower Seed, Super Delicious, 347
    Peanut Salvage Bars, 334
    Quaker company, 360
Oatmeal Cookies
    Black Walnut and, 342
    -Coconut, Chewy, 361
    and Fig, 258
    Pineapple-, 301
Ogden, Bradley, 15
Ohsawa Sauce, Tempura Roots in, 160–161
Oils
    about, 467–472
    avocado, 69
    basil, 381
    fats in, 467
    health benefits of, 468–469, 471
    in margarine, 472
    mass-produced, 467–468
    from nuts and seeds, 319, 329, 333, 334, 346
    smoking point, 470
    soybeans in, 353
Okra
    about, 151–153
    flowers, 119, 152
    Gumbo, Chicken Filé, 153–154
    locally grown, 17–18
    North African Style, 153
    Slaw, -Mirliton, 154–155
    varieties, 152, 492
Oldways Preservation and Exchange Trust, 3
Olive(s)
    about, 283–284
    Caponata with Chives, 388

to cure, 284
    Marinated, Rosemary and Lavender, 284
    Salad Niçoise, 285
    varieties, 507
Olive oil, 468, 470
    health benefits of, 469, 471
    mail order sources, 523
Omelet, A Fine, 448–449
Onion(s)
    about, 155–158
    Pearl, Peas, Braised with Lettuce and, 165–166
    pesticide levels in, 40
    Pico de Gallo, 158
    to roast, 158
    tearing from, 155, 156
    varieties, 156–157, 492
    See also Chives; Leek(s); Scallion(s); Shallot(s)
OPX (Organic Price Index), 49
Orach, red, 400–401
Orange(s)
    about citrus fruit, 242–243
    Chicken, Asian-Style, 244
    Chicken with Citrus and Cumin, 391–392
    French Toast, The Ultimate, 246
    Nectarine-Viognier Fizz, 282
    nutrients in, 41–42
    Panna Cotta, Citrus, 440
    Rice, Almond and, 244
    varieties, 501–502
    Vinaigrette, Red and Yellow Beet Salad with, 75
    Vinaigrette, Vanilla-, 245
    Wakame Salad, 182–183
    Watercress, and Beet Salad, 207
Oregano, 401–402
    flowers, 119
Oregon Tilth, 430
Organic Caucus, congressional, 31
Organic Consumers Association, 31, 517
Organic cooking
    Chefs Collaborative, 16
    Chef's techniques, 15
    everyday, 22
    gourmet-style, 21–22
    recycling process in, 51
Organic farming
    animal husbandry, 24, 27-28, 30, 50, 418–421, 424, 427

biodynamic, 475
    cacao plantations, 458
    certification and, 10, 33, 35, 39, 47, 422
    coffee, 455
    composting process in, 4, 22–24, 33, 46, 225
    dairy, 437, 439, 441
    environmental benefits of, 5–6, 41
    expansion of, 32, 43
    fluctuations in crop quality, 47
    genetically diverse crops, 18–19, 39, 41
    green manure in, 46
    heritage breeds, 419, 429, 430
    large growers, 37
    National Standards (USDA), 30, 32, 33–35
    pest control. *See* Pest control, nontoxic
    pest and disease resistant plants, 24–25
    questions to ask farmer, 46
    research, 36, 37–38
    small farmers, 5, 18, 39, 45–47
    sustainability and, 10, 33, 41
    thrifty plants and animals, 24
    variety names, 6–8
    wineries, 475
    See also Agriculture; Animal husbandry
Organic food
    versus corporate food products, 1–3
    health benefits and safety of, 39–43
    information sources on, 517–518
    market and sales, 14, 17, 32, 37, 43
    price index, 49
    "price lookup" stickers on, 38
    reasons for buying, x–xi, 29, 39
    site-specific flavors in, 3–4
    terminology, 35, 36
    USDA seal, 27, 30, 32–33, 35–36
    See also Certification; *specific foods*
Organic food sources
    Community Supported Agriculture, 13–14, 48–49, 518
    farmers and farmers' markets, 6, 9–12, 45, 48, 518
    information on, 518–519
    mail order, 519–524
    pick-your-own operations, 6
    purveyors, 47–48
    roadside stands, 6, 12–13

supermarkets and chain stores, 14, 33, 36, 38, 430
wholesale distributors, 524–526
Organic Gardening, 21, 36, 37, 363
Organic Materials Research Institute, 41
Organic Trade Association, 30, 36, 420, 519
Organochlorines, 29
Oxalic acid, 135, 173, 186
Oyster mushroom, 491

P

Paella, 368–369
Palladin, Jean-Louis, 15
Palm fruit oil, 472
Pancakes
    Amaranth Popcakes, 304
    Potato, Scandinavian, 170
Panna Cotta, Citrus, 440
Papaya(s)
    about, 285–286
    dried, 462
    pesticide levels in, 40
    Salad, Green, 287
    seeds, 286
    varieties, 507
Parsley
    about, 402–403
    Chimichurri Sauce, 404
    Green Goddess Dressing, 404
    Green Sauce, Walnut, 341–342
    juice, 18
    persillade, 403
    Pesto, 337
    Pesto, Rosemary, 407
    Tabbouleh, 203
Parsnip(s)
    about, 159–160
    Sauté of Chestnuts, Brussels Sprouts and, 161
    Tempura Roots in Ohsawa Sauce, 160–161
    unpeeled, 281
    varieties, 493
Pasilla chile, 105
Passionfruit
    about, 287–288
    Pavlova, 288–289
    varieties, 288, 507
Pasta
    Angel Hair, with Summer Squash, 190–191
    with garlic, 129

with Hunter's Sauce, 194–195
    Penne with Broccoli and Fava Beans, 77–78
Pastry flour, 372
Pavich, Steve, 37, 260
Pavlova, 288–289
Pea(s)
    about, 162–165
    blossoms, 119
    Braised with Lettuce and Onions, 165–166
    in Kale Soup, Portuguese, 137
    pesticide levels in, 40
    shoots, 163
    snow, 163–164, 493
    Soup, Scandinavian, 166
    sugar snap, 163, 164, 493
        Baked, 165
        Green Papaya Salad, 287
    varieties, 163, 493
Peach(es)
    about, 289–291
    to blanch and freeze, 291
    dried, 462
    Melba, 292
    pesticide levels in, 40
    Pie, 292
    and Plum Cobbler, 306
    Pork Loin, Hazelnut-Crusted, 330
    and Strawberry Succulence, 316
    unpeeled, 281
    varieties, 289–290, 508
Peanut(s)
    about, 332–333
    fats in, 321
    Gado Gado Sauce, 395
    to roast and salt, 333
    safety of, 332
    Salvage Bars, 334
    Sauce, Thai, 333
Peanut butter
    -Dark Chocolate Sauce, 460
    to make, 333
    Peanut Salvage Bars, 334
Peanut oil, 333, 468
Pear(s)
    about, 293–295
    Bartlett Pear Salad, 295
    Comice, with Prosciutto and Baby Greens, 295–296
    Crosnes, and Hazelnut Salad, 114
    dried, 462
    pesticide levels in, 40

unpeeled, 281
    varieties, 293, 294, 508
    See also Asian pear(s)
Pearl onions, 157, 492
Pecan(s)
    about, 334–335
    fats in, 321
    Lace Tulips, 268–269
    Pie, Southern, 335
Penne with Broccoli and Fava Beans, 77–78
Peperoncini, 105
Pepino Snack, Mexican, 296
Pepper(s). *See* Chile(s); Sweet pepper(s)
Peppermint, 399
Pequin chile, 105
Perilla, 404–405
    Salad, Green, 405
Persillade, 129, 403
Persimmon(s)
    about, 296–298
    Bread, Sweet, 299
    dried, 298, 462
    Sundae, 299
    varieties, 297, 508
Pest control, nontoxic
    Bacillus thuringiensis (Bt), 46–47, 82, 121
    beneficial insects, 25, 131, 392, 475
    diatomaceous earth, 162
    in fruit growing, 217, 225
    physical barriers, 121, 131, 206
    water sprays, 162
Pesticide Action Network, 28–29
Pesticides, 40, 54, 92, 225
    genetically engineered crops and, 26
    health risks from, 24, 28–29, 39
Pesto, 337
    with fennel, 126
    Rosemary, 407
Petaluma Poultry Processors, 430
Petunia, 119
Pfeffernüsse, 379
Pickles, pickled
    Beets, 73, 74
    cucumber, 116
    Kim Chee, 63
    Pepino Snack, Mexican, 296
Pickling cucumbers, 115, 486
Pick-your-own operations, 6
Pico de Gallo, 158
Pie(s)
    Apple, American, 220

Blueberry, 236
Cherry, 242
Crust, Double, 236
Crust, Single, 211
Gooseberry, 251
Ground Cherry, 134
Huckleberry, 266
Peach, 292
Pecan, Southern, 335
Pizza, Thyme, 415
"Pumpkin," Made with Butternut
    Squash, 211
Rhubarb-Huckleberry, 174–175
See also Tart(s)
Pilaf, Quinoa, 363
Pineapple(s)
    about, 299–301
    dried, 462
    -Oatmeal Cookies, 301
    pesticide levels in, 40
    Sauce, Chicken in, Indonesian,
        301–302
    varieties, 509
Pine mushrooms, 491
Pine nuts, 321, 336–337
    See also Pesto
Pistachio(s)
    about, 338
    fats in, 321
    Stuffing, Turkey, 339
    Veggie Burgers, Grilled, 338–339
Pita Bread, 374
Pizza, Thyme, 415
Planet Organics, 13, 99
Plantains, 226–227, 499
Plum(s)
    about, 302–305
    Jam, Damson, 307
    and Peach Cobbler, 306
    SugarPlums!, 306
    unpeeled, 281
    varieties, 303–304, 509
Pluots, 304
Poblano chile(s), 105
    Tacos of Creamy Braised Chard, 98-
        99
Polyoxyethylene amine (POEA), 27
Polyphenols, 55
Polyunsaturated fats, 321, 467, 468
Pomegranate(s)
    about, 307–309
    Duck Stew with Walnuts and,
        309–310

juice, 306–307
Tapioca, 310
varieties, 509–510
Porcini, Beef Stew with, 150–151
Pork
    about, 426–427
    Caraway-Infused, with Sauerkraut
        and Apples, 383
    Chops, Cider-Glazed, with Prune-
        Armagnac Confit, 305
    Coriander, 390
    Feijoada, Brazilian, 350
    Garlic Rub for, 130
    heritage breed of, 419
    Loin, Hazelnut-Crusted, 330
    Loin Roast with Dried Fruit and
        Sweet Spices, 428
    New England Boiled Dinner, 83
    organic, about, 426–428
    trichina infection and, 426
    See also Bacon; Ham; Prosciutto;
        Sausage
Portobello mushrooms, 150
Portuguese Kale Soup, 137
Potato(es)
    about, 166–169
    Artichoke Stew, Moroccan-Style, 57
    and Eggplant Stew, Indian, 122–123
    Gratin, Fingerling Potato and
        Chanterelle, 169
    Mashed, Garlic and Celery Root, 96
    New England Boiled Dinner, 83
    Pancakes, Scandinavian, 170
    Patties, Sweet Marjoram, 402
    pesticide levels in, 40
    Pork, Caraway-Infused, with
        Sauerkraut and Apples, 383
    Salad, German, 411–412
    Savory Roasted, 411
    Soufflé, 169
    Soup, -Lovage, 398–399
    unpealed, 281
    varieties, 7, 168, 493–494
Poultry
    free range label, 14, 16
    humanely raised certification, 418
    organic, about, 429–431
    See also specific types
Prawns, Tarragon, 413
Pregnancy, pesticide exposure during,
    28
Preserves
    Apricot, 222–223

Cherries, Brandied, 240
Cranberry Relish, 248
Quince Marmalade, 311
Violet Jelly, 120
See also Chutney; Jam
Preserving and canning, 241, 281
Price index, organic, 49
Primrose, 119
Processed food, 452–453
Prosciutto
    Comice Pears with Baby Greens and,
        295–296
    Saltimbocca, 409
Prostate cancer, 26, 438
Prune(s), 462
    -Armagnac Confit, Cider-Glazed
        Pork Chops with, 305
Ptucha, Greg, 11
Pudding
    Figgy, 259
    Indian, 112
    Pomegranate Tapioca, 310
Puffball mushroom, 491
Pullet eggs, 447
"Pumpkin" Pie Made with Butternut
    Squash, 211
Pumpkin seed(s)
    about, 343–344
    fats in, 321
    to toast, 344
    Winter Squash Soup with, 344–345
Puntarella, 102, 485
Purdy, Tuddie, 330
Purveyors, 47–48

Q

Quail, 429
Quality Assurance International (QAI),
    33, 456
Quark, 444
Quiche, Chard, Savory No-Crust,
    99–100
Quince(s)
    about, 310–311
    Marmalade, 311
    varieties, 510
Quinoa
    about, 361–363
    flour, 362–363, 372
    Pilaf, 363

R

Rabbit ranchers, 433
Radicchio
  about, 101
  Salad, Red and White, 103
  varieties, 485
Radish(es)
  about, 170–172
  Daikon Stir-Fry, 172–173
  flowers, 119
  Salsa, 172
  unpeeled, 281
  varieties, 171, 494
Raisin(s)
  about, 462
  grapes for, 262
  Sauce, Sweet-and-Sour, 461
Raita, 187–188
Ramps, 387, 487
Raspberry(ies)
  about, 312–313
  Charentais Melon Cockaigne,
    279–280
  Clafoutis, 313
  Peach Melba, 292
  pesticide levels in, 40
  varieties, 510
  Vinaigrette, Intense, 314
  wineberries, 312
  See also Black raspberry(ies)
Reading Terminal Market, Philadelphia,
  11–12
Red cabbage, 82, 483
Red currants, 249, 251
Red orach, 400–401
Red raspberry(ies). See Raspberry(ies)
Reed, Lorene, 13
Refried Beans, Mexican, 349–350
Reindeer meat, 433
Reiners, Steve, 7
Relish
  Caponata with Chives, 388
  Cranberry, 248
Research, organic, 36, 37–38
Rhubarb
  about, 173–174
  -Huckleberry Pie, 174–175
  Stewed, 174
  -Strawberry Crisp, 317
  varieties, 173, 494
Rice
  about, 364–365
  Carrot Soup with, 88

and Celery Root, Bulgarian Style, 95
and Cheese Frittata, 369
Chicken, Asian-Italian Style, 394
Chicken Marvels on, 432–433
Grape Leaves, Stuffed, 263–264
Gumbo, Chicken Filé, 153–154
mail order sources, 522
Orange and Almond, 244
Paella, 368–369
Risotto Supreme, Shrimp, 436
United States-grown, 366–367
varieties, 365, 368
  See also Wild rice
Ricotta, sheep's milk, 444
Risotto Supreme, Shrimp, 436
Roadside stands, 6, 12–13
Roberts, Glenn, 366–367
Rock Cornish chickens, 429
Rodale, Bob, 363
Rodale, J. I., 440
Rodale Institute, 49
Rodale Press, 363
Rolls
  Cinnamon, 373
  Whole-Wheat and Black Walnut
    Quick, 466–467
Romaine
  Caesar Salad, The True, 143–144
  nutrients in, 142
  varieties, 490
Romanesco (broccoletti), 76
Roots of Change Fund, 13
Rosemary
  about, 406–407
  Chicken Toscana, 407
  flowers, 119
  Lamb, Rack of, Garlic and, 425
  Olives, and Lavender Marinated, 284
  Pesto, 407
  varieties, 406
Rouille, 129
Roundup, 27
Routt, Allen, 15
Rub, Garlic, for Meat, 130
Rum
  Grapefruit Cooler, 246
  Mojito, 400
Rutabaga
  about, 175–176
  Bashed Neeps, Sonoma Style,
    176–177
  unpeeled, 281
  varieties, 494

S

Safflower oil, 468
Sage
  about, 408–409
  flowers, 119
  Saltimbocca, 409
  Stuffing, Turkey, 409–410
  tea, 408
Saintsbury, George, 276
Salad(s)
  Arugula and Mesclun, with
    Grapefruit and Avocado, 60
  Bartlett Pear, 295
  Beet, Red and Yellow, with Orange
    Vinaigrette, 75
  Caesar, The True, 143–144
  caprese, 444
  Comice Pears with Prosciutto and
    Baby Greens, 295–296
  Crosnes, Pear, and Hazelnut, 114
  Fennel and Tomato, 126
  Greek, 116–117
  Looseleaf Lettuce and Roasted Beet,
    144
  Niçoise, 285
  Papaya, Green, 287
  Perilla, Green, 405
  Potato, German, 411–412
  Red and White, 103
  "Spring Tonic," with Sweet Dressing,
    147–148
  Tabbouleh, 203
  Wakame Orange, 182–183
  Watercress, Beet, and Orange, 207
  See also Slaw(s)
Salad dressing
  Bacon, Warm, Winter Green Slaw
    with, 99
  Blue Cheese, 144–145
  Carrot-Juice, 88
  Green Goddess, 404
  Sweet, "Spring Tonic" Salad with,
    147–148
  See also Vinaigrette
Sales, organic food, 14, 17, 32, 37, 43
Salmon
  Dilled, 392
  Fillets with Horseradish Crust, 306
  genetically engineered, 434
  nutrients in, 435
Salmonella bacteria, 42
  antibiotic resistant strain of, 27–28
  in diary, 441

542 · THE ORGANIC COOK'S BIBLE

in eggs, 446–447
Salsa
  Extra Hot, 107
  Fresh, Hot, 389
  Molcajete, 107
  Pico de Gallo, 158
  Radish, 172
  Verde (Green), 107, 199
Salsify
  about, 177–178
  Gnocchi, 179
  unpeeled, 281
Saltimbocca, 409
Santa Fe grande chile, 105
Saturated fats, 321
Sauce(s)
  apple-horseradish (*apfelkren*), 396
  Béarnaise, Chervil, 386–387
  Berbere, 385
  Black Currant, Lemon Bavarian with, 251–252
  Cashew, 326
  Chimichurri, 404
  Chocolate, Dark, -Peanut Butter, 460
  deglazing, 185
  Gado Gado, 395
  Garlic, Ancient Greek, 130
  Green, Walnut, 341–342
  Harissa, 107
  "Hollandaise," Healthy, 68
  Hollandaise, Steamed Asparagus with, 67–68
  Huckleberry Game, 266
  Hunter's, Pasta with, 194–195
  Ohsawa, Tempura Roots in, 160–161
  Peanut, Thai, 333
  Pesto, 337
  Pesto, Rosemary, 407
  Pineapple, Chicken in, Indonesian, 301–302
  Raisin, Sweet-and-Sour, 461
  Sherry-Shallot, Veal Scallops with, 185
  tomato, canning, 202
  Tzatziki, 116
  See also Salsa
Sauerkraut
  Homemade, 84
  with kohlrabi, 138
  nutrients in, 82
  Pork, Caraway-Infused, with Apples and, 383
Sausage

Feijoada, Brazilian, 350
  Gumbo, Chicken Filé, 153–154
  Sage Turkey Stuffing, 409
  and Sweet Pepper Frittata, 195
  and Turnips in Their Shells, 205
Savory(ies)
  about, 410–411
  flowers, 119
  Potatoes, Roasted, 411
  Potato Salad, German, 411–412
Savoy cabbage, 82, 483
Scallion(s)
  about, 156–157
  Frittata, 159
  Gazpacho, Green, with Shellfish, 199–200
  Green Goddess Dressing, 404
  Kim Chee, 63
  Sukiyaki, 64–65
  Tabbouleh, 203
Scandinavian Pea Soup, 166
Scandinavian Potato Pancakes, 170
Scarlet runner bean flowers, 119
Scotch Bonnet chile, 105
Scotch Lamb and Barley Soup, 356
Scowcroft, Bob, 31, 36, 37
Seafood. *See* Fish; Shellfish
Sea lettuce, 182
Sea palm fronds, 182
Seaweed
  about, 180–182
  Hiziki with Vegetables, Braised, 183
  Wakame Orange Salad, 182–183
Seckel pears, 293
Seeds
  fats in, 321
  fennel, 125
  flaxseed, 343
  nutrients in, 319
  to sprout, 346–347
  to toast, 51, 344, 346
  See also Pumpkin seed(s); Sunflower seed(s)
Semolina flour, 372
Seniors' Farmers' Market Nutrition Pilot Program, 12
Serrano chile(s), 105
  Pico de Gallo, 158
  Salsa, Extra Hot, 107
  Salsa, Fresh, Hot, 389
  Salsa Verde, 199
Sesame oil, 468
Shallot(s)

about, 157, 184–185
  -Sherry Sauce, Veal Scallops with, 185
  varieties, 495
Sheep milk cheese, 442
Shellfish
  about, 434
  Celery and Seafood Consomme, 93–94
  Crab and Squash Soup, 212
  Green Gazpacho with, 199–200
  mercury in, 434
  Paella, 368–369
  See also Shrimp
Shepherd, Renee, 142
Sherry
  -Shallot Sauce, Veal Scallops with, 185
  Shrimp, Brussels Sprouts and, 81
Shiitake mushroom, 491
Shortening, 472
Shrimp
  Celery, and Seafood Consomme, 93–94
  Gazpacho, Green, with Shellfish, 199–200
  organic certified, 435
  Paella, 368–369
  Risotto Supreme, 436
  Sherry, Brussels Sprouts and, 81
  Tarragon, 413
Simian immunodeficiency virus, 26
Sinskey, Robert, 43
Skordalia, 129
Slaw(s)
  Cole Slaw, Midwestern Sweet-and-Sour, 83–84
  Okra-Mirliton, 154–155
  Winter Green, with Warm Bacon Dressing, 99
Sloppy Joes, 423
Slow Food movement, 3, 419
Slow Food USA, 35, 425, 429, 430, 442
  contact information for, 517
Smith, Bob, 41
Smithsonian Institution, coffee certification of, 456
Snail, The, 35
Snap beans, 131, 132, 488
Snow peas, 163–164, 493
Soil Association (UK), 34, 41
Soil fertility, 4, 22–24, 33, 225
Sonoma Style Bashed Neeps, 176–177

Sorbet, Kiwi-Lime-Strawberry, 268–269
Soufflé
    Corn, Cheesy, 112
    Potato, 169
Soup(s)
    Canned and mixes, 452
    Carrot, with Rice, 88
    Celery and Seafood Consomme,
        93–94
    Crab and Squash, 212
    Gumbo, Chicken Filé, 153–154
    Kale, Portuguese, 137
    Pea, Scandinavian, 166
    Potato-Lovage, 398–399
    Watercress, 208
    Winter Squash, with Pumpkin Seeds,
        344–345
    See also Gazpacho; Stock
Sourdough bread, 466
Southern-Fried Chicken, 432
Soybeans
    about, 348, 352–353
    dried, to cook, 349
    genetically modified, 26, 32
    Tempeh, Barbecued, 353
    Tofu, Homemade, 354
    varieties, 488
Soy Milk, 353
Soy oil, 468
Spaghetti Squash with Tomato and
    Basil, 213
Spanish-Style Cardoons, 86
Spearmint, 399–400
Spelt, 372
Spices, about, 377–378
    See also specific spices
Spinach
    about, 186–188
    Chinese, 62, 481
    Creamed, 188
    juice, 18
    pesticide levels in, 40
    and Sweet Potato Flan, 197–198
    varieties, 187, 495
Spirulina, 371
Spreads. See Dips and Spreads
Spring Hill Farms, 444
Sprouts, seed and legume, 346–347
Squash. See Summer squash; Winter
    squash
Star anise, 379
Steiner, Rudolf, 475
Stevia rebaudiana and stevioside, 473

Stew
    Artichoke, Moroccan-Style, 57
    Beef, with Porcini, 150–151
    Duck, with Walnuts and
        Pomegranates, 309–310
    Eggplant and Potato, Indian,
        122–123
    Lamb and Cauliflower, 91
Sticky rice, 365
Stock
    Chicken, 454
    commercial, 452
    Vegetable, 453
Stonyfield Farm, 16, 40
Strawberry(ies)
    about, 314–316
    Charentais Melon Cockaigne,
        279–280
    Crepes, 317
    dried, 462
    fraise des bois, 316
    -Kiwi-Lime Sorbet, 268–269
    and Loquat Jam, 271
    and Peach Succulence, 316
    pesticide levels in, 40
    -Rhubarb Crisp, 317
    varieties, 510
    wild, 315, 316
Stuffing
    Pistachio Turkey, 339
    Sage Turkey, 409–410
    Wild Rice and Cornbread, 375
Sucanat, 473
Succotash, Lima Bean, 146
Sugar, 473
Sugarloaf endive, 101
Sugar snap peas. See Pea(s), sugar snap
Sukiyaki, 64–65
Summer savory. See Savory(ies)
Summer squash
    about, 189–190
    Angel Hair Pasta with, 190–191
    Battered and Fried, 191
    blossoms, 119, 190
    Blossoms, Stuffed, 191–192
    varieties, 189, 495–496
    See also Zucchini
Sunflower, 119
Sunflower oil, 346, 468
Sunflower seed(s)
    about, 345–345
    fats in, 321
    Granola, Super Delicious, 347

    to sprout, 346–347
    to toast, 346
Supermarkets, organic food sections in,
    14, 33, 38
Susser, Allen, 15
Sustainability, 10, 16, 33, 41
Sustainable Agriculture Network, 13
Sweet-and-Sour Coleslaw, Midwestern,
    83–84
Sweet-and-Sour Raisin Sauce, 461
Sweet Dumpling squash, 209
Sweeteners, 473
    Vanilla Ice Cream, Sugarless, 474
Sweet pepper(s)
    about, 192–194
    Hunter's Sauce, Pasta with, 194–195
    pesticide levels in, 40
    Ratatouille, 123–124
    to roast, 194
    and Sausage Frittata, 195
    varieties, 193, 496
Sweet potato(es)
    about, 195–197
    candied, 197
    locally grown, 17–18
    and Spinach Flan, 197–198
    varieties, 196–197, 496
Sweet woodruff, 119
Swiss chard. See Chard

T
Tabbouleh, 203
Tacos
    of Chard, Creamy Braised, 98–99
    Corn, Kasha, and Bean, 357–358
Tahini, Hummus, The Best You've Ever
    Tasted, 351
Tapioca, Pomegranate, 310
Tarragon
    about, 412
    Chicken, 413
    Green Goddess Dressing, 404
    Prawns, 413
    vinegar, 412
Tart(s)
    Key Lime, 245
    Tarte Tatin, 219–220
    See also Pie(s)
Tarte Tatin, 219–220
Tauxe, Robert, 42
Tea
    Moroccan Mint, 400
    sage, 408

Tempeh, Barbecued, 353
Tempura Roots in Ohsawa Sauce, 160–161
Texas A&M University, Vegetable and Fruit Improvement Center at, 16–17
Thai chile, 105
Thai Peanut Sauce, 333
Thrifty plants and animals, 24, 42–43
Thyme
    about, 413–414
    Chicken with, Grilled, 414–415
    flowers, 119
    Pizza, 415
Tiramisù, 457
Tofu
    Homemade, 354
    in Sukiyaki, 64–65
Togarashi chile, 105
Tomatillo
    about, 198–199
    Gazpacho, Green, with Shellfish, 199–200
    Salsa Verde, 107, 199
    varieties, 198, 496
Tomato(es)
    about, 200–202
    and Fennel Salad, 126
    Frittata, Scallion, 159
    Gazpacho, Untraditional, 202–203
    Greek Salad, 116–117
    Hunter's Sauce, Pasta with, 194–195
    insalata caprese, 444
    Pico de Gallo, 158
    Ratatouille, 123–124
    to roast, 202
    Salad Niçoise, 285
    Salsa, Fresh, Hot, 389
    Salsa Molcajete, 107
    Salsa, Radish, 172
    sauce, canning, 202
    Spaghetti Squash with Basil and, 213
    Tabbouleh, 203
    varieties, 201, 496–497
Transfair, 455, 456
Trichinosis, 426
Triticale, 372
Trout, Macadamia, 331
Truffles, Oregon white, 491
Trypsin inhibitors, 26
Tulips, Pecan Lace, 268–269
Tuna, in Salad Niçoise, 285
Turkey, 419, 429, 430–431
    See also Stuffing

Turnip(s)
    about, 204–205
    and Sausage in Their Shells, 205
    Tokyo cross, 204
    unpeeled, 281
    varieties, 204, 497
Tuscan White Beans, 351
TV dinners, 2
2, 4-D, 27
Tzatziki, 116

U

Union Square Greenmarket, New York, 11
United Natural Foods, 32
U.S. Department of Agriculture (USDA), 9, 10, 13, 429
    National Farmers Market and Direct Marketing Association, 518
    dairy farming and, 439
    fish farming and, 434
    food stamps, 12, 518
    National Organic Program (NOP), 34, 36, 38, 418, 422
    National Organic Standards, 30, 32, 33–35, 421
    organic research funding, 36, 37
    retail rules of, 38
    Organic seal, 27, 30, 32–33, 35–36, 430

V

Van Aken, Norman, 15
Van En, Robyn, 13
Vanilla Ice Cream, Sugarless, 474
Vanilla-Orange Vinaigrette, 245
Veal
    Demi-Glace, 453
    humanely raised, 419, 423–424
    organic, about, 424
    Saltimbocca, 409
    Scallops with Sherry-Shallot Sauce, 185
Vegetable(s)
    Asian. See Asian vegetables
    genetically modified, 26
    Hiziki with, Braised, 183
    juicing, 18, 73
    locally grown, 17–18
    mail order sources for, 520
    New England Boiled Dinner, 83
    nutritious cultivar development, 16–17

pesticide levels in, 40, 54, 92
protein, 371
Ratatouille, 123–124
ripe-picked, 6
roasted root, 160
site-specific flavor in, 4
Stock, 453
unpeeled, 281
variety names, 7–8, 45, 49, 479
    See also Organic food; specific vegetables
Vegetarian diet, B12 deficiency and, 371
Veggie Burgers, Grilled, 338–339
Vinaigrette
    Bartlett Pear Salad, 295
    citrus, 243
    Comice Pears with Prosciutto and Baby Greens, 295–296
    Orange, Red and Yellow Beet Salad with, 75
    Raspberry, Intense, 314
    Vanilla-Orange, 245
Vinegar, herb, 381, 412
Violet
    flowers, 119
    Jelly, 120
Vivid Picture project, 13–14, 517

W

Wakame, 182
    Orange Salad, 182–183
Wal-Mart, 36
Walnut(s)
    about, 339–341
    black, 340
    Black, and Oatmeal Cookies, 342
    Black, and Whole-Wheat Quick Rolls, 466–467
    Candied, Hot, 342
    Cinnamon Rolls, 373
    Duck Stew with Pomegranates and, 309–310
    fats in, 321
    Green Sauce, 341–342
    mail order sources for, 521
Walnut oil, 468
Washington State Apple Commission, 218
Watercress
    about, 206–207
    Beet, and Orange Salad, 207
    Soup, 208

Waterfowl farming, organic, 429
Watermelons, 278, 506
Waters, Alice, 49, 141, 142
Wax beans, 131, 488
Weber, Kathleen, 463
WebMD Medical News, 27
Wheat, 370–372
Wheat germ, 372
White Beans, Tuscan, 351
White currants, 250
Whole foods, defined, 355
Whole-grain flour and meal, 463
Wholesale distributors, 525–526
Whole-Wheat and Black Walnut Quick
    Rolls, 466–467
Whole-wheat flour, 370, 463
WIC coupons, 12, 518
Wild plants. *See* Foraging
Wild rice
    about, 374–375
    and Cornbread Stuffing, 375

Williams, John, 43
Wilson, Dan and Colin, 427
Wine
    Coq au Vin, 477
    Nectarine-Viognier Fizz, 282
    organic, 474–476, 524
    site-specific flavor in, 4
    sulfites in, 476
    See also Sherry
Wineberries, 312
Winter savory, 410–411
Winter squash
    about, 208–210
    -Mango Chutney, Spicy, Seared Duck
        Breast with, 431
    "Pumpkin" Pie Made with Butternut
        Squash, 211
    to roast, 210
    seeds, to toast, 51
    soup, 51
    Crab and, 212

Soup with Pumpkin Seeds, 344–345
Spaghetti Squash with Tomato and
    Basil, 213
varieties, 17, 209, 498
See also specific squash
Wynne, Bob, 31

Y

Yogurt, in Tzatziki, 116

Z

Zaiger, Floyd, 304
Zamboni, Luciano, 102
Zucchini
    about, 189, 190
    Ratatouille, 123–124
    varieties, 495–496
    Veggie Burgers, Grilled, 338–339
    See also Summer squash